The Animal and the
Daemon in Early China

SUNY Series in Chinese Philosophy and Culture
David L. Hall and Roger T. Ames, editors

The Animal and the
Daemon in Early China

Roel Sterckx

State University of New York Press

The cover image shows a rubbing of a stone representing a "Man Hugging a Bear" from the tomb of Han general Huo Qubing (d.117 B.C.E.), Xingping County, Shaanxi. (Rubbing made by Dr. Lawrence Sickman, property of Ann Paludan).

Material adapted from Roel Sterckx, "Transforming the Beasts: Animals and Music in Early China." *T'oung Pao* 86, 1–46, copyright © 2000 by E. J. Brill, used with permission. Selections from David R. Knechtges, *Wen xuan or Selections of Refined Literature*, copyright © 1982 by Princeton University Press, are reprinted by permission of Princeton University Press.

Published by
State University of New York Press, Albany

©2002 State University of New York

For information, address State University of New York Press,
90 State Street, Suite 700, Albany, NY 12207

Production by Dana Foote
Marketing by Fran Keneston

Library of Congress Cataloging-in-Publication Data

Sterckx, Roel, 1969–
The animal and the daemon in early China / Roel Sterckx
p. cm. — (SUNY series in Chinese philosophy and culture)
Includes bibliographical references and index.
ISBN 0-7914-5269-7 (alk. paper) — ISBN 0-7914-5270-0 (pbk. : alk. paper)
1. Human-animal relationships—China. 2. Animals and civilization—China.
I. Title. II. Series

QL85 .S79 2002
306.4—dc21
2002021655

10 9 8 7 6 5 4 3 2 1

To my parents

CONTENTS

Acknowledgments   ix

Introduction: Contextualizing Animals   1
    The Animal and the Daemon   5
    Animals as Images   8

Chapter One: Defining Animals   15
    Problems of Definition   16
    Animals in Texts   21
    Naming Animals and Animal Names   29
    Conclusion   42

Chapter Two: Animals and Officers   45
    Managing Animals   46
    Ritual Animals   56
    Animals and Spirits   61
    Calendrical Animals   64
    Conclusion   67

Chapter Three: Categorizing Animals   69
    Qi and Blood   73
    Yinyang and the Five Phases: Correlative Taxonomies   78
    Toward a Moral Taxonomy   88
    Conclusion   91

Chapter Four: The Animal and Territory   93
    Animal Patterns as Social Patterns   96
    Animals and Territory   101
    Animals beyond Territory   110
    Conclusion   122

Chapter Five: Transforming the Beasts   123
    Animals and the Origins of Music   124
    Animals, Music, and Moral Transformation   129
    The Transformation of Animals through Virtue   137

Moral Hybrids 153
"Speaking with Birds and Beasts" 158
Conclusion 162

Chapter Six: Changing Animals **165**
A Cosmogony of Change 167
Demonic Transformations 171
Functional Metamorphosis 173
Autonomous Transformations 177
Symbolic Metamorphosis 186
Portentous Transformations 194
Metamorphosing Agents 198
Critique of Change 200
Conclusion 203

Chapter Seven: Strange Animals **205**
Defining the Strange 206
Interpreting the Strange 211
Confucius Names the Beasts 216
When the Grackos Nest in Lu 225
The Dog as Daemon 231
The Capture of the White Unicorn 233
Conclusion 237

Conclusion 239

Notes 245

Bibliography 321

Index 353

ACKNOWLEDGMENTS

Several people and institutions have contributed to the genesis and completion of this book. My greatest intellectual debt is to Mark Edward Lewis who initiated me in the study of early China at Cambridge and has been an inspirational teacher and mentor ever since. For comments and criticisms on earlier versions and parts of this work I thank Glen Dudbridge, Robert Chard, Sir Geoffrey Lloyd, and the anonymous readers for SUNY Press. I am especially grateful to Ken Brashier who read through the entire manuscript alerting me to many errors in style, language, and content. David McMullen, Joseph McDermott, and John Moffett provided formative guidance and assistance during the early stages of the project. I am grateful to Roger Ames for inviting me to submit my text for publication in this series. While the expertise of these scholars, colleagues and friends has been invaluable in sharpening my understanding in many ways, all errors and inadequacies are my own.

For institutional support I am indebted to the Faculty of Oriental Studies at Cambridge University, the Needham Research Institute, and the staff at the Cambridge University Library and Bodleian Libraries. The Institute of Chinese Studies at Oxford provided a stimulating working environment during my tenure as a junior research fellow at Wolfson College. I should also like to thank the Institute of History of the Chinese Academy of Social Sciences at Beijing and the Department of Chinese Studies at the National University of Singapore for their hospitality during several visits. Colleagues in the Department of East Asian Studies at the University of Arizona provided supportive company during the final reincarnation of the manuscript. This work would not have been possible without the financial support of the Board of Graduate Studies at Cambridge University, Clare Hall Cambridge, the British Academy, the Spalding Trust, and Wolfson College Oxford. Finally I thank Qingying for her support while I was working on these pages when necessary, and for taking me away from them, also when necessary.

INTRODUCTION
CONTEXTUALIZING ANIMALS

This book examines animals in early China, not the animal that forms the object of study for the zoo-historian, archaeologist, fabulist, or literary critic, but the perception of animals and the animal world as a signifying exponent of the world of thought in Warring States and early imperial China. It does not attempt to offer (for reasons I will explain below) a natural history of animals nor does it provide an analysis of the protoscientific inquiry of animals in China. Instead, it seeks to contribute to a cultural history of the perception of animals as a window for the investigation of early Chinese views of the world and explores the ways in which the early Chinese sought to explain the human-animal relationship. This study will thus link the perception of animals with enquiries into the human self-perception and relate the discourse on animals in early China to the creation of human forms of social, political, and intellectual authority.

A great deal of scholarly effort in the study of ancient China has been devoted to the examination of the ideas and activities of its people(s). This pre-occupation with the study of the world of man reflects the traditional charac-terization of ancient Chinese thought and society as human centered. Most scholarly treatments endorse the predominance of a humanistic orientation among the masters of philosophy in Warring States and Han China. A focus on the social order and a desire to establish the parameters of human conduct are generally recognized as the philosophical core of early Chinese thought. The in-clination to clarify the workings of human society, the development of statecraft, the cultivation of the self, and the ways in which the individual figured within the social community and the cosmos at large, characterizes not only the dominant Confucian ideology but also constitutes a significant element in most other schools of thought. Even in its most contrary form—namely, the Daoist asser-tion that man should eschew any constructive role in the ordering of society— philosophical debate in early China was primarily concerned with the place of the human individual and the organization of human society. While, as Donald Harper has reiterated, the natural world was not entirely ignored, the extant writ-ings of the masters of philosophy of the Warring States and Han period rarely displayed an interest in nature outside of its utility as an analogy for particular philosophical arguments.[1]

Scholarly research that takes the culture of human beings as its main focus for the study of the past has proven pivotal to our understanding of the formative economic, political, military, and intellectual developments in War-ring States and early imperial China. The assessment of material life and the re-construction of important historical events, as well as the close scrutiny of important individuals, their texts, and their ideas, have enlightened our under-standing of the mentalities of the elites whose writings provide the primary source materials for this period. It is perhaps, and somewhat paradoxically, to the credit of historians of science and technology that students of China have been encouraged to step away from the notion that human activity provides the sole fruitful point of departure for the study of early China. To be sure, many assumptions and conclusions about the existence of a scientific or naturalist tradition in premodern China still fail to gain scholarly consensus. Neverthe-less, monuments of scholarship such as the work of Joseph Needham are to be commended for redirecting the focus of investigation away from the human protagonist and toward an interest in Chinese perceptions of the natural world. This study has been inspired by questions that have arisen in the wake of these inquiries into Chinese views of the natural world. However, by placing the study of animals at the heart of cultural history, it departs from the aspirations of historians of science to establish a natural history of animals or trace a science of animals in China. While this project was originally conceived as a study of animal lore in texts from the Warring States and early imperial periods, it soon became clear that the exploration of materials on animals would prompt me to address a range of issues beyond the actual animal reference.

Studies of animals in past and contemporary societies have shown that perceptions of nature manifest human self-perception in several ways. In the European tradition, where boundaries between nature and human culture tended to be delineated in a more explicit manner than in China, investigations into the natural world were, at various stages in history, predicated by the social, religious, and philosophical climate of the time. Perceptions of the natural world were linked to human aspirations affectively, aesthetically, and intellectually. In Tudor and Stuart England for instance, as Keith Thomas points out, the human ascendancy over a world of inferior animal species that were to be exploited and subjected to man's commands was generally accepted. Such confident anthropo-centrism however had given way by the end of the eighteenth century when the "rigid barriers between humanity and other forms of life had been much weak-ened."[2] The interplay between the human self-perception and the perception of animals gained momentum in nineteenth-century Britain when Darwin had de-throned God as the creative impulse behind evolution and substituted divine creation with the forces of natural selection. While Darwinian theory itself had bridged the gulf that divided reasoning humankind from the irrational animal world, the evolutionary debate was still seen by many of its participants as occur-ring within natural theology, and animals remained symbols of various orders within human hierarchies and objects of human control.[3] In short, as Walter Burkert notes, the study of nature and human self-knowledge should no longer be separated, even if Socrates long ago insisted that it was right to do so.[4]

In every society, past and present, humans have coexisted with populations of animals of one or many species. The motives that have impelled humans to attribute certain symbolic significances to animals are closely intertwined with the perception of their place among the living species and the way in which the boundaries between the realms of culture and nature, man and beast, are conceived. Animals figured in several ways in Warring States and early imperial China. In addition to their practical role in husbandry, hunting, transport, and human consumption, animals were used as victims in sacrificial religion, figured as agents and objects in ritual practice, and served as symbols and metaphors in the creation of social models of authority. The animal world also provided a rich thesaurus for the expression of fundamental social, moral, religious, and cosmological ideas. Most studies that deal with the perception of animals and the human-animal relationship in ancient societies deal with the history of individual species and the socioeconomic role of animals, or they focus on the question of representation, image, and metaphor. Scholarship dealing with China is no exception to this trend. There is no systematic analysis of how animals and the natural world figured in the generation of sociopolitical, religious, or philosophical models of authority, and there has been no substantial examination of how the perception of the animal world shaped and reflected the intellectual discourse that sought to determine man's place among the living species in China. The study of animals can play several roles for the inquiry into the human self-perception. I see at least four such roles and will briefly outline each of them.

First, animals are a natural or biological category, and as such, philosophers, scientists, and artists throughout history have attempted to distinguish animals from the human world on the basis of their biological otherness. The physical separation of animals from humans and the great variety and physical uniqueness among animal species have rendered the animal as a favorite medium to represent the realm of the other, the non-human world. Furthermore, as a biological category animals have prompted explanation and classification. These classifications reflect how human societies have viewed the internal structures of the natural world and the relationship among its living creatures. The proto-scientific and scientific study of animals—from Aristotle to Linnaeus to modern animal genetics—also shows how the perception of nature and the biological boundaries among species, including humans, are historically contingent and ever changing.[5]

Second, animals function as a social category. As objects of social practice—breeding, domestication, hunting, sacrificing, and consuming—the manipulation and management of animals reflect and/or influence social organization. Hierarchies within human society may reflect attitudes and preoccupations of different member groups toward the natural world. Modern anthropology claims that "animals are good to think with," a statement that also applies to ancient societies where categories drawn from a classification system of the natural world also served to express the nature of categories and relations among humans and vice versa.[6] Attitudes toward the animal world are encoded in the social context in which humans and animals have interacted. Both in ancient and contemporary societies, humans have organized themselves on the basis of their social, religious, and economic need for animals as well as their emotional attitudes toward them. Even within individual societies, the social perception of animals need not be univocal and can be contradictory. In what she described as "one of the outstanding paradoxes of the Roman mind," Jocelyn Toynbee referred to the fact that the Romans had an active interest in the beauty of the animal kingdom and displayed a high degree of devotion to their pets but at the same time took pleasure in the public sufferings and slaughter of thousands of exotic creatures in the public arena.[7]

Third, animals function as objects and mediums of power. Nations aspiring for political hegemony and dominance have traditionally adorned their flags, armor, and crests with images of stalwart creatures such as the eagle, lion, or dragon. But more important, throughout human history the economic exploitation of animals has itself been a feat of social and political power. The symbolic appropriation of the wilds and control over the animal world figured among the paraphernalia of rulership. In Roman games and in Victorian zoos alike, the combat and exhibition of animals was inextricably linked with empire and the celebration of conquest and dominance. The keeping of menageries was a trait of superior civilization. Parks and zoos (and modern-day museums) combined a sense of order with a desire to exhibit the wild and exotic. With animals in their role as representatives of what is "other," exogenous, strange or nonhuman, the establishment of knowledge and control over the animal world has figured prominently as an indicator of political power, intellectual supremacy, and socioreligious dominance.[8]

Finally, animals are adjuncts of human thought and function as images and symbols. Animal categories played an important role in the abstraction of images of human society. Being biologically distinct from humans, animals figured frequently as the archetypal cultural "other."[9] Animals and the world to which they belong are opinionated in that the human mind tends to select and represent rather than reproduce what it observes. Through selecting, discussing, and encoding animals in text or image, the animal reference therefore reveals as much about human concerns as about animals themselves. Whether their function be material, symbolic, didactic, or decorative, animals are a vehicle for the perception of human society.

The Animal and the Daemon

The general argument developed in this book can be outlined as follows: the classic Chinese perception of the world did not insist on clear categorical or ontological boundaries between animals, human beings, and other creatures such as ghosts and spirits. The demarcation of the human and animal realms was not perceived to be permanent or constant, and the fixity of the species was not self-evident or desirable. Instead animals were viewed as part of an organic whole in which the mutual relationships among the species were characterized as contingent, continuous, and interdependent. Consequently the animal world, in several ways, provided normative models and signs for the guidance of human society. The interpretation of animal behavior and response to signifying patterns in the animal world were mediated by the figure of the human sage or ruler-king. The sage's hermeneutic of the natural world did not consist of analyzing the animal world as a distinct and separate reality ruled by internal and independent biological laws; rather, he explained animals through integrating their appearance and behavior within the encompassing structure of a human-animal congruity. Through linking the comprehension of animals with the ruling of human society, the early Chinese presented the animal world as a normative model for the establishment of sociopolitical authority and the ideal of sage rulership.

Despite the substantial volume of material on animals preserved in writings from Warring States and Han China, these texts rarely sought to analyze the living species following a systematic biology, zoology, theology, or anthropology. The absence of an "ology" seeking to differentiate humans, animals, and other creatures into fixed ontological categories suggests that, in order to understand the way in which the Chinese reflected on the multifarious fauna that surrounded them, one should attempt to identify culturally specific factors that influenced the early Chinese construction of biological reality and the ways in which relationships among the living species were viewed. While it may be considered well established that early Chinese thought perceived a continuity between the world of nature and the realm of human culture, the ways in which this continuity was expressed and its role in the creation of models of sagehood, as well as its implications for the early Chinese understanding of the natural world, have not received adequate scholarly treatment. Three key themes therefore appear throughout this study.

First, the status of the biological animal will be assessed. If most preserved writings from early China show little interest in determining ontological boundaries between the living species, this has implications for the degree to which animals were seen as natural creatures. If both the human and animal world were conflated within a larger continuum in which natural and moral categories converged, animals were less likely to be singled out as natural objects of (protoscientific) inquiry but, instead, were subjected to predominantly cultural or social classifications. This however does not entail that Warring States and Han thought was solely concerned with human-centered values or that the discourse on animals merely focused on mythical, fantastic, or sacred animals that exemplified human virtues.

Second, the relative absence of fixed categories and the recognition that species boundaries are to some extent amorphous implies that other theories were formative in the perception of the animal world in early China. This study will argue that the notions of change and transformation were pivotal to the perception of animals and the conception of the human-animal relationship. If, as I hope to show, a paradigm of change and transformation functions as an appropriate hermeneutic tool to read the animal reference in early China, then this very notion of change and transformation needs to be specified and explicated in its different facets.

Finally, this study will assess the status of the human observer in relation to the animal world and evaluate his or her place within the model of change. To do so it needs to explore the contexts associated with the observation, interpretation, explanation, and mastery of the animal world, and identify the ways in which the continuous correlation and interchange between human society and the natural world were mediated.

These three themes will be examined by approaching animal material in texts from four perspectives: the animal world as a textual category, the interrelation between humans and animals, the species relations within the animal realm itself, and the realm of the supernatural or strange. Chapters 1 through 4 deal with the question of order in the animal world and are mainly concerned with the first part of my proposition; namely, the relative absence of a theory of animals in early China and its implications for the protoscientific, lexicographic, and cultural classification of the animal world. Chapters 5 through 7 deal with the transgression of fixed orders between the living species and advance a model of change and transformation as instrumental in the perception of the human-animal relationship.

Chapter 1 is a structural analysis of the organization of animal material in texts. It explores the spurious attempts made at defining animals in early China and shows how the merging of animals as a natural and cultural category is reflected in the status and organization of animal material in texts. Instead of being the object of zoological debate, the animal world was subsumed within a universe of names. Rather than being concerned with the analysis of animals as biological creatures, many Warring States and Han texts evince a preoccupation with the attribution of names to creatures. Much of the protoscientific analysis of animals therefore occurred within the framework of the lexicographic analysis of animal nomenclature. The act of naming animals and ordering animal names not only constituted a feat of political and intellectual control, it also provided an authoritative model to map out and order the animal world itself.

Chapter 2 examines how animals were subsumed within the control of the human polity through ritual, calendar, and human office. The management of animals in early China was firmly linked to bureaucratic control. The association of human office with the management of the natural world occurs across a number of Warring States and Han texts and was formulated in its most idealized form in the description of the ideal state in the *Zhouli* 周禮. Ritual hierarchies, reflected in the use of animals as gifts and as sacrificial victims, influenced the classification of animals. The subsumption of animals within a human bureaucratic model was also reflected in the conception of animal spirits and in calendrical prescriptions regarding the management of animals.

Chapter 3 explores traces of animal taxonomy in early China. Three models of animal classification are identified: classifications based on the notion of blood or "blood and *qi*," the correlation between the living species according to the notions of *yin* and *yang* and the five phases, and moral taxonomies. I will discuss the internal structure of these classifications and assess the motives behind classification.

Chapter 4 argues that the early Chinese perception of order in the animal world was based on the notion of space and territory rather than the concept of species. Against the background of legends claiming that the sages had made patterns (*wen* 文) in the animal world explicit to mankind, order in the animal world was primarily seen as territorial. A physical unity, as well as a moral unity, characterized the relationship between animals and the soil or territory that formed their habitat. Transcending this sociobiological order through collecting exotic animals into parks and maintaining a system of animal tributes was a way through which rulers ensured symbolical dominance over territories beyond the epicenter of their physical power.

Chapter 5 explores the human-animal relationship and introduces the philosophy of moral transformation as an identifying feature of this relationship. Warring States and Han texts did not merely present the man-animal relationship in simile or metaphor but, rather, characterized this relation as being interdependent and mutually transformative. The sage had a pivotal function in mediating the relationship between the human and animal world and was portrayed as an agent capable of morally transforming the natural world and turning beasts into cultured animals. Through the mastery of music, which was thought to originate with sound and motion in the animal world, and through cultivating virtuous human governance, the sage asserted his authority over the natural world. This sociopolitical ideal of a sage-ruler asserting dominance over the world through moral transformation rather than physical domination had its parallel in the discourse on the ruling of barbarians who were presented as the nearest in kin to animals.

Chapter 6 deals with the topic of species change and animal metamorphosis. Based on cosmogonic theories that saw the emergence of all things as the result of a process of permanent transformation, Warring States and Han texts made frequent reference to a dialectic of physical change in the animal world. Certain texts explained animal metamorphosis as the result of moral retribution; others advocated that species change was entirely functional or spontaneous in accordance with the cycle of the seasons and changes in animal habitat. Furthermore, the capability of animals to undergo physical changes was instrumental in the association of numinous or daemonic power with certain species.[10] The discourse on animal metamorphosis also provided models for the perception of human sagacity, which was qualified as the capability to comprehend physical changes in the animal world.

Chapter 7 examines the discourse on animal prodigies. Many Warring States and Han writings firmly attributed the occurrence of animal anomalies to flaws in the workings of human affairs. The explanation of freak animals and animal behavior exemplified a fundamental congruity between the world of man and the animal realm. The human sage, epitomized by the figure of Confucius, functioned as a mediator of the strange seeking to discern patterns of order in a constantly permutating world of hybrids, monsters, and freaks. Through assigning names to unknown creatures and explaining anomalous animal behavior within receptive categories, the human sage emerged as a master of the strange. Anomalous animal behavior itself was often explained as a transgression of physical and geographical boundaries in the natural world.

Animals as Images

Animal imagery abounds across a wide range of early Chinese writings, from the *guan-guan* 關關 chanting ospreys of the *Shijing* 詩經, to Zhuangzi's 莊子 animal allegories, to the mongrels and monsters in the *Shanhaijing* 山海經 bestiary. While no systematic study has dealt with the perception of animals in this corpus of texts, a number of studies in Western, Chinese, and Japanese scholarship have treated one or more aspects of this rich animal thesaurus. Without claiming to do justice to all of the issues raised in these treatments, two main frames of analysis have characterized the study of the animal theme in premodern China. A first approach has focused on explicating animal imagery within the framework of a particular text or literary genre such as mythological epos, poetry, songs, narrative fiction, and fable. These studies interpret portrayals of animals in view of the internal objectives of a particular text, a poem, a narrative, and its author(s), and they identify animal imagery as a referential medium to allegorical truths beyond the original animal reference.[11] A second group of studies has adopted what could be called an ethnohistorical approach.

These studies analyze animal references in the context of a particular regional folklore, its social and religious customs, its origin myths and legends.[12]

While any effort to understand the cultural significance of animals inevitably prompts the reader to oscillate between the view that one is dealing with real creatures, and the contention that the animals in question function as agents of certain symbolical values, most scholarship that touches on the animal theme in China has confined its approach to analyzing the animal world as an analogous referent to human society. This has resulted in a tendency to assign animal references to interpretative categories such as the allegory or the metaphor. A few words need to be said regarding this explanatory logic as it has dominated the secondary literature on the subject.

It goes without saying that many references to animals in early Chinese texts can be explained as imagery, some of which may or may not be inspired by the observation of actual animal behavior in the natural world. To mention a few recurrent examples: the disgorging of food (*fan bu* 反哺) by certain birds taken as a sign of their sense of filial piety; the cuckoo's "unfilial" conduct of having its eggs hatched by other birds; or the owl's unfilial instinct to devour its own mother.[13] Other beliefs, images, and representations are abstractions of such observations: for example, the saying that, as a sign of benevolence, foxes will upon death turn their head in the direction of the mound where they were whelped to demonstrate that they have not forgotten their origins.[14] In addition to sometimes being rooted in empirical observation, the interpretation of animal behavior was also shaped through textual precedent and layers of commentary and annotation. In many Warring States and Han writings, an identification mechanism is at work similar to what Edward Schafer has described in his study of Tang fauna and flora; namely, that most Chinese writers "were hardly different from our medieval Latinists, who, though they often wrote of birds, never looked at nature, but drew on a conventional fund of bird metaphors and allegories which their readers would recognize instantly."[15]

In the Warring States and early imperial period, we witness the emergence of a series of imagined animals, each portrayed with standard biological and behavioral features, which became shared knowledge. Such archetypal animal imagery was taken up by authors and applied to serve the purpose of the texts they wrote. Hence, strings of uniform animal imagery developed, among which the most famous examples (such as the dragon, phoenix, and tortoise) are well known. To sketch one example, the *qilin* 騏驎, often referred to as a unicorn, whose physiology is already moralized in a poem in the *Shijing*, turns into an even more powerful archetype when it moves Confucius to tears at the end of the *Chunqiu* 春秋.[16] By the time of the Han the appearance of a *qilin* becomes virtually synonymous with the arrival of a virtuous reign, the interest in the interpretation of animal omens increases, and miraculous animal appearances lend their names to several imperial reign dates in Western Han chronology.[17] A few centuries later, Shen Yue's 沈約 (441–513 C.E.) dynastic history of the Liu-Song 劉宋 (420–479 C.E.) devotes an entire essay to the unicorn and its counterparts, accompanied by a list of their numinous appearances in history.[18] From being a singular record in a Warring States historical chronicle, repetitive references to such numinous animals had gradually become rhetorical devices used by the historiographer to mark out the alternating phases of prosperity and decline in the course of a dynastic history. References to ominous animals had become emblematic signposts for pending social and political events.

That animal iconography can be fruitfully interpreted as a symbol of social reality has also been shown by art historians and archaeologists. For instance Chang Kwang-chih has argued that Shang and early Zhou art motifs may reflect changes in the man-animal relationship that run parallel with changes in mythology and the transition from ancestor worship to the worship of Heaven. Chang detects changes in zoomorphic iconography around the mid-tenth century B.C.E., from awe-inspiring animals forcing humans in a subordinate and submissive role to more conventionalized animal figures and hunting scenes wherein man challenges and subdues mythical animals.[19] Ann Paludan notes how conventional artistic attributes in tomb statuary were used to represent a standard set of social values. When representing the supernatural properties of certain creatures, artists drew on a repertoire of customary attributes such as wings, horns, scales, flames, or outstretched tongues, such that "real animals were portrayed in conventional poses emphasizing the values they symbolized."[20] Yet in an analysis of hybrid birds and beasts in Han art, Martin Powers notes that animal iconography should not be interpreted as a *direct* symbolism of social values. "The visual omen," for Powers, "is rarely a mere symbol of a social ideal. More often, by means of metaphor or metonymy, it is a close analogue of the social ideal it represents."[21]

One could filter an extensive animal lore from early Chinese writings, and—with the appropriate blind eye for text generic tropes—reconstruct "views on animals" or images evoked or symbolized by particular species. This study will take into account several such standardized animal images. However while animal categories certainly played an important role in the abstraction of images of human society in China, the question remains whether one can interpret references to the animal world in Warring States and Han texts invariably as allegorical or metaphorical representations for the purpose of comparison with or clarification of the human world. Not only is the applicability of notions such as metaphor and allegory in the context of early Chinese literature much debated, definitions have also varied profusely according to the body of texts under scrutiny and/or the literary environment that produced them.[22]

One early text that stands out for the volume of discussion its use of natural imagery has spawned is the *Shijing*. The function and meaning of animal imagery in the *Shijing* have been discussed at length by exegetes ever since the Han.[23] The use in many poems of a "stimulus" or "evocation" (*xing* 興) of nature images juxtaposed to human events has sparked a long exegetical wave of commentators and scholars seeking to connect social ideologies to particular natural images, some more convincing than others. While this exegesis has proven fruitful for the elucidation of the poesis of the *Shijing,* by singling out animal imagery and by assuming that it needs to be unveiled to reveal a social ideology behind the image, efforts to clarify the use of animals or the nature of the human-animal relationship that may be gleaned from these poems have remained marginal. To be sure, both in the case of the *Shijing* as well as in later Warring States and Han writings, the role of the author as a mediator of natural imagery and the moral semantics of his text should certainly not be dismissed. Yet assuming that an author or observer merely functioned as a bridge between two distinct orders, nature and the human world, would amount to a rather narrow assessment of early Chinese affinities toward the natural world. Even in the poesis of the *xing,* as Pauline Yu has suggested, the selection of categorical correspondences between natural imagery and human events rarely involves the complete otherness of reference. "Natural object and human situation were believed literally to belong to the same class of events (*lei* 類): it was not the poet who was creating or manufacturing links between them."[24] The view that the Chinese merely digested the natural fauna in order to illustrate a human or social principle therefore only sheds partial light on early Chinese perceptions of nature, since this approach makes projections from one realm to explicate the other and vice versa.

In sum, without intending to minimize the symbol-evoking qualities of animals, animal imagery need not always be substitutive for human behavior. This would entail that the early Chinese maintained a conceptual distinction between two independent, self-functioning worlds—the animal realm on the one hand and the human order on the other—which they then juxtaposed and explicated following literary or artistic convention. Even when an allegorical digestion of animal imagery contributes to the elucidation of human principles and social morality, the acknowledgment that many authors "looked at the animate inhabitants of their environment as reflections of their own personal and public selves" can only be a partial reflection of the ways in which the early Chinese may have conceived the human-animal relationship.[25]

This study is not the first attempt to investigate animals or aspects of the animal theme in China. Several scholars have made valuable contributions, and they will be cited where my analysis is indebted to them. Two preliminary remarks need to be made regarding the methodology I have adopted. The first concerns my choice to base this study primarily on texts, and the second is a note regarding the internal coherence and spatiotemporal diversity of the sources.

This study relies primarily on textual sources. I have not confined the scope of investigation to a particular set or genre of texts but attempted to draw on a wide corpus of received texts and archaeologically recovered manuscript evidence. Undoubtedly numerous potentially relevant passages may have been overlooked or not given the length of analysis they deserve. While I make occasional reference to archaeological evidence, a systematic discussion of material culture is beyond the scope of this study. Such a task requires the professional care of scholars of archaeology and art history. It has been my aim to focus primarily on animals as evinced in the textual world of Warring States and Han China. No doubt a systematic study of archaeological, pictorial, and other physical evidence will modify, question, and hopefully complement some of my findings. Animal remains and artifacts as well as portrayals of scenes involving "birds and beasts" on tomb murals provide a very important source for the study of the role of the animal in early Chinese society. Many pictorial scenes in Han murals for instance were inspired by episodes from the classics and other contemporary literature.[26] The methodological debate of how word and image intersect or how literary subjects are visualized is ongoing, and the dialectic approach between text and picture has proved fruitful.[27] However, the absence of a subject-specific textual corpus on animals combined with the richness and diversity of pictorial material documented in tombs has led scholars to neglect the scrutiny of texts.[28] Animal material has not been analyzed across different genres of texts and, as will be clear from the titles in the appended bibliography, there has been a tendency to limit the scope of inquiry to one text or text genre or, alternatively, to a particular animal or species.

My second caveat concerns the spatial and temporal diversity of the sources I have taken into consideration. Warring States China, and by extension the unified early empire, was a mixture of several regional cultures, each characterized by a particular climate, flora, fauna, and human habitation. This is reflected in the textual record which, on several occasions, leaves no doubt as to the fact that certain animals and animal-lore are associated with particular regions. We must therefore assume that regional variation is reflected in the way sources which link their textual ancestry to a specific region document the perception of animals. It is unlikely that the realm of animals, hybrids, demons, and spirits was uniform across the entire political entity traditionally referred to as Warring States and early imperial China. Archaeological evidence for example increasingly shows that the main Eastern Zhou states each had their own culture and some animal-lore is clearly geographically specific.[29] A good example of this is the association in texts of reptile lore with the south, or, in material culture, of "tomb-quelling" animal figurines (*zhenmushou* 鎮墓獸) with Chu 楚 culture.[30] Although the study of the perception of animals would surely benefit from regional case studies, I hope that my conjuncture of sources will illustrate that the model in which I propose to read the animal reference shows an element of consistency and applicability that transcends regional diversity traditionally associated with some sources. Attempting to map out a geo-history of animals in

Warring States and early imperial China based on the textual record currently available would be a highly speculative enterprise.

Finally, a word regarding the temporal diversity of the sources. Any account dealing with aspects of the cultural history of a society in the past falls prone to the strains of established methodologies. A theoretical bone of contention in dealing with ancient societies is the tension between a desire to historicize ideas and social practice, "to set the record straight," and a tendency on the other hand to treat societies such as ancient China and its thought as being virtually untouched by chronology. Both approaches are bound to leave a taste of dissatisfaction. This study does not attempt to provide a linear or chronological analysis of the animal theme for two reasons. First, it is my contention that the subject itself does not lend itself for analysis within a fixed diachronic frame. Second, both the social as well as the physical nature of many of the sources concerned make it difficult to date these texts or parts of texts with firm precision. As a general guideline, I have taken into account texts datable within the time frame from the Spring and Autumn period to the Eastern Han, supplemented with later sources that date evidence to the Warring States and early imperial period. Questions regarding the dating, authorship, authenticity, and transmission of certain texts or chapters are kept to a minimum. While my collective contextual reading of text fragments that span several centuries may not give due account of potential chronological developments in the perception of animals or transmissions of specific animal imagery in individual texts, I hope it will shed some light on the perception of animals within the overall mental universe of the period.[31]

CHAPTER ONE

DEFINING ANIMALS

Provided that one is prepared to allow for certain fundamental generalities that apply to most if not all living species, notions of humanity and animality, like the concept of nature itself, are to be perceived as cultural constructs. The boundaries between what is seen to belong to the realm of human culture and what is assigned to the natural world are variable and historically contingent. Whether one's focus of enquiry lies in tracing developments in the history of a science of nature, or whether one wishes to examine the cultural roots behind natural imagery, any investigation into the perception of animals in ancient and contemporary societies must take stock of this variability. In exploring the perception of animals in early China, we must therefore give heed not to assign the animal kingdom to a context of analysis that remains absent from early Chinese writings. While the modern Western mind may be impelled to view animals as subjects or objects belonging to a natural world detached from human concerns, such naturalist perception of the animal world may not have been present in the minds of the Chinese authors who compiled the texts that make up our source material. As Geoffrey Lloyd recently observed, "what we must at all costs avoid is the assumption that there is a single concept of nature towards which both Greeks and Chinese were somehow struggling, let alone that it was *our* concept of nature as in 'natural science.'"[1]

One term frequently associated with Chinese concepts of nature is *zi ran* 自然, which can be translated as "so of itself" or "so of its own accord." This term implies an emphasis on spontaneity rather than on physical and objectifiable reality. "So of itself" is in essence an adjectival qualification, it describes a state of being rather than an essential quality and is therefore not equivalent to nature as a physical world that exists of itself and by its own laws. From the outset, any investigation into Chinese perceptions of the natural world requires dealing with an ambiguity innate in its object of study itself. First, if what is natural is conceptually formulated as the mere spontaneous existence of things "of themselves," the natural world does not necessarily constitute the equivalent of what we understand as the physical world. While the world of physis can be understood as the physical world, the world of *zi ran* is just the way of things as they are and does not exclude elements one would habitually assign to the realm of human society or culture in general. Second, if the natural world is perceived as the world of that which spontaneously exists rather than a biological reality functioning according to a set of natural laws, it need not prompt definition, analysis, or explanation. In short, the natural world is a negotiated reality. As Claude Lévi-Strauss has pointed out, the researcher never engages in a dialogue with a uniform and pure concept of nature but with "a certain condition of the relationship between nature and culture, defined by the historical period in which he lives, his own civilization, and the material means he has at his disposal."[2] In several ways the analysis of Chinese animal references in this study will therefore necessitate a methodological as well as a conceptual compromise: methodological in that my analysis and interpretation of animal material in Chinese texts has been guided by structural imperatives either innate to or absent from the body of texts under investigation; conceptual in that I am trying to explicate something which in the Chinese sources has remained implicit; namely, the animal notion itself.

Problems of Definition

The initial step of an investigation into the perception of animals within the cultural context of early China may seem obvious; namely, to address the question of how Chinese authors have tried to define the animal and examine the available theoretical discourse on animals. Such exercise however does not prove to be very fruitful. Whereas the philosophical treatment and textual documentation of animals in ancient Greece began at least as early as Pythagoras (sixth cent. B.C.E.), Chinese texts from the Warring States and early imperial era remain relatively silent on animal theory.[3] Questions regarding the physiology of animals, the classification of species, the interpretation of animal behavior, or the economic and social relationship between humans and animals figured in the margins of Warring States and Han philosophical discourse. While the surrounding world of the Chinese observer, like that of his Greek or Roman counterpart, was dotted with an equally rich fauna of flying, running, swimming, and crawling creatures, the motivations behind the observation of the natural world and the way in which these were recorded and put to analytical scrutiny were of a different nature. In early China, the notion of the animal was generally not a self-evident category, and observations of animals and animal behavior did not find their way into a collective body of analytical writings.

One area that illustrates the low share of theoretical discourse on animals in early China is that of the basic terminology used to refer to animals as either a generic category or a collective of different species or groups. The classical Chinese language lacks a linguistic equivalent for the term "animal." "Animal" or "animated being," with its origins in the Platonic notion of "zoon" (ζῷον), implies a notion of animacy and inanimacy as a distinctive criterion. As a concept including everything that partakes of life, including humans and animals, as opposed to inanimate mineral and plant life, it may not be entirely compatible with classical Chinese equivalents such as *wu* 物, *shou* 獸, *qin* 禽, *chong* 蟲, or even the modern generic term for animals, *dongwu* 動物 ("moving being").[4] The difficulty in tracing the ontological status of animals as evinced in the writings of early China is reflected in the bleached terminology used to denote an animal or animal group in Chinese. Compare the following entry for "animal" in the *Oxford English Dictionary,* which provides a tentative summary of definienda associated with animals in the Western tradition. Echoing Aristotelian gradualism in biology, it contains elements such as the inferiority or superiority of species, generic typicality, and formal differentiation from opposites:

> A living being; a member of the *higher* of the two series of *organised beings,* of which the *typical forms* are endowed with life, sensation, and voluntary motion, but of which the *lowest forms* are hardly distinguishable from the lowest *vegetable forms* by any more certain marks than their *evident relationship* to other *animal forms,* and thus to the animal series as a whole rather than to the vegetable series.[5]

No one single denotative definition that summarizes the essential ontological properties of a being that approximates the Greek or Western notion of an animal can be found in early Chinese writings. Even if one is prepared to stretch semantic categories, it remains problematic to build a consensus around a graph or word in classical Chinese that covers a concept similar to the "animal" in the aforementioned dictionary entry. This is not to say that a Chinese terminology for animals is absent or less developed. The opposite is true. Several graphs in classical Chinese function as generic referents that approximate the category animal. However a general feature of most of these graphs is that they embrace plural meanings, often partly overlapping with each other.

Perhaps the most general referent to a living being is comprised in meanings associated with the graph *wu* 物. Although the *wu* graph stands out as one of the most polysemantic terms in Chinese, its origins and some of its definienda in early texts appear to link it with animals. In the *Shuowen jiezi* 說文解字, Xu Shen 許慎 (30–124 C.E.) gives the following gloss:

> [*Wu*] means the ten thousand beings (*wan wu* 萬物). The ox is a big being (*da wu* 大物). The calculation of heaven and earth (*tian di zhi shu* 天地之數, i.e., the astronomical record of the universe) starts from the Cowherd constellation. Therefore the graph consists of the element *niu* 牛 and the sound *wu* 勿.[6]

If we read this gloss through the eyes of later commentaries, the analogy between *niu* 牛 and the graph *wu* is that between the physical size of an ox and the all-encompassing semantic range of *wu* as a denominator for indeterminate "things." Likewise the function of the cowherd constellation as a primal point of orientation in the astronomical description of the cosmos is compared to the function of *wu* as the most common and functional linguistic referent to phenomena in general. The direct association with the ox element is probably Xu Shen's own fictitious rationalization as the archaic *wu* graph is linked more generally with the emblematic use of animals as early as the Shang and Zhou.[7] Some scholars have interpreted the *wu* graph as a pictographic representation of a man holding a knife and killing an ox. This has lead to the suggestion that it may represent a sacrificial animal or animal offering.[8] The *locus classicus* for *wu* in the sense of an animal offering is a *Guoyu* 國語 passage explaining the role of shamanic mediums using ritual vessels and animal offerings to communicate with the spirits.[9] Additional early evidence that may link *wu* to animals occurs in a *Zuozhuan* 左傳 passage that mentions armor decorated with animal designs, and another passage advocating the presentation of animal sacrifices to a spirit.[10] Other more generalizing statements can be found in Warring States texts, none of which however relate *wu* exclusively to animals. The *Zhuangzi* for instance paraphrases *wu* as "everything that has appearance, image, sound and color."[11]

Other characters used to denote animals reflect a similar polysemy. First there are the graphs *shou* 獸 and *qin* 禽, traditionally translated as "beasts" and "birds." Again, a uniformity of definition is hard to trace. In its gloss for *shou* the *Shuowen* states that creatures with two feet are called *qin,* and quadrupeds are called *shou.*[12] According to another early lexicon, the *Erya* 爾雅, a creature is called a *shou* when it has four feet and hair, and a *qin* if it has two feet and feathers.[13] Xu Shen further defines *qin* as a common denomination for "walking beasts" (*zou shou* 走獸).[14] A text fragment ascribed to a Han compilation known as the *Bohutong* 白虎通 defines *qin* in a pun on its secondary meaning as a verb "to capture" and states that the graph is "a general name for birds and quadrupeds, illustrating that they are 'imprisoned' (*qinzhi* 禽制) by man."[15] According to Zheng Xuan 鄭玄 (127–200 C.E.) *qin* denotes birds and quadrupeds that are not yet impregnated.[16] While these sets of definienda refer to the number of feet and the presence or absence of feathers or hair, other definitions are mere paronomastic glosses. Thus Xu Shen further qualifies *shou* as "that which guards and protects" (*shou bei* 守備), a definition based on the homophony of the characters 獸 *sjeu and 守 *hrjegwx, and the inclusion of the dog radical (*quan* 犬), the dog being the exemplary guardian animal.[17] He Xiu 何休 (129–82 C.E.) glosses the graph referring to the winter hunt, *shou* 狩, as 獸, the idea being that in winter game animals are fat and ready to be hunted.[18] *Shou* 獸 is also connected with the idea of the wilds. The *Erya* for instance distinguishes *shou* "wild animals" from *chu* 畜 "domesticated animals" in two separate chapters. Kong Yingda 孔穎達 (574–648 C.E.) comments elsewhere that what is fed at home is called a *chu* "domestic animal," while what lives in the wilds is called a *shou* "wild animal."[19] Together with the isolation of domestic animals as a distinct group the use of the term *liu chu* 六畜 "six domestic animals" emerges. The origins of the term *liu chu* are uncertain. The expression occurs as early as the *Zuozhuan* but may be older. It is specified regularly into six concrete animals in sources from the third century B.C.E. onward.[20] The Qin daybooks or *rishu* 日書 (dated ca. 217 B.C.E.) excavated at Shuihudi 睡虎地 (Hubei; discovered in 1975–1976) contain a list including the horse, ox, sheep, pig, dog, and chicken, and frequently use the term *liu chu*.[21] The *Zhouli* mentions the terms *liu shou* 六獸 "six beasts," *liu qin* 六禽 "six birds," and *liu chu* 六畜. According to Zheng Xuan *liu chu* refers to the same set of animals as those covered by the term *liu sheng* 六牲 "the six sacrificial animals," with *liu chu* referring to animals during the initial process of breeding and *liu sheng* to animals that are about to be used in sacrifice.[22] No further information on the origins of these collective terms for wild and domesticated animals is preserved in contemporary sources.

Another red herring is the character *chong* 蟲, which is a polysemantic word comprising animals in general, insects or invertebrates in particular. The earliest etymological definition of the graph *hui* 虫 occurs in the *Shuowen*, where it is glossed as the name for a viper and explained as a term for any small animal that creeps or flies, is hairy or naked, and has a shell or scales.[23] The polysemantic nature of *chong* is further illustrated by its usage in early medical literature where it can cover anything from bugs, worms, reptiles, and insects to other parasitic vermin.[24]

Finally there is little evidence that the binome *dongwu* 動物 "moving beings," which also functions as the generic name for animals in modern Chinese, was used as a consistent referent to animals in early China. Possibly the earliest occurrence of *dongwu* as a generic reference for animals occurs in the *Zhouli*, where it is juxtaposed against plants (*zhiwu* 植物) and humans (*min* 民).[25] To my knowledge there are no other passages where this binome distinguishes animals from plants and human beings, or where it exclusively refers to animals rather than moving phenomena in general.

This brief survey of terminology is not exhaustive. Several other classifying terms that refer to specific groups of animals could be added such as *lin* 鱗 for scaly animals, *jie* 介 for armored species, *mao* 毛 for hairy animals, *yu* 羽 for feathered species, and *luo* 裸/蠃 for naked animals. Yet as is the case with the definitions surveyed above, diverging opinions exist among early commentators and modern scholars as to the precise body of creatures these terms refer to, not in the least as to whether humans are consistently referred to as naked animals.[26] It may be clear from the above outline that the early Chinese corpus, or at least those texts which have survived, contains few attempts at authoritative definition or at developing a univocal animal terminology that sought to delineate the formal and behavioral characteristics of the main animal groups. Chinese writings of the Warring States and Han periods rarely collect observations from nature in order to evaluate that knowledge with a view to establishing a vocabulary that could claim universality and contribute to a theoretical model of the animal world.[27]

One way of circumventing the problem could be to side with scholars who seek to attribute the absence of denotative description to the particularity of the Chinese language, which may or may not provide the linguistic tools to articulate formal definitions. Philosophers and linguists have argued that the notion of definition itself needs to be qualified in the Chinese context. In a recent study Christoph Harbsmeier notes that "the Chinese tended to be interested in definitions not in a Socratic way and for their own sake as descriptions of the essence of things, and they were very rarely interested in definition as an abstract art in the Aristotelian manner."[28] David Hall and Roger Ames express a similar caution against the search for natural essences in Chinese definitions:

> The Chinese don't seem to know what a definition is! . . . The confusion is easy enough to overcome, however. Once we recognize that there is no basis for appeal to objective connotation in the sense that there can be no effort to characterize all of the essential properties common to the members of a class, then we shall understand that there can be no objective denotation in which, presupposing the connotative properties, we could point out all the members of a class. Once we understand this, we shall avoid demanding a definition and remain content with asking for concrete examples and models.[29]

While definitions, even when presented in their culturally specific reincarnation as exemplary models, may provide a source of knowledge of the Chinese conceptual world, one should note that their absence, as in the case of generic animal terminology, can be an equally rich source of insight. In short any attempt to address animals as a category runs the inherent danger of resorting to a terminology that is not paradigm-free, and colored Greek or Western for that matter. Any endeavor to integrate precarious notions such as "definition," "classification," or "species" should therefore be veiled in a cautious *caveat*. While one should try to avoid imposing modern schemes of biological and philosophical logic on ancient Chinese texts, the lack of a compatible terminology for the study of animals will on occasions necessitate the use of Western, culturally specific terminology. In this study I will have to revert to terms such as "animal," "animated being," or "creature," although such choice of words might not always accurately reflect the original Chinese concepts they intend to represent. My reservation is that they be used in as much a paradigm-free manner as possible.

Stepping away from the issue of definition in early Chinese epistemology, another test to measure attitudes toward the definition of animals in early China and assess the reception of animal terminology is to examine how later Chinese scholars themselves perceived the issue. It then appears that not only do we find comments on the subject to be extremely scarce, but also that observations regarding the absence of a theory of animals are not exclusive to the Western observer. For instance, in a work entitled *Bian wu xiaozhi* 辨物小志 ("Short Treatise on the Discrimination of Things"), the Ming scholar Chen Jiang 陳絳 (fl. ca. 1530) points at the polysemy of terms used to refer to the main animal groups. The following extract illustrates his confusion regarding the ways in which the ancients used animal terminology:

> Bipeds with feathers are called *qin* 禽. Quadrupeds with hair are called *shou* 獸. Thus a *shou* can also be called a *qin* [having four feet implies having two]. The *Changes* (*Yi* 易) states that if one approaches deer without a hunter, one follows the *qin*. A deer hence is also a *qin*. In the Quli 曲禮 (chapter of the *Liji* 禮記) it is said that although the ape can talk, it is not different from the *qin* and *shou*. An ape hence is also a *qin*. The *Yili* 儀禮 takes *qin* to constitute the six gifts. In the case of a minister the gift is a lamb; a lamb is therefore also a *qin*. The duodenary animals in Cai Yong's 蔡邕 *Yueling wen da* 月令問答 ("Questions and Answers about the Monthly Ordinances")—being the rat, ox, tiger, rabbit, horse, sheep, monkey, chicken, dog, pig, dragon and snake—are all *qin*. . . . A *qin* is also called a *shou*. According to the *Zhouli* . . . there are five classes of big *shou* under heaven, including the naked, feathered and scaly animals. This means that birds, dragons and snakes are all *shou*.[30]

Chen constructs a circular argument in order to demonstrate that *qin* and *shou* are mutually overlapping categories. Rather than making a statement on the natural world, his method is lexicographic and follows a model often used by modern scholars trying to explain classical animal terminology; namely, tracing the occurrence of certain key terms and comparing the semantic fields of similar graphs in different contexts. The results are, as can be seen in Chen's statement, equally variant and confusing. His statement suggests that in order to gain any understanding of early Chinese animal theory, one must start by recognizing its low share within Warring States and Han intellectual discourse and acknowledge the polysemantic nature of many of the basic animal terms.

Animals in Texts

From animal terminology, we proceed to the textual record of animal theory. One only needs to take a bird's-eye view of the transmitted Warring States, Qin, and Han textual corpus to determine that the received record has hardly transmitted any textual material that deals with animals in a systematized or exclusive manner. As in the case of the absence of a denotative animal terminology, the fact that early Chinese writings did not single out animals as an autonomous topic of discussion or topos in itself reveals much about the status of animals as subjects of intellectual debate. While animal material is omnipresent in early Chinese texts, this material did not evolve into systematized zoological theorization. This relative scarcity of zoological theory and the absence of a (proto)zoological corpus implies by no means that the physical fauna was a topic not worthy of disputation. It does however reflect on the biological and sociological standing of animals and their relationship with the human world in early Chinese thought. Both individual comments on the kind of knowledge a human observer can draw from the animal kingdom as well as the genre of texts in which animal material has been recorded show that the protoscientific inquiry of animals remained secondary to discussions of their practical use and explanations of animal nomenclature.

     Few early Chinese texts engage in a theoretical discussion on whether and how the human observer should gather information about and organize data from the natural world. On the contrary, an expertise in the detached observation and analysis of the natural world does not appear to be considered a trademark of the human sage. A passage in a Han work known as the *Chunqiu fanlu* 春秋繁露 ("Luxuriant Dew of the Spring and Autumn") states that "being able to explain the species of birds and beasts (*shuo niaoshou zhi lei* 說鳥獸 之類) is not the desire of a sage. The sage wants to explain benevolence and righteousness and regulate those. . . ."[31] This rare epistemological statement on the human sage's approach toward the animal world suggests that the human sage should not engage in taxonomic definition and in the differentiation of categories in the animal world. Instead the sage should devote his efforts to regulating and elucidating human values. The sage here is said not to be preoccupied with the explanation of categories (*lei* 類) in the natural world but with the clarification of ethical principles in human society. That the author traditionally associated with this text, Dong Zhongshu 董仲舒 (179–104 B.C.E.), may have been renowned for his agnostic attitude toward the animal world is exemplified in an apocryphal anecdote. It accounts that Dong was so earnest in his study that, during a period of three years, he did not throw a glance at the parks, and when riding a horse he did not know whether it was a mare or a stallion.[32]

     At first reading, the *Chunqiu fanlu* statement seems to suggest that the animal realm was a topic not worthy of a sage-ruler's scrutiny. However, this is not necessarily the case. The text states that the sage does not "explain" (*shuo* 說) the species of birds and beasts. The verb *shuo* has the connotation of "analysis" and is glossed by Xu Shen as *shi* 釋, "to explain, unravel (a meaning)."[33] A constituent graph in this last character, *bian* 釆, likewise conveys the meaning of "discriminating" or "separating one (category) from another." Xu Shen glosses it as "to discriminate and separate" (*bianbie* 辨別) and suggests that its pictographic origins resemble the "distinction and separation of animal toes and claws," an image that echoes Cang Jie's 蒼頡 legendary invention of the character script based on the foot tracks of birds.[34] The etymologies underlying the use of *shuo* here may therefore refer to one particular notion of discrimination; namely, a process in which the differentiation between animal categories or species consists of the enumeration of *differentiae* between species A and B. In other words, while the sage may not preoccupy himself with distinguishing species differentiae, the author by no means infers that sages should simply disregard the animal world. In fact the *Chunqiu fanlu* devotes considerable attention to the classification of animals and sacrificial victims within its correlative models.[35] Implied in the *Chunqiu fanlu*'s agnostic statement is the idea that taxonomic differentiation constitutes only one particular and, hence, partial way of gaining knowledge of the animal world. As we will see, taxonomy is a hermeneutic process which, in early China, was deeply entrenched in lexicography, as can be seen, for instance, in the titles of the "zoological" chapters of the *Erya* (*shi chong* 釋蟲, *shi yu* 釋魚, *shi niao* 釋鳥, *shi shou* 釋獸, *shi chu* 釋畜).

A second significant reference that comments on the relationship between sagacity and the *episteme* of the natural world needs to be addressed. In the *Lunyu* 論語, Confucius admonishes his pupils to study the *Shijing* and argues that through the study of the Odes one would acquire, among other qualities such as the capacity for observation and communion, a "wide knowledge of the *names* of birds and beasts, plants and trees" (*duo shi yu niaoshou caomu zhi ming* 多識於 鳥獸草木之名).[36] Confucius alludes here to the rich body of animals and plants used as rhetorical "stimuli" or "comparisons" (*bi* 比) in the Odes. While the identification of animal and plant names constitutes only one element in a longer series of human qualities one can obtain by studying the Odes, this passage remains important both in terms of its advocacy of the Odes as a source of exegesis of the natural world and in its indication as to how natural imagery is "knowledgeable." First, Confucius notes that the Odes are to be taken as a basic thesaurus and authoritative lexicon for the understanding of the animal world. Second, such knowledge is not specified as a process of discrimination between species but as a recognition of names (*ming* 名). Rather than referring to an act of differentiation between species and kinds, Confucius proposes an epistemology of the living species that consists of knowing their names. Joseph Needham has argued that this quote should oblige us to believe that "in the closing years of the sixth century B.C., canons of botanical and zoological nomenclature were being actively discussed by the learned."[37] This proposition is questionable. The *Shijing* is certainly the oldest extant and most extensive textual source of animal lore. This is already noted by Sima Qian 司馬遷 (ca. 145–86 B.C.E.) who qualifies the Odes as a record of "mountains and rivers, valleys and gorges, birds and beasts, herbs and trees, female and male animals, and female and male birds."[38] The importance of the Odes as a source of botanical and zoological lore is also reflected in titles of later lexicons, encyclopedic treatises, and dictionaries that focused on classifying and annotating its rich fauna and flora. The earliest among these is Lu Ji's 陸璣 (ca. 222–280 C.E.) *Mao shi caomu niaoshou chongyu shu* 毛詩

草木鳥獸蟲魚疏 ("Explanatory Notes on the Plants, Trees, Birds, Quadrupeds, Insects and Fish in Mao's *Shijing*"), which sparked the compilation of many similar works in later periods.[39] The first lexicons and their commentaries as well as later commentaries to historical and ritual texts by Eastern Han and post-Han exegetes primarily based their explanations of animal nomenclature on precedents from the *Shijing*. However, two other significant points follow from Confucius's observation; namely, the question of the genre of literature in which this animal imagery was incorporated, and the emphasis put on animal nomenclature and the act of naming.

While Needham presumed that scholars actively discussed animal nomenclature and possibly wrote them down in zoological compendia now lost to us, it seems to me that Confucius's instruction reveals a more important point. As a primary reference tool for the knowledge of animals, Confucius refers to a book of poetry and folk songs rather than to a zoological compendium or analytical treatise of some kind. This suggests that, rather than being an exercise in the recognition of animals and plants, the identification of animal and plant names in the Odes was more likely, as Steven Van Zoeren has pointed out, "a natural outgrowth of the sort of textual exegesis that went on in a pedagogical setting."[40] In other words, if animal nomenclature were actively discussed by the learned, why write them down in poetry? Although active discussions of animal nomenclature were part of a larger project of poetical exegesis, they present rather weak evidence to authenticate the existence of a living tradition of protozoological enquiry.

The qualification of a textual genre by Confucius is significant, since the nature of the surviving literature available for the study of the animal in early China reveals something about the animal concept itself and the place of animals as a topic of intellectual discourse. As I have already indicated, the corpus of surviving Warring States and Han texts has transmitted hardly any records dealing with topics that approximate the concerns of early Greek or Roman zoological writings.[41] Zoology, in its sense of a science or protoscience that deals with the animal world and its members as individuals and classes, and with animal life and morphology, does not form an autonomous topic of scholarly discourse in received early Chinese writings. Chinese philosophers did not develop a body of texts that systematized or articulated empirical data from the animal kingdom.[42] This is not to say that, as will be shown in chapter 3, certain texts do not contain a considerable amount of animal data or that a naturalistic interest in the animal world is entirely absent in the works of the masters of philosophy in Warring States and early imperial times. To give one example, a work such as Wang Chong's 王充 (27–ca. 100 c.e.) *Lunheng* 論衡 ("Disquisitions Weighed in the Balance") contains large sections as well as several chapters that deal specifically with animal topics ("Encountering Tigers," "Discussing Insects," "Untruths about Dragons," and others).[43] However, to identify these text passages as zoological or objectivity-oriented discussions of the animal world would be problematic. Most of Wang Chong's argumentation aims at refuting popular beliefs and superstitions regarding certain animals and daemonic creatures. While much valuable information regarding the perception of animals is transmitted in Wang's rebuttals, the prime motivation of his discourse does not stem from an intrinsic interest in analyzing animals.

With the masters of philosophy remaining largely silent on the collection and interpretation of data from the animal world and with protozoological works virtually nonexisting, what about more practical and technical works on animals? The analysis of data from the natural world and natural philosophy in the Warring States period was predominantly the domain of natural experts such as astrologers, physicians, diviners, the makers of almanacs, and practitioners of related specialties. The excavation of new manuscripts over the past three decades increasingly reveals the wide range of specialist literature in which magicoreligious and naturalistic views of the world are blended. New discoveries are sure to follow and shed new light on the contents of these specialist texts and the extent to which they circulated.[44] It is noteworthy however that among this body of technical texts, writings dealing with animals and animal material in general are relatively scarce. Texts and manuals dealing with the mundane preoccupations of the Warring States farmer or herdsman—such as animal breeding, animal domestication and husbandry, animal physiognomy, and animal medicine—have only been preserved in small number. While this may partly be due to the selective survival of texts, the limited reference to a technical literature on animals in the received corpus suggests that such literature did not flourish or, alternatively, that the technical discourse on animals may have been deemed unworthy of canonical survival.

Judging from the reproduction of Liu Xin's 劉歆 (46 B.C.E.–23 C.E.) catalogue of the imperial library at Chang'an 長安 preserved in the *Hanshu* 漢書, few substantial writings on animals other than lexicographic materials (surveyed below) and a series of technical works dealing with animal physiognomy, tortoise divination, and fishing appear to have circulated or gained the recognition that earned them a place in the imperial bibliography. These include a lost work entitled *Xiang liu chu* 相六畜 ("Physiognomizing the Six Domestic Animals") in six scrolls,[45] and a text entitled *Zhao Mingzi diao zhong sheng yu bie* 昭明子釣種生魚鼈 ("Zhao Mingzi's [manual] on Fishing, Planting, and Raising Fish and Turtles") in eight scrolls.[46] Zhao Mingzi is unknown in the received record. The first text is listed under the bibliographic division "Xing fa" 形法 ("Configuration Models"), the second under the division "Za zhan" 雜占 ("Miscellaneous Divination").

A similar work on fishing entitled *Yangyujing* 養魚經 ("Classic on Fish Farming"), whose putative authorship is attributed to Fan Li 范蠡, is mentioned in the bibliographic treatise of the *Jiu Tangshu* 舊唐書.[47] The figure of Fan Li, a grandee from the state of Yue 越 active during the first half of the fifth century B.C.E., is also linked to manuals on fish breeding under his honorific name of Taozhu Gong 陶朱公. A work entitled *Taozhu Gong yang yu fa* 陶朱公養魚法 ("Taozhu Gong's Methods for Fish Farming") is preserved in fragments in a sixth-century C.E. manual on agriculture.[48] Fan Li's association with aquatic creatures is further attested in an exchange in the *Guoyu*, where he puts the people of Yue rhetorically on a par with animals and refers to his Yue ancestry as unaccomplished vassals of the royal house of Zhou living on the shores of the eastern sea amidst tortoises and fish.[49]

In a section entitled "Shi gui" 蓍龜 ("Milfoil and Turtle"), the Han bibliographic catalogue further contains a series of works related to tortoise divination.[50] Tang bibliographic treatises contain other titles on animal physiognomy, some of which are attributed apocryphally to earlier authors. They include a work entitled *Xiangniujing* 相牛經 ("Classic on Cattle Physiognomy") whose putative author was Ning Qi 甯戚, a grandee at the court of Duke Huan 桓 of Qi 齊 (685–643 B.C.E.);[51] a work entitled *Xianghejing* 相鶴經 ("Classic on the Physiognomy of Cranes") attributed to the legendary immortal Fu Qiugong 浮丘公; and anonymous technical works such as a *Xiangbeijing* 相貝經 ("Classic on the Physiognomy of Shells"), a *Yingjing* 鷹經 ("Classic on Falcons/Falconry"), and a *Canjing* 蠶經 ("Classic on Silkworms").[52] A shepherd from Henan by the name of Bu Shi 卜式 (fl. ca. 111 B.C.E.) is accredited with the authorship of a work entitled *Yang yang fa* 養羊法 ("Methods for Sheep Farming").[53]

Although no body of early veterinary literature has been transmitted, reference to animal healers as well as to the medicinal treatment of animals in several texts suggests that such technical literature may have been circulating. The idealized description of the offices in the royal state of Zhou preserved in the *Zhouli* includes the office of an animal doctor and a horse sorcerer.[54] In addition to the use of animal physiognomy, which may have been part of early veterinary practice, animal practitioners most likely used a combination of shamanic and medicinal healing.[55] A mural depicting the castration of a bull has been recovered from an Eastern Han tomb in county Fangcheng 方城 (Henan).[56] Reference to animal healing occurs most frequently in relation to the horse, which confirms that in Warring States and Han China, as elsewhere, horses were considered a particularly valuable asset.[57] One legendary horse healer was Ma Shihuang 馬師皇 who was allegedly active at the time of the legendary Yellow Emperor. According to one account, his healing skills were so efficient that a dragon spontaneously gave itself up to receive Ma's needle treatment.[58] In general, animal doctors were probably deemed quite low on the social ladder. Xunzi 荀子, for example, accuses those who adhere to paradoxical sophist theorems as being stupid by stating that their attitude does not even amount to making a reputation for oneself by physiognomizing chickens or dogs.[59] A story in the *Liezi* 列子 mentions a horse doctor together with a beggar and suggests that both professions received the scorn of the nobility.[60]

Other, less technical writings may have included substantial information on animals, animal lore, and magicoreligious beliefs and practices associated with animals. These include titles of lost works such as the *Ren gui jingwu liu chu bian-guai* 人鬼精物六畜變怪 ("Human and Demonic Spectral Entities and the Mutant Prodigies of the Six Domestic Animals"),[61] and a work entitled *Za qinshou liu chu kunchong fu* 雜禽獸六畜昆蟲賦 ("Miscellaneous Rhapsodies on Birds, Beasts, the Six Domestic Animals and Various Insects").[62] This last work presumably included poetic expositions on the animal theme or didactic morality tales such as the one that appears in a recently discovered late Western Han manuscript recovered from a tomb at Yinwan 尹灣 (Jiangsu; excavated in 1993). In this piece, entitled *Shen wu fu* 神烏賦 "Rhapsody on the Spirit Crows," crows are praised for their sense of benevolence as they egorge their food to their parents, practice righteousness, and grasp the way of humans. It tells the story of a bitter rivalry between a foraging pair of crows diligently searching for materials to build their nest and a robber crow attempting to steal their nest provisions. Despite having chosen to build their nests in a tree at the residence of an official whose "kindness reached to the insects and worms," the couple is not spared from the robber crow's intrusion. A bitter fight ensues in which the female crow gets injured. The male bird is left to wail because it cannot follow its partner in death.[63]

The titles of technical literature transmitted in the received canon can be supplemented with a series of recently excavated manuscripts. The excavation of two manuscripts on dog physiognomy have been reported at the sites of Yinqueshan 銀雀山 (county Linyi 臨沂, Shandong; second century B.C.E., discovered in 1972) and Shuanggudui 雙古堆 (Fuyang 阜陽, Anhui; burial dated ca. 165 B.C.E., excavated in 1977).[64] The Yinqueshan manuscript is severely damaged. One scholar has speculated that it mainly deals with hunting dogs.[65] Furthermore, mention should be made of a text known as the *Xiangmajing* 相馬經 ("Classic on the Physiognomy of Horses") excavated at Mawangdui 馬王堆 (Hunan).[66] An early Western Han manuscript assigned the title *Wanwu* 萬物 ("Myriad Things") excavated at Fuyang in Anhui contains technical and medical material and includes devices for catching animals and expelling venomous pests. The Mawangdui medical corpus likewise contains a rich thesaurus of animal drugs.[67]

Finally data on animals have been preserved in administrative and legal texts. Among Han administrative documents excavated in the northwestern frontier region of Juyan 居延, a fragmentary cattle register has been recovered from a site at Taralingin-durbeljin (Dawan 大灣).[68] Considerable attention is given to animals in the Qin daybooks and legal documents excavated at Shuihudi and Longgang 龍崗 (Hubei; discovered in 1989–1991). Calendrical and legal texts comprised a broad set of topics pertaining to daily life, and legal disputes regarding animals covered a wide range of issues. The Qin legal codes refer to the theft of animals, dissatisfactory results or malpractice in the breeding of cattle and horses, the suitability of horses for the army, rules regarding the breeding of chickens and pigs, animals in private parks, the tiger hunt, and the wounding of carriage horses.[69] The Longgang slips contain legislation on private parks and the management of horses, sheep, and cattle. For instance one article that deals with trespassing animals stipulates that the attribution of legal liability to animals should depend on the status of the owner and the behavior of the animals: "When dogs belonging to the black-haired (common) people enter into the Forbidden Parks but do not chase nor kill its (resident) animals, they do not (need to be killed). But if they do chase and catch animals . . . kill them."[70]

Compared with the output of other technical Warring States and Han writings—texts that deal with astronomy, medicine, calendrical calculation, and divination—this is a relatively small number of texts, many of which are now lost or have been preserved only in fragmentary manuscript form. It is difficult to assess whether such specialized literature might perhaps not have survived the 213 B.C.E. burning of the books. I believe that the output of both "zoological" and "zootechnical" literature was probably relatively small. Writings that dealt with the practical observation and management of animals would hardly have been considered a potential danger to Qin's legalist ideology. If writings on animal husbandry, animal physiognomy and divination, or veterinary practice were in circulation in large numbers in pre-Qin times, they were likely to survive the bibliocaust along with works on medicine, divination, arboriculture and agriculture. To be sure, the chance survival of texts does not provide a sufficient explanation for the absence of a zoological corpus or clarify why, to paraphrase Edward Schafer, in ancient China goat antelopes hobnobbed with gibbons as if modern ecology did not exist.[71] But while absence of evidence does not necessarily constitute evidence of absence, the record currently available suggests that it is unlikely that a large body of systematized textual material dealing with animals was in circulation in the period in question. As such, the early Chinese corpus contrasts with the situation in ancient Greece where, by the late fourth century, Aristotle (384–322 B.C.E.) had compiled a considerable body of zoological treatises,[72] still predating the first Chinese dictionaries that contained entries according to "zoological" headings—mainly the *Erya* and *Shuowen jiezi*—by more than two hundred years.

Another reason for the scarcity of transmitted animal material may be the absence of a record of animal domestication in early China. Animal husbandry played a minor role in traditional Chinese agriculture. Livestock was certainly kept by Chinese farmers, but in far smaller numbers than in Europe. Among the domesticated animals, dogs and pigs have the longest history.[73] Meat itself constituted a relatively minor share in the traditional Chinese diet, in which grains and vegetables constituted the main food.[74] While evidence suggests that a large variety of hunted game was consumed, one can assume that these products predominantly ended up in the kitchens of the elites and the nobility. Food remains and stomach contents from Mawangdui suggest that a wide variety of hunted animals were thought to be fit for human consumption. These include wild rabbits and sika deer, pheasants, cranes, turtledoves, wild geese, partridges, magpies, and ringed pheasants.[75] But even allowing for the consumption of game animals among elites, the Chinese diet was nowhere as carnivorous as its European counterpart.

From a zoohistorical point of view, the omnipresence of animals in the received record as well as in archaeological and art historical evidence indicates that this scarcity of specialized or systematizing texts does not suggest a priori that the animal was a marginal subject in early Chinese texts, nor that the use of animals in early China was somehow peripheral. Apart from multiple animal references in literary, historiographic, lexicographic, and technical sources, a detailed attention to animals is also attested in ritual canons (mainly the *Zhouli, Liji,* and *Yili*). As chapter 2 will show, ritual texts document in great detail the use of animals as sacrificial viands and their presentation as exchange gifts or as symbols of social and ritual status, and they reflect a detailed attention to the role of animals in early Chinese religion.

In sum, if we are to gain a balanced picture of how animals were perceived in early China, they should be examined through the lens of the various textual genres in which they appear. We should refrain from confining our conclusions to the small number of texts or text fragments which at first sight approximate "zoological" writings, a concept which in itself is culturally specific.[76] Given the number and nature of transmitted textual sources or title references from the Warring States and early imperial period, there is room to infer that the vast majority of the extant texts are characterized by the absence of a conscious effort to dissociate animal nomenclature and specialized discourse regarding animals from the literary contexts in which they appear by integrating them into separate canons. This is a significant background for the further study of the animal theme in early Chinese texts. Not only does it indicate that concepts of what was perceived as an animal or animalistic being have to be derived from a variety of sources including literary, historiographical, and philosophical texts, the absence of an elaborate attempt at (proto)zoological theorization also suggests that animals and their relation to the other living species were viewed within different paradigms. The next section will show that a model of names deeply influenced the early Chinese representation and interpretation of the animal world.

Naming Animals and Animal Names

As indicated in the aforementioned *Lunyu* quote, Confucius's exhortation to study the *Shijing* as a window on the animal world was an appeal to study their names. According to Confucius, knowledge about animals was to be acquired through the exegesis of their names in a literary text. While the detached analysis

of animals appears to have been of minor importance to scholars and philosophers, the role of naming and the mastery of animal nomenclature were central
elements in the early Chinese perception of the animal world. Rather than
studying animal behavior, animal physiology, or the mutual relationships
among species in the natural world, scholars focused on taxonomizing the textual thesaurus used to represent this world. This is reflected first and foremost
in a recurring emphasis on the etymological classification of animal nomenclature. It can also be seen in passages that present the comprehension of names as
the epistemological means to comprehend and control the workings of the animal world. While this focus on the clarification of nomenclature did not relegate the biological animal to the margins of protoscientific interest, identifying
animals through names and naming, in addition to providing the underlying
principle for the lexicographic classification of animal graphs, also figured as a
way in which one could exert an intellectual command over the natural world.

Texts that filtered animal lore out of their literary contexts were mainly
lexicographic in nature and not discursive or argumentative. In several of these
works, explaining animals is synonymous with explaining their names. A brief
survey of the *status quaestionis* of transmitted texts and text chapters dealing with
animals as a more or less autonomous subject matter up to the end of the Eastern
Han will illustrate this. Works such as the *Erya* 爾雅, *Ji jiu pian* 急就篇, *Fangyan*
方言, *Shuowen jiezi,* and *Shanhaijing* illustrate how the early Chinese "zoology"
of the natural world amounted to a "nominology" of the textual referents available to describe its animal inhabitants.

The main and oldest transmitted lexicon that devotes substantial sections
to animal nomenclature is the *Erya*. Scholarly consensus situates its compilation between the fourth and second centuries B.C.E. It contains five chapters on
animals dealing with insects, fish, birds, wild animals, and domestic animals,
and it may be the first source that dissociates domestic animals (*chu* 畜) from
others as a separate category.[77] Following the research of Naitō Torajirō 內藤虎
次郎, Joseph Needham submits that its chapters on natural history were composed between 300 and 160 B.C.E., with the chapter on domestic animals slightly
later between 180 and 140 B.C.E. He further notes the close association of its animal nomenclature with the Odes, the Mao Heng 毛亨 commentary of which
reached its definite form around the same time (ca. 220–150 B.C.E.).[78] In the
preface of the principal subcommentary to the work, Xing Bing 邢昺 (932–1010
C.E.) emphasizes its importance as a compendium of animal nomenclature by
alluding to Confucius's canonical *Lunyu* quote on the *Shijing.* He states that the
work "enables one to have a broad comprehension of things and be without
doubts. For an extensive knowledge of the names of birds, beasts, plants, and
trees, nothing comes near the quality of the *Erya*."[79]

Although clearly distinguishing between five groups of animals in its chapter titles as well as utilizing the classifier *shu* 屬,[80] the *Erya* gives no definitions of

the principal classifying terms *chong* 蟲, *yu* 魚, *niao* 鳥, *shou* 獸, and *chu* 畜. One of its rare generic comments is included in the chapter on *chong*, which ends with a statement that "those with feet are called *chong* 蟲, and those without feet are called *zhi* 豸."[81] The *Erya* is predominantly a list of names and focuses on the explanation of graphs/names. Its main preoccupation lies, as Wang Guowei 王國維 (1877–1927) has pointed out, with the explanation of *ming* 名.[82] Most entries are definiendum-definiens pairs (e.g., 蟬 *tan* [is/means] [a/the] 白魚 "white fish") and thus much of the *Erya* is in fact a synonymicon.[83]

The *Erya* animal chapters do not provide a zoological differentiation of the animal world. Its general categories appear to be distinguished on the basis of a mixture of biological and lexicographic criteria. Recurring biological criteria include differentiae such as male-female, great-small, and the use of *zi* 子 to indicate the young or fledglings of a species.[84] The *chong* chapter includes reptiles, amphibians, crustaceans, piscines, and turtles, as well as insects.[85] The *yu* chapter includes tortoises, snakes, and geckos, as well as several graphs with a *chong* radical.[86] The chapter on *shou* includes a reference to humans.[87] The *niao* chapter includes the bat (*bianfu* 蝙蝠) and the *wushu* 鼯鼠 rat, presumably because both have wings. Because of their wings bats were known as "immortal rats" (*xianshu* 仙鼠) in the state of Qi. Other dialectal variants in the eastern part of the empire included *feishu* 飛鼠 "flying rat" and *laoshu* 老鼠 "old rat."[88]

Occasionally, the *Erya* includes a short biological generalization or description of an animal's behavior. Although this is usually limited to a record of color, size, shape, or habitat, in some entries more detailed information is given.[89] For instance we learn that the *guanzhuan* 鸛鶉, or *furou* 鶝鶔 bird, looks like the magpie, has a short tail and, when being shot at, will catch the arrow in its beak and shoot it off at humans. Elsewhere a list is included of terms describing mastication and, in the case of birds, ways of flying.[90] The chapter on birds also contains a statement on how to distinguish male from female birds:

> In case one cannot distinguish between female and male birds, do it by means of the wings; if the right wing covers over the left wing then it is a male bird, if the left wing covers over the right then it is a female bird.[91]

The main emphasis in the *Erya* animal chapters however is on the recognition of an animal and the association of the right name (graph) with the appropriate creature, rather than on the cognition of the biological properties of the animals themselves. The latter is further illustrated by an entry on the identification of a bird and rat that share the same biotope: "If a bird and a rat reside in the same hole, the bird is a *yu* 鵌 and the rat is a *tu* 鼵."[92] This gloss gives data on particular animal behavior in order to assist the reader to connect a name with two creatures in the same habitat. Knowledge of the name of one animal leads to knowing the name of the other. No comment is given as to why these two creatures choose to live together. Throughout the *Erya* biological information is subjected to the explanation of nomenclature.[93]

A second, much overlooked, source is a short work with the title *Ji jiu pian* 急就篇, identified by Needham as a "Handy Primer."[94] The bibliographic treatise in the *Hanshu* lists it (in one scroll) under the category of the "Minor Studies" 小學 (i.e., language, text, and script studies, "philology") and attributes its compilation to Shi You 史游 (ca. 48–33 B.C.E.), who was active at the Han court as Director of Eunuch Attendants under Emperor Yuan 元帝 (49–33 B.C.E.).[95] Judging from the extant version, the book consists of a series of mnemonic character lists in tri-, tetra-, and heptasyllabic verses often ending in alternating end rhymes. Interspersed throughout the text are mnemotechnic lists of animals. In line with the primer's objectives indicated in its introduction—"to set out and order the names, surnames, and styles of all things" (*luo lie zhu wu ming xing zi* 羅列諸物 名姓字)[96]—the structure of the entries is aimed at the recitative memorization of various groups of names including animals, plants, cloths, tools, titles, and diseases. A few examples illustrate the format in which its animal material appears:

> Among the six domestic animals are nourished:
> sucking pigs, hogs, swine,
> boars, gelded pigs, hounds and dogs,
> wild chickens and chicks . . .

> When pigeon, dove, quail or speckle bird hit the net they die.
> Kites, magpies, harriers and owls stare at each other in alarm . . .

> Flying Dragon and Phoenix follow each other.
> Child Demon Shooter (*sheji* 射支 / 魅) and Expeller of Evil (*bixie* 辟邪)
> will eradicate all bane.

> What can be brought about by accumulated study
> is not a question of ghosts and spirits.[97]

The first two extracts are couplets enumerating domestic and wild animals. The third example deals with two well-known sacred animals whose names also refer to constellations. The next example deals with two fabulous monsters known from demonographic literature. The last extract reveals some of the pedagogical philosophy behind the work. The young reader is advised not to rely on the favors of the gods to achieve wealth and social status and instead to depend solely on diligent study. By appealing to the power of recitative learning, the reader will not be deluded and seek recourse to ghosts or spirits. The understanding of the world is translated as the mastery of nomenclature. As one would expect for a primer addressed to a young readership, the *Ji jiu pian* does not offer any theoretical discussion on the nature of the creatures or their mutual (zoological) relationships, nor does the text relate the animal terms to the recognition of animals in the natural world. The manual is centered around the mastery of names.

The enumerative and evocative use of animal nomenclature as a powerful literary device had precedents in the pre-Han period, notably in early poetry. One example is a hymn from the state of Lu 魯 ("Jiong" 駉, Mao 297), preserved in the *Shijing*, which lists no less than sixteen different terms to denote horses. Each stanza is introduced by an evocation of the physical well-being of Duke Xi's 喜 (659–627 B.C.E.) horses. This is followed by an enumeration of all the colored varieties of horses.

> Fat and sturdy are the stallions, in the distant open grounds;
> among those stallions, fat and sturdy,
> there are white-breached black ones and light-yellow ones,
> there are pure black ones and bay ones,
> with their chariots they go bang-bang,
> he thinks of them endlessly,　思無疆
> may these horses be good!　　思馬斯臧

> Fat and sturdy are the stallions, in the distant open grounds;
> among those stallions, fat and sturdy,
> there are grey-and-white ones and brown-and-white ones,
> there are red-yellow ones and black-mottled grey ones,
> with their chariots they go strongly,
> his thoughts are without end,　　思無期
> may these horses be strong!　　思馬斯才

> Fat and sturdy are the stallions, in the distant open grounds;
> among those stallions, fat and sturdy,
> there are flecked ones and white ones with black manes,
> there are red ones with black manes and black ones with white manes;
> with their chariots they go grandly,
> his thoughts never weary,　　思無斁
> may these horses be active!　　思馬斯作

> Fat and sturdy are the stallions, in the distant open grounds;
> among those stallions, fat and sturdy,
> there are dark-and-white ones and red-and-white ones,
> there are hairy-legged ones and fish-eyed ones;
> with their chariots they go vigorously,
> his thoughts do not swerve,　　思無邪
> may these horses be swift![98]　思馬斯徂

The final couplet of each stanza ends with a mnemonic act: the duke thinks of his horses, and thus they become good, fine, active, and swift. The enumerative recital of horse terms vivifies the strength of the stallions and the duke's mnemonic act of channeling his mind (*si*) empowers their strength. The recitative character of the poem together with its elaborate horse terminology has led some to speculate that the poem was chanted as a prayer during a sacrifice to a horse spirit.[99] Its style prefigures a use of language common with that of later incantatory literature. The association of quasi-magical effects with mnemonic namegiving, which will be discussed in more detail in chapter 7, are commonplace in early demonographic texts. Word magic also figures prominently in the Han rhapsody, which draws its strength from the linguistic power of naming. Wang Yanshou's 王延壽 (fl. mid-second cent. B.C.E.) *Meng fu* 夢賦 ("Nightmare Rhapsody") is a prime example of a text built around the apotropaic use of names.[100] The perfunctory use of namegiving as an attribute of empowering control has its counterpart in the early Christian West, notably in the role of Adam as ultimate "nomothete" (namegiver) of all creatures. Among the popular depictions of animals in early Christian art is the portrayal of Adam naming the beasts. Once God has given Adam dominion over the animal world, Adam shows that, by naming all creatures, he understands their nature and is able to control and use them.[101]

A focus on names is perpetuated in the only extant dialectal lexicon of the early imperial period. Yang Xiong's 揚雄 (53 B.C.E.–18 C.E.) *Fangyan* 方言 devotes one chapter (*juan* 8) to regional variants of animal names. It contains seventeen entries, starting with the regional variants for "tiger" (*hu* 虎). All entries follow the same idiomatic format: [in region A] [animal] X "is called" (*wei zhi* 謂之) [animal] Y. Little additional information is given on the behavior or appearance of the animals and all is focused on the listing of dialectal variants and synonyms that could aid in the recognition of animal names in the languages of different regions.[102]

As China's oldest preserved comprehensive character dictionary, Xu Shen's *Shuowen jiezi* is a source of paramount importance for the identification and explanation of animal names. Since explaining the pictographic origins and phonetics of a graph entails the attribution of semantics to a character, the elucidation of a graph's origin often implies the explication of its use as a name. Moreover, in a large number of animal entries Xu Shen includes additional data beyond the etymological analysis of a graph. For a number of animal graphs he supplies details concerning the appearance and behavior of the animal in question, and often this information stems from a concern to explain its name. In many cases, animal names reflect the natural behavior of the creature they denote. Explaining a name frequently consists in identifying characteristic features of the creature such as its color, size, alimentary habits, its morphology or physiognomy, and the nature of its locomotion. For instance the graph *shi* 鼫 is glossed as the "Five Skills Squirrel" (*wujishu* 五技鼠):

It can fly but cannot fly over house roofs. It can climb but cannot reach the top of a tree. It can swim but cannot cross a gorge, it can dwell in a hole but cannot conceal its (entire) body, it can walk but not in front of (i.e., faster than) humans. These are called its five skills.[103]

For his information Xu Shen relies on textual sources, and we may assume that a number of glosses were inspired by personal observation or hearsay. Xu Shen's etymological classification according to 540 graphic classifiers ("radicals") includes a large number of graphs that are representations or pictograms of animals, many of which have origins dating back to the Shang oracle bones.[104] As in the case of the *Erya*, zoological analysis in the *Shuowen* is subsumed within the framework of lexicography. In a sense, Xu Shen's etymological analysis could be seen as a "zoo-taxonomic" statement since it organizes animal graphs into subgroups based on the animal classifiers. Occasionally the *Shuowen* includes generic biological statements such as the observation that animals which do not suckle are oviparous.[105]

Despite the informative value of the animal lore accompanying Xu Shen's graph analyses, the information he provides is motivated mainly by lexicographic concerns rather than biology. The composition of the *Shuowen* as a project and its inclusion of large numbers of animal graphs were driven not by an intrinsic interest in the analysis of animals, but a desire to render the classics free of doubt.[106] Xu Shen is concerned first and foremost with the analysis of graphs representing the names of animals. This is clear from those entries that define the basic animal graph classifiers. Few of these animal classifiers are followed by a generic (biological) statement. *Yu* 魚 "fish," is defined as an "aquatic animal"; *niao* 鳥 "bird," as a "collective noun for birds with a long tail"; *hu* 虎 "tiger," as the "superior among the mountain animals"; and *shu* 鼠 "rat," as a "common noun for crevice animals."[107] However in many cases the *Shuowen* does not define the animal represented by the graph, but explains the pictographic semblance of the graph that represents the animal. Rather than stating that a *yang* 羊 is an animal with physical and behavioral characteristics A and B, Xu Shen states that the graph 丫 represents the horn of a sheep. Similarly when the entry for "tiger" states that its feet resemble human feet, Xu refers to the graphic semblance between the character *ren* 人 and the bottom part of the *hu* 虎 graph rather than to a biological similarity between the two species.[108]

In other cases the animal classifiers are defined by moral or cultural characteristics associated with the animal in question, with biological descriptions as secondary complements. *Ma* 馬 "horse" is explained as *nu* 怒 "fury" and *wu* 武 "martiality," a definition inspired by the horse's role in military affairs.[109] *Niu* 牛 is explained as *shi* 事 "to serve" and *li* 理 "to order," reflecting its servant role as a means of transportation and its use in agriculture (plowing).[110] *Hu* 狐 "fox" is defined as a prodigious animal on which demons take a ride.[111] Finally *gui* 龜 "tortoise" is glossed as *jiu* 舊 "old," related to divinatory practice and reflecting the belief that tortoises grew old and were able to foresee the future.[112] According to the *Liji,* tortoises were placed in front of other offerings during sacrifices because of their knowledge of the future. Regulations for setting out items in preparation for banquets and products presented as tribute stipulated that the tortoise was given priority because of its gift of prior knowledge.[113]

In discussing the role of nomenclature for the establishment of what he accepted to be a Chinese natural science, Joseph Needham remarks that this must have required "a scientific, or at least protoscientific, tradition in which men were interested in debating exactly what it was that someone else was talking about." He calls this a self-consciousness concerning appellations and points out its close analogy with the Confucian doctrine of the rectification of names.[114] While, as we will see, Needham's observation of the importance of nomenclature and its link with political philosophy is certainly justified, his assumption that there was a widespread protoscientific debate underlying the preoccupation with names is, at least with reference to the nomenclature of animals, unsubstantiated. It is highly questionable whether the aforementioned *Shuowen* glosses for the horse, ox, fox, or tortoise were the result of a widely shared protoscientific deliberation. The *Shuowen*'s animal nomenclature are, first and foremost, subject to lexico-graphic deliberation. Xu Shen was active during an age when the world was viewed as a reality in which all phenomena were interrelated within an encompassing hierarchy, a world in which human activity and the cycle of the natural world were thought to interact in consonance. This search for harmony among all things was reflected in the Han view of language and the work of the lexicographer who, through quasi-etymological associations such as paronomasy and other linguistic puns, attempted to relate different aspects of reality to each other by glossing them together as the explanation of a graph.

Finally, a work that is not strictly lexicographic but surely encyclopedic and systematizing in nature is the *Shanhaijing*. This text is difficult to assign to any single category of writing and has been variously described as a handbook on prodigies, a geographical gazetteer, or even a set of explanatory notes accompanying tribute maps.[115] An important ingredient of the *Shanhaijing* is the identification of unknown zoomorphic and theriomorphic creatures and their inherent dangers or advantageous properties. In the majority of the cases the descriptions are variations of a standard formula: In place X, there is an animal [有獸/鳥/魚 焉] Y; it is shaped like [其狀如...] Y; its name is [其名曰...] Y; its sounds are like [其音如...]. Whenever the appearance of the creature is ominous the formula reads: "If you observe (this creature), then (it means)... [見則...]." Riccardo Fracasso has argued that these formula had a divinatory function seeking to enable the observer to foretell future events by observing animals, monsters, and spirits ("teratoscopy").[116] In the text, the emphasis is put on the recognition of the creature's name, and this is often supported by providing the sound it makes. The importance of namegiving in the *Shanhaijing* is further evinced in the structure of the entries. The description of an animal's shape or its physical resemblance to a more commonly known creature virtually always precedes the attribution of the name. So rather than providing the name first, which is then explicated by a physical and/or behavioral definition of the creature in question, the name itself is presented as an identifying feature of the creature. The text is therefore as much about the attribution of names to unknown creatures as it is preoccupied with the descriptive narration of a creature's shape, sound, diet, and behavior. The performative force of naming an unknown creature suffices to give the user of this text the power to control it. By naming a monster it is given a taxonomic status within the bestiary. The animal and its name are isomorphic.[117]

The role of the *Shanhaijing* as a source of names is also reflected in an anecdote preserved in Liu Xin's preface to the text. It tells the story of Dongfang Shuo 東方朔 (fl. ca. 130 B.C.E.) naming a strange bird that had been offered to Emperor Wu 武帝 (141–87 B.C.E.) and identifying its diet. In his explanation Dongfang Shuo credits the *Shanhaijing* as the source of his information.[118] The *Shanhaijing*'s concern with naming can also be seen in another example which distinguishes birds in "name categories":

> [Beyond the northwest sea] . . . there are three kinds of pentachromatic birds (*you wucai niao san ming* 有五采鳥三名): one is called the *huang* 皇 bird, one the *luan* 鸞 bird, one the *feng* 鳳 bird.[119]

A number of names in the *Shanhaijing* are derived from animal sounds and often the creatures identify themselves by shouting out their own name. This is variously recorded with formulas such as "the creature makes a sound like its name," "its call sounds like its name," or "it calls out its own name."[120] In some cases an animal name reflects a physical or behavioral feature of the creature concerned. Thus the name of the ape or *xingxing* 狌狌 (猩猩) may be an indirect allusion to or a phonetic pun of 行行 reflecting its ability to walk or behave like a human being.[121] As was already shown by the "five skills squirrel," the allusion to an animal's behavior in its name is a pattern that occurs regularly. The *Yilin* 易林, an Eastern Han divination guide, contains another example in a verse on a bird known as the *pojia* 破家 or "destructor of households":

> On the wall sits a bird,
> which names itself (*zi ming* 自名) the "Destructor of Households."
> Its summoning cry is like deadly poison,
> and brings calamity and disaster to the state.[122]

The recurrent reference in the *Shanhaijing* to animals naming themselves or calling out their own name echoes the theme of "forms and names" (*xing ming* 刑 [形] 名) in the works of the masters of philosophy where a preoccupation with names figured prominently in theories regarding the exercise of administrative control in the political realm. The human equivalent of the *Shanhaijing* animals calling out their own names occurs in the *Han Feizi* 韓非子, where officials are said to identify their qualities and "name themselves" to the ruler.[123] The equation of sound and name is also made in the Mawangdui *Jingfa* 經法, which states that "forms and names produce sounds; and sounds and realities should tally with each other (*xing ming chu sheng, sheng shi diaohe* 刑 [形]名出聲, 聲實調合)."[124] Like the ruler who prompts his officials to declare their aims or announce their tasks and verifies whether their achievements match their name, the user of the bestiary lets the *therata* identify their shapes and behavioral properties, whereupon he can respond accordingly to their appearance and control the monsters by protecting himself against their dangerous aspects or making use of their advantageous (medicinal, nutritional) properties. Finally, the *Shanhaijing* makes no attempt at categorizing the animal species it describes. In fact, one of its rare generic statements points at the changeability of animal categories according to regionality. The section on the "southern lands beyond the sea" states that in this region insects are considered to be snakes, and snakes are called fish.[125]

The animal entries in the above described systematizing texts suggest that animal names were based on a variety of features such as color, shape, sound, and behavior. No statement is given in these works as to whether there exists a linguistic or philosophical principle that underlies the naming of animal creatures. The lexicographic identification of Chinese animal names remains a bugaboo in historical linguistics. It is difficult to determine whether a particular creature was originally named after its behavior, or whether semantics were imposed on a graph based on homophonic puns used to verbalize its behavior.[126] Most likely a combination of phonetic and semantic processes were at work. A rare theoretical statement on the origins of animal names appears in a later source, the *Kong Congzi* 孔叢子, where an interlocutor states that "the names of dogs and horses all derive from their shapes and colors (*xing se* 形色)."[127] The eclectic and selective nature of the aforementioned works, most of which collect and classify terms that are sifted out of a body of texts or originate in orally transmitted lore, may partly account for the absence of theorization regarding biological species in general. The naturalist considers it his task to relate the appearance and behavior of a specific animal to a larger group or species by identifying formal and behavioral similarity or difference. The lexicographer considers it his task to explain extraordinary animal names by relating them semantically or phonetically to a common graph. While the former's task consists in explicating shared behavior among creatures in the natural world, the latter operates as an exegete of heterogeneous graphs within a textual realm. While the naturalist is concerned with real creatures, the lexicographer imposes a nominalist order on the world. Hence linguistic authority and textual precedent rather than the direct witness of nature may have been more important in determining the inclusion of an animal entry in a selective compendium. Furthermore there may have been a bias to provide a written record for "noteworthy," exemplary, or anecdotally renowned specimens only. The skeptic Huan Tan 桓譚 (43 B.C.E.–28 C.E.) dismisses the necessity of a textual record for ordinary members of the animal kingdom:

> As for domestically bred animals, they are base. But whenever there are especially fine specimens among them, they have been recorded in texts (*jian ji shi* 見記識). Therefore there are the horses named Hualiu 驊騮 and Jilu 驥騄, and oxen that were praised with the names Guojiao 郭椒 and Dingliang 丁櫟 .[128]

Huan Tan suggests that common animals are not deserving of a textual record; what is ordinary is not noteworthy. Only animals that have gained reputation through virtuous conduct or extraordinary physical achievements, animals whose names come with fame, merit a place in the written record. When the qualities of such famous species are evoked, the intrinsic power of their names appears to be as important as their actual physical description. For instance the enumerative listing of the fancy names of King Mu of Zhou's 周穆王 (956?–918? B.C.E.) legendary horses—Blossom Red, Green Ears, Red Thoroughbred, White Offering, Tall Yellow, Outstripper, Dull Sable, Son of Hills—proves at least as powerful and evocative as the statement that these horses were in fact fast runners.[129]

As suggested above, a preoccupation with animal nomenclature has to be seen against the background of a broader concern with language, words, and names in Warring States and Han thought. Theories about the "rectification of names" (*zheng ming* 正名) figured in the agenda of most Warring States schools of philosophy. The focus of discussion varied, ranging from the Legalists' advocacy to verify deeds against official titles as a premise for bureaucratic control, to a more logical fascination with the relationship between name and object in Later Mohist writings. However despite diverging views as to what constitutes a name and its referent, a common denominator of most schools was the acknowledgment that there should be clarity in the attribution of names to realities, and the idea that the mastery and understanding of names engenders practical and intellectual control over the cosmic and sociopolitical world they represent.[130]

In its origins as a sociopolitical philosophy, the Confucian doctrine of the "rectification of names" held that, in order to maintain social harmony and advance the effective ruling of society, names and social functions need to correspond. Confucius had linked efficient rulership with the capability to verify the concordance between official titles and their corresponding functions. By being able to name (*ming* 名) things the sage-ruler commanded (*ming* 命) a grasp over those realities. Not only did names issue from the sage, the correct use of names also established a prerogative to assert one's authority over the socio-political realm.[131] As such the act of naming itself was invested with sociopolitical power. As Angus Graham puts it:

> The sage, however much or little he may analyze, in the first place distinguishes, classifies, and fixes by naming. . . . What each in his position in cosmos and community would spontaneously incline to do in perfect awareness thus follows for Confucius immediately from correctness in naming, that is, from naming which correctly assimilates, contrasts, and connects.[132]

Attributing names to realities in both human society and the natural world and using those names in a perfunctionary and performative way was a means to order the world. While philological motives provided the foundation for lexicographic attempts to classify the natural world, this meticulous attention to nomenclature and namegiving was closely linked to a philosophical attempt to grasp or taxonomize the cosmos.

A preoccupation with names can be expected in lexicographic materials; yet, the paradigm of names was not confined to lexicographic classification only. Just as the lexicographer sought to establish a semantic concordance between a *ming* 名 "name" and a *wu* 物 "referent," ritual texts prescribed that in the practical management of animals proper names had to be connected with the proper creatures. Thus both on the level of the explanation of graphs as well as that of the social or ritual use of animals, early Chinese attempts to categorize species divisions (*fen lei* 分類) were dominated by concerns to attribute proper names to the various species and establish their identity by means of their name (*bian ming wu* 辨名物 "distinguishing name and species").[133] Descriptions involving practical and mundane dealings with animals often linked the manipulation of animals together with the association of names with specific creatures.

A number of passages in the *Zhouli* suggest that the ritualist or officiant differentiated animals through the attribution of names. The cook (*paoren* 庖人) who prepares the six domestic animals, the six wild animals, and the six kinds of wild birds for the kitchens is said to "distinguish their names and kinds" (*bian qi ming wu* 辨其名物).[134] Jia Gongyan's 賈公彥 (fl. ca. 650 C.E.) subcommentary adds that all birds and beasts have a name (*ming hao* 名號) and a color (*wu se* 物色). Possibly the text suggests that the cook should attempt to categorize all game animals under one of the three "six" categories. More plausible is the idea that a cook does not prepare victim animals he cannot name (i.e., identify by name and color). Unidentified animals are not to be consumed. Similarly, the hunter (*shouren* 獸人) responsible for supervising hunting expeditions and surveying the game "distinguishes their names and kinds." The same commentator notes that all wild animals have a name and color.[135] In order to determine which particular animals should be used for specific sacrificial procedures, the vice minister of rites (*xiaozongbo* 小宗伯) selects the six classes of sacrificial victims according to the color and texture of the hides and "distinguishes their names and kinds."[136] The chicken officer (*jiren* 雞人) responsible for the sacrificial chickens, "distinguishes their kinds."[137] The entry on the tortoise keeper (*guiren* 龜人) comprises the treatment of six kinds of tortoises "each having a name [associated] with their kind (*ge you ming wu* 各有名物)." The commentaries again suggest that *wu* may refer more specifically to the animal's color thereby reaffirming name and color as important distinctive criteria.[138] This use of *wu* referring to the color of an animal occurs as early as the *Guoyu*, where it is stated that the hair of a sacrificial victim serves to demonstrate its color (*mao yi shi wu* 毛以示物), while blood serves to announce the act of killing.[139] As these *Zhouli* passages suggest, identifying species by name and appearance according to their social use constituted a central task of those concerned with the management of animals.

The important role of naming was further attested in the existence of a ritual nomenclature for sacrificial animals. A specific generic term, *sheng* 牲, was used to denote victim animals in general. According to the *Zuozhuan* an ox could only be called a victim when the animal and the day of its sacrificial slaughter had been divined. In a commentary Du Yu 杜預 (222–84 C.E.) adds that on obtaining a favorable day, "the name of the ox is changed into *sheng*."[140] Failure to obtain a favorable divination could result in the victim not being slaughtered. So when on one occasion (in the year corresponding to 566 B.C.E) diviners failed to obtain an auspicious response after three divination sessions the bull was set free.[141]

The transformation of an animal into a sacrificial victim went parallel with a change in its name. The received term for this name was *shenghao* 牲號, or "appellation for a sacrificial victim." According to the *Zhouli* a high priest, or "great invocator," distinguished the "six appellations," which included the names of spirits, demons, numinous emanations, sacrificial animals, sacrificial grains, and jades.[142] The sacrificial appellations of victim animals are specified in the *Liji* and some are preserved in other texts. For example ritual prescription held that during rites at or in the ancestral temple the sacrificial ox was known as "the creature with the large foot."[143] A variant of this name occurs as the sacrificial appellation for an ox in a covenant text excavated at Houma 候馬 (Shanxi, early fifth cent. B.C.E.). Warring States covenants were oaths in which several parties made a pledge by slaughtering a sacrificial victim, smearing the lips with the animal's blood, and burying the inscribed covenant tablets together with the victim in a pit.[144] Victims used in covenants may have varied with the occasion and the rank of the covenantors and included sheep, oxen, pigs, dogs, horses, chickens, and cockerels. The covenant fields excavated at Houma and Wenxian 溫縣 (Henan, ca. 497 B.C.E.) rendered remains of mostly sheep with occasional oxen and horses.[145]

Other sacrificial appellations for victim animals included "stiff bristles" for a pig, "fatling" for a sucking pig, and "soft hair" for a sheep.[146] The sacrificial name for a cockerel was "red shriek," a dog was called "broth offering," a pheasant was known as "wide toes," and the hare as "the clairvoyant."[147] According to commentaries by Zheng Xuan and Kong Yingda most of these names find their origin in the fact that the victims were expected to be fat and glossy for sacrifice. Hence when an ox is well fed, its feet grow big and will leave large footprints. Fat pigs are said to get hard hair and whiskers, and the distance between a pheasant's toes was taken as an indication that the bird had been well nourished. The eyes of a hare were believed to open when it grew fat.

The color red in the sacrificial appellation for the chicken is linked to its association with the sun, the *yang*, fire, and the south. An allusion to this appellation is preserved in an exorcismal spell that invokes the apotropaic power of the color red and the sound of a chicken's cry indicating the time and announcing dawn or the conquest of light over darkness. Xu Shen and Ying Shao 應劭 (d. ca. 204 C.E.) note that during the suburban sacrifices in the state of Lu red chickens were used to sacrifice to the sun. During the ritual a brief incantation was performed stating: "By means of (this cockerel's) cry at dawn and its red feathers we ward off the calamities for the Duke of Lu."[148] The association of fowl, chickens, or cockerels with the color red is also attested in a story explaining that the call to beckon chickens is *zhu-zhu* 朱朱. This was based on a legend that the bird had descended from a human ancestor, Zhu Gong 朱公 (The Vermilion Lord), who had changed himself into a chicken.[149]

According to Zheng Xuan, sacrificial appellations were used to distinguish the status of victim animals from those that were destined for human use. Cai Yong (133–92 C.E.) maintained that sacrificial victims (as well as other sacrificial implements) were given a different name during sacrificial rituals as a means of respect for the spirits. This would distinguish them from animals used for human consumption.[150] In other words, through the use of sacrificial names the status of the animal transformed from profane into sacred. Sacrificial appellations were a form of word magic, they endowed sacrificial animals with special powers. We can therefore assume that the act of naming an animal or animal victim was perceived by the participants and officiants of such ceremonies as a gesture of ritual control or power. Just as a concern with names influenced the textual classification of animals, the assignment of sacrificial appellations contributed to the ritualization of the animal.

Conclusion

Warring States and Han writings make few attempts to define in a theoretical fashion the notion of the animal. In a world view that did not distinguish a structure of immutable and archetypal essences behind visible realities, the search to delineate a fixed formal and behavioral essence of each and every living creature did not develop into a major issue of intellectual inquiry. A noticeable feature of the early Chinese text corpus therefore is the absence of a body of protozoological texts. While a number of writings collated and classified animal material in function of the etymological clarification of graphs or the cosmographic description of all things under heaven, the analysis of data on the animal world did not spark a genre of writings that debated animals in a systematized and exclusive manner. While animals were discussed in practical and technical works dealing with agriculture, divination, the calendar, or medicine, none of these writings sought to analyze data on animals with a view to explain animal behavior or investigate the internal workings of the animal world itself. The biological animal did not provide a topic for widespread intellectual debate, neither did it inspire the development of a textual canon that took the natural world as its main subject of discussion. Textual records of activities involving the direct observation of the animal world are an exception rather than the rule. As we will see, this was also reflected in the idea that the sages, rather than being naturalists, were observers of human behavior and morality.

Instead of being concerned with the collection and classification of animal data and the analysis of the differentiae between animals and other living creatures, the analytical exposition and classification of animals in early China was motivated by a concern with the classification of animal names. Much of the protoscientific discourse on animals occurred within the framework of lexicography. This detailed attention for animal nomenclature was part of a wider concern with textual exegesis and lexicographic classification. Defining animals revolved around the attribution of names to unidentified creatures, occasionally linking the origins of an animal name to its behavior or sound, or connecting the names of unusual species to more generally known animal kinds. This ambition to project an order of names onto the natural world or equate the explanation of animals with the elucidation of animal graphs was linked to sociopolitical theories on the "rectification of names," which had presented clarity of naming as a means to establish mental and practical control over a world of multiple realities. That lexicographic collectanea of animal nomenclature originated just prior to or during the Han may therefore not be coincidental. Political unification, and consequently, the merging of the real and imaginary fauna of a largely expanded empire, prompted the creation of order among these new data by means of texts. The gradual expansion from feudality to empire with its influx of exotic spoils from distant regions to the Chinese heartland gave rise to a growing realization of the immense variety of fauna and flora "under heaven." The compartmentalization of this new world in dictionaries or its acclamation in rhapsodic prose poetry may have been an answer to an existing need for rulers and scholars alike to "visualize" this newly extended bestiary through texts and hence establish symbolical and intellectual control over all species.

CHAPTER TWO

ANIMALS AND OFFICERS

While the classification of nomenclature and the attribution of names provided one way to establish order in the animal realm, the social and ritual use of animals by humans provided another. Central to the Warring States and Han view of the natural world was the notion that its internal order was deeply affected by the course of human affairs. Hence patterns of organization and classification within the animal world were rarely presented as based on biological premises. The ascendancy of human categories over laws of nature influenced the classification of animals. In model descriptions of the ideal royal state such as the one preserved in the *Zhouli*, otherwise known as the "Office(r)s of Zhou" (*Zhou guan* 周官), the identification, management, and treatment of animals were subsumed into offices that were part of an all-encompassing human polity. Data about the appearance and behavior of animals were paired with information about the human agent who dealt with them. While the wilderness was not wholly on the defensive, human control over the animated species also affected the extra-domestic sphere. Animals in the wilds were also subsumed within the human realm, and minute details pertaining to the habitats and activities of nondomestic species were brought under the aegis of human administrative control. This desire to project a human administrative model onto the natural world was further attested in stories that praised the ancients for being successful administrators of the natural world or criticized contemporary rulers for being inadequate at it. In the same way that names had to be connected with all creatures under heaven in order to enable the human subject to wield authority over that world, so too a human office was to be assigned to each aspect of the animal world for the ruler to be able to assert his dominance over the natural world.

Ritual texts prescribed how specified officers were to be assigned to care for specific species or charged with specialized functions involving animals. The integration of the animal world within a human model led to the development of animal classifications that were inspired by ritual and socioreligious criteria such as sacrificial practice or the ritual exchange of gifts. Calendrical texts instructed the ruler how to subsume observations in the animal world and the practical management of animals within the bounds of administrative control. These texts explained the workings of the animal world in concordance with human activity and the temporal and spatial frameworks that shaped it such as the agricultural cycle or various cycles of ritual practice. Thus while the lexicographer classified, explicated, and debated animal names in systematizing lexica and glossaries, the ritualist classified animals according to social criteria and compartmentalized the animal world within the overall structure of the ritualized state.

Managing Animals

Evidence suggests that as early as the late Shang period kings charged special officers with the procurement, breeding, training, and welfare of animals. Oracle bones record officials charged with the keeping of hunting dogs and the breeding of horses. Shang inscriptions also contain a number of graphs related to husbandry such as words for animal enclosures, stables, fish ponds, and corrals for the breeding of rabbits, oxen, and deer. In addition the oracle bone inscriptions preserve a substantial vocabulary on activities involving the hunt. Together with preserved faunal remains, these records bear early testimony of the Shang's advanced level of organization in confronting its natural environments. Similarly officials in charge of herding cattle, training horses, and supervising dogs appear in Zhou bronze inscriptions.[1]

Warring States and Han writings document a great number of officials in charge of animals, several of which may have already existed in early Zhou times. One of the richest sources to provide information about animals in early China, the *Zhouli,* presents a cosmological model in which every aspect of human activity pertaining to the natural world is subsumed within an order of "offices" (*guan* 官). The world view emerging from the *Zhouli* is one that compartmentalizes the whole of reality and human activity into what essentially amounts to a bureaucratic order. The text, originally known as the *Zhou guan,* provides a description of the administrative structure of the royal state of Zhou and includes detailed accounts of the various governmental officials and their tasks. Among its officials there are a substantial number of "animal officers." They are spread proportionally across each of the primary sections of the currently transmitted *Zhouli* (namely the offices of heaven, earth, spring, summer, and autumn), which suggests that the management of the natural world was viewed as part of the administrative domain of each main government department. The *Zhouli* provides many valuable insights into the Warring States perception of animals. To be sure, the received text may not necessarily reflect actual Zhou institutions and presents a rather idealized Han view of the court functions in the state of Zhou. Yet, given that a substantial number of its "animal officers" appear (some with variant titles) in other, less systematizing Warring States texts, many of these offices most likely existed in some form prior to their incorporation into the *Zhou guan.*[2] The *Zhouli* also incorporates functions from a more popular sphere of technical experts. These included specialists who dealt with animals, such as physiognomists, healers, and animal trainers.

The *Zhouli* descriptions of office follow a standard format stating the name of the office followed by the specification of its duties. The following entry, for example, describes the duties of the *chong ren* 充人 or "fatteners" [of sacrificial animals]:

> They are in charge of tethering the sacrificial victims. When a sacrifice is held to the Five Emperors they tether the animals in the stables and feed them during a period of three months. They do the same for sacrifices offered to former kings. For other, separate sacrifices, they tether the animals to the gates of the capital and have them fed there. When the sacrificial victims are presented for selection they announce which ones are perfect. When the best ones have been decided upon, they assist (their lords in leading the animals to the sacrificial spot).[3]

The "fatteners" were part of a larger chain of officers who managed the animals from birth until they ended up in the sacrificial stands. These included herdsmen, stable and park attendants, and keepers of sacrificial meats. For instance, the tasks of another official, the ox officer or "cowherd" (*niu ren* 牛人), consisted of raising the oxen for public use by the state, which involved providing and feeding those oxen used as sacrifices, as offerings on the occasion of the reception of state guests, as provisions for the army or as sacrificial victims at funerals.[4] Another official was responsible for decorating oxen as sacrificial victims, placing vertical sticks on the horns to prevent the animals from goring, attaching a rope through the nose to lead the oxen, and presenting water for ritual washing and wood for ritual cooking.[5] Other functionaries in the *Zhouli* are commissioned with a wide range of duties such as gathering exotic species, collecting sacrificial meats, breeding, herding and training domestic animals, taming wild species,[6] the veterinary treatment of animals, the management of animal tributes and parks, the care of the animal stables, the preparation of animals for ritual occasions,[7] the tax collection of animal horns and bird feathers,[8] the settlement of legal disputes involving animals,[9] the expulsion of venomous species, the organization of the hunt and the fishing season,[10] and the expulsion of demonic and prodigious animals. A human office was connected to every aspect of the animal world. Thus a corollary of the *Zhouli*'s presentation of the ideal state as a replica of the entire cosmos was the idea that the natural world itself was subject to bureaucratic control.

An important consequence of the subsumption of the animal world into an overarching model of the bureaucratic state was that the preoccupation with animals fundamentally merged with the sociopolitical and ritual sphere. The *Zhouli* officers are not charged with the observation, gathering, and interpretation of empirical data regarding the living species. Rather, they are commissioned with tasks that integrate animals and animal-related phenomena within the power of the social polity. Furthermore, by incorporating the treatment of animals within a bureaucratic model, the animal world was also made part of a ritual order. In its descriptions of human office, as Mark Lewis has pointed out, the *Zhouli* does not dichotomize the practical handling of routine tasks from the cultic and religious roles assigned to each office. The text pairs administrative tasks with religious rites and ritual responsibilities, and presents the ideal state as a sphere in which the practical management of the duties of office is doubled with roles in religious ritual.[11] Similarly the natural world to which a great number of offices are assigned and a wide array of tasks devoted, was doubled as a ritual and religious realm. Descriptions of officials dealing with animals frequently combine mundane tasks such as the herding or breeding of animals with the management of animals for the purpose of state ritual or religious sacrifices. Thus the aforementioned ox officer in charge of feeding the state's cattle also provided beef for the army, sacrificial meat for the ancestral spirits, and prepared sacrificial implements such as a basin to collect blood and a rack to suspend the sacrificial meats. The fishing supervisor not only regulated all fishing activity within the royal domain but also supplied fresh and dried fish products for sacrificial ceremonies.[12] State officials were in charge of practical as well as more symbolic activities involving animals, from menial tasks such as the cooking of animal meats or the provision of animal fodder to the mantic destruction of nests made by ominous birds.

By assigning a human officiant to deal with every aspect of the management of the animal world, the manipulation and treatment of animals only became important as long as it affected the human realm. Consequently, animals became part of social and ritual categories that shaped human society. This human matrix imposed on the natural world entailed that, in many instances, the formal description of animal species was modeled on their social use rather than on their biological properties. The natural world in the *Zhouli* does not form the object of naturalist enquiry; instead it is the object of administrative control. The registering and classification of animal species grew out of social imperatives such as the preparation of food, the procurement of ritual victims, or the use of animals as tax commodities or tokens of personal and communal wealth.

That socioritual motives influenced the classification of animals is illustrated by the *Zhouli*'s specification of different types of horses. Horses, as is clear from references to technical literature on horse physiognomy and veterinary treatment, constituted a valuable commodity in Warring States and early imperial China. This was mainly so because of their value in transport and warfare. Sima Qian repeatedly describes the state of economic affairs in the empire by its presence or absence of horses. For instance the emperor's inability to find horses of the same color to draw his carriage or the necessity of generals and ministers to ride about in ox carts are presented as indications of the absence of prosperity.[13] The abundance of horses indicated the contrary. Thus Sima Qian writes that after the consolidation of the Han, "there were horses even in the streets and alleys of the common people or flocking in droves along the paths between the fields. And anyone so poor as to being reduced to riding a mare was rejected by his neighbors and not allowed to join village gatherings."[14]

In the *Zhouli* these social assets of horses inspire the classification of these animals. Hence the commander of the stables (*xiaoren* 校人) is said to distinguish the royal horses into six categories (*bian liu ma zhi shu* 辨六馬之屬). The text defines each category (*shu*) by mentioning the horse term first, followed by the qualifier *yi wu* 一物 "one kind" or "group." The actual categories distinguished are horses suited for breeding (*zhongma* 種馬), warfare (*rongma* 戎馬), ceremonial display (*qima* 齊馬), travel (*daoma* 道馬), the hunt (*tianma* 田馬), and labor horses (*numa* 駑馬). The stable officer thus differentiates horses into appropriate categories for equine usage. The criteria used to qualify the horses do not consist of biological differentiae but rather feature characteristics that determine the animal's use within the human polity.[15] Another official, the horse appraiser (*mazhi* 馬質), responsible for the procurement of horses and the valuation of their prices, uses a different classification in function of their cash value and distinguishes horses into three classes (war horses, hunting horses, labor horses).[16] A similar pattern can be seen for other officers that are said to engage in some act of differentiation or classification of animals or animal victims. In most cases the differentiation of animals is inspired by ritual or socioreligious imperatives.[17]

Another consequence of the association of human agents with specific animal species in the *Zhouli* is a general tendency not to engage in the explanation of how animal species behave, but rather of how humans deal with them. Hence, a prominent number of the *Zhouli* animal officers are engaged in apotropaic and exorcistic activities, activities that aim at keeping the animal fauna at a distance or manipulating animal species for the benefit of humans. The worm specialist (*shushi* 庶氏) expels venomous species by means of verbal exorcismal blows. The officer of predatory birds (*shishi* 翨氏) attacks wild birds; the bird killer (*sheniaoshi* 射鳥氏) shoots birds of ill omen that appear during sacrifices; the nest destroyer (*zhecushi* 柞蔟氏) destroys the nests of unpropitious birds; the exterminator (*jianshi* 翦氏) expels venomous insects by fumigating them with herbs; the frog officer (*guoshi* 蟈氏) expels turtles and toads; the "water jug sprinkler" (*huzhuoshi* 壺涿氏) expels water bugs; and the palace protector (*tingshi* 庭氏) shoots birds of ill omen that appear in the state.[18]

To summarize, instead of ordering the animal world into a protozoological project based on their natural qualities, the author(s) of the *Zhouli* integrate the animal world into a social zoography in which every single aspect of an animal's natural behavior was classified within the province of human office. The description of the animal realm in the *Zhouli* does not focus on animals or innate animal behavior *in se* but reflects on those aspects of animal behavior that affect humans. In this respect, it seems to me hardly justifiable—as some Chinese scholars in the history of the sciences tend to do—to sift out parts of this text that contain what may appear to be zoological data at first sight, and present these as evidence for the existence of or inclination toward a scientific investigation of animals in early China.[19] For instance one passage in the *Zhouli* that could approximate a biological description is a section that deals with the physiognomic examination of horns or antlers.[20] The text analyzes in considerable detail the length, color, internal composition, and flexibility of the ox horn. The context of this passage however—it is incorporated in the "Kaogong ji" 考 工記 , which substitutes the original section on the offices of winter—suggests no zoological or biological motives.[21] It aims at instructing bow craftsmen on the proper use of animal horns for the fabrication and decoration of bows. The biological information conveyed in this passage is thus subsumed in a context that is ultimately concerned with a human craft. Another passage frequently quoted as evidence of scientific zootaxonomy in early China is the entry on the *ziren* 梓人 "woodcarvers."[22] Although this entry, which divides the animal kingdom into two main groups ("large" and "small" animals), each with its separate subdivisions, reflects a degree of biological specification, the context of the passage should be taken into account. It deals with the decoration of musical instruments, and its principal aim is to establish a correlation between the nature of the animal used as decoration and the sound of the musical instrument on which it is depicted.[23] Another passage qualifies animal physiognomy and the observation of animal behavior within the frame of culinary and sacrificial practice by establishing a relationship between an animal's outer appearance, its conduct and its taste:

> When an ox bellows at night, its meat tastes like rotten wood. When a sheep has long and felted fur, its hair has a frowzy odor. If a dog has red thighs and a hasty walk, (its meat) has a putrid smell. When a bird loses its color and sings with an exhausted voice, (its meat) is fetid. When a pig looks blind and squint-eyed, its flesh is measly. When a horse is black over its spine and striped on the legs, it tastes like rotten crickets.[24]

As in the aforementioned cases, the collection of observational data on animals here serves a human purpose; namely, the selection of the ideal sacrificial viands for ritual ceremonies and royal banquets.

While the incorporation of animals within the human polity is exemplified most prominently in the *Zhouli,* other Warring States and Han texts corroborate similar perceptions. Two narratives in the *Zuozhuan* suggest that both the idea of associating human bureaucratic nomenclature with the natural world as well as the management of animals by designated officers may have predated the ideal-ized system portrayed in the *Zhouli*. A first narrative stages the Lord of Tan 郯 (fl. ca. 524 B.C.E.) visiting the court of Lu and explaining why his ancestor, the legend-ary emperor Shaohao 少皞, had used the names of birds for his officers. He ex-plains that each of the legendary five emperors in antiquity had regulated their calendar and fixed their official titles following the natural omen that had an-nounced their rule: clouds, fire, water, a dragon, and a phoenix. The emblematic use of bird names was inspired by the appearance of a phoenix when Shaohao succeeded to the throne. Next a list is given of Shaohao's officers each carrying a bird title. In charge of the calendar was an official named Phoenix Bird (*fenghuang-shi* 鳳凰氏); the officer of the equinoxes was named Dark Bird (*xuanniaoshi* 玄鳥氏); the officer of the solstices Shrike (*bozhaoshi* 伯趙氏); the officer of the commencement of spring and summer Green Bird (*qingniaoshi* 青鳥氏); the officer of the closing of spring and autumn Cinnabar Bird (*danniaoshi* 丹鳥氏); the officer of instruction Partridge (*zhujiushi* 祝鳩氏); the minister of war Vul-ture (*qujiushi* 鴡鳩氏); the minister of works Wood Pigeon (*shijiushi* 鳲鳩氏); the minister of crime Hawk (*shuangjiushi* 爽鳩氏); and the minister of affairs Falcon (*gujiushi* 鶻鳩氏). The passage goes on to state that officials known as the Five Pigeons (*wujiu* 五鳩) assembled the people, the Five Pheasants (*wuzhi* 五雉) regulated the five classes of crafts people, while the Nine-Tailed Birds (*jiuhu* 九扈) regulated the nine departments of agriculture.[25] This passage is concerned with the association of animal names to human offices. The fact that Shaohao's official nomenclature consisted of bird names is of secondary importance since his predecessors all named their offices after other natural omens. At the core of the story lies the idea that the legendary sages had drawn on natural phenomena to organize the calendar and titles on which their governments were based. That it emphasizes the importance of clarity regarding the origins of bureaucratic titles is clear from a comment following the Lord of Tan's explanation in which Con-fucius is said to have studied bureaucratic nomenclature with him. The same idea is confirmed in a later source, the *Bao Puzi* 抱朴子, which alludes to Confucius in this *Zuozhuan* passage stating that "since (Confucius) had to ask the Lord of Tan about the bird offices, there was something he did not understand about officialdom."[26] Confucius is not said to be ignorant of birds; rather he is unable to connect bird names with officialdom. He cannot make the connection of a *wu* 物 with a *guan* 官 and wishes to learn why and how bird names came to denominate offices. The logic behind the latter, which consists in pairing bird behavior with the function of the official in question, is the main topic of the *Zuozhuan* com-mentaries. For instance the *shuangjiu* is identified as the predatory eagle or hawk pouncing on criminals. The *bozhao* is said to sing from the summer solstice until the winter solstice, and the *fenghuang*'s knowledge of the seasons explains its name being used for the calendar. Underlying this narrative is the message that the mastery of the natural world translates in the mastery and comprehension of the human offices that were connected with it and the natural signs that provided the source of their nomenclature. The story ends with the statement that Shao-hao's successors no longer could draw on distant natural omens but instead based themselves on human affairs to organize their calendars.

A second passage in the *Zuozhuan* is a narrative on the raising of dragons.[27] In response to the appearance of a dragon in the capital of Jin 晉 (allegedly in 513 B.C.E.), its head scribe-astrologer Cai Mo 蔡墨 recounts how the ancients raised dragons and how the state used the services of two clans known as the Dragon Rearers (*huanlongshi* 豢龍氏) and the Dragon Tamers (*yulongshi* 御龍氏). The story sketches the fate of these offices over the course of time. It states that the breeding of dragons during the reign of Emperor Shun 舜 and several genera-tions after him was successful. Dragons kept appearing and for this reason Shun's officer in charge of dragons was awarded the (clan) title (*shi* 氏) "Dragon Rearer." Under Emperor Kong Jia 孔甲, the thirteenth ruler of the Xia 夏, the pedigree of successful dragon breeders disintegrated. When the Thearch gave Kong Jia two sets of dragons, the latter was not able to feed them and members of the clan of the Dragon Rearers could no longer be deployed. Instead a descendant of a differ-ent clan who had learned his skills from the Dragon Rearers was put in charge of Kong Jia's dragons and awarded the (clan) title Dragon Tamer. This officer how-ever failed in his duties and was therefore no longer deserving of the office and its name since he had fed one of the sacred dragons as food to his ruler. Up to this point the story seems clear. Kong Jia is presented as the first ruler who fails to look after the sacred dragon. This failure to look after dragons is a sign of his incom-petent rule. As a response, dragons stop appearing to nonvirtuous rulers.[28] How-ever an interesting turn in the narrative follows. To the question why no dragons currently appear, Cai Mo answers:

> As for the creatures [phenomena of the world], each has its own office/officer (*fu wu, wu you qi guan* 夫物, 物有其官). The officer cultivates his methods for tak-ing care of them (*guan xiu qi fang* 官修其方), and from dawn to dusk thinks of them. If he neglects his duties for one day death will be the result. He would lose his office and not receive a salary.[29] When officers cherish their duties, the crea-tures [phenomena of the world] come to them. When they abandon and neglect their duties, they cease to appear and go into hiding.

Cai Mo proceeds by stating that for this reason the ancients had established "offices of the five phases/ processes" (*wu xing zhi guan* 五行之官) and lists these offices with their presiding spirits. He identifies the dragon as a creature belong-ing to the phase of water (*shui wu* 水物) and states that since the office of water (*shuiguan* 水官) had been abandoned, dragons could no longer be obtained alive. Therefore the reason why Kong Jia is blamed for the disappearance of drag-ons is his failure to employ an expert dragon breeder. Kong Jia had failed to connect the appropriate office (*guan* 官) with the appropriate creature (*wu* 物) and thus failed to subsume the treatment of dragons successfully into his court.

Because of its importance in the history of the development of *wuxing* thought, this passage has received much scholarly attention. According to Benjamin Schwartz, the story portrays a state analogy in which spirits are said to "preside" over each of the five elements. Jean Lévi speaks of a bureaucracy as "a symbolical reproduction of the universe." Mark Lewis sees the story of Shaohao's bird offices as a "parable of the shift from religious authority to administrative government through the agency of rites and cosmology" and the Kong Jia episode as an early example of the transformation of a politicized spirit world defined by genealogy to a politicized spirit world defined by office.[30] While I agree that the narrative on the dragon rearers indicates the emergence of a genealogy of office and projects the maintenance and transmission of office onto the spirit world, the bureaucratic parallel between the human and spirit world presented in this story has been overemphasized. In my view, the passage does not indicate that the natural world was simply viewed as a mirror of the human state bureaucracy. Rather it suggests that natural phenomena and spirit creatures are subsumed within human control via the agency of a human office. In the case of Kong Jia, successful rulership would have entailed the management of dragons by an appropriate officer.[31] This premise underlies two themes that will be discussed in chapters 5 and 6; namely, the idea that the disintegration of an efficient officialdom would result in the animals from the wilds taking over, and the association of the appearance of ominous animal portents with virtuous and efficient government.

The terminology used for many of the animal officers encountered so far is noteworthy. In both *Zuozhuan* passages, the officials carry the suffix *shi* 氏 in their title. Many Chinese scholars still refer to these narratives as standard examples for the existence of animal totemism in archaic times, claiming that the addition of this suffix indicates a link between the office and an archaic animal totem.[32] There is however no convincing evidence linking the origins of the aforementioned animal offices to primitive animal worship. Nor is there any other form of ritual behavior that links certain animal species to certain social groups. Animals, together with other celestial and natural phenomena, may certainly have been used in an emblematic way in early China. In a passage in the *Shangshu* 尚書 for instance Shun requests to see "the emblematic figures of the ancients (*gu ren zhi xiang* 古人之象): the sun and the moon, the stars and the constellations, the mountains, the dragon, and the flowery animals (variegated pheasants) that are depicted on the upper sacrificial robes of the emperor."[33] However theories which seek to assign the origins of these animal titles to an ancestral totem are unsubstantiated.[34]

More plausible than indicating a totemic origin or a mythical dragon clan is the idea that the suffix *shi* 氏 in these *Zuozhuan* narratives refers to a clan or lineage. Allen J. Chun has argued that "*shi* was quite explicitly linked with political rank and ritual maintenance of the feudal state . . ., *shi* was conferred upon an individual largely in response to some act of virtue which could only be defined in relation to political favor and subsequent ritual obligation."[35] The term *shi* in this period also refers to a specialist, a technical expert whose skills are devoted to the management of a specialist activity. Without necessarily maintaining its aristocratic connotation of a land-based polity loyal to a sovereign, this interpretation is closely linked to the idea of a clan or guild. Specific technical tasks were transmitted through the members of a lineage, and clans were formed around groups who shared common technical skills, in the *Zuozhuan* case "rearing" and "taming" dragons. The link between the hereditary transmission of a profession and recognized state office is clarified elsewhere in the *Zuozhuan* by a grandee from the state of Lu: "When an office has been held successfully for generations, then the (name of) that office may become the clan-name (*guan you shigong, ze you guanzu* 官有世功則有官族)."[36] When we turn to the *Zhouli* depiction of the offices in the idealized state, no fewer than fifty-five officers carry the suffix *shi* in their title. Among these several are associated with the treatment of animals (the *fubushi* 服不氏 "animal tamer," *sheniaoshi* 射鳥氏 "bird killer," *luoshi* 羅氏 "bird netter," *mingshi* 冥氏 "nighttime trapper," *xueshi* 穴氏 "officer of crevice animals," and others). The *shi* suffix in the *Zhouli* denotes a specialist (or a clan of specialists) whose services were recognized and employed by a ruler. It is therefore likely that many of the animal officers attested in the *Zhouli* originated from clans or lineages of technical experts who passed on their skills in animal treatment.

The dialectic between officialdom and the maintenance and control of the natural world and its living species is illustrated again in a later anecdote dated to the early Han. The story involves the keeping of an animal register. It stages Emperor Wen 文帝 (180–157 B.C.E.) who asks his commander of the Shanglin 上林 preserve for the register of the birds and beasts kept in the park (*qin shou bo* 禽獸薄). After having repeated his request over ten times without obtaining a response from the park commander or his assistants, a petty official in charge of the tiger cages steps in and replies to the emperor instead of his superiors. The lad is said to be very thorough and detailed in his reply regarding the animal register the emperor had requested and wants to demonstrate this by endlessly rattling off the register. As a result the emperor decides that the commander in charge is incompetent and orders that the petty official be promoted director of the Shanglin park. Next however Emperor Wen is catechized and reprimanded by one of his advisers who criticizes him for relying on "oral eloquence" rather than "substance"; that is, the emperor ought to rely on the written register and the proper official.[37] Again this story deals with the topic of governance through officialdom. In this case a ruler is admonished to respect the hierarchy among his officials. Secondly, the anecdote stresses the impor-

tance of the assignment of the proper official for the management of the preserve animals, and thirdly, it illustrates bureaucratic record keeping of animal
stocks and the predominance of the written record over oral instruction. The
emperor informs himself about his animal stock via a record-keeping official.
Only this designated official, even when subordinates might be better versed to
do so, is allowed to brief the emperor on his animal stock. Hence a proper *guan*
官 or "controlling office" needs to be connected with the corresponding duties.
Otherwise the management of the Shanglin animals would falter, and as a consequence the ruler's authority would wane.

The idea that matters pertaining to animals were the domain of the appropriate human officer, in other words the rectification of office as a mirror
image of the rectification of names, also forms the subject of a story preserved
in the *Huainanzi* 淮南子 in which Confucius's horse wanders off in the wilds
and gets lost:

> Once when Confucius was travelling, his horse went missing and was eating away
> the grain of a farmer. The rustic (*ye ren* 野人) was infuriated, took the horse and
> tied it up. Zi Gong 子貢 went over to persuade the farmer [to return the horse]
> but finished his statement without being able to recover the horse. Confucius
> said: "Well, explaining things to human beings using concepts they cannot un-
> derstand is like offering the three sacrificial animals to the animals in the wilds or
> playing the *jiu shao* 九韶 music to please flying birds. I am at fault here; it is not
> the farmer's mistake." Next Confucius sent a stable officer over to explain the sit-
> uation. The stable boy arrived, saw the rustic and said: "You are cultivating the
> lands from the eastern sea to the western sea. My (master's) horse got lost, so how
> could it do anything else but eat from your grain sprouts?" The rustic was greatly
> delighted, untied the horse and gave it back.[38]

Several themes run through this story. First Confucius's stratagem to deal with
the seemingly trivial affair of recovering a stray horse consists of indirect communication, first via a disciple and next via a messenger with an even lower status. The story insinuates that the whereabouts of horses and animals are no
immediate preoccupation of the sage, as can be seen elsewhere in a *Lunyu* passage where, following a conflagration of horse stables, Confucius is said to en-
quire about the welfare of the people but not that of the horses.[39] As will be
shown in chapter 5, this stance of indirect contact with the animal world also
typifies the sage's attitude toward sacrificial victims as well as barbarians, who
were considered to be close to animals. Secondly, the anecdote deals with the
theme of the rectification of office by illustrating that a sage-ruler deals with the
animal world through the assignment of the proper human office. Matters concerning horses are to be left to the care of a stable officer, and only this official
possesses the skills, language, and inborn adeptness to get through to the mind

of a farmer since, in the eyes of Confucius, both the stable boy and the farmer approach the level of animals. In fact an earlier version of this story preserved in the *Lüshi chunqiu* 呂氏春秋 speaks of a "rustic type" (*bi ren* 鄙人) instead of a stable officer.[40] Rather than dealing in a direct way with the recovery of his horse, Confucius appears to be concerned primarily with the correct orchestration of the proper agents of communication to achieve his end. His attitude is reminiscent of the sage's informed avoidance to engage in the direct analysis of the natural world. Just as the sage refrained from investigating the biological animal but instead ordered the animal world through the assignment of names, so the immediate management of animals is substituted by the assignment of a mediating role to a corresponding human office.

Ritual Animals

The task descriptions of the animal officers in the *Zhouli* indicate that various kinds of socioreligious practice were responsible for the subsumption of animals within the human polity. Ritual codes specified the different areas of social use of animals by prescribing how humans and animals should relate to one another within a ritual context. They stipulated when, how, and which animals were to be used by specific officiants in sacrificial procedures and ritual exchanges. While such ritual prescriptions primarily sought to establish differentiae, status, and hierarchies within human society, the detailed attention to the ritual use of animals at the same time enhanced the compartmentalization of animals in ritual and social categories. Animals were selected and differentiated according to their ritual functions, and an animal's status among its species' peers was frequently determined by its ritual service to humans. So while animals contributed to the creation of human hierarchies, the social use of animals in turn also influenced the way in which animals were perceived.

   Seen through a lens of ritual hierarchies, animals were ranked within various social taxonomies. Such social classifications were often more elaborate than the traces of biological taxonomy preserved in Warring States and Han writings. Human hierarchies were reflected in hierarchies of animals and vice versa. The aforementioned task of many *Zhouli* officials to "distinguish names and kinds" among animal victims served to align the proper use of the proper animal with the proper function by the proper office. Numerous examples occur in the received record. In the *Zhouli*, the minister of rites is said to "use animals to demarcate the six gifts in order to classify the officials." Each official grade is connected with a specific animal kind used as gift.[41] Another official, the vice minister of rites, selects and names the six animal victims and "issues the distribution of the animals to the five officers." The Eastern Han exegete Zheng Sinong 鄭司農 elaborates on this statement by listing the officials and the animals over which they preside: the Minister of Education presides over the ox, the Minister of Rites over the chicken, the Minister of War over the horse and sheep, the Minister of Justice over the dog, and the Minister of Works over the pig.[42]

Another ritual practice reflecting the dialectic between human and animal hierarchy was the system of exchange gifts. The *Yili* contains the following formula for such presentations:

> The lower order of great officers, upon visiting each other, take a (living) wild goose as a present. They embellish it with cloth and bind its feet with a cord, carrying it as if one holds a pheasant. The upper grades of officers, upon visiting each other, take a (living) lamb as present. They embellish it with cloth, bind its four feet and tie it up at the front with its head to the left, the lamb being held as one holds a fawn.[43]

A chapter in the *Chunqiu fanlu* entitled "Gifts to Superiors" (*zhi zhi* 執贄) explains this use of a particular animal by a specific officer in more detail. The text reiterates that in the presentation of gifts to superiors or friends, a minister should use a lamb and a senior officer a goose. Next it clarifies the use of these animals by pairing their natural behavior to the social disposition and the expected conduct of the human officer in question:

> A goose is of the same kind as the honorable man. An honorable man stands above the people and must, in a reserved manner, follow the order of first and last. He ought to be reverent and possess the capability of controlling rank and order. Therefore the senior official uses the goose as a gift.
>
> A lamb has horns but does not use them; it sets out preparations but never uses them; and it resembles someone who likes benevolence. If one catches a lamb it does not cry; if one kills it, it does not wail. It resembles someone who dies for righteousness. When lambs feed from their mother, they have to kneel to get (the milk). This resembles someone who knows the rites. Therefore the word for "sheep" (*yang* 羊) also means "propitious" (*xiang* 祥). Hence a minister uses it as a gift.[44]

The same examples occur elsewhere. In the *Shuoyuan* 說苑 and *Bohutong* the list is broadened to include both the common officer (*shi* 士), who is associated with the pheasant because it cannot be inveigled by food or subjected by force, as well as the common people who are associated with the tame duck, which cannot fly away.[45] The comparisons inferred here are quite clear. The goose serves as an image for orderly conduct in society, and the lamb evokes the idea of pious and moral conduct by individual administrators. The image of the honorable man "standing above the people" may allude to the idea that geese on seasonal passage fly at higher altitudes than common birds. "Following the order of first and last" refers to the image of geese flying in an orderly formation, an image also reflected in other texts where precision formations of flying birds are used to name army formations.[46]

Yet more important than the choice of specific animals such as the lamb and the goose is the nature of the context in which these animals' behavioral characteristics are described. These passages are concerned with a ritual topic—namely the hierarchy of gifts. The data regarding the biological behavior of the goose and the lamb are interwoven with and inferred from the imperatives of proper ritual conduct by each official in question. In other words, in order to exemplify the use of the lamb and goose as gifts, the author of this passage reads human conduct and human morals into the behavior of the animal. He is not concerned with reporting empirical data on these animals but with explicating animal conduct in function of their use within a ritual order. He has transformed the lamb and the goose into a minister and a senior official.

This social hermeneutic of animal behavior allows for a degree of polysemy in description, since each social use of a specific species can lead to new or slightly adapted associations linked with the same animal. While, above, the goose was linked to a ruler's capability to control rank and order, elsewhere it is singled out as the ideal wedding gift because of its sense for orderly and subject obedience:

> As for the use of the goose as a present [at marriage], it is chosen on the basis of its seasonal (migration to) the south and (return to) the north and its never missing regular timing. This clarifies that a girl is not deprived of her right time. (The goose) is also a bird that follows the *yang* (sun), as in the principle of a wife's duty to follow her husband. Furthermore (geese) are chosen on the basis of (their characteristic of) forming rows and ranks in flight and while resting. This clarifies the rites of marriage according to which old and young have their proper order and do not trespass on each other.[47]

Another way of differentiating between animal species or distinguishing between individual animals within a particular group resulted from their function as sacrificial victims. By far the most frequent reference to the practical use of animals in early China occurs within the context of the ritual slaughter. In addition to the hunt which, in China as well as in other ancient civilizations, was often viewed as an act of organized ritual slaughter on a large scale, the inspection, killing, distribution, and ritual consumption of animals and animal parts was a widespread reality in ancient China.[48] Specified animal victims as well as the context in which they were killed are documented as far back as the Shang. Oracle bone inscriptions mention ancestral offerings that appear to have primarily consisted of domestic animals including pigs, sheep, cattle, and dogs. Domestic animals also figured prominently among offerings in Shang mortuary ritual.[49] Data on the sacrificial use of animals also occur, albeit in smaller numbers, in Zhou bronze vessel inscriptions as well as text passages datable to the early Zhou period. Similar sets of domestic animals provided the main source of sacrificial meat in the Warring States period. For instance, sacrificial victims in the Chu manuscripts excavated at Baoshan 包山 (Hubei; burial dated ca. 316 B.C.E.) include the horse, the pig, the ox, the sheep, and the dog. The Baoshan texts also contain an elaborate terminology for victim animals within these main groups.[50]

The use of animals for ritual slaughter during ancestral sacrifices and state ceremonies entailed that certain animal species were subsumed within a sacrificial taxonomy. Victimal hierarchies reflected the status of the persons who were allowed to sacrifice. The ritual canon of the state of Chu reserved the sacrifice of oxen for rulers and members of the nobility while commoners were told to offer fish.[51] According to the *Liji* the emperor used a bull, a ram, and a boar (i.e., a set of victims known as the *tailao* 太牢 or "greater lot") in the sacrifice to the altars of the spirits of land and grain. Feudal lords were only entitled to a ram and a boar (the *shaolao* 少牢 or "lesser lot").[52] In the sacrifices to the Five Deities (*wu si* 五祀), the emperor and his feudal lords used a bull, while ministers and grandees used a ram.[53] Another code stipulated that the bull was the victim offered by the feudal lords, the sheep by the grandees, and the pig by common officers.[54] A victim hierarchy according to social status also applied during sacrifices following the birth of a son.[55]

Besides being determined by the rank or standing of the performer and recipient of the sacrifice, an animal species could also be differentiated according to sacrificial criteria of a more physical nature. This is exemplified in the case of the most prominent sacrificial victim in early China, the ox or bull.[56] Detailed information about the physical properties of the bull occurs in the context of sacrifice. Several texts provide information on the ox as an ideal sacrificial victim. In general, factors taken into account for selecting a sacrificial bull were color, purity of the hide (i.e., whether it has spots or is monochrome), the bull's size, and the condition of its horns. The breeder of sacrificial animals (*muren* 牧人) in the *Zhouli* is said to "distinguish the victims by hide" (*mao zhi* 毛之); that is, to select those with a uniform hide and distinguish among red, black, spotless, and variegated animals.[57] According to the *Mozi* 墨子, the sage-kings of antiquity selected victims among the six domestic animals by their fatness and the perfection and color of the hide.[58] The sacrificial killing of the wrong victim, or of victims that were physically deformed, is considered unorthodox in several texts. Reference is made to sick or wounded animals that must be removed from the sacrificial altar and replaced, and to cases in which a sacrifice is abolished or modified because of the unfortunate physical condition of the animal victim.[59] One story tells of a cock performing self-mutilation by picking out its own tail feathers in order to avoid being selected as a sacrificial victim.[60] In general preference was given to young sacrificial animals.[61]

Sacrificial criteria functioned as a kind of taxonomic different in their own right. Hence when officers of different ranks were permitted to sacrifice an ox, distinctions were made according to the physical appearance of the animal: "The Son of Heaven uses an ox of one color, pure and unmixed; a feudal prince uses a fattened ox and a grandee a thin ox . . .".[62] An alternative classification differentiated oxen according to the features of their horns:

> Bulls used in sacrificing to Heaven and Earth have horns (no longer than) a cocoon or a chestnut.[63] Those used in the ancestral temple have horns that can be grasped with the hand, and oxen used for feasting guests have horns one (Chinese) foot long.[64]

The quality of the victim also reflected the hierarchy of the deities or natural forces that were addressed during a sacrifice:

> If there was anything unpropitious about the ox intended for a sacrifice to the Thearch (*di niu* 帝牛), it was used as an ox sacrificed to the spirit of the grain (*ji niu* 稷牛). The Thearch's ox had to be kept in a cleansed stable for fattening during three months. The spirit of the grain's ox only needed to be perfect in parts. This is how a distinction was made between the spirits of heaven and the ghosts of man.[65]

In this passage the qualification of two kinds of oxen is inspired by the status of the addressee to which they are to be sacrificed. The addressed spirit becomes an adjectival qualifier of the category "ox." Sacrificial imperatives thus serve as taxonomic referents.

Differentiating animals according to a socioreligious criterion such as sacrificial practice transformed the animal into a socioreligious category rather than a biological species. The secularized animal victim is no longer a biological animal. Its practical use is tabooed, and it can no longer serve as ordinary food. The latter is illustrated in a story from the mid-first century c.e., which relates how the excessive use of cattle in sacrifices had caused severe economic hardship among a local community. People who ate ox meat destined to propitiate local spirits would die from disease and make a mooing sound before they passed away.[66] Wang Mang 王莽 (r. 9–23 c.e.) was also known for depleting animal resources in a prolific number of cults. At more than seventeen hundred different cult centers he used over three thousand different kinds of sacrificial birds and beasts. When these could no longer be afforded, chickens were used instead of ducks and geese, and dogs were used as substitutes for elaphures and deer.[67] In its sacralized status, the animal's biological name, as was shown in the previous chapter, was replaced by a sacrificial name or appellation. It was separated from the ordinary flocks and subsumed within a social taxonomy. In its sacralized or ritualized state, it has become a social category, and its status is no longer determined by biological properties but by ritual principles that guide human society. For instance, the *Liji* stipulates that a ruler should descend from his chariot when passing a ritually cleansed sacrificial ox.[68] Likewise, a sacrificial victim was not to be sold at the market together with common animals.[69]

In sum, ritual procedures prescribing the preparatory treatment and use of sacrificial animals could be described as a chain of physical and symbolical transformations. The segregation of animals from the herds for sacrifice transformed the animal into a victim. The ritual preparations that followed (fattening, cleansing, decorating), together with the special treatment of the victim, turned the animal into an ideal sacrificial victim. Finally the slaughter and blood shedding of the animal transformed the animated victim into deanimated sacrificial meat, from an entity that was "animal" to one that becomes "edible."[70] And every stage of this process was managed by a human officer: the herdsman, the fattener, the butcher, and the priest.

Animals and Spirits

Zoolatry or the sacrificial worship of animals and animal spirits is documented only sporadically in the received textual record of ancient China. Unlike in ancient Egypt, Greece, Rome or Gaul, outspoken zoomorphism appears to have been less widespread in Warring States and Han religion. While evidence suggests that the sacrificial worship of agricultural spirits was part of religious practice since Zhou times and possibly earlier, early China was less familiar with the systematic manifestation of deities as animals, or animals that functioned as standard attributes, emissaries, or servants to the gods.[71] There is also little evidence of spirits wielding their authority as master domesticators of the animal world. With the exception of a number of animal acolytes associated with the Queen Mother of the West (Xiwangmu 西王母) in the Han—the three-legged crow, a nine-tailed fox, a toad, and a hare pounding the elixir of immortality—the Chinese pantheon did not include gods that were invariously identified with emblematic animals such as Dionysos and the bull, Zeus and the eagle, or Athena and the owl.[72] Since ancestral worship was the single most important motive behind organized religious activity in ancient China, references to alliances between gods and animal acolytes or divine epiphanies through the medium of animals or spirits who lived in a realm detached from the human world are scarce.

Despite occasional descriptions of animals as the seat of a sacred presence and scattered references to the cultic worship of animal spirits, it is difficult to ascertain whether animal spirits formed the object of regular religious devotion. Oracle bone evidence suggests that divinations concerning silkworms and the mulberry as well as invocations of and sacrifices to tutelary silkworm spirits occurred in the Shang.[73] The *Guoyu* records an incident in the seventh century

B.C.E. when the appearance of an ominous bird on the city gate of Lu sparked off a cult. The bird cult however was criticized on the basis that it did not belong to the orthodox canonical sacrifices.[74] Other Warring States, Qin, and Han sources contain records of sacrifices to horse, dragon, chicken, cat, and tiger spirits.[75] During the Han sheep and pigs were sacrificed to the silkworm spirit just prior to the ceremonial feeding of the imperial silkworms in the spring.[76] Emperor Xuan 宣帝 (73–49 B.C.E.) is recorded to have built a shrine for the worship of a tributary gift consisting of the skin, teeth, and claws of a white tiger captured in the southern commanderies where tigers may have been worshiped.[77]

The presence of auspicious animal days in calendars from the state of Qin could be testimony of the sacrificial worship of domestic animal spirits.[78] It is more plausible however that certain days were considered more or less auspicious than others for activities involving particular animals. Both daybooks excavated at Shuihudi for instance contain lists enumerating auspicious or tabooed days for engagements involving animals connected with the domestic sphere such as horses, cows, sheep, pigs, dogs, chickens, and silkworms.[79] With the exception of a prayer addressed to a horse spirit discussed below, no liturgy for the worship of animal spirits has so far been transmitted.

While zoolatry may not have played a dominant role in early sacrificial religion, it is noteworthy that, judging from evidence currently available, the association of animals with human office was replicated in the early Chinese perception of the spirit world. Evidence increasingly shows that the Warring States spirit world had a strong bureaucratic component. As Donald Harper has shown, by the end of the fourth century B.C.E. the underworld already resembled a bureaucratic state, and dealings with the spirit world conformed to the norms and procedures of the human bureaucracy. A pantheon of spirits once defined by sacrificial cycles was gradually being redefined along bureaucratic lines over the course of the fourth century.[80] That a dialectical relationship between popular religion and state bureaucracies also affected the perception of spirits connected with the animal world is illustrated in a section entitled "Horses" (*ma* 馬) in one of the Shuihudi daybooks. This text fragment constitutes a unique piece of liturgical evidence describing a sacrificial rite performed for the benefit of young foals and corroborates that the spirit world worshiped by elites and commoners in the third century B.C.E. included tutelary animal spirits. It further indicates that the relationship between the worshiper and the addressed animal spirit was perceived in a bureaucratic fashion. The incantation-prayer, performed at the onset of the herding season when the animals are released onto the pastures, is addressed to the Horse Begetter (*mamei* 馬禖), a fertility spirit that echoes the office of a sexual intermediary (*meishi* 媒氏) attested in the *Zhouli*.[81] The officiant addresses the horse spirit as "The Ruler-and-Lord" (*zhujun* 主君) and presents himself in a hierarchical relationship with the spirit by referring to himself as "Grandee" (*dafu* 大夫):

I, the Grandee, have first spread out the buffalo mat,
today is a favorable day.
Fat suckling pigs, pure wine and excellent white millet
have arrived at the place of My Lord.
My Lord, we have trapped and fenced off these excellent horses.
Chase away their afflictions,
exorcise their baleful influences.
make their mouths be fond of [food],
and [their tongues] be fond of drink.
(Make them) stay in line, move by themselves without [being ridden],
and come forth of their own accord without being chased.
Make their noses able to savor the smells,
make their ears sharp and their sight clear.
Make their heads be (positioned) horizontally on their bodies,
their spines provide strength for their bodies,
their forelegs be [. . .] for their bodies,
their tails be good in chasing off [insects],
their stomachs become sacks for the hundred grasses, and
their four feet be fit for walking.
My Lord, we urge you to drink and eat (the sacrificial offerings).
I, annually, shall not dare to neglect you.[82]

A manuscript from the late Warring States or early Qin period excavated from a tomb at Fangmatan 放馬灘 (Tianshui 天水, Gansu; burial dated ca. 230–220 B.C.E.; excavated in 1986) reveals another aspect of the bureaucratic subsumption of animals in the spirit world—namely, their role as acolytes of spirit-world officials. It presents a white dog as the agent of an underworld official entitled *simingshi* 司命史 "Scribe of the Director of the Life-mandate." According to the account, a man named Dan 丹 is released from the tomb by the underworld authorities to join the world of the living again. The underworld official orders the white dog to dig up the burial pit to let him out. Mediating on the threshold of the realm of the living and the dead, the dog here executes an order from a record-keeping afterlife official.[83]

Other sources mention animal creatures charged with bureaucratic functions in the spirit world or animals as acolytes in the celestial bureaucracy. According to the *Shanhaijing*, a quail presides over the affairs of the Thearch, and phoenixlike yellow birds are said to guard the Thearch's immortality drugs on mount Wu 巫.[84] The three-footed crow (*sanzuwu* 三足烏), believed to reside in the sun, acts as a messenger of the Queen Mother of the West and also appears as a judgmental arbiter of human affairs.[85] In the *Guoyu* Rushou 蓐收, a spirit with a human face, white hair, tiger claws, and grasping an axe, is identified by an oneiromancer as Heaven's penal spirit.[86]

Calendrical Animals

The subsumption of the animal world into the mental universe of a human-controlled sociopolitical realm was epitomized in calendrical texts. Aiming at accommodating and harmonizing human activity with the cycles of the surrounding physical world, calendars pigeonholed observations of animal activity in the natural world into temporal units and paired human activity with seasonal animal behavior.[87] Prescriptive texts known as *yue ling* 月令, or "monthly ordinances," contained detailed information on animal behavior. Yet rather than explaining the causes of animal behavior and systematizing internal relationships within the natural world, calendrical texts grafted animal information onto a human model and designed the temporal and spatial organization of human affairs according to patterns in the natural world. Calendrical models integrated animal observations with the cyclic rhythms of human activity. With the management of the natural world being subject to the control of the all-encompassing bureaucratic state, calendars focused primarily on the collection of those data that were pertinent to the regulation of human society.

An early example of a calendrical sequence predating the received state calendars preserved in the *Lüshi chunqiu, Liji, Da Dai Liji* 大戴禮記, *Huainanzi,* and *Yi Zhoushu* 逸周書 can be found in an ode from the state of Bin 豳 preserved in the *Shijing* ("Qi yue" 七月, Mao 154). The poem refers to the month during which the mulberry branches are stripped of their leaves as the "silkworm month" (*can yue* 蠶月). It further details a temporal schedule for the observation of animal behavior as well as activities related to them. Animal behavior significant within the agricultural cycle includes the singing of orioles and shrikes, the chirping of cicadas and the movement of locusts and grasshoppers. The poem further connects the tenth month with the smoking out of rats, and the first month with the hunt for badgers, foxes, and raccoon dogs.[88] Animal behavior also inspired the timing of sacrificial activities. A passage in the *Zuozhuan* delineates the seasons according to hibernation patterns:

> In the case of sacrifices in general, the suburban sacrifices were held at the time of the "opening and awakening" (*qi zhi* 啓蟄, i.e., when the hibernating animals re-emerged). When the dragon (constellation) appeared, the rain sacrifice was performed. At the "commencement of killing" (*shi sha* 始殺) the autumnal fruit sacrifices were offered (to the ancestors). At the time of "closing and lying dormant" (*bi zhi* 閉蟄, i.e., when the hibernating animals hide away in their burrows) the winter sacrifice was held. If a sacrifice was held in discord with these dates [which were determined by divination], this was put down in a written record. [89]

Calendrical animal observations were predominantly inspired by human needs. This is illustrated in the case of a rat exorcism. The observation of rats shedding their tails in the twelfth lunar month (winter) was to be taken as a sign for humans to start their extermination in the first month of the new lunar year. During that month at dawn before the sun came out, the head of the household was to "behead" or cut open a rat, suspend it in the middle of the house and chant an exorcistic prayer.⁹⁰ In addition to being a measure for pestilence control, the movements of rats and other rodents were monitored for other purposes. The Shuihudi daybooks contain an entry in which good fortune and misfortune are divined depending on the month and day during which rats creep onto the window frames.⁹¹

In addition to linking seasonal animal behavior with the temporal organization of human activity, the calendar also associated human office with the management of the natural world. The chapter on "seasonal rules" (*shize xun* 時則訓) in the *Huainanzi* includes numerous instructions regarding the management of animals via the intermediary of a specified officer. Several of these officers recur, with slight variations, in the other received state annuaries. Their activities are described as follows: in the sixth month the officer of fisheries is ordered to spear scaly dragons, capture alligators, fetch turtles, and capture sea turtles;⁹² in the ninth month the master of sacrifices offers some of the game animals caught in the hunt to the four directions;⁹³ in the eleventh month a superintendent of uncultivated land instructs people to hunt wild birds and beasts;⁹⁴ and in the twelfth month an official known as the master of fisheries is ordered to commence fishing.⁹⁵ In the third month the emperor orders bulls to be mated with cows and stallions with mares; two months later he promulgates rules regarding the breeding of horses, rules known as his "horse policy" (*ma zheng* 馬政). This last expression illustrates the ruler's bureaucratic control over the treatment of horses. One commentator even suggests that the term *ma zheng* refers to the name of a particular official.⁹⁶

The "monthly ordinances" illustrate how the ruler wielded an indirect authority over the natural world through monitoring its cyclic phases of production, growth, and harvesting via a human bureaucracy. At nodal points in the calendar an official exercized the ruler's orders regarding the living species. While the final authority to align human events with the course of nature ultimately issued from the sage-ruler himself, it was the assignment of specialized officials to the management of agriculture, hunting, and sacrifice that enabled him to attune (*guan* 官) human activities to the course of nature.

Regulations such as the promulgation of a "horse policy" were more than just a prescriptive item in the calendar. This is clear from their inclusion in the domestic and foreign policy agenda of the early Han rulers. For instance when Empress Lü 呂 (r. 187–180 B.C.E.) prohibited livestock trade with the Southern Yue 越, an edict specified that in the exceptional circumstance when the trade of horses, cattle, and sheep proved indispensable, only male animals were to be traded in order to prevent the barbarian animal stocks from propagating.⁹⁷ In the

spring of 146 B.C.E. Emperor Jing 景帝 approved a memorial proposing that
horses "over five feet and nine inches with teeth that are not yet smooth (i.e.,
horses below the age of ten)" should not be allowed to be exported through the
custom barriers.[98] The same emperor also expanded the area of pasture land for
horses in order to increase public resources.[99] His successor, Emperor Wu, was
equally serious in promulgating detailed horse policies. In order to attract immi-
grants to settle in the northern border regions, permission was given in 113 B.C.E.
to residents of those districts to raise horses. Government officials lent out mares,
which had to be returned after a period of three years with an interest of one foal
for every ten mares.[100] In order to strengthen his cavalry, feudal lords and high
officials were ordered the following year to supply a specified number of stallions
to the government depending on their rank. In village posts throughout the empire, people were set to breeding colts for which an annual interest was received
each year.[101]

Despite the detailed nature of the animal data displayed in the "monthly
ordinances" and the importance attached to the practical implementation of
such calendrical prescriptions, it is important to note that these empirical observations ultimately served to regulate human activities such as gathering wood,
spinning silk, planting, and harvesting. Animal behavior is interpreted first and
foremost as an indicator for human activity. Animal activity that does not pertain to the organization of human activities forms a lesser part of the calendar.
The animal of the calendar is a socialized animal. Its activities are not explained
with a view to analyzing the natural world but are subsumed within a scheme of
human "monthly ordinances" or "daybooks." Within such a scheme, human
and animal activity needed to be balanced. Therefore if animal activity was seen
to take place at an untimely phase within the annual cycle, it was believed that the
human schedule based on it would disintegrate. Harvests would fail, and famines
and other natural disasters would ensue. If a ruler failed to incorporate accurately
the activities in the surrounding animal world into the model of human affairs,
this model itself would fall prey to decomposition. Likewise the ruler's adept
command of society would ensure seasonal security within the natural world.

> If the way of society is properly structured, then the myriad things all acquire their
> appropriate place, the six domestic animals each obtain their proper growth, and
> all living things obtain their allotted fate. Therefore, just as the six domestic ani-
> mals will multiply if they are nurtured and bred according to the seasons, and just
> as plants and trees will flourish if they are cut and planted with the seasons, so too,
> if the acts and orders of government are according to the seasons, the hundred
> families will be united and the worthy and good will offer their allegiance.[102]

Finally, a series of emblematic animals came to be associated with the calendrical year cycle. These were the so-called twelve animals or animal signs,

more popularly known later as the animals of the Chinese zodiac (*shi-er sheng xiao* 十二生肖): rat, ox, tiger, rabbit, dragon, snake, horse, sheep, monkey, rooster, dog, and pig. The duodenary animal cycle matched each of the earthly branches (*di zhi* 地支) with a patron animal. The origins and original use of the animal cycle are uncertain. Their image may have been based on archaic astronomical associations. A century ago, Edouard Chavannes proposed that the cycle originated among Turkish people in central and north Asia and that it seeped into China during the first century C.E.[103] At the time of Chavannes the *Lunheng* provided the earliest transmitted example of a complete duodenary animal cycle.[104] Tracing correspondences between animal graphs in names and years of birth, Peter Boodberg has speculated that the chronogrammatic use of the twelve animals may have been in practice as early as the sixth century B.C.E.[105] The discovery of two new examples in calendars found at Shuihudi and Fangmatan suggests that the appearance of the cycle in China should be dated back to the late Warring States period at least. The Shuihudi and Fangmatan animal cycles appear in a calendar aimed at identifying thieves by sight and name. They may provide early evidence for the practice of name selecting according to the day of birth.[106] Given that the three preserved cycles differ slightly (for instance the dragon is absent in the Shuihudi and Fangmatan versions), they were probably part of a developing system.

Conclusion

In their treatment of the animal world, Warring States and Han writings primarily focused on the selective collection and organization of those data regarding animals that affected human society. Rather than describing the internal workings of the natural world as a reality dissociated from human affairs, these texts firmly linked the identification, management, and classification of animals with offices and officials that were part of the all-encompassing bureaucratic state. As a consequence the perception of the natural world was largely subject to a human model in which socioreligious criteria and practices such as the exchange of gifts, the ritualized slaughter of animals, the role of animals in the spirit world, and the use of calendars provided an important framework for the way in which animals and animal behavior were classified.

Texts dealing with the organization of ritual and the ordering of the duties of human officialdom therefore provided a formative context for the classification of animals as well as the explanation of animal behavior in early China. Descriptions of the royal offices of Zhou, portrayals of the ideal sacrificial victim and its role within ritual hierarchies as well as calendrical prescriptions confirm that the interest in the biological animal was determined by the degree to which it could be incorporated in and controlled by the human polity. While, as the next chapter will show, the subsumption of the animal world within a human, social model did not preclude the development of more detached attempts at ordering the animal world, categorizing animals in early China often amounted to describing and ordering the usage of animals according to their human functionality. This implied that animals were perceived to be sociocultural creatures as much as natural beings. It also meant that through projecting human categories onto the animal world and defining animals in social contexts that where guided by human principles, the animal kingdom came to be seen as a moral realm ruled by laws similar to those that governed the world of man.

CHAPTER THREE

CATEGORIZING ANIMALS

The examples of animal classification encountered so far have shown that the hermeneutic of the animal world in early China tended to blend biological and socioreligious models. Rather than dissociating the biological properties of animals from their social perception, both were taken as complementary. While we must assume that the Warring States and Han observer was also encouraged to differentiate real animals from the more fantastic and monstrous creatures that inhabited the worlds of demonographies and bestiaries, the overall picture is one in which a clear distinction between biological and culturally constructed animals remains absent. In their double role as both habitual and ordinary companions to humans in daily life as well as objects instilling fear and awe in the minds of commoners and elites alike, animals in early China, as in other ancient societies, were creatures laden with both biological veracity and symbolic significance.

The previous two chapters have shown how both the lexicographer and the ritualist, each in their own way, sought to formulate various models of order in the animal world. In the case of the former, animal classification figured within the greater enterprise of ordering a universe of graphs and names and obtaining a sense of cosmic security through the attribution of names to unknown creatures. For the latter, animal classification was inspired by imperatives that originated from the various social usages of animals in human society. This chapter examines whether early texts provide information regarding the differentiae between humans and animals or among the animal species other than their distinctiveness by name or their functional incorporation within the human polity. I will propose to distinguish three contexts of classification—a physical, functional, and moral model—and discuss how each of these classificatory schemes sought to relate or distinguish the living species.

Three observations regarding classification in ancient societies need to be kept in mind when approaching the Chinese material. First, anthropologists and scholars of early science have argued at length that taxonomic theorization in "primitive" or "prescientific" civilizations encompasses ideas that transcend the mere observation of the natural or biological world. Interests other than the gathering of biological knowledge about specific species usually preceded the development toward a more detached observation of the natural world. In ancient Greece and China, as well as early modern Europe, practical and utilitarian motives contributed to the desire to study and classify the natural world. For instance a curiosity to gain insight into the medicinal properties of plants and animals sparked a growing interest in botanical and zoological classification in medieval and later imperial China when encyclopaedists increasingly integrated data about animals and plants in practical writings such as pharmacopoeia, travelogs, gardening manuals, or books on farming and veterinary medicine.

Second, the scientific and symbolic observation of the animal world should not be strictly separated, neither can the two attitudes be ranked in sequence with the latter representing a so-called more primitive stage that preceded and conditioned the discovery of the former. The reverse can be true, as is shown for instance in the Christian medieval period where illustrated bestiaries interpreted animal lore both as allegories and as actual accounts of the miracles of God's creation while drawing substantially on the pagan "scientific" writings from Greek and Roman antiquity.[1] While symbolic classification and biology do not preclude each other, neither wholly requires the presence of the other to form a system that lends itself to a meaningful analysis of the natural world. Whenever societies in the past have attempted to make sense of the internal structures and external workings of the natural world by developing a set of categories to classify its visible and invisible components, empirical observation has only been one constituent part of an overall taxonomy. As Geoffrey Lloyd notes in a discussion of early Greek zoology, many nonobservational elements enter the equation.

> The very marking of the contrasts between animals, men, divine creatures and demigods of various kinds, and the gods themselves, is itself evidence that animal taxonomy is subsumed in a much wider framework. The objects to be encompassed in the classification span both what we should call the natural and the supernatural domains, and the interest is as much in establishing the external relations of the groups as in the internal divisions between, for example, the various kinds of animals themselves.[2]

In early China animal classification was certainly embedded within a "wider framework," and it is the nature of this framework itself, including the motivation behind the impulse or refusal to formally taxonomize nature, that needs to be addressed to clarify the origins and directions of early Chinese attempts to classify the living species.

Third, apart from structuring the natural species, taxonomic systems, regardless of their internal cohesion, in turn also reflect the world view of the observer and the cultural context in which the observations are rooted. Ethnozoologists have shown that folk-biological classifications, despite the fact that they often provide a stable framework for inference and an inductive compendium of biological information, are incongruent with scientific animal taxa.

The cultural perception of natural classes or kinds and biological taxa are not isomorph.[3] The prevalence of animal nominology as well as the detailed descriptions of animals in the context of ritual in early China corroborate the idea that particular cultures or societies tend to select only certain differentiae between animal species as being relevant for their own classificatory models.[4] Taxonomic systems thus implicitly convey sociocultural meanings and values since any logos detected in the natural world both structures and is structured by that sociocultural logos. Situating the place of an animal within a socioreligious universe goes beyond identifying its place within the natural fauna.[5]

No claim can be made that early Chinese texts contain unified theories that developed out of a scientific motivation to classify the animal world. Lexicographic clarification, the treatment of animals in ritual practice, and practical concerns stemming from the daily usage and treatment of domestic and wild animals appear to have been more formative in the perception of the animal world than the detached observation of nature. Few passages in Warring States and Han writings decontextualize animals from their social or literary environment or reflect a desire to taxonomize animals according to protoscientific criteria. A fragment in the *Xunzi* that figures within a broader discussion of the rectification and distribution of names could be (and indeed has been) misread as such:

> Therefore although the ten thousand things are manifold, there are times when one wishes to refer to them all, and thus one calls them "things" (*wu* 物). "Things" is a great general term (*da gong ming* 大共名). . . . There are times when one wishes to selectively speak of them, so one says "birds and beasts" (*niao shou* 鳥獸). "Birds and beasts" is a great classifying term (*da bie ming* 大別名). One extends this process and divides them again and again. When one reaches a point where no further division is possible, then one stops.[6]

At first sight, this excerpt could function as a nice prolegomenon to a more detailed scheme of species division in the animal world. However, its context indicates that we are not dealing here with a missed attempt at zootaxonomy. In the passage from which the above quote is taken, Xunzi merely argues how through a process of differentiation (*bie* 別) one can carve up the world and narrow down general categories to specific subcategories. Xunzi points out that birds and beasts are a particular differentiation of the general category of "things" (*wu*), but makes no attempt to elaborate on the "classifying terms" (*bie ming*) that differentiate the "birds" and "beasts." As Robert Eno has pointed out, although Xunzi in his taxonomical portrait of reality conceives of the world as naturally structured by categories and relationships, the categories themselves are a blend of an ideal and empirical world. They ultimately figure as the analogue or grounding force of a ritual or ethical order and not as a logic of objective natural entities.[7]

While discourse on the classification of the living species is present in certain Warring States and Han texts, the evidence is fragmentary and lacks detail and consistency. In general the object to be classified into subcategories is the cosmos as a whole with the animal world figuring as only one constituent part. The hermeneutic path followed then is one that seeks to narrow down every existing reality from a primal unity. Several texts picture a differentiation of "all things" from a monadic unity into more concrete physical categories ranging from heaven and earth, mountains and rivers, to human beings, birds, and beasts. Such imagery of a cosmomorphism in which the natural world diversifies itself through a process of dyadic and correlative opposition had philosophical roots in cosmogonies of a proto-Daoist signature such as those found in the *Daodejing* 道 德 經, the *Huainanzi,* and the *Wenzi* 文 子. The archetypal statement on the diversification of the cosmos into smaller entities is an aphorism in the *Daodejing* stating that "the *Dao* begets one; one begets two; two begets three; and three begets the myriad creatures."[8] The *Huainanzi* speaks of birds, fish, and quadrupeds as subcategories or "differentiated creatures" (*fen wu* 分物) of a primal unity. However a consistent vocabulary of "division" (*fen* 分) or "differentiation" (*bie* 別) of the animal species remains absent.[9]

The above observations are not to imply that attempts at protoscientific taxonomisation did not exist in early China. Several text fragments evince an interest in the classification and differentiation of the animated species that goes beyond explaining their name or their use within the social order. Some traces of classification are put in explicit terms, others are implicit. There is however insufficient ground to infer a unified ontology of the living species from this material, which is quite disparate in itself. While some systems of animal classification appear to be based on physical—that is, biological—principles, a strong moral component underlay the distinction between humans and animals. Many statements on the physiological relationship between humans and animals, or among specific animal groups, form part of moral theories on the proper societal ethos propounded by individual thinkers or philosophical schools. In general three main paradigms of classification can be distinguished. First, certain texts indicate that the classification of the living species was based on the notion that living creatures possessed "blood and *qi*" (*xueqi* 血 氣), which was perceived as both a physiological and a moral agent in its function as seat of the emotions. Second, a number of sources proposed a structuring of the internal relationships among living creatures according to the correlative notions of *yin* and *yang* and the five phases. These texts sought to incorporate the classification of living creatures within a functional description of the structure of the cosmos as a whole by pairing animal categories with objects and attributes that were not strictly animal. Finally, distinctions between humans and animals were made according to moral principles. In this model the appropriation and mastery of certain feats of ritual and social behavior defined the boundaries between human and animal nature. Frequently these three models, which I distinguish here mainly for the purpose of presentation, amalgamated into various combinations leaving animals being categorized according to a variety of parameters.

Qi *and Blood*

Attempting to trace a physiological theory on the basis of which the early Chinese sought to explain the differences and similarities between humans and animals remains a precarious enterprise. This is due not only to the fact that no systematic exposition on the subject has survived in the sources, but also because, in stringing together fragmentary evidence to elucidate certain key terms that may have been instrumental to the formulation of such theories, one has to remain skeptical as to whether they were part of a shared vocabulary. Certain terms that evoke predominantly physiological connotations in one context (for instance "*qi*" as "breath" in medical texts) may not have the same meaning in a different context (for instance "*qi*" as omnipresent "stuff" in cosmology). Despite these reservations this section will show that, in the minds of Warring States and Han thinkers, there was at least an implicit awareness of a physiological model that distinguished living creatures from inanimate things.

In the "Tai shi" 泰誓 chapter of the *Shangshu,* a chapter widely held to be a forgery of Han times, a human being (*ren* 人) is identified as the sole creature among the myriad beings to be endowed with "spiritual energy" (*ling* 靈). In his commentary Kong Anguo 孔安國 (ca. 156–ca. 74 B.C.E.) glosses *ling* as *shen* 神 and explains that human beings are the most noble creatures produced by heaven and earth.[10] The idea that human beings are distinguished by their possession of *shen* or *jingshen* 精神—that is "refined (essential) spirit"—occurs elsewhere, but it is hard to ascertain to what degree there existed a common understanding of these terms. Wang Fu 王符 (90–165 C.E.) states that "what makes a human being into a human being is not its having an eight-foot-high body but the fact that it possesses essential spirit (*jingshen*)."[11] The attribution of *ling* (a term also linked with sacred animals) as distinctive to humans only appears to be an isolated reference. Furthermore the attribution of *ling, shen,* or *jingshen* to humans may simply mean that humans have more "wits" or possess a greater intellectual awareness than nonhuman creatures.

A more common way in which early texts distinguished humans and animate beings from the inanimate world or differentiated species within the animate world was based on the notion of *qi* and blood. *Qi,* blood, and "blood and *qi*" (*xueqi* 血氣) were perceived as a distinctive criterion of animacy. Given its use in early medical literature, *xueqi* is best understood as a compound term rather than blood *and qi.* Its meaning approximates what Manfred Porkert has called "configurational energy," being an agency in which "*qi* represents the active aspect, and *xue* the structive one. . . . The vital functions depend not on the presence of *xue* but on its particular intrinsic quality and its harmony with the other forms of energy, especially *qi*."[12] The combination of "blood and *qi*" as an essential component of animated life can be dated back to the fourth century B.C.E.[13] The idea that *qi* flows along with blood through vessels inside the body occurs around the first half of the third century B.C.E., the first reference to blood vessels possibly occurring a century earlier in a *Zuozhuan* description of a distraught horse.[14]

Among the species endowed with *qi,* or "blood and *qi*," the difference between animals and humans depends, according to some sources, on a degree of fineness or subtlety of *qi.* The *Huainanzi* states that "coarse *qi* forms animals, and refined *qi* forms humans."[15] This juxtaposition of coarse (*fan* 煩) versus refined (*jing* 精) indicates that the physiological basis of animals and humans was perceived to be made up from the same basic stuff, while physical and behavioral differences were thought to originate primarily from the way in which a creature's *qi* is structured. The *Wenzi* contains a similar distinction maintaining that animals are formed by coarse *qi* (*cuqi* 麤氣).[16] Animality was also linked to varying degrees of order or disorder of a creature's "blood and *qi*." Hence the *Guoyu* states that the Rong 戎 and Di 狄 barbarians resemble wild animals because their "blood and *qi*" is not regulated.[17] Here animalistic or barbaric conduct is equated with the inability to control one's "blood and *qi*."

While acknowledging external physical differences between humans and animals based on the organization and refinement of the basic stuff that makes up all creatures, more often the possession of "blood and *qi*" is said to unite them. The *Liezi* defines human beings as "anything with a skeleton seven feet high, hands different from its feet, hair on its head and teeth inside the mouth, standing upward as it runs." Birds and beasts are defined as "anything with wings at its side or horns on its head, teeth apart and claws spread out, flying upwards or walking bent down."[18] The text then proceeds by stating that "the species endowed with blood and *qi*" comprises demons, spirits, animals, and human beings:

> The fact that the sages gathered the ghosts, spirits and *chimei* 魑魅 first, next summoned the human beings of the eight quarters and finally assembled birds, beasts and insects, implies that there are no great differences in mind (*xin* 心) and intelligence (*zhi* 智) between the species endowed with blood and *qi* (*xueqi zhi lei* 血氣之類).[19]

Here the sage is said to be able to summon all blood species because they share a heart-mind and intelligence.[20] Although different species may have varying physical shapes, the possession of "blood and *qi*" makes each of them susceptible to the moral authority of the sage, which transcends species boundaries.

According to Wang Chong, human beings live by the agency of refined *qi* (*jingqi* 精氣) which is made possible by the blood vessels.[21] He further defines blood as the "*jingqi* during one's life period" and describes "blood and *qi*" as the seat of one's *jingshen*, hereby again associating the development of spiritual energy with the presence of a physiological substrate of blood vapor.[22] Wang also refers to the living species as "the species that contain *qi*" (*han qi zhi lei* 含氣之類) and "the species that contain blood" (*han xue zhi lei* 含血之類).[23] In one passage he distinguishes humans from wild birds that contain blood (*han xue zhi qin* 含血之禽) and beasts that have bodily form (*you xing zhi shou* 有形之獸).[24] Still according to Wang, there exists no major difference between human birth and that of the six domestic animals, both being creatures that possess "blood and *qi*."[25] Likewise birds and beasts are said not to differ from humans in their possession of emotions and desires. All blood creatures for instance are conscious of hunger and cold.[26]

From its association with mental functions such as the heart-mind and spiritual awareness, it is clear that the notion of "blood and *qi*" was more than a biological or physical property. In a number of texts "blood and *qi*" is said to underlie the faculty of the emotions. This correlation is significant since it attributes a faculty similar to human emotions to nonhuman living beings. The notion that nonhuman creatures were receptive to impulses other than those needed to guarantee their physical subsistence enhanced the idea of a moral contingency between the animal world and the human realm. Animals, as will be discussed later, were often pictured as creatures susceptible to human virtues and morality. According to the following excerpt from the *Liji* (informed by a similar passage in the *Xunzi*), all creatures that possess "blood and *qi*" are subject to emotions. This includes birds and beasts who also mourn for the loss of one of their kind.

> In general, all creatures that live between heaven and earth and have "blood and *qi*" are certain to possess awareness (*zhi* 知). Among those having awareness, there is none which does not love its kind (*lei* 類). Consider the case of large birds and beasts: when they lose a mate or are separated from their group, then even after a month or a season has passed, they are certain to circle around their old home and fly about there. They are crying and calling, moving to and from, gazing about uncertainly and hesitantly, before they are able to leave the place. Even small birds like swallows and sparrows chatter and cry for a while before they are able to leave.[27]

The text goes on to argue that human beings possess the highest degree of awareness among the "blood and *qi*" creatures and therefore must show filial piety until death. Still according to the *Liji* all creatures with "blood and *qi*" respect their kin, an idea that echoes Xunzi's proposition that humans who forget their deceased relatives on the day they die ought to be considered lower than birds and beasts.[28] As the passage above suggests, the distinction between human and beast is only frail with regard to the awareness of the well-being of species' consorts as well as the inclination to preserve one's own species. The distinction between humans and animals is not "speciest"; it is perceived as a differentiation in degree rather than kind. Feats of animal behavior aimed at preserving the species are explained as a less refined expression of filial piety and the universal desire to maintain proper kinship relations. A sense of mourning for one's kind befalls all "blood and *qi*" creatures, and the idea that "kind loves kind" applies equally to the animal kingdom.[29]

Several passages suggest that emotions and temperament were seen as faculties innate to all "blood and *qi*" creatures across the species divide. "Blood and *qi*" is identified as an agent for aggression at least as early as the *Zuozhuan,* and similar ideas occur in the Mawangdui *Jingfa* and among the Chu bamboo manuscripts discovered at Guodian 郭店 (Jingmen, Hubei; excavated in 1993).[30] In the *Huainanzi,* species with "blood and *qi*" are said to possess the temperaments of joy and anger and the inclination to advance toward benefit and shun danger in the same way as humans. The same text links climate with human temperament in an analogy in which "blood and *qi*" are presented as the bodily equivalent of rain and wind.[31] Similarly all creatures with "blood and *qi*" are said to have an inclination to play with each other when pleased or hurt each other when angry.[32] The *Shiji* notes that animals having blood, teeth, and horns will resist when being opposed.[33] In the *Liezi,* a tiger rearer qualifies "blood and *qi*" as the psychosomatic base of a living creature's temperaments by stating that "it is in the nature of all creatures with 'blood and *qi*' to be pleased when one complies with them and to get angry when one is obstinate to them."[34]

The identification of animated beings as creatures that possessed blood or "blood and *qi*" was also reflected in the discourse on sacrificial practice. The oblation of blood occupied a central role in sacrificial religion where the concept of blood was often presented as a life-giving force or agency of animated life. The graph 血, which in origin represents a drawing of a filled sacrificial vessel, is glossed in the *Shuowen* as "the blood of victim animals offered during sacrifice."[35] The presentation of blood to feed the spirits together with the inspection of a victim's hair or hide were standard components of sacrificial procedure. According to a description of an ancestral sacrifice in the *Shijing,* the ritualist first opened the hair layers of the animal with a *luan* 鸞 knife (a knife with bells on its handle) to verify the pureness of the victim's hide, in this case a red bull. Following the slaughter the officiant "takes its blood and fat" to feed the spirits.[36] The important and visible role of blood shedding is borne out in a description of a blood consecration ceremony conducted after the completion of a new temple:

> The sacrificial butcher rubs the sheep clean, the priest chants a prayer (to bless the victim) and the cook while facing north takes the animal to the stone pillar and

places it to the south of it, the highest officiant standing to the east. The butcher then lifts up the sheep and climbs onto the roof at the middle-point (between east and west). In the centre on the roof, he faces south, stabs the animal and lets the blood run down in front of him. Then he descends. At the gate of the temple and at each of the two side rooms a chicken is used, first at the gate and then at the side rooms. The hairs and feathers around the ears are pulled out under the roof (before the killing). When the chickens are cut, at the temple gates and the rooms on each side of it, officers stand opposite to the respective gate and room and face north. When the ritual is over, the priest announces that it is finished, following which everyone retires. Then a message is returned to the ruler saying: "The blood consecration of such-and-such a temple has been completed."[37]

During sacrifices at the ancestral temple, oxen were led forward and fastened to a pillar. Officiants then bared their arms and inspected the hair with particular attention to the growth around the ears. Next the victim was killed and cut open with a *luan* knife.[38] The inspection of the hair tufts behind the ears, according to one commentator, was linked to the idea that the ear governs the faculty of hearing, and therefore the animal's ears were presented to induce the spirits to lend their ear to the sacrificial requests of the supplicants.[39] The symbolism of the victim's ears was also apparent at sacrificial killings during covenants where the left ear of the animal was cut off, a custom similar to the practice of cutting off the left ear of an enemy killed in battle or animals killed in ceremonial hunts.[40] The rationale behind blood shedding and the removal of the hair tufts is further explained in the *Guoyu:*

> Inspecting the hair of a victim animal serves to demonstrate its color. Bleeding it serves to announce the act of killing. One receives the spirits in trust by pulling out the hair and collecting the blood and presents it together with the other offerings as a rule of respect.[41]

Ritual instructions on the orthopraxis of sacrifice justified moderation in sacrificial killing on the basis that both the human sacrificer and the animal victim were creatures of "blood and *qi.*" Extravagant and unnecessary shedding of animal blood was seen as an infringement of the respect that the gentleman should demonstrate toward all blood species. Needless killing of animals amounted to a symbolic slaughter of the self and one's moral integrity. The *Liji* states:

> The gentleman does not kill oxen without a reason, the grandees do not kill sheep without a reason, and the officer does not kill dogs and pigs without reason. The gentleman keeps a distance from the kitchen (i.e., the place where animals are killed); in general (the gentleman) does not personally trample on (i.e., kill) the species that contain "blood and *qi.*"[42]

Evidence suggests that the perception of "blood and *qi*" as animating principles also influenced the selection of animal parts used in sacrifice to the spirits.
In ritual codes, prominence is given to the position of the lungs in the sacrificial
layout of animal parts and to those organs which contain blood and/or *qi*. The
Liji for instance indicates that during a sacrifice to the souls of the departed,
blood and *qi* were an important criterion in the presentation of offerings: "Blood
is offered because of the *qi* contained in it; by offering the lungs, liver and heart
one honors (those organs as) the home of *qi* (*qi zhu* 氣主)."[43] With blood and *qi*
believed to be agents of vitality, the oblation of blood was a visible presentation
of *qi* with the organs being the physical media containing this energy. Thus the
act of slaughtering and bleeding a victim constituted a process of transformation
during which the animal transformed from an animate blood creature into
sacrificial meat. Bleeding an animal is, as Noëlie Vialles points out,

> to take away life itself, the vital principle, therefore to de-animate. As such it is an
> inevitably radical act, allowing of no degrees, and it is what makes the subsequent
> transformations possible. For those transformations we might reserve the less
> radical term "de-animalisation," for they do not in fact concern the vital *principle*
> but rather the bodily *form* of the animal, re-forming it and thus turning it into
> something edible, something quite different from a living body.[44]

In Warring States and Han China, the killing of a living creature could be described
as a process of de-animation, which consisted of the dissolution of blood and *qi*.

To summarize, rather than radically distinguishing animals from humans,
the discourse on blood and "blood and *qi*" provided a theoretical background fa-
voring the presence of psychological and physical similarities between humans
and animals. In linking instinctive temperaments and emotions to all "blood and
qi" creatures, Warring States and Han writings classified humans and animals
together as animate creatures possessing a sense of awareness and moral potentiality. The prominent symbolism of blood and *qi* in sacrificial ritual confirms its
role as a principle of animacy associated with humans and animals alike.

Yinyang *and the Five Phases: Correlative Taxonomies*

A second significant mode of classification of the animal world was its subsumption within the correlative models of *yinyang* and the five phases (*wuxing*
五行). The origins and developments of correlative thinking and its pervasive
influence on late Warring States and Han thought have been studied in detail
and need not be rehearsed here.[45] What concerns us here is how these models
perceived the organization of the animal world, or more importantly, how *yinyang* and correlative thinking related the animal world to the phenomena in the

cosmos at large. Through its attempts to find homologies between natural and human phenomena, and through its assumption that the natural world was deeply implicated in human affairs, correlative thinking subsumed natural phenomena into schemes that ultimately served to regulate human society by adjusting its workings to patterns in the natural realm. As Benjamin Schwartz states: "Paradoxically, what correlative cosmology offers is both a sense of the human's dependence on all levels of his being on cosmic forces and yet the exhilarating promise of the capacity on the part of some minds to comprehend these forces which seem to be eminently 'knowable' and the power to use this knowledge to achieve an 'alignment' between the human and natural worlds."[46] The description of the relations among the living species within correlative schemes can thus be seen as another way in which Warring States and Han thinkers projected the organization of the animal realm within the bounds of human control. In its aspirations to encompass both natural and cultural phenomena within a comprehensive classificatory scheme based on assumptions of interrelatedness and interdependence, *yinyang* and correlative thinking supplied much of the rationale behind the rejection in early China to view the animal world as a separate sphere of knowledge.

From the mid-third century B.C.E. onward, when correlative thinking had gradually filtered into the works of the philosophers, the most frequently recurring scheme approximating a zoological classification was a differentiation of all living species into five categories. This standard model described the living species according to their external shape, more specifically the covering of the skin, and divided animals into scaly, feathered, naked, hairy, and armored species.

Animal category	Phase	Season	Direction	Color
scaly 鱗	wood	spring	east	green/blue
feathered 羽	fire	summer	south	red
naked 臝	earth	late summer	center	yellow
hairy 毛	metal	autumn	west	white
armored 介	water	winter	north	black [47]

Although subject to occasional debate, most versions of this scheme identify human beings as the central class of naked animals.[48] It has been suggested that the introduction of humans as "naked" or "scantily haired" species was a later addition prompted by the increasing influence of *wuxing* thought during the Western Han, but this is by no means certain.[49] Evidence suggests that a generic category of hairless animals may have been known in pre-Han times. The "Xuan gong" 玄(幼)宮 calendar in the *Guanzi* 管子 mentions (in its section on the center) that fire produced by hairless animals (*luo shou* 倮獸) is used for cooking.[50] Furthermore, color correspondences applied to animals already existed before

Han's systematization of five-phase theory.[51] Regardless of its origins the inclusion of human beings within the framework of five-phase theory can be seen as a systematizing attempt to position humans along with other animal species within one and the same frame of analysis.

While the aforementioned discourse on "blood and *qi*" singled out human beings as creatures generated by a more refined residue of *qi,* the five-phase paradigm placed human beings as central creatures in a circular zoography. Rather than speaking of a zoological taxonomy, I would suggest the term "zoography" here since this model primarily describes the relationship between the animal groups and other cosmic sequences such as time, space, and color rather than analyzing the individual animal groups themselves. Within this cyclical zoography, the constituent elements therefore need to be explained by "locating them within the pattern."[52] Hence the association of spring with scaly animals, summer with feathered animals, autumn with hairy creatures, and winter with the armored species need not be seen as a biological statement but rather as an attempt to align taxonomic categorization with a temporal logic based on the seasons. The same applies to other combinations inferred from this scheme, such as the association of human beings with yellow earth, or birds with the color red and the sun.

Correlative classifications thus attempted to interrelate disparate categories within an overarching model that encompassed realities outside the animal world. This process of classifying the universe by induction or extrapolation through detecting systematic correspondences between remote phenomena was sometimes formulated in the idea that one could "push" or "project" (*tui* 推) meanings over the boundaries of different categories or "species" (*lei* 類).[53] While *tui lei* is usually described as an epistemological method associated with five-phase and *yinyang* thinking, in general it refers to a process in which visible realities in the natural world are identified and categorized in order to "push" or extrapolate this explanatory logic to realms beyond the visible. As such it has been theoretically accredited to Zou Yan 鄒衍, an influential scholar who was active at the Jixia 稷下 academy in Qi in the middle of the third century B.C.E. His method is summarized by Sima Qian:

> First [Zou Yan] had to examine small phenomena, then he expanded and magnified (his scope), until he reached what was without limit. . . . He began by classifying China's famous mountains, great rivers and connecting valleys; its birds and beasts; the fruitfulness of its waters and soils, and its rare products; and from this extended (*tui*) his survey to what is beyond the seas, and men are unable to observe.[54]

The origins of the particular deductive conjunctions that link each of the five phases to an animal group are uncertain. They may have resulted from the idea that the condition of an animal's skin covering was determined by varying degrees of density or sparsity depending on the seasons. This explanation is suggested by a Qing scholar, Li Yuan 李元 (fl. 18th century), who describes the seasonal change of dominant animal categories in the "monthly ordinances" as a process of "dispersion" and "coagulation":

> The *yang* disperses and the *yin* coagulates. Spring and summer are *yang*. There-fore armored shells disperse (*san* 散) into scales, scales disperse into feathers. Au-tumn and winter are *yin*, therefore feathers coagulate (*ning* 凝) into hair and hair coagulates into armored shells.[55]

According to Li this pattern of dispersion and coagulation of *yang* and *yin* ex-plains why, according to traditional calendars, hawks transform into pigeons in mid-spring, field mice transform into quails in late spring, small birds enter the big waters to transform into bivalves in late autumn, and fowl enter the big wa-ters to change into molluscs in the beginning of winter.[56] Thus the prominence of a specific animal species during one particular season is explained by match-ing its physiology and behavior to a continuously changing annual *yinyang* pat-tern. These animal metamorphoses in the calendar will be discussed in more detail in chapter 6.

An important consequence of the incorporation of humans as a functional group within an overarching reality, rather than as an essential category that was ontologically differentiated from everything nonhuman, was the absence of a lin-ear notion that perceived the living world as a hierarchy of more or less developed species. At least on the basis of biology, correlative models did not position human beings as the most developed specimens at the apex of an evolutionary progres-sion; neither were humans differentiated on the basis of superior or inferior phys-ical features or ontological properties innate or unique to their species. Instead the human animal was categorized by its functional properties in correlation with other creatures and the cosmos at large. Early Chinese categories, or "groups of beings that resemble each other" (*lei* 類), were rarely identified by appealing to "a shared essence or 'natural kinds,'" but by a functional similarity or relationship that obtains among unique particulars."[57] Herein lies a fundamental difference with the Aristotelian perception of animals for Aristotle saw animals as part of a hierar-chy of existence in a scale of perfection with man at the top. As Roger French sum-marizes, for Aristotle, "the natural world was a collection of natures-of-things, each a principle governing the development and behavior of the individual thing. That is, there was no external set of principles by which natural things developed or interacted, no wisdom of a maternal Nature."[58] The integration of animal cate-gories within correlative schemes in early China did precisely the opposite. Exter-nal sets of principles such as time or season, space or biotope, color, and human activity were instrumental in delineating animal classes and their mutual relation-ships. As the subsequent chapters will illustrate, the supremacy of human beings over other animal classes—epitomized in the pivotal role of the sage- or ruler-king—was not seen as the result of a natural supremacy or gradual biological perfection; rather, it was presented as the result of the human species' ability to adapt to each of the other animal "phases" and its ability to change according to changing circumstances. Rather than being celebrated as the most perfected outcome of an evolutionary progression, the human animal occupied the center within a cyclical hierarchy. What differentiated humans from the other living species within the five-phase model was the fact that the human animal encompassed features of all animal species and could change its habitat and biorhythm according to the seasons. As such the naked animal was a microrepresentation of the entire animal species, the embodiment of a universal species that distinguished itself from others not by a quintessence called "human" but by its capacity to move and act correctly according to the changing parameters of the cosmos.

This characterization of the central human ruler is most clearly evinced in the calendar where, at each particular phase of the annual cycle, the human ruler accommodated his activities with that of the prevailing animal species. Not only does the ruler sacrifice and consume animals appropriate to each season, he also tallies his choice of animal game, as well as his clothes and other ritual paraphernalia with the animal species associated with a specific season. In spring he eats mutton, in summer chicken, in late summer beef, in autumn dog meat, and during the winter months pork. He also sacrifices the animal proper to the season and gives precedence to a different animal organ during each phase of the sacrificial cycle.[59] Finally, as will be discussed in chapter 6, the image of the ruler-king or human sage as the "ultimate animal" encompassing all other species was corroborated by his identification with metamorphosing creatures such as the dragon and other hybrids and was further epitomized by the advent of numinous animals in response to his actions.

Turning to some textual materials, it is no great surprise to find the more elaborate descriptions of animals and animal activity according to *wuxing* and *yinyang* models in works of a Han signature. The most detailed correlative systematization of the animal world is preserved in the syncretistic *Huainanzi* (compiled ca. 140 B.C.E.). The discourse on animals in this work is scattered across different chapters and does not form an independent section within the transmitted version of the *Huainanzi*. Another common trait of the *Huainanzi* descriptions of animals is that they figure as part of a larger cosmogonic and cosmological portrait and therefore do not appear to have grown out of a systematizing attempt to develop zoological theory. The first elaborate statement on animals appears in a chapter dealing with astronomy. The passage correlates animals and their locomotion in a *yinyang* paradigm:

> As for the hairy and feathered animals, they belong to the species which fly and
> run. Therefore, they belong to the *yang*. As for the armored and scaly animals,

they belong to the species which hibernate and hide. Therefore they belong to the *yin*. The sun is the ruler of the *yang*, hence in spring and summer the herd animals shed hair, and at the solstice elaphures and deer shed their antlers. The moon is the ancestor of the *yin*. Therefore, when the moon wanes, the brains of fish deplete, and when the moon dies, the swollen oyster shrinks. Fire goes up and trails, water goes down and flows; therefore birds flying up go high, the fish when stirred go down. Things which are of a kind stir each other.[60]

Elsewhere in a chapter on topography, the *Huainanzi* differentiates the living species according to their diet or the produce they take in from the soil. It distinguishes creatures that feed on water, earth, wood, grass, (mulberry) leaves, flesh, *qi*, and grain, and ends with the class of the spirits (*shen* 神), who are said to be immortal and need not feed themselves.[61] Later in the same chapter follows a passage sometimes quoted as proof for the existence of a zoological tradition in early China. The passage combines observable data with *yinyang* classification, asserts that all creatures upon birth are differentiated into different categories, and specifies species differentiae based on diet and anatomy:

Birds and fish are all born of *yin* but belong to the class of *yang* creatures. Therefore birds and fish are oviparous. Fish swim through water; birds fly in the clouds. Thus at the beginning of winter swallows and sparrows enter the sea and turn into clams. The myriad living creatures are all born as different kinds. Silkworms eat but do not drink. Cicadas drink but do not eat. Mayflies neither eat nor drink. Armored and scaly creatures eat during the summer but hibernate in winter. Animals that eat without mastication have eight bodily openings and are oviparous. Animals that chew have nine bodily openings and are viviparous. Quadrupeds do not have feathers or wings. Animals that have horns do not have upper (incisor) teeth.[62] Hornless animals have soft fat [lard] and do not have incisor teeth (?). Some animals with horns have hard fat [suet] but do not have molar teeth (?). Creatures born during the day resemble their fathers; those born at night resemble their mothers. Extreme *yin* produces females, extreme *yang* produces males. Bears hibernate, and birds migrate seasonally.[63]

John Major has characterized this passage as "an attempt to create a systematic and consistent taxonomy of animals on the basis of data obtained mainly from the close observation of nature and then refined with reference to yin-yang principles." The *Huainanzi* here, according to Major, gives a system that "can be described as genuinely scientific, in that it makes use of valid data, is systematic, and is objective rather than normative."[64] I concur with Major's acknowledgment of the internal sophistication displayed throughout this passage. It contains one of the most detailed protoscientific descriptions of animals currently transmitted. In that respect this fragment and its variant preserved in the *Da Dai Liji* stand out

among the overall corpus of Warring States and Han writings. However the isolated nature of such passages should also encourage us to modify their importance and representativity as evidence for an early Chinese science of animals.
Although "many creditable observations," to use Needham's words, are evinced
in these fragments, one should not overlook the fact that descriptions such as
these form part of an overall cosmography and are subsumed within a system of
symbolic correlations. On this count it may be asked whether a process of deductive, anormative or objective observation of nature was the prime motivation for
the author(s) of this passage. The same applies to a description preceding the
fragment quoted above in which the birth and gestation period of animals is cal-
culated following a numerological model. Rather than aiming to achieve biological accuracy, this scheme seeks to interrelate all phenomena (including celestial
bodies, pitchpipes, winds, and the seasons) within an all-encompassing numerological framework. The main ideological lead for the topographist at work in
this chapter consists of matching his creditable observations with the internal
logic of his correlative frame. More important than the correct observation of
taxonomic hints among animals is the maintenance of a creditable set of correlations. Without precluding the role of direct observation, in correlative descriptions of the natural world the accuracy and comprehensiveness of system often
prevails over the reliance on verifiable data.

A final passage of interest in the *Huainanzi* is part of a description of the
evolution of animals and plants. It pictures an evolutionary scheme in which
primordial ancestors beget ("give birth to," *sheng* 生) five classes of animals via
the intermediary of a dragon specimen (in the case of humans, an aquatic
"Oceanman," *hai ren* 海人).

> Downyhair gave birth to Oceanman. Oceanman gave birth to Ruojun 若菌. Ruo-
> jun gave birth to the sages; the sages gave birth to ordinary people. Thus creatures
> with scanty hair are born from ordinary people.
>
> Winged Excellence gave birth to Flying Dragon. Flying Dragon gave birth to
> the phoenix (*fenghuang* 鳳皇). The phoenix gave birth to the simurgh (*luan niao*
> 鸞鳥), and the simurgh gave birth to ordinary birds. In general feathered crea-
> tures are born from ordinary birds.
>
> Hairy Heifer gave birth to Responsive Dragon. Responsive Dragon gave birth
> to Establish-Horse. Establish-Horse gave birth to the *qilin*. The *qilin* gave birth to
> ordinary beasts. In general hairy animals are born from ordinary beasts.
>
> Scaly One gave birth to Scaly Dragon. Scaly Dragon gave birth to Leviathan.
> Leviathan gave birth to Establish-Apotrope. Establish-Apotrope gave birth to or-
> dinary fishes. In general scaly creatures are born from ordinary fishes.
>
> Armored Abyss gave birth to First Dragon. First Dragon gave birth to Dark Sea-
> Turtle. Dark See-Turtle gave birth to Divine Tortoise. Divine Tortoise gave birth to
> ordinary turtles. In general armored creatures are born from ordinary turtles.[65]

Two elements in this description are noteworthy. First, there is the presence of a dragonesque creature in the genealogy of each of the five classes of animals. This corroborates the image of the dragon as an all-encompassing animal that influences all species. The *Huainanzi* scheme suggests that there is a demiurgic dragon at the origins of each of the five animal classes. The same idea is also confirmed in a twelfth-century reading of this passage that underlines the ancestral role ascribed to the dragon: "As for the myriad creatures be they feathered, hairy, scaly or armored, they all find their ancestry in the dragon."[66] A second noteworthy element in this evolutionary passage is the occurrence of the denominator *shu* 庶 "ordinary, common" in the term for the penultimate "begetter" in each series. While a series of ancestral creatures with fantastic names are said to produce offspring within each animal class, it is not until the evolution has devolved to the stage of the "ordinary" creatures that the five classes of animals are said to reproduce themselves. So winged creatures are born from "ordinary" birds (*shu niao* 庶鳥), hairy creatures from "ordinary" beasts (*shu shou* 庶獸), and so forth. The passage correlates formal attributes to each *shu* category: *ren* 人 (remains) *ren* 人, *shou* 獸 is qualified by *mao* 毛, *niao* 鳥 is qualified by *yu* 羽, *yu* 魚 is qualified by *lin* 鱗, and *gui* 龜 is qualified by *jie* 介.

Contrary to another evolutionary scheme found in the *Zhuangzi* (and discussed in chapter 6) in which all living creatures are said to emerge from and return to a germinal state, in the *Huainanzi* a pedigree of numinous creatures act as precursors to the ordinary generic animal groups. The *Huainanzi* scheme does not recognize sharp boundaries between natural and ordinary species on the one hand and mythical or divine creatures on the other.[67] While a degree of evolutionary specification is clearly present in the above passage, it would be, as John Major comments, "absurd to suggest that one is dealing here with an ancient Chinese anticipation of Darwin." The passage was not intended as a zoological reflection on the origin of species, nor does it uniquely focus on animals, as the text continues with a similar scheme for plants and trees. Apart from the fact that it links the idea of evolution with five-phase correlation, its most revealing aspect lies in the suggestion that all animals ultimately emerge from one. Rather than seeking an ontological differentiation of the living species, the text suggests that all five animal classes emerge from an undifferentiated state and go through a dragon phase. It discloses a view of the cosmos as a structured pattern of energy in which each creature is endowed with a higher or lesser degree of refinement. This idea of the emergence of all species from one primal force or energy provides a significant background for the understanding of animal metamorphosis, which will be discussed in chapter 6. Finally, my assumption that the development of a zoological taxonomy may not have been the prime aim of the author of this passage is further supported by the fact that in no other Warring States, Qin, or Han text zoological specification goes beyond a classification into five classes.

While the *Huainanzi* provides a rich thesaurus of *yinyang* and *wuxing* discourse on animals, remnants of similar discussions are scattered across a number of other late Warring States and Han texts including the *Lüshi chunqiu*, *Chunqiu fanlu*, *Da Dai Liji*, and *Lunheng*. Similar classifications also occur in newly excavated manuscripts. Among the Western Han bamboo slips recovered from tomb no. 1 at Yinqueshan, a text reconstructed as the *Cao Shi Yinyang* 漕是 (氏) 陰陽 ("Master Cao's Yin and Yang") contains evidence in which a taxonomic order is given according to the degree of *yin*-ness or *yang*-ness of a specimen within its affiliated group. In addition the text also provides a *yinyang* order for the six domestic animals:

> The most *yin* among the armored animals are the tortoise, the *jiao* 蛟 dragon and the turtle. The most *yin* among the scaly animals are the *long* 蠪 dragon, the snake, and the [. . .].[68]
>
> The most *yin* among the naked animals is the frog/toad (*rana rugosa*).[69]
>
> Of the six domestic animals, ox and sheep are *yin;* horse, dog, pig and chicken are *yang*. Now the ox and sheep value . . . [the rear?] . . . the dog, the horse, and the pig value the front and have soft fat (lard). The chicken is pure vermilion red and so its share of *yang* is especially quintessential.[70]

A fragment in the *Da Dai Liji* combines the notion of five classes of living species with *yinyang* thought and the concept of seminal energy (*jingqi* 精氣):

> As for the hairy animals, they are hairy and then are born (i.e., hairy animals are born with hair). The feathered animals are born with feathers. Both hairy and feathered animals are produced by *yang qi*. The armored animals are born with shells, the scaly animals are born with scales. Both armored and scaly animals are produced by *yin qi*. Only human beings are born naked. They are the seminal essence of both *yin* and *yang*. The essence of the hairy animals is the unicorn. The essence of the feathered animals is the phoenix, the essence of the armored animals is the turtle and the essence of the scaly animals is the dragon. The essence of the naked animals is the Sage.[71]

This passage argues that all living species emanate from the generative workings of *qi*, which, in its refined or pure form, produces the representative sacred animals of each species. A similar idea is expressed by Wang Fu who presents *qi* as a generative principle of all creatures ranging from sacred animals that embody virtuous principles to ordinary insects and vermin: "As for the unicorn, dragon, simurgh, phoenix, fly, grub, locust larvae and locust, there is none that does not come about by the means of *qi*."[72] Significant in the *Da Dai Liji* passage is the portrayal of human beings as the central species encompassing both *yin* and *yang*. Together with the inclusion of sacred animals as the most essential or refined exemplars within each species group, the human sage figures as the most accomplished type among the naked creatures. Each of the five classes of animals—be it *yin, yang,* or *yinyang*—is headed by a "seminal" representative of this class. Similar to the idea encountered earlier where the human-animal difference was attributed to the degree of purity or coarseness of *qi,* this passage argues that out of every field of *qi* arises an animal that is a more refined specimen (*jing* 精) and therefore encompasses all features of its representative animal category.

In assessing the value of animal classification according to correlative systems based on *yinyang* and the five phases, one could point out that the data included in these schemes are not always uniform and contain inconsistencies and variations. For example while amphibians are usually classified with scaly or fishy creatures, the Yinqueshan fragment treats them as naked animals. Another example is that of the horse, which elsewhere can be seen to be associated with *yin*—the earth and the female—rather than with *yang.*[73] However the degree to which these classifications are consistent should not be the main criterion in judging whether we are dealing with a relevant taxonomy. Several correlations and five-phase placements were debated by Han scholars themselves. The fundamental question here is whether or not the correlative systems are applied to the animal world out of zootaxonomic consideration, or whether the animal world was subsumed into a theoretical framework of classification in order to illustrate the all-encompassing applicability of *yinyang* and five-phase categorization to every aspect of the physical world. The information preserved in Warring States and Han writings supports the latter hypothesis. These texts are primarily concerned with model thinking. Rather than the taxonomic model being derived from data gathering about the animal species, animals are fitted into the model to enhance the functionality of the model itself.

In sum, the *yinyang* paradigm—and the same applies to *wuxing* thought—is a classificatory system of functional relations rather than of ontological quintessences. Explaining or inferring in such a correlative system is filling a place within an overall pattern rather than assigning its constituent elements to essentialist categories.[74] Hence the assertion that an animal can be defined as belonging to *yin* or *yang* depends on the relational context in which it figures. The preoccupation of the observer or taxonomist lies in defining the contours of the category and assigning each element a due place within these wider situational frameworks rather than to engage in the internal analysis of its constituent elements. Just as the lexicographer related animals to the world of written graphs or the ritualist described animals according to socioreligious criteria, so the cosmologist's impulse to study animals as biological creatures was dominated by a tendency to categorize them within the wider context of reality as a whole. As chapter 7 will illustrate, this was also reflected in the idea that the human sage was first and foremost a figure who engaged in the mental process of interrelating and bringing forth unifying categories to analyze the phenomena of the world as well as the doctrine that a comprehension of the bigger picture of reality ought to prevail over the call to scrutinize individual elements in the natural world. Summarized in the jargon of the contemporary life sciences, *fenleixue* 分類學 has traditionally prevailed over *dongwuxue* 動物學.

Toward a Moral Taxonomy

While attempts to define the relationship among the living species on the basis of physiological theories and correlative thinking bear witness of a considerable level of analytical interest in the natural world, classificatory schemes inspired by animal physiology never became the mainstay of the early Chinese discourse on living creatures. Instead efforts to characterize the distinctions between humans and animals gained front stage within the context of debates on human nature and human morality. Just as physiological theories suggested that faculties such as emotions and feelings of piety toward one's kin were shared by animals and humans alike, so the identification of an innate sense of morality became a prominent element in determining the status of animals in relation to humans. Throughout the Warring States and early imperial period, references to human-animal distinctions in terms of varying standards of social morality outnumber discussions based on biological differentiation. The association of a moral consciousness or moral potentiality with the nonhuman living species had important implications for the determination of the place of the animal among the living species and the wider sociopolitical realm. It gave way to a moralization of the physical animal and its biobehavior and meant that the animal kingdom was rarely perceived as a purely physical world that functioned according to its own independent laws of nature.

A maxim in the *Mengzi* 孟子 claims that "what differentiates man from birds and beasts is but trifle. Ordinary people cast it aside, only the gentleman preserves it."[75] Mencius recognizes a distinction between the human and animal species, but likewise emphasizes the frailty that characterizes this distinction. Secondly, Mencius infers the prerequisite of human comprehension and sagacity as a means to uphold or obliterate the discrimination between the human and the beast. In the *Lunyu,* Confucius had pondered on a similar question. Disappointed by a criticism of his own refusal to turn his back on human society he states: "I cannot flock together with the birds and beasts. Am I not a member of this human species? With whom, then, can I associate myself?"[76] Although Confucius dissociates himself from the birds and beasts (i.e., the natural companions of the hermit or recluse), by indicating that he would only associate with morally superior specimens of the human species, he implies that the divide between the human and the bestial does not run parallel with the biological distinction between animals and human beings. Confucius's moral teaching tallies with the prevailing tendency in the above-discussed physiological and correlative philosophies to view the human-animal difference as a difference in degree rather than in kind. While most philosophical schools in Warring States and Han China assumed a degree of polarity between the categories of man and animal, they did not invariably regard animals to be inferior or judged all humans to be ethically superior. Since the difference between man and beast was as much of a moral as well as a biological nature, the notions of bestiality and humanity were believed to be subject to change. In his capacity to separate moral conduct from immoral behavior, the human sage mediated the boundaries of what was considered proper to humans as opposed to what ought to be seen as bestial. What made a man really human, said Xunzi, was not primarily his being a hairless biped, but his ability to draw boundaries.[77] As Hall and Ames put it: "The classical Confucian notion that the difference between beast, human being, and gods is simply cultural, means that while those human beings who are important sources of culture have a claim to divinity, human beings who resist enculturation are, quite literally, animals."[78] Reversibly, animals were sometimes portrayed to be superior to morally defunct humans. A consequence of this bias toward moral differentiation was that the necessity to isolate humans as distinctive from animals on a natural basis became secondary.

A most articulate theoretical distinction between humans and animals in moral terms occurs in Xunzi's much quoted "ladder of souls" passage. Here humans distinguish themselves from the biological and cognitive condition of the nonhuman world by a moral sense for righteousness.

> Water and fire have *qi* but do not contain life (*sheng* 生). Herbs and trees contain life but have no knowledge (*zhi* 知). Birds and beasts have knowledge but no righteousness (*yi* 義). Man has *qi*, contains life, has knowledge and also has righteousness, therefore he is the most valuable creature in the universe.[79]

In his discussion of this passage, Joseph Needham makes a parallel between Xunzi's view of moral righteousness as a distinguishing feature of humans and the Aristotelian attribution of a rational soul (ψυχὴ διανοητική) to humans in addition to a vegetative and sensitive soul common to animals: "It is typical of Chinese thought that what particularly characterised man should have been expressed as the sense of justice rather than the power of reasoning."[80] While Needham could be criticized here for overstating his case in pitching morality against rationality, it is significant indeed that Xunzi places the power for moral reasoning before the mere faculty of cognition, a degree of perception of which animals are equally capable in his view.[81] Xunzi goes on to argue that a sense for social organization (*qun* 群) enables humans to subdue and use animals that surpass them in physical strength. This capability to form social flocks is said to originate from man's capability to "draw (social) distinctions" (*fen* 分) which in turn originates from his sense for righteousness (*yi* 義).[82] The idea that social organization makes humans superior to animals despite their physical weakness also occurs in the *Lüshi chunqiu*.[83] A few centuries later Cui Bao 崔豹 (fl. 290–306 C.E.) provides a variant of Xunzi's scheme that does not include humans, omits a sense for moral righteousness as a distinguishing factor to humans only, but concurs with Xunzi in attributing cognition to animals:

> Among beings (*wu* 物), there are those who have life (*sheng* 生) and knowledge, there are those who have life but no knowledge, there are those who don't live (*bu sheng* 不生) and have knowledge, and there are those who don't live and have no knowledge. In general those who live and have knowledge are the animal species (*chong lei* 蟲類). Those who live but have no knowledge are the plants and trees. Those who don't live and have no knowledge are water and earth. Those who do not live but have knowledge are the ghosts and spirits.[84]

The human capacity to organize oneself socially was also attributed to the perception that humans, as opposed to animals that exist in various kinds, belonged to one and the same group. For instance the *Guanzi* notes that "although relations among a flock of crows may seem good, they are never really close," and other texts point out that animals of prey do not flock.[85] According to the *Huainanzi* birds and beasts cannot form flocks because their species are different (*qi lei yi* 其類異), and tigers and deer cannot gambol about together because their strength (*li* 力) is unequal.[86] Animals here are said to lack a sense for kin affinity reaching beyond their own species.

The adoption of a clan name as well as the acceptance of social distinctions based on gender and marriage were attributes that separated humans from a state of primordial bestiality. A neglect of appropriate gender distinctions and segregation between male and female would relegate the human order to the level of an animal society. When rulers and ministers overindulge in their desires, the *Guanzi* states, men and women will no longer be kept separate but revert to animal behavior.[87] Xunzi argues that relationships of parenthood and pedigree among animals lack the integrity of a human father-to-son relation. Although the distinction between male and female exists among animals, it does not induce a separation between the sexes. He also underlines that the petty man has a heart like that of tigers and wolves and the behavior of wild beasts, and states that failing to respect a worthy amounts to acting like a wild beast.[88] The *Bohutong* points out that one of the reasons why humans adopt a *xing* 姓 or clan name is because they wish to remove themselves from birds and beasts.[89]

Several texts present ritual propriety as a tool to curb the supposedly animal aspects of man. They indicate that the human-animal difference was centered around the thesis that animals possessed physical power (*li* 力); whereas, humans were endowed with a sense of morality and ritual propriety (*li* 禮). Mencius compares people who enjoy a full stomach, warm clothes, and "dwell in idleness without instruction" with beings that "approximate birds and beasts." He also states that people who fail to reciprocate ritual propriety, benevolence and loyalty are mad and do not differ from birds and beasts.[90] The *Guanzi* identifies physical power as a distinctive property of animals by stating that "heaven serves with its seasons, earth with its material resources, man with his virtue, the spirits with their omens, and animals with their physical strength."[91] The *Yanzi chunqiu* 晏子春秋 equates a gentleman who has lost his ritual propriety with common folk, and common folk without ritual propriety with birds and beasts. It further states that "following the beasts and not returning is called wildness."[92] Han Ying 韓嬰 (fl. 150 B.C.E.) differentiates the petty man from the gentleman as someone "whose structure of limbs and body is joined like that of birds and beasts."[93] In several texts the lack of ritual propriety or *li* is exemplified by the observation that animals and petty humans alike flock together and have instinctive physical intercourse failing to make a distinction between young and old, species or kin. One recurrent expression holds that deer lack ritual propriety because stag and calves go with the same doe.[94] Finally some texts extended gradations in moral consciousness and virtue to certain animals and argued that not all animal species occupied the same place on the moral ladder. Animals were thus diversified as a conceptual support for the differentiation of various degrees of morality. The *Da Dai Liji* for instance points out that the phoenix "by birth" has a sense of benevolence and righteousness while the tiger and wolf "by birth" have a covetous and violent heart, "each being different because of its mother."[95] The different susceptibility to morals here is said to be innate. While all humans may be potential sages because they share the same physiology, not all birds and beasts can become phoenixes and unicorns.

Conclusion

While Warring States and Han writings did not develop elaborate natural philosophies of the living species, these texts nevertheless displayed various degrees of theoretical interest in the differentiation of the species and the formulation of the human-animal relationship. A number of text passages described the differences and similarities among the living species on the basis of physiological determinants such as the possession of blood or "blood and *qi*." Other passages invoked moral principles as the main element that separated or, in some cases, united human beings and animals. Toward the late Warring States period, descriptions of the various components of the animal world were increasingly incorporated in classifications based on the correlative principles of *yin* and *yang* and the five phases. While we can only speculate whether or to what degree these models rearranged or reworked notions of classification that may have developed during the centuries preceding the upsurge of correlative thinking, it is clear that these models were preoccupied primarily with the act of classifying rather than with the search for clarity about the structures of the animal world itself. More important than exposing the rudimentary principles of the biological features of the different species, early Chinese taxonomies sought to integrate particular animal observations within a unitary scheme that encompassed all human actions, natural phenomena, and moral principles in the world. That natural empiricism remained secondary to the desire for comprehensiveness and totality in classification was reflected in the fact that the most enduring taxonomy of the living species was limited to five main animal groups—feathered, hairy, naked, armored, and scaly—a number inspired by five-phase theory rather than nature.

However all these attempts at classification, regardless of their eclectic and fragmentary nature, had one element in common; rather than emphasizing the radical difference in kind between the living species, they underlined their common origins and explained difference as a difference in degree. Classification based on explicating similarities between the species prevailed over classification through differentiation. Physiological theories maintained that both humans and animals were "blood and *qi*" creatures, correlative models positioned humans as one constituent group among all other species, and moral theories analyzed animal behavior according to the same standards and principles that governed human society. The boundaries between animals as representatives of the natural world and animals as part of an all-encompassing order that included humans and human culture were therefore not clear and distinct.

CHAPTER FOUR

THE ANIMAL AND TERRITORY

In addition to structuring the animal world as a world of names and subsuming the living species and their mutual relationships within various social, ritual, and protoscientific categories, early Chinese writings also developed natural philosophies that sought to relate animals to humans, explain their habitats, and clarify their behavior. While several narratives presented the origins of civilization as a process in which humans separated themselves from animals, natural patterns in the animal world were also thought to be part of the inspiration behind the invention of cultural devices such as the trigrams, writing, and clothing. The masters of philosophy addressed the human-animal relationship primarily on moral grounds, yet, other Warring States and Han writings at the same time sought to relate humans to animals according to natural criteria such as geography, climate, and biotope. Underlying these explanations was the idea that the animal world was structured according to a "sociobiological" order based on the concept of soil or territory, a category that comprised both physical and moral features.[1] Through linking animals to notions of locality or territoriality, an initial order within the animal world was conceived. This perception of a structural order in the natural world based on territorial habitat in turn sparked the creation of models of authority within the animal kingdom and inspired the animal realm being used to generate images of sociopolitical power. Both the real and imaginary movement of animals—as could be seen in the collection and hunt of animals in parks—as well as changes in an animal's location or alterations to its habitat—as was evinced in the use of animals as tributary gifts—served as images for the ruler-king to assert his dominance in the sociopolitical realm.

In many cultures, the domestication of the wilds and its fauna and flora is portrayed as a process in which humankind distinguishes and elevates itself from the instinctive nature of the surrounding wilds through a process of gradual civilization. Civilization is presented as a course of successive cultural transitions, a process that evolves from a state in which wild animals dominate humans who rely on them through hunting and gathering, to a state in which humans breed, domesticate, and train wild animals who in turn become dependent on the human pastor or farmer for their welfare. Traces of the gradual emergence of humankind out of a primal state of wildness are preserved in several narratives from the Warring States and early imperial periods. They relate

how divine sages transformed a hunting-and-gathering society into an agricultural community and describe how human society developed from a pristine
state of peaceful cohabitation or fiendish antagonism with the animal world
into an ordered community ruled by the grace of a moral code and sustained by
the appropriation of agricultural technology and pastoral skill.

Most writings associated with the masters of philosophy of the Warring
States and early Han period comment on how the organized breeding, domestication, slaughter, and consumption of animals redefined the relationship between human beings and the surrounding natural world. While each school
defined its ideal of society by emphasizing different innovations as the crucial
ones that set men apart from beasts, the idea that humanity resulted from the
work of the sages was common to most philosophical schools of the period.[2] As
the previous chapter has shown, several passages in the *Mengzi, Xunzi, Guanzi*,
and other Warring States writings emphasized that the separation of man and
beast was in the first place a moral emancipation. Xunzi argued that a call for
social organization and ritual propriety set men and beasts apart. Mengzi's
claim that the difference between humans and animals is only small implied
that it required constant moral cultivation to be maintained. The idea that humans differ from animals by their innate response to moral cultivation occurs
in another passage in the *Mengzi* that states that Shun, on hearing about the virtues of goodness, left the mountains and abandoned his deer and pig consorts
to become a human ruler.[3] The *Mozi* argued that humans had separated themselves from animals primarily through technological inventions. In their quest
to emancipate humankind from its aboriginal bestial existence, the sages, according to Mozi, had invented weapons to counter wild beasts. Humans here
are said to differ from animals in their need for agriculture and manufacture.[4]

Several Warring States and Han writings presented the origins of human
culture, the transformation from raw to cooked, and the transition from naked
to dressed as a "refinement of the animal world occasioned by the modelling
efficacy of its cultural leaders."[5] A host of legendary patron sages were accredited with the virtue of having lifted human culture out of a primitive natural-
ism. The *Zhuangzi* and *Han Feizi* 韓非子 describe how humans were taught to
protect themselves from the wilds by "nesting" together:

> In the age of remote antiquity, there were few human beings while birds and beasts
> were numerous. Since mankind was unable to overcome birds, beasts, insects and
> serpents, there appeared a sage who made nests by putting pieces of wood together
> to shelter (the people) from harm. The people were delighted and made him the
> ruler of All-under-Heaven and called him the Nest Dweller (*youchaoshi* 有巢氏).[6]

Several sources account how sages from antiquity engaged in acts of cultural
creation or revealed to humankind feats of a civilizing potentiality that was em-

bedded in the structures of nature and the cosmos. Sages instructed the people to use knotted cords to make nets and baskets for hunting and fishing. The Divine Husbandman, Shennong 神農, turned wood into plowshares and plow handles, taught the people the principles of tilling the soil, and educated them about the market exchange of agricultural goods. The Spirit of the Grain (Hou Ji 后稷) instructed the people on how to sow, reap, and plant the five grains. Legendary cultural heroes such as the Yellow Emperor, Yao, and Shun turned tree trunks into boats and paddles, tamed the ox and harnessed the horse and thereby opened up communication and transport between distant regions. By stringing together pieces of wood, the sages made bows and arrows that granted humans a dominating power over the wilds. Civilization brought a change in the habitat of both the living and the dead. Under the transforming efficacy of the sages, the common people left their caves and forests for constructed houses and started to bury the dead in inner and outer coffins. The sages further introduced writing and the written document and asserted governmental authority through the establishment of officialdom.[7] One appraisal of the civilizing endeavors of the sages was a saying that, were it not for Yu's legendary dyking of the floods that reclaimed land over sea, all creatures in the world would be fish.[8] Certain animals were praised as contributors to agricultural society. One Han text lauds the ox as "the foundation of tilling and agriculture" determining the "strength or weakness of the state."[9] The domestication of animals and the tilling of the soil were hailed as the ultimate victory of humanity over wildness.

The wilds and its animal inhabitants did not disappear from the histories of civilization after the sages had differentiated human society from its pre-human animal state, nor did their transformation into domestic(ated) animals dissolve their bestial nature. While in the Judeo-Christian tradition the biblical creation narrative in Genesis glorified man's mission to subdue the animal world and presented "agriculture as standing to land as did cooking to raw meat,"[10] a universally accepted theory that granted divine approval to the dominion over animals by a superior human species did not exist in early China. As this chapter and the next will show, Warring States and Han texts exposed different views on how to accommodate, assimilate, or differentiate human beings from animals. Yet there are no textual sources that give a detailed history of the domestication of animals. While a number of culture heroes figure as "first domesticators" such as Cheng Ya 乘雅 who harnessed the horse or Wang Hai 王亥 who tamed oxen, the origins and development of a term such as "the six domestic animals" (*liu chu* 六畜) remain difficult to trace with certainty.[11]

The absence of a uniform origin myth of animal domestication or an orthodox doctrine of human supremacy that won acclaim across different schools of thought was significant in that it also provided a background for more naturalist views of the world that saw cultural creation as a transgression of an original and perfect natural order. It underlies a recurring tension in early Chinese

texts between on the one hand voices that sought to justify the human dominion of animals and, alternatively, strands of thought that advocated a harmoni-
zation with the rhythms and patterns of the animal realm as the best means of
achieving a balance between humans and the natural world.[12] Some equated the
primitive origins of civilization with the raw and the bestial, others interpreted
this precivilized naturalness as a condition of harmony between man and his
brute natural environment. While each school of thought in the Warring States
and Han period espoused its own view of the past, the origins of civilization and
the emancipation of humankind, both those who equated primitivism with
bestiality, and those who hailed primitive naturalness as superior to cultural
edifice insisted on varying forms of natural and cultural harmony between humans and animals.[13] Natural philosophies that sought to detect patterns of initial order in the animal world by linking the living species to their
sociobiological environment provided the formative background to these portrayals of the human-animal relationship.

Animal Patterns as Social Patterns

The observation of animal culture was part of the narratives describing the origins of cosmological organization. A famous passage in the Great Commentary
to the *Zhouyi* (Appended Statements, *Xici* 繫辭), a text written just prior to or
early in the Han, describes the origins of the trigrams:

> Anciently, when Baoxi 包犧 (= Fuxi 伏犧) ruled the All under Heaven, he looked
> up and contemplated the images in heaven; he looked down and contemplated the
> patterns on earth. He contemplated the markings of birds and beasts (*niaoshou zhi
> wen* 鳥獸之文) and the properties of the earth (*di zhi yi* 地之宜). He proceeded
> directly from himself and indirectly from other things. Thereupon he invented the
> eight trigrams in order to enter into connection with the virtue of spiritual bright-
> ness (*shenming* 神明) and categorise the innate nature of all beings.[14]

In the *Zhouyi* the eight trigrams (*ba gua* 八卦), whose combinations form the
sixty–four hexagrams used to divine and prognosticate future events, figure as
basic building blocks in the communication with and description of the cosmological order. They provide a medium to determine man's place within the universe and give guidance to his or her actions. Rather than being the result of a
purposeful act of creation, the invention of the trigrams by Fuxi was, as the
Great Commentary indicates, based on the observation of patterns inherent in
nature, both in the heavens as well as on earth.

Whether or not the origins of the trigrams, which most likely predate the
compilation of the *Zhouyi* as a coherent text in the ninth century B.C.E., may be

assigned to "the herding and hunting stage in Chinese civilization,"[15] the Great Commentary suggests that the observation of "markings" (*wen* 文) in the animal world was part of the inspiration behind their organization. Animal patterns are here presented as the counterpart of celestial phenomena.[16] At the same time, the text firmly connects these animal *wen* with the principles (*fa* 法) of the earthly realm and the soil. The image evoked is that of celestial and earthly counterparts marked by readable celestial bodies and markings on the soil that provide a grammar for the sages allowing them to derive the lines of the trigrams. Just as the stars and other celestial bodies were the primal coordinates to describe heaven (uranography), so animal culture and the characteristics of the soil were a first point of focus for the sages when they mapped out the structures of the terrestrial universe (geography). The comprehension of the universe was linked with the sages' capacity to observe all species that move on and above the earth.[17]

Linked to the image of the sages as observers of *wen* in the animal world was the idea that they gave birds and beasts a proper name. An apocryphal text associated with the *Chunqiu* 春秋 states that Fuxi and Suiren 遂人 (燧人) initiated the naming of insects, birds, and beasts.[18] While, to my knowledge, no textual evidence prior to the Eastern Han apocrypha (*chanwei* 讖緯) specifically credits Fuxi or any other cultural hero with the invention of animal nomenclature, this reference seems almost certainly inspired by the Great Commentary's portrayal of Fuxi as the "reader" of the markings of birds and beasts. The ability to observe, name, and discriminate creatures was also embedded in the semantics of the *fu* 伏 graph used in Fuxi's name, which was glossed by Han scholars as *bie* 別 "to distinguish" and *bian* 變 "to transform."[19] This gloss echoes the identification of Fuxi as the divine sage who distinguished names and transformed patterns into meaningful images, the trigrams. Fuxi's image as a cultural hero capable of mastering the animal realm is also attested by his role as the inventor of the hunt instructing the people how to deal with wild beasts.[20]

Another significant issue underlies the Great Commentary quote. The observation of bird and beast patterns is described as a means to an end rather than an end in itself. For the sage, animal patterns served as a model that could be used in order to categorize the nature of the "ten thousand beings." As such, natural behavior and relationships within the animal world are implicitly interpreted as meaningful beyond the boundaries of the natural world. The observation of animal characteristics by the sages is extrapolated and transposed in terms of the social organization and behavior of human beings. Animal *wen* thus came to be perceived as a structure of social *wen*.

This transposition of animal patterns into human society is reflected in several direct references and allusions to the Great Commentary passage in subsequent texts. A number of writings quote the Great Commentary passage as an authoritative precedent in arguments maintaining that the structures of the animal world also percolated into human society. In the Eastern Han, Xun Shuang

荀爽 (fl. ca. 166 C.E.) quotes a version of the Great Commentary passage in an argument about the need for compliant behavior of women, which in his view ought to be modeled on submissive conduct of females as can be observed in the animal kingdom:

> When we look at the patterns amongst birds and beasts, in the case of the birds, it is the male who cries at the young ones, and the females follow and subject themselves. In case of the beasts, it is the male who roars proudly and leads, and the females then follow.[21]

The integration of animal patterns into the social world also applied to material culture. According to the preface of the treatise on chariots and robes in the *Hou Hanshu* 後漢書, the decorative design and coloring of clothes were inspired by animals. The text recalls the image of a primitive society and states how in remote antiquity human beings lived in caves and in the open wilds, dressed themselves in animal furs, were covered in hides, and subsisted without the rule of law or social regulations. Then the following passage precedes the Great Commentary quote:

> The sages of later generations changed this for the use of silk and hemp. They observed the patterns of the variegated pheasant and the colors of blossoming flowers. Then they dyed silk in order to imitate these. For the first time they made the five colors and made clothes with them. They saw that birds and beasts had a system of crests, horns, whiskers and dewlaps, hence they made hats, ceremonial caps, throat-bands and fringes in order to make decorations for the head.[22]

This passage argues how animal *wen* in the form of feather patterns and plumage colors provided the initial model for the invention of clothing. The invention of clothes, often hailed as the innovation that set men and beasts apart, was inspired by the physical appearance of those creatures from which humans aspired to differentiate themselves.

The origins of the character script itself, the basis of writings and social communication, were also inspired by the observation of signs in the animal world. The observation of animal markings already figured in the origin myth of Fuxi's invention of the trigrams. Another legend claimed that the inventor of the written script and scribe at the court of the Yellow Emperor, Cang Jie, imitated bird tracks to invent the written graph.[23] Natural philosophies of writing reflected in the works of Xu Shen and others presented the written character in the first place as an organic entity. This was emphasized by the idea that graphs derived from the traces of birds and beasts—living creatures in the natural world rather than inanimate objects.[24] The relationship between the animal world and the origins of writing was further illustrated in an anecdote claiming that animals feared the invention of writing, in the attribution of animal names to various kinds of script and calligraphic styles, in the revelation of written signs on the animal body, and in the role of animals as intermediaries transmitting or revealing sacred writings.

A story in the *Huainanzi* relates how, at the time when Cang Jie invented writing, Heaven poured down millet while demons started wailing at night. According to Gao You's commentary, the demons feared the invention of the written word, which would be used to impeach or expel them. The same commentator links the graph for demon (*gui* 鬼) with the graph for rabbit (*tu* 兔) and notes that rabbits feared the invention of writing because their fur would be used to make writing brushes.[25]

The association of writing with animal movement was reflected in the description of calligraphy. A calligraphic style referred to as "animal script" (*chong shu* 蟲書) was known at least from the Qin dynasty onward.[26] By the end of the first century B.C.E., a style known as "bird and animal script" (*niao chong shu* 鳥蟲書) was used to write on banners and inscribe tallies.[27] The Eastern Han scholar Cai Yong refers to various postures of the hands to describe the patterning of calligraphy brushing after bird traces and animal tracks.[28] As Kenneth DeWoskin has suggested, the hand movements in making calligraphy may have been seen as correlative to animal movements leaving their markings. Later calligraphic manuals and texts explaining the various hand postures adopted to play the zither often correlate the position of the hands to natural scenes expressing motion such as trailing geese formations, leaping fish, or pecking birds.[29] More recently Lin Yutang (1895–1976) has commented on the image of animal movements as the inspiring motive behind calligraphic scripts in the animal style:

> One can understand Chinese calligraphy only when one's eyes have been opened to the form and rhythm inherent in every animal's body and limbs. Every animal body has a harmony and beauty of its own, a harmony which grows directly from its vital functions, especially the functions of movement. The hairy legs and tall body of the draught-horse are as much a form of beauty as the more neatly formed outline of the racing-horse. That harmony exists in the outline of the swift, springing greyhound, as it exists also in that of the hairy Irish terrier, whose head and limbs end almost in square formations—strikingly represented in Chinese calligraphy by the blunt *li-shu* [隸書] style. . . . The important thing to observe is that these plant and animal forms are beautiful because of their suggestion of movement.[30]

A number of sources attributed the origin of the written script (*wen* 文) to the observance of patterns on the physical animal body. As will be discussed in chapter 5, a similar logic establishing a link between patterns in the form of written graphs on the animal body and the animal's character formed a guiding principle in the physiognomy of sacred animals. The *Chunqiu yuanming bao* 春秋元命包 gives an apocryphal version of Cang Jie's creation of the character script as a parallel to Fuxi's invention of the trigrams:

> [Cang Jie] . . . thereupon scrutinized the transformations of heaven and earth. He looked upward and contemplated the round and crooked shape of the Kui 奎 constellation. He looked downward and examined the markings on the shells of tortoises, bird feathers, mountains and rivers, and then guided his palm to create the written character.[31]

Associated with the idea that the markings on the bodies of animals inspired the invention of the script was a tradition that identified sacred writings as signs revealed through the medium of animals, a belief that echoed the appearance of writings on animal parts in archaic plastromantic and scapulimantic practice. Shang plastromancy, as Léon Vandermeersch has suggested, was based on the premise that the diviner could detect *li* 理 ("principles, raison") in the structure of the bone tissue that enclosed an animal creature endowed with numinous powers (*ling* 靈).[32] The turtle shell used in divination was itself laden with symbolism; it has been suggested that its plastron resembled the Shang vision of the cosmos, with the undershell being roughly square like the earth and the domed and round uppershell resembling heaven. As such the turtle carapace was a microversion of the universe.[33] The reading of the marks on turtle shells also served to identify turtle species and their suitability for divination. In a chapter on turtle divination incorporated in the *Shiji*, Chu Shaosun 褚少孫 (?104–30 B.C.E.) distinguishes eight famous turtle species and states that "the tortoise diagrams (*gui tu* 龜圖, i.e., the designs on the shell plastron) in each case comprise *wen* (patterns, writings, markings) beneath the abdomen. When the markings say so-and-so, this (determines) that it is such-and-such a tortoise."[34] Eastern Han apocrypha portrayed the invention of the trigrams as a revelation through the medium of a divine amphibian. According to their versions of the legend, Fuxi had based the design of the trigrams on the designs he observed on the back of a tortoise emerging from the river Luo 洛 (i.e., the so-called *Luo shu* 洛書 "Luo Writing"). One source states that "Fuxi's virtue penetrated the upper and lower realms. Heaven responded with patterns and designs of birds and beasts. Earth responded with the River Chart and the Luo Writing. (Fuxi) then standardised these images and composed the Changes (*Zhouyi*)."[35] Other texts refer to the Luo writing as "scales and shells forming graphs."[36] These origin tales each established a close relationship between the detection of animal markings and the foundation of the pictographic script.

The examples discussed above all variously show how early Chinese narratives on the origins of civilization presented animal culture as an inherent part of the "readable" surface of the observable world before the sages set out to develop cultural devices such as the trigrams, clothing, color, and writing. The image of animal footprints and bird tracks on the earth symbolized a primitive era before the sages would set man apart from the beasts. At the same time animal markings inherent in nature were made explicit by the sages to serve the purpose of cultural edifice. The image is taken up by Mencius, who pictures the primitive state as an era in which wild animals roam on the surface of the earth and leave their signatures on the soil. Birds and beasts, Mencius states, flourished in abundance at the time of Yao. Animals impinged on humans, and paths made by animal footprints and bird tracks ran criss-cross the Middle Kingdom.[37] The next section examines how the sages established order among the animal paths on the soil of the Middle Kingdom and will show that the creation of this sense of order consisted in pairing the soil with its appropriate animal inhabitants, and in establishing a physical and moral concordance between local territory and the creatures that dwelled on its surface.

Animals and Territory

The important role of animal life and soil characteristics as an identifying feature of territorial locality prevails in early references to the geographic organization of the earth. Such descriptions almost invariably contain a statement on the animal presence in a specific territory and the suitability of the local soil as a habitat for certain plant, animal, or human species. The "Yu gong" 禹貢 chapter of the *Shangshu,* a text traditionally dated to the time of the semilegendary emperors Yao and Yu but possibly compiled as late as the Qin, presents Yu the Great devising a geographic scheme of China that divides the known lands into nine territories or provinces (*jiu zhou* 九州). A late chapter in the *Yi Zhoushu* ("Zhi fang" 職方) takes up the same model and, with each territorial division, lists the animals that conform to its soil with the idiom *qi chu yi* 其畜宜 —"as for the (domestic) animals, this (territory) is suitable for such-and-such animal."[38] Similar descriptions are preserved in the *Zhouli* and the geographical treatise of the *Hanshu.*[39] Elsewhere the *Zhouli* elaborates this scheme and distinguishes five categories of soil, each of which is characterized by its appropriate animals (*dongwu* 動物), plants (*zhiwu* 植物), and human inhabitants (*min* 民). In certain cases physical features such as color or skin covering are said to be common to humans and animals that share the same soil:

> The first (category) is called mountains and forests. It is appropriate for hairy animals . . ., and its people are hairy and rectangular. The second is called rivers and marshes. It is appropriate for scaly animals . . ., and its people are black and fat. The third is called hills and slopes. It is appropriate for feathered animals . . ., and its people are round (?) and long. The fourth is called banks and plains. It is

appropriate for armored animals . . ., and its people are white and lean. The fifth
is called plains and marshes. It is appropriate for naked animals . . ., and its people
are fleshy and short.[40]

The connection between the soil and the living creatures who inhabit it was
apparent in various forms of social communication such as tallies and seals for
the passage into different territories and military symbols such as army banners.
The *Zhouli* distinguishes the realms of water, plains, and mountains. It states that
tallies for circulation (*jie* 節) used by states in mountainous regions carried the
image of a tiger, the states of the plains carried tallies with human images, and the
states located near lakes or marshes carried dragon tallies.[41] As a potent military
symbol, the tiger likewise graced tallies used to raise troops (*hufu* 虎符, "tiger
tallies").[42]

Similar symbolism appeared on banners of an army on the march. The
"Bing fa" 兵法 ("Methods of Warfare") chapter in the *Guanzi* includes among
nine symbols the dragon for marching through water, the tiger for marching
through forests, the crow for marching up slopes, the snake for marching
through swamps, the magpie for marching over dry land, and the wolf for
marching through mountains.[43] Dragon emblems may have been used as apotropaic images to ward off aquatic monsters. Several texts speak of troops meeting with water monsters. Sima Qian for instance records how a water goblin
known as the "azure rhinoceros (or water buffalo)" (*cangsi* 蒼兕) was invoked
to urge King Wu's 武 (1049/45–1043 B.C.E.) troops to cross the Meng 孟 ford in
his campaign to conquer the Shang.[44] Wang Chong identifies this creature as
the *cangguang* 倉光, a nine-headed monster that capsizes boats.[45] Another
chronicle records that in the sixteenth year of King Zhao 照 (r. ca. 977/75–957?
B.C.E.) troops met with a huge rhinoceros while crossing the river Han 漢.[46]

The link between animals and territory is further attested in the *Liji*,
which lists a series of animal designs on signal flags that vary according to the
nature of the obstacles a funerary troop was facing:

> When there is water in front, the flag with the green bird should be displayed.
> When there is dust in the front, the flag with the screaming kites is shown. When
> there are chariots and horsemen in front, the banner with the flying wild geese is
> shown. For a body of troops, a flag with tiger skin is shown. When a predatory
> beast is in front, a flag with a leopard skin is shown. On the march, the banner
> with the Vermilion Bird is in front; that of the Dark Warrior behind; that with the
> Green Dragon on the left; that with the White Tiger on the right.[47]

In this passage several creatures are linked to military symbolism and representations of territory. According to Zheng Xuan the relation between water and a
blue-green bird refers to an aquatic bird named *qing que* 青雀 ("green water

fowl"?). The image of the kite to indicate dust is said to originate in a belief that the kite's screech causes an upsurge of wind. Geese fly in formations similar to an army troop, their image therefore serving to warn the coming of a hostile army. The use of tiger skin to indicate the passing of an infantry troop echoes a common identification of brave soldiers as tiger-men or tiger-warriors.[48] Martial symbolism was also associated with the use of tiger skin. For instance the *Zuozhuan* account of the famous battle of Chengpu 城濮 (632 B.C.E.) between the state of Chu and an alliance led by Jin records how a Jin general had his battle horses cloaked in tiger skins.[49] The use of a white leopard (*pixiu* 貔貅) hide to signal the presence of dangerous animals on the way may be based on the idea that the awesome leopard would scare away predatory animals. The Vermilion Bird, Dark Warrior, Green Dragon, and White Tiger were also known as the "four spirits" (*si shen* 四神) and refer to stellar constellations known by the same names.[50] Commentators state that the configuration of different army divisions was sometimes based on such astronomical configurations.[51] According to Wang Chong, these four spirits were the heavenly counterparts of four numinous animals also known as the *si ling* 四靈 (i.e., the dragon, unicorn, phoenix, and tortoise): "Heaven contains the essence of the four constellations and sends them down to produce the bodies of the four (numinous) animals."[52] The *si ling* also came to symbolize the four quadrants of the earth or any other microspace. Throughout this *Liji* passage the talismanic display of animal symbols appears to be based on the animal's correlation to the terrain on which the procession was advancing.[53]

The congruence between the soil and its inhabitants, both animals and humans, figured in a broader natural philosophy in which different regions were conceived as being subject to different "airs" (*qi*). In chapter 3 we saw how several texts presented the agency of "blood and *qi*" as the physiological basis or substrate for the emotions and temperament of living creatures. *Qi* was also thought to influence the temperament and character of living beings in its tangible form of wind (*feng* 風). This dialectic between *qi* and human behavior, for instance, figured as a key notion in Warring States theories of violence that argued that human physique, political action, climate, and natural environment were closely intertwined. Both social and physical aggression among living creatures were attributed to the nature of the configured cosmic or regional energies that influenced them.[54]

A similar notion of territorial *qi* underlay perceptions of *locus* and human and animal habitat. Local customs, human passions, and animal instincts were believed to be stimulated by regional "airs." The soil on which humans and animals lived provided the primary material for the formation of their physiology and character. The *Huainanzi* summarizes the idea that the nature of the soil determines the physical shape of its living inhabitants by stating that "each category of land generates according to its kind (*tu di ge yi qi lei sheng* 土地各以其類生)." Following this logic mountainous *qi* is said to produce mainly males, while the *qi* of swamps will produce many females. The *qi* of hot places produces many premature deaths while that in cold places produces longevity, and so on.[55] In an argument on the origins of avian features such as feathers and wings traditionally associated with immortals or "bird-people," Wang Chong reiterates this soil congruence by stating that "the hairy and feathered people are the produce of the shape of the soil."[56] The image of the earth as the progenitor of the creatures that dwell on its surface is also illustrated in Xu Shen's gloss for the graph *tu* 土 "earth," which is defined as *tu* 吐 "to spew" and explained as "the spitting of the earth which begets the myriad things." This gloss evokes the image of the earth "exhaling its vapors" (*tu qi* 吐氣) to produce fauna and flora.[57]

As was the case with the influence of *qi* on human beings, "soil *qi*" not only influenced the shape and natural instincts of animals, it also determined their moral qualities. This idea is reflected in a number of passages that link animal behavior to the native territory of both animal and human inhabitants. The necessity to maintain a unity between regional soil and its animal inhabitants is explicated in a chapter in the *Shangshu* entitled the "Hounds of Lü" (*Lü ao* 旅獒). This text relates how, following the conquest of the Shang, the Zhou established contacts with the nine wild and the eight barbarian tribes. One of these tribes, the western Lü, had sent a tribute of their famous hounds to King Wu, which led his Grand Protector, Duke Shi 奭 of Shao 召, to compose this piece as a way to instruct his ruler on the issue of tributary goods. The text starts by stating how enlightened kings in the past had spread their virtues and subdued the barbarians. Each tribe had made offerings of regional products (*fang wu* 方物) to the king, who in turn had displayed these goods as tokens of his power. Next follows a remonstrance in which King Wu is dissuaded from accepting strange animals and advised to employ only those species that share a common "territorial nature" (*tu xing* 土性) with its human inhabitants. The admiration for exogenous breeds from faraway regions is portrayed as a sign of hubris on behalf of the ruler when consolidating his state:

> [A ruler] should not engage in what is unprofitable to the harm of what is profitable, and then his merits will be completed. He should not value strange things (*yi wu* 異物) and despise useful things (*yong wu* 用物), and then his own people will suffice (to deliver what he needs). If dogs and horses do not share the nature of his local territory (*tu xing*), then he does not raise them. Exotic birds and strange animals shall not be nourished in his state. If a ruler does not consider things from afar as precious, then foreign people will come to him. If the only thing he considers to be precious are worthies, then the people near to him will be at peace.[58]

Parallel to the suggestions in the *Zhouyi* and *Zhouli* where animal patterns and animal physiology were linked to the nature of the soil, theories developed asserting that a particular "soil ether" or *qi* in general would produce a specific category of creatures or species (*wulei* 物類). The nature of the soil, its climate and "winds," its inhabitant living species, and its prevailing human custom(s) figured as standard elements in descriptions of territory or locality. This is particularly clear in the terminology used to describe foreign regions that commonly juxtapose territory (*tudi* 土地), wind vapors (*fengqi* 風氣), and human or animal species (*wulei* 物類).[59] The introduction to an Eastern Han compendium on customs (*fengsu* 風俗 "winds and customs") explains that regional and ethereal influences befall all blood creatures, thereby linking the susceptibility to social and environmental influences with the idea that living creatures can "draw" regionalized *qi* into their blood:

> By "wind" we mean the cold or warmth of the Heavenly *qi,* the difficulty or ease of the Earthly terrain, the excellence or pollution of waters and springs, and the hardness or softness of grasses and trees. By "customs" we mean the way in which creatures with blood imitate these and live.[60]

In addition to linking animals with the local soil, its climate, and its "airs," theories of territoriality emphasized the premise that animals would not instinctively transcend the boundaries of their natural habitat. Judging from the few passages received, it is not unlikely that the perception of a territorial unity of humans, animals, and the soil had fermented into a basic principle in early Chinese geography. Traces of a world view that sought to divide the earth into static unities of locality each marked by their own human and animal fauna are preserved in the geographical theories of Zou Yan. While no major writings by Zou Yan are extant, a brief description in the *Shiji* gives a fragmentary insight into his ideas. According to Sima Qian's account, Zou Yan positioned China as the ninth part of one of nine large continents, all separated by encircling seas. He further pictured the Middle Kingdom, also called the "Spiritual Country of the Red Region" (*Chi xian shen zhou* 赤縣神州), as "only one of the real Nine Zhou" and held that "around each of these lies a small encircling sea, so that people, birds and beasts cannot pass from one to another."[61] The people and animals on Zou Yan's nine continents are said to be separated by water in order to prevent them from mixing among each other (*xiang tong* 相通). Zou Yan suggests that in its original territorial layout among the continents of the world, China's people and animals were segregated from human and animal creatures beyond its boundaries.

The idea that humans and animals cannot transgress their habitat or change locality without significant physical, social, or symbolical consequences constituted a type of sociobiological order in early China. Several texts note that the idea not to cross one's natural boundaries was a fact of nature. The *Huainanzi* states that the mynah (or gracko) and the parrot never cross the river Ji 濟 and that the badger dies when crossing the river Wen 汶. It goes on to explain the cause of these creatures' deaths by stating that "their nature (*xingxing* 形性) cannot be altered, their habitat (*shiju* 勢居) cannot be moved."[62] Virtually identical passages appear in the *Zhouli* and the *Liezi*. In both these variants, not the animal's nature or habitat but the "soil ether" (*tu qi* 土氣) or climate is offered as an explanation.[63] The *Liji* extrapolates this philosophy to the barbarian tribes that surround the Middle Kingdom and states that each of these different tribes have a nature that cannot be altered. Zheng Xuan notes that this is due to the soil vapor (*di qi* 地氣).[64] Both barbarians and animals are thus firmly linked to the soil and the "soil ether" they share with plants and other humans of the same locality.

The image of fierce and powerful animals coming to their end because they leave their natural environment frequently served as an analogy in criticisms of a ruler's indulgence to engage in activities beyond the reach of his own capabilities or the bounds of his own political domain. One saying held that while net or hook are unable to control the mighty "boat-swallowing" fish when it roams in the seas, this huge medusa would fall prey to animals as minute as ants when it strands upon a dry shore.[65] Another saying applied the same motif to the image of the dragon and the human sage and suggests that maintaining a root in one's habitat serves as a necessary condition to exert one's power: "If a dragon does not even have one foot of water, it has no means to ascend to heaven. If a sage does not even have one foot of soil, he has no means to rule the empire."[66]

Criticisms against dissolving the environmental unity of humans and animals based on territoriality are also attested in passages asserting that particular animals can only be consumed by people who share the same habitat. Han Ying notes that the meats consumed by the southern Miao 苗 tribes can be poisonous for the Han Chinese: "The (flesh/hides) of the strange animals of the Nan Miao is like that of dogs or sheep, but if you give it to a human being (i.e., a Chinese) it is a lethal drug. It is thus because custom changes the disposition, and habit alters the nature."[67] A similar distinction between a Chinese-versus-barbarian taste of animals is made in the *Huainanzi*. It states that while the southern Yue people considered the catch of a "whisker snake" (*ranshe* 髯蛇) to be a delicacy, people in the Middle Kingdom considered it useless and threw such snakes away.[68] Other taboos on the consumption of animals on regional grounds have been received. One of these was a rumor, presumably in circulation during the Han, that, while all over the empire cranes were eaten, this was banned in the three capital districts since people believed outbreaks of thunder would ensue from the capture of cranes.[69]

The importance of the unity of soil and habitat also appears in stories in which a sage master attempts to refute the anomalous character of a species in its natural habitat. The *Yanzi chunqiu* relates how Yanzi dismissed Duke Jing 景 of Qi's (547–490 B.C.E.) suspicion that his observance of tigers in the mountains and snakes in the marshes could be inauspicious. Yanzi argued that mountains and crevices are the natural habitat of tigers and snakes respectively, hence their observance in these places could not be ominous.[70] Yanzi reassures the duke by reaffirming the link between an animal's appearance and its natural environment. Elsewhere we read that the plains are the habitat for strange birds and beasts, mountain forests house strange tigers and leopards, and gorges and streams house snakes and dragons.[71]

It is possible that the notion of a congruence between the soil and its animal life left a trace in early agricultural thought, notably in the idea that manure or fertilizers were more effective if they were the product of indigenous animals. The *Zhouli* documents the office of the Plant Officer (*caoren* 草人) who is said to be responsible for the "methods of soil transformation (*tu hua* 土化)." His tasks include "taking into consideration the qualities of the soil, assessing its suitability, and determining the appropriate seeds (to be used on those soils)." Then the text proceeds with a list of specified animal concoctions used as manure, each of which is designed to fertilize (i.e., transform) nine different types of soil:

> In general they dress the seeds as follows: for red and hard soil they use ox (fat, liquid, broth?). For red and light-reddish soil they use a sheep.[72] For heaped-up and granular soil they use elaphures. For dried up marshy soil they use deer. For eroded and dry soil they use a badger. For granular soil they use the fox. For sticky (black) soil they use the pig. For hard and solid soil they use hemp, and for light dry soil they use the dog.[73]

Although attempts at developing a typology of soils can be found in several Warring States texts, it is uncertain to which corresponding types of soil this passage may refer.[74] Yet in pairing different animals with different soil types, it may suggest a belief that soil transformation or fertilization is enhanced by the use of excrements or products of animals that were native to the targeted soil. Both textual and pictorial evidence confirms an advanced knowledge of the use of animal fertilizers in early China. The dressing or dipping of seeds in liquid manure was practiced as a preventive measure against insect plagues. Wang Chong refers to a technique attributed to Shennong and Hou Ji that consisted in "decocting horse excrements and using the fluid to soak the seeds."[75] A Han commentary to the aforementioned *Zhouli* passage mentions the treatment of seeds by boiling various kinds of animal bone for decoction. The use of animal bones, bombyxine and ovine excrements for the treatment of seeds and soil is further attested in a manual on farming attributed to the agriculturalist Fan Shengzhi 氾勝之 (fl. first cent. B.C.E.), and in Han murals depicting farmers scooping up dung behind their horses.[76] While these materials do not provide conclusive evidence that theories on the correspondence between animals and the soil occupied the minds of Warring States farmers and tillers, they do suggest a link between the use of animals and animal products and the treatment of particular soils.

Naturalist explanations were not the only principles to furnish the rationale for the view that animals should ideally abide in their own environment. Some texts argued against transcending one's habitat on the basis that sharing a particular soil determined not only an animal's physical or natural disposition, but also its moral character. The recognition that an animal's locality and behavior were intricately linked echoes similar views on the relationship between an animal's "topos" and "ethos" noted by Aristotle.[77] According to such theories, there existed a kind of moral and emotional affinity or congruence between animals and human beings that shared the same soil or soil vapor. Hence the relationship between home-bred animals and their human counterparts would be more harmonious than that between humans and animals from different regions, both in physical and moral terms. Barbarian tribes for instance were not only seen as skillful animal tamers because they shared the heart-mind of animals, their skills also differed according to the natural environment and customs in their native lands. Nomadic tribes inhabiting the steppe lands such as the Xiongnu 匈奴 were said to be more adept in handling horses, while southern tribesmen knew their ways in hunting tigers, handling snakes, or attacking alligators in the tropical swamps.[78] The boundaries of a soil-habitat could also be of a political nature or coincide with the frontiers of a state or fief. In the *Zuozhuan*, the Marquis of Jin is advised not to use foreign horses in his battle against Qin. Horses, his remonstrator argued, should only be deployed for a military or political cause that serves their native "waters and soils":

> Anciently, during important battles, one was required to ride horses bred in one's own state. They are native to its waters and soils and know the hearts of its people. They are docile to instruction and accustomed to the roads; whatever place one directs them to, there are none who won't abide by (their driver's) will. Now for the battle that is before us, you are using horses of a different state [i.e., Zheng 鄭]. These horses will become afraid, their behavior will change and they will run contrary to the will of their driver. Their confused *qi* will make them wild and excited. Their timorous blood will flush through their whole body, and their veins will stand out everywhere. Externally they will appear strong, but internally they will be weak. They will not be able to advance or withdraw, and they will be unable to turn round. Your lordship is sure to regret this.[79]

The marquis however failed to heed the advice and, on the day of the battle, his horses got stuck in the mud.

The explanations encountered so far variously sought to assign physical and moral properties of living creatures to their relationship with territory and the soil. Territorial theories also influenced the perception of animals in religious practice. Both the numinous power engendered by animals in religious ceremony as well as their suitability as sacrificial victims were often justified on the basis that there existed a territorial bond between the animal, the ritual officiant, and the sacred locus where a ritual would be conducted. To the early Chinese a territory, locality, or landscape was a numinous space inhabited by localized spirits who through various means exerted numinous power over this physical realm. Spirit powers influenced the soil, its crops, and its animals.

Together with ancestral sacrifices and sacrifices offered to the gods of the grains, the altars of the gods of locality, or spirits of the soil (*she* 社) also fostered political authority. In origin these altars were heaped-up mounds of soil. Feudal lords established ritual and political allegiances by mixing a gift of soil from the altar mound of the central ruler into their own mound.[80] The altars of the soil and the grain symbolized the social, political, and religious heart of the feudal state, while offerings to the spirits of the four directions (*fang* 方) served to delineate the borders of each territorial polity and its spirits.[81] Landscapes, their mountains, and their rivers, figured as sacred spaces. They were, as the *Liji* states, able to produce clouds and cause the emergence of wind and rain, and inhabited by "strange beings" called "spirits."[82]

According to the *Liji*, spirits would only savor those sacrificial victims that are tied to the soil or territory with which their spiritual influence is connected.

> What has not been produced by heaven (i.e., in the proper season) and has not been nourished by the (proper) soil shall not be used in ritual (sacrifices) by the gentleman. The spirits do not appreciate those offerings. If inhabitants of mountains sacrifice fish or turtles, or if inhabitants on the shore of a lake sacrifice deer or pigs, the gentleman would say that they do not know the (proper) rites.[83]

It is not unlikely that beliefs in the territorial kinship between spirits and their animal offerings were inspired by sacrificial codes stipulating that spirits do not appreciate offerings which do not belong to their own category, kin, or species.[84] The link between the performative effect of an animal sacrifice and the territorial nature of the numinous space that was addressed is also attested in instructions on sacrificial techniques. Spirits of the land were worshiped by burying the animal remains in the soil; spirits of the watery realms by drowning the animal victim. The *Yili* stipulates that "in sacrificing to heaven, the offering is burnt on a pile of firewood; when sacrificing to the hills and the peaks, the victim is elevated (on a mound). In sacrificing to the rivers, it is drowned, and when sacrificing to the earth, it is buried."[85] The goddess of the earth, Houtu 后土, was worshiped by the burial of a yellow calf, and until late in the Han, horses were drowned during sacrifices to the river god Hebo 河伯.[86] The ritual horse prayer found at Shuihudi is accompanied by an instruction for the officiant to pile up earth and fashion a horse figurine. It is likely that this use of sanctified soil was aimed at propitiating the soil spirits of the pastures the herds were to occupy.[87]

The importance of the notion of regionality in the selection of animal victims is further documented in passages dealing with sacrifice where both a directional symbolism as well as the regional color constituted an important sacrificial criterion. The *Zhouli* stipulates that for the performance of sacrifices to mountains and streams victim animals have to be chosen according to the color of that region.[88] The importance of color and territorial order is also reflected in the treatment of tortoises used in divinatory procedures. An officer known as the Tortoise Keeper (*guiren* 龜人) was instructed to "distinguish the animals according to the color of their region and the shape of their body." The color details are supplemented by Zheng Xuan in accordance with five-phase theory: the heavenly tortoise should be dark black, the earthly tortoise yellow, the eastern species blue-green, the western white, the southern red, and the northern black.[89]

The idea that animals and territory constituted a fixed unit may even have influenced economic thinking. In a chapter in the *Guanzi* dealing with methods for insuring fiscal control, Master Guan proposes to put barren lands unsuitable for agriculture to economic benefit by establishing a government monopoly on the procurement and sale of sacrificial victims that hail from these pastures. Guanzi bases his argument on the assumption that people may refuse to have their own sheep and cattle mate with wild and exogenous herds. By allowing only those animals that have been cross-bred with animals from infertile neighboring lands to be used in spring and autumn sacrifices, the government could stimulate demand and increase the revenue gained from these animals. Thus the people's sense for ritual and ceremony could be made to prevail over their hesitancy to have local breeds mate with imported herds.[90]

To summarize, the territorial connection between the soil and its animals was believed to be more than just a physical link. Animals figured as part of a *couleur locale* comprising natural characteristics, moral connotations, and spirit power. In this sense the typology of the natural world in early China was closely linked to the idea that all living creatures had to be assigned a place within an encompassing and fixed topology. Animal behavior, the suitability of animal meats for consumption, the social and economic use of animals, as well as their efficacy as mediums in sacrificial religion were determined by their native link with a particular soil and their territorial disposition in general. This insistence on a fixed sociobiological order provided an important framework for the identification of animals that embodied special sociopolitical and numinous powers. It also formed the background for the explanation of portentous and anomalous animal behavior. For it was precisely the transgression of territorial boundaries and the capability to transcend one's fixed sociobiological order, both physically or in its more abstract guise of *qi,* that inspired the portrayal of certain animals as numinous. Species that were able to encompass the *qi* of various regions, change habitat, and transgress their biotopical confines were identified as numinous animals.

Animals beyond Territory

With territory viewed as part of a regular sociobiological order based on a moral and physical congruence between the soil and its living creatures, the transcendence of territorial boundaries and the movement of living creatures between localities constituted a significant alteration to this regular order. Traditionally rulers asserted their social, political, and economic command by traveling their lands and exchanging tributary goods with neighboring peoples, and through hunting and the ritual consumption of game animals at various stages during such itineraries. Equally important to the chase of animals as an act of conquest was the hunter's spatial movement, which served as a real or symbolical act of territorial creation. Surpassing the bounds of one's geographical polity was a gesture of sociopolitical and religious authority.

Together with the human ruler's exodus from his own political epicenter on processions to the outskirts of the empire, a whole range of goods including animals and various animal products traveled along. These functioned as objects of exchange or targets of organized hunts during such missions. As part of the establishment of political ties across different localities, animals from different regions were gathered as memorabilia and tokens of power in the courtyards and animal parks of the central ruler. Both the manipulation of animal species within the confines of animal enclosures and hunting parks, as well as the exchange of animal tributes as symbols of their respective territorial habitat and its human rulers, contributed to the generation of sociopolitical power. Through transcending the regular geographical order in which both human and animal species would dwell on their regional soil without crossing territorial boundaries, both the human subject and the animal object were invested with real and symbolic authority.

The importance of the hunt and the hunting park lay in its symbolism rather than its economics. Economic considerations behind the organization of large-scale hunts and the seclusion of animals in parks included the provision of a variety of meats for the royal or imperial kitchens, and availing the ruler with a sufficient supply of sacrificial victims to conduct state and ancestral sacrifices and entertain prominent guests.[91] The *Liji* specifies three as the maximum number of seasonal hunts permissible each year. Each of these hunts served a particular purpose: providing for the sacrificial offerings, providing for guests, and providing for the kitchens.[92]

It is uncertain when exactly the establishment of hunting parks became a regular practice. According to the *Huainanzi*, Shang founder Tang 湯 established parks to provide his ancestral temples with "living and dead meat."[93] Given its Han provenance, this statement need not be accepted as historical fact. At least one reference in the *Zuozhuan* suggests that kings during the Eastern Zhou period set up hunting parks. After assuming the throne in 675 B.C.E. Zhou Hui Wang 周惠王 reportedly turned a private orchard into an animal preserve.[94] Other references mention a lord shooting geese in his park and a suggestion to use elaphures and deer gathered in a park as relief provisions.[95] Besides indicating that animal parks existed in one or more of the feudal states during the Spring and Autumn and early Warring States period, the available textual evidence remains inconclusive about the size or contents of these animal preserves. More reliable is the evidence for the Han period which confirms that hunting parks were used for the provision of sacrificial meats. For instance within the annual cycle of state ceremonies during the Han, a sacrifice known as the *chuliu* 貙劉 ritual took place at the onset of autumn. In essence the *chuliu* ceremony was the killing by the emperor of game, usually young deer, whose meat was then offered to the ancestors at the imperial tombs and the ancestral temple within the capital. It functioned both as a hunting festival and military exercise.[96]

More important than the park's role as a breeding ground for the ruler's culinary and sacrificial needs was its symbolic role. The seclusion of wild animals into a confined space such as a park or a court garden was in the first place an endeavor to sanctify the numinous powers of the ruler. In imperial times, parks provided "the most tangible image of the emperor as a cosmic figure, an earthly simulacrum of the all-embracing Heaven."[97] Quests for animal exotica to fill these preserves as well as the organization of territorial hunting campaigns to celebrate a ruler's political authority are already associated with the Shang and Zhou rulers. While some voices condemn an overindulgence in the hunt for animal exotica as a sign of dynastic extravagance on the part of the ruler, others present it as an endorsement of a ruler's all-encompassing powers. According to Sima Qian Shang tyrant Zhou 紂 not only fought wild animals with his bare hands, his insolence was further shown by the fact that he "collected an excessive number of dogs, horses and strange creatures to fill his palace, expanded his pastures and terraces at Shaqiu 沙丘, and gathered many wild beasts and birds to put in them."[98] One account describes how the conquest of the Shang was accompanied by the bloody capture of great numbers of wild animals including tigers, panthers, rhinoceros, yaks, bears, boars, badgers, and numerous herds of stag and deer. The campaign was sealed with the sacrifice of over five hundred oxen to Heaven and Hou Ji as well as offerings of nearly three thousand sheep and boar to other spirits.[99] The observation, hunt, and sacrifice of strange creatures as a tour de force of the ruler can be seen most notably in the description of the itineraries undertaken by Zhou King Mu (956?–918? B.C.E.). At several stages during his legendary journey King Mu is reported to have participated in hunts. In one campaign he is portrayed catching white foxes and black badgers and sacrificing them to the spirit of the Yellow River. On another occasion he surveys a mountainous landscape with its multifarious birds and beasts during a period of five days. Often the king receives pastoral goods and herds of cattle and sheep in exchange for precious artifacts from the Chinese heartland.[100] A contemporary of King Mu, King Yan 偃 of Xu 徐, is also described as a lover of exotica. One source states that he would dive into deep waters to find strange fish and enter the depths of the mountains to find strange animals, which he would then display in his courtyard.[101]

While both elites and common people in Warring States and Han China engaged in animal sports such as cockfighting, bullfighting, racing hounds and horses, and setting dogs on hares, the collection of exotic breeds in nature preserves and the wild animal chase were more than a testimony to a devotion to rural pursuits among its leading social classes.[102] Parks served as scenes in which rulers staged symbolical conquests of the natural world through the means of ritual hunts and staged animal combats. Hunts in animal enclosures and pens as well as the ritual killing and consumption of game during banquets afterward constituted important insignia of ritual and political prowess.[103] Such acts assisted rulers in the symbolic assertion of their dominance over distant regions and their human and animal subjects. Similar to natural landscapes and their inhabiting wildlife, parks and artificial gardens were a sacred space, and engaging in the pursuit of exotic creatures within its boundaries amounted to partaking in the sacred aura of this topographic microcosm.

The sacred character of animal enclosures can be seen in an ode in the "Greater Elegantiae" (*Da ya* 大雅) section of the *Shijing* where the royal park of King Wen 文, founder of the Zhou, is described as a *ling you* 靈囿, a "numinous" or "divine" park:

> The King was in the Divine Park,
> Where does and bucks were lying down.
> The does and bucks, so sleek and fat;
> White birds were glistening.
> The King stood by the Divine Pond;
> How full was it of fishes leaping about! [104]

The Mao preface to this poem states that when King Wen received his mandate from Heaven, the people rejoiced in the fact that he possessed numinous virtue (*ling de* 靈德), which reached the birds, beasts, and insects.[105] In the *Mengzi* the ode is quoted in an answer to an inquiry by King Hui 惠 of Liang 梁 (370–319 B.C.E.) as to whether sages should find pleasure in the seemingly trivial observance of geese and deer. Mencius argues that a ruler has to be good and wise first before he can enjoy these sights. He also suggests that a ruler's subjects should be able to share the delight of observing the ruler's exotica: "Even if one possesses towers, ponds, birds and beasts, how could they be enjoyed alone?"[106] In this sense Mencius portrays the spontaneous labor devoted by his subjects to the construction of parks as a celebration of a ruler's virtue and thus attributes the emergence of such parks to moral leadership rather than the violent conquest of the animal world. While King Wen's park spanned a surface of seventy *li* square, it was only natural according to Mencius that his people thought it too small. This was the result of the king's willingness to share it with woodcutters and catchers of pheasants and hares alike.[107] Jia Yi 賈誼 (201–169 B.C.E.) comments on King Wen's virtue reflected in this poem by stating that "at the place where sage rulers are present, fish, turtles, birds and beasts also find their place. How much more then should this be the case for the human populace!"[108]

     The symbolic function of parks as microcosms celebrating the ruler's en-
compassing power over all living creatures came to the forefront in early imperial
times. Han political imperialism went coterminous with the biological expansion of empire, and parks in the capital region gathered representative species
from every region of the emperor's universe.[109] Rhapsodic descriptions of Han
Wudi's Shanglin park by Sima Xiangru 司馬相如 (ca. 180–117 B.C.E.) and Zhang
Heng 張衡 (78–139 C.E.) portray these preserves as a microcosm of all fauna and
flora under heaven. They describe how strange animal species from all quarters
were concentrated into an enclosed space in the metropolitan Chang'an 長安 region, the epicenter of the empire.[110] In the newly emerging genre of the Han rhapsody, novel fauna and flora were celebrated with a novel vocabulary. As Yves
Hervouet has pointed out, a great deal of the animal nomenclature in Sima
Xiangru's poems consists of imaginary species that Sima could hardly have seen
himself. Some animal names are neologisms, and small-sized species, such as insects or worms, are remarkably absent. Hence the majesty and grandeur of the
emperor and his park are reinforced by the enumeration of large and awesome
animals, rocks, plants, and the like.[111] In the same style, the *Hanshu* records Han
Wudi's expansionist glory in the western regions with a vivid depiction of his
newly acquired animal mirabilia. Upon hearing about the famous heavenly
horses and after having established a corridor to Dayuan 大宛 and Anxi 安息
(ca. 101 B.C.E.), "the *pushao* 蒲梢, dragon-stripes, fish-eye, and blood-sweating
horses filled the Yellow Gate; groups of great elephants, lions, ferocious hounds
and ostriches were reared in the outer parks; and exotic goods from different directions were brought from the four quarters of the world."[112]
     With the increase of empire over a vastly expanded territory, some exog-
enous creatures presented to the Han court underwent a process of sinicization.
Certain animals were adapted, in image and in name, to the indigenous and familiar fauna. Han jade carvings of felines for example may have been Chinese
versions of the western Asian lion, as Jessica Rawson has suggested. Late Warring States and Han artisans turned the image of animals originating from the
steppes in the border areas into tigers or other local creatures to fit local perceptions.[113] Descriptive enumerations of animal exotica generally emphasized that
these animals came from remote places and had crossed or covered large territories. Ban Gu's 班固 (32–92 C.E.) "Western Capital Rhapsody" mentions imperial enclosures and a "forbidden park" that housed unicorns from Jiuzhen
九眞, horses from Dayuan, rhinoceros from Huangzhi 黃支, and ostriches
from Tiaozhi 條枝, "crossing the Kunlun 崑崙 mountains, traversing the vast
seas, strange species from various directions arrived from thirty thousand *li.*"[114]
     Having crossed territorial boundaries over vast distances, within the parks
the spatial distribution of these animals was linked to their place of origin. Accounts of royal hunts within the preserves describe how game animals symbolically represented all species within the ruler's realm.[115] For example, in an

exposition of the ancient hunting rituals, Ma Rong 馬融 (79–166 C.E.) states that before the hunt "animals from the nine marshy preserves were gathered together," hereby reiterating the connection with the Nine Provinces.[116] By roaming through a park and contemplating or hunting exotic beasts in artificial landscapes, the ruler symbolically paced through his empire in the same way that he engaged in "inspection tours" (*xunshou* 巡守) of his political realm. The collection of exotic animals provided "a vivid rhetorical means of re-enacting and extending the work of empire."[117] It was a ritual display of the physical symbols of conquest and acquisition. Within the parks, Edward Schafer notes, a sense of cosmic and geographic order prevailed. "Mammals are distinguished in the poems by their places of origin, especially as to whether they represented the north or the south, and seem to have been placed symbolically in the corresponding parts of the park."[118] Watery creatures are associated with the east in Sima Xiangru's rhapsody on the Shanglin park:

> In the vast lakes of the east . . .
> horned dragons and red female dragons,
> Sturgeon and salamanders,
> Carp, bream, gudgeon, and dace,
> Cowfish, flounder, and sheatfish
> Arch their backs and twitch their tails,
> Shake their scales and flap their fins,
> Diving towards the deep crevices;
> The waters are loud with fish and turtles,
> A multitude of living things.[119]

A number of passages suggest that distinctions were made between the symbolic value of killing animals from the wilds as opposed to slaughtering domesticated breeds. The catch of game animals from the wilds was mainly a prerogative of the ruler. He exerted his authority beyond his domestic realm through hunting nondomestic animals. In the *Zuozhuan,* Zi Chan 子產 (d. ca. 522 B.C.E.) refuses to grant leave to an official for a hunting expedition in preparation of a sacrifice arguing that only the ruler is permitted to use "fresh animals" (*xian* 鮮); that is, wild animals caught in nature.[120] The *Zhouli* contains a statement stipulating that among the common people those who do not raise animals are not permitted to use animal victims in sacrifice.[121] It is plausible that such taboos were associated with the idea that hunting was a form of sacrifice and therefore subject to ritual regulations of hierarchy. This is not to say that the lower classes, servants and slaves stayed away from the breeding of meats and fish or the hunt of animals for domestic consumption. A slave contract dated to 59 B.C.E. for example gives a long list of instructions for a domestic servant that includes hunting and raising animals. While not being allowed to mount a horse or ride in a carriage, the contract stipulates that the servant should make bird nets to trap sparrows and crows, weave fishing nets, shoot geese and wild ducks, climb mountains to shoot deer, and dive into the waters to catch turtles. Further the slave is ordered to raise several hundreds of geese in the backyard, expel malign birds such as owls, herd swine, rear piglets and colts, feed cattle and horses, plaster the stable walls, and engage in other menial jobs.[122] That the unauthorized chase of animals in the wilds and in parks was punished is attested in legal codes. Several articles regarding "forbidden parks" (*jin yuan* 禁苑) among the Qin legal documents excavated at Longgang (Yunmeng county) deal with trespassing in parks and with hunting.[123]

Descriptions of animal parks suggest that the condensation of various animal species into one geographical space figured as a testimony of a ruler's numinous power. Similar ideas applied to the use of animals in ritual. On at least one known occasion, a collection of animals was released on the mountain top where a ritual sacrifice took place. This occurred in 110 B.C.E., when Han Wudi performed the *feng* 封 and *shan* 禪 sacrifices on Mount Tai 泰.

> To complete the ritual all sorts of strange animals and flying creatures, white pheasants and other animals from distant regions were set free. Animals such as rhinoceroses and elephants where not set free, but brought to Mount Tai and taken away again (after the sacrifices).[124]

Emperor Wu symbolically released exotic animals from cages on Mount Tai, thereby creating an omen in the hope that the good fortune that correlates with such omen would be stimulated. The omen created symbolizes the idea that the radiance of an emperor's virtue causes the arrival of exotic animals from all quarters of the empire to flock spontaneously around the sacrificial *locus*. Geographical boundaries diffuse and all animal species mix and roam the peaks of Mount Tai to celebrate the emperor's virtue. As in descriptions of parks and animal enclosures, free and unbound movement rather than *stasis* characterizes the animal portrayals.

Similar symbolism can be found in decorative motifs on the so-called Han hill censers (*bo shan lu* 博山鑪) used to burn incense. In addition to depicting domestic and hunting scenes in which humans and animals interact, these mountain censers displayed a microcosm of freak and magical animals that swirl around a mountain peak shrouded in clouds. The earliest textual reference to these hill censers emphasizes both the exotic nature of the animals represented and the naturalness and spontaneity of their movements: "Carved on this (censer) are exotic birds, strange animals. Exhaustively represented are all spiritual prodigies. All these move in a spontaneous manner."[125] Confined to a single microcosmic space, the compact assemblage of animals evoked numinous influence and magical power. The spirit mountain presents itself as a cosmic wilderness where all creatures intermingle in the intermediary space between heaven and earth. The same image inspired depictions of animals on walls of palaces, temples, and tombs. A good example occurs in Wang Yanshou's *Lu Lingguang dian fu* 魯 靈光殿賦 ("Poetic Exposition on the Numinous Radiance Basilica in Lu"), which presents a pictorial exposition on the decorations of the pillars and roof of a palace built by a son of Emperor Jing (r. 157–141 B.C.E.).[126] The poem guides the spectator's eyes on an upward voyage along the columns to the roofs of the palace. It first depicts a moving jungle of bipeds, quadrupeds, tigers, dragons, red birds, snakes, deer, reptiles, hares, monkeys, and bears curling around the palace pillars. Higher up the column, barbarians are pictured. Again higher up between the ridge-poles, spirits and immortals dwell on mountain peaks. The poem proceeds:

> Suddenly all turn hazy like echoes and shades,
> and mingle and disperse like ghosts and spirits.
> Portrayed in picture are Heaven and Earth,
> all species and classes of living beings,
> various creatures and prodigies,
> mountain spirits and sea phantoms.
> Recorded in sketch are their shapes,
> embodied in vermilions and greens.
> A chiliad transformations and myriad changes,
> all and each in different forms.[127]

This finale concludes a progressive description that debouches into a realm where all species are blurred and where animals, ghosts, and spirits diffuse in a universal rhythm of transformation. Concrete species turn into spiritual categories, physical territory becomes a numinous space. Another less detailed account is recorded for the Jianzhang 建章 palace constructed by Han Wudi in 113 B.C.E. In this immense palace complex, a tall "phoenix tower" was placed in the east, a tiger park in the west, a great lake to the north with replica of islands, holy mountains, tortoises, and fish, and a Jade Hall to the south with gigantic bird statues at the gates.[128]

Another consequence of rulers transcending the boundaries of their political habitat was the traffic of animals as tributary tokens of exchange between states. This exchange of animal tributes shared similarities with organized hunts during which it was common to reserve the most precious animals as game for the ruler and his guests or as food for the spirits. Descriptions of rulers traveling their real and imaginary empires such as King Mu's journey in the *Mu Tianzi zhuan* further suggest that the exchange of goods and animals often occurred in conjunction with hunting and sacrifice. As a result of the system of animal tributes, animals were made to transcend their regional habitat, albeit passively. While tributary exchanges sometimes had a considerable economical role, their symbolic function was very similar to the collection of animals in enclosures and parks. The tributary offering of exogenous breeds to a central ruler sealed a ruler's political dominance by exemplifying that his influence encompassed geographical boundaries and extended to human and animal species beyond the visible territorial epicenter. By accepting the gift of representative exotic species and mirabilia from all directions, the ruler claimed dominion over their indigenous habitats.

A passage in the *Xunzi* describes the perfect world order or "Great Divine Order" (*da shen* 大神) as one wherein the central kingdoms would put to use the indigenous products of the barbarian periphery:

> It is by the Northern Sea that there are fast horses and barking dogs; nonetheless the Central States acquire them, breed them, and put them to work. It is by the Southern Sea that there are feathers and plumes, elephant tusks, rhinoceros hides, copper ores, and cinnabar; still the Central States obtain and process them. It is by the Eastern Sea that there are purple-dye plants, fine white silks, fish, and salt; nonetheless the Central States acquire them and use them for food and clothing. It is by the Western Sea that there are skins and hides and multicolored yak tails; still the Central States obtain them and put them to use.... Therefore, even though the tiger and leopard are ferocious beasts, the gentleman can have them skinned for his own use. Thus, all that Heaven shelters and Earth supports is brought to its ultimate refinement and its fullest utility; so that the refined is used to adorn the worthy and good, and the useful is employed to nourish the Hundred Clans and peace and contentment are brought to them.[129]

This passage portrays the successful use and deployment of exogenous animals and goods as a hallmark of moral civilization. While recognizing that a fixed geographical order befalls all species, the Central States, and by extension its sage ruler, are capable to put to good use everything that lies beyond its immediate periphery. The wild, bestial, and unknown can be "skinned" to serve the development of the civilized center, and barbarians, who are compared to ferocious beasts, will submit to the civilizing control of the center.

In the *Zuozhuan,* the concept of a ruling center that exerts a socioreligious dominance over its wild periphery is traced back to Yu the Great's original division of the world into nine regions and his casting of the nine talismanic cauldrons. The following passage provides the earliest description of a process in which "animalia" beyond the ruling center are symbolically centralized:

> Anciently, when the Xia (territory) was marked by virtue, the distant regions made pictorial (representations) of the creatures (in their region), and tributes of metal (were sought from) the Nine Herdsmen. Tripods were then cast with those creatures represented on them. All creatures (being thus revealed), (instructions were

given) of preparations (to be made), so that the people would know these spirits and evils. Therefore when people would enter rivers, marshes, hills and forests, they would not meet nor follow them, and the *chimei* or *wangliang* 罔兩 would not meet with them. Hereby they could harmonize high and low, and enjoy the favors of Heaven.[130]

Parallel to the aforementioned mapping out of the Nine Provinces with their fauna and flora, this passage describes how the ruler commissioned ambulant rulers ("shepherds") of the periphery to identify (con-tribute) images of unknown creatures to the center. These strange images of demons and spirits cast in bronze function as the iconic key to the ruler's knowledge and control of the inhospitable surrounding domains. The central region symbolically encompasses its distant surroundings and its creatures. Once represented in name or image by the center, symbolical power and control has been established over the unknown.[131]

The image of pastors or shepherds gathering images from the wild periphery and tributing them to a sedentary heartland further reflects a view of geographical space that pictured the center as static, domesticated, and in a state of sociopolitical permanence, while its concentric outskirts, both the nomadic borderlands in the north and the neighboring jungles in the south, were viewed as increasingly unstable, wild, and in a state of motion.[132] A similar division between a fixed center and a moving periphery that echoes the aforementioned notion of a soil habitat is reflected in the terminology used to distinguish between sedentary tribes who are aboriginal and "stick to the soil" (*tu zhu* 土著) and nomadic people who "move with or follow their domestic animals" (*sui chu mu* 隨畜牧).[133] The emperor or ruler-king was portrayed as a cosmic shepherd of all under heaven. This image of shepherding frequently occurs as a craft analogy for ruling a state. One Han text links a ruler's tour of inspection (*xun shou*) with the image of shepherding and refers to Tang and Yu as shepherds.[134] The tribute of animals as well as the explanation of the appearance and behavior of new creatures that had been imported from these distant territories or could be encountered on expeditions beyond the heartland constituted a practical and mental attempt to ascertain the social, political, and religious supremacy of the ruler-king who saw himself as the center of the universe.

A similar link between rulership and cosmographic collection through the representation and ordering of the world in image or text has been associated with the composition of the *Shanhaijing*. This work, which dates at least partly to the Warring States or Qin period, is presented in one source as a written record of the unknown creatures Yu confronted on his demiurgic tour of the empire. The *Wu Yue chunqiu* 吳越春秋 states that Yu summoned the spirits of famous mountains and great marshlands to "question them about the mountain ranges, river courses, metals and jades, the species of birds, beasts and insects present there." Next he ordered Bo Yi 伯益 to explain (*shu* 疏) and record them in writing (*ji*

記).¹³⁵ The preface accompanying Liu Xin's edition of the *Shanhaijing* reiterates the link between Yu's ordering of the universe and its classification into a written record. Topography is here characterized as a mental act of pacing through unknown lands, and identifying and controlling its creatures by incorporating them by name in a text.¹³⁶ The *Shanhaijing* therefore embodies the idea that the world can be ordered through naming on two levels: first, in the act of naming unknown creatures in the text itself (discussed in chapter 1) and, second, in the textual representation of the world as a whole. As an enterprise of textualization, the entire work presents itself as a continuation of the cosmic act of naming and recording, a project that had been initiated by sages such as Yu and Bo Yi.

Evidence suggests that throughout the Warring States and Han period contending views were at play as to whether or not rulers should engage in the deployment and collection of foreign animal species. The celebration of exotic animals in Han parks appears to be far removed from the admonitions against the import of foreign or extraterritorial breeds in the "Lü ao" or Sima Qian's condemnation of tyrant Zhou's indulgence in exotica. Criticisms against an overzealous devotion to the collection of exotic animals were often part of discussions on human and economic expenditure, not in the least during the Western Han when the tributary system had started to contribute considerably to the depletion of Han's treasuries. A written account of a court conference summoned in 81 B.C.E. to discuss contemporary political problems and recorded by Huan Kuan 桓寬 as the "Discourses on Salt and Iron" (*Yantie lun* 鹽鐵論) contains a telling critique:

> In ancient times one did not use human strength in favor of birds and beasts, and one did not deprive the people of their resources in order to feed dogs and horses. Therefore resources were plentiful, and there was abundant physical strength. But wild animals and exotic beasts cannot be used to cultivate the land; instead they cause those who should be plowing and weeding to devote their efforts to raising and feeding them. While the common people don't even have short sleeves to wear, dogs and horses are dressed in ornate embroidery. While the black-haired people don't even manage to get the chaff and dregs of grain, birds and beasts are eating millet and meat.¹³⁷

Elsewhere in the *Yantie lun* the use of exotic animals is the subject of a dispute between the great secretary representing the Han government and worthies staged as critics of Han's policies. The spokesman for the government argues that the display of strange animals and exotic goods serves to impress the barbarians and demonstrates the virtues of the emperor, but his critics retort that the establishment of imperial authority should depend primarily on upholding the rites and practicing virtue. The Duke of Zhou, according to the worthies, was able to bring the barbarians to submission by showing them the virtues of filial piety rather than by offering them the spectacle of wild beasts and bears. Next the notion of exoticism itself is questioned:

> Rhinoceros, elephants, water buffaloes and tigers exist in great numbers among the southern barbarians. Mules, donkeys, and camels are raised on a permanent basis by the northern barbarians. Animals looked upon as being rare by the Middle Kingdom are looked down upon by foreign states.[138]

Another caution for frugality in the gathering of strange animals within the confines of the ruler's domain reverberated toward the end of the Western Han. Among measures proposed in a memorial issued in 7 B.C.E. designed to curb excess government expenditure was the stipulation that commanderies and kingdoms should no longer be allowed to present "famous (wild) animals" (*ming shou* 名獸) to the imperial court.[139] Since the tributary system required the Han court to reciprocate such gifts, the underlying motive for the prohibition on the import of exotica here seems mainly economical. Implicit in these criticisms is a moral undertone suggesting that a devotion to animals at the expense of human welfare undermines moral government. As chapter 5 will show, the same theme was a topic of debate in critiques on hunting.

Both arguments in favor of and against the deployment of animals and other mirabilia from foreign lands indicate an underlying tendency to view the regular order in nature as being based on territoriality. One text that elaborates on the importance of territoriality in tributary missions is the chapter on "Royal Meetings" (*Wang hui* 王會) in the *Yi Zhoushu*.[140] This chapter contains a detailed description of the layout of exotic animals and other products sent as tribute to the Zhou court by peripheral countries and foreign tribes following a directional symbolism. Each animal is named, and often its physical shape and behavior are identified.[141] This is followed by a subsection, possibly added later, in which Shang founder Tang instructs his minister Yi Yin 伊尹 (fl. 1542?–1536? B.C.E.) on a general principle regarding court tributes:

> When the feudal lords come to present tribute, some of them (come from regions) where no horses and cows are born, yet they present things (animals) from distant places. This practice contradicts reality and is not beneficial. Now I wish that they would present tributary goods that are innate to their physical regions (*yin qi dishi suo you* 因其地勢所有). When they present something, it must be easy to obtain and not precious (*yi de er bu gui* 易得而不貴).[142]

Next Yi Yin is commissioned to create "Statutes on the tributary goods from the Four Directions," which would regulate their content and decree which specific tributes should be donated by each region (east-south-west-north). Tang's statement implies that the tribute of exotic beasts and products should be organized according to the notion of territory. While maintaining the ideal that a ruler should gather exotica around him, Minister Yi is charged to rectify the arbitrary tribute of exotic animals according to the principle that they should be distinctive and native to each particular region. Although the collection of species that transcended the territorial habitat was a device to ascertain the ruler's symbolical power over their native regions, this text suggests that a notion of territorial order should apply even to the tribute of these exotica, an idea reminiscent of the topographical layout of the various animal species in parks and preserves. Only when exogenous breeds and products were perceived to be representative of the soil or region they came from—hence "easily obtainable and not precious" for the indigenous inhabitants—did their symbolical collection make sense, since it was through the collection of "moveable" animal species that the ruler symbolically exerted his power over "fixed" territorial regions beyond his central polity.

Conclusion

Writings from the Warring States and Han period often insisted on the idea that there existed an immediate correspondence between the internal organization of the animal world and the creation of order in human society. While the origins of human culture were viewed as the direct result of the physical or moral conquest of a primitive or bestial order by legendary sages and heroes, patterns derived from the animal world at the same time provided the inspiration for cultural foundations such as the trigrams, writing, and clothing.

Central to the perception of an initial order in the natural world was the notion of territory. The natural world in early China was ordered on spatial rather than speciest principles. Consequently the early Chinese perceived a close physical and moral concordance between the soil and the living creatures that shared the waters and airs of the region. This congruity between animals and territory was reflected in various practices such as the consumption of animal meats, the use of animals as sacrificial victims or for military purposes, and even agricultural thought. Animals that transcended the boundaries of their native localities were instrumental in the creation of social models of authority. The collection of animals in hunting parks and the exchange of animal tributes by kings and rulers provided the political symbolism for claims to cosmic rule. Hence the symbolic and numinous powers associated with certain animals were not seen as a the result of magical or transcendent properties inherent to the species; rather, they resulted directly from the perception of a fixed territorial unity between each living creature and its native soil, and from the belief that a transgression of this territorial order empowered these creatures to the benefit or awe of the human ruler and his subjects.

CHAPTER FIVE

TRANSFORMING THE BEASTS

Perceptions of locality and territorial habitat did not provide the only rationale behind the explanation of natural and cultural links between humans and animals. In addition to advocating a moral consonance between events in the animal world and human activity, Warring States and Han writings also sought to unveil this congruence as part of a philosophy that placed the concept of change and transformation at the heart of the human-animal relationship. The idea that civilization emerged from the separation of humans from the wilds meant that the fundamental distinctions between humans and animals were based on moral rather than biological premises. Descriptions of the interaction between humans and animals therefore often maintained that biological animal conduct could be appropriated into the world of the social or, reversibly, that human ethics could influence the workings of the animal realm. Accordingly, a proper understanding of the contingency between the human and animal world was said to be instrumental for a sage-ruler to achieve a moral dominance over the natural world. Just as wild animals could be domesticated to be employed in husbandry, transport, and sacrifice, they could also be civilized and transformed into cultured beings. Hence the domestication of the animal world and the triumph of human governance over the natural world at large were presented as a process of moral transformation rather than an act of physical conquest. Like their human counterparts, animal instincts, so it was claimed, were subject to changes that could be instigated by the laws of nature, human principle, or both. The same moral devices that transformed human beings into civilized creatures would exert their influence over the animal realm.

The idea that one could draw the bestial into the social or extrapolate social values from the animal world reflected a mode of organic thought that focused on condensing or expanding the categories of the human and the bestial. Instead of picturing the animal world as the allegorical or metaphorical double of human society, theories of change and transformation emphasized the interdependence and mutual influence among all animated species. This hermeneutic process was also crystallized around the idea that one could "expand the categories" or "extrapolate the species," an idea which, as I mentioned in chapter 3, was sometimes understood as a process of *tui lei*. Several Warring States and Han texts insisted that events and feats of behavior among one group of living creatures would have a spontaneous or induced impact on others. Likewise it was claimed that changes in the human realm would enhance changes in the animal world and vice versa.

The notion that the understanding and control of the natural world depended on the sage-ruler's capability to morally transform the animal world was reflected in two prevalent themes debated across a number of Warring States and Han writings. First there was the belief that music, like wind, territorial "airs," or climate, exerted a moral influence over the animal world. This was reinforced by the view that music originated from animal sounds and movements in the natural world. Secondly the discourse on moral transformation was anchored in a doctrine which held that the human cultivation of virtue would cause animals to behave in a moral way. Such theories were prominent in narratives on the original human-animal condition, the discourse on the hunt and predatory animal behavior, on the training and domestication of the wilds, and, finally, on sacred animals and hybrids. It also resonated in traditional portrayals of barbarians as animals.

Animals and the Origins of Music

The idea that the natural world was subject to the transformatory influence of human governance runs throughout much of the early Chinese discourse on music. The early Chinese thought of music as a moral force. The mastery of music enabled the sage-ruler to transform the morals of his human subjects and create social harmony. Human sagacity was associated with the ability to penetrate the masses through the medium of sound.[1] Music was also a means to reach the spirits. It sought to enhance the spirit world's responsiveness to sacrifices or induce a fortuitous resonance by the gods on behalf of the supplicant. Finally music served as a civilizing force and provided the means through which foreign lands and unruly barbarian "winds" and "customs" could be transformed. Since the concept of "winds and customs" (*fengsu*) comprised a locality's human activity, as well as plant and animal life and its territorial *qi*, the power of music to "change the winds and alter customs" (*yi feng yi su* 移風易俗) could also affect its nonhuman creatures.[2] And since local climates could influence the character of a region's human and animal inhabitants, local musical "airs" or "winds," viewed as an exponent of the indigenous natural environment, were the embodiment of the morals and customs of a particular people or community.

Just as the observation of animal patterns (*wen*) was linked to the creation of culture and human artifice, Warring States and Han writings related the origins and practice of music and dance to the observation of patterns of sound and movement in the animal world. Music did not emerge as a technological invention or an aesthetic phenomenon created out of nothing by legendary first musicians or sages. Instead, patterns such as tone, rhythm, and melody were thought to be inherent in nature. In the same way that the sages had emancipated humans from the wilds by turning bird tracks into writing, the skillful musician assumed the task of discovering and observing the patterning of sound and movement in nature in order to make these explicit to mankind. With musical patterns viewed as part of nature, the origins and inspiration for melody and rhythmic movements were therefore attributed to the observation of animal sounds and movements.

The "Gu yue" 古樂 chapter in the *Lüshi chunqiu* records how, at the time of the legendary ruler Ge Tianshi 葛天氏, music originated when people grasped an ox tail and sang melodies while stamping with their feet.[3] The same narrative relates how the twelve pitch standards were distinguished according to the cries of the phoenix: six tones were derived from the calls of the male phoenix, and six tones were based on the sounds of the female.[4] The phoenix was linked with the tuning of musical instruments and seen as the originator of wind instruments. Its image as the embodiment of wind is evinced in the cognate etymology of the characters *feng* 鳳 and *feng* 風. Its cries were likened to that of pan-pipes, bells, and drums.[5] A passage in the *Guanzi* identifies musical tones as homophones of the cries of birds and beasts. It associates each note on the pentatonic scale with animal sounds stating that they resemble the sounds produced by squealing piglets, neighing horses, lowing cows, sheep separated from the flock, and the song of ringed pheasants.[6] The transformation of wind into sounds was associated with the legendary emperor Zhuan Xu 顓頊 (fl.? 2514 B.C.E.) who commissioned Flying Dragon to give form to the sounds of the eight winds and then ordered Salamander to conduct by drumming with its tail on its belly.[7]

Besides tone or melody, the origins of drumming were also linked to the animal world. The image of a drumming reptile bears testimony to the use of reptile skins to cover drums. This practice can be traced to archaic China. Alligator drums have been excavated from Neolithic sites in Shanxi and Shandong, and a *Shijing* ode describes how King Wen's construction of the royal park was celebrated by musicians rolling alligator drums (*tuo gu* 鼉鼓). This type of drum was also used in the hunt.[8] Drums were also covered with the hides of horses, oxen, and deer.[9]

Aquatic creatures and reptiles were frequently affiliated with drumming or rhythmic motion.[10] One creature said to "drum on its belly" was the thunder spirit (*leishen* 雷神) described in some sources as a hybrid with a dragon body and a human head.[11] The use of reptile skins on drums and the use of amphibian animal imagery to provoke rain and thunder may have been inspired by the idea that amphibians take both water and land as their habitat and therefore mediate between arid and moist zones. The *Shanhaijing* associates the origins of the drum with the figure of Kui 夔, also known as Shun's legendary music master. Kui is portrayed as a fabulous aquatic beast whose emergence from the Eastern Seas stirs up rain and wind. Skinned and made into a drum, the Yellow Emperor drummed on it with the bones of the Thunder Animal (*lei shou* 雷獸).[12] Reference is also made to the sounds of the drum as a mimicry of thunder as well as to the thalassic origins of thunder.[13]

The association of Kui and the origins of drumming with the east tallies with the traditional identification of the east (*dong* 東) as a progenitor of movement (*dong* 動).[14] According to the *Zhouli,* skins or hides were stretched on drums on the day when the hibernating animals reemerged. This was in early spring, when, following Zheng Xuan, the hibernating animals could hear the thunder and started "moving" (*dong*), precisely the performative effect drums were expected to bring about.[15] That animals respond to the emergence of thunder is also noted by Cai Yong who records that in late winter pheasants crow in response to thunder. In early spring, when things start moving on the soil surface of the earth, hibernating animals respond and get into action.[16] Beating drums covered in animal hides, an act of sympathetic magic, may have been perceived as an effective medium to induce changes in climate or movement among the creatures or spirits that were addressed. Furthermore calendrical texts identify the spring season as the period when animals awake from hibernation and start "moving." The character for spring itself, *chun* 春, is frequently glossed as *chun* 蠢, "to wriggle like worms," suggesting an archaic connection between spring and animal movement.[17] The "Lesser Annuary of the Xia" (*Xia xiao zheng* 夏小正)—a text which is incorporated in the *Da Dai Liji* but as seen in its title claiming origins back to the Xia dynasty—confirms that alligators were caught in the second month to make drums.[18]

While animals were known to be receptive to thunder, their response to thunder was also portrayed as an act of drumming. In the *Xia xiao zheng* the observation of the pheasant "drumming its wings" is taken as an indication of the emergence of thunder.[19] The idea that an animal's sensory faculties could predict climatological phenomena such as thunder, rain, lightning, or earthquakes is well documented. Certain birds were known to be prescient of the arrival of storms, and fish were said to be sensitive to impending rain.[20] The animal's sense for movement is attested in the description of Zhang Heng's famous bronze seismograph, which had an outer surface that was ornamented with designs of mountains, turtles, birds, and beasts: "Outside the vessel there were eight dragon heads, each one holding a bronze ball in its mouth, while round the base there sat eight (corresponding toads) with their mouths open, ready to receive any ball which the dragons might drop."[21] A bronze ball dropping from a dragon mouth into a toad underneath indicated a movement of the earth. It is plausible that the decorative choice of reptiles and amphibians on the domed cover and body of the seismograph was based on the idea that these animals were capable to sense movement and transmit its vibrations.

The belief that drumming caused motion in the animal world also recurs in references to the organized hunt where drums were used to startle animals from their natural habitat. Several officers in the *Zhouli* are said to use drums in order to hunt, expel or exorcise animals. The "Night-time Trapper" (*mingshi* 冥氏), who was responsible for setting nets and snares to catch night-prowling animals, is said to use a spirit drum (*ling gu* 靈鼓) to expel and lure wild animals into falls and traps. An officer entitled "Water Jug Sprinkler" (*huzhuoshi* 壺涿氏) was charged with beating a drum made from baked soil in order to expel aquatic vermin.[22] Other evidence is preserved in inscriptions found on ten stone drums from the state of Qin (unearthed in Shaanxi, provisionally dated to the fifth cent. B.C.E.). While the exact relation between the actual inscriptions and the events that led to the manufacture of these drums remains uncertain, it is worthwhile noting that several inscriptions deal with the hunting theme of the animal chase. One piece lauds the martial courage of hunter and chariot driving the game to exhaustion:

> Our chariots are well crafted,
> Our horses are well matched,
> Our chariots are in order,
> Our horses are sturdy.
> Our lord goes hunting, goes roaming about,
> The does and deer so alert and agile,
> Our lord seeks them out.
> Well adjusted are our horn bows;
> With bow and string we await [the animals].
> We drive away the bulls who
> approach with clattering hoofs,
> scampering and moving in droves.
> Now we drive, now we stop.
> The does and deer tread warily,
> Their advance is ever so wild.
> We drive out the tall ones;
> They come with thud of hoofs.
> We shoot the full-grown ones.[23]

Sima Xiangru describes how drums were used to instigate an attack during a hunt in the Shanglin park.[24] Thus while the act of drumming was associated with animal movement, drumming itself was believed to cause a responsive physical motion ("com-motion") in the animal realm.

In addition to linking drumming with animal motion, animal motion itself was seen as a source for musical resonance. References to the *luan* 鸞 (鑾) and *he* 和 bells that were attached to the steeds that pulled the royal carriages of the Zhou suggest that the pace of the horse was perceived as the source for the tolling of the bells: "The *luan* bells are attached to the horse's bit, the *he* bells to the carriage railing. When the horse moves, the *luan* bells cling. When the *luan* bells clang, the *he* bells resonate. This is the pattern of the pace."²⁵ The *Zuozhuan* mentions that bells on the horse's forehead and bit display a ruler's "sound" or reputation (*sheng* 聲).²⁶ A similar passage occurs in the *Xunzi*: "There are the sounds of the *he* and *luan* bells (on the horse's trappings); the chariot moves along with the 'Martial' and 'Imitation' airs and (the horses) gallop along with the 'Succession' and 'Protection' music in order to nurture the (Son of Heaven's) sense of hearing."²⁷ Elsewhere it is stated that such bells sound harmoniously only when the charioteer drives in the correct manner: "If the (driver) relaxes the pace then they won't sound; if he hastens the pace they will lose (the right) tone."²⁸ By "pacing" the horse, the charioteer regulates the clinging of the bells. By controlling the unbound instinctive motion of the horse, the ruler controls the sounds and hence maintains a grasp on the rhythm of the universe. Only when the motion of the horses was properly mastered by the driver would the ruler's reputation reverberate through the euphony of these bells.

The close connection between animal sounds and the origins of music was also attested in aesthetic theories concerning the decoration of musical instruments. A passage in the "Kaogong ji" describes the tasks of the woodcarvers and deals with decorative animal motifs carved on clocks, bells, and their stands or suspension bars. First, the text classifies the "large animals under heaven" into five groups: animals with firm layers of fat (oxen and sheep), animals with soft fat (pigs), naked animals (short-haired species such as tigers and leopards), feathered animals, and scaly species (dragons and snakes). The last three of these groups are said to be used as decoration on music stands. Next a list is given of animals used as decorative carvings on instruments and ritual vessels. They are differentiated according to their bone structure, their way of locomotion, and the way in which they produce sounds: animals that produce sounds by means of the throat (e.g., water lizards), the mouth, the flanks (e.g., crickets), the wings, the thighs (e.g., grasshoppers), and the chest. Finally animal sounds are connected with the appropriate musical instrument. Naked animals produce sounds that are loud and have a spacious echo and are therefore said to be the appropriate decoration for the stands of bells. Feathered animals produce sounds that are light, rising, and far reaching, hence they are the appropriate decoration for the stands of musical stones.²⁹ The passage suggests that the sound produced by the instrument should reflect the natural sounds of the animal(s) depicted on it.

Finally animal movements were also linked to the origins of dance. The mimetic nature of music and dance in early China suggests that certain animals were the subject of imitative dances. For instance in several sources an eponymous Confucius mentions a magical rain dance associated with the southern state of Chu in which the one-legged *shangyang* 商羊 bird is imitated. According to one description, children performed this dance by leading each other two by two on a rope, bending one foot, and jumping while saying: "Heaven is about to send down a huge rainfall, the *shangyang* bird starts dancing."[30] The use of bird feathers in the dance was also associated with the procurement of seasonal fecundity. Liu Xi 劉熙 (died ca. 219 C.E.) glosses the graph *yu* 雨 "rain" as *yu* 羽 "feather," suggesting that when bird feathers are in motion, they will disperse like rain.[31] The performance of dragon dances whereby models of dragons were manipulated in order to invoke the downfall of rain may be seen as another example of such imitative animal dances.[32]

Animals, Music, and Moral Transformation

While Warring States and Han texts linked the origins and performance of music with animal sounds and motion, the grounding of the origins of sound and motion in the natural world also provided the background for theories on human governance through music. A sage-ruler's sociopolitical authority was frequently associated with his ability to respond to motion in the animal world and his capacity to transform the animal world through the mastery of music. While being part of the inspiration behind music, animals were also portrayed as a receptive audience.

In describing the civilizing influence of music on the governance of human society, the treatises on music in the *Liji* and *Shiji* comment on the relationship of animals with both the production of sound and their susceptibility to melody. Animals are said to have a knowledge of sound (*zhi sheng* 知聲), but lack a knowledge of tones (*bu zhi yin* 不知音). The music treatises also point out that sound patterns can only be cultivated and systematized into music by the gentleman or sage, thereby identifying the capability to refine rough sound into patterned melody with human sagacity. Only the gentleman or sage is able to master music and comprehend its inner workings.[33] According to Zheng Xuan the difference between humans and animals with regards to the understanding of melody is that "birds and beasts know music only as sound but they do not know the transformations (*bian* 變) into *gong* 宮 and *shang* 商 notes."[34] Melody is described here as the product of a series of sound transformations or modulations (chromaticisms) and the ability to comprehend this process of transforming sound into melody is said to distinguish humans from animals.

So while the origins of music and dance were attributed to the existence of sounds, movement, and rhythm in the animal world, without the sages' transformation of such "uncarved" sounds into musical patterns, animals would not experience these bare sounds as music, and, consequently, would not be affected and moved by the aesthetics and, most importantly, the moral influence music was believed to exert on all living beings. The mastery of music therefore presented itself as another means enabling the sage-ruler to subsume the animal world under human control: the sage observes sound and rhythm in the animal world, transforms these into music and dance, which, in its turn, exerts a transformatory influence on animals. Through modeling himself on patterns inherent in the animal world in order to emulate humankind from its instinctive level by means of music, the human sage likewise transformed the animal world itself and lifted it into the moral cosmos which constituted the habitat of humans and animals alike.

The domestication of the wilds through music was based on the premise that animals were receptive to similar emotions as human beings and spirits. Even the skeptic Wang Chong subscribed to this observation on one occasion when writing that birds and beasts are also susceptible to mournful sounds, "their ears being similar to human ears."[35] Wang here merely reformulates a theme that can be traced in several earlier and contemporary texts. In the *Shangshu*, the performatory effect of music and dance is presented for the first time as a device to transform and domesticate the wild animal world. The "Shun dian" 舜典 and the "Yi Ji" 益稷 speak of Yu leading the animals to dance and music master Kui sounding the chimes that caused birds and beasts to frisk and gambol.[36] This narrative associates the origins of music and its civilizing influence with the gradual emancipation of humankind from the wilds. In the words of Ying Shao commenting on the *Shangshu* passage: "If even birds and beasts have a sense of (musical) resonance how much more then is this the case for humans."[37]

Several texts document famous music masters whose performance could affect or spellbind animals. Frequently the musical mastery displayed by these individuals is presented as a craft analogy for the art of successful government. The tunes produced by lute player Hu Ba 瓠巴 allegedly caused fish to come out of the ponds to listen and Bo Ya 伯牙 played the zither so skillfully that horses looked up and forgot about their fodder.[38] The melodies produced by music master Shi Kuang 師曠, court musician of Duke Ping 平 of Jin (557–532 B.C.E.), set two rows of eight black cranes to dance.[39] A compassionate response of birds to human sounds is recorded in the *Yantie lun,* where mountain birds come fluttering down in response to the desperate humming cries made by the unhappy Zengzi 曾子. This text also notes that whenever music master Kuang plucked his lute, all animals would come dancing up to him.[40] Another story is that of Xiao Shi 蕭史, who lived at the time of Duke Mu 穆 of Qin (659–621 B.C.E.) and whose pan-pipe play could summon white cranes and peacocks. According to one account Duke Mu married off his daughter to the pan-pipe player who taught her to imitate the cry of the phoenix on the flute. Several years later a phoenix perched on their roof, an event that inspired the duke to order the construction of a Phoenix Pavilion. Husband and wife stayed in the pavilion for several years without coming down until one morning they followed a phoenix and soared off. To commemorate the episode, the people of Qin erected a "Shrine of the Phoenix Girl."[41]

Underlying these tales of famous music masters was the recognition that music had a performative effect on the animal world and nature in general. Central to the identification of the influence of musical performance on the natural world was the perception that the animal world functioned within a larger moral biology based on the correspondence between animal behavior and a ruler's conduct. Echoing the image of music as the refined result of a process in which bare sounds are transformed into melody, human sagacity and successful governance were presented as one's capability to morally transform the wilds through music. According to the author(s) of the "Yue ji," refined music instills a harmonious resonance in the natural world and exerts a fructifying influence on all living creatures:

> Feathered and winged animals will be active; horns and antlers will grow, torpid insects will come to the light and revive; birds will brood and incubate (their eggs); the hairy animals will mate and nourish (their young); mammals will have no stillborns and oviparous species no broken eggs. And so this will be attributed to the way of music.[42]

A prose poem by Wang Bao 王褒 (fl. ca. 60–50 B.C.E.) known as the "Rhapsody on the Pan-pipes" describes how the transformative effects of the pan-pipe tunes reach all the way down to the lowly insects and reptiles:

> Thus, the cricket and measuring worm
> Slow their crawl, gasping and panting.
> The molecricket, ant, and gecko
> Creeping along, languid and listless,
> Move to and fro, back and forth,
> Goggling like fish, gaping like fowl.
> Lowering their mouths, they whirl and twirl,
> Staring intently, forgetting to eat.
> How much more would this affect humankind, which is stirred by
> the harmony of *yin* and *yang*,
> And transformed by moral custom![43]

As the last lines in this stanza indicate, the transformatory influence of music in the animal world equaled that of moral transformation in the human world. Music had a sociopolitical range. It was a mediating force that radiated the virtuous influence of the ruler into the wilds and caused all living creatures to resonate with his moral authority. Music transformed the "winds and customs" of all species, as is illustrated in the following extract from Ma Rong's 馬融 "Rhapsody on the Long Flute," a piece written ca. 126 C.E.:

> Thus, noble and mean, pretty and plain,
> Wise and foolish, brave and timid,

Fish and turtles, birds and beasts,
All who hear it prick up their ears, skittish as deer.
Hanging like bears, stretching like birds,
Gawking like owls, looking backwards like wolves,
Hooting and howling, jumping and leaping.
Each attains his proper measure.
Every person satisfies his desires,
And all return to central harmony,
And thereby improve customs and mores . . .
Sturgeon poke out their heads by the riverbank to listen,
Horses look up from their grazing and black cranes begin to dance.[44]

The image of musical resonance in the animal world provided a classic metaphor for the idea that a sage-ruler commands and instructs through moral transformation (*jiao hua* 教化) rather than physical dominance. In an allusion to the *Shangshu* image of Yu and Kui leading the animals in the dance, the following passage describes court music as an encompassing force that induces a wild periphery to submit and merge with a civilized center:

> When all the sages harmonise in the courts, then the myriad creatures will harmonise in the fields. Therefore when the *shao* 韶 music of the pan-flutes is performed nine times, the phoenix will come and show its respect. When the music stones are struck and the chime stones are slapped, all the animals will lead each other in the dance.[45]

This passage presents the concept of music as the cosmic equivalent of the domestication of wild animals through physical violence.[46] Music is said to affect the "bestial in the beast," its civilizing influence transforms the predatory instincts of wild animals. The same idea occurs in narratives that oppose the mastery of violence to the mastery of music. Conquest through violence was embodied by the figure of the Yellow Emperor, who gathered and tamed wild bears, leopards, panthers, lynxes, and tigers and employed them as fierce warriors in the battles against his adversaries.[47] Music master Kui typified the conquest of animal instincts through music. Thus a passage in the *Liezi* contrasts the Yellow Emperor with music master Kui by stating that the former summoned animals through physical force (*li* 力) while the latter attracted birds and beasts through the medium of sound (*sheng* 聲).[48]

Music not only transformed the predatory instincts of wild animals, it ultimately served to transform the bestial *mores* of society as a whole. Being itself a static composition of continuously changing modulations, music aimed to modulate the disposition of all living creatures. Such is the interpretation given by an eponymous Confucius in response to a query by Duke Ai 哀 of Lu (fl.

494–477 B.C.E.) about the *Shangshu's* laudatory reference to music master Kui and his dancing animals:

> These words refer to the transformatory effects of good government (*shan zheng zhi hua* 善政之化). When the emperors and kings of antiquity accomplished their deeds, they composed music. . . . If this music was harmonious, then Heaven and Earth would indeed respond to it. How much more so (was the reaction of) all animals![49]

The *Shangshu da zhuan* 尚書大傳 takes up the topic of bells and resonance in the animal world and presents a system of direct correlations between the performance of a certain pitch and the resonating animal category. While the ruler figures as the fountainhead of all sound, each animal species responds to a different modulation:

> When the emperor is about to go out, the "yellow bell" pitch is struck and the five chimes to the right (of the emperor) all resonate (*ying* 應). The horses (pulling the chariot) will neigh in the correct pitch. . . . (To) the sound of the *ruibin* 蕤賓 pitch dogs bark and pigs grunt. When it reaches the naked and armored animals, there are none that do not stretch their neck to listen to the *ruibin* tone.[50]

Just as the concept of motion through the medium of drums and dance was inspired by animal movement, the civilizing influence of music on the wild nature of animals was in its turn closely related to the idea that music literally "moved" living creatures and stirred up (e)motions in their behavior. To "transform through motion" (*dong hua* 動化) was a musical concept, a process described in the *Huainanzi* as "soundlike" (*sheng ran* 聲然).[51] The same text describes the transition from physical motion or dance to moral emotion: "When there is joy there is movement, movement gives rise to the trampling of the feet. This again leads to commotion, which leads to song. When there is song, there is dance. When song and dance are in accordance, wild birds and beasts will jump about."[52] The same principle of correspondence between music and motion is explicated in the *Shangshu da zhuan,* which states that "when perfect music is in mutual harmony, the living beings will move and produce each other, this being the principle that similar sounds mutually respond to each other."[53] In other words musical harmony instigates movement that sparks off cycles of generation and transformation in the natural world. In another apocryphal work entitled *Yue dong sheng yi* 樂動聲儀 ("Musical Motion and the Principle of Sound"), Confucius compares the effects of the ancient pan-pipe music to movement (*dong*) induced by climatological, moral, and material phenomena.[54] Musical theories of human governance thus synthesized the notion of social and cosmic harmony as the result of a process of perpetual transformation in which each component in the natural world was both the recipient as well as the source of *dong* 動 "movement." The categories of physical motion ("nature") and moral emotion ("culture") in response to music amalgamate.

Since harmonious music was thought to reflect social and cosmic harmony, the lack of moral cultivation would result in musical cacophony, which ultimately portended social disintegration and cosmic chaos. Moral integrity therefore constituted a precondition for the successful execution of transforming musical airs. Music would only be morally operative when performed by or for the benefit of a virtuous and sage ruler. A narrative in the *Han Feizi* deals with this subject. It stages music master Kuang who disapproves of a superior melody being played for Duke Ping of Jin on the grounds that the duke's reign had been insufficiently virtuous to merit such gracious melody. In his remonstrance Master Kuang refers back to the Yellow Emperor's composition of this tune:

> In former times the Yellow Emperor gathered demons and spirits together at the top of Mount Tai 泰. He drove an elephant carriage pulled by six *jiao* dragons. Bifang 畢方 (walked) parallel with the linch-pin (of the wheel), Chiyou 蚩尤 marched in front, Fengbo 風伯 ("Wind Sire") swept the dirt (in front of the carriage), Yushi 雨師 ("Rain Master") sprinkled water on the road. Tigers and wolves were at the front, demons and spirits were following behind, mounting serpents crawled on the ground, and phoenixes sheltered (the procession) from above. In such great unity with the demons and spirits (*da he guishen* 大合鬼神) the Yellow Emperor composed the *qingjiao* (清角) tune. Now however, my Lord's virtue is shallow and not sufficient to (be permitted to) hear (this tune). If he would hear the tune, I fear there will be ruin.[55]

This passage links the composition and reception of music to an approval by the spirit world. Accompanied by a pantheon of animals, demons, and spirits ranging from the wolf to the virtuous phoenix, the Yellow Emperor is said to have composed the tune "in great unity with demons and spirits." The creation of superior music is linked here with the natural resonance of those animals and spirits who were the acolytes of the Yellow Emperor. As such, the susceptibility of animals and daemonic creatures to music is tied to their presence at the time of the origin of musical melody. Being the reflection of a sage-ruler's accomplished rule through virtue, nothing less than perfected music would attract sacred animals to his court. The latter is exemplified by another creature said to perch within the human realm as a response to musical performance. The fabulous *luan* 鸞 bird, or "simurgh," whose sounds were associated with the aforementioned *luan* bells on chariots, had a singing range that included the five notes. Hence it would only appear in response to hymn music, a highly refined form of musical accomplishment normally only executed to eulogise virtuous rulers.[56]

The premise of a moral resonance that encompassed all species through the transformatory power of music could also produce adverse effects. In such a model, a ruler's misapprehension of music would lead to anomalous transformations in the natural world. Musical disharmony, often expressed as a ruler's failure to select the right music for the right occasions, would cause disharmony among the creatures resonating with his music. The unbalancing cosmic effects caused by rulers who do not apprehend music would result in climatological anomalies, social disorder, humans adopting the heart-mind of birds and beasts, and the reversal of normal species behavior.

> Dodders give birth to fowl, fowl also give birth to quails, moths gather in the city sounding like humming crowds. Snakes crawl through the city in a west-east direction, horses and cattle start talking, dogs and pigs have intercourse, wolves enter the city, people fall down from heaven, there are dancing owls in the market, pigs fly through the city, horses grow horns, roosters grow five feet, pigs are born without hoofs. Many chickens lay empty eggs, earth altars move place and pigs give birth to dogs.[57]

While the performance of refined music could transform the beast into a cultured animal, the misapprehension of music turned animals into specters or dysfunctional hybrid creatures.

The impulses to movement associated with music not only implied the physical movement of animals. Music also extended its influence to the spirit world. A *Guoyu* passage describes music as wind or air that "opens up mountains and rivers." The text further speaks of music as a means to radiate one's virtue over all living beings (*feng wu* 風物) and suggests that, by causing one's virtue "to breeze forth" over living creatures, contact can be established with the spiritual forces that share the habitat of these creatures.[58] Since animals could be moved by music, they could also function as messengers of musical resonance with the spirit world. A passage from the entry on the "Great Director of Music" (*da si yue* 大司樂) in the *Zhouli* elaborates this idea to the full:

> In general the six kinds of music are used [as follows]: With one change of melody (*bian* 變) one reaches the feathered animals (*yu wu* 羽物) and the spirits (*shi* 示) of the rivers and marshes. With a second change of melody one reaches the naked animals (*luo wu* 臝物) and the spirits of mountains and forests. A third change in melody affects the scaly animals (*lin wu* 鱗物) and the spirits from the hillocks and slopes. With a fourth change in melody one reaches the hairy animals (*mao wu* 毛物) and the spirits of the embankments and the flats. A fifth change in melody affects the armored animals (*jie wu* 介物) and reaches the spirits of the earth. A sixth change of melody reaches the four sacred animals (?) (*xiang wu* 象物) and the spirits from heaven (*tianshen* 天神).[59]

This passage portrays a spirit world that is stratified according to the receptiveness of each spirit category to the performative effects of musical melody. Each realm within this spirit geography—rivers, mountains, slopes, plains, earth, and heaven—is linked with the animal kind by which it is inhabited. Communication with the spiritual forces connected with each of these realms is enacted through provoking a response or movement in the mediating animals by means of music. The communication through music is portrayed as a series of successive "transformations" (*bian*, "alterations, modulations, mutations") of melody, as a result of which each of the respective spiritual forces responds. The more modulations executed on this score (or the more changes in melody), the further its influence is said to reach, and the higher the category of responding spirits.

The *Zhouli* passage above describes how through the medium of the movement of animals, modulations in a musical score ultimately reach the spirit world. In reverse, just as sound and drums were used to startle or scare off animals, the medium of music could also be used as a demonifuge to counteract the spirits. This is attested in the apotropaic use of music in early demonographic and ritual literature. For example an entry in the *jie* 詰 ("Spellbinding") section of the Shuihudi daybooks prescribes the use of drums, bells, and voice to exorcise humans and animals that are possessed by spirits:

> When people or birds and beasts as well as the six domestic animals continuously walk into a person's home—these are spirits from above who are fond of those below and enjoy entering. Have men and women who have never entered the home [a euphemism for sexual intercourse] beat drums, ring clappered bells, and screech at them. Then they will not come.[60]

While the wide range of sources documenting the transformative power of music over the animal world suggests that the idea was generally accepted by the schoolmen and philosophers of Warring States and Han China, the compatibility of the human and animal world has also been the subject of skepticism. A passage in one of the outer chapters in the *Zhuangzi* doubts the dialectic between ritual music and the spontaneous response of animals:

> If one would display the *xianchi* 咸池 music or the *jiushao* 九韶 melodies in the wilds of lake Dongting 洞庭, the birds would fly off upon hearing it, the quadrupeds would run away and the fish would hide in the depths. Human beings, on the contrary, would gather and come back to look at the performance. Fish live in the water, human beings die in the water. Fish are necessarily different (from humans), and their likes and dislikes are therefore different. Hence the former sages did not consider their capabilities as one (and the same) and did not consider (both species') affairs alike.[61]

This passage is part of a critique of the temple worship of a bird. Zhuangzi suggests that ritual music is a cultural creation incompatible with sounds in the natural world. Though not specifically refuting the fact that animals can be susceptible to music, Zhuangzi argues that different species react differently and that the performance of ritual music only exerts a transformatory influence if performed in its proper environment—that is, the ancestral temple or any other ritual space. By arguing that musical resonance does not transcend the species habitat, Zhuangzi questions whether musical harmony necessarily induces social harmony across the species divide. However, the crux of his critique lies in his refutation of the performance of ritual music for the benefit of an animal. The notion of spontaneous resonance is not put into question; instead, the moral effect of music as a ritual creation is said to affect only its creators. As such these comments tally with remarks throughout the *Zhuangzi* maintaining that genuine sages do not engage in conscious acts of cultural creation that might contravene with the natural disposition of the various species.

The Transformation of Animals through Virtue

The identification of music as a force of moral transformation was based on the notion that animals and the natural world at large were susceptible to moral laws and human virtues. Parallel with the philosophy that nature could be morally transformed by winds and music (*feng hua* 風化), theories developed asserting that virtuous human conduct and exemplary rulership exerted a transformatory influence on the animal world and the cosmos as a whole (*de hua* 德化). Narratives on the origins of the human-animal relationship suggest a tension between a tradition that pictured the original man-animal condition as a situation of fundamental antagonisms between incompatible species, and another which saw this "Urzeit" as an age of harmonious man-animal cohabitation. Yet an overarching feature of both narratives was their insistence on the idea that the modus vivendi between humans and animals was based primarily on moral principles rather than biological law.

Several passages in proto-Daoist texts maintain that humans and animals shared an original state of naturalness. They present the ability of humankind to merge with the world of the birds and beasts as its highest moral accomplishment. In the *Zhuangzi* this original order is described as an age of "perfect virtue" (*zhi de* 至德), a time when "birds and beasts could be tied to a leash or bridled and led about." The original understanding between humans and animals was so unspoiled that one could climb up a tree and peep into the nests of crows and magpies, all because "humans lived the same way as birds and beasts, and grouped together side by side with the myriad creatures."[62]

The *Daodejing* links this vision of an original age of simplicity in which predatory animals would desist from infringing on humans with the cultivation of virtue (*de*). In one aphorism it states that "one who possesses virtue in abundance is comparable to a newborn baby: poisonous insects will not sting it; ferocious animals will not pounce on it; predatory birds will not swoop down on it."[63] A passage in the *Liezi* presents the idealized era of a harmonious man-animal oecumene as a time when animals, like humans, were susceptible to moral instruction:

> The divine sages of extreme antiquity fully knew the desires and manners of the myriad beings, and comprehensively interpreted the cries of all the different species. They gathered them together for meetings and gave them instructions, which they received as if they were human.[64]

Other narratives portrayed the observation of animal behavior as a barometer of the dialectic of decline and prosperity in the history of humankind. According to the *Liezi*, humans and animals lived together and walked side by side in antiquity but were frightened away and scattered for the first time during the period of the legendary Five Emperors and the Three Kings.[65] A more detailed account of how animal behavior changed according to the phases of degeneration and renaissance in human history occurs in the *Huainanzi*. It notes that during the rule of the Yellow Emperor dogs and pigs would spit out grain and millet on the roadside as a sign of abundance and prosperity. Tigers and wolves would not bite recklessly, and predatory birds did not strike at random. During the same era, the phoenix roved over the courtyard, and the *qilin* roamed about in the suburbs. Green dragons came forward spontaneously to be yoked to carriages, and excellent horses such as the Flying Yellow 飛黃 reclined in the stables.[66] The sequence is followed by a period of decline, following which the goddess Nü Wa 女娃 mends the sky and restores cosmic order. The animal world responds in return: "Among the wild birds and beasts, vipers and snakes, there were none that did not hide away their claws and teeth, or stored away their venomous poisons. No animal displayed predatory and voracious instincts."[67] However such virtuous animal conduct reversed with the advent of the tyrannous regime of Jie 桀 of the Xia dynasty when "dogs flocked together howling and entered deep pools, pigs held rushes in their mouths and berthed themselves in dark corners.... Flying birds injured their wings, and running animals crippled their feet.... Foxes and racoon dogs headed to their dens. Horses and cattle escaped and went lost."[68] By moralizing animal behavior as a consequence of human actions, such tales provided the mythological background for the belief that moral government had a profound impact on the animal world.

The moralization of animal biology emerged most prominently in the discourse on the hunt and in accounts of violent animal behavior. The idea that decadent government was a prime cause of human-animal antagonism was epitomized by the practice of the hunt. The unbridled physical chase of animals was interpreted in the first place as a transgression of a moral code. In a passage in the *Zuozhuan*, the concept of virtue as a principle of balance between man and beast is read into the *Shangshu* narrative of Yu pacing out the Nine Provinces and contrasted with the lavish animal hunt. The passage is staged as an exhortation spoken by a forester responsible for hunts at the time of King Wu of the Zhou:

> Far and wide Yu's footsteps reached.
> As they lined out the Nine Provinces,
> and traversed them to open up the Nine Paths,
> the people possessed chambers and temples,
> the animals flourishing grasslands,
> each of them (man and beast) had a place to dwell,
> and because of virtue (*de*) there was no distress.
> Then Archer Yi 夷羿 took over the emperor (Yu's) place,
> he coveted a desire for (the chase of) wild animals,
> neglected the care of his state,
> but (instead) thought of its does and stags.[69]

According to this narrative, the initial pattern of harmony and order between man and beast as well as each species' habitat flourished through the moral authority of the ruler. All species possessed their own dwelling place. The living had their houses, the dead their temples, and the animals their grasslands. Yu's virtuous rule which, as mentioned before, caused the animals to dance up to him, inspired humans and animals not to trespass on each other's domains. Yu's organization of the lands into nine geographical units respected the unity of all living species with their appropriate biotope. This harmony however lasted only until bow and arrow replaced government through virtue, and a desire to chase and kill animals redefined the man-animal relationship.

The Archer Yi in this passage is presented as the archetypal embodiment of the idea that overindulgence in the hunt results in the neglect of political duty. This theme occurs in a number of other stories. One story tells how Yanzi reprimanded Duke Jing of Qi for not having returned from a hunt for seventeen days. Yanzi argued that the people of Qi would come to think of their lord as someone who despises his people and loves wild animals instead. The duke is warned of the pernicious consequences of his attitude: "Fish and turtles who reject the deep springs and come to the dry surface are therefore trapped by hook or net. Birds and beasts who abandon the dense mountains to come down to the cities and plains are therefore caught by hunters."[70] According to Yanzi the duke's habitat should be his state, and venturing into the wilds is compared with animals leaving their own native lands to get caught by hunters. A similar story is that of Duke Xian 獻 of Wei 衛 (576–599, 546–544 B.C.E.), who disgraced his guests by abandoning a banquet to go off and shoot wild geese.[71] Xunzi uses similar imagery as a state analogy by arguing that just as rivers and springs, mountains and forests form the natural habitat for dragons and fish, birds and beasts, so the nation should be the natural dwelling place for literati and people. When a nation loses its government, its people will abandon it just as dragons would leave a dried-up pond or animals would flee from forests with sparse vegetation.[72] Criticism of a ruler's fondness of animals above affairs of state also forms the theme of a tale in the *Zuozhuan*, which tells of a lord who was so fond of cranes that he had them ride about in his carriage. When the time to mobilize for war had come, his people told him to mobilize his cranes to fight instead.[73] An exemplary life story of Fan Ji 樊姬, wife of King Zhuang 莊 of Chu (613–591 B.C.E.), describes how she demonstrated her protest against her husband's overindulgence in hunting by refusing to eat the meat of birds and animals.[74]

Violent and predatory animal behavior was explained following the same moral biology. Rather than being ascribed to a purposeful evil nature innate in animals, predatory killings and attacks on humans were explained as the result of a distorted balance within human society or between human activity and animal life. When sages ruled human society, the influence of good government would spontaneously transform the predatory disposition of wild animals so that "tigers and leopards could be pulled by the tail, and vipers and snakes could be trod upon."[75] The *Da Dai Liji* reiterates the *Daodejing* image of predatory animals who refrain from following their instincts in the face of human virtue:

> When sages are ruling the state . . . rapacious beasts forget to attack, and (predatory) birds forget their spurs. Wasps and scorpions don't sting young babies. Mosquitoes and gadflies don't bite young foals.[76]

Such moral correspondence also accounted for its reverse. Reports on ravaging raids by tigers and wolves on human settlements, also known as "tiger and wolf calamities" (*hu lang bao* 虎狼暴), centered on the idea that a bestial government or irresponsible ruler turned animals into predators and stressed that the lavish hunting of animals would cause animals to chase humans. A prose poem attributed to Wang Su 王肅 (195–256 C.E.) entitled "Rhapsody on Remonstrating against Engaging with Tigers in Combat" articulates this theme. Echoing Sima Xiangru's lengthy descriptions of hunts in the imperial parks, an interlocutor criticizes his lord's overindulgence in hunting on the grounds that it distorts both the habitat of humans and animals: "You drive people into the forest glens and attack tigers in their realm."[77] As in the edifying anecdote of Master Yan reprimanding Duke Jing for his devotion to the hunt, the moral failure of human rule here is said to reverse the disposition of the species: the (human) hunter becomes the (animal) victim; and just as humans trespass on animal habitats, animals inflict similar bestial calamities in the human habitat. The unbridled intrusion of animal territory blurred the proper physical and moral distinctions between man and beast.

Mencius extrapolates this analogy and argues that if a ruler allows his animals to feast on provisions destined for humans while his human subjects are dropping dead from starvation, he is "leading the animals in the devouring of men." When the path of morality is obstructed, a ruler shows animals the way to devour man, which eventually leads to cannibalism.[78] While King Xuan 宣 of Qi's bounty may be sufficient to reach the animals, Mencius still criticizes the king for failing to have the merits of his government reach to his people.[79]

The moral interpretation of animal violence is the rule rather than the exception in Warring States and Han writings. The first-century philosopher Wang Chong devotes a special chapter to the ravaging tiger theme entitled "Encountering Tigers" (*Zao hu* 遭 虎). In this piece Wang attempts to refute at length the correlation between tiger attacks and the depravity of officials in government. While ascribing men being devoured by tigers to an arbitrary accidental encounter, he acknowledges that tigers enter human settlements as soon as human rule has degraded to the bestial level of the wilds (i.e., the tiger's natural habitat). Although Wang can be accused of inconsistencies in his argumentation, his meticulous attention to the subject reflects contemporary beliefs that tiger attacks followed from negligence in government.[80]

The idea that animal violence should be attributed to the course of human actions is well illustrated in two cases referring to events which occurred in the mid-Eastern Han. One account relates how in the 110s C.E. a southern commandery was plagued by tiger and wolf attacks. In an edict its governor explained that the human intrusion on the natural habitat of these animals combined with the extravagant hunt was the cause behind the plagues:

> In general, the residence of tigers and wolves in the mountains and forests is like the residence of human beings in cities and markets. In antiquity, in the age of complete transformation, wild animals did not cause any trouble. All this originated from the fact that grace and trust were wide ranging and abundant, and benevolence reached the avian and running species. Although I, your governor, possess no virtue, how could I dare to neglect this righteous principle. (Therefore) when this note arrives, let cages and pit-traps be destroyed, and do not recklessly go trapping in mountains and forests.[81]

As a result of the edict, the tiger plagues waned, and the people regained their peaceful existence. Just as the *Zhuangzi* had referred to a golden age of peaceful man-animal cohabitation as a time of "perfect virtue," this account describes it as an age of "supreme transformation" (*zhi hua* 至 化), a time when the human virtue of benevolence had morally transformed wild animals. A similar tiger plague story features Song Jun 宋均 (fl. mid first cent. C.E.), a figure who was known as a critic of shamanistic practices and ardent opponent of popular superstitions. Song was sent off to become governor of Jiujiang 九 江 (Anhui), a commandery plagued by tiger calamities and paralyzed by the burdens of tax and corvée labor levied in order to stop these tiger raids. Upon his arrival he issued the following edict:

> Tigers and leopards live in the mountains, turtles and alligators in the water, each have their entrusted habitat. The presence of wild beasts in the Jiang-Huai region is similar to the northern territories having chickens and pigs. Now (the tigers) harm the people, and the malign influence behind this lies with low-hearted officials who put all efforts into catching them. This is not the basis of showing sympathy. If these officials were to devote their attention to removing detrimental poverty and think about promoting loyalty and goodness, then they could at once remove traps and pits, discharge taxes and restore order.[82]

Following Song's intervention, rumor held that the tigers moved together with him to the east and crossed the Jiang. In his edict Song first reiterates the congruence between territorial habitat and its animal presence. Next he argues that wild beasts are endemic to the Jiang-Huai region and attributes their anomalous behavior to the officials' indulgence in the pleasure hunt. The moral of the story is clear: Song's exemplary rule as governor had transformed the tigers' bestial nature, and as a consequence they "cross the Jiang" and leave their natural habitat. All wild animals, so his biography ends, "stood in awe of his virtue."[83] Moral authority had transformed their bestial instincts and led them to transcend the boundaries of their own biotope.

The susceptibility of animals to human laws is the subject of another anecdote dating to the Eastern Han. It stages magistrate Tong Hui 童恢 who reprimands two tigers for attacking humans: "Heaven has produced the ten thousand beings, and among them humans are the most honorable. Tigers and wolves should prey on the six domestic animals, but you instead injure and harm humans." Tong then orders the tiger guilty of preying on humans to bow its head and receive punishment. The latter obeys and is executed while the innocent tiger is set free.[84] Wang Chong questions such moral compatibility between humans and animals. His critique quotes a story about a hawk who spontaneously repents before a virtuous prince for having preyed upon a pigeon. Wang concludes that "the sage is not capable of inducing birds and beasts to righteous conduct."[85]

Accounts seeking to explain the roots of violent animal behavior in the workings of human society frequently invoked an idealized ancient tradition in which hunting regulations were devised by sage-kings with a view to balance the human need for game animals with the preservation of the rhythms in the animal realm. Criticisms of and justifications for the transgression of the balance between the ritual need for hunting, the consumption of meats, and the preservation of natural reserves were underpinned by moral imperatives. Descriptions of hunting campaigns and hunting techniques recognized the ambiguous nature of the hunt as both an act of killing and a moral gesture of preservation. For instance the complementary relationship between hunting and preservation was evinced in the etymological explanation of the graph used for the "winter hunt" (*shou* 狩), which was glossed paronomastically as "to preserve" (*shou* 守). One Han text defines the winter hunt as "preserving the soil and taking (the products) from it."[86]

Prescriptions on the techniques used to kill game as well as explanations of the seasonal logic for banning or encouraging the killing of animals aimed to reflect the moral integrity of the hunter. Sima Qian praises Shang founder Tang for encouraging hunters not to extinguish the game and allowing a fair number of animals the chance to escape the nets:

> Once Tang went out of the city and saw someone who had set nets on all four sides in a field praying, "from all four sides under heaven may [birds] fall into my nets." Tang said, "Hey! This would exhaust them!" Then he took the nets away from three sides and prayed, "If you want to go to the left, go to the left. If you want to go to the right, go to the right! If you don't listen to this order, you will fall into my net!" The feudal lords heard of this and said, "Tang's virtue is the highest. It even extends to birds and beasts!"[87]

Similarly the Son of Heaven would never encircle an entire flock and feudal lords would never catch an entire herd.[88] The poet Zhang Heng also invokes the image of Cheng Tang as a moral hunter and describes various "compassionate" techniques displayed during an imperial hunt. These include respecting the hunter's horses, the selective killing of game, and the release of animals from nets and traps. Reference is also made to the so-called *san qu* 三驅, rendered by David Knechtges as the "three-sided *battue*," a hunting technique in which the quarry is flushed out on three sides only, allowing the animals an escape route on one side:

> In shooting, they do not tear the fur.
> As offerings they present the six birds;
> In season they supply the four fats.
> The horses' legs are never run to exhaustion;
> The coachmen never tax their strength.
> The emperor fulfils the rites and orders a three-sided *battu* [*sic*],
> Unties the nets and releases the great deer.
> He does not excessively indulge himself and thus teaches moderation;
> He does not slaughter everything and thus displays kindness.
> He admires Tianyi 天乙 (=King Tang) who loosened the net,
> And who through instruction and prayer won the people's allegiance.
> He emulates Chief Ji 伯姬 (=King Wen of Zhou), who north of the Wei 渭

Lost his bears but caught a man.
His grace seeps down to the swarming insects;
His might shakes the eight corners of the world.
"He loves pleasure, but never to excess."[89]

Ritual codes stipulated that animals killed out of season were not to be sold on the markets, and that the Son of Heaven should not eat or sacrifice pregnant animals.[90] According to Xunzi, the sage-kings of antiquity would never disturb the creeks and waters of breeding tortoises and fish with their nets or poisonous medicines.[91] Mencius states that if close-meshed nets were not used in large ponds there would be more fish and turtles than anyone could eat.[92] Confucius praises one of his disciples for throwing back undersized fish.[93] Calendars prescribed that during the spring season hatching and breeding animals were to be left undisturbed and nests were to be left uncovered.[94] A passage in the *Guoyu* preserves a detailed account of the seasonal logic behind hunting taboos which are again associated with an idealized era in antiquity:

When Duke Xuan 宣 went to cast his nets in the springs of the river Si 泗 in the summer, Li Ge 里革 cut them up and threw them away saying: "In antiquity whenever the great colds were over and the soil awoke from hibernation, the officer of fisheries went to investigate the nets and traps in order to catch the best fish. He reaped wild shell animals from the rivers, offered them at the ancestral temple, and had this carried out throughout the state. This was known as 'assisting the spreading of the (*yang*) vapors.' At the time when birds and beasts were pregnant (i.e., in spring) but aquatic animals were fully grown, the hunting officer issued a ban on setting up nets (for birds and quadrupeds) and speared fish and turtles in order to store them as dried meats for the summer. This was known as the 'assisting of growth.' When birds and beasts were fully grown and the aquatic animals pregnant, then the officer of fisheries issued a ban on the casting of fishing nets but set up animal and bird traps and snares in order to fill the kitchens of the ancestral temples. This was the 'storing of the products of the seasons for (later) use.' Furthermore in the mountains tree shoots were not trimmed, in the swamps sprouting plants were not cut down. As for fish there was a ban on collecting fish roe and young fish, among animals deer foals had to be allowed to grow, birds had to be allowed to brood over their eggs and fledglings, and with regards to insects it was not permitted to collect the larvae of ants and locusts. This was known as 'letting grow the ordinary creatures.' Such are the instructions from antiquity. But now, instead, the fish (you are catching) have not yet spawned and are not allowed to grow. Furthermore you have (already) cast your nets. This is a sign of unbridled greed."[95]

Evidence suggests that hunting and gathering from the wilds or in parks were also subject to legal measures. Such laws stipulated the number of predatory beasts that could be caught, determined their cash value, and established rules on the management of animal enclosures. For instance the following entry from the "statutes on agriculture" in the Qin legal codes is concerned with trespassing by hunting dogs:

> In settlements close to corrals and other forbidden parks, in the season of young animals one should not venture to take dogs to go hunting. When dogs of the common people enter forbidden parks without pursuing and catching animals, one should not venture to kill them; those which pursue as well as catch animals are to be killed. Dogs killed by wardens are to be completely handed over to the authorities; of those that are killed in other forbidden parks the flesh may be eaten, but the skin is to be handed over.[96]

While economics and practical animal management appear to be the main concern in legal literature, a common feature of the ritual and philosophical discourse on the hunt was its moral bias. Establishing the edifying virtue of the hunter appeared to be at least as important as the concern for the hunted animal. This is clear from passages suggesting that inflicting harm on the natural world ought to be perceived as an indirect violation of human moral values. For instance Confucius is said to have claimed that the unseasonable killing of one single animal was "contrary to filial piety."[97] Elsewhere the unrightful slaughter of the six domestic animals is said to cause retribution affecting one's relatives.[98] Like the provision of ancestral meats through the hunt, the ruler's personal inspection of sacrificial victims was an act of filial piety according to the *Liji*.[99] The *Lüshi chunqiu* notes that the maltreatment of herbs, trees, chickens, dogs, cattle, and horses would result in a requital on human beings.[100] The *Lunyu* states that Confucius used a fishing line but not a net, and that he used a stringed arrow but never aimed at roosting birds.[101] Literati likewise are said not to use stringed arrows.[102] Emperor Han Wudi is reported to have refrained from catching cranes on one occasion since it was the spring season during which the use of nets was not permitted.[103] As a response to the appearance of spirit birds during the previous summer and spring, Emperor Xuan issued an edict in 63 B.C.E. instructing the metropolitan areas not to search out nests for eggs during those seasons or fire pellet shots at overflying birds.[104]

A passage in the *Zuozhuan* stresses the ritual imperative that underlies the killing of animals. It condemns the pleasure hunt by stating that in ancient times the dukes would not engage in the killing of animals unless their meat was used in the context of ritual sacrifice:

> When the duke was about to go to Tang 棠 to view the fishing, Zang Xibo 臧僖 伯 remonstrated, "The ruler does not pursue any creature that is not of use in the practice of the great services of state or whose substance cannot be used to supply

implements (for sacrifice). . . . Therefore one uses the spring hunt, the summer hunt, the autumn hunt, and the winter hunt, all in the intervals between agricultural activity, to practice the services (of state). . . . According to ancient rule a lord would not shoot a bird or beast whose flesh was not offered in the sacrificial pots or whose hide, teeth, bones, horns, fur, or feathers were not used in the sacrificial vessels. The creatures which fill the mountains and forests, streams and swamps and the provision of tools are the task of underlings and the care of the lowly officers; the ruler has nothing to do with them."[105]

Other stories portray animal compassion as a sign of an innate sense of benevolence, virtue, or kindness. One anecdote tells of Duke Jing of Qi, who robbed a sparrow's nest but put the fledglings back when noticing that they were too weak.[106] Another story tells of Qin Xiba 秦西巴, who was ordered to bring home a fawn that had been caught by his master during a hunt. Followed by the crying mother deer and unable to bear its lamentations, Qin released the fawn.[107] Another virtuous character, Tian Zifang 田子方, offered to buy an old horse worn out by years of public service. He argued that deploying a horse's strength while young but casting it aside when old was breaching the rules of benevolent conduct.[108]

Finally the moral contingency between the activities of the human hunter and the hunted animal was also embedded in depictions of animals in systematizing calendrical texts. Prescriptions on when and how to hunt a particular animal species served to maintain a moral balance between the human and animal realm over a temporal sequence of changing natural habitats—that is, the seasons. Hence according to the "monthly ordinances" the hunting season was opened when the game animals themselves displayed their innate moral disposition. Fishermen are advised to start fishing only when "the otters sacrifice fish." The image of sacrifice is used to indicate that there is an abundant catch so that remains of prey are scattered around on the river banks as if the otters were sacrificing to the four directions. Hunts would start only "when the wolves sacrifice prey." And the nets were set out only "when doves transformed into eagles," one way of saying that seedeaters assume a carnivorous condition.[109] So rather than justifying the opening and closure of the hunting season in terms of the observation of certain natural laws, it is the hunter's respect for the animal's innate sense of sacrifice that determined his choice to catch game. The hunter's regard for the animal's inborn inclination to perform seasonal offerings is portrayed as a way to prevent these predatory animals from preying upon humans as their sacrificial meat. Respecting the prescriptive cycle of the calendar provided the rationale that would prevent human morals from being sanctioned by the natural world.

While the discourse on the hunt and the descriptions of moral hunting techniques sought to justify the taking and preservation of animal life on the grounds that it reflected the hunter's sense of moral propriety, the premise behind these theories was a belief in the transformatory power of humans over the natural world in general. There were several ways in which this idea was formulated. These included the notion that a sage-ruler's virtue could reach all animal species, the use of craft analogies that emphasized the spontaneous moral understanding between humans and animals, the image of domestication and shepherding as an analogy for the ruling of human society, and the portrayal of animals showing their allegiance to virtuous individuals.

Virtue Reaching Birds and Beasts

Just as the attraction of exotic animals to the ruler's center exemplified his moral authority, the capability to transform the wilds through moral virtue rather than physical or technological dominion was a testimony of the sage-ruler's moral authority over all species.

> Confucius said: When Shun was a ruler, in government he respected life and despised killing. In assigning offices he engaged worthies and dismissed the unworthy. His virtue was as tranquil and pure as heaven and earth. He could change like the four seasons and transform things. Therefore everything within the four seas was subject to his influence, which permeated the different species (*yi lei* 異類). Phoenixes were soaring about, unicorns came, birds and beasts complied to his virtue.[110]

This passage from the *Kongzi jiayu* presents Confucius associating Shun's moral authority over all species with his image as a source of moral transformation. The *Huainanzi* notes that the sage-kings in antiquity could "shape and transform birds, beasts and insects" and quotes this as a precedent to acknowledge their capability to implement social laws in human society.[111] The expression that a sage-ruler's virtue "extended to birds and beasts" figured as a standard topos acknowledging his all-encompassing moral authority over all living species. One of the *Yijing* manuscripts found at Mawangdui states that "Tang's virtue reached even the animals and fishes, and therefore there were more than forty states that sent in pelts and cloth to submit to him."[112] Emperor Qin Shihuang 秦始皇帝 had expressions stating that his kindness and appraisal "reached cattle and horses" immortalized in stone on at least two occasions.[113] And the *Chunqiu fanlu* repeatedly presents a ruler's authority over the animal world in a sequence following the five phases suggesting that with each season the ruler's benevolence should reach its corresponding animal species.

1. Wood/ spring
   • the ruler's grace reaches the scaly animals (*en ji lin chong* 恩及鱗蟲)
   • result: abundance of fish, whales do not appear, dragons descend

2. Fire/ summer
    • the ruler's grace reaches the feathered animals (*en ji yu chong* 恩及羽蟲)
    • result: abundance of birds, yellow geese appear, the phoenix roams about
3. Earth/ late summer
    • the ruler's grace reaches the naked animals (*en ji luo chong* 恩及倮蟲)
    • result: sages come near, immortals descend
4. Metal/ autumn
    • the ruler's grace reaches the hairy animals (*en ji yu mao chong* 恩及於毛蟲)
    • result: abundance of bi/quadrupeds, the *qilin* 麒麟 arrives
5. Water/ winter
    • the ruler's grace reaches the armored animals (*en ji jie chong* 恩及介蟲)
    • result: abundance of sea turtles, the spirit tortoise emerges.[114]

The idea that virtuous rulership generated a moral disposition in animals that could transform their instincts is further illustrated in a rhapsody on the crane attributed to Lu Qiaoru 路喬如(second cent. B.C.E.?). The poem describes cranes wading at the edge of a pond, presumably in a park or courtyard of a ruler. The cranes—renowned as symbols of escapism and freedom—are described in all their natural movements. The poet suggests that despite their natural inclination and capability to fly off, the birds remain in the surroundings of the pond:

> Therefore we know that
> These wild birds with their wild instincts
> Have not yet escaped their cage.
> Relying on the magnanimous love of our king,
> Even wild birds cherish his grace.
> While prancing they sing and dance,
> the vermilion railings are their reason of joy.[115]

While the cranes retain their instinctive inclination to soar off and are free to leave the king's park, the king's moral government makes them stay, their captivity ("vermilion railings") is their reason of joy. In sum, whereas sages attracted animals through virtuous conduct, hunters chased and subdued animals through physical violence. An anecdote about a hunter in the Mencius illustrates this contrast between moral achievement and brute force. It tells how Feng Fu 馮婦 had been renowned for being an expert in seizing tigers. However when, having become an "eminent gentleman," he once bared his arms to assist a crowd to catch a tiger "the crowds were delighted whereas those who were gentlemen laughed at him."[116] The moral of the story is clear: a gentleman does not bare his arms to counter a wild beast.

Natural Harmony and Moral Understanding

Craft analogies involving animals—such as charioteering, the bridling of horses, archery, or fishing—all emphasized that such techniques were successful through harmony between man and animal rather than through physical domination. The legendary archer Bo Juzi 蒲且子 and the famous angler Zhan He 詹何 were able to "connect with birds flying a thousand feet above," and "cause fish (to dart toward the hook) from the depths of the great springs," because they had obtained an all-pervading harmony with the Dao.[117] Another legendary archer, Skinbone, could draw his bow, fire it with no arrow attached on the string, and bring down a wild goose.[118] Yang Youji 養由基, a general in the service of King Gong 共 of Chu (590–560 B.C.E.), focused on hitting his target, a divine white monkey, by aiming at the place where the moving ape had not yet arrived before releasing the arrow. As a result the monkey "responded" to his arrow and fell down.[119] Superiority in skill due to a natural rapport between man and animal also figures in the well-known *Zhuangzi* story of cook Ding 丁 who had attained such a familiarity with the anatomy of oxen that fleshing out their carcasses had become an effortless and natural activity.[120]

Rather than seeking recourse to brute force, technology, or the implementation of the yoke, the transformation of the inhospitable wild animal world was to be accomplished through harmony with the animal's natural instincts. The skillful tiger trainer is successful since he neither gives the animals their way nor thwarts them:

> Now in my heart I neither oppose them nor comply with them; thus the birds and beasts regard me as their equal. Therefore when they roam in my garden, they do not think about their lofty forests and desert marshes, and when they sleep in my courtyard, they never desire to be deep in the mountains or hidden away in the valleys. This principle is only natural.[121]

Similarly, the *Zhuangzi* proposes that the animal breeder should accord himself (*shun* 順) with the natural disposition of his animals. Only then would wild tigers fawn on the person who rears them.[122] A passage in the *Huainanzi* argues that horses are docile to instruction if one connects with their temperament:

> That fish leap about and magpies are piebald is similar to the reason why man and horse are man and horse. Muscles, bones, shape and body is what they receive from Heaven. It cannot be changed. From this point of view they belong to different species. But when a horse is a grazing foal, it jumps and leaps with its hooves up in the air, it hoists its tail up in the air and runs about. Man cannot control it. . . . Until the stable officer trains it to obedience and the skilful cavalier instructs it. . . . Therefore, although its outward appearance makes it a horse, and this "horse-ness" cannot be transformed, the fact that it can be driven is due to instruction. A horse is but a daft animal. But if one connects with its energy and intent (*tong qizhi* 通氣志), it will likewise await instruction and accomplish itself. How much more is this the case for humans![123]

The perfect physical maintenance of horses contributes to the creation of a bond between cavalier and horse, as is emphasized in a Warring States military treatise. Its putative author, Wu Qi 吳起 (ca. 440–ca. 361 B.C.E.), instructs the Marquis of Wu as follows:

> Now the horses must be properly settled with appropriate grass and water and correct feeding so as to neither be hungry nor full. In the winter they should have warm stables, in the summer cool stables. Their manes and hair should be kept trimmed, and their hooves properly cared for. Blinders and ear protectors should be used so as to keep them from being startled and frightened. Practice their galloping and pursuit; exercise constraint over their advancing and halting. Men and horses must be attached to each other (*ren ma xiang qin* 人馬相親); only thereafter can they be employed.[124]

Other passages describe how the skillful charioteer or cavalier should aim to connect with his horses in a moral way by following rather than manipulating the movement of the animal. A good charioteer is advised to align himself with the natural movement of his horses, so that "the horses' bodies are attuned to the chariot, and the driver's heart is in harmony with his horses."[125] According to one source, "the horse knows that behind there is a chariot but considers it to be light. It knows that there is a man in it but loves him. The horse adores (the charioteer's) righteousness and likes being used by him."[126]

The idea that successful man/animal cooperation depended mainly on a mutual moral understanding rather than a relationship of physical domination or subordination is epitomized by a statement of Confucius in the *Lunyu* arguing that "a swift horse is not praised for its physical strength but for its virtue."[127] Confucius does not respect the animal in its bare animal state. When his stables catch fire he inquires whether any human being was hurt, but "did not ask about the horses."[128] For Confucius the use of animals is subject to a moral and ritual imperative. When Zi Gong wishes to abolish the sacrificial sheep used at the announcement of the new moon, Confucius reprimands him for loving the sheep rather than being concerned with the disappearance of the rite.[129] Another passage relates how Confucius prefers animals in their ritualized state. When presented with a carriage and horse, he refused to bow because it was not as worthy as sacrificial meat.[130] Confucius's predilection for the moral interpretation of animal behavior is further exemplified in his judgment of tiger calamities:

> When Confucius was passing the side of Mount Tai, there was a woman wailing at a grave in mourning. He leant on his chariot bar and listened, and sent Zi Lu 子路 to inquire, "Your cries tell me that you really must be in deep pain." She said, "Yes. Previously my father-in-law was killed by a tiger, my husband also found his death this way. Now my son has been killed by a tiger." Confucius said, "Why then do you

not leave this place?" "Because," said the woman, "there is no oppressive government here." Confucius said, "Remember, my disciples, that an oppressive government is worse than tigers."[131]

Shepherding the World

Accomplished skill in animal domestication provided a craft analogy for skillful political rulership. Charioteering was often compared with ruling a state and domesticating animals became an archetypal image for models of social organization and subordination.[132] The *Huainanzi* compares the "shepherding of the people" or ruling of a state to the raising of domestic animals. By locking off an animal enclosure and hindering the animals in their natural movements, one only induces them to be "wild at heart."[133] The *Shizi* 尸子 states that Shennong was able to possess the empire for seventy generations because the shepherding of the people was easy.[134] According to Mencius, winning over the people consists in refraining from imposing on them what they dislike: "People turn to benevolence in the same way as water flows downwards or as animals head for the wilds. Therefore the otter is the one who drives the fish into the depths, the hawk chases the birds to the bushes, Jie and Zhou drove the people to Tang and King Wu."[135] Tallying successful statesmanship with an expertise in herding animals is further illustrated in the story of Bu Shi 卜式, a successful farmer and shepherd from Henan who briefly made it to imperial counsellor in 111 B.C.E., and who, as mentioned in chapter 1, is eponymously accredited with the authorship of a work on sheep farming. Sima Qian accounts how Bu Shi on repeated occasions wished to donate all his possessions to the court in support of the border defense campaigns against the Xiongnu. When finally lured to court by Han Wudi to take care of the emperor's sheep in the Shanglin park, Bu Shi compares administrative success with the herding of animals: "It not only applies to sheep. Governing people is the same thing. You make them get up and rest at the right time, and if there are bad ones, pull them out at once before they have a chance to spoil the flock."[136] Given that nomadic barbarians were customarily put on a par with their animal flocks, it is no coincidence that this story casts a herdsman as a successful advisor and model for the committed struggle against the Xiongnu.

Animals Reciprocate Moral Virtue

The notion that sages were able to exert a moral authority over the animal world also underpinned references to the spontaneous guardianship by wild animals of future cultural heroes and sage-rulers. Shun's virtue was of such a nature that tigers, wolves, vipers, and snakes would leave him unharmed when he entered the forests.[137] As an abandoned baby, the Spirit of the Grain, Hou Ji, was protected from the ice by a bird covering him with its wings. Sheep and oxen would not tread on the child.[138] Zhang Qian 張騫 (fl. ca. 125 B.C.E.) relates how the young leader of the Wusun 烏孫, the Kunmo 昆莫, was fed by birds and suckled by a wolf in the desert.[139] Another foundling Zi Wen 子文 (fl. ca. 600 B.C.E.) was suckled by a tigress and later became a chief minister in Chu.[140] Legend held that a barbarian infant named Dongming 東明 was saved by pigs and horses. Fish and turtles formed a floating bridge to lead him across a river to the country of Fuyu 夫餘 where he eventually became king.[141]

In addition to these miraculous infancy stories, several texts record instances in which animals in turn display their moral conduct in respect for individuals who led exemplary lives. The *Hanshu* records that following the king of Linjiang's 臨江 (mid second cent. B.C.E.) suicide, several tens of thousands of swallows picked up earth in their beaks and piled up his grave mound.[142] Swallows also came down to fill up the burial pit of Empress Ding 丁 after Wang Mang had ordered to desecrate her tomb.[143] Another case is that of the Yang 楊 clan, whose members were associated with the appearance of spirit birds from the late Western throughout the Eastern Han. One story tells how several days before the burial of Yang Zhen 楊震 (d. 124 C.E.) a big bird settled in front of his coffin, wailing and shedding tears. After the burial it flew off. Later a stone bird statue was erected at the tomb site. The appearance of this funeral cortège of birds was immortalized in stone on Yang's stele.[144]

Instances of filial animal piety perpetuated beyond death are recorded. Legend held that elephants spontaneously tilled the tumulus of Shun, and that crows labored the fields where Yu was interred and hence became his animal tenants.[145] Immortals likewise attracted the spontaneous attendance of animal acolytes. The legendary Pengzu 彭祖, alleged to have lived eight hundred years, was associated with the presence of tigers. Another most virtuous immortal was known as Zhuji Weng 祝雞翁 or "The Old Man Who Beguiled Chickens." According to one account, the old man had raised chickens for over a hundred years, had given surnames and styles to each bird of his thousand-odd flock and would summon them by name. In his reclusion, he was said to be flanked constantly by hundreds of white cranes and peacocks.[146] The association of white animals with immortality recalls Sima Qian's and Ban Gu's descriptions of the islands of immortality, which were inhabited by "creatures, birds and beasts completely white."[147] Another story is that of Liu An 劉安 (180–122 B.C.E.), whose domestic animals obtained immortality together with their master so that "his dogs were barking up in Heaven, and his roosters crowing in the clouds."[148] The ascension of domestic animals with their immortal master is also attested in the stele of the immortal Tang Gongfang 唐公房 (fl. ca. 9–25 C.E.). This stele inscription accounts how Tang Gongfang was given an elixir that enabled him to understand the language of birds and beasts, portrays him as a rat hunter using magic to imprison and kill rats, and records how his animals went up to heaven with the whole household. At the end of the Han, a local cult developed around Tang Gongfang, who came to be worshiped as a rat expeller.[149]

Moral Hybrids

With animals susceptible to the transformatory influence of music and human virtue, the animal realm as a whole could be read as an exponent of a moral cosmos. The protagonists of this moral bestiary were real and fabulous animals which exemplified that a transformation from "beast" to "animal" mirrored principles similar to those which distinguished sages and virtuous rulers from the common herds in human society. Moral animals differed from those that had retained their bestial instincts in the same way that the sage had differentiated himself from the commoner. With human principles deeply implicated in the workings of the animal world, the moral biology of the natural world was typified by hybrids and sacred animals that had ceased to be ordinary animals since they embodied behavioral and physical features that transcended the species. Certain animals were credited with the possession of similar transformatory powers to those of the human sage, other animals were physiognomized as numinous creatures that manifested outward signs of virtue on their physical body.

As was noted in chapter 3, a set of four creatures known as the "four numinous animals" (*si ling*) were considered to be the superior members of the species they represented (hairy, feathered, scaly, and armored). Being the most refined exemplars of their species, their moral supremacy was paralleled to the edifying virtue of the sage in human society (with the human sage being the fifth sacred animal presiding over the naked animals according to five-phase logic). Interaction between the human world and the animal realm was often described as a contact of some sort between the ruler and one of these sacred animals. The locus classicus on the *si ling*, preserved in the *Liji*, notes how the human sage is able to reach all living species through the domestication of the sacred animal that represents them:

> Therefore when the sages established rules, they thought it necessary . . . (to rear) the four sacred animals as their domestic animals . . . .What are the four sacred animals? They are the *qilin*, phoenix, tortoise, and dragon. Therefore, if one takes the dragon as a domestic animal, fish and sturgeon won't conceal themselves (from man). If one takes the phoenix as a domestic animal, birds will not fly off in distress. If one takes the *qilin* as a domestic animal, the beasts won't scatter away. If one takes the tortoise as a domestic animal, the feelings of men won't lose themselves.[150]

Given that the text further states that through the domestication of the four sacred animals "drink and food have their origin," this passage could be interpreted as a theoretical statement or origin narrative on the use of animal domestication in relation to husbandry. Its essential message however has a wider philosophical implication for not only does it present the sage as the source of the domestication of the animal world but it also attributes similar powers to representative creatures within the animal realm itself. The sacred animals relate to the animal species in the same way the sage relates to human beings. This analogy can also be seen in the suggestion that the human sage is to the people what the unicorn is to the beasts, or the phoenix to the birds.[151] Like the sage, the sacred animals exerted their virtue over other animals. In turn the human sage's control over the birds and beasts was determined by the degree with which he could exert his influence on each of the four sacred animals. His conduct was endorsed or sanctioned by the presence or absence of the four *ling* animals. The latter is reflected in a standard expression that occurs throughout the corpus of Warring States and Han writings:

> If you cut wombs and kill foetuses, the *qilin* will not come to the suburbs. If you exhaust the marshes and its fish, the *jiao* dragon won't reside in its springs. If you trample nests and smash eggs, the phoenix won't fly over the region.[152]

Just as ordinary humans were surrounded by a natural fauna of birds and beasts, the sage was surrounded by a set of numinous animals. And just as virtuous conduct and moderation in the hunt appeased the temperaments of wild and predatory beasts, the display of sagacity and moral rule would cause the numinous animals to join the ruler's moral universe. Parallel with the civilizing influence of the human sage over the wilds, the presence of the sacred animals would transform other animals' predatory instincts. For instance, in a passage appended to the *Shiji*, Chu Shaosun describes the origins of the spirit tortoise used in divination. As its natural habitat the text refers to a "Felicity Forest" (*jia lin* 嘉林), which is identified as a place where no predatory tigers, wolves, owls, or poisonous insects would abide. It further states that turtles with divine powers could be found in the waters of the Yangzi river. The regional inhabitants bred and consumed these animals on a regular basis because they believed it could induce the onset of vital *qi* and provide a remedy against old age. Rumor held that aged people in the south used turtles to prop up the feet of their beds.[153]

As was suggested in the *Liji* passage quoted above, the transformative power of the sage on the animal species as a whole was exerted through the medium of numinous animals or animals that possessed *ling* power.[154] The four numinous animals illustrate another aspect of *tui lei* thinking. Within each animal category the *ling* animals "push" their moral influence onto the animal creatures subject to them. The sage transforms the sacred animals, who in turn transform their representative species. A passage transmitted in the *Shuoyuan* further connects the origins of *ling* power to movement. Describing the dragon, it states that "when (the dragon) moves or causes movement, it generates *ling* power by means of which it exerts transformatory influences (*dong zuo ze ling yi hua* 動作則靈以化)."[155] Similar to the discourse on the transformation of the animal world through music, this statement combines the notion of spirit power and transformation with the idea of movement, and indicates that the sacred animals' appropriation of spirit power depends on their capacity to transform other animals. A hierarchy among animals according to their *ling* capacity could therefore be conceived of as a spirit geography consisting of a series of concentric circles surrounding the central *ling* specimen within each animal group.[156] Species that are removed further from the *ling* epicenter are endowed with less spirit power. Hence Xu Shen for instance refers to five directional spirit birds consisting of the phoenix at the center surrounded by four avian phoenix-like birds: the *faming* 發明 to the east, the *jiaoming* 焦明 to the south, the *sushuang* 鷫霜 to the west, and the *youchang* 幽昌 to the north.[157] Wang Chong refers to a "Record on the Five Birds" (*wu niao zhi ji* 五鳥之記), which held that each of the four directions as well as the center were graced by the presence of giant birds that were followed by flocks of other birds whenever they roamed about. Their size and plumage color is said to resemble that of the phoenix.[158] A similar "tortoise circle" is transmitted in the *Zhouli*, where four directional tortoise species supplement the heavenly and earthly tortoise.[159]

The idea that certain sacred animals exerted spiritual energy or *ling* power over their subject species may not have been confined to symbolism only. Traces in later writings on animal husbandry suggest that beliefs connected with the sacred bestiary shaped in preimperial times also found their way into practical husbandry concerns. A nice example relates to the guardian function of the spirit tortoise and is preserved in the *Qimin yaoshu* 齊民要術 ("Essential Techniques for the Peasantry"), an agricultural manual dated to ca. 535 C.E. In its instructions on carp breeding the farmer is advised to construct a lagoon or pond within which nine divisions are to be distinguished (equivalent to the "nine provinces" or *jiu zhou* in early geography). The manual then states that from the fourth month onward turtles called "Spirit Guardians" (*shen shou* 神守) are to be put in the pools to prevent *jiao* dragons from leading the carp to fly off once they have multiplied to the number of 360.[160] So the spirit tortoise confines the fish to their watery habitat and prevents them from transcending their watery nine provinces to become immortal and lost for the fish market! The *ling* tortoise exerts numinous power over its piscine subjects. This practice of putting spirit tortoises in fish ponds is recorded in numerous later writings and widely spread in Chinese aqua farming up to the present day.[161]

The "four sacred animals" were not the only creatures that exerted a cardinal role in the moral bestiary that encircled the sage-ruler. Similar functions were associated with a series of moral hybrids whose functional physical deformity symbolized the presence of humanlike virtue within the animal realm. The

hybrid composure of these animals embodied the integration of social values in
the natural world. Hybrids participated in both the human and animal worlds.
The following excerpt from the *Han shi waizhuan* 韓詩外傳 depicts a moral
universe in which the sage-ruler is surrounded by moral hybrid animals in the
four cardinal directions. It features imaginary animals who have to transcend
their instinctive behavior in order to survive. The human ruler, being the head
of the naked species positioned in the center, is admonished to "hybridize" or
combine the worthy "limbs" in his society in the same way the moral hybrids
harmonize their individually dysfunctional body parts:

> Among the fish in the eastern sea there is one called the *die* 鰈. They move around
> combining their [single] eyes. Unless they are two together, they cannot get anywhere.
> In the north there is a beast called the *lou* 婁, one of which eats while the other
> keeps watch. Unless they are two together they cannot eat their fill.
> In the south there is a bird named *jian* 鶼. They combine their [single] wings
> when they fly. Unless they are two together, they cannot take off.
> In the west there is a beast called *jue* 蟨. Its front legs are those of a rat, its hind
> legs those of a rabbit. When it gets sweet grass it always takes it in its mouth and
> gives it to the *qiongqiong juxu* 蛩蛩距虛. Not that by instinct it loves the *qiong-
> qiong juxu*, but because it could avail itself of its legs. [It has long forelegs and
> short hindlegs and is unable to ascend hills without carrying the *jue* on its back].
> Now if even birds, beasts, and fish depend on one another, how much more
> should a ruler of ten thousand chariots do so.[162]

A similar scheme is incorporated in the *Erya*. It is noteworthy that the *Erya* does
not list these hybrid creatures in one of its chapters on animal nomenclature
but in the chapter entitled "Explaining Earth." Reflecting the aforementioned
emphasis on territoriality and the directional character of numinous animals,
this suggests that hybrids, like their normal animal counterparts, were perceived as part of a spirit geography rather than as members of an autonomous
bestiary. The *Erya* authors further add a fifth hybrid assigned to the center—the
two-headed "bramble-head snake" (*zhi shou she* 枳首蛇)—and conclude by
stating that these hybrids are "the strange vapors of the four directions and the
Middle Kingdom."[163] This final phrase qualifies moral hybrids as emanations of
a regional *qi* and suggests that, similar to the association of soil *qi* with animal
habitat, moral hybrids were innate to specific regions and subject to local airs.
A similar principle is exemplified in the *Shanhaijing*, which presents a magical
landscape marked by local animals, hybrids, and spirits.[164]

In addition to interpreting hybrid animals as the embodiment of social values, the identification of a moral potentiality with certain animals was also linked
to the concept of *wen* 文. The previous chapter has shown how animal patterns in
the natural world were transposed into the human realm and how this process de-

termined the formation of a cultural order inspired by the animal world. An inverted process characterized the identification of sacred animals. A number of writings literally projected moral values onto the anatomy or physiognomy of certain animals and argued that an animal's character traits were to be inferred from external bodily signs. Plumage texture, bodily structure, and skin patterns were read as social *wen*. These physical "animal *wen*," as will be discussed in chapter 6, were also interpreted as indicators of change and numinous power.

The projection of moral patterns onto the physical animal body was most noticeable in the practice of animal physiognomy, which consisted of finding a correlation between the physical organization of the animal body and its qualities for human use. In essence physiognomy was a process which drew natural patterns into a social discourse. It assumed no separation between the physical and moral. While the physiognomist's prime concern was to recognize animals with superior physical qualities for practical use, the examination of the animal body was not inspired by protoveterinarian concerns only. The identification of physical features on an animal's body also provided a locus for the understanding of the cosmos. Just as early Chinese medical texts sought to draw parallels between the human body, the state, and the cosmos at large, physiognomical analysis inferred moral principles from the physical body. Thus several slips among the readable parts of the Mawangdui manuscript on horse physiognomy map out a terrestrial geography on the horse's head and body and suggest that the lines and curves on the horse should be understood as a body landscape. A later manual on horse physiognomy projects a state analogy onto the anatomy of the horse through linking the horse's various body parts with officials in the human bureaucracy:

> Bo Le said: 'The head of the horse is the king, so one desires it to be square. The eye is the chief counselor, so one wishes it to obtain clarity. The spine is the general, so one wants it to be strong. The stomach is the city fortification, so one wants it to be extended. The four feet are the commanders, so one wants them to be senior."[165]

Alternatively bodily patterns were read as symbols of moral virtues. Occasionally such interpretations were based on the resemblance of body lines with written graphs. The physical qualities or inborn nature of an animal were then literally read of the animal body through the recognition of ideographs on the skeleton structure or skin texture.[166]

A similar explanatory logic based on the recognition of virtues or *wen* on the physical body inspired the identification of other animals as numinous creatures. The anatomy of the phoenix for instance was associated with Confucian virtues: its head carried virtue, its cranium manifested righteousness, its back supported benevolence, and its heart was entrusted to knowledge.[167] A description of the phoenix in the *Shanhaijing* is even more explicit and uses the term *wen* repetitively:

[the phoenix] is pentachromatic and patterned (*wen* = cultured): . . . the pattern
on the head says "virtue," the pattern on the wings says "righteousness," the pattern on the back says "ritual deportment," the pattern on the breast says "benevolence," the pattern on the belly says "trustworthiness."[168]

An apocryphal work associates righteousness, trust, ritual conduct, benevolence,
and wisdom with the body, head, throat, and back of the four avian phoenix acolytes mentioned earlier.[169] The physiognomy of the chicken, which stands out
among its avian peers for its timely crow that determines day from night and induces the bird species to resonate, was also associated with Confucian virtues: it
is marked by the virtues of culture (*wen* 文) symbolized by the crest, martiality
(*wu* 武) embodied by the spurs, bravery (*yong* 勇) because it fights its enemies,
benevolence (*ren* 仁) because it calls its companions when it finds food, and
trustfulness (*xin* 信) because its crows are perfectly timed.[170]

   To summarize, the analogy between the daemonic nature of sacred animals and the pervasive qualities of the human sage was epitomized by the notion
of *wen* 文 in its multiple sense of culture, writing, as well as "decorative texture"
or "pattern." The ways in which the patterns and texture of an animal's skin or
hide were articulated were thought to indicate its sagacity. Just as the human sage
distinguished himself from the masses by his capability to fall back on cultured
behavior and the ability to create writings (*wen*), so the numinous animals distinguished themselves within their species by displaying various patterns (*wen*)
on their skin, hides, or scales. Sacred animals, to quote Wang Chong, were thus
seen as the cultured counterparts of the sages in the animal kingdom:

> Worthies distinguish themselves through writings. If one (cannot) differentiate
> dull individuals from eminent individuals, one must (take their) writings to es-
> tablish a distinction. This is not only true in the case of humans, it is also true in
> the case of animals. The dragon has patterns on its scales, and (therefore) is more
> numinous than snakes. The phoenix's plumage has five colors, (therefore) it is the
> leader among birds. The tiger is fierce, and its pelt (combines the colors) of the
> field mouse and the salamander. The tortoise has (fore)knowledge, on its back it
> carries patterns (written characters). As for these four animals, (although) their
> bodies have no (special) inner disposition, compared to other animals they are
> sage and wise. . . . Animals display patterns (*wen*) at the outside, human beings
> take writings (*wen*) as their foundation.[171]

"Speaking with Birds and Beasts"

In addition to presenting music and moral cultivation as a means to transform
the animal world, a number of texts refer to the mastery of animal language and

the adoption or simulation of instinctive animal behavior as a way to communicate with animals. Several individuals were associated with the auspicy of animal sounds. There is music master Kuang who is portrayed as a master of bird language. An episode in the *Zuozhuan* accounts how Master Kuang interprets the sight of joyfully cawing crows as a sign of a retreating army. Elsewhere a report that birds were circling around the soldiers' tents is taken as a sign of the army's surrender.[172] Similar observations of animal activity occur regularly in a military context.[173] An apocryphal tradition held that Qin Zhong 秦仲 (ninth cent. B.C.E.) was able to speak to birds, who then responded to him.[174] The esoteric master Zhan He could divine the lowing of cows.[175] Yang Wengzhong 楊翁仲 understood the neighing of horses, and Qin ancestor Bo Yi 伯益, also known as Shun's forester, could talk to the birds. Tradition held that Bo Yi was the first figure to tame and domesticate animals.[176] The divination of bird calls and animal sounds occurs mainly in texts and titles of manuals from the post-Han period. Judging from the bibliographic treatise in the *Hanshu*, it did not belong to the standard mantic practices of the time.[177] The earliest well-documented "ornithophonist" was Guan Lu 管輅, a diviner who lived during the third century C.E.[178]

These scattered references to the human understanding of animal language and animal behavior not only figured as metaphors for the extraordinary perspicacity of human sages, they also become significant in the light of contemporary descriptions of barbarians as the nearest in kind to animals. Numerous sources portray barbarians who shared the habitats of the exotic bestiaries in the periphery of the Chinese cultural epicenter as having the inner disposition of animals. The bodily functions and behavioral features of foreign tribes and exogenous peoples were said to have undesirable animal associations. Their temperaments and desires were equated with those of animals.[179] A number of tales account how certain barbarian tribes originated from the sexual union of a human with an animal.[180] The difference between distant tribes and the civilized Chinese heartland was also symbolically expressed in terms of their skin covering: "armored and scaly" barbarians (*jielin* 介鱗) were to be distinguished from civilized people dressed in "clothes and robes" (*yishang* 衣裳).[181]

In the same way that natural philosophies had pictured a moral concordance between territoriality, local airs, and the human-animal habitat, the animal tendencies among foreign tribes were attributed to the fact that they were subject to a different ethereal influence.

> As for the Rong and Di barbarians, they are a strange *qi* from the four directions. They squat on their heels and crouch down in a haughty manner and differ in nothing from birds and beasts. If they would live scattered within the Middle Kingdom, they would confuse and bring into chaos the Heavenly *Qi* and pollute and corrupt good-hearted people.[182]

In this passage, which is part of an argument against further campaigns against the Xiongnu, the court Confucian Lu Gong 魯恭 (32–112 C.E.) advocates a strict segregation between a civilized center and a barbarian periphery on the grounds that territorial *qi* should not be blurred. Barbarians are said to be subject to strange and abnormal vapors (*yi qi* 異氣) that make them live like animals, while the Middle Kingdom is endowed with virtuous "heavenly *qi*" (*tian qi* 天氣).

Another characteristic associated with barbarians was their foreign tongue, which was known as the language of birds and beasts.[183] Some tribes were said to be able to communicate in animal speech. According to the *Zhouli* the "Convicts of the Yi 夷 tribes," who were attached to the office of the herdsmen, raised cows and horses, and could speak with birds. Similarly the "Convicts of the Mo 貉 barbarians" were attached to the office of the "animal tamer." They raised and trained wild animals and were in charge of "speaking with wild animals."[184] The *Zuozhuan* contains the story of Ge Lu 葛盧, chieftain of the Jie 介 tribe, who divined a cow's lowing to indicate that her three calves had all been used as sacrificial victims. The same eastern country of Jie was known as a place where people understood the language of the six domestic animals.[185]

The bestialization of barbarians also explained their identification as expert hunters. According to one account set during the reign of King Zhaoxiang of Qin 秦昭襄王 (fl. 306–251 B.C.E.), accomplished bowsmen belonging to the Ba 巴 tribe were rewarded with tax relief and reduced penal sentences for killing a voracious white tiger that had been terrorizing the region. Han emperor Gaozu 高祖 is reported to have engaged the Board Shield Man-barbarians (Banshun Man 板楯蠻) for shooting white tigers in exchange for tax exemptions. Their skills earned them the title of White Tiger Exempted Barbarians (Bai Hu fu Yi 白虎复夷).[186] Elsewhere a general describes barbarians as people "who make saddled horses their home, and hunting their occupation."[187]

Together with barbarians, individuals lacking in virtue were identified as animals. Villains who disguised themselves in dog fur to intrude on a private property were known as "dog-thieves" (*goudao* 狗盜).[188] This identification of scoundrels with animals is illustrated in great detail in daybooks excavated at Shuihudi and Fangmatan that include a calendar for the identification of bandits according to the duodenary animal cycle. With each animal sign, the bestial features of the villain are outlined. At the end of each item, their names are listed. For instance, the Shuihudi entry for the twelfth cycle states:

> On *hai* 亥 days, corresponding to the pig: Those who steal have a big nose and a hasty walk. They have the spine of a horse and their face is not complete. They have a mole on their waist and hide in pig pens and under walls. In the early morning you can get them but at dawn you cannot catch them. Their name(s) is (are) *tun gu xia gu* [. . .] *hai*.[189]

While it is not obvious for each entry in the thief calendar, there is a relationship between the animal sign and the robber's external appearance and behavior. For instance the villains active on days that correspond to the tiger sign are said to have whiskers and black spots, those active on rat days have whiskers and a pointing mouth, and those active on days corresponding to the reptile sign have snake eyes, a yellow color, and hide under tiles and vessels.

Since barbarians were presented as closely related to birds and beasts, they were subject to the same model of human governance as the animal world. Barbarians were distinguished from ordinary humans because they interacted with the wilds in a direct way. This is illustrated in references to their physical animal resemblance and their superior skills in herding, raising, and domesticating animals. But whereas barbarians master the animal world in a physical and direct way, the sage wields an indirect, nonphysical, and moral authority over the beasts through the medium of music and the cultivation of virtue. The sage does not engage in direct contact with animals, even if they outwardly share similarities with humans: "Contacting parrot and ape does not secure one's glory. . . . Contacting parrot and ape means to share the side of birds and beasts."[190] The same moral distance is maintained in the context of sacrifice. Ritual prescription held that a ruler should not taste the meat of those animals whose sounds he had heard. The idea is exemplified in the Mencius, where King Xuan of Qi cancels the slaughter of a bull for the blood consecration of a bell because he had seen the animal alive. Not being able to bear its frightened appearance he orders the bull to be replaced by a sheep. Whether or not one wishes to interpret King Xuan's gesture as an act of animal compassion (in which case changing a bull for a sheep is difficult to explain) or as an act of frugality in sacrifice (replacing a large victim by a small one), the story suggests that a sage-king should keep a moral distance from the act of killing.[191] This is confirmed in other passages that note that the sage-ruler shows his benevolence and righteousness by keeping away from the kitchens or abattoirs.[192]

The discourse on the transformation of the animal world also had its counterpart in the idea that the sage-ruler should exert a transformatory influence over the bestial barbarian periphery surrounding his sociopolitical heartland. For if the transformatory power of music and the radiance of moral virtue exerted a civilizing effect on the beasts and birds, it would have a similar effect on barbarians, who were their nearest in kind. Therefore in the same way that animals who were susceptible to music and virtue would gather and perch within the central realm to figure as acolytes of the virtuous ruler, barbarians could be transformed to shed off their bestial instincts and trade their animal hides for Chinese clothing. Therefore in Warring States and Han discourse sinicizing the outer regions often became tantamount to domesticating barbarians as one domesticates animals, or to transforming the beasts into cultured subjects of the central sage-ruler.[193]

Conclusion

In many Warring States and Han writings the relationship between the human world and the animal realm is described as a moral continuum. Man and beast were perceived as interacting in a field of contingency, and the animal world was believed to be subject to the influence of human morality. Central to the early Chinese perception of the animal world was the notion that human governance exerted a transformatory influence over the natural world. Being part of a moral cosmos, animals were susceptible to laws other than those which determined their instinctive behavior in their natural environment.

Two themes were at the heart of a philosophy that conceived of the sage-ruler as an agent capable of exerting an encompassing moral control over the wilds: first, the idea that music affected the nonhuman world, and second, the idea that the cultivation of virtue exercized a transformatory power over the animal world. By associating the origins of music and dance with the observation of sounds and movement in the animal world, the discourse on music provided a rationale for the explanation of a sage-ruler's influence over animals. Music changed the instinctive disposition of wild animals and transformed the beasts into moral animals who would abandon their bestial instincts to become animal acolytes of a virtuous ruler. Through subsuming animals among the audience receptive to the moral influence of music, Warring States and Han writings also inferred a conceptual proximity between the idea of physical motion in the animal world and moral emotion. Likewise, the cultivation of virtue in human society was seen as a condition for the spontaneous and orderly working of the animal world. Animals could sanction human society for a lack of moral rule by reverting to predatory instinctive behavior.

An important consequence followed from the idea that animals were susceptible to human virtue. It meant in the first place that instinctive animal behavior was often interpreted as being determined by moral principles that originated in human society and, secondly, it entailed that changes in human society would spontaneously induce behavioral changes in the animal world. Idealized descriptions of the organized hunt, the apparatus of hunting techniques and hunting taboos, as well as the ways in which to domesticate and train wild animals all shared the assumption that both humans and animals functioned according to the same moral biology. The latter was further exemplified by the idea that a sage-ruler wielded authority over the animal world through the medium of hybridized sacred animals. These animals were credited with similar transformatory powers as the human sage, and their physiognomy was associated with moral virtues.

Since barbarians were portrayed as the next of kin to animals, the same rhetoric that sought to justify human moral dominance over the wilds through transformation provided the vocabulary to justify central ("Han," "Chinese") control over peripheral barbarian tribes. While all animal species and barbarians could become potential tributaries subject to the deanimalizing transformatory powers of the Middle Kingdom, an equally strong countercurrent insisted on animalizing and demonizing wild animals and foreigners by deeming them unworthy to be considered part of humanity, which was embodied by the figure of the sage-ruler. The discourse on the transformation of the animal world thus provided a model for the way in which humans could assert their social, political, and moral dominance over the entire cosmos.

CHAPTER SIX

CHANGING ANIMALS

In addition to presenting the natural world as susceptible to moral transformation and changes induced by human behavior, the early Chinese also pictured the world of plants, trees, birds, and beasts as a continuously changing physical reality. The previous two chapters were mainly concerned with the changing interactions between the human and animal world. This chapter will shift its focus "within the species" and link the dialectic of transformation to the ways in which the physical animal world itself was perceived. While the natural world as a whole served as a source for literary allusion and philosophical imagination ever since the compilation of the Odes, the animal realm in particular inspired a great deal of discourse on the broader notion of change, ranging from ideas about physical metamorphosis to sociopolitical discussions of dynastic change.

The association of animals with ideas on change partly derived from the observation of animal physiology and animal behavior. Both to the Warring States observer and his or her modern counterpart, a number of events in the animal world present themselves as activities of change. For instance the adaptation of certain animals' physical disposition according to the cycle of the seasons, the alteration between night and day (diurnal versus nocturnal animals), or the passage to and from different habitats all constituted activities that presented the natural world as a changing reality in a state of continuous motion. Besides acknowledging these observable changes in the natural world, early Chinese writings also contain numerous references to cross-species changes and human-animal transformations. Given the low share of zoological theory in early China and the acceptance of an intricate interdependency between animal behavior and the workings of human society, the frequency of animal references related to change and metamorphosis may not be coincidental. The fact that observations of change or metamorphosis in the animal world were persistently interpreted as significant beyond the boundaries of the physical world suggests that such ideas were central to the ways in which the early Chinese understood the living world and the way in which the animal world figured in the sociopolitical and religious sphere of early Chinese society.

The notion of species change, as this chapter will show, was also crucial in the conception of numinous authority and power among the living species. The idea that all living species were subject to a fundamental rhythm of change in their micro- or macro-habitat had important consequences for the ways in which animals were perceived as daemonic beings in China. In the Judeo-Christian tradition, as Ohnuki-Tierney points out, transgressing the demarcation line between humans and animals was against the order created by God and therefore blasphemous. Species transformations or metamorphoses between animals and humans were seen as transgressions against a sacred order.[1] In medieval and early modern Europe philosophers and theologians had cast man as the sole proprietor of the right to dominate and subjugate the natural world. The biblical prerogative claiming that the differences between man and beast were unbridgeable had caused, to quote Keith Thomas, an "anxiety, latent or explicit, about any form of behaviour which threatened to transgress the fragile boundaries between man and the animal creation."[2] In ancient China, where the idea of a hierarchical creation was absent and where change and flux constituted the normal order, transgressions of the human-animal boundaries conveyed different meanings. The early Chinese spirit world was not conceived as a pantheon of gods and demons detached from the world of humans, populating heavens and hells, and interacting with each other on the basis of divine principles solely reserved for the gods. Even in the mythological tradition, myths in which gods interact with each other in a world of their own are the exception rather than the rule.[3] The absence of a strict separation between a realm of the divine and an immanent world of natural creatures also meant that the early Chinese did not insist on theological theories that sought to classify gods, demons, and spirits into classes such as zoomorphic versus anthropomorphic. A pantheon of animal-gods remained absent.

Scholars past and present have acknowledged the amorphous nature of the boundaries between the living species in Chinese thought and noted that metamorphosis rather than stasis was the order of things. A century ago, the Dutch sinologist J. J. M. De Groot observed that

> Chinese philosophy has never occupied itself seriously with the matter of zoanthropy. Quite satisfied with its all-explaining theory of migration of souls in the Universe . . . it has simply referred to the popular ideas on zoanthropy as plain matters of fact. . . . But we may admit unreservedly, that the doctrine that the Universe is one compound of an infinite number of *kwei* (*gui*) and *shen*, continuously effused into men and animals equally, has always much helped to uphold the belief in a transition of souls from men into beasts and from beasts into men, as that doctrine, on account of its being a production of the mind of the infallible ancients, never lacked absolute authority.[4]

While De Groot's reference to soul terminology needs to be read with care, his basic observation of an effusive, changing universe in which animals and human beings transform constantly, still holds. Species change and the transcendence of biological boundaries are a prominent theme throughout early Chinese texts. In what follows I will discuss the various ways in which ideas about species change were formulated. An analysis of the semantics behind species change will clarify its influence on early Chinese perceptions of the animal world. The aptitude to metamorphose or transcend one's species was often seen as a source of daemonic power. Metamorphosis and hybridity figured as regular occurrences that provided models for authority, sagacity, and spirit power. Physical transformations in the natural world were believed to influence the cultured society of man, and the appearance of transforming beings was integrated in a larger sociopolitical philosophy which explained animal metamorphosis as an indication of social and cosmological change.

A Cosmogony of Change

Based on cosmogonic theories of the emergence of all things from a primal unity or undifferentiated field of energy (*qi*), several texts elaborated theories that pictured the development of the various animal species, plants, and minerals through a process of metamorphosis in which all species mutated from primal types. These texts maintained that the boundaries between the animated species were vague and indistinct. Rejecting the idea of progressive creation or linear hierarchies among the living species, they also emphasized that all species in the world came into existence through laws of change and transformation.

The opening passage of the "Yi ben ming" 易本命 chapter in the *Da Dai Liji* describes how all living species came into existence through an underlying principle of change or alteration (*yi* 易). It also identifies sagacity and an insight in the rhythms of the Dao as a precondition for the understanding of the origins and subsequent mutations of the living species:

> The Master said: [The principle of] change (*yi*) has brought into existence humans, birds, animals, and all the varieties of creeping things, some living solitary, some in pairs, some flying and some running on the ground. And no one knows their true nature. Only he who profoundly masters the virtue of the Dao can grasp their basis and their origin.[5]

The idea that a principle of change, alteration, or transformation operates as the "begetter" of all species is developed in more detail in works of a proto-Daoist nature. A passage in the *Zhuangzi* describes the genesis of animated beings in stages of spontaneous generation starting with the seed or germ (*zhong* 種 and *ji* 機) and resulting in the birth of man out of a horse. The text suggests that minerals, plants, animals, and human beings come forth from the smallest germs through a process of continuous mutation and transformation:

Seeds contain germs. Upon contact with water they enter into a continuity of stages. Reaching the edge between water and land, they become the "envelopes of frogs and oysters." If they germinate on the slopes they become *lingxi* 陵舄 plants. When the *lingxi* gets into contact with dung, it becomes the *wuzu* 烏足 "crowfoot." The roots of the crowfoot become *qizao* 蠐螬 "maggots," its leaves become butterflies. The butterfly suddenly transforms into an insect that lives under the stove. It has a shape of shed skins, and is named *qutuo* 鴝掇. After a thousand days the *qutuo* becomes a bird named the *ganyugu* 乾餘骨. The saliva of the *ganyugu* becomes the *simi* 斯彌 bug, the *simi* bug becomes a *shixi* 食醯 "wine-fly." The *yilu* 頤輅 is born from the wine-fly. The *huangkuang* 黃軦 is born from the *jiuyou* 九猷. *Mounei* 瞀芮 "gnats" are born from rotten *huan* 蠸. The *yangxi* 羊奚 plant couples with bamboo that has not sprouted for a long while and produces the *qingning* 青寧 plant. The *qingning* gives birth to the *cheng* 程 "leopard" which begets the horse. The horse gives birth to man. Man again returns to his germinal state. The myriad creatures come out of germs and return to germs.[6]

This fragment does not develop an apparent taxonomy portraying a different ontology for creature, species, or gender. Animate and inanimate species are said to mutate continuously, and in many phases of the generative process, species boundaries are crossed. Change and transformation here are not expressive of a teleological striving for biological fulfillment or species perfection; rather, they constitute the essential process of generation itself. Amphibian animals become insects, insects turn into birdlike creatures, plants generate mammals. As Needham notes, the fixity of biological species is firmly denied. "What is celebrated here," to quote Benjamin Schwartz, "is the delightfully inexhaustible and protean transformations of nature."[7]

Spontaneous generative change and transformation in the animal world also provided imagery for the description of cosmological patterns of change. The opening passage of the transmitted *Zhuangzi* exemplifies the idea of species change with the well-known image of the leviathan *kun* 鯤 who turns into a gigantic *peng* 鵬 bird:

In the North Ocean there is a fish, its name is the Kun; the Kun's girth measures who knows how many thousand miles. It changes into a bird; its name is the Peng; the Peng's back measures who knows how many thousand miles. When it puffs out its chest and flies off, its wings are like clouds hanging from the sky. This bird when the seas are heaving has a mind to travel to the South Ocean. The South Ocean is the Lake of Heaven.[8]

The *kun* metamorphosis, from fish to bird, symbolizes a change in realm— from the dark, northern, amorphous *yin* waters to the southern ocean, the *yang* pool of Heaven—and suggests that dynamic species transformation befalls all beings. One could look for naturalist explanations behind this metamorphosis such as a traditional belief that fish and birds belonged to the same species, or, as one scholar has speculated, the image of a bird eating a fish, which may have inspired a fish-to-bird metamorphosis.[9] The *kun* metamorphosis also symbolizes a transformation from the smallest entity—*kun* 鯤 originally means "fish roe"—to the most giant being.[10] Regardless of which natural explanation one seeks behind the image, the *kun* metaphor typifies how the idea of transformation was exemplified by animal metamorphosis and suggests that species change was thought to be a fundamental part of the cosmogonic process. Even if one wishes to read this narrative as nothing more than an imaginative evocation of metaphor, one must assume that, in order to be powerful, the image itself was rooted in a belief that many animal species metamorphose. The *Liezi* supplements Zhuangzi's animal transformations with another series:

> Sheep's liver changes into the goblin sheep underground. Horse blood turns into demon fire and human blood turns into wild fire. Kites become sparrow-hawks, sparrow-hawks become cuckoos, cuckoos after a while turn again into kites. Swallows become bivalves, moles become quails, rotten melons become fish, old leaks become sedge, old ewes become monkeys, fish roe becomes insects.[11]

Metamorphosis and transformation here are not viewed as anomalous or abnormal but as a genuine and spontaneous natural process. As Angus Graham points out, it is unnecessary to look for a historical process of generation or a particular order in such transformation series.[12] The main aim of these fragments lies in demonstrating that the boundaries between the species are blurred.

Other passages in the *Zhuangzi* cunningly exemplify the idea that the basic law of physical transformation befalls all living kind upon death. In one story the sickened Ziyu 子輿 claims not to be troubled by his physical deformity: "If [the force that brings about change, *zao hua zhe* 造化者], borrows my left arm to transform it into a cock, I will crow to announce dawn . . . if it transforms my spirit into a horse I will ride it." Another figure Zili 子犁 reprimands the relatives of the bedridden Zilai 子來: "Do not make him fear transformation. . . . What will it turn you into? A rat's liver or a fly's leg?"[13] Here the metamorphoses do not follow sequential stages, but merely serve to illustrate Zhuangzi's disbelief in species fixity of any kind. The final passage of the "Tian yun" 天運 ("Movements of Heaven") chapter stages a dialogue in which Laozi instructs Confucius on the basic law of transformation. Again generation through transformation in the animal world is taken up as the point of comparison:

> [Laozi said] . . . when white herons look at each other, the pupils in their eyes do not move, and they undergo a "wind transformation" (*feng hua* 風化) [i.e., impregnate each other]. As for insects, the male insect buzzes in the air above (*shang feng* 上風),

and the female responds in the air below (*xia feng* 下 風), and impregnation (*feng hua* 風化) takes place. The *lei* 類 are both male and female, therefore they [auto-generate] through "wind transformation."[14] One's nature cannot be altered, one's fate cannot be transformed, the seasons cannot be halted, the Dao cannot be obstructed. If you get hold of the Dao there is nothing that cannot be done of itself, if you get lost in the Dao, nothing will be possible of itself. Confucius did not leave his home for three months. Then he saw Laozi again and said: "I have got it. Crows and magpies generate by hatching, fish by the exchange of saliva, small-waisted wasps by transformation (*hua* 化). When there is a baby brother, big brother cries. For a long time I have, as a human being, not been going along with the process of transformation! If one does not go along with transformation as a person, how can one transform others?" Laozi said: "Good Qiu, now you've got it!"[15]

The generation of offspring is here described in terms of a "wind transformation" (*fenghua*), implying that the correspondence of *qi*, in the form of wind, functions as an agent that generates without physical or bodily intercourse. Furthermore man's generation through transformation is seen as the physiological basis that enables him to morally transform other humans. A similar image occurs in another passage in the *Zhuangzi*: "the *pen* 奔 wasp is not able to metamorphose [=beget] the bean caterpillar. A Yue chicken cannot brood over the eggs of a snow-goose but a chicken from Lu is certainly capable to do so. . . . Now my talents are too little and do not suffice to transform you."[16]

In the fictitious dialogue between Laozi and Confucius, "wind" or "air" are presented as a generative agent that begets through transformation, an idea parallel to the perception of music as a wind that morally transforms the natural world. Perhaps the earliest occurrence of "wind" expressing the mutual attraction between male and female species occurs in a passage in the *Zuozhuan* where two lords are said to be separated from each other by such a large distance that even the "wind-heat" cannot make their horses and cattle entice each other.[17] Other texts link wind with the idea of "germination" (*meng* 萌), or present insects (*chong* 虫) as the seminal essence of wind.[18] Xu Shen states that the movement of wind results in insects being born and transforming after eight days. Wang Chong notes that insects are produced by the vapors of wind and confirms the same transformation period of eight days. Still according to Wang the fact that insects take their *qi* from the winds inspired Cang Jie to compose the graph *feng* 風 as a composite of the elements *fan* 凡 and *chong* 虫.[19] Other texts link generation through wind transformation with the notion of wind as a musical air. The *Huainanzi* states that the male mounting snake cries in the upper airs while the female cries in the lower airs. When this occurs "transformation turns (the air) into bodily form."[20] Oviparous generation and the maturation process of a bird fetus inside the egg were also known as a transformation (*hua*) from egg to chick.[21] In short, the generative relationship among living creatures was often perceived as a process of transformation.

To be sure, this picture of amorphous species boundaries did not imply that no attempts were made to distinguish the living species on a biological or sociological basis, or that no attention was given to an animal's different aptitudes. This is clear from the attempts at lexicographic, ritual, and correlative classification discussed before. However just as the interest in individual animal morphology was relegated in favor of the inclusiveness of classification, the boundaries between the species in early China were not fixed. Instead they were formulated according to various typologies of change.[22] Furthermore references to changing animals were not confined to cosmogonic statements that saw their transformations as merely part of a greater cosmological pattern. Physical and symbolical animal metamorphoses also figured prominently in the social and political discourse of Warring States and Han China. Against the background of a philosophy that accepted the notion of change and transformation as a basic paradigm, the reference to "changing animals" conveyed several subsidiary meanings. While certain texts pictured a moral causation behind human-animal metamorphoses, others viewed animal metamorphosis as a functional adaptation to a temporal cycle or attributed it to the spatial distribution of different animal groups. In the case of certain animals, metamorphosis and spontaneous transformation were considered to be an inherent and autonomous property. Animal metamorphosis was also enacted on a symbolical level in shamanic practices, ritual dances, and the ritual use of animal skins. Finally, metamorphosis came to be viewed as a portentous indication for sociopolitical and cosmological change. I will discuss each of these types of metamorphosis next. For the purpose of argumentation, I refer to metamorphosis in a broad sense and take it to indicate both changes in physical composition (color, size, and shape) and partial or complete change of species and/or gender.

Demonic Transformations

One group of narratives featuring "changing animals" could be brought together under the heading of demonic metamorphosis. These are cases in which a transformation of some kind occurs as a result of a numinous sanction by an anonymous power (for instance Heaven). Alternatively the human-to-animal or animal-to-human change is occasioned by a specific demonic agent such as a malign spirit, a disease, or an attack by wild animals. A common feature of these stories is their etiologic nature evinced in the implicit or explicit presence of a specific reason or external cause behind the metamorphosis. The cause of change can be an ethical one such as misconduct or, alternatively, a natural cause such as disease or premature death. The physical change is imposed or provoked and is usually recorded in a story explaining the intent and consequence of the metamorphosis (for instance the expiation of a former crime or the vengeance for ethical misconduct).

Two well-known metamorphosis cases are recorded in the *Zuozhuan*. The first is that of Gun 鯀, father of the legendary Yu, who was transformed into a yellow boar for failing to dike the floods.[23] Scholars have given various interpretations to this story, ranging from the suggestion that Gun's metamorphosis is a metaphoric account of a life-and-death cycle, to the view that Yu and Gun were two manifestations of the same deity, which had changed body.[24] Another *Zuozhuan* story foreshadows an avenging ghost scenario, a theme that appeared increasingly in texts such as the *Shiji* and the dynastic histories of Han and became popular as a literary genre in the early medieval period. The story tells of Peng Sheng 彭生 (fl. ca. 690 B.C.E.), who avenges his unjust death by transforming into a pig and causing his assassin, Lord Xiang 襄 of Qi, to be injured during a hunt. The wound ensuing from this hunting incident would eventually cause his death.[25] Similar cases of moral animal metamorphoses occur elsewhere. In the *Shanhaijing* the Thearch puts Gu 鼓, who was the son of a mountain spirit, together with another spirit named Qin Pi 欽䲹 to death for an unjust killing, whereupon the latter transformed into an osprey and the former into a *jun* 鵕 bird.[26] The same text recounts how the goddess Nü Wa, daughter of the legendary Red Emperor, was drowned in the East Sea, following which she transformed into a *jingwei* 精衛 bird, devoting the rest of her life to the Sisyphean task of carrying stones and wood from the western mountains to dike the East Sea.[27] The *Shanhaijing* further mentions ten entities named "The Bowels of Nü Wa," which allegedly had been transformed into spirits. Guo Pu provides the background to their origin stating that Nü Wa underwent seventy metamorphoses a day and that these spirits had transformed out of her abdomen.[28]

An early imperial episode figures Han Empress Lü and is set in the format of an avenging ghost story. It tells how Empress Lü poisons the heir to Gaozu's throne (Ruyi 如意, the prince of Zhao 趙) and gets bitten under her left arm by a dog. People believed that the spirit of the prince had transformed itself into a grey dog to take its revenge. The wound under the empress' arm fails to heal and she dies as a result.[29] The presence of an explicit moral cause behind such metamorphosis cases suggests that this type of animal metamorphosis was related to the wider belief in demons (*gui* 鬼) as ghosts of deceased human beings. The origins of the *gui* character itself have been linked with a simian creature resembling a human-cum-animal hybrid. In Warring States and Han times demons were often identified as creatures that changed into or out of other creatures. A graphic illustration of this idea occurs in the morphology of the composite character *hua* 傀, which is glossed by Xu Shen as "demonic transformation" (*guibian* 鬼變).[30]

A moral cause connecting the state before and after a human-to-animal or animal-to-human transformation is however not a universal feature. The *Huainanzi* recounts the metamorphosis of Gongniu Ai 公牛哀 as a consequence of disease. He turns into a tiger and kills his brother without any apparent reason.

The story suggests that each bodily form entails an inherent natural behavior and that there need not remain a mental or physical link between the creature before and after the metamorphosis:

> Hence (Gongniu Ai's) cultured behavior became that of a beast. His nails and teeth had altered. His will and heart-mind were transformed and his spirit and bodily form were changed. When he was a tiger, he did not know he had been a human being before. And when he was a human being he did not know he would become a tiger. The two [states of being] drove each other out, both having pleasure in their assumed forms.[31]

Gao You comments that while someone may turn into a tiger, such metamorphosis can be reversed as long as one has not started to devour humans, in other words, as long as the instinctive faculties of the animal are not fully adopted. In another story, set as a remonstrance by Wu Zixu 伍子胥 (sixth cent. B.C.E.) to the king of Wu 吳 criticizing the latter's desire to follow the common folk in their drinking habits, the *Shuoyuan* recounts the moral tale of an unfortunate dragon-to-fish metamorphosis. In the story the Lord of Heaven reprimands a white dragon for lamenting being shot in the eye by a fisherman after having assumed the shape of a fish. The Lord of Heaven criticizes the dragon's metamorphosis itself, which led to its unfortunate injury. The dragon, described as the "precious domestic animal of the Lord of Heaven," may well inspire awe and respect in its dragon state, but once transformed into an ordinary fish it had become an easy target for the fisherman. A change in form had implied a change in the way others treated it. Just as the dragon had lost its spirit power by turning into a fish, the king would lose his reputation by associating with commoners.[32]

Functional Metamorphosis

Whereas demonic transformation stories presented human and animal metamorphoses as sometimes the consequence of a moral sanction, calendrical texts asserted that species transformations were functional and belonged to the regular course of nature. The underlying philosophy here was that time, space, and changing biological environments compelled the living species to adapt different shapes in order to be in harmony with the greater rhythm of the cosmos which, as was illustrated above, was associated with continuous change and motion. The calendar provided a schematized framework that monitored the actions of human society according to the changing rhythms in nature, its fauna and its flora. Calendars articulated how changes within the human world could be aligned with the changing patterns in the natural world; in other words, they sought to establish stasis in a continuously changing Umwelt. As the previous chapters have shown, texts such as the "monthly ordinances" or "Lesser Annuary of the Xia" were a rich repository of animal data and provided a detailed guide to seasonal animal behavior.[33] Since the observation of motion in the animal world constituted an important ingredient in the development of calendars, these texts also preserved a detailed record of "changing" animal behavior.

The "monthly ordinances," as mentioned in chapter 3, indicated the alterations of the seasons and the annual *yinyang* cycle with a standard set of animal metamorphoses. Mid-spring was viewed as the time when the hawk (*ying* 鷹) would transform into a pigeon (*jiu* 鳩). In late spring field mice (*tianshu* 田鼠) would transform into quails (*ru* 鴽). In late autumn small birds (*jue* 爵) entered the big waters to transform into frogs (bivalves, *ge* 蛤), and at the beginning of winter, fowl (*zhi* 雉) entered the waters to change into molluscs (*shen* 蜃).[34] Scholars and commentators have given various explanations for these particular metamorphoses, some more plausible than others. For instance the *Da Dai Liji* attributes the pigeon-to-hawk metamorphosis to a dual disposition innate to one and the same bird species. Following this logic the bird would manifest itself as a hawk in its predatory condition and as a pigeon when it was not hunting. As one nineteenth-century scholar paraphrased, "the hawk-existence of the bird is when it is carnivorous, and the dove-existence is the period of its non-carnivorous state."[35]

Zheng Xuan connects the transformational powers of pigeons with their symbolic role to regenerate, rejuvenate, and nourish the aged. In Han times pigeons were distributed to the elderly in mid-spring because it was believed that these birds never choke on their own food.[36] During an annual ceremony performed in the eighth month in the Eastern Han, "pigeon staffs" (a staff with the end shaped in the form of a pigeon) were distributed to the aged. Their association with the procurement of longevity is described in a Han verse:

> The pigeon-staff supports the aged,
> and clothes and feeds a hundred mouths.
> It adds to their longevity,
> and [thus] calamities will not arise.[37]

The idea that ageing was a form of transformation adds another explanation to the symbolism associated with transforming pigeons and the distribution of pigeon staffs. Zheng Xuan explains:

> Spring birds are those which, having hibernated, then first come forth, such as the yellow sparrow of the South Commandery. At this time hawks change to become pigeons; the pigeons and (other) spring birds transform the old to become new, so that it is appropriate to use them for nourishing the aged. They help the generative ethers to circulate.[38]

The belief that birds transformed with the seasons may have been based on the observation that certain bird species migrate seasonally. A work known as the *Qinjing* 禽經 or "Classic of Birds"—attributed to Shi Kuang (sixth cent. B.C.E.) but surviving as an apocryphal text with commentary by Zhang Hua— concludes with the statement that "the transformations of the feathered animals rotate according to the seasonal ordinances."[39] It is not implausible that the animal transformations in the calendar originated from an observational point of view. The idea would then be that the observer saw two different animals in different seasons but assumed that these were two shapes of the same animal. The change of an animal's seasonal habitat may have been perceived as a change in animal kind, and the dialectic of absence and reemergence of certain animals (as seen for example in hibernation and seasonal migration) may have been interpreted as a metamorphosis of species.[40]

Winged creatures entering the waters and transforming into clams or fishlike creatures may be attributed to the perception that both birds and fish belonged to the *yin* species (both fish and birds are oviparous, do not chew, and have a similar form of locomotion):

> Birds and fish are born from *yin* but belong to *yang*. Therefore birds and fish are both oviparous. Fish swim in waters and birds fly among the clouds. Therefore in winter swallows and sparrows enter the waters and transform into mussels.[41]

Wang Chong makes a similar observation: "Fish and birds belong to the same species. Therefore birds can fly, and fish also. Birds lay eggs and fish also. Vipers, adders, bees, and scorpions all lay eggs and have a similar nature."[42] One report dated to the late first century C.E. notes that the virtue of the local governor of Guangling 廣陵 was of such a nature that locusts that had been plaguing the region entered the rivers and sea to turn into fish and shrimp.[43]

Noteworthy in a number of these calendrical metamorphoses is the image of water as a transforming agent. With water being part of the natural environment of metamorphosing animals such as piscines, reptiles, and amphibians, frequent reference is made to transformations induced by contact with water. This was reinforced by the belief that water was a generating force, an idea that had cosmogonic precedents. The "Water and Earth" ("Shui di" 水地) chapter of the *Guanzi* develops a cosmology based on water. Described as the "blood and *qi*" of the earth, water is said to be the primal stuff (equivalent to *qi* in other cosmologies) from which humans, fauna, and flora emerge. Furthermore, the *Guanzi* also identifies water as a daemonic force (*shen* 神). Hence the *jiao* dragon would only maintain its divine status among the watery creatures by the grace of water. When deprived of water, its divine nature fades. Similar to the influences attributed to regional "soil *qi*," the *Guanzi* attributes regional temperamental differences to local waters. Thus the sage is said to transform the morals of his people by ensuring that the water throughout the state is the same and pure. The sages' transforming influence over the world lay in understanding the waters of the various regions and how these influenced the morals of its inhabitants.⁴⁴ The image of rivers as the guiding channels of *qi* occurs in the *Guoyu*.⁴⁵ A manuscript recovered from Guodian tomb no. 1—dubbed "Taiyi sheng shui" 太一生水 after its first line—suggests that ideas about the cosmogonic power of water may have been current by the late fourth century B.C.E. It opens with the statement that "Grand One begets the Waters," which is followed by the subsequent phases in the formation of the world.⁴⁶ It is not unlikely that a belief that water could physically transform living creatures had its conceptual roots in cosmologies that presented water as a generative force transforming the customs and temperaments of living creatures.

An early example of the transformatory power of water on reptiles and fish occurs in the *Shanhaijing*:

> In Hu Ren 互人 Land . . . , there is a fish with one side dried up (partially shriveled), called the Fish Woman (*yufu* 魚婦). (This is) Zhuan Xu, who after dying, revived again. When the wind comes from the north, the heavens are a great spring. Snakes then transform into fish. This is the Fish Woman Zhuan Xu dying and reviving again.⁴⁷

The damp and swampy climate of the south reinforced the perception that southern people were related to reptiles and piscines. The *Huainanzi* refers to the grave mound of Hou Ji in the south, and states that the people there resuscitate after having died. Among them there were demifish. Gao You comments that people in southern regions would revive after death or transform into fish.⁴⁸ The belief in the transformatory power of water over fish and reptiles is also attested in a ritual instruction in the *Liji* which stipulates that during a period of heavy rainfall fish and turtles should not be used as food offerings.⁴⁹ One explanation was that, since rainfall could induce reptiles and snakes to transform temporarily into fish and turtles, servants had to be careful not to offer these transformed aliens as food to their masters.⁵⁰ Similarly, the identification of amphibians as demons was based on the perception that they could live on land or hide in water and hence were never completely visible. Early evidence for this occurs in a poem in the *Shijing* where an animal known as the *yu* 蜮, a kind of torpedo that hides in sand and mud and blinds or narcotizes humans by spitting sand at them, is paired with a *gui* because it cannot be hooked: "If you were a ghost or a spit-sand, you could not be caught."⁵¹

While none of the explanations of the calendar metamorphoses surveyed above is conclusive, it is likely that the notion of animals changing shape according to the passage of the seasons was also inspired by *yinyang* thinking. In chapter 3 we discussed how some texts sought to classify animals as being of a *yin* or *yang* nature. It was noted that these classifications were primarily functional and part of an overarching description of the cosmos as a whole, rather than constituting a systematic or widely accepted *yinyang* animal taxonomy. The functional nature of *yinyang* classification is also apparent in the explanatory logic behind the calendar metamorphoses that indicate that there is a *yin* and a *yang* aspect to each animal and suggest that mastering the seasonal changes through physical metamorphosis was part of the maintenance of the regular course of nature. Animal transformations in the calendar are perceived as the readable part of the seasonal patterns of change.

Just as the moral transformation of the animal world through music and virtuous governance was a hallmark of the sage, reading these metamorphoses in the animal world was the task of the sage-ruler. This can be inferred from references that link the comprehension of functional animal metamorphosis with human sagacity. Only a sage is said to be able to fathom the functional transformations of all creatures and understand that they are a genuine part of the natural process.

> Macrura turn into quails, and the water-scorpion becomes a dragon fly. They all give birth to a creature that does not belong to their own species, and only the sage knows their transformations.[52]

By linking the understanding of animal metamorphoses with human sagacity, the discourse on changing animals hence provided a model of intellectual authority that pictured the understanding of change as the highest accomplishment of the sage-ruler. As the next section will show, the assertion that sagehood was determined by one's ability to grasp change was also reflected in the interpretation of signs of physical change on the animal body.

Autonomous Transformations

Within the fauna of animals certain groups were more apt to metamorphose than others. Because of their natural disposition, amphibian and reptile creatures—including the dragon and the snake—figured prominently in metamorphosis cases. Their association with metamorphosis was inspired by their mutant nature; they slough their skin, live in water or tunnel beneath the ground, and move constantly between land and water.[53] The hybrid "mutant serpent" (*hua she* 化蛇), named for its ability to change, was a portent for floods.[54] The etymology of the graph *yi* 易 used to express change or alteration was explained as a drawing of a lizard. Xu Shen identifies it as a kind of gecko, which led Joseph Needham to suggest that its meaning is derived either from color changes or rapid shifts in position.[55] The image of reptiles and amphibians as paragons of change also occurs in descriptions of the Way, or Dao. Both the *Lüshi chunqiu* and the *Huainanzi* describe the workings of the Dao as "now dragon, now snake" (*yi long yi she* 一 龍 一 蛇).[56] Similar imagery occurs in the *Guanzi*:

> What is profound does not issue from the mouth or appear on the face.
> At one moment like a dragon, at another like a serpent,
> it may transform itself five times a day.[57]

Yet the attribution of sacred power to certain animals was not confined to observable, reptilelike natural qualities. Central to the association of daemonic power with particular animals in early China was the notion that these creatures were able to undergo physical, biotopical, spatial, and temporal changes. Numinous animals were described as creatures able to commute from one realm into another and change color, shape, or behavior according to the laws of nature and the laws of human society. The daemonic animal was able to transgress boundaries within its own species and the natural environment in which it was living. It could move from land into the sea, from the mountains to the plains, from the underground onto the surface, from the earth up to the heavens, or from the distant western regions into the Chinese cultural sphere.[58] These animals encompassed physical beauty, human virtue, and numinous power in one single body. In the same way that a hierarchy of spirit power was perceived within the various species following their ability to transform other creatures, a numinous hierarchy was also conceived according to their degree of formal "mutability."

The four sacred animals headed the list of their species, and the human sage shared a similar position among the naked animals. Each of these creatures has a composite composure and many among them are capable of changing their bodily features. A classical description of the unicorn held that it had "the body of a deer, the tail of an ox, and a horn on its round crane."[59] The phoenix, king and queen among birds, was "a swan at the front and a unicorn at the rear with the neck of a snake and the tail of a fish . . . having the texture of a dragon, body of a turtle, and the beak of a swallow that pecks like a chicken." The phoenix's encompassing power to represent all bird species is also confirmed in the statement that it "copies a hundred (all) shapes."[60] The sacred turtle is described as having a pentachromatic texture, a snake's head, and the neck of a dragon. It was also believed to have passed through a thousand years of transformation.[61] A passage preserved in the *Shiji* adds that the turtle "changes with things" and "transforms its colors according to the seasons" (spring-azure, summer-yellow, autumn-white, winter-black). Born in the deep springs and growing up on the yellow earth, the turtle was believed to know the ways of heaven and to understand the past. It symbolized permanence and surpassed human transience as its longevity outlasted that of ordinary mortals. As such the turtle transcended the normal boundaries of time. As a storehouse of fore-knowledge and wisdom it provided the material source for the divination of timeless truths in human affairs.[62]

The fabulous *luan* bird, or simurgh, encompassed various categories of color and sonority. According to the *Shuowen* it had a pentachromatic feather pattern, the shape of a fowl, and mastered a singing range that included all five tones.[63] The simurgh was also associated with the idea of transformation in the etymology of the 鸞 graph, which was linked to *bian* 變. Zhang Hua states that upon birth the bird resembles a phoenix and that after a while its five colors gradually change and alter (*bianyi*).[64] The simurgh has also been connected with solar symbolism and the image of the "soul-bird," an archetypal image of a bird representing the soul of the deceased.[65] Such theories on birds as representations of the soul remain inconclusive. However the idea that birds and the flight of birds symbolized transcendence into another realm, such as the transition from life to death or the flight to immortality, is well attested. Moving in a void between heaven and earth, bird flight embodied the cyclical alterations of *yin* and *yang*:

> The sounds of geese, an impressive sight!
> They rise up high and transform like spirits.
> Turning their backs to the darkness they face the light,
> through the Dao they are blessed and meritorious.[66]

This verse, preserved in an Eastern Han divination manual, evokes the image of the light-dark/*yang-yin* alternation scheme of the Dao symbolized by the southward migrating geese that glide over the earth (*yin*) heading toward the bright sun (*yang*). The goose is portrayed as the pivot of the *yinyang* alternations. As a *yang* bird—that is, a bird that flies away from the *yin* (shadow) toward the *yang* (sun)—its upward movement is compared to a spirit flight which, together with the alteration between light and darkness, evokes the image of the changing rhythms of the Dao.[67]

The champion of metamorphosis among early China's sacred animals was the dragon. Central to descriptions of dragons and other dragonesque creatures was the idea that they underwent physical changes. The expression "to transform like a dragon" (*long bian* 龍變) also provided an epithet for sagehood, authority, and encompassing virtue.[68] The following excerpt from the *Guanzi* summarizes the repertoire of metamorphosing qualities associated with the dragon:

> The dragon lives in water and, covered in the five colors, it roams about. Therefore it is *daemonic* (*shen* 神). If it wants to become small, then it transforms like a silk-worm or a caterpillar. If it wants to become big, then it conceals all under heaven. If it wants to ascend, then it rises with the cloudy vapors. If it wants to descend, then

it enters into the deep springs. There is no (fixed) day for its transformations and no (fixed) season for its ascending and descending. Thus it is called *daemonic*.[69]

As John Hay has suggested, in this passage the dragon is portrayed as "transformational both in constitution and habit, synchronically and diachronically."[70] An even more explicit exposition on the transformational character of the dragon forms the subject of the opening fragment in the *Ersanzi wen* 二三子問 ("The Several Disciples Asked"), one of the *Yijing* manuscripts found at Mawangdui. The text opens with Confucius praising the greatness of the dragon. He uses familiar imagery describing the dragon as the ultimate shape shifter encompassing *yin* and *yang* and enjoying the protection by the spirits of wind, rain, and thunder as well as the respect of all other animals.

> The several disciples asked, saying: "The *Changes* often mentions dragons; what is the virtue of the dragon like?" Confucius said: "The dragon is great indeed. The dragon's form shifts. When it approaches the Lord in audience, it manifests the virtue of a spiritual sage. . . . Into the deep currents, the fishes and reptiles surround it and of those beings of the watery currents there is none that does not follow it; perched up high, the god of thunder nourishes it, the wind and rain avoid facing it, and the birds and beasts do not disturb it." (He said): "The dragon is great indeed. While the dragon is able to change into a cloud, it is also able to change into a reptile and also able to change into a fish, a flying bird or a slithery reptile. No matter how it wants to transform, that it does not lose its basic form (*ben xing* 本形) is because it is the epitome of spiritual ability (*shen neng* 神能).[71]

This passage articulates in detail how the assumption of other animal shapes constitutes an expression of numinous power or "spiritlike capability." The sacred dragon is portrayed as an original shape or body that can manifest itself as every other species in the animal kingdom, be it avian, reptile, or piscine. In later sources this hybrid composition of the dragon became known as the "nine resemblances" (*jiu si* 九似), a definition ascribed to Wang Fu, who claimed that dragons incorporated the bodily parts of nine other animals.[72] The dragon's bodily composure combined parts of all other animal species, and its habitat and forms of locomotion encompassed those of swimming, winged, and running creatures alike. The dragon epitomized the image of the sacred animal as the embodiment of change. It encompassed the boundaries of species, space, and time, and represented all animals in one without losing its "original shape," its permanence or constancy within change.

The association of numinous powers with an animal's capacity to transform and incorporate physical parts of various species into one single body did not apply only to the most virtuous exponents of the animal kingdom such as dragons, phoenixes, and unicorns. Other animals were distinguished from the common herd following a similar logic, and spiritual authority was associated with creatures that displayed a composite physiognomy, complex texture, or variegated color. One example is that of the parrot. In his "Rhapsody on the Parrot," Mi Heng 禰衡 (fl. ca. 173–198 C.E.) portrays this bird as an exogenous creature that had come to China covering vast distances, a "holy bird (*ling niao* 靈鳥) coming from the Western Regions." Together with its qualification as a "holy bird" comes the statement that the parrot combines various colors and textures and that it surpasses its own kind in knowledge: "Although the parrot socializes with other feathered and hairy creatures, it surely has a different mind and heart."[73] As the allegorical double of the poem's exiled author, the caged parrot is described as an extraordinary bird with physical and behavioral features matching those of the familiar sacred animals. The idea that the parrot transcended the ordinary animal species was also reinforced by the belief that it could imitate human speech.[74] Other avian species with special powers include ominous spirit birds (*shen niao* 神鳥, *shen jue* 神爵). Han texts frequently depict these birds as multicolored or pentachromatic in accordance with five-phase theory (they are also known as "five-color birds," 五色鳥). The phoenix is presented as their master:

> Spirit birds are pentachromatic,
> The phoenix is their leader,
> They gather in royal valleys,
> and cause the ruler to obtain his position.[75]

The image evoked by the multicolored plumage of these spirit birds recalls the association of numinous power and virtue with the appearance of extraordinary physical patterns on the animal body. The previous chapter showed how several texts presented a parallelism between the daemonic nature of animals and hybrids and the pervasive qualities of the human sage expressed through the concept of *wen*, meaning both "cultured writing" as well as "decorative texture" or "pattern." The same notion of *wen* was apparent in the perception of "changing animals" as numinous beings. Animals with a changing skin texture provided the inspiration for discourse on change. Wang Chong draws a comparison between an animal's skin covering and the notion of *wen*:

> The fact that humans have "cultured writings" [*wen*] is like the beasts having hair. Hair exists in five colors and all grow on the body. (But) if one has (only) *wen* but no substance, this would be like pentachromatic animals whose hair grows disorderly.[76]

Wang compares belletristic writings without substance to a variegated hide which, although it contains the five colors, lacks an orderly texture. In the *Shizi* a passage arguing for a worthy's inherent nobility uses a similar comparison. It criticizes the idea that there should be a link between the development of an animal's skin and plumage patterns and the development of its natural instincts. As in the case of young beasts and birds, the worthy's instincts, that is, his potential sagacity, are said to be innate even prior to the development of any outward signs during the course of his life:

> Before the cubs of the tiger and leopard have developed their striped patterns, they are possessed with an "ox-devouring" impulse. Before the feathers of wild swan fledglings are fully developed, they have a heart of the four seas [i.e., fly everywhere]. As for the life of a worthy, it is similar.[77]

The patterning on an animal's skin also provided imagery used to express sagacious responsiveness to changing conditions. A good example of this is an analogy that compares the texture or pattern on the pelts of a series of felines with various degrees of responsiveness to change and the potential to metamorphose. Among its explanations of hexagram forty-nine—*ge* 革—the received text of the *Zhouyi* states that "the great man transforms like a tiger" (*da ren hu bian* 大人虎變) and has markings (*wen*) that are distinct, whereas "the gentleman transforms like a leopard" (*junzi bao bian* 君子豹變), having markings that are more obscure.[78] The text alludes to the fact that the stripes of the tiger skin are more refined and readily distinguishable than the texture of spots on a leopard skin. Given that the original meaning of *ge* is the molting of an animal's pelt, the idea of transformation here may have been inspired by the observation of a tiger and leopard skin.[79] Perhaps the patterns and stripes on these animals' pelts evoked the image of the constantly shifting lines in the hexagrams. While this interpretation remains speculative, the image was certainly powerful enough to inspire Yang Xiong to add a third animal to the series and clarify its internal order:

> The sage is distinguishable like a tiger: its patterns [*wen*] are clear. The gentleman is distinguishable like a leopard: its patterns are (more) obscure. The pedant is distinguishable like the wildcat: its patterns are densely (positioned) to each other. If the wildcat transforms, then it becomes a leopard; if the leopard transforms, then it becomes a tiger.[80]

This passage is part of a discussion on how one's outside patterns (*wen*) ought to relate to one's inner basis or substance (*zhi* 質)—"If one has the substance of a sheep but the skin of a tiger, then one is delighted upon seeing grass but perturbed upon seeing a jackal. One has forgotten the 'tiger-ness' of one's skin." Just as the distinct nature of its skin patterns makes the tiger easily distinguishable from other animals, so the sage is said to distinguish himself from ordinary people and petty intellectuals through his "cultured" or "civil" (*wen*) behavior.

Successive stages of moral transformation will turn a commoner into a sage: the wildcat's blurry pelt texture can transform into a spotted leopard skin pattern, which in turn can transform into the pattern of clear and distinct stripes of a tiger skin. The petty disputer can become a gentleman after one transformation, and the gentleman in turn can become a sage.[81] A classical precedent for the image of animal hides to distinguish inner disposition from outward appearance occurs in the *Lunyu*:

> Ji Zicheng 棘子成 said: As for the gentleman his substance (*zhi*) suffices. What does he need refinement (*wen*) for? Zi Gong said [. . .] refinement is no different from substance, substance is no different from refinement. The hide of a tiger or leopard, stripped of its hair, is no different from a dog's or sheep's hide, shorn of hair.[82]

In the analogy the difference between a tiger or leopard and a dog or sheep lies both in the color and patterns of their fur and in the stuff they are made of. *Wen* and *zhi* are said to be complementary and only theoretically different. The idea that external appearance (*wen*) without inner substance should be avoided also occurs in statements claiming that the stripes and spots on the tiger or leopard skin are the very reason for their death.[83]

The use of patterned animal hides to symbolize moral transformation and social principles in general was also evinced in the decoration on a ruler's chariot. According to Cai Yong a leopard tail was attached to the last in a row of chariots during the Han.[84] A post-Han source that dates the use of these "Leopard Tail Chariots" (*baoweiche* 豹尾車) back to the Zhou, states that these chariots were "the means by which was symbolised (the fact) that the gentleman transformed like a leopard; the tail meaning 'modesty.'"[85] The patterned stripes on an animal's skin also served as a physical comparison to social patterns or principles in human society. The *Taixuan jing* 太玄經 for instance states that "Ornate patterns are over embellished. If tiger and leopard were patterned thus, it would not please Heaven, it would be bad."[86] Finally, the metamorphosing abilities of the dragon were also linked with the concept of *wen* ("markings"). This is illustrated in the Mawangdui *Yi zhi yi* 易之義 ("The Significance of the Changes"):

> Confucius said: "The sage is trustworthy indeed. This is said of shading one's culture (*wen*) and keeping tranquil, and yet necessarily being seen. If the dragon transforms seventy times and yet is not able to lose its markings (*wen*), then the markings are trustworthy and reach the virtue of spiritual brightness."[87]

In addition to attributing numinous powers to animals that displayed extraordinary markings on their skins or plumage, creatures that underwent a complete physical metamorphosis were also linked with the image of encompassing sagehood. Given the omnipresence of sericultural activity in early China, the sight of silkworms transforming into spinning cocoons must have been quite common. A rhapsody on the silkworm (*Can fu* 蠶賦) preserved in the *Xunzi* presents the silkworm's biology as a metaphor for the sage's responsiveness to constantly changing conditions. Like the *bambix mori,* which transforms into a silk cocoon after twenty-two days, the sage is described as "continuously transforming like a spirit," "continuously transforming without growing old," and encompassing gender distinctions. Just as the silkworm eats the mulberry leaves and emits them as threads of silk, so the sage transforms chaos into order. The same rhapsody describes the silkworm as having "a feminine charm and a head resembling that of a horse."[88] Its metamorphic character was also evinced in a legend about the goddess of sericulture who was believed to have a horse head. An early medieval source tells the story of a girl who promised to marry her stallion if he could find her missing father. The horse did so but was slaughtered and skinned by the girl's father. Wrapped up in the skin of her stallion, she was found in a mulberry tree where she had metamorphosed into a silkworm.[89]

An equine creature that played an important role in the symbolical creation of sociopolitical and religious authority was the so-called heavenly horse (*tianma* 天馬), which was introduced at the court of Han Wudi around the turn of the first century B.C.E. The quest for and conquest of these fabled horses from the far western region of Ferghana served to demonstrate Han military strength. But more important than its practical use was its symbolical and religious significance. Obtaining the long-expected, dragonlike horse, said to be born from the waters, was part of the symbolic affirmation of Han Wudi's all-encompassing virtue and power.[90] Like other sacred animals, the heavenly horse derived its numinous powers from its ability to metamorphose and transcend the boundaries of species and geography. In one hymn it is described as a creature resembling a tiger with two spines which gallops on the clouds and "transforms like a demon."[91] The heavenly horse traverses the earthly and heavenly realms, roars over endless distances, comes and goes, appears and disappears. Furthermore, it was believed to match the spiritual powers of the dragon and represented as an avian creature with wings, or as a hybrid serpentine creature with a horse head.[92] As alter ego of the heavenly dragon, this horse was also known as the "dragon horse" (*longma* 龍馬) and harbinger or manifestation of the dragon (*long zhi mei* 龍之媒).[93] In Zhou times a horse taller than eight Chinese feet was called a dragon.[94] Behind such imagery of heavenly horses and winged dragon horses lurks a metaphor for imperial authority. Transforming dragons and heavenly horses embodied the ideals of the sage-emperor whose powers reached both the natural and supernatural realms. Like the composite dragon or heavenly horse, the emperor transgresses the boundaries of the ordinary human species. To no great surprise horses and dragons figured as standard escorts in descriptions of spirit journeys and quests for immortality.

The image of wings as a vehicle for the transition into another realm thus obtained its counterpart in the animal realm in the shape of avian horses and winged dragons that accompanied human immortals. And just as the animal acolytes connected with the immortals had metamorphosing powers bestowed on them, so human immortality was linked with the idea of bodily transformation and the belief that immortals grew wings and feathers. For instance the legendary immortal Wang Ziqiao 王子喬, who became the subject of cultic worship by the late Han, was alleged to have turned into a bird and flown off. He is also documented as rising to heaven on a white crane. According to a stele inscription, possibly compiled by Cai Yong, immortal Wang appeared at his family tomb next to which the stele was erected. Wailing noises were heard at the tomb during the *la* 臘 festival of 137 C.E. Upon investigation people noticed tracks of a large bird in the snow near the grave.[95] Max Kaltenmark has suggested that in the spirit geography of the *Shanhaijing* such winged immortals and barbarian bird-people with a physiognomy resembling that of immortals were located on the eastern edges of the Chinese cultural sphere, near the lands of immortality.[96]

If numinous power among animals was identified with the ability to metamorphose, transcend one's habitat, and respond to changing circumstances, these were precisely the features associated with the human sage. The *Shuoyuan* notes a parallel between the idea of change and locomotion claiming that, just as "there is none among the supreme spirits that does not change, there is none among the supreme worthies who does not move place."[97] This image echoes Confucius's ideal of the itinerant scholar-politician who crosses the boundaries of states to offer advice to different rulers: "A gentleman who cherishes a settled home is not worthy of being a gentleman."[98] It also tallies with imagery of transforming animals who cross habitats and temporarily alight in the courtyards and gardens of virtuous rulers.[99] A text fragment attributed to Ying Shao defines someone who "transforms like a dragon" as someone with the capability to transcend local custom:

> Man must rise transforming like a dragon. One should not be tied to one's village or hamlet. If a person is restrained by and tied to local custom, he will not change residence upon seeing something good, and therefore will be called a commoner (*suren* 俗人).[100]

"Transforming like a dragon" here distinguishes the commoner from the sage, who is said to be capable of transcending the local airs and alight at the palaces of foreign rulers who will solicit his counsel. Elsewhere the sage's flexibility to changing circumstances is compared to the phoenix's reliance on the winds: the phoenix rides on the winds, whereas the sage relies on the seasons.[101] Yet the power to transcend local custom was also a source of frustration. Like the sage, the sacred animal had no fixed abode. Its distant journeys between heaven and earth and its travels between remote regions and domestic heartlands evoked the perpetual peregrinations of the sage whose enlightening wisdom was the source of his transformatory influence while at the same time containing the kernels of his eventual demise and misunderstanding. Whereas the "common birds all have their roosting-places, only the phoenix hovers distractedly with nowhere to alight."[102] Like the sage, the sacred animal roamed over vast distances and constantly changed habitat.

While sacred and fabulous animals may have been more influential in breaking down the species barriers than the ordinary animals of the manors and peasant communities of Warring States and Han China, the faculty of metamorphosis was not confined to creatures that signified sagehood, virtue, and good fortune. As we have seen, several texts note how lesser specimens such as worms, clams, rats, and doves could turn into or change out of other animals. Documentary evidence such as demonographies and divinatory records further indicate that the capability to assume different shapes applied equally to baleful animals and demons in the narrow sense of the word.[103] These texts do not theorize regarding the moral nature of such creatures and are mainly concerned with how humans should counter them. That transforming animals were not always virtuous or auspicious can also be seen in references to parasitic worms and vermin, which cause disease by invading the healthy body and transforming it into a diseased body. The physician engages in the task to diagnose change in the body and respond accordingly. For instance in one medical case history preserved in the *Shiji* the famous physician Chunyu Yi 淳于意 (second cent. B.C.E.) diagnoses "bowel bug (pinworm) conglomeration" as the pathogen for an illness resulting in the swelling of the abdomen and an epidermic rash. The physician attributes the occurrence of the malign bug to a density of cold and moist, which prevents the *qi* from escaping from the body where it then transforms into intestinal worms. The patient's symptoms are identified as being caused by "worm vapor."[104]

Symbolic Metamorphosis

The references to changing animals discussed so far attempt to explain physical metamorphosis in the animal world by coupling the notion of change with the generation of power or, alternatively, by linking the archetypal characterization of the sage as a master of change with the idea of metamorphosis in the animal kingdom. Another form of metamorphosis documented in Warring States and Han texts was the exertion of spirit power through the assumption of an animal form or the adoption of animalistic characteristics.

Studies on contemporary shamanism have led several scholars to address the role of the animal as a representational medium in early China. The question whether or not animals functioned as mediums in the communication with the spirit world in early Chinese religion and ritual has been, and will no doubt remain, an issue of debate. Various interpretations have been given to the zoomorphic motifs on Shang and Zhou bronze vessels and artifacts. Chang Kwang-chih has argued that the animal iconography on these bronzes was not merely decorative but served the function of assisting the shamans to communicate with the spirit world. According to Chang, offering animals in bronze vessels may have been a concrete means of achieving contact with the other world, and animal designs on ritual vessels could be interpreted in the same context. If animals were seen as acolytes of shamanic powers, the possession of animal-styled bronzes may have symbolized the possession of the means to communicate with the spirit world.[105]

The exact meaning of the major motif on Shang bronzes, an animal face often seen as two dragons facing one another and known as the *taotie* 饕餮, remains an enigma. While an early reference to the *taotie* occurs in the *Zuozhuan,* where it is identified as one of four evil creatures during the time of the Yellow Emperor, it is a passage in the third century B.C.E. *Lüshi chunqiu* describing the *taotie* as a bodiless glutton trying to devour a man which has traditionally been linked to the bronze animal mask.[106] Although most scholars accept that, in addition to their decorative function, these motifs must have been iconographically meaningful, there is less agreement as to whether such zoomorphic imagery alluded to real or imagined animals and, more importantly, how it should be interpreted in terms of Shang and Zhou myth and cosmology. Sarah Allan has argued that the primary allusion in these zoomorphic motifs is to transformations of state. The recurrent bronze motif of the gaping mouth and the tiger devouring humans may allude to the sacrificial feeding of the spirits, the passage of death, or the transition from the human world to the realm of the spirits.[107] Others have argued that the *taotie* represented a kind of spirit mask aiding shamans in their communication with the spirit world. Elisabeth Childs-Johnson has suggested that animal imagery on Shang bronzes can be identified as a symbol of supernatural or daemonic transformation from the human to the animal realm, symbolizing "access to supernatural power through transformational identification with the hunted wild animal."[108] While none of these theories on the role of animal imagery in the archaic religion of the Shang and early Zhou are conclusive, they do suggest that animals, either in their function as food for the spirits, or as imagery on masks and bronze vessels, played a role in facilitating communication with the spirit world. That this process may have been linked to varying representations of human-to-animal or animal-to-spirit metamorphosis is therefore not implausible.

More solid is the textual evidence from the Warring States and early imperial period that strongly suggests that the symbolical identification with animals was perceived as a source of numinous power. The enactment of representational metamorphosis can be seen in late Warring States and Han shamanic practices and is illustrated by the role of the spirit mediator and the function of the spirit mask. The physical identification with animals was further evinced in the ritual use of animal skins and hides as well as in magico-religious practices during which ritual officiants adopted animal postures or imitated animal behavior.

According to the *Zhouli* a spirit medium or functionary known as the *fangxiangshi* 方相氏 covered his face with an animal mask and wore a bearskin during annual exorcismal rites at the *nuo* 儺 festival.[109] These bearskin hoods reportedly had four golden eyes, which led Kaltenmark to suggest that they revealed the double human-cum-animal nature of the shaman. In his classic study of the *nuo* ritual exorcism, Derk Bodde suggests that the four eyes symbolized the shaman's ability to scrutinize evil spirits in all four directions.[110] Judging from descriptions of the way in which these annual *nuo* processions were conducted during the Han, at the heart of the ceremony was a shaman brandishing a lance and shield to drive away noxious influences from the palace. The shaman was accompanied by twelve attendants disguised as spirit beasts wearing fur, feathers, and horns. A spell was chanted to urge these costumed actors to devour a host of evils and expel dreams. Various other officials put on wooden animal masks to participate in the exorcisms. The identification with animal powers enacted by disguising the face with an animal mask or by wearing its skin reinforced the officiant's power to deter malign influences through the medium of a monstrous facial expression. In a list describing the physical countenance of past sages, Xunzi even likens Confucius's face to an exorcist's mask. By comparing Confucius's facial complexion to an animalistic spirit mask, a device used to repel evil influences and enhance communication with the spirit world, Xunzi links human sagacity with spirit power and physical ugliness or deformity.[111]

Evidence suggests that animal skin itself was thought to be endowed with metamorphosing powers and that the enactment of a metamorphosis into animal form required wearing an animal skin and mimicking animal sounds.[112] A received gloss for the graph for skin or hide, *pi* 皮, was *bei* 被 meaning "to cover the body."[113] The skin itself may have been considered as the essence of an animal, its "vital wrapping."[114] Wang Chong notes that when birds and beasts die, their flesh is completely exhausted while skin and hair remain.[115] Ying Shao records a custom in which a concoction of burnt tiger skin was administered to exorcise evil forces.[116] Other sources suggest that the association of spirit power with an animal's hide applied to clothes in the case of humans. For instance an anomaly account dated to 20 C.E. reports that the tiger-striped grave clothes of the deceased Emperor Xuan left the inner coffin in his tomb and planted themselves upright outside the inner chamber. A similar event allegedly happened at Emperor Ai's 哀帝 funerary chamber twenty years earlier.[117] Possibly coverage by an animal skin or hide was believed to symbolize or induce metamorphosis. This is attested in a reference in the *Mu Tianzi zhuan* where the Son of Heaven's spirit drum (*ling gu* 靈鼓), a drum covered with a reptile or animal skin, is said to transform into a yellow snake. Such spirit drums were used to summon the spirits of the earth, hence the color yellow.[118]

Just as shamans exerted their influence over the spirit world by wearing animal hides and masks, so barbarians mastered the animal world by clothing themselves in animal hides or imitating animal patterns or designs on their skin. This lore is particularly rich with reference to southern tribes. Traditionally the southern regions inhabited by tribes such as the Yue were associated with a folklore that was rich in magic and demonic beliefs. Yue people, according to Sima Qian, customarily believed in demons and engaged in divination by means of chicken bones. People from Chu and Yue were said to be strong believers in omens.[119] Furthermore the air of the south was thought to be malignant and have a detrimental influence on the creatures that had to live in it. The exiled general Ma Yuan 馬援 (14 B.C.E.–49 C.E.) noted that the poisonous waters of the south functioned as a natural barrier even to animals. The river Wu 武 was rife with virulent plague so that "birds could not fly across, and beasts were unable to come to its banks."[120] Southern animals were also associated with poison. Most notable among them was the *zhen* 鴆 or "secretary falcon" whose feathers were decocted to brew a deadly poison. People reportedly dreaded entering the southern seas because the *zhen* falcon lived there, and anyone who would drink fluids that had been in contact with this bird was sure to die.[121]

Southern people living in these tropical and swampy climates were identified with fishy creatures. The Yue tribes were equated with reptiles and watery creatures because of their custom to tattoo their naked bodies with reptile patterns (*wen shen* 文身). Tattooing the body, together with cutting off the hair, served to avoid being wounded by alligators and dragons.[122] By imitating scaly animals southerners thus acquired superior powers in handling aquatic creatures. They were employed as swimmers who entered the waters to attack and hunt scaly creatures and water monsters. Yang Xiong lauds their fiercesome hunting skills in his "Rhapsody on the Barricade Hunt":

> Next the tattooed men display their skill;
> they wrestle scaly reptiles in the water.
> They cross the solid ice,
> defy the awesome pools.
> They search the rocky shore and twisting banks,
> seeking out dragons and crocodiles.
> They step over otters and muskrats,
> Grab turtles and alligators,
> Seize the magic tortoises . . . ,
> they mount huge sea monsters,
> ride giant whales.[123]

This portrayal of tattooed fishermen illustrates again how the adoption of physical animal *wen* was believed to engender power over the wilds. In the case of another barbarian tribe the adoption of external animalistic features is set against a myth of origin which features a metamorphic genesis involving a miraculous birth from an animal. The Ailao 哀牢, whose ancestor was impregnated by a drifting tree that had transformed into a dragon, tattooed their bodies with dragon patterns and wore clothes to which they attached animal tails.[124] Snake imagery and portrayals of shamans wielding their powers over the spirit world through handling snakes were prominent in Chu religion.[125]

Another form of symbolical metamorphosis related to shamanic animal impersonation was the mimicry of animal movements. A number of Warring States and Han texts make reference to the adoption of animal postures as an act of engendering magic power. A southern dance for the invocation of rain in which children imitated a one-legged bird was mentioned in the previous chapter. In oracle bone and bronze inscriptions the graph for Kui 夔, the legendary master of music and dance, possibly represented a drawing of an apelike creature or a shaman disguised in animal skin and wearing a mask.[126] The assumption of animal postures was also believed to have a magical efficacy in the treatment of demonic illness comparable to the apotropaic effects produced by exorcistic animal dances.[127] Bodily animal postures as well as therapeutic animal pantomimes also occur in early physical cultivation literature. For instance sexual manuals found at Mawangdui contain lists of sexual positions and movements such as the "roaming tiger," "cicada clinging," "monkey's squat," and "rabbit bolts." Names of physical exercises associated with *daoyin* 導引 ("guiding and pulling") on a chart found at Mawangdui and in a manuscript excavated from a tomb at Zhangjiashan 張家山 (Jiangling, Hubei, mid-second cent. B.C.E.) refer to animal postures such as the "bird stretch" and the "bear ramble."[128] While such names no doubt functioned as an imaginative terminology for gymnastic exercises, it is not implausible that they grew out of a belief that the assumption of animal postures engendered therapeutic effects on the body.

The mimicry of animal postures was also attested in a military training ritual known from the Qin onward as "horn butting" (*juedi* 角抵). During these sessions wrestling contestants wore horns on their heads, presumably to identify themselves with the powers of bulls.[129] While it is difficult to establish with certainty the exact symbolism behind these horned dances, there is strong evidence that horn butting as well as the wearing of a cap named after the horned *xiezhai* 獬豸 beast were linked with legal procedure. One source credits this animal with an innate sense of justice: "In ancient times there was a *xiezhai* beast which butted the treacherous and cunning. Therefore, those who maintain the law base themselves on the shape of its horn to make a cap."[130]

There is evidence of other imitative animal dances. One Han dance in which actors played animal roles was known as the "ballet of the Manyan monster, the fish and the dragon (*manyan yu long zhi xi* 漫衍魚龍之戲)." According to a Tang commentator this performance began with one actor dancing at one end of the courtyard dressed as a *sheli* 舍利 beast, a "fish-dragon" reportedly known for its habit of spitting gold. When this act was finished the creature entered the front hall of the palace and splashed into water to transform itself into a paired-eyed fish. The fish then emitted nebulae obscuring the sun, and by the time the clouds had dispersed, it had turned itself into a yellow dragon, which came out of the pool to dance in the courtyard.[131] Zhang Heng's "Rhapsody on the Western Capital" gives a vivid description of a similar performance in which actors enact the roles of a whole range of fabulous animals:

> There was a giant beast one hundred *xun* long;
> This was the *manyan*.
> A sacred mountain, tall and rugged,
> Suddenly appeared from its back.
> Bears and tigers climbed on, grappling one another;
> Gibbons and monkeys leaped up and clung to a high perch.
> Strange beasts wildly capered about,
> And the great bird proudly strutted in.
> A white elephant marched along nursing its calf,
> Its trunk drooping and undulating.
> A great sea-fish transformed itself into a dragon,
> Its form writhing and wriggling, twisting and twining.
> The *hanli* [*sheli*], mouth gaping,
> Changed into a sylph's chariot,
> Which was harnessed to a four-deer team,
> And carried a nine-petal mushroom canopy.
> The toad and tortoise were there,
> And water denizens played with snakes.[132]

These pantomimic dances and mimicry displays may have been arts most skillfully practised by barbarians. The histories of the Later Han speak of barbarian tributes including musicians and magicians who were able to metamorphose and transform, spit fire, dismember their own limbs, and change around the heads of oxen and horses.[133]

As in human rituals such as hunting and sacrifice where participants may take on the appearance of prey or predator by the use of masks, costumes, and animal skins, the ritual movements of the pantomimic animal dance were another expression of the symbolical identification with the nonhuman world. The symbolical transformation into an animal detached the subject from the normal classificatory schemes and engendered in it spiritual powers that bridged the categories of the human, the supernatural, and the divine. The idea of a person being possessed by the spirit of the animal he is mimicking has also been explained as an expression of a transition of the regular world into a world of chaos.[134] This psychological stratum—physically identifying with an animal implies becoming one—could give further ground to transformation stories.

In addition to aiding shamans, dancers, and ritual officiants in their communication with the animal world and the realm of the spirits, the collection, tribute, and targeting of animal hides and skins also served to celebrate the symbolic subjugation of the animal world. It was Marcel Granet who drew special attention to the fact that the character *fu* 服, apart from its use in the sense of "subjugating vassals" or "domesticating wild animals," also carries the secondary meaning of "wearing clothes" or "to put on a disguise."[135] That the parallel proposed by Granet was not far-fetched is corroborated in text passages that interpret one's external disguise (such as clothes, animal furs, masks) as a reflection of one's inner character. An early example of a parallel between one's external (dis)guise and one's heart or inner disposition, which also incorporates the image of *wen,* occurs in a passage in the *Guoyu*:

> Clothes are the expression of one's heart (*fu xin zhi wen ye* 服心之文也). It is like the tortoise [shell], if you stick a burning pole in it, there must emerge an expression (*wen* 文) on the outside.[136]

This passage compares the reading of someone's character to a diviner's cracking of a tortoise shell and suggests that in the same way that divinatory cracks on a plastron shell manifest the tortoise's foreknowledge of affairs, one's external *wen,* or embellishments in the form of clothes, are a reflection of one's internal nature.

Similarly animal hides were symbolical representations of the wilds and its inhabitants. As was noted in chapter 4, kings and emperors maintained parks and menageries to assert their sway over nature and empire. Animal hides figured prominently as tokens of political submission. According to the *Liji* the ritual display of tiger and leopard skins served to demonstrate a ruler's power to "subdue" the wildly natured (*fu meng* 服猛, that is, "subjugate the barbarian vassals").[137] The decorative exhibition of exotic animal hides and their use as clothing were an assertion of a ruler's power, not only over the animal specimen from which they were stripped, but also over the human populations sharing their habitat with these wild animals. Just as adopting animalistic features endowed the ritual officiant with numinous powers and empowered him to communicate with the spirit world, so collecting the hides of wild and exotic animals and occasionally donning oneself with its most potent physical symbol, the skin or hide, engendered a subjugating power in the figure of the hegemon. Adopting *fu* (guise) enabled one "to *fu*" (subdue).

This enactment of power through the symbolic appropriation of animal hides can also be seen in descriptions of archery ceremonies. According to Han ritual manuals, archery targets and tally holders used during shooting rituals were decorated with animal motives:

> As for targets, the Son of Heaven's target has a (picture) of a bear's (head) on a white background; the feudal lord has an elaphure target on a red background; a great officer has a cloth target background, with (the heads) of a tiger and a leopard drawn on it; the ordinary officer a cloth target, with (the heads of) a deer and a pig drawn on it.[138]

Jeffrey Riegel has suggested that the skins of the bear, tiger, and leopard used to cover target stands were meant, together with the humanoid configurations in which the targets and their stands were cut, to be "manifestations of the erratic malcontents who dared to challenge the king's sovereignty."[139] Elaphures (*mi* 麋), according to one explanation, were targeted to keep deceitful (*mi* 迷) vassals at a distance, and shooting deer and pig targets would rid the fields and crops of harmful animals.[140] Elsewhere reference is made to animal hides and skins as the representation of the beast's essence on the targets they cover or decorate. The *Zhouli* mentions the office of the Manager of Furs whose task it was to provide animal skins that served as targets during archery ceremonies. This officer is said to supply tiger skin targets, bear and leopard skin targets, and deer skin targets according to the rank of nobility of the participants (royal: tiger, bear, leopard; feudal lords: bear, leopard; grandees: elaphures).[141] Here the status of the marksmen is symbolized by the animal(s) drawn on their target(s). By exerting his skillful dominance over the target hide, the marksman controlled the forces of the represented animal. In the same way that weaker animal species are dominated by more fierceful predators, the most ferocious animal specimen (tiger-bear-leopard) were targeted during royal archery contests to enable the ruler to symbolically assert his dominance over his subordinate officers and vassals. The *Shuowen, Bohutong,* and *Lunheng* describe the targeting of these hides as a method to "subjugate the ferocious" (*fu meng*), the same function the *Liji* had associated with the collection of animal hides as tribute. These statements corroborate the symbolical link between animal furs, hides, or skin and the notion of *fu* 服. By aiming at the skin, the marksman aimed at the whole animal and at the whole animal species it represented, thereby symbolically transferring some of the animal forces associated with his target onto himself. From shooting at his target, to quote the *Bohutong*, "each (marksman) takes on the power that enables him to subdue (*fu*)."[142] That the act of shooting itself was associated with the demonstration of power is further attested in statements claiming that, on important ritual occasions, a ruler or sacrificial officiant was expected to "personally shoot" (*zi she* 自射, that is *ipso manu*) the wild animal or sacrificial victim involved.[143] Finally the targeting of animal hides was also linked with the idea that there exists a relationship between external guise and inner disposition and the rhetoric that equated barbarians with animals on the basis that they were dressed in animal hides. By shooting at animal hides, the ruler transformed the animal targets (*hou* 候) into yielding vassals (*hou* 候).[144]

Evidence suggests that these ritual shootings were accompanied by the performance of songs intoning the fearsome image of these animal targets. Ballads known as the *zouyu* 騶虞 and a piece entitled *li shou* 貍首 ("Head of the Wildcat") were performed during archery ceremonies.[145] While the latter piece is lost, the former was inspired by a *Shijing* ode that compares the ruler-hunter with a fabulous beast known as the *zouyu*.[146] This creature has been variously described as a virtuous animal, a white tiger with black stripes which does not eat other living creatures or tread on living grasses, or a strange beast with a tail double the length of its body. The poem describes how the ruler-hunter kills five wild boars discharging only one arrow. Whether, as the Mao preface suggests, the *zouyu* was a righteous beast appearing as a response to King Wen's transformatory government and heralding the completion of the "kingly way," or whether it was the name of a hunting officer or park supervisor, both interpretations support the image of a ruler exerting his authority through "targeting" the wilds.[147]

Portentous Transformations

"Changing animals" also inspired sociopolitical discourse in preimperial and early imperial China. Animals that undergo transformations were often perceived as indicators of social or political change. The observation of change among the living species, both physical and behavioral, became part of a wider philosophy of social and dynastic change. In the same way that early Chinese animal classifications combined biological and cultural criteria in their explanation of mutual species relationships, the interpretation of changing animals portending social or political changes exemplified how the hermeneutic of the natural world was firmly rooted in the discourse on the governance of human society.

Metamorphic animal imagery was part of the rhetoric indicating a change in dynastic power or shifts in political fortune. After the conquest of the Shang dynasty by Zhou King Wu a cloud of fire allegedly assumed the shape of a red crow as a sign of the consolidation of the Zhou.[148] The dynastic transition from Qin to Han was also colored with metamorphic animal imagery. The first Han emperor Gaozu, born from the union of his mother with a dragon, killed a white snake in a spell of drunkenness. The snake was the son of the White Emperor, who had metamorphosed himself into a white snake to block the road of Gaozu's conquering troops. The act of killing this ominous animal symbolized the end of the Qin line, the opening of the "road to Han," and the conquest of red over white, Han over Qin.[149]

Theories that sought to establish cosmological justifications for empire, sovereignty, and rulership proliferated during the early imperial period. Together with the increasing importance of philosophies that perceived systematic correspondences between the workings of human society, the natural world, and the cosmos as a whole, growing attention was paid to the observation and interpretation of unusual events in the natural world such as physical meta-morphoses among the living species. While early imperial sources provide the richest thesaurus of animal transformations as portentous indicators of change, the recording of such species changes was certainly not a new Han phenome-non. For instance the *Zhushu jinian* 竹書紀年, parts of which predate the East-ern Zhou period, mentions a woman changing into a man, a horse turning into a human being, and a horse turning into a fox.[150] The *Mozi* records a woman turning into a man as a consequence of the untimely sacrifices of Shang tyrant Zhou.[151] Lisa Raphals has argued that such references should be seen against the background of other passages in the *Mozi* that correlate the disintegration of human civilization with the transgression of the sexes, "human failures in the correct construction of gender have been transposed onto the external world it-self."[152] Few of these pre-Han references to species and gender change, however, received contemporary social or political interpretations.

It was not until the Han that elaborate interpretative schemes emerged in which physical metamorphoses of living beings were classified into groups and systematically interpreted as indications for social or cosmological change. Metamorphoses in the natural world were interpreted as anomalies, meaningful flaws in the balance of nature or the course of history.[153] The canonization of these portentous metamorphoses culminated in Ban Gu's "Treatise on the Five Phases" ("Wuxing zhi" 五行志) which set a precedent for similar treatises in later dynastic histories.[154] Metamorphic imagery in the Treatise includes animal mutations and human gender changes, sexual union between creatures of a dif-ferent species, miraculous births, and the appearance of hybrids and physically deformed creatures. A substantial number of these cases are drawn from earlier sources. In the Treatise however they are given a new social, political, or cosmo-logical explanation by Han interpreters such as Jing Fang 京房 (the second, died 37 B.C.E.), Liu Xiang, Liu Xin, Dong Zhongshu, Ban Gu and others. In addition to the sociopolitical clarification of animal transformations, attempts were also made to categorise animal anomalies under separate headings. Hence the Trea-tise refers generically to prodigies involving insects and footless reptiles as *nie* 孽 "calamities," those involving the six domestic animals are called *huo* 䄆 (禍) "misfortunes," and those concerning human beings are called *e* 痾 "sickness."[155] Further Liu Xiang speaks of "chicken calamities," "cow calamities," "dog calami-ties," "sheep calamities," "fish adversities," "pig calamities," "dragon and snake adversities," "snake adversities," and "horse calamities."[156] While in many cases an anomalous animal event referred to in the Treatise was in origin no more than an isolated occurrence in a Warring States source, by reorganizing and interrelat-ing unusual contemporary and past animal events within generic categories, the

Han interpreters had extolled physical transformations in the animal world as a statement on the workings of human society and the entire cosmos itself.

The metamorphoses in the *Hanshu* portent treatise do not constitute isolated demonic transformations or a spontaneous change of form in accordance with the rhythms of nature. Instead, the physical changes documented in the Treatise forebode events and changes that pointed beyond the particular metamorphosis case. Portentous metamorphoses are presented as either the result of or an indication of sociopolitical changes to come. They are the physical translation of the changing course of human affairs. Some examples will illustrate this. The portent treatise elaborates on three cases involving a chicken transformation. These cases are interpreted as portending the gradual rise to power of the Wang 王 clan toward the end of the first century B.C.E. In 49 B.C.E. a hen was reported to transform into a rooster, "its plumage covering had transformed but it did not crow, nor lead its flock, and it had no spurs." A year later another hen was reported to gradually transform into a rooster while brooding over its chicks; this time the rooster had a crest, spurs, was crowing, and led its flock. The final case in the sequence was a report that during the Yongguang 永光 reign (43–38 B.C.E.), someone had donated a rooster that had grown horns.[157] The interpretation of the chicken-to-rooster transformations all center around imperial concubines and their families taking power. The first transformation is said to prefigure the Wang imperial concubine (Zhengjun 政君) becoming empress (12 April 48 B.C.E.). The reference to the rooster not crowing, leading, or growing spurs would indicate that the gradual "transformation" of the Wangs to power had so far only reached its germinal stage. The second transformation signalled the gradual enfeoffment of the Wangs and their rise to high posts, the hen "brooding over its chicks" indicating that there were more Wang scions to come. Finally the rooster growing horns prefigured the establishment of Wang Feng 王鳳 (regent, 33–22 B.C.E.), which heralded the start of the Wangs' gradual usurpation of power culminating in the reign of Wang Mang (9–23 C.E.).[158]

Sima Biao's 司馬彪 (240–306 C.E.) treatise on the five phases preserved in the *Hou Hanshu* reports a similar chicken transformation for the year 178 C.E., in this case a hen that was in the process of turning into a rooster. The plumage on its body already resembled that of a rooster but its head and crest had not yet been transformed. In the interpretation of the event, Cai Yong refers to the chicken transformations portending the rise of the Wang clan at the end of the previous dynasty. He then advises the emperor: "If your government does not introduce reforms, the chicken's head and crest might complete (the metamorphosis), and the calamities that will ensue will be even worse." The latter refers to the impending Yellow Turbans rebellion (184 C.E.).[159] In another memorial Cai Yong states that the downfall of winter cicadas and chicken metamorphoses all come about when women usurp government.[160]

The *Hanshu* treatise further documents human females changing into males predicting the victory of the power of *yin* and incompetent people usurping political power.[161] Animals giving birth to animals of a different species or to human beings are interpreted as portents for a break in the succession or a change in ruling clan. A report of a swallow giving birth to a sparrow in 7 B.C.E. concludes with an explanation that "if the new-born is not of the same species, the son will not be heir."[162] Again precedents for such events occur in other sources. For instance the *Zhanguo ce* records that at the time of King Kang 康 of Song 宋 (337–286 B.C.E.), a hawk was hatched in a sparrow's nest. The omen was explained as a sign that the small had given birth to the great, and that Song should reign over the empire (a task the king failed to accomplish).[163] Horses giving birth to human beings are compared to Qin's reliance on violence, which ultimately led to its self-destruction. Qin's political hubris was frequently compared with unruly bestial behavior.[164] Numerous references are made to animals that interbreed or cross-breed with pernicious consequences.[165] Such anomalies were said to announce the breakdown of lineage relations and the topsy-turvy nature of human hierarchy.

> When pigs give birth to fish and bream,
> And rats dance around in courts and halls,
> Villainous flattery will spread its venom,
> The notion of superior and subordinate will blur,
> And the ruler will lose his state.[166]

While hybrid animals, as was noted in the previous chapter, often embodied the idea of virtue and sagacity, Ban Gu's portent treatise also explained a number of hybrids and deformed creatures as physical conglomerates of *yin* and *yang* in one single body. Creatures that assumed shapes in between the species provided physical representations of disturbances in human society, flaws in a historical process, or the derailment of a dynastic cycle. Features of anatomical deformity were explained either in general terms or applied to a specific historical event. For instance a deformity whereby the lower part of the body grows on the upper part is explained as prefiguring the emergence of lower-rank officials over a careless ruler. Horns or antlers sprouting on dogs, horses, and human beings are taken to be indications of violence or armed rebellion.[167] Yang Xiong alludes to the portentous significance of horns by stating that "oxen (without horns) and horses with horns do not exist in the present nor did they in the past ... Hornless oxen and horned horses alter Heaven's constancy."[168] The following extract from the *Hanshu* portent treatise illustrates the extent to which physical changes and deformity were detailed. It follows a report of the birth of a deformed child in Chang'an (anno 1 C.E.):

> Jing Fang's *Yi zhuan* 易傳 states: "Perverse solitude: seeing a pig carrying mud on its back." Its prodigy will be people growing two heads. . . . If in the case of human

beings and the six domestic animals head and eyes grow below, this means that they neglect superiors and that what is regular will be changed. Whenever a prodigy comes about, it is there to reprimand the loss of regularity, each of them signifying according to its category. "Two heads" means that the subordinates are not united. "Many feet" means that what one is in charge of, is of an evil nature.[169] "Few feet" means that subordinates cannot handle their responsibilities, or that (the ruler) does not take responsibility over his subordinates. In all cases where lower body parts grow above, it means a lack of respect.[170] When the upper body parts grow below, it means that one commits an outrage to women and is rude. If one gives birth to what is not one's species, this means illicit chaos. If a human being upon birth is big, then superiors will speedily accomplish themselves. If upon birth one can speak, then one will like empty talk. In the case of all prodigies these categories can be extrapolated. If one does not reform then they will turn into misfortune.[171]

The last sentence implies a message to the ruler and human society in general. Symptoms of physical change have to be read as indications of anomalous human behavior and ought to be responded to by the world of man. The ruler has to change to meet change, or as Lu Jia suggests, the worthy gentleman possesses a sense of knowledge that "follows these transformations and causes him to reform."[172] Understanding the hidden meanings behind physical changes among the living species and responding correctly with human changes—that is, virtuous government—constituted a model for political authority. It was a way to preserve the social polity from sinking down to a bestial existence.

Through subsuming the metamorphosis of living creatures into an overarching model that sought to explain changes and misdemeanors in human society, Han discourse on changing animals had reduced the last vestiges of a naturalistic logic behind animal metamorphosis to a debate on human governance. While commentators to the metamorphoses in the calendar still attempted on occasions to give naturalistic explanations to the phenomena, the portent interpreters of Han equated changing animals with social and political changes in the world of man. Through the compilation, rearrangement, and categorization of physical animal anomalies from past and present into a unitary catalogue that provided a model for the analysis of portents in later times, the Han interpreters had shifted the analysis of natural anomalies to the realm of textual exegesis and substituted the investigation of regular and irregular events in the natural world with the scrutiny of textual records *about* nature.

Metamorphosing Agents

It is hard to establish with certainty how the internal mechanics behind animal metamorphosis were understood. One factor that makes any hypothesis on the issue troublesome is the polysemantic nature of the key terms used to express change or transformation such as *yi*, *bian*, *hua*, and others. While in many cases *bian* appears to refer to gradual or partial changes and *hua* to more sudden and profound transmutations, upholding strict semantic differences between these terms across different texts does not always accurately reflect their intended significance. Nathan Sivin has cautioned readers to keep general discussions of this terminology within the internal scope of the text under investigation.[173] Angus Graham proposed the following generic meanings for the main terms denoting change: *yi* 易, "substitute, exchange": X replacing or changing places with Y; *hua* 化, "transform": X changing into Y; *bian* 變, "alter": X changing but remaining X.[174] While the semantic nuances of these terms should certainly not be overlooked in the context of the philosophical or lexicographic analysis of individual texts, they fail to shed light on how animal metamorphosis was understood other than that it entailed a condition of change and nonpermanence, a basic idea associated with each of these terms. In a subcommentary to the *Liji*, the Tang commentator Kong Yingda attempts to explain the concepts *bian* and *hua* in terms of old versus new. He uses the seasonal animal transformations in the calendar as examples:

> The initial flow is called *bian*. When something is *bian*-ing, both the new and the old body are in existence together. The *bian* process terminates the old body and brings into existence the new body, this is called "causing *hua*" [*wei hua* 爲化]. It is as in the Monthly Ordinances (which say that) the pigeon *hua*-s into a hawk. This means once it has become a hawk it cannot become a pigeon again, just like a good man cannot have a bad character again.[175]

A few scattered references indicate that a soul or a similar entity may constitute the agent that makes a creature turn into another being. The Appended Statements in the *Zhouyi* (*Xici* 繫辭) refer to the "wandering *hun* soul" (*you hun* 遊魂) as a transforming agent: "Seminal vapors make up beings, the wandering *hun*-soul makes up transformations."[176] The dynastic history of the Later Han mentions the origin story of the Ba tribe who descended from a king whose *hun* 魂 and *po* 魄 souls had transformed into a white tiger after his death.[177] J. J. M. De Groot, the first Western scholar to treat the subject of zoanthropy, sought to classify metamorphoses in two categories: those based on soul mutation into a different species, and the purely corporeal metamorphosis.[178] His analysis however draws mainly on post-Han sources and the emerging *zhiguai* 志怪 literature from the third and fourth centuries C.E. The value of his thesis lies in the suggestion that metamorphosis did not necessarily imply a transition of a transcendent or immanent soul or spirit.

There is insufficient evidence in Warring States and Han texts to substantiate the existence of a soul mutation theory. Distinguishing a unified soul concept remains an even more precarious matter. Furthermore, the attribution of a soul to animals is rare. One example occurs in a Han ballad where a crow's *hun* and *po* are said to fly off to Heaven after the bird had been shot dead.[179] Another passage in Yang Xiong's "Rhapsody on the Barricade Hunt" states that the startled and exhausted game animals have "their *hun* lost and their *po* gone," although this expression might just refer to the fact that the animals had lost their spirit to resist the hunters.[180] Zhang Heng's "Rhapsody on the Southern Metropolis" states that the *hun* of both humans and animals can be shaken by sad music, and in his "Rhapsody on the Western Capital" animals are said to lose their way, "bereft of spirit, devoid of soul (*sang jing wang hun* 喪精亡魂)."[181]

There is evidence that, by Han times at least, it was thought that old age could transform creatures into other creatures, demons, or spirits. In his famous "Owl Rhapsody" Jia Yi describes dying as changing into an alien thing: "A thousand changes, a myriad transformations with never any end. If by chance one becomes human, how could that be a state to cling to? If one transforms into another creature, what cause is that for regret?"[182] Related to this was the belief that demons were spiritual remainders of old beings. The fact that the first-century critic Wang Chong argues at length that humans are endowed with an unchangeable body that is not subject to metamorphosis, and that bodily metamorphosis does not increase one's life span, could be indicative of the widespread acceptance of such beliefs at the time.[183] Finally, reference is made to the transformation of blood. The blood of humans, horses, and oxen that had died on the battlefield could, according to several sources, turn into a lightening blaze known as "demon fire."[184]

Critique of Change

The question whether or not the causes for animal transformations were deeply implicated in the course of human affairs was subject to a lengthy evaluation and criticism in the work of Wang Chong, who recapitulates many of the aforementioned metamorphosis references. Wang Chong firmly denied the possibility that heaven could interfere purposefully in the affairs of men. As a result, throughout the *Lunheng* the social interpretation of animal transformations is met with skepticism. However the main tenet of Wang Chong's criticisms did not center on the denial of the phenomenon itself, rather it consisted in questioning its interpretation. Wang accepted the existence of animal metamorphosis as a phenomenon and also recognized its sociopolitical basis. In a chapter on omens he acknowledges the fact that seasonal metamorphoses befall all species:

> Sometimes when human government is at peace and the *qi* is in harmony, various living creatures transform and change. There is spring when the hawk transforms

into a pigeon and autumn when the pigeon changes back into a hawk. The species of snakes and rats abruptly turn into fish and turtles, frogs turn into quails, pheasants into bivalves. Living species transform according to their *qi*. One cannot deny this. . . . Sometimes in times of universal peace and when the *qi* is in harmony, a hornless river-deer may turn into a unicorn and a snow-goose into a phoenix. This surely is the nature of their *qi*; they transform and change with the seasons. Why should there necessarily be a species that remains permanent?[185]

Elsewhere in a rebuttal against the belief in human immortality, Wang argues that frogs can indeed change into quails, and that sparrows dive into the water to turn into clams. He attributes this to their original nature while at the same time refuting the fact that transformation can be attained through artificial means such as studying the Dao.[186] According to Wang's analysis, at times of sociopolitical harmony (thought to be a precondition for a peaceful man-animal cohabitation) animal transformations are not anomalous but natural and indicate that the cosmic pattern of constant change has not been disturbed by human behavior. Animals that turn into other animals should thus be seen as the physical hallmarks of cosmological harmony.

Wang makes a distinction between humans and other creatures with regard to their innate aptitude to metamorphose. Humans are said to possess an unchangeable body; whereas it lies in the nature of animals such as dragons and cicadas to transform: "Creatures which by heavenly nature do not metamorphose cannot be induced to metamorphose again. Creatures that metamorphose cannot be induced not to do so." In Wang's view human males turning into females and vice versa is a phenomenon that is not predetermined by heaven but emerges as a response to a human intervention. He considers these to be induced transformations, which form no part of a human being's regular nature.[187] While Wang's argumentation suffers from inconsistencies to the point of being plainly contradictory at times, his attention for the subject of animal transformation bears testimony to the currency of two popular assumptions that may have been held at the time: first, the idea that animals can change into and out of each other and, second, a predominant tendency to explain this phenomenon not according to a natural logic but following a sociopolitical model.

Wang Chong is also critical of the interpretation of interbreeding species. As an example he discusses the case of Bao Si 褒姒. As the favorite of Zhou King You 幽 (781–771 B.C.E.), Bao Si's extravagance is said to have played a major role in the ruin of the Western Zhou. Legend held that she was born out of the sexual union of a palace girl and a black sea turtle. This turtle was the product of a metamorphosis out of the saliva of two dragons that battled at the end of the Xia dynasty.[188] While Wang acknowledges the influence of this concubine's illicit behavior on the downfall of the Western Zhou, he is hesitant to accept the idea that a family history in which the interbreeding of different species had occurred necessarily needs to be interpreted as prefiguring a break in succession or genealogy. Since turtles and humans are a different species, a turtle would never be attracted by a palace girl to "emit its vapor":

> Having intercourse with a black turtle was not regular. Therefore Bao Si caused calamities whereby the Zhou perished. When one has reckless intercourse with (a creature) that does not belong to one's species, there will be offspring which is un-principled and mischievous. Now the mothers of Yao and Gaozu had illicit inter-course [with dragons]; why then did these two emperors become worthy and sage men? Is this any different from the Bao Si case?[189]

Finally Wang Chong's critique links physical metamorphosis with the idea of immortality and the preservation of the body. For instance, in his inter-pretation of Gongniu Ai's transformation into a tiger, he states that animals can metamorphose into a human body only if this body is still alive with quintes-sential *qi*. Once the body is dead and has decayed "no strength of a rhinoceros, nor a tiger's ferocity could make it change again."[190] When creatures have meta-morphosed they will not return to their previous state: "Once a chrysalis has changed into a cricket, and once its wings are fully developed, it cannot change into a chrysalis again."[191] Despite its internal inconsistencies Wang's skeptical evaluation of the subject reflects the gradual development of a belief in bodily transformation connected with immortality throughout the late Warring States and early Han period and prefigures the intensified growth of such beliefs throughout the Eastern Han into early medieval times.[192] The image of reptiles, metamorphosing amphibians, and cicadas emerging from the pupa would soon be linked to escapist aspirations for immortality, transcendence, bodily transformation, and ideas about the "release from the corpse" (*shi jie* 尸解).[193] Thus testify the opening lines of a poem by Zhong Changtong 仲長統 who wrote at the end of the Eastern Han:

> Flying birds leave behind their traces,
> Cicadas shed off their exuviae (skin),
> Mounting snakes leave behind their scales,
> The spirit dragon drops off its horn,
> The perfect man is able to metamorphose,
> The comprehensive gentleman transcends the vulgar.[194]

Indeed, documentary evidence of animal transformations in the ancient texts shaped a precedent for theories developing in the post-Han era which claimed that humans, like their counterparts in the animal world, could undergo bodily transformations leading to physical immortality. Thus while references to animal metamorphosis in the original texts may have been lapidary, fragmentary, and scattered within different contexts and genres of writings, they never-theless provided a canonical patchwork from which later authors would select and conjecture examples in support of their theories of physical change and bodily transformation. To illustrate this, I end this chapter with a passage from Ge Hong's 葛洪 (ca. 280–342 c.e.) *Bao Puzi*, a text that recollects many of the animal transformations documented in Warring States and Han writings.

> If you claim that all creatures endowed with *qi* have one and the same fixity, your thesis cannot be sustained, for the pheasant turns into a bivalve, the sparrow into a clam, earth worms assume wings, river frogs come to fly, oysters become dragon-flies, *xingling* 行苓 plants become maggots, field mice become quail, rotting grass turns into fireflies, alligators become tigers, and snakes become dragons. If you claim that humans, unlike ordinary creatures, have a regular nature . . . how can you account for cases where Niu Ai became a tiger, the old woman of Chu a tortoise . . . the dead coming back to life and males and females changing sex?[195]

Conclusion

Against the background of a cosmogony largely devoid of ontological separa-tions or structural differences between living beings, several texts from the Warring States and Han period asserted that living creatures in the natural world, along with plants and minerals, originated through a process of constant transformation and metamorphosis. As a result, the observation of "changing animals" and metamorphic imagery in the natural world was firmly embedded in these texts. The observation that living species could undergo varying forms of metamorphosis was not an isolated theme. It figured within a broader dis-course on change and transformation that pervaded early Chinese thought.

Various forms of animal metamorphosis were documented in early China. They ranged from demonic human-to-animal transformations result-ing from moral retribution, to animals that metamorphosed according to the cycle of the seasons or changes in their habitat. Other forms included species whose physique was subject to spontaneous mutations, hybrids who incorpo-rated bodily parts of different species in one, and humans who identified them-selves with the animal world through the symbolical enactment of animal behavior and the use of animal masks and animal hides. Finally a number of animal transformations were identified as portents signaling changes in the course of human events or impending alterations to the cosmic cycle.

To be sure, the thematic distinction between these forms of metamor-phosis as presented in this chapter—demonic, functional, autonomous, sym-bolic and portentous—is sui generis rather than the product of a theoretical classification in the texts themselves. The contexts in which reference was made to "changing animals" varied, and certain cases can be explained by combining different aspects of the working typology proposed here. One element however characterized most of these interpretations of changing animals; namely, the idea that physical metamorphosis and the transgression of the species were connected with numinous power and concomitantly had meaning beyond the mere perception of animal transformation in the natural world. Animals that were apt to metamorphose were signifying animals. Within the internal confines of the animal kingdom, animals that metamorphosed or incorporated characteristics of various species into a single body were perceived to possess numinous power sometimes compared to human sagehood. Similarly, physical bodily changes in the animal world had a warning or reprimanding power with implications beyond the natural order.

Metamorphosis in the animal world also figured in the creation of ideals of sagehood. The sage-ruler was expected to comprehend patterns of change in the animal realm and read meaning in these physical transformations. He was a mediator of change who had to distinguish natural balance from physical anomaly and accordingly respond to these with human changes. Since the notion of change and transformation was a principle simultaneously operative in both the human and animal world, metamorphosing animals were seen as the physical embodiment of a changing universe that also constituted the habitat of the human animal. However, as the final chapter will show, the prevalence of a world view in which species boundaries were blurred did not preclude that certain animals were identified as strange and abnormal prodigies.

CHAPTER SEVEN

STRANGE ANIMALS

If one looks upon prodigies as not being prodigious, then their prodigious nature will annihilate itself.

—Xie Zhaozhe 謝肇淛 (1567–1624).[1]

The dialectic of moral transformation that linked the world of man to the animal world, the association of metamorphic animal behavior with sagacity and numinous power, and the portrayal of metamorphosing animals, crossbreeds, and hybrids as indicators of cosmological and sociopolitical change, all contributed to the conflation of the animal as a natural and cultural category in early China. The tangent line between human culture and the physical animal world was marked by a continuous flux that blurred the notion of a fixed species. In addition the discourse on changing animals insisted that human society was firmly dependent on signs from the natural world for the self-sanctioning of its own workings. By tallying natural changes with changes in the sociopolitical realm, human society and the animal world were projected as parallel worlds subjected to the same cosmic laws. While both physical or biological as well as symbolical imperatives provided the rationale for the explanation of the animal world as a changing reality, the categories of "culture-man-morality" and "nature-animal-bestiality" were not perceived as two independent realities. Instead both worlds were viewed as interdependent spheres subject to constant change and mutual influence. Animals therefore rarely existed "an sich," but were perceived as signifying creatures inspiring meaning beyond the physical order to which they belonged.

Despite the widely received notion that the amalgamation of species boundaries was part of the regular course of nature, certain animals and animalistic creatures that displayed physical deformities or hybrid features were singled out and set apart as being "strange," ominous, or anomalous. While changing animal behavior, as we have seen, was frequently left unquestioned and accepted as a normal pattern embedded in nature, a number of animal observations were given particular attention in the written record of Warring States and early imperial China. Unnatural animal behavior and anomalous events in the animal world were registered in detail as many of these occurrences were believed to be pregnant with social significance. This final chapter will deal with the discourse on these white ravens and examine the semantics behind the interpretation of "strange" animals.

As had been the case with theories that sought to relate animals to human office, ritual, music, territory, and metamorphosis, the perception of strange animals likewise drew the physical animal firmly into the realm of the observer and the human polity. And in the same way that the human sage had been cast as the source of moral transformation of the natural world, numerous texts presented the sage as the unspoken expert in the explanation of strange creatures. The interpretation of strange animals thus constituted another pillar in the generation of a model of sagehood. Furthermore the discourse on strange animals reinforced the perception that the animal world was not to be understood as a purely natural realm separated from a world inhabited by ghosts and spirits. Both worlds merged in varying composite or daemonic creatures that prompted interrogation, interpretation, and response. The interpretation of such strange creatures was a prerogative of the sage who mediated the notion of strangeness through subsuming the interpretation of freaks into receptive categories. And, as had been the case in descriptions of the human-animal relationship and the mutual rapport among the various animal species, the idea of change was a central theme in the interpretation of anomalies in the animal world.

Defining the Strange

Throughout the previous chapters I have argued that the early Chinese did not devote much energy to the protoscientific classification of the animal world and its components and did not insist on describing and analyzing patterns of biological universality or differentiation that applied to one or more animal groups. A question that arises then is whether categorical notions of anomaly, abnormality, or "strangeness" can be defined when a unified and univocal classificatory system, an explicit nomos of the animal world itself, is left unarticulated or, more importantly, is not conceived of as strictly biological in nature.

Anthropological research has shown that anomaly is an essentially taxonomic affair and that categories of anomaly are not necessarily factual but constitute representations and experiences of abnormal events to an implicit or explicit audience. Anomalies are cultural constructs accessible only against the background of an implicit and shared notion of order and normality.[2] Every system of classification therefore produces its own anomalies. Since the early Chinese understanding of the animal world was not rooted in the analysis of an objectified biological reality, abnormalities that reflect or affect specific animal behavior did not necessarily require explanation within a framework of biological normality. The absence of explicit zoological theories did not preclude the early Chinese from developing a systematizing discourse on crossbreeds, freak animals, and hybrids. While in many cases the symbolic value of particular animals was linked with their taxonomic anomaly, Warring States and Han writings often remained silent on the "regular" or "normal" classificatory framework against which unusual animal appearances were judged. What was regular or normal often remained implicit and was left unsaid.[3] On the other hand, the extraordinary gets into the written record because the observer assumes that it is "note-worthy" and needs clarification. What is textualized and transmitted to the contemporary historian is the anomaly rather than the system that generates it—here we may find another reason why ordinary animals receive less textual attention than fabulous species. Even with an implicit understanding of normality, what is perceived to be strange ultimately still depends on the mindset of the observer. The motivations underpinning the observer's justification to interpret and record certain natural kind as anomalous also depend on other factors such as the circumstance in which the observation is made or the audience to which it is reported. The idea that anomalous animal kind or freak animal behavior solely came to the observer out of nature and its biological orders can be laid aside.

Several passages in Warring States and Han texts assert that freak appearances and animal anomalies are not embedded in nature but develop from particular features of classificatory schemes that originate with the observer or the human subject in general. While the appearance of ominous animals had since long found its way into texts—most notably in the *Shijing* where the observation of certain animals and animal sounds frequently provides a "comparison" or "stimulus" that runs through the rest of the poem—we must wait for China's oldest historical chronicle, the *Zuozhuan*, to find more detached comments on the causes, workings, and status of strange appearances in the natural world.[4] In the following passage, a grandee from the state of Jin defines anomalous events in terms of a "contravention" (*fan* 反) against the temporal, physical, and moral order:

> When Heaven goes against (the normal course of) the seasons it causes calamities (*zai* 災); when Earth goes against (the normal nature of) its creatures it causes prodigies (*yao* 妖); when people go against virtue they cause chaos (*luan* 亂); when there is chaos then calamities and prodigies are produced. Therefore in the written language the character for "regularity" (*zheng* 正), when reversed, gives the character for "deficiency" (*fa* 乏).[5]

This passage firmly denies the existence of a natural cause that may occasion prodigious events. At the heart of this definition is the premise that human disorder and a lack of virtue, through its pernicious influence on the course of heaven and earth, are the first cause for the occurrence of prodigies. The argument is further reinforced by invoking the idea of the inversion (*fan*) of normality in the world of written graphs.

　　Another early theoretical remark that focuses more specifically on the nature of an anomaly involving animal behavior is preserved in the *Zuozhuan*. It accounts how at the time of Duke Yan 嚴 of Lu (fl. ca. 679 B.C.E.), two snakes— one from inside the city (*neishe* 內蛇) and one outsider (*waishe* 外蛇)—fought each other in the southern gate of the capital of Zheng. The "inner snake" is reported to have lost the fight and died.[6] According to the chronicle this remarkable event would prefigure the return of Duke Li 厲 of Zheng (679–673 B.C.E.), represented by the outer snake, to claim his throne after having been forced out of his state six years earlier. Han interpreters saw this prodigy as a sign for mistrust when establishing a successor.[7] More important for our purpose than its inclusion in a specific historical narrative is the *Zuozhuan*'s explanation of the general principle underlying this mysterious event. In response to a question whether Duke Li's restoration had indeed ensued from this prodigious event, a grandee named Shen Xu 申繻 gives the following reply:

> When people fear something, their *qi* flames up and takes hold of them. Prodigies (*yao* 妖) come forth from man. If people have no pretext for strife, prodigies do not come about by themselves. When people neglect constancy, prodigies arise. Therefore prodigies exist.[8]

While acknowledging that the snake fight was a prodigious event, Shen Xu denies that freak animal behavior is embedded in the natural order and attributes the appearance of such events to the human subject—namely, misdemeanor and rivalry among humans. Like the previous passage which ascribed the inversion of regularity to human chaos, the cause for the animal anomaly is firmly attributed to irregularities in the human order. The lack of "constancy" or "normality" (*bu chang* 不常) is caused by the human subject, hence its translation into an animal anomaly.[9] Furthermore the prodigy is linked to an emanation of *qi* which is said to "overheat" and take possession of the person in which it lodges. Centuries later Wang Chong would argue that the snakes were not real snakes but merely prodigious vapors that resembled snakes fighting each other.[10]

　　This basic principle illustrated in the *Zuozhuan* according to which anomalies are to be attributed first and foremost to the mental state or social behavior of the human observer underwent no major conceptual shifts in the following centuries. In texts of the early imperial period, similar ideas are reported in speeches and memorials that sought to explain unusual events. For instance Lu Jia ascribed the emergence of calamities and freak events to "malign *qi*" that originated from bad government.[11] *Yinyang* specialist Yi Feng 翼奉 (fl. ca. 45 B.C.E.) held that anomalies were caused by the obstruction of *qi* in human beings:

I have heard that when a human being's *qi* internally counter-flows, it stirs up motion in heaven and earth. Heaven's transformations appear in the *qi* of the stars and the solar eclipses. Earth's transformations manifest themselves in strange creatures and quakes.[12]

The association of freak events with the disintegration of human government and the counterflow or obstruction of *qi* was reiterated by court officials in the Eastern Han. Responding to the appearance of a green snake on the imperial throne in 172 C.E. Yang Si 楊賜 maintained that "harmonious *qi* brings about good fortune while obstinate *qi* brings about disaster." He then quotes from the *Shangshu*, from an ode in the *Shijing* ("Si gan" 斯干, Mao 189) that associates snakes with signs for the involvement of women, and refers to the snake fight in the *Zuozhuan* as a precedent.[13] A similar explanation is given by Xie Bi 謝弼 (ca. 169 C.E.) to the appearance of a snake together with torrential storms. According to Xie, harmonizing one's *qi* corresponds to the presence of virtue while prodigies and freaks originate from a flaw in government. Furthermore snakes are said to be produced by *yin* and scaly animals are to be interpreted as presages for armed rebellion. Among examples from the past, the same verse from the "Si gan" ode is quoted.[14] Common to these scholars' explanations was the desire to detect a direct relation between human government and animal anomalies through establishing a typology of physiognomic or physical correspondences. In this respect Wang Chong ridicules the calendar specialists for claiming that insects with red heads would emerge as a response to demeanors by military officials while black-headed vermin would be produced by civil officials.[15]

In addition to assigning the causes for the emergence of strange creatures to the human order, their appearance was also attributed to the observer's misapprehension of a cosmogony of change that was thought to influence every creature and event in the world. Such explanations aimed to rationalize freak occurrences by asserting that they would lose their "strangeness" when viewed as part of a greater pattern of change and transformation. In a much-debated chapter on the nature of Heaven ("Tian lun" 天論), Xunzi contends that order and chaos ought to be attributed to man's actions and that ill omens and prodigies do not automatically bring about misfortune. Since Heaven is morally neutral, prodigies can only be seen as the outcome of its regular operations and thus require a naturalistic explanation. Xunzi advises humans not to fear strange appearances or freak events since they are merely part of the "normal" natural course. This normal course of nature is defined as an order of change and transformation:

> When stars fall down or trees groan the people in the state are terrified. They ask me for the reason behind this, and I reply that there is no specific reason. They represent the transformations of heaven and earth (*tian di zhi bian* 天地之變),

the changes of *yin* and *yang* (*yin yang zhi hua* 陰陽之化), and constitute rare appearances in the world of things. We may consider them strange, but we should not fear them.[16]

Xunzi goes on to argue that only calamities precipitated by humans should be feared, and among these prodigies caused by the human order he includes poor agricultural practice and unseasonable labor causing cows and oxen to interbreed, and the six domestic animals to give birth to monstrosities. The notion that a comprehension of the deep structures of heaven would erase fear and confusion over strange appearances in the visible world reverberates elsewhere. Such ideas were part of a philosophy which held that the world could be unfolded into different levels of reality: on the one hand a deep structure that remains unnamed and is comprehensible to the prescient and clairvoyant sage only, and, on the other hand, a common reality of delusive visible perceptions. In an attempt to dissuade Emperor Cheng 成帝 (33–7 B.C.E.) from his increasing reliance on superstitious practices and beliefs in ghosts and spirits, Gu Yong 谷永 argued that a comprehension of the basic workings of the universe would bleach away the illusion of anomalous appearances: "I have heard that if one understands the nature of Heaven and Earth one cannot be deluded by spirits and prodigies; if one knows the nature of the myriad creatures, one cannot be misled by anomalies." He ends his memorial by invoking the *Lunyu*'s portrayal of Confucius as a sage who does not talk about oddities and spirits.[17]

The correlation between the observer and the conception of the strange has been articulated most eloquently by Guo Pu 郭璞 (276–324 C.E.) in his preface to the *Shanhaijing*. In an attempt to debunk contemporary skepticism regarding the fantastic nature of the creatures and events featured in this text, Guo argues that anomaly or strangeness (*yi* 異) does not emerge out of the inherited nature of objects themselves but springs from the perception of the subject.[18] Guo maintains that people become accustomed to frequently observed objects and find strange those things which rarely meet the eye. As historical precedent he refers to King Mu's legendary cosmic peregrinations and collection of exotica suggesting that these accounts, for which a textual record had just been recovered from a tomb in 297 C.E., had not met with the same disbelief or scrutiny by contemporary scholars. Although writing almost seven centuries after the report on the snake fight in the *Zuozhuan*, Guo Pu's comments still conform with the understanding of prodigies as it had been upheld by scholars in the Warring States and early imperial period. Both Guo Pu's explanation and the above selected comments, which resurface as an elitist response to commonly held beliefs in omens and fears of anomalies, signal two main points. First, animal anomalies originated with the observer, their degree of strangeness depended on the observer's ability to unravel their cause as rooted in the human polity. Second, coping with the strange therefore depended on a perspicacity to see beyond what appears strange, and to explain the strange as normal, that is to de-anomalize the animal prodigy.

Interpreting the Strange

As we have seen, central to Warring States and Han perceptions of sagehood was the notion that the sage was able to explain or question the continuity between the workings of human society and the patterns that governed the natural world. This interpretative role of the sage was also reflected in the early Chinese discourse on animal anomalies. Just as human sagacity was associated with the power to morally transform the animal realm and parallel with the identification of the sage or ruler-king as the agent who responded to change in the animal realm, the sage mediated the confines of anomaly in the animal world.

A general characteristic of early Chinese narratives on the strange is that the anomalous nature of a particular creature or event appears as a negotiated concept. It is the result of a process in which an observer questions a particular observation and "thinks it strange" (*yi zhi* 異之, *guai zhi* 怪之), followed by an explanation or interpretation by a sage, a worthy minister, or a master. The stratagems used by the sage to explain strange appearances rarely consist of a straightforward disapproval or denial of the prodigy or its occurrence. Rather the interpreter attempts to "de-anomalize" the strange through classifying it within receptive categories. In the clarification of strange occurrences the primacy of the sociopolitical over the miraculous is upheld. The sage does not doubt or refute the sociopolitical origins of animal omens or the signifying message behind anomalous animal behavior but questions the commoner's perception of the event as being strange. The sage explains the strange "as if it is normal" and criticizes the observer for perceiving a prodigy as being prodigious. Through specifying the catenary relationship between human activity and animal behavior, the sage disrobes the prodigy of its abnormality.

A description of the "Great *Ru*" (*da ru zhe* 大儒者) in the *Han shi waizhuan* summarizes the pivotal role of the sage as a master of the strange:

> When it concerns matters of benevolence and righteousness, even in the case of birds and beasts, he makes distinctions [as clearly as] between black and white. When strange creatures and mutant prodigies which he has never seen or heard of suddenly emerge somewhere, then he brings up a comprehensive category (*tong lei* 統類) in order to respond to them; having no doubts, he brings forward a model and measures them as exactly as [two parts of] a tally fit together.[19]

This passage justifies the sage's comprehensive grasp of reality by appealing to his ability to apply unifying categories to the unknown. The sage is said to possess the innate capability to respond to moral (*ren yi* 仁義), natural (*niao shou* 鳥獸), and supernatural (*qiwu bianguai* 奇物變怪) occurrences by slotting them into appropriate categories. His reaction is not the result of a premeditated process of deliberation but rather a spontaneous and instantaneous "knack" to respond to the emergence of the unknown. Furthermore the sage is said to bring order to unusual appearances by putting forth a comprehensive or controlling category (*tong lei*) as a framework of explanation. He comprehends the natural and super-natural worlds through the application of unifying categories and the revelation of deep structures. This image accords with a general skepticism in early China regarding the assumption that knowledge of the natural world is attainable through the differentiation, division, and subdivision of species or kind. While engaging in the act of differentiation (*bie* 別) between what constitutes human or bestial behavior in the realm of morality ("the sage distinguishes between benev-olence and righteousness even in the case of animals"), when faced with un-known occurrences in the natural world, the sage's performative response consists of bringing forward a unifying typology. At the heart of the sage's mental mastery of all phenomena in the world lies his ability to assess whether and to what degree one ought to carve up the world into recognizable realities, and when to bring up unifying categories in order to interrelate all phenomena, in-cluding those which appear incomprehensible at face value. The sage thus pos-sesses the ability to shift the framework of explanation and broaden the range of reference in his explanation of prodigies: he attempts to assign a unifying cate-gory to a variety of different physical appearances, extrapolates from observation to explanation, and clarifies the prodigy's image by relating it to a more familiar appearance.

This identification of the sage as an agent able to assign visible animal prodigies to a broader cosmic picture concealed from the eyes of ordinary men appears in several texts. A passage in the *Huainanzi* argues that the sage has the perspicacity to see beyond what appear to be strange creatures because he grasps the basic notion of change that underlies their emergence. While ordi-nary people are alarmed by prodigies, the sage remains unperturbed.

> Moreover there are no strange creatures of heaven and earth. When male and fe-male mate, and *yin* and *yang* blend together, in the case of the feathered species it produces chicks and fledglings; in the case of the hairy species it produces foals and colts. The soft element becomes skin and flesh, the solid element becomes teeth and horns. People do not consider this strange. Water gives birth to sea shells and clams, mountains produce gold and jade. People do not consider this strange. Old ash-trees produce fire and old blood becomes demon fire. People do not consider this strange. Mountains emit the *xiaoyang* 梟陽. Water gives birth to the *wangxiang* 罔象. Wood gives birth to the *bifang* 畢方. The well produces the *fenyang* 墳羊.[20] People consider these strange because they rarely hear or see them

and because their knowledge of things is shallow. As for strange creatures under heaven, only the sage sees them. The ups and downs of their benefit and harm are only clearly apprehended by a knowledgeable person.[21]

According to this passage sages, unlike the common people, need not rely on frequent observation of the natural world since they possess an innate knowledge and insight in the *yinyang* patterns through which the various species emanate into the world. Anomaly is said to be a subjective interpretation which originates from the frequency or rarity of perception by the observer. This is illustrated later in the text when it states that pigs are valued most as sacrificial victims not because of their intrinsic value but because they are a familiar and easily obtainable commodity. Furthermore the passage also refers to the habitat or "field" (mountains-water-wood-well) that produces strange creatures and suggests that the same pattern that begets the ordinary hairy and feathered species familiar to the common people is also at the base of the emergence of prodigies from water, soil, wood, and mountains. Gao You's commentary identifies these hybrid creatures as the refined essence or "genie" (*jing* 精) of their habitat, hereby associating the sage's comprehension with his ability to grasp the nature of the most "essential" creatures or those that may be perceived to be prodigious by the common people.

The sage's power over the unfamiliar is attributed to his ability to master "shape-shifting" creatures while ordinary people merely grasp the image and appearance of familiar creatures and relegate the unfamiliar to the realm of ghosts and spirits. In an anecdote in the *Han Feizi*, a painter explains to the king of Qi that dogs and horses are harder to draw than ghosts and demons since people know them and see domestic animals on a daily basis. Ghosts and spirits have no shapes and are therefore easier to represent since they permit room for interpretation.[22] Implicit in this anecdote is a critique that unfamiliar creatures are too easily explained away as ghosts and demons. Since representation in image amounts to "imagination," the incapability to differentiate image from reality is commonplace among those who are disturbed by unusual appearances. This incapacity to distinguish image from reality is also illustrated in the story of Zi Gao 子高 (fl. ca. 523 B.C.E.), the Duke of She 葉, who was so fond of dragons that he had his lodgings decorated with carvings of dragons. When one day a real dragon descended in front of his residence he ran away in fear. The duke's fashioning of dragon images had prompted the arrival of a real dragon. The duke did not like real dragons but merely their resemblance.[23]

A passage in the *Han Feizi* links the concept of imagination with a lack of familiarity or visualization in a pun on the character *xiang* 象, meaning both "elephant" and "image":

> People rarely see living elephants, but when they find the bones of a dead elephant, they base themselves on the structure of the bones in order to imagine it as a living

elephant (*an qi tu yi xiang qi sheng* 案其圖以想其生). Therefore the means by which people are able to have ideas and imagination are called "elephants/ images (*xiang*)." Although the Way cannot be heard or seen, the sage grasps its visible functions in order to determine a vision of its bodily form. Therefore the [*Dao de jing*] states: "The formless form, the 'substance-less' image."[24]

This passage pictures the sage as an agent capable of interpreting images as a referent to a reality that is not visible to the common eye. The sage makes present what is absent in its bodily or physical form. He need not see the whole animal "in flesh" in order to explain its appearance and fix its visible manifestation but grasps the essential skeleton structure of an appearance to make manifest the "fleshed-out" parts that may give rise to imagination. The image is reminiscent of the butcher in the *Zhuangzi* whose skill is superior because he possesses a comprehensive grasp of the essential anatomy and skeleton structure of his animal and no longer visualizes a real ox in front of him. The same idea is expressed in the statement that a sage is able to know the entire length of a snake when it lifts up its head by only one foot, or the saying that a sage needs only to see the tusks in order to assess an elephant's size.[25]

To summarize, in describing the stratagems of a sagacious response to uncanny creatures the above passages present the sage as an agent who reduces the shapeless and changing prodigy to fixed and familiar categories. They suggest that deducing the true nature of an event or a physical appearance when it is still in its germinal stage and assessing a proper response to it constitute the hallmark of the sage. To recapitulate with the *Huainanzi*:

> Therefore the sage is someone able to be *yin* or *yang*, weak or strong; he moves or remains tranquil according to the times; he establishes merits relying on natural disposition. When creatures move he knows their return (*wu dong er zhi qi fan* 物動而知其反); by attending them in their germinal stage he examines their transformations (*shi meng er cha qi bian* 事萌而察其變); when they change he establishes an image for them (*hua ze wei zhi xiang* 化則爲之象); when they circulate he establishes a response to them (*yun ze wei zhi ying* 運則爲之應). Therefore during his lifetime there is nothing that troubles him.[26]

It is this imperturbability in the face of physical mutations which is also praised in Guo Pu's preface to the *Shanhaijing*: "The Sage or August One goes to the origins of change (*yuan hua* 原化) in order to get at the heart of transformation (*ji bian* 極變), he connects an 'image' to creatures (*xiang wu* 象物) in order to respond to the uncanny."[27]

One recurrent context for the explanation of animals as daemonic creatures was the dream. This may be explained from the nature of the dream concept itself, which was closely linked to the idea of transformation in Warring States and Han China. Just as prodigies were explained as ephemeral appearances, dreams were said to deal with images (*xiang* 象). The dream swayed on the brink of what was portrayed as real, actual, and normal as opposed to what was imagined by the observer or the person who dreams.[28] The ephemeral nature of the boundaries between a real experience and the experience in a dream is epitomized in the well-known parable of Zhuangzi who did not know whether he had dreamed he was a butterfly, or a butterfly dreaming he was Zhuang Zhou. This story also suggests that a distinction of some kind exists between the butterfly and Zhuangzi and calls this "things changing" or "the transformation of things" (*wu hua* 物化), which refers to a continuous changeover between dreamer and dream object.[29] That a work preoccupied with the description of the transient nature of human life and the nonfixity of physical and mental categories selects the metamorphosing butterfly to symbolize the ever-changing state of things may not be a coincidence.

The dream is linked with changing images elsewhere. In the *Liezi* dreaming is identified as a situation in which "the spirits connect with something" or a "spiritual encounter," dream objects are identified as "sensory transformations" (*gan bian* 感變). People who trust in dreams are said not to grasp "the coming and going of the changes of things" (*wu hua zhi wanglai* 物化之往來).[30] According to Wang Fu the original meaning of the word for dream (*meng* 夢) was "a denomination for a difficult and unconscious observation, a name for the unclear and diffuse." Wang further characterizes the strange dream (*qi yi zhi meng* 奇異之夢) as a phenomenon in which images constantly transform and take each other's place with the dreamer not being able to trace them. One of the diviner's tasks consists in "scrutinising the reasons of its transformations and investigating its signs and symptoms."[31] In other words, divining a dream is explained as the interpretation of the changing of images, an idea reminiscent of the sage's interpretation of changing appearances in the real world. The dream interpreter therefore needs to clarify the "transformative membrane" that "hangs between the dream world and the waking world."[32] Like the appearance of the prodigy in the real world, its appearance in dreams is a negotiated concept between the informant and the oneiromancer. And as in the case of animal prodigies in the real world, there usually exists a causal and moral reciprocity between a creature's appearance in the dream and the dreamer's fortunes in real life.

Early evidence for the practice of divining animal lore in dreams occurs in the *Shijing*. One poem divines the dream appearance of bears as the auspicious signs for the birth of sons while cobras and serpents are interpreted as portents for daughters.[33] In another poem the dream image of multitudes of fish, among other imagery, is interpreted as a sign for a prosperous year. Several other poems in the *Shijing* associate the image of fish with fertility, an abundant harvest, spring, generative energy, and marital bless.[34] Animal dreams occur elsewhere. The *Fengsu tongyi* tells the story of Duke Wen 文 of Jin (636–628

B.C.E.), who meets with a giant snake during a hunt. After realizing that a Son of Heaven should cultivate virtue when confronted with a prodigy, the duke repents for his shortcomings in government. Later during the night a servant who was guarding the snake has a dream vision in which Heaven kills the snake saying: "Why did you obstruct the path of a sage-ruler?!" At dawn the snake had rotted away.[35] The message here is that prodigies are to be countered through self-examination and the cultivation of human office. This dream echoes another story in which the child Sun Shu-ao 孫叔敖 (sixth cent. B.C.E.) meets with a two-headed snake, kills and buries it, and goes home crying. When his mother asks him why, the child explains that seeing a two-headed snake would lead to death. His mother comforts him saying that someone with *yin* ("hidden") virtue would be compensated by heaven. The boy became a successful official. Sun's innate virtue, which made him cope with the snake prodigy as a child, foreshadowed his later success as minister in Chu.[36]

Like their counterparts in the real world, animal portents in dream accounts are often mediated by a diviner and lead to corresponding actions in the state of awakening. When Duke Wen of Qin (765–716 B.C.E.) had a dream vision of a yellow snake dangling down from heaven to earth with its mouth positioned on mount Fu 鄜, the omen was interpreted as a sign of the Thearch, and an altar was erected to sacrifice to the White Emperor.[37] Sima Qian accounts how emperor Qin Shihuang, after being told by his magicians that large fish blocked the access to the isles of immortality, dreamed of a battle with a sea spirit in the shape of a human being. After an oneiromancer had divined that this evil water god manifests itself in the form of a gigantic fish or dragon, the emperor went off to personally shoot a giant fish.[38] Emperor Er Shi 二世 (fl. ca. 209 B.C.E.) dreamed of a white tiger killing one of his carriage horses and, following the advice of a diviner, performed a river sacrifice by drowning four white horses.[39] When one of Emperor Gaozu's concubines reported a dream in which a green dragon came leaning on her abdomen, Gaozu interpreted this as an auspicious sign that he wished to complete. The story goes that the emperor had intercourse once with his concubine resulting in the birth of a male offspring, the future Emperor Wen.[40] The founding ruler of the Eastern Han, Emperor Guangwu 光武帝 (r. 25–57 C.E.), dreamed that he ascended to heaven on a red dragon. After awakening, he felt "perturbed in his heart" following which one of his officials explained that the dragon that had appeared to him in his dream was in fact the mandate of heaven manifesting itself in his spirit.[41]

Confucius Names the Beasts

As the paragon of wisdom and the archetypal sage, the figure of Confucius was frequently associated with the comprehension and transformation of the natural world and its inhabitants. As we have seen, in the *Lunyu* Confucius admonished his disciples to study the animal nomenclature of the *Shijing*. Elsewhere he praised the virtuous governance of the ancient kings which incited the animals to dance, and in several passages we have encountered Confucius giving moral instructions on the killing of wildlife or commenting on the human-animal relationship and the maintenance of a balance in the natural world. The Confucius figure was also identified with changing animals and sacred hybrids. Confucius lauds the powers of the transforming dragon in the *Zhouyi*, and weeps over a wounded unicorn in the final moments of the *Zuozhuan* chronicle, thereby identifying himself with both the king and uncrowned hero of the animal kingdom.

Several Warring States and Han texts reinforce Confucius's image as the paragon of sages by casting him in the role of an agent who de-anomalizes prodigious animal appearances. They show Confucius confronting strange occurrences in the animal world, identifying monsters by name, and administering advice on how human society ought to respond to such events. A locus classicus is a story that stages the Master identifying a marvelous beast in an urn as a clay sheep. Its oldest version is recorded in the *Guoyu*:

> Ji Huanzi 季桓子 was digging a well when he found something resembling an earthen jar which contained a sheep inside. He sent for someone to consult with Confucius on this matter and said: "While I was digging a well I found a dog, what is this?" Confucius replied: "According to what I have heard this is a sheep. I have heard the following: the prodigies of the woods and stones (i.e., the mountains) are the *kui* and the *wangliang*; the prodigies of the water are the dragon and the *wangxiang*; the prodigy of the earth is the *fenyang* 獖羊 'burial sheep.'"[42]

The origins and identification of the creature referred to as a *fenyang* in this passage and its connection with the earth are uncertain. Reference to a sheep or goat in connection with the earth occurs in the duodenary animal cycle in the "calendar for thieves" found at Shuihudi. There an "old sheep" is linked to the eleventh phase of the animal cycle, which, interestingly, corresponds to the dog in later versions of the cycle. The villains identified in this entry are said to hide in the ground: "On *xu* 戌 days, corresponding to old sheep: those who steal have a red color. As people they are hard in their actions. They have a mole on their cheeks and hide in dung and weeds or in the ground. In the early morning you can get them but at night you cannot get them. Their names are. . . ."[43] The *Shizi* mentions a dog that lives in the earth and was known as a *di lang* 地狼 or "earth wolf."[44] Whether there exists a link between these creatures and the buried object in the *Guoyu* story remains speculative. Perhaps the *fenyang* was just a dug-up clay burial figurine.

More important than the tentative identification of the creature in question is the way in which the *Guoyu* story depicts Confucius and the stratagem by which he identifies the animal in the jar. The anecdote displays the defining features of the sage in the face of the unknown. By recognizing the creature as a *fenyang* and dismissing its identification as a dog—that is, a common and familiar animal to most people—Confucius identifies and names a creature that is anomalous in the perception of the common people. The same strategy of naming appeared in the story mentioned in chapter 5 in which children imitated a strange bird in a rain dance. There the Duke of Qi observes a bird with one foot jumping about, "thinks it very strange," and asks Confucius who replies: "This (creature) is named a *shangyang* (*ci ming shangyang* 此名商羊)."[45] Although the Confucius in the *Guoyu* story admits he has never personally seen a similar creature (the source of his hearsay is not identified), he relates the creature to receptive categories by classifying it among other prodigies connected with water, earth, stones, and wood. Whether these other prodigies belonged to the received knowledge of the observer is left unanswered. The prodigy or monster remains, as Michel Foucault puts it, "a shady, mobile, wavering region in which what analysis is to define as identity is still only mute analogy; and what it will define as assignable and constant difference is still only free and random variation."[46] By relating the *fenyang* to other creatures and identifying their respective habitat, Confucius brings up a comprehensive category that abates the *fenyang*'s singular, hence anomalous nature. Confucius's display of an extensive and comprehensive knowledge of all phenomena in the world is therefore rooted in his ability to extend the category of a singular appearance by adding comparable occurrences to it. An Eastern Han source records a variant of the *fenyang* story in an explanation for the presence of cedar trees near graves. It accounts how someone, while digging up earth, finds a creature like a sheep. Next the creature is identified by two children on the street who figure as the mantic equivalent of Confucius as the source of names. The children identify the creature by name and state that it usually resides in the earth where it eats the brains of dead people. Finally they give advice on how to counter the beast by thrashing its head with bushels of cedar.[47]

The idea that the sage attributes the strange to a lack of perception and innate knowledge and looks beyond what appears to be uncanny at first sight is illustrated in another edifying Confucius story preserved in the *Liezi*, *Huainanzi*, and *Lunheng*. Here a family in the state of Song which had been unremitting in its virtuous conduct for three generations is confronted "without any reason" by a black cow giving birth to a white calf. They consult Confucius who, against their expectation, thinks it is a good omen and advises them to sacrifice the calf to the spirits. As a result the father of the family turns blind a year later. When the cow gave birth to another white calf and Confucius is once again consulted by the son of the family, the Master sticks with his opinion and again calls for the calf to be sacrificed. Following this, the son too loses his eyesight for no obvious reason. In the end however Confucius's persistence in interpreting the white calves as auspicious omens is vindicated when the city of Song comes under siege by Chu and all able-bodied men are called to its defence. Being crippled and useless in battle, both father and son manage to escape the fighting. Their blindness had saved them. When the siege was over, they regained their eyesight. Confucius's interpretation of the white calf omen had been proved beneficial after all.[48]

The theme of Confucius as namer and interpreter of anomalous animals is a recurring topos. The famous capture of the unicorn at the end of the *Chunqiu* (481 B.C.E.) stages Confucius identifying an injured monoceros with a fleshy horn as a *lin* 麟, an animal thought to herald the advent of a virtuous ruler.[49] A later version of this story preserved in the *Kong Congzi* gives a more dramatic account of the event underlining the dichotomy between the common man's ignorance and the sage's power to identify a creature as being ominous:

> The lad Chu Shang 鉏商, one of Shu Sun's 叔孫 charioteers, gathered firewood in the wilds and caught an animal. None of his men could identify it, hence Shu Sun thought the creature was inauspicious, and he abandoned it in Wufu lane. Ran You 冉有 told the Master about it and said: "This creature has the body of a hornless deer but with a fleshy horn. Can this be other than a prodigy from Heaven?" The Master said: "Where is this creature now? I must see it." He then went to see it, saying to his charioteer Gao Chai 高柴: "Judging from what Qiu 求 has said, this creature must be the *lin*." When they arrived and looked at it, it was in fact so.[50]

As was the case with the *fenyang*, Confucius identifies and names a creature whose appearance had been reported to him before he actually sees it. His capability to give the unicorn its proper name distinguishes the Master from his informant. The narrative is reminiscent of the format of texts such as the *Shanhaijing* and demonological literature where frequently the physical features of a creature are outlined first, only then followed by its name. As in some of the aforementioned accounts, this story also reiterates the idea that there exist different levels of comprehension of natural and unnatural appearances: first, that of the commoner whose apprehension is limited to the observable physical world, and, second, that of the sage whose knowledge extends to the realm of the invisible, the world that can be known through names and does not require direct witness. A critique by Wang Chong underlines this dichotomy between the sage's wisdom to de-anomalize the unknown through naming as opposed to the popular misconception of considering what is unknown to be strange. In his view only common people associate the capability to name strange creatures with sagehood. Wang ridicules the idea that a sage's comprehension of strange beings should therefore be thought of as an inborn faculty or supernatural quality of some kind.

(Compare this with) Confucius who, when he saw an animal, named it a *xingxing* 狌狌 . . . Confucius had never before seen a *xingxing*, but upon its arrival he immediately was able to give it a name. . . . If ordinary people had heard of this, then they would say that Confucius was spirit-like and prescient. However Confucius was able to name the *xingxing* because he had heard the songs of the mountain people[51]. . . . Ordinary people . . . upon noticing worthies or sages giving creatures their proper names, consider them spirit-like.[52]

The Confucius stories above emphasize the Master's role as a source of names and add another aspect to the central place of naming in the early Chinese perception of the animal world. The role of naming, which had pervaded Warring States thought in its philosophical and political incarnation as a theory on the rectification of names, found its performative and magic double in the realm of the strange. This empowering function of naming emerged against the background of the prominent use of names and titles as a way of administrative control in early China.[53] Just as the ruler matched office against name, the sage engaged in the act of naming prodigies in order to secure mental control over their appearance.

It is plausible that the performative use of names grew out of a tradition of shamanic invocations and ritual prayers in which demons, spirits, and other supernatural forces were called upon to come and assist its supplicants. Naming as a therapeutic act of controlling uncanny creatures figures prominently in the context of healing and demonic medicine in Warring States texts. Calling out the name of a disease-causing parasite, bug, or demon was thought to have an apotropaic healing power. An episode in the *Zhuangzi* accounts how Duke Huan of Qi falls ill after spotting a demon during the hunt. The diagnosis concluded that the duke's illness was self-inflicted and resulted from his "angry and anxious *qi*," an idea that echoes the belief that prodigies appear as a result of overheated or inflamed *qi*. Next the duke inquires as to whether demons exist. His shaman gives an affirmative answer following which he lists a series of names of demonic creatures as well as the places they hide. In the end a marsh demon named *weiyi* 委蛇 is identified as the specter seen by the duke. After being told that this creature appears only to future hegemons, the duke recovers instantly.[54]

Therapeutic namegiving is also found in more practical manuals such as the Shuihudi demonography and the items that deal with demonic illness in the Mawangdui medical corpus. Most entries in the Shuihudi demonography are structured in an identical format: first demonic symptoms are identified, next a demon is named, and, finally, an apotropaic instruction is given. An illuminating passage dealing with "naming the unknown" in the context of medicine occurs in the Mawangdui *Za liao fang* 雜療方 ("Recipes for Various Treatments"), which contains several entries on how to protect oneself from attacks by the aforementioned *yu* 蜮 "spit-sand," a poisonous invertebrate water creature associated with sex and the south.[55]

If by misfortune you are shot by the *yu*, venomous snakes, and bees, chant an incantation and spit at it thrice. Name the creature that did the shooting with its name, saying: "So-and-so. You five brothers, so-and-so knows all your names. You who dwell in the water are the fish-*qi*. You who dwell on the land are the bug-*qi*. Those lodged in trees are the bee and *ransi* (caterpillar). The one who flew to Jing-in-the-South is the *yu*. . . . "[56]

In this recipe, the officiant's power over the demonic vermin that causes disease is based on name magic. Similar to the sage in the aforementioned *Huainanzi* passage who identified prodigies and their habitat in the mountains, water, woods, and pits, the officiant in this recipe identifies disease-causing creatures by name and habitat in order to expel them from the body. Another example of mantic control over strange creatures through name magic occurs in the *Guanzi*, where a creature named *qingji* 慶忌 is identified as the genie of the dry marsh. According to the text one can dispatch this creature beyond a thousand *li* by shouting out its name and have it report back in a single day. Similarly, by shouting out the name of the serpentine *wei* 蟡, identified as the genie of the dry river, one can catch fish and turtles.[57] In sum, political and philosophical theories on the rectification of names had their practical counterpart in the exorcistic act of naming to counter prodigies and the use of name magic in shamanic healing.

While the role of naming appears to be central to the typification of Confucius as a master of the strange, these stories rarely present Confucius engaging in theoretical expositions on freak occurrences. Confucius's reticence to engage in a discourse on strange phenomena is canonized in the *Lunyu*'s so-called agnostic characterization of the Master as someone who "did not speak (*bu yu* 不語) about prodigies, feats of strength, chaos and spirits."[58] Implied in this statement is the idea that the sage refuses to "talk about" prodigies at random or engage in an argumentative exposition on uncanny creatures.[59] The *Lunyu* passage suggests that the sage does not speak about the uncanny "as if it *is* uncanny." As is shown in stories featuring Confucius facing the strange, his attitude is not one of indifference but of "studied avoidance."[60] The sage avoids talking about freak events, an act which merely stirs up doubt and confusion in the minds of the people. Yet by performing his role as the ultimate nomothete of all phenomena in the world he keeps these creatures at bay. Confucius's agnosticism therefore implies that he does not engage in explanatory discourse on these phenomena but controls the proliferation of the belief in such creatures by giving them a proper name and by relating them to known categories. While the sage respects the appearance of monsters as "monstra," omens showing a divine sanction or approval, he keeps them at a distance. As we will see shortly, this discursive silence with regard to the strange epitomized in Confucius's attitude toward prodigies was mirrored in the purported refusal of the classics to explain animal prodigies other than providing a mere record of their occurrence.

The idea that a sagacious response to prodigies ought to be achieved through indirect avoidance and the application of receptive categories is further clarified in Ying Shao's introduction to a chapter on marvels and spirits ("Guai shen" 怪神) in the *Fengsu tongyi*. In his justification of the motives for the compilation of the chapter, Ying Shao reiterates the so-called agnostic attitude of Confucius toward prodigies:

> The tradition holds that what is spirit-like (*shen* 神) means "to extend" (*shen* 申) and what we call strange (*guai* 怪) is in fact "doubt" (*yi* 疑). Confucius gave the strange phenomena of the earth the name "burial sheep" (*fenyang*). The *Lunyu* states that the Master did not speak about prodigies, feats of strength, disorder and spirits. Therefore I have selected the most obvious cases and called this chapter "On Marvels and Spirits."[61]

By suggesting that he has selected the most illustrative cases among prodigious phenomena for the compilation of his chapter, Ying Shao portrays himself and his text as a substitute for Confucius's silence on these matters. In other words, through de-anomalizing a series of prodigious events in his stories, he aims to discard remaining doubts that may have been evoked in the reader's mind by Confucius's agnosticism. Ying thus presents his text as a more articulate verbalization of the Master's aphoristic silence on these matters. He reiterates received glosses for the terms *shen* and *guai* and, by doing so, indicates that the sage's capacity to comprehend uncanny phenomena lies in his ability to "extend" his knowledge and conquer doubts. Furthermore Confucius's act of naming the *fenyang* is juxtaposed to his refusal to "speak about" uncanny phenomena. In the footsteps of Confucius, Ying Shao suggests that both a preoccupation with and neglect of spiritual powers and anomalous events are dangerous for the ideal ruler. Throughout the chapter, he associates the psychology of the common folk with the notion of doubt and portrays the sage as someone who can extend his cognitive categories. To Ying Shao, writing at a time when the Han dynasty was succumbing to an irreversible decline, the sagacious response to strange appearances was embodied in the ideal of the Confucian scholar-official who relies solely on the classics and cultivates virtue and human office in the face of events which terrify and confuse ordinary people.

These themes are exemplified throughout the "Guai shen" chapter. In one story the protagonist slays a fox demon and is promoted as "filial and incorrupt," and in several other anecdotes personalities who are able to either explain or neglect a strange appearance end up achieving brilliant official careers. In one story two red snakes appear as auspicious signs to a general. While the general initially doubts the diviner's positive interpretation of the omen, the ensuing successes of his military and public career eventually confirm the auspicious character of the snakes' appearances. The implied message suggests that even if a spectral appearance is interpreted as an omen, it is only an initial indication of eventual good fortune and still requires a proper human response to yield concrete beneficial results.[62] The issue is no longer whether a strange appearance is genuine or not— "the Master doesn't speak about . . ."—but whether the human response to it can be considered to be authentic, firm, and morally correct.

The Confucian classics, and by extension Ying Shao's own text, are thus presented as a "unifying" or "controlling" category (cf. the idea of *tong lei*) in the realm of texts and provide a textual parallel to the sage's act of de-anomalizing strange creatures. The latter occurs literally in a story in which Dong Zhongshu wards off a shamanic curse at the court of Han Wudi by reciting from the classics, which causes the curse to rebound and kill the shamans.[63] In the same way that Han lexicographic compendia had sought to do away with the confusion over the names of strange creatures through the analysis of graphs, so Ying Shao presents the Confucian classics as the textual remedy to counter the appearance of such creatures. As Robert Campany has suggested, Ying Shao's text seeks to rectify "manners and customs" in the same way the sages rectified names and the lexicographer collated and explained unknown graphs.[64] Like the lexicographer who explained apparent neologisms through relating them to familiar graphs and retracing the textual locus in which the graph appeared, so the sage named unknown creatures and drew them into the realm of the familiar by identifying their habitat, explaining their behavior, and clarifying their physical appearance.

This role of the Confucian classics as the means through which strange appearances can be neutralized or rectified and the archetypal portrayal of Confucius as the interpreter of animal appearances is also reinforced by the image of Confucius as lexicographer deciphering animal graphs and explaining their shapes and origins. On several occasions in the *Shuowen*, Xu Shen invokes the authority of Confucius for the explanation of graphs. For instance the entry for the graph *quan* 犬 includes Confucius commenting on its pictographic origins by stating that "if one looks at the written sign *quan*, it is like when one draws a dog (*gou* 狗)." In the following entry Confucius goes on to identify the *gou* graph. Elsewhere he identifies the graphs for oxen and sheep and defines the graph for crow as an onomatopoeia of its cry.[65] Similarly, the *Shuowen* also stages music master Shi Kuang in the explanation of a bird graph.[66]

The image of Confucius as a wise statesman who opposes improper responses to extraordinary events and refuses to welcome divine forces to interfere with human affairs is echoed in descriptions of other sages. A notable figure is that of Zi Chan who, according to the *Zuozhuan*, disapproved of his people offering a sacrifice in response to the appearance of two dragons fighting in a pool. The event occurred after a flood had inundated Zheng (in 523 B.C.E.):

> Dragons were fighting in the Wei 洧 pool outside the Shi gate. The people of Zheng requested to perform a deprecatory sacrifice to them. Zi Chan refused to

give permission and said: "When we are fighting, the dragons do not look at us; when dragons are fighting, why should it only be us looking at them? If we perform an expulsion sacrifice then we are in fact driving them out of their own abode. If we don't seek anything from these dragons, they will not seek anything from us." Following this the request was withdrawn.[67]

In the same way that Yanzi, whom we encountered in chapter 4, reassured Duke Jing that mountains formed the normal habitat for tigers, Zi Chan's argument is based on the idea that each creature is assigned its proper environment. By indicating that the springs form the natural habitat for dragons and by questioning the efficacy of humans sacrificing to a realm not their own, Zi Chan indirectly dismisses the dragon fight as an abnormal event. Zi Chan's attitude toward the proposed dragon sacrifice may have foreshadowed the image of Confucius as a sage who advises to be reverent to the spirits while keeping them at a distance.[68] It also echoes a theme occurring elsewhere in the *Zuozhuan* that one should not sacrifice to spirits that are not one's own, as well as Confucius's observation in the *Lunyu* that sacrificing to a spirit not one's own amounts to flattery.[69]

Another figure who was praised for his "spiritual luminance" after having de-anomalized strange animal behavior was Shi Kuang, the legendary music master and diviner of bird cries. A story preserved in the *Shuoyuan* describes how Shi Kuang demystifies the misinterpretation of two animal appearances by his lord, Duke Ping of Jin. During a hunt the duke observes a young tiger lying low without moving. He reports his observation to Shi Kuang assuming that what he had just witnessed was a case of wild animals not daring to raise themselves when a hegemon goes out. Shi Kuang replies: "A magpie feeds on hedgehogs, hedgehogs feed on *junyi* 鷒鸃 birds, *junyi* birds feed on leopards, leopards feed on the *bo* 駮 panther who feeds on tigers." He then notes that *bo* panthers resemble piebald horses (*bo ma* 駮馬). Therefore since piebald horses were mounted during the hunt, the tiger had remained motionless out of fear for these horses, and not as a response to the duke's virtue and righteousness. This story is followed by a similar anecdote. When, during another hunt, a bird circles Duke Ping constantly, he presumes it is a phoenix descending on him foreboding the advent of his hegemony. Shi Kuang then corrects the duke and identifies the bird as a *jianke* 諫珂, an eastern bird known to "detest other birds but love foxes." Since the duke was wearing fox furs during the hunt, the bird had circled him because it was attracted to the fur and not because of his virtue.[70] In both cases Shi Kuang's redress contains a veiled political criticism of his superior (both piebald horses and fox fur are symbols of a lavish life style), whom he accuses of calumniating himself.

The passages discussed above were mainly concerned with clarifying the reasons why prodigies emerge and the human response to such occurrences. A question remaining to be addressed is whether a common mechanism or structure underlies the prodigious events themselves. In other words, what caused an animal appearance to be thought of as strange, which patterns of behavior in the natural world were generally seen as anomalous? The remaining pages of this chapter will show that animal anomalies in early China figured in the first place as the embodiment of changing circumstances. As was the case with the symbolic role associated with metamorphosing creatures, the notion of change provided the conceptual framework that determined the identification and explanation of freak events in the natural world. The early Chinese discourse on animal prodigies revolved around the notion of a transgression of boundaries and implicitly accepted categories. It focused on patterns indicating a transcendence of or flaw within the socio-biological order and was expressed in conceptual dichotomies such as inner versus outer, central versus peripheral, the wilds versus the domesticated order.

While defining anomaly as a transgression of boundaries may seem axiomatic, it is noteworthy that notions of change and transformation provided a tool of explanation for both the conception of virtuous or sacred animals as well as the understanding of anomalous species. This suggests that contending views on how to explain feats of change in the animal world may have been at work. I suspect that, while an elitist and philosophical discourse emphasized, in various ways, the virtues of change in the animal world as signs of sagacity or numinous power, such views emerged against the background of a more popular or commonly held discourse that saw similar phenomena as anomalous, strange, and undesirable. Yet in either case the motivation to distinguish categorically between the human and animal world or develop conceptual distinctions between phenomena as requiring either a physical or a moral explanation were subordinate to a world view that saw both humans and animals as exposed to the same laws. While the susceptibility to moral causation may have been perceived to be more subtle in the case of the human sage than that of the savage animal, the difference was one of degree rather than kind. In the eyes of the Warring States and Han observer the same cosmic laws that applied to the enlightened sage and his sacred animals applied to the commoner, his domestic animals, and the predators in the wilds.

To illustrate some of the ways in which animal prodigies were linked to the idea of change, I present three cases extracted from sources that span most of the period discussed in this study: first, the discourse on a bird anomaly recorded in the Spring and Autumn Annals; second, the perception of the dog as a daemonic animal; and, finally, a Han memorial on the capture of a white unicorn.

When the Grackos Nest in Lu

An animal anomaly that has received significant attention in several Warring States and Han sources is recorded in the Spring and Autumn Annals. Under the year corresponding to 517 B.C.E., the *Chunqiu* reports that birds known as *quyu*

鸜 鵒 came to make their nests in the trees on the banks of a river in the state of Lu.[71] The *quyu*, more commonly known as the Chinese crested mynah or gracko (*acridotheres cristatellus*), is a black bird spotted white under the wings. Contemporary descriptions of this bird are scant but later sources provide more information. According to the sixteenth-century pharmacologist Li Shizhen, the *quyu* was also known by its alternative names *baba niao* 八八鳥 and *ba ge* 八哥. Li states that the bird loves bathing in water and nesting in magpie nests, in the hollows of trees, or in the rafters of houses. He further notes that mynahs fly in flocks when snow is about to fall; hence they are referred to by yet another name, *hangao* 寒皋(告) "Announcer of the Cold." The mynah was also said to be able to imitate the call of other birds as well as human speech when the tip of its tongue was cut short.[72] A few points of reference regarding its original biotope may be gathered from contemporary texts. The "Section on the Central Mountains" in the *Shanhaijing* refers twice to a habitat of the mynah: one on mount Youyuan 又原, and another on mount Heng 衡. The precise location of these mountains however is uncertain.[73] More reliable evidence is provided in Han statements that claim that the *quyu* did not transgress the river Ji 濟, although it is possible that this observation was inspired by the *Chunqiu* and *Zuozhuan* record.[74] Based on these few data, we may speculate that the region south of Jinan 濟南 commandery formed the boundary of the mynah's natural habitat. In late Zhou times, the river Ji ran eastward from county Jiyuan 濟源 in the state of Han 韓 (present-day Henan) and, cutting through the states of Lu and Qi, discharged in the Bohai 渤海 gulf north of the Shandong peninsula.[75]

While the *Chunqiu* limits itself to a brief statement that "mynahs came to nest," subsequent interpretations of this event exemplify how late Warring States and Han authors linked animal anomalies with the notion of territory, the dichotomy between inner and outer, and the transgression of the natural and human order. The historical event linked with the appearance of the mynahs was Duke Zhao 昭 of Lu's (541–510 B.C.E.) forced departure from his state. Ousted by the Ji 季 clan, symbolized by the mynahs, and banned to the barren wilds, the duke fled Lu and set up camp at Ganhou 乾侯, an arid settlement in Jin, where he died eight years later. His body was brought back to Lu for burial. In its description of events, the *Zuozhuan* begins by noting that the unusual phenomenon of the nesting mynahs was recorded in the *Chunqiu* because such an event had never before been documented (*shu suo wu ye* 書所無也). It then stages a Lu grandee named Shi Ji 師己 who, expressing his marvel at the nesting mynahs, quotes a children's ditty that allegedly was sung during the time of dukes Wen 文 (626–609 B.C.E.) and Cheng 成 (590–573 B.C.E.), both predecessors of Duke Zhao.[76] This ditty from the past would have predicted Duke Zhao's imminent flight from Lu:

> Here come the mynahs,
> A duke will leave in disgrace.

Look at the mynahs' wings,
A duke will flee to the outer wilds (*wai ye* 外野),
as provision one brings him a horse.
Look how the mynahs leap about,
A duke will stay at Ganhou,
asking for garments and a jacket.
Mynahs will make their nests,
and far away (a duke) will rest,
Zhoufu 稠父 will lose the fruits of his efforts,
Songfu 宋父 will become haughty.[77]
Look at these mynahs!
Someone will leave while we sing,
and return while we weep.[78]

Two notions of anomaly are singled out in this story: first, the fact that the mynahs or grackos appear in a geographical region that is not their natural habitat; second, the idea that by nesting high up in trees rather than hidden in holes in walls or banks, the birds do not follow their normal instinctive behavior. The *Gongyang* commentary qualifies both elements of anomaly:

> [Question] Why is this event documented in the records? [Answer] Because it is strange. [Question] Why is it strange? [Answer] Because these are birds that do not belong to the Central States (*fei Zhongguo zhi qin ye* 非中國之禽也), and they normally nest in dens but (in this case) perch (in trees).[79]

Similarly the unicorn captured in the very last entry of the *Chunqiu* is identified as a creature that does not belong to the Central States and its inclusion in the textual record is justified on the same basis—namely, "because it is strange."[80]

Numerous references to the nesting mynahs occur in later texts. Liu Xiang identifies mynahs as birds that nest in caves among the Yi and Di barbarians and interprets the fact that they came to the Middle Kingdom and perched in trees instead of crevices as a sign of *yin* taking over the *yang* position (a sign prefiguring Duke Zhao's expulsion from the palace to the outer wilds).[81] Wang Chong, on the contrary, held that the mynahs' appearance had no relation to Duke Zhao's bad ordeal and that it was mere coincidence.[82] The equation of exogenous birds with exogenous people is articulated in at least two apocryphal sources which state that while mynahs have a flying locomotion that makes them belong to *yang*, as birds from barbaric regions they reside in crevices in the *yin*.[83] Other apocryphal texts present Confucius explaining to Zi Xia 子夏 that mynahs are non-Chinese birds.[84] He Chang 何敞 (fl. ca. 84 C.E.) refers to both the mynah case and the capture of the unicorn when arguing that auspicious omens arrive on the basis of

228

Strange Animals

virtue, while calamities and freak appearances originate in government.[85] As this case illustrates, prodigious animals appeared as creatures that crossed their natural habitat, often abiding in unnatural proximity to humans. In the *Zuozhuan*'s account of events, the birds' change in habitat portends the duke's change in political fortune. While wild birds leap about in the domestic sphere of Lu, the duke is banned to the outer wilds.

Similar cases are recorded in other Warring States and Han texts most of which include the crossing of a physical boundary as a standard feature in the identification of animal behavior as anomalous. The Shuihudi demonography for instance contains numerous remedies against demonic entities intruding the domestic sphere of humans (*ru ren shi* 入人室, *ru ren gong* 入人宮). It prescribes exorcistic blows with a bamboo whip to be performed when one is met by birds, beasts, and bugs that are entering a person's house. Another feat of demonic intrusion are birds, beasts, and domestic animals constantly entering a person's home or crying inside human mansions. The latter can be halted by burning loose head hair and the fur and whiskers of the six domestic animals at the places where they stop. Other acts of domestic intrusion include a wolf shouting at a person's door saying "Open up, I am not a demon," or wildfire in the shape of bugs entering the house.[86]

The transgression of the boundaries between inner and outer or wild and domestic is illustrated in numerous other examples: a bear from the wilds entering the palace,[87] wild animals playing in the courtyards and wild birds perching on the trees of courtyards, wild birds entering the ancestral temples or palaces,[88] pigs breaking out of the pen or stable and entering residential halls, snakes emerging from a palace or entering the capital, rats dancing at the palace gates and inside the court, and rats nesting in trees.[89] These can be supplemented with references to inauspicious birds singing or moving around in places that normally constitute the domain of human civilization such as ravens singing in the courtyard or crows fighting with magpies in a palace pond. In one story preserved in the *Yanzi chunqiu,* the presence of a crying owl in a newly built pavilion leads to a deprecatory sacrifice with white woolly grass. Following the exorcism the owl faced the throne, spread its wings wide open, prostrated, and died.[90] As was the case in hunting accounts and the discourse on predatory animal behavior, images of animals transgressing their habitat were signs of the most radical change that could affect the human order—namely, a situation of a "world turned upside down" in which animals ventured into the domain of human civilization. The substitution of human rule by the law of the wilds, the implosion of the human moral order together with the inversion of the natural instincts of animals and the intrusion of wild animals or barbarians into human settlements and cities of the Middle Kingdom were variants of one leitmotif—namely, the idea that the realms of civilization and wilderness were not eternally fixed but subject to periodical changes.

The above examples pictured animal anomalies in terms of a transgression of space by identifying unusual animal movement as the transgression of the dichotomy between the domestic sphere and the wilds. The topsy-turvy relationship between inner and outer or the sphere of the domestic versus the wilds was further attested in accounts of animals that assumed human characteristics. The Shuihudi demonography contains an entry in which birds and animals that adopt human speech are said to be "prodigious" (*yao* 夭/妖). In order to ward off this freak behavior, the text prescribes corresponding magic which consists of increasing the number of humans standing around. Another entry deals with wild animals and the six domestic animals meeting people to speak with them.[91] The role reversal of humans and animals was also exemplified by daemonic animals being aware of the human calendar, the ultimate symbol regulating the human order. The *Zhouli* documents the office of a "nest destroyer" who was in charge of destroying the nests of ominous birds. His tasks included suspending tablets inscribed with the names of the ten-day cycle, the twelve hours, twelve lunar months, twelve Jupiter stations, and twenty-eight lunar lodges on top of the nests of unpropitious birds to exorcise them.[92]

To summarize, records such as that of the nesting mynahs and other animal prodigies mentioned above illustrate how the blurred distinctions between the human and the animalistic were seen as signs of daemonic influence. They sketch a dichotomy between the spheres of the domestic and the wilds, the inner and the outer, the human and the nonhuman, and indicate how a transgression of these boundaries challenged the well-being not only of the state and its ruler but also of the individual household, which is advised to answer demonic intrusion with proper human responses. While canonical texts propounded theories arguing that a sage-ruler should respond to these flaws in nature through the cultivation of virtue and the moral force of transformation, more practical texts such as the Qin daybooks show how local elites and commonfolk resorted to a mixture of popular beliefs and magic to deal with such events.

The episode on the nesting mynahs and later commentaries on this event also indicate something about the status of animal prodigies in the textual realm. We saw that the *Gongyang zhuan* justified the recording of the mynah case in the *Chunqiu* by appealing to the anomalous nature of the event. The event was put to record because it was strange. The record itself however is annalistic and short. Its causes and consequences, its hidden and deeper meaning are left unexplained. The *Zuozhuan* gives a similar justification for the canonization of prodigious phenomena in its commentary on the occurrence of a cockroach plague in the autumn of the year corresponding to 665 B.C.E. It states that "in all cases in which (such) things do not amount to a calamity, they are not recorded."[93] As with the mynah case, the *Gongyang* commentary concurs: "[Question] Why is (this plague) recorded? [Answer] Because it is strange."[94] Similar justifications are given for recording the appearance of elaphures in the winter of 677 B.C.E. and "spit-sands" in the autumn of 676 B.C.E.[95] While the occurrence of a strange appearance is recorded in the actual *Chunqiu* chronicle, its explanations occur outside the chronicle in the *zhuan*. The *Chunqiu* thus links the justification for a textual record with the anomalous nature of the event and the observer's perception of it being "note-worthy." In a memorial addressed to Emperor Huan, *yinyang* specialist Xiang Kai 襄楷 (fl. ca. 166 C.E.) explains Confucius's observation of the unicorn along the same lines. Commenting on the occurrence of contemporary portents, he remarks that such events "are like the unicorn in the *Chunqiu* which should not have appeared but appeared anyway. Confucius recorded it because he thought it was extraordinary."[96] The mediation of an event as being anomalous (*yi* 異) and its inclusion in a textual record (*shu* 書) are closely intertwined.

In a lucid analysis Mark Lewis has shown how in the late Warring States period the canon or classics gradually came to be seen as the textual double of the sage who possessed supreme intelligence, while commentaries emerged as the textual parallel of worthies devoted to explaining and transmitting the subtle and hidden meanings that were anchored in the classics.[97] Above we noted how the sage's attitude toward strange appearances, exemplified by Confucius, was marked by a reticence to engage in disputation on these matters. The *Chunqiu* anomaly records and their explanation in the *Gongyang, Guliang,* and *Zuo* commentaries suggest that the sage's refusal or "studied avoidance" to engage in discourse on prodigies was reflected in the status of animal prodigies in the realm of texts. Just as the sage refrains from entering a lengthy analytical discourse on prodigies that would lead to confusion and social disintegration, so the classics limit themselves to recording these occurrences but leave the explanation to be dealt with by commentators and extracanonical writings such as lexicographies or apocryphal texts. Some passages assert that the classics, or the written record in general, ought to make note of prodigies without explaining them. Xunzi's "Tian lun" chapter contains a statement claiming that according to tradition "prodigies among the myriad things should be recorded but not explained" (*wan wu zhi guai, shu bu shuo* 萬物之怪書不說). (Or in an alternative reading, "are not explained in the books").[98] In the *Huainanzi,* the explanation of animal prodigies and other miracles is consigned to books on prognostication (*chan shu* 讖書): "When the six domestic animals grow many ears and eyes, this is not auspicious, the books on prophecies illustrate this."[99] Similarly, the "Treatise on the Five Phases" in the *Hanshu* discussed in chapter 6 was structured as a commentarial exegesis of strange occurrences in writings from the past and sought to establish causal links between contemporary portents and precedents from the past by juxtaposing them within a five-phase framework. Just as the sage limited his discourse on the strange to the attribution of names while leaving speculative explanations to worthies, disciples, diviners, and court officials, so the classical canon limited its discourse on extraordinary creatures to providing an elementary record of the event while leaving the elucidation of events to historians and commentarial traditions.

The Dog as Daemon

The association of anomaly with the notion of change is also illustrated in references to the dog, an animal that receives a great deal of attention in late Warring States and Han texts. Archaeology has shown that dogs had a prominent socioeconomic role in daily life as early as the Shang period and possibly earlier. Traditionally three main functions were associated with the dog: hunting, guarding, and the use of dogs as foodstuff.[100] In addition to these more profane aspects associated with dogs, many texts document the use of dogs in religious rituals and present dog behavior in the context of anomaly accounts. This prevalent role of the dog as a daemonic animal was linked to the idea that dogs mediated change and lived on the threshold of the human-animal divide. The dog embodied familiarity and proximity between the human and animal world, and its mediating role is evinced in several contexts, most prominently, in demonology, in sacrificial practice, and in the use of dogs in exorcistic rites.

Mediating on the boundaries between domesticity and wildness, inner and outer, the human and the bestial, dogs in China and elsewhere were associated with the threshold of the house.[101] The dog's dual nature, inspired by the fact that it belongs to the human household without being equal to its human inhabitants, is well attested in several sources. Xu Shen identifies dogs as animals that "know the hearts of humans and can be employed by them."[102] In the *Fengsu tongyi* Ying Shao captures the image of the dog as an animal that attracts in its function as a familiar domestic animal and guardian of the household, while at the same time protecting the household against baleful creatures and dangerous influences. The dog is said to be a companion to humans as well as an apotropaic animal:

> It is commonly held that dogs can distinguish visitors from the house owner and that they are good in keeping guard. Therefore they are attached to the four gates to ward off thieves and robbers.[103]

The dog's peculiar relationship to humans inspired a number of dog demon stories in connection with the household and the domestic sphere. These include cases of dog intrusion and feats of cynanthropic behavior—that is, occasions when dogs are portrayed behaving like humans. The demonography in the Shuihudi daybooks mentions a spirit dog who assumes the shape of a demon to enter people's houses at night, seizing the men and sporting with the women.[104] Ying Shao records the appearance of dog demons several times. In a story criticizing the belief that the dead can reappear as spirits, an old dog is found after the spirit of a dead man who terrorized his household had dispersed. The dog was caned to death immediately.[105] Another story tells of a dog walking upright and behaving like a human, wearing a cap and sitting in front of the hearth while tending the fire.[106] Elsewhere a diviner foretells by means of the hexagrams that a chambermaid was possessed by an old black dog. The advice is to kill the dog and send the girl back to her home village.[107] A story preserved in the *Hanshu* (dated to 28 B.C.E.) tells about two males "lodging in the same room" when a humanlike shape appeared. The men beat at the phantom whereupon it turned into a dog and ran out.[108] Such stories not only document dog transformations but also present the house or domestic sphere as the main scene of such events.

Besides the image of the dog as a daemon of the household sphere, the perception of the dog as an agent of change was also attested in its role as a protective spirit accompanying the transcendence of geographical or spatial boundaries. The role of the dog as guardian or mediator for the passage into different territory was reflected in the use of dog sacrifices to the road. Dogs were dismembered or crushed by royal chariots before setting out on a journey (the so-called *ba* 軷 or driving-over sacrifice). Sometimes sacrificial dog blood was smeared on the wheels of a chariot.[109] Manuscripts excavated in the ancient region of Chu at Wangshan 望山 (County Jiangling, Hubei) and Baoshan corroborate the use of white dogs in sacrifices to the roadside, gates, and paths close to human residences.[110] Chariots that brought people beyond the threshold of their own state or region into foreign regions may also have been decorated with dog imagery. The *Liji* states that when a grandee or officer leaves his state the chariots are covered with white dog skins while the horses have disheveled manes.[111]

Finally, the dog functioned as a demonifuge of the domestic sphere and mediated on the threshold of the living and the dead whose "domus" was the grave or tomb. The former is attested in the slaughter of white dogs and the apotropaic appliance of dog blood on doorposts and windows to ward off baleful events caused by *gu* 蠱 poisoning, a practice which, according to Sima Qian, was initiated by Duke De 德 of Qin (677–676 B.C.E.).[112] Dogs also appear as psychopomps or guardians of the soul in the afterlife. According to a record in the *Hou Hanshu*, the Wuhuan 烏桓 people, a tribe belonging to the eastern barbarians who lived in what is currently known as Inner Mongolia, had a custom of burning a dog fattened for the occasion during the burial of their worthy soldiers to guard the spirit-soul of the deceased on its return to Red Mountain (i.e., the residence of the souls).[113] A story collated in the *Xinlun* (but probably of a later date) tells of a mother who returns from the dead in the shape of a green dog to wash her child's hair.[114] The Fangmatan story discussed in chapter 2, in which a white dog is presented digging up a man who had died prematurely, provides another example of the link between the dog and the underworld. In addition to references to dogs as guardians of the deceased, their mediating function on the threshold of the dead may also be seen in the use of dog skins on funerary chariots. The *Zhouli* documents a series of funerary chariots used when the ruler was in mourning. Several of these chariots are said to be covered with a dog-skin carpet.[115] The use of dog sacrifices at the gates and doors of the living and the dead as well as its use in travel sacrifices suggest that dogs were perceived as daemonic animals operating in the liminal or transitory realm between the domestic and the unknown, danger-stricken outside world.

The Capture of the White Unicorn

A third example that serves to illustrate the prevalence of transformatory thinking and the role of the rhetoric of change in the interpretation of anomalous animal appearances is a memorial submitted by Zhong Jun 終軍 on the occasion of the capture of a white unicorn in 122 B.C.E. According to Ban Gu's account of events, Zhong Jun had joined the entourage of Emperor Wu on a sacrificial procession to the altars of the five directional emperors at Yong 庸 when a unicorn was captured. The report of the capture echoes the appearance of a unicorn to Confucius at the end of the *Chunqiu*.[116] The significance of this event at the time can be derived from the fact that it led to the renaming of the reign title, which became *yuan shou* 元狩 "Principal Capture."[117] The creature in question was reported to have one horn and its hooves were cloven in five segments. It was found together with a strange tree that had branches sticking outward and joining again on the trunk.

The account of this remarkable incident and its interpretation preserved in the *Hanshu* follow the familiar structure of an anomaly episode as discussed earlier. At first, the emperor holds the two phenomena to be strange (*yi ci er wu* 異此二物), and next he solicits advice from his ministers, upon which Zhong Jun presents a reply:

> The southern Yue sneak away and screen themselves off in the reeds and rushes. They flock together with the birds and the fish and (the first day of) our lunar calendar does not apply to their customs. We have established control over the neighbouring borders and the region of Dong Ou 東甌 has been appended to the inside (of the empire); the king of the Min 閩 has accepted surrender and the southern Yue have been overtaken and secured. The northern Hu 胡 follow their animals and frequently move their settlements. They display the conduct of birds and beasts and have the hearts of tigers and wolves, and therefore nobody has yet been able to pacify them since antiquity. . . .
>
> When the Mandate of Heaven is settled for the first time, the myriad things start to develop until they reach the point at which, in the six directions, customs (winds) are unified and the nine provinces share the same habits. It is necessary to wait for an enlightened sage to establish the culture, and then the merits of the

ancestors will be transmitted infinitely. Thus it took the Zhou until King Cheng 成 before their government was settled, and refined signs appeared in response. Our emperor has replenished the brightness of the sun and the moon. He has handed down sagacious thoughts by engraving them in stone and displayed his distinguished respect to the spiritual luminances. He has offered burnt and interred sacrifices to the suburban altars (of Taiyi and Houtu). The essence of his offerings has joined with the spirits, and his accumulation of harmonious *qi* has responded to their enlightened powers. That a strange animal has arrived now to be captured is nothing but appropriate. Formerly when King Wu 武 was in the midst of crossing a stream, a white fish jumped into the royal boat. The king bowed, took the fish and sacrificed it by burning. And all his dukes said "It is fine!"[118] Now, the suburban sacrifices have not yet been introduced to the spirits of heaven and earth, and (already) we have obtained an animal to fill the sacrificial stands. This is the way in which Heaven shows its appreciation, a matching omen for its understanding with you. It is therefore appropriate to illuminate these times and this delightful day by declaring a new reign period. Let mats of white woolly grass from the Jiang Huai region be made, and let the *feng* and *shan* sacrifices be displayed on Mount Tai to respond to this bright countenance. Give orders to those who write down the events to put them on record.

For when the six fishhawks flew backwards, this was a sign of opposition.[119] When the white fish jumped into the boat, that was a sign of compliance. As for presages of enlightenment and gloom, above this is seen in disorder amongst the flying birds, below it is seen in movement among the fish in the springs. Each can be extrapolated according to its category. Now this animal from the wilds has united its horns to clarify its common root (with you). All the branches that adhere to the inside (of the tree) demonstrate that there is no outside. When there are responses such as these, there are bound to be those who will untie the hair-knot, cut off the left sleeve, wear caps and belts, dress in (Chinese) garments,[120] and receive a "cultural transformation."[121]

The symbolism at the heart of this memorial was reiterated in the opening lines of an accompanying sacrificial hymn composed to mark the occasion and entitled "Song of the White Unicorn" (*Bai lin zhi ge* 白麟之歌):

> While holding court on top of Mount Long,
> We gaze across the western boundaries,
> Thunder and lightning accompany our burnt offerings,
> We have captured a white unicorn!
> Thus: it has five toes
> to manifest the virtue of Yellow.
> We planned against Xiongnu bestiality,
> and have decimated the *Xunyu* (=Xiongnu).[122]

In seeking to explain the appearance and shape of the captured unicorn, Zhong Jun's memorial combines several themes analyzed in the previous chapters. First, there is the identification of barbarians with animals and the portrayal of barbarian conquest as a victory of humanity over bestiality. Such linking of animal omens with the submission of barbarian tribes was of course not new to the image building of emperors in the Han. Similar omens had already been associated with the investiture of late Shang and early Zhou rulers. A frequently cited example is the story of a wild pheasant alighting on the ears of the sacrificial tripods during a sacrifice by King Wu Ding 武丁 (?–1189 B.C.E.) to King Tang.[123]

Second, in projecting a sociopolitical discourse onto natural events, the memorial uses visual images of change. In the same way that changing animals reflected social, dynastic, and cosmological change, the hybrid in Zhong Jun's memorial embodies the merging of the animallike barbarian tribes with the empire of Han. The composite nature of the animal symbolizes the unification of different human tribes. The annexation of the foreign periphery to the Han empire is described as a metamorphosis on a cosmological scale. Han Wudi's conquest of the barbarian tribes is portrayed as a transformation from animal to civilized Han subject. The image resembles a similar expression describing the domestication of barbarians as a "transformation through ritual" (*li hua* 禮化)—that is, turning "bestial" barbarians into "human" Chinese vassals.[124] This animal-to-human transformation is further symbolized by the shedding of barbarian hides and the adoption of Chinese clothing, an image reminiscent of the role of skin symbolism in the perception of metamorphosis. The five tribes, symbolized by the five toes of the unicorn, coagulate into one single antler symbolizing Han's unification. Underlining this same idea of unity, Sima Xiangru refers to the captured unicorn as "the beast whose pair of antlers butt as one."[125] Zhong Jun suggests that sinicizing the outer regions is tantamount to domesticating the barbarians as one domesticates animals.[126] The tribes are compared to wild animals (*ye shou* 野獸), a category that implies both location and character, and parallels the language that dichotomizes animals from the wilds from cultured and domesticated animals. Just as the virtue of the individual sages reaches down to the birds and the beasts, so the cultivating and transformative power of empire reaches down to the bestial barbaric tribes on its distant periphery.[127]

Third, the passage illustrates how freak creatures were interpreted through integrating their appearance within received categories. Zhong Jun emphasizes that, whenever a virtuous ruler is established, the arrival of strange animals (*yi shou* 異獸) should not be understood as unusual or anomalous but, on the contrary, as self-evident and appropriate (*yi* 宜). The freakiness or hybridity of this strange creature is "de-anomalized" on the premise that what is "different-in-form" or abnormal (*wai* 外) will be integrated into the sphere of the interior (*nei* 內), since the virtue of the ruler encompasses its freakiness and internalizes such appearances into a recognizable metaphor for imperial authority (note that the text speaks about "appending barbarians to the inside of the empire"). As was the case with Confucius's identification of the clay sheep, the possibility whether a creature with one horn and cloven hoofs actually exists remains unquestioned; instead it is de-anomalized. In the same way that the sage accommodates the appearance of changing animals with human changes, the interpreter in this memorial accommodates the hybrid's strangeness through reaffirming the continuum between its natural appearance and the course of human affairs. Finally, in his exhortation to write down the events and preserve them on record following historical precedent, Zhong Jun also reaffirms the link between the recognition of an event as anomalous and noteworthy and its preservation in a textual record.

In a chapter on omenology Wang Chong criticizes the *ru*'s self-made claim that "upon seeing a phoenix or unicorn, they know them" because they rely on pictures or images of these animals and the textual precedent of the *Chunqiu* which identifies a deer with one horn as a unicorn. Literati, Wang argues, claim to be able to judge whether or not a bird with a variegated plumage or a one-horned deer are in fact a sacred phoenix or unicorn by "examining these cases by means of pictures and images" and "verifying them by past and present traditions."[128] Wang proceeds with a series of criticisms, some construed more resourcefully than others. He insists that ominous animals cannot be identified by their physical features, and that people arbitrarily attribute names to unusual creatures.[129] Wang further denounces the idea that animals which transcend their habitat should be thought of as ominous. If creatures can be identified as a phoenix or unicorn simply on the basis that they do not live in the Middle Kingdom but come from the outer wilds, then the sacred phoenix and unicorn would unrightfully be put on a par with ordinary mynahs.[130] Wang Chong also disputes the belief that the phoenix and unicorn, surrounded by their acolyte species, are omens for peace, and he denies the extrageneric distinctiveness of ominous creatures on the premise that classes and species should not be seen as fixed or permanent in the first place.[131]

By juxtaposing the phoenix and the unicorn with the human sage as a basic axiom of his analogies, Wang Chong however does not refute the existence of ominous animals but merely denies that a knowledge of these creatures depends on the recognition of external physical features. In the end the only valid criterion accepted by Wang to verify, differentiate, and judge animal omens is "the virtue of the government and the ruler at the time."[132] Wang's skepticism often remains founded on the assumption that there exists a sociopolitical base or, more general, an aetiology of human morals that correlates the interpretation of the animal world to the course of human affairs. His critique has thus come full circle: ominous animals are not species determined but stem from classificatory schemes that ultimately take human government as their parameter. The understanding of strange animals therefore depends on the comprehension of the correlation between human government and animal behavior.

The mere analysis of a creature's forms, shapes, or guise provides insufficient ground to deem it anomalous:

> A goat originally has two horns, the *xiebi* 觟䚦 has one. Its body is disadvantaged when compared with the flocks and it does not match its species group; why then should it be considered strange? A turtle with three legs is called a *nai* 能, and a tortoise with three legs is called a *fen* 賁. If neither a *nai* nor a *fen* can be more spiritlike than four-legged turtles and tortoises, why should a goat with one horn be wiser than animals with two horns?[133]

> Speaking from the point of view of wisdom and sagacity, sage birds and sage beasts and common birds and ordinary beasts alike all have strange features. Sage birds and beasts can possess benevolence, goodness, modesty, and purity, without there being any bodily peculiarity.[134]

Conclusion

Writings from the Warring States and Han periods firmly linked the perception of anomaly in the animal world with the idea that freak animals and anomalous animal behavior embodied change in the affairs of human society. In the same way that human sagacity was paralleled to imagery of metamorphosis in the animal realm, the sage was perceived as the agent who de-anomalized strange animals by relating their physical shape and appearance to receptive categories. As a cosmic agent able to change and accommodate to changing circumstances, a salient feature of the sage-ruler's disposition toward the nonhuman world was his perspicacity to unveil the prodigy as a category of normality.

When faced with the occurrence of strange events and the appearance of prodigious creatures in the natural world, the explanatory strategies applied by the sage consisted first of all in assigning the causes for the appearance of animal prodigies to misapprehensions on behalf of the human observer or to flaws in the workings of the human realm. Second, the strangeness of an animal appearance was controlled and hence explained by positioning the prodigy within a framework of known categories, and through attributing names to the uncanny. By naming unknown creatures and relating their appearance and behavior to familiar observations, the sage controlled the appearance of strange phenomena in the physical world in the same way as the lexicographer glossed rare and unknown animal graphs in the world of texts. In the end animal anomalies were clarified and neutralized through reiterating the interdependent and congruent nature of the human-animal relationship. In this sense, the sage explained change as a matter of permanence or constancy by underlining that the permutations of the living species were the outward signs of the fundamental hybridity of the world of man and the animal world.

CONCLUSION

We should note that no creature holds anything dearer than the kind of being that it is (lions, eagles, dolphins value nothing above their own species) and that every species reduces the qualities of everything else to analogies with its own. We can extend our characteristics or reduce them, but that is all we can do, since our intellect can do nothing and guess nothing except on the principle of such analogies; it is impossible for it to go beyond that point.

—Michel de Montaigne (1533–1592)[1]

One of the Outer Chapters in the *Zhuangzi* entitled "Horses' Hoofs" (*ma ti* 馬蹄) contains an edifying story featuring Bo Le 伯樂, China's legendary horse physiognomist. The text begins by evoking the natural instincts of horses in their normal environment, away from the stable and human manipulation. Horses' hoofs are there to tread the frost and snow; their coats serve to protect them against wind and cold. Horses are naturally inclined to graze, drink from a stream, and gallop around, twining their necks together and rubbing when pleased, and turning their backs on each other to kick when angry. Then comes Bo Le, who claims to know everything about horses and pretends to possess the skills to put them to optimal use. He singes them, shaves them, pares them, brands them, yokes them, and ties them up in stable and stall. He starves them and makes them go thirsty, races them, makes them run side by side in front of a carriage, and forces bit, whip, and rein onto them. As a result many horses succumb to his drill, die, or learn to resist their human instructor.

In many ways this study has been about Bo Le and his horse. It has examined the ways in which animals in their natural setting were yoked into cultural submission by the encompassing skills of the craftsman, the human observer, and the sage. It has also explored Bo Le's horses in their natural environment as creatures whose biological fate remained firmly distinct from the human world and whose natural instincts provided the ultimate measure to test the nature of Bo Le's skills. In other words, it has dealt with the ways in which the early Chinese appropriated the animal world to create ideals of human sagehood and socio-political authority. An ubiquitous theme throughout the previous pages has been a preoccupation with the ways in which the bounds between the horse's instincts and Bo Le's skills, nature and culture, were delineated in early Chinese thought.

What is clear first and foremost in this analysis is that Warring States and Han texts posit a general contingency and continuum between the human realm and the animal world. As signifying living creatures surrounding the human observer, the animal kingdom provided models for authority in human society and functioned as a catalytic medium for the conception of human morality. It has proven difficult to articulate a dichotomy between moral and natural (hence scientifically investigateable) animals in early China or to unveil a development toward systematized theoretical discourse on the physical animal. The reference to animals in Warring States and Han writings conflated moral and physical categories and illustrates again that perceptions of nature are socially constructed. In a recent anthropological essay Philippe Descola states that

> a common feature of all conceptualisations of non-humans is that they are always predicated by reference to the human domain. This leads either to sociocentric models, when social categories and relations are used as a kind of mental template for the ordering of the cosmos, or to a dualistic universe, as in the case of western cosmologies where nature is defined negatively as that ordered part of reality which exists independently from human action. Whether it operates by inclusion or by exclusion, the social objectivation of non-humans thus cannot be disjointed from the objectivation of humans; both processes are directly informed by the configuration of ideas and practice from which every society draws its concepts of self and otherness. Both processes imply establishing boundaries, ascribing identities and devising cultural mediations.[2]

The conceptualization of animals in ancient China clearly reflects a model that was predominantly sociocentric. The Chinese tended to think of their animals with morality without this ever having sparked a scientific impetus to get clear about animals themselves. The fact that discussions of the animal world were deeply implicated in the formulation of the human self-perception, ideals of sagehood, and human governance suggests that the predominant concern of its authors was to understand morality rather than animals. As such, animals, more than any other object in the natural world, provided a lens through which the natural realm and the social order of human society converged. Unlike their counterparts in the Greco-Roman world, the ancient Chinese did not develop a terminology of differentiating categories in order to analyze the animal realm as "a world of birds and beasts."

This aporia on the animal world as the object of a distinct realm of knowledge implied that knowledge of and control over the natural world was primarily qualified as the capability to detect signifying patterns in the animal realm in order to align human activity with the cycles detected in the surrounding fauna. Animals were viewed as a constituent part of an overarching organic whole that encompassed all living species. Explaining animals therefore entailed clarifying their place within this overall structure rather than seeking to delineate their ontological distinctiveness. The animal world was subsumed within a moral cosmos that constituted the habitat of both humans and animals. The notion that both realms were separated and functioned according to internal and mutually incompatible principles was firmly denied. Instead of seeking to delimit its boundaries within the fixity of ontological definition, the early Chinese primarily sought to explain what animals meant and signified to the human observer. However, the fact that the Chinese did not insist on developing a *theoria* of animals and the living species did not imply a humanistic disinterest toward everything nonhuman; rather it reflected a willingness to discuss animals as part of a larger natural world of which humans themselves constituted but one unstable part.

Indeed the question of how animals related to humans, in other words a concern with the human-animal correlation, was perceived to be more important than the preoccupation with the ontological conditions that determined that relationship. This concern for correlation applied to both real and imaginary animals. This study has shown that not only symbolically powerful and sacred animals acted to mediate the social world of man with the world of nature and the cosmos, but that a fundamental continuum between the human and animal world underpinned most contexts of textual discourse on animals, ranging from practical agricultural instructions in the calendar to edifying verses on sacred animals. This hermeneutic impulse to detect mutuality, congruence, and correlation between all living species reinforced a perception of animals as daemonic beings, that is, creatures which functioned as signifying exponents of a larger cosmic pattern rather than creatures conceived as purely biological species.[3]

If the main concern lay with correlating animals, humans, and daemonic creatures rather than with a search for ontological clarity about the biological differentiae among the living species, a fundamental ingredient of this correlation was the idea that this relationship was subject to change and transformation. The notion of change and transformation, as I have tried to show, profoundly shaped the way in which humans and animals were thought to relate to each other in early China. It percolated into the discourse on the human-animal relationship, inspired the view that species boundaries were blurred and that living creatures were subject to various forms of metamorphosis, and influenced the explanation of the supernatural animal anomaly. More importantly the changing correlations between man and beast and the image of physical transformation in the animal world provided models for human sagehood and daemonic power. To be sure the theory of change that runs through several chapters of this book is, to a certain degree, no more than a heuristic model composed from the perspective of a modern reader and based on a corpus of disparate references to the animal world in admittedly wide-ranging and variegated genres. However it is clear that the majority of its data, not in the least the direct textual discourse on change and transformation in relation with animals, find their origin in the sources themselves. The perspective gained at this point then is one in which the absence of an "ology" in the perception of the living species in early China, as indicated in the introduction, can be substituted by a category of change. And, paradoxically, it is this notion of change that has provided the ingredients for conceptual fixity in our reading of early Chinese references to the natural world.

How far, we may now ask, does this model of change relate, in turn, to the broader political, social, and philosophical paradigms that characterized Warring States and Han thought? The comprehension of the animal world was clearly not seen as an act of objectivation of the natural world but rather as an act of integration based on the acquisition of insight into the changing parameters of the man-animal relation. Here the window on the animal kingdom in early texts reveals as much about the human observer as about animals themselves in that it corroborates a fundamental feature in early Chinese thought: the primacy of change and process over permanence and substance, transformation over ontological fixity. Perhaps these features are well reflected in the notion that animals are primarily "moving beings" that prompt human movement and response. Should we look here for the semantic pedigree of the modern Chinese generic term for animals, *dong wu* 動物?

Against the background of a nature-culture continuum and a human-animal correlation that was subject to change, it is no surprise to find a prominent presence of the human sage or ruler-king in the discourse on animals. Mediating the interface between man and beast, and grasping the ever-changing conditions of their mutual relationship, the sage stands at the crossroads of the human-animal contingency, a crossroads with numerous paths radiating from it. One of the most salient features of the sage is that he is not prone to explicate what an animal is but rather how to deal with it or respond to signifying patterns in the animal realm. The mastery of animals consisted in the attribution of names to creatures and the subsumption of animals within the human ritual order. If the empirical observation that animals are named in all of the world's languages is considered a truism, the idea that the act of naming animals and explaining their behavioral features belonged to the domain of the sage or ruler-king rather than the technical expert, philosopher, or naturalist may distinguish early China from the Greek world. In the interface between the human and the bestial, the sage was said to morally transform the animal world through music and virtue. The sage further figured as the agent who grasps and explains manifestations of metamorphosis within the animal realm and relates these patterns of physical change to the human realm. Finally the sage determined the boundaries of the supernatural through attributing names to strange creatures, and through subsuming anomalous animals within receptive categories. In sum, the prominent role of the human sage in relation to textual discourse on animals epitomized the overarching tendency to subsume the animal into the human realm. In the idealized environment of a modern zoo, the ancient Chinese sages would probably choose to stroll along with the animals inside the cages rather than observe and analyze their behavior through a separating fence.

Finally the picture presented in this book remains inevitably incomplete. The relative scarcity of sources, both textual and material, which may provide testimony of the ways in which ordinary peasants and village dwellers in Warring States and Han China perceived the nonhuman species suggests that the mentalities reconstructed in this study are likely to reflect the views of those strata within society capable of creating, reading, preserving, and circulating texts. If reconstructing the meaning of animals in a particular society entails outlining the contours of its "entire system of collective representations, and of how animals enter into the social practices and cultural concerns of a people in their lives, in both everyday and extraordinary events," this book has been but a first step.[4] Nevertheless I hope it has illustrated that the study of the animal theme can provide a framework of explanation for a wider variety of phenomena and ideas beyond the reference to animals. It is precisely here that the study of animal references across different genres of texts may have some lessons to offer on how the inquiry into the animal kingdom reflects the way in which humans view their place among the living species. If this study has been successful in showing that, for this reason at least, Chinese attitudes toward the nonhuman species are worth examining, it will have achieved more than its purpose.

NOTES

Introduction. Contextualizing Animals

1. Harper (1998), 10. Rodney Taylor describes this consensus as a "prevailing tendency to classify the Confucian ethic as just another species of humanism." See Taylor (1986), 237.

2. Thomas (1983), 301.

3. Young (1985), 1–19; Rivo (1990), 39–42.

4. Burkert (1998), x. Annie Schnapp-Gourbeillon writes in an introduction to a study of animals in Homer: "L'animalité alors s'intègre à une entreprise plus vaste de réflexion de l'homme sur lui-même, recherche introvertie où l'altérité ne figure guère qu'en contrepoint." See Schnapp-Gourbeillon (1981), 11.

5. On this issue see the essays collected in Torrance (1992).

6. Tambiah (1985), 169–211; R. Tapper, "Animality, humanity, morality, society," in Ingold (1988), 47–51; Albert-Llorca (1991), 270–73.

7. Toynbee (1996), 21.

8. For a discussion of how the collection, classification, maintenance, study, and hunt of captive wild animals served to demonstrate human mastery of the natural world and British dominion over remote territories in the nineteenth century see Rivo (1990), 205–209, 217–26, 232–43, 243–88. For the use of animals as tokens of political submission and exhibits of imperialism see also Tuan (1984), 72–80; and Malamud (1998), 57–104.

9. On the rhetoric of animality as a discourse on the other see Baker (1993), 89–116.

10. I use the term "daemonic" to express the "signifying" or "numinous" in general, in the sense proposed by Angus Graham. See Graham (1981), 35, note 72.

11. Such studies include work on animals in myth by Rémi Mathieu (1984a, 1984b, 1984c, 1990) and Anne Birrell (1993), and studies on animal imagery in poetry and prose by Robert J. Cutter (1989a, 1989b), Madeline Spring (1988, 1993), Paul Kroll (1984), Robert Hightower (1959), William Graham (1979), James Hargett (1989), Suzanne Cahill (1987), and others (see note 23).

12. To this group belongs a wide range of studies by Chinese scholars discussing animal references according to theories of totemism including Liu Chungshee H. (1932, 1940–41), Ling Chunsheng (1957, 1971), Zhang Mengwen (1982), Zhou Qingming (1984), Liu Hong (1988), Liu Fude (1990), Wang Dayou (1988) and others. In Western scholarship the ethnohistorical approach is reflected in the works of J. J. M. De Groot (1892–1910), Marcel Granet (1926), Wolfram Eberhard (1968), Edward Schafer (1956, 1967, 1991), and Derk Bodde (1959, 1975). Dragon studies constitute a field in itself. Among its

most valuable contributions are studies by De Visser (1913, chapters 1 to 7), Jean-Pierre Diény (1987), Raymond Dragan (1993), John Hay (1994), Izushi Yoshihiko (1928), Shiratori Kiyoshi (1934), He Xin (1990), Liu Zhixiong and Yang Jingrong (1992), and Du Erwei (1966). A general survey of Chinese animal lore is included in Tournier (1991), 27–33, 43–217. This work however lacks scholarly depth and apparatus. The same applies to a survey of animals in art in Sowerby (1940), 19–128.

13. For an example of a moral analogy involving the owl, which devours its mother as it grows up, and young crows disgorging food to feed their mother see *Xinlun*, 6b, 21b–22a. See also *Shuowen jiezi zhu*, 6A.66a. Another unfilial beast believed to devour its father was the *pojing* 破鏡 "Mirror-breaker," allegedly offered during exorcismal sacrifices in spring. See *Hanshu*, 25A.1218; *Shiji*, 28.1386; and Eberhard (1968), 162–63. For the image of the crow as a filial bird disgorging its food see also chapter 1, p. 27 and note 63.

14. See for instance *Chuci*, 4.14b ("She jiang" 涉江), 13.13b ("Yuan si" 怨思); *Huainanzi*, 10.325 ("Miu cheng" 繆稱), 17.555 ("Shuo lin" 說林); *Liji zhushu*, 7.1a ("Tan gong shang" 檀弓上); *Shuowen jiezi zhu*, 10A.36a; *Bohutong shu zheng*, 9.433 ("Yi shang" 衣裳); *Qianfu lun*, 5.333 ("Shi bian" 實邊); *Wenzi*, 1.37a ("Shang de" 上德); *Hou Hanshu*, 16.631.

15. Schafer (1967; rpt. 1985), 236. Madeline Spring concludes in a more recent study: "Animals, whether of the lowest or highest orders, are only rarely featured or celebrated in their own right in T'ang literature. [T'ang writers] . . . were observers of the natural world (sometimes keenly so), but they were not naturalists. They saw most plants and animals as carrying significance for one's own moral life, owing to a well-developed literary tradition that conditioned the way they looked at the natural world around them, or at least how that world was to be reflected in literature." See Spring (1993), 150.

16. *Mao shi zhengyi*, 1C.11a–12a, "Lin zhi zhi" 麟之趾 (Mao 11).

17. Ominous animals lend their names to several reign dates in the Western Han: *yuan shou* 元狩 (122 B.C.E., following the capture of a unicorn), *yuan feng* 元鳳 (110 and 80 B.C.E.), *shen jue* 神爵 (61 B.C.E.), *wu feng* 五鳳 (57 B.C.E.) and *huang long* 黃龍 (49 B.C.E.). Wang Mang designated the year 14 C.E. *tian feng* 天鳳. No animals appear in Eastern Han reign dates.

18. *Songshu*, 28.791. It mentions seven Han cases. The unicorn essay is followed by a detailed catalog of portentous animals. See *Songshu*, 28.791–29.870.

19. Chang (1976), chapter 9, esp. 176–84, 195–96. See also Loewe (1978), 98–100.

20. Paludan (1991), 9.

21. Powers (1991), 247.

22. Recent discussions include Saussy (1993) and Yu (1987).

23. For a list of works dealing with the explanation of the fauna and flora in the *Shijing* from Han to Qing see chapter 1, note 39. In modern scholarship mention should be made of the work by Ishikawa Misao (1976, 1977a, 1977b, 1983). Fish imagery in the *Shijing* is treated in Wen Yiduo (1948) and Inoi Makoto (1975). On the golden oriole and other bird motives in the *Shijing* see Heian Shinshirō (1978); and C. H. Wang (1974), 114–25.

24. Yu (1987), 57–65.

25. Spring (1993), 152.

26. See Finsterbusch (1952); Wu Hung (1987), (1989); Powers (1983), (1991). For reference to animal material in Han murals see Shenzhen bowuguan (1995), esp. 61–70. An extensive chronological list with bibliographic references to excavated animal drawings and artifacts is included in Chen Wenhua (1994), ch. 4, pp. 426–563.

27. On the complex issues involved in the interpretation of animals encoded in prehistoric art and the problem of representation, identification, and meaning in general see Morphy (1989), 1–17. See also the remarks on "recognisable animals" in Hicks (1993), 5–9.

28. A recent comment claiming that the reading and interpretation of textual materials regarding animals "a de quoi plonger le chercheur dans la perplexité," and the suggestion that "les seules bases solides sur lesquelles, dans un premier temps, nous puissions asseoir une histoire renouvelée des animaux en Chine sont des bases matérielles," reflects the undervaluation of textual sources for the study of animals. See Elisséeff (1993), 21. For a survey of recent Chinese scholarship related to "anthropozoology" (defined by the author as a discipline that "studies the perception of animals by humans, and the psychical and physical relationship the latter maintains, willingly or unwillingly, with other living species") see Elisséeff (1998), 273–81.

29. Wolfram Eberhard's approach in the field of Chinese folklore studies reflects this in its adoption of an ethnological "geo-action" perspective over chronology. See Eberhard (1968).

30. The exact meaning of such figurines remains the subject of debate. Recurring features include deer antlers and a long tongue. Often these tomb guardian beasts grasp and devour snakes. In general they were put in the head compartment of medium-sized and large Chu tombs. It is uncertain whether they were produced exclusively for tombs, or whether they were actual representations of regional deities. Opinion differs as to whether the figurines were apotropaic psychopomps aimed at protecting the dead's spirit in the tomb or on its journey to the hereafter, or whether they were meant to ward off intruders from the world of the living. It has also been suggested that the figurines should be connected with the earth spirit *tubo* 土伯. For the state of the field see Salmony (1954); Wang Ruiming (1979); Chen Yaojun and Yuan Wenqing (1983); Peng Hao (1988); Wu Rongzeng (1989); Jiang Weidong (1991); Hasegawa Michitaka (1991); Qiu Donglian (1994); Zhang Jun (1994), 62–126; Zheng Shubin (1996); and Major (1999), 132–33. Dr Alain Thote (private communication, 7.1.1997) questions whether they exclusively belonged to Chu culture since most wooden objects buried in tombs outside Chu have decayed and leave us with no artifacts for comparison.

31. Animal names are glossed and annotated when relevant to the discussion. Latin nomenclature are based on Du Yaquan (1933), Han Li (1992) and the *Chinese Materia Medica* series by Bernard E. Read. Although technical nomenclature conveys authoritative specificity and common name translations are not always the best solution for culture-specific fauna, ordinary language may be closer to the original perception of the animals in question. In many instances I will not translate the Chinese animal name or

term in order to avoid the problem of translating language-specific words. As a rule, I have tried to use terms or definitions extracted from collective contextual meanings, rather than those imposed by modern zoology or biology.

Chapter One. Defining Animals

1. Lloyd (1996a), 7.

2. Lévi-Strauss (1962), 29.

3. Richard Sorabji (1993) has shown that debates about animal language and mind are at the heart of the Western philosophical tradition.

4. Plato's category of the "zoon" is described in *Timaeus*, 77B. See Bodson (1978), ix–x.

5. *Oxford English Dictionary* (2d ed.; Oxford: Clarendon, 1989), vol. 1, p. 474 [my italics].

6. *Shuowen jiezi zhu*, 2A.10a. See also Wang Guowei, "Shi wu" 釋物, in Wang Guowei (1923), 6.13b–14a.

7. Vandermeersch (1977–80), vol. 1, 223–28; Yang Xiaoneng (2000), 144.

8. K. C. Chang (1981), 537–40; Ai Linong (1985), 28.

9. *Guoyu*, 18.560 ("Chu yu xia" 楚語下).

10. Yang Bojun, *Zuozhuan zhu*, pp. 251–52 (Lord Zhuang, year 32), p. 1582 (Lord Ding, year 10).

11. *Zhuangzi jishi*, 19.634 ("Da sheng" 達生).

12. *Shuowen jiezi zhu*, 14B.18b–19a.

13. *Erya zhushu*, 10.11a.

14. *Shuowen jiezi zhu*, 14B.17a.

15. *Bohutong shu zheng*, 12.591 ("que wen" 闕文).

16. See his commentary in *Zhouli zhushu*, 4.6b.

17. *Shuowen jiezi zhu*, 14B.18b. Phonetic transcriptions refer, where possible, to Li Fanggui's 李方桂 reconstructions of Old Chinese as represented in Schuessler (1987). *Shou* 守 is a common variant for *shou* 獸 in Warring States manuscripts. For examples see *Guodian Chu mu zhujian*, "Zi yi" 緇衣, slip 38 (plates, p. 20); "Liu de" 六德, slip 43 (plates, p. 72); "Er san zi wen" 二三子問 in *Boshu Zhouyi jiaoshi*, 348. For an argument refuting Duan Yucai's 段玉裁 (1735–1815) interpretation of the graph 嘼 as "sacrificial victim" see Yang Shuda (1955b).

18. See his commentary in *Chunqiu Gongyang zhuan zhushu*, 4.11b. See also Fan Ning's 范甯 (339–401 C.E.) commentary in *Chunqiu Guliang zhuan zhushu*, 3.9a.

19. See his commentary in *Shangshu zhengyi*, 11.18b ("Wu Cheng" 武成); and *Chunqiu Zuozhuan zhengyi*, 51.10a–b.

20. *Zuozhuan zhu*, p. 1457 (Lord Zhao, year 25).

21. *Shuihudi Qin mu zhujian*, 192, 194, 195, 212, 213, 233, 237. The same animals are listed in the *Erya*. See *Erya zhushu*, 10.25b.

22. *Zhouli zhushu,* 4.6b, 13.1a. See also *Zuozhuan zhu,* p. 116 (Lord Huan, year 6).

23. *Shuowen jiezi zhu,* 13A.40b–41a. The confusion in defining *chong* 蟲 is illustrated in Fèvre (1993). This study neglects the use of animal terms in non-lexicographic texts and does not include *qin* 禽 among the general terms that denote animals.

24. Harper (1990), 225–30; and Harper (1998), 74.

25. *Zhouli zhushu,* 10.3b–4a. See also Zou Shuwen (1982); Gou Cuihua (1989), 95.

26. Opinion differs regarding the definition of the "naked" or "scantily haired" species, i.e. animals without any natural covering apart from the skin. Zheng Xuan states that *luo chong* refers to short-haired animals such as the tiger and the leopard. See his commentary in *Liji zhushu,* 16.14a ("Yue ling" 月令); and *Zhouli zhushu,* 41.13b. Gao You's 高誘 (fl. 200 C.E.) commentary to the *Lüshi chunqiu* notes that the *qilin* is the head of the naked animals. See *Lüshi chunqiu jiaoshi,* 6.323 note 29 ("Ji xia ji" 季夏紀). These identifications continue to be an issue of debate among Chinese zoohistorians. See Gou Cuihua (1958).

27. The relative absence of denotative definition and categorization of the natural world in China has prompted comments by Western sinologists on earlier occasions. While Marcel Granet's contention that the Chinese "n'ont aucun goût pour classer par *genres* et par *espèces*" referred to a hesitation in Chinese thought to define ideas without evoking concrete examples, J. J. M. De Groot was more categorical in concluding that "Chinese authors have roundly avowed themselves altogether unable to discover any real difference between men and animals." See Granet (1934; rpt. 1999), 125; De Groot (1892–1910; rpt. 1964), vol. 4, 157.

28. Harbsmeier (1998), 54.

29. Hall and Ames (1995), 253.

30. *Bian wu xiaozhi,* pp. 3–4, referring to *Zhouyi zhengyi,* 1.30b; *Liji zhushu,* 1.11a; *Cai Shi Yueling wen da,* 5a; *Zhouli zhushu,* 18.22b–23a ("the six gifts"), 41.13a–16a ("Ziren" 梓人).

31. *Chunqiu fanlu jinzhu jinyi* (*Chunqiu fanlu* hereafter), 5.140 ("Zhong zheng" 重政). The same statement occurs in *Da Dai Liji,* 5.8a ("Zhong zheng").

32. *Yiwen leiju,* 93.1617. The story is based on Dong's reputation as a reclusive erudite of the *Chunqiu* who lectured to his students from behind a curtain. See *Shiji,* 121.3127.

33. *Shuowen jiezi zhu,* 3A.15a.

34. *Shuowen jiezi zhu,* 2A.4a. The link between animals and the origins of writing is discussed in chapter 4.

35. Such diverging views within the *Chunqiu fanlu* may derive from the fact that it is a composite work with many of its chapters, especially those dealing with *yin-yang* and five-phase thought, no longer credited with Dong's authorship. See Queen (1996), 93–104.

36. *Lunyu zhushu,* 17.5a ("Yang Huo" 陽貨) [my italics]. According to one count, 109 animal species occur throughout the *Shijing*. See Wang Zichun and Cheng Baochao (1997), 15.

37. SCC, vol. 6, part 1, 191.

38. *Shiji,* 130.3297. See also *Hanshu,* 62.2717.

39. Lu Ji's work, which is extant, is mentioned in Sui and Tang bibliographic treatises. See *Suishu,* 32.917; *Jiu Tangshu,* 46.1971; and *Xin Tangshu,* 57.1429. This last work further mentions a *Mao shi caomu chongyu tu* 毛詩草木蟲魚圖 in 20 scrolls. See *Xin Tangshu,* 57.1430. Works dealing with zoological and botanical nomenclature in the *Shijing* similar to that of Lu Ji as well as commentaries and supplements to Lu Ji's work proliferate in later periods. These include titles such as Cai Bian's 蔡卞 (1058–1117) *Mao shi ming wu jie* 毛詩名物解 (its glosses on animals comprise chapters 6 to 14); and Mao Jin's 毛晉 (1599–1659) *Mao shi caomu niaoshou chongyu shu guangyao* 毛詩草木鳥獸蟲魚疏廣要 or *Mao shi Lu shu guangyao* 毛詩陸疏廣要. A work entitled *Mao shi cao chong jing* 毛詩草蟲經, possibly compiled during the Six Dynasties period, was extant at least until the Northern Song. Fragments of four chapters are preserved in Ma Guohan's 馬國翰 (1794–1857) *Yuhan shanfang ji yishu* 玉函山房輯佚書 (Changsha, 1883), fasc. 17. Other works include (Anon.?) *Mao shi yu ming jin kao yi juan jiayu kao yi juan* 毛詩魚名今考一卷嘉魚考一卷; Xu Shijun's 徐士俊 *San bai pian niaoshou caomu ji* 三百篇鳥獸草木記 (1699); Yao Bing's 姚炳 *Shi shi ming jie* 詩識名解 (1708); Xu Ding's 徐鼎 *Mao shi ming wu tu shuo* 毛詩名物圖說 (1772); Fang Huan's 方瓛 *Du shi shi wu* 讀詩釋物 (1783); Mao Qiling's 毛奇齡 (1623–1716) *Xu shi zhuan niao ming* 續詩傳鳥名; Chen Dazhang's 陳大章 (fl. ca. 1700) *Shi zhuan ming wu jilan* 詩傳名物集覽; Jiao Xun's 焦循 (1763–1820) *Mao shi caomu niaoshou chongyu shi* 毛詩草木鳥獸蟲魚釋 and *Lu Shi caomu niaoshou chongyu shushu* 陸氏草木鳥獸蟲魚疏疏; Mou Yingzhen's 牟應震 (ca. 1800) *Mao shi wu ming kao* 毛詩物名考; Mao Yuanding's 茅原定 *Shijing ming wu jicheng* 詩經名物集成 (1803); and Huang Chunkui's 黃春魁 (Qing) *Shijing niaoshou caomu kao* 詩經鳥獸草木考 (preface dated 1848).

40. Van Zoeren (1991), 45.

41. Compare for instance the brief survey on China in Petit and Théodoridès (1962), 15–22, with its data on Greece and other areas.

42. Cf. Métailié and Fèvre (1993), 99.

43. "Long xu" 龍虛 (ch. 22), "Luan long" 亂龍 (ch. 47), "Zao hu" 遭虎 (ch. 48), "Shang chong" 商蟲 (ch. 49), "Jiang rui" 講瑞 (ch. 50).

44. The best account of the sources, disciplines (astrology, divination, medicine), and activities of these natural specialists is Professor Harper's chapter "Warring States Natural Philosophy and Occult Thought," in Loewe and Shaughnessy (1999). For a survey of manuscript evidence up to 1993 see Harper (1997).

45. *Hanshu,* 30.1775. Xie Chengxia suggests that this work was lost between the end of the Han prior to the Sui. See Xie Chengxia (1980), 358.

46. *Hanshu,* 30.1773. For an extensive bibliographic survey of later works on horses, other equines, cattle, ovines, poultry, fish, and silkworms, see Wang Yuhu (1979).

47. *Jiu Tangshu,* 47.2035.

48. See the section on fish farming in the *Qimin yaoshu.* Taozhu Gong became an eponym for individuals associated with economic success and material welfare. See *Shiji,* 129.3257.

49. *Guoyu*, 21.657 ("Yue yu xia" 越語下).

50. *Hanshu*, 30.1770. Titles include *Guishu* 龜書, *Xia gui* 夏龜, *Nan guishu* 南龜書, *Ju gui* 巨龜 and *Za gui* 雜龜 .

51. Reign dates for the pre-imperial period follow those given in Loewe and Shaughnessy (1999), 25–29 (table 1).

52. *Jiu Tangshu*, 47.2035; *Xin Tangshu*, 59.1538. According to the bibliographic treatise in the *Suishu*, works entitled *Xiangyajing* 相鴨經 ("Classic on the Physiognomy of Ducks"), *Xiangjijing* 相雞經 ("Classic on the Physiognomy of Chickens") and *Xiangejing* 相鵝經 ("Classic on the Physiognomy of Geese") were in circulation during the Liang 梁 period (502–587 C.E.). It also mentions another work on crane physiognomy attributed to the Eight Lords of Huainan (Huainan Ba Gong 淮南八公). See *Suishu*, 34.1039 (division on the five phases).

53. The *Yang yang fa* is preserved in fragments in *juan* six of the *Qimin yaoshu*. It is also collated in Ma Guohan, *Yuhan shanfang ji yishu*, vol. 14, fasc. 69. On Bu Shi see also chapter 5, p. 151.

54. *Zhouli zhushu*, 5.8b–9a (*shouyi* 獸醫), 33.6b (*wuma* 巫馬). See also Zhongguo chumu shouyi xuehui (1992), 2–21.

55. On physiognomy see Sterckx (1996), 72–75. For animal medicine see for instance *Shanhaijing jiaozhu*, 2.29, 4.114, 5.158 (plants said to improve the gait of horses). Itō Seiji suggests a link between the appliance of red herbal juices to horses and the image of the "blood-sweating" Ferghana horses. See Itō Seiji (1959), 110–12.

56. Xia Henglian and Lin Zhengtong (1996), 100, plate B36.

57. Compare for instance the attention devoted to the veterinary treatment of horses in ancient Rome. See Hyland (1990), 49–60; and R. E. Walker, "Roman Veterinary Medicine," in Toynbee (1996), 303–23. The importance of the horse in Zhou China is evident in the *Shijing*. According to one count, no less than eighty poems mention horses and/or chariots. See Yang Wensheng (1996).

58. Kaltenmark (1953), 47–48. For Ma Shihuang see also *He tu ting zuo fu* 河圖挺佐輔 in *Weishu jicheng*, 1109.

59. *Xunzi jijie*, 4.124–25 ("Ru xiao" 儒效).

60. *Liezi*, 2.9a–b ("Huang di" 黃帝).

61. *Hanshu*, 30.1772, in the division "Za Zhan" 雜占 ("Miscellaneous divinations").

62. *Hanshu*, 30.1753, in the division "Za fu" 雜賦 ("Miscellaneous rhapsodies").

63. The manuscript (21 slips, ca. 664 characters) is dated to the Yongshi 永始 and Yuanyan 元延 reign periods, 16–8 B.C.E. The tomb occupant has been identified as Shi Rao 師饒 (cognomen Junxiong 君兄), chief of the Labor Service section of Donghai 東海 commandery. See Teng Zhaozong (1996). A transcription appeared in Lianyungang-shi bowuguan (1996). For the excavation report, photo reproductions of the slips, and an updated transcription see *Yinwan Han mu jiandu*, 148–150 (transcription), 114–33 (plates). Annotations and recent discussions include Qiu Xigui (1997); Liu Lexian and Wang Zhiping (1997); Yu Wanli (1997); Fu Junlian (1997); and Wang Zhiping (1999).

The benevolent and filial nature of the crow egorging its food to feed its mother is eulogized in a stone inscription on a Han pillar gate recovered in 1964 at Babaoshan 八寶山 in the western suburbs of Beijing (dated between 89 and 113 C.E.). See Beijing shi wenwu gongzuo dui (1964); Shao Mingsheng (1964); and Guo Moruo (1965). An apocryphal text associates flying with *yang*, states that *yang* vapor forms benevolence, and claims that therefore the crow egorges its food. See *Chunqiu yun dou shu* 春秋運斗樞 in *Weishu jicheng*, 722. See also *Shangshu wei* 尚書緯 in *Weishu jicheng*, 391.

64. Fuyang Han jian zhengli zu (1983), 23; Li Ling (1993a), 78–81; and Li Ling (1993b), 11–12.

65. Xie Chengxia (1980), 360. Slips that may have belonged to the original text include nos. 0315, 0208, 0221, 0242, 0261, 1639, 1808, 1826, 2289, 2790, 3483, 3889, 4047, and 4233 in *Yinqueshan Han jian shiwen*.

66. For a transcription of the 5200 character text see Mawangdui Han mu boshu zhengli xiaozu (1977); and Li Ling (1993b), 1–10. See also Xie Chengxia (1977). Major parts of the text focus on the physiognomy of the horse's eyes and head. The editors suggest that it was written in Chu during the late Warring States period. According to He Runkun it should be dated to the early second century B.C.E. See He Runkun (1989a), 66. The problematic nature of the text is reflected in the remarkable silence of secondary scholarship on this manuscript since its excavation. Zhao Kuifu (1989) has speculated that the actual manuscript consists of three distinct parts (a main text and two commentaries). The bibliographic treatise of the *Suishu* (completed in 656 C.E.) mentions a *Xiangmajing* 相馬經 in one scroll. See *Suishu*, 34.1039. Both *Jiu Tangshu* (47.2035) and *Xin Tangshu* (59.1538) mention a *Xiangmajing* in one scroll attributed to the famous horse physiognomer Bo Le whose inspections allegedly increased the value of a horse ten-fold. See *Zhanguo ce*, 30.1092. A physiognomic treatise entitled *Tong ma xiangfa* 銅馬相法 is attributed to the Eastern Han warlord Ma Yuan 馬援 who became a horse spirit in Tang times. See *Hou Hanshu*, 24.840–41; Schafer (1967; rpt. 1985), 99; Xie Chengxia (1980), 362–63. Some early veterinary manuals are attributed to animal physiognomers such as, for example, a work entitled *Bo Le zhi ma zabing jing* 伯樂治馬雜病經 ("Bo Le's Classic on the Treatment of Various Horse Ailments"). See *Suishu*, 34.1048. Further discussions of horse physiognomy include Zou Jiezheng (1959); Chen Enzhi (1987); and Gou Cuihua (1989), 18. For a survey of post-Han sources related to the horse see William Y. Chen (1993), 223–45.

67. For a transcription and discussion of this text see Fuyang Han jian zhengli zu (1988); Hu Pingsheng and Han Ziqiang (1988). The language in *Wanwu* is very similar to passages in the *Shanhaijing*. For its botanical nomenclature see Dong Yuan (1995). On its role as an antecedent of materia medica literature see Harper (1998), 33–34. The early Chinese use of animals as drugs and foodstuffs, a subject still awaiting a more systematic treatment, falls beyond the scope of this study.

68. Loewe (1967), vol. 2, 302–307.

69. For theft see *Shuihudi Qin mu zhujian*, 100, 103, 104, 105, 151, 152; A. F. P. Hulsewé (1985), D24, D35, D36, D37, D38, D39, D40, E10, E11; on animal breeding see *Shuihudi Qin mu zhujian*, 22, 24, 74, 76, 86, 87; Hulsewé (1985), A7, A9, B20, B27, C18, C19; on army horses see *Shuihudi Qin mu zhujian*, 81; Hulsewé (1985), C6; on chickens and pigs see *Shuihudi*

Qin mu zhujian, 35; Hulsewé (1985), A34; on private parks see *Shuihudi Qin mu zhujian*, 47; Hulsewé (1985), A64; on the tiger hunt see *Shuihudi Qin mu zhujian*, 85; Hulsewé (1985), C16; on wounding horses see *Shuihudi Qin mu zhujian*, 86; Hulsewé (1985), C17. For reference to hunting and fishing in the Shuihudi slips see He Runkun (1989b).

70. *Yunmeng Longgang Qin jian*, 33, lines 48–49. A similar law occurs in the Shuihudi legal codes. See chapter 5, p. 145. Legal provisions regarding animals and their treatment occur throughout later legal codes. The Tang code contains numerous articles on public stables, herdsmen, sacrificial victims, and government animals, as well as legal measures to punish owners for the aggressive behavior of their domestic animals. See *Tang lü shu yi*, 15.275–88 (arts. 196–209, 279, 399, 408, 422); tr. Johnson (1997), 178–97. The laws related to the board of war in the Qing Code (*Da Qing lü li* 大清律例) contain a section entitled "Stables and Herds" (*jiu mu* 廏牧). It deals with issues such as the verification of livestock, the treatment of sick and emaciated animals, injuries inflicted to animals, slaughter, the reporting of newborns, etc. See Jones (1994), 218–24.

71. Schafer (1967; rpt. 1985), 206.

72. *Historia Animalium, De Partibus Animalium, De Generatione Animalium, De Motu Animalium, De Incessu Animalium*. For a survey of the main principles of Aristotle's analyses of animals see French (1994), 43–81. In contrast with its contemporaries of Han, the Roman world too witnessed the compilation of encyclopaedic works on biology and natural history such as Pliny the Elder's (23–79 C.E.) *Historia Naturalis*.

73. Francesca Bray comments: "the chapters on stock-raising in the agricultural treatises are short and usually tucked away at the back of the volume. . . ." See Bray (1984), 3–7. For an assessment of the role of pasture husbandry and fish farming in Qin and Han times see Yu Huaqing and Zhang Tinghao (1982); and Yu Huaqing (1982). For bibliographic surveys of sources on animal husbandry see Wang Yuhu (1958); Zhang Zhongge and Zhu Xianhuang (1986).

74. See K. C. Chang (1977), 25–83.

75. Hunan nongxueyuan (1978), 42–83.

76. A volume on the history of Chinese zoology has appeared recently (in Chinese) claiming to fill the gap in the section on the biological sciences of the *Science and Civilisation in China* project. See Guo Fu, Li Yuese (Joseph Needham), and Cheng Qingtai (1999). This volume, published in Beijing by Kexue chubanshe, is a collaborative effort by Chinese historians of science and zoology supplemented with materials collected by Dr. Needham in preparation for a planned study on zoology. This work deserves to be commended as a detailed survey of the state of scholarship in the history of zoology among Chinese scholars. However as a plea for the existence of a biological science of animals, and especially with reference to the pre-imperial and early imperial period, this project remains unconvincing. Its conception is illustrative of a prevailing trend among Chinese scholars in the history of zoology to infer a (proto) scientific ideology from early Chinese sources by collating only those data which evince a zoological interest in animals while disregarding the context of the sources, their share in the overall body of preserved texts, or the social context in which these writings may have circulated. Rather than making a strong case for the existence of a

scientific interest in the animal world in early China, its authors focus predominantly on the association of modern zoological nomenclature with ancient Chinese terminology. In doing so they perpetuate a long Chinese tradition in which the explanation of the natural world is equated with the textual exegesis of the nomenclature that represent it. The position of the human observer and the question whether or not the early Chinese collected animal data with a view to analyzing the workings of the animal world itself are left ignored.

77. See W. South Coblin, "Erh ya," in Loewe (1993), 94–99. It has been suggested that the *Erya* chapters on wild and domestic animals originally formed one chapter. See Zou Shuwen (1982), 512.

78. Needham, SCC, vol. 6, part 1, 186–94.

79. *Erya zhushu*, 1.5a.

80. *Erya zhushu*, 10.18a (*shu shu* 鼠屬), 10.23a (*ma shu* 馬屬), 10.23b (*niu shu* 牛屬), 10.24b (*yang shu* 羊屬, *gou shu* 狗屬), 10.25a (*ji shu* 雞屬).

81. *Erya zhushu*, 9.17a.

82. See the preface to his *Erya caomu chongyu niaoshou shilie* 爾雅草木蟲魚鳥獸釋列 in Wang Guowei (1923), 5.1a–2a. See also Gu Yanlong (1990), 166.

83. *Erya zhushu*, 9.13b.

84. Generic terms include *xiong-pin/ci* 雄-牝/雌 ("cock and hen"): 10.3b, 10.4a, 10.6b; *pin-mu* 牝-牡: 10.11b, 10.12a, 10.21b; *da-xiao* 大-小: 9.17b, 9.18a, 9.21b, 9.23a, 10.25a; *zi* 子: 9.12a, 9.14a, 9.18a, 10.10b, 10.11b, 10.12a, 10.12b, 10.14a. *Mu-pin* 牡-牝 together with the "cock and hen" mode occur as a gender distinction among animals in an early chapter of the *Mozi*. See *Mozi jiaozhu*, 1.48 ("Ci guo" 辭過). Liu Xiang 劉向 (ca. 77–6 B.C.E.) notes that *yin-yang* is manifest among birds as "cock and hen," among quadrupeds as *mu* and *pin*. See *Shuoyuan jiaozheng*, 18.450 ("Bian wu" 辨物). See also Yang Shuda (1955a).

85. See for example *Erya zhushu*, 9.13b, 9.14b. On the polysemantic nature of *chong* in the *Erya* see further Gu Yanlong (1990), 23–26, 59–60.

86. *Erya zhushu*, 9.19b, 9.20a–b, 9.22a–b. For annotations of the *Erya* insect and fish names see Shi Xiaoshi (1990); Liu Shipei 劉師培 (1884–1919), *Erya chong ming jinshi* 爾雅蟲名今釋 (in *Liu Shenshu xiansheng yishu* 劉申叔先生遺書 [Shanghai: Jiangsu guji, 1997], pp. 446–59). See also Huang Kan's 黃侃 (1886–1935) *Erya zheng ming ping* 爾雅正名評; and Cheng Yaotian's 程瑤田 (1725–1814) *Shi chong xiao ji* 釋蟲小記. The latter is discussed in Métailié (1992), 171 ff.

87. *Erya zhushu*, 10.19a–b.

88. See the commentaries by Guo Pu 郭璞 (276–322 C.E.) and Xing Bing in *Erya zhushu*, 10.7b, 10.8a. See also *Shuyiji*, 2.20b, where a text entitled *Xianjing* 仙經 ("Classic on Immortality") is quoted as a source for this name. For dialectal variants see *Fangyan jianshu*, 8.287.

89. For a chart reconstructing the animal categories of the *Erya* against a modern zoological taxonomy see Gou Cuihua (1989), 94.

90. *Erya zhushu*, 10.10a, 10.19a. According to Duan Chengshi 段成式 (803?–863 C.E.), the *guanzhuan* or *furou* was also known as the *duoyi* 墮羿 "Shed-feather." See *Youyang zazu*, 16.155 (no. 625).

91. *Erya zhushu*, 10.10b. See also *Bowuzhi*, 2.3b.

92. *Erya zhushu,* 10.9b. Guo Pu comments that the burrow is three to four Chinese feet in the ground with the rat staying inside while the bird remains outside. A mountain called "Bird-rat Common Cave" 鳥鼠同穴 is mentioned in the "Yu Gong" 禹貢. See *Shangshu zhengyi,* 6.28a ("Yu gong"). See also *Shanhaijing jiaozhu,* 2.64; *Shiji,* 2.70; *Huainanzi,* 4.152 ("Di xing" 墜形); *Hanshu,* 28A.1532, 1533, 1534; *He tu kuo di xiang* 河圖括地象 in *Weishu jicheng,* 1099.

93. The *Guangya* 廣雅 (compiled by Zhang Yi 張揖, ca. 230 C.E.) follows the *Erya* organization into nineteen semantic chapters including five animal chapters (ch. 15–19). Although new graphs are included, a similar emphasis on nomenclature/ synonimity is maintained. The *Xiao Erya* 小爾雅, which comprises all of chapter 11 in the *Kong Congzi* and contains about 650 target characters, includes a subchapter on birds (*guang niao* 廣鳥) and a subchapter dealing with domestic and other animals (*guang shou* 廣獸). For a reconstruction see Ariel (1996), 138–67. The *Piya* 埤雅, compiled by Lu Dian 陸佃 (1078–1085 C.E.), comprises twelve chapters dealing with animals.

94. SCC, vol. 6, part 1, 194 ff. See also Hervouet (1964), 335–36.

95. *Hanshu,* 30.1720, 1721. The *Suishu* refers to the work as *Ji jiu zhang* 急就章 (1 scroll). See *Suishu,* 32.942. The *Jiu Tangshu* adds a *Ji jiu zhang zhu* 注 (1 scroll) attributed to Yan Zhitui 顏之推 (ca. 531–591 C.E.). See *Jiu Tangshu,* 46.1985. The transmitted version contains commentaries by Yan Shigu 顏師古 (581–645 C.E.) and Wang Yinglin 王應麟 (1223–1296 C.E.).

96. *Ji jiu pian,* 1.33.

97. *Ji jiu pian,* 3.247–48 (according to the commentators *jiao* dogs are a species of big dogs bred by the Xiongnu 匈奴), 3.193, 4.257–59, 4.322, 4.295. Some animal nomenclature are also preserved in the *Cang Jie pian* 倉頡篇, an orthographic primer attributed to Li Si 李斯 (280?–208 B.C.E.) which has been partly recovered from tombs in Juyan (Gansu) and Fuyang (Anhui).

98. *Mao shi zhengyi,* 20A.5b–10b; translation adapted from Legge (1871; rpt. 1991), 611–13; and Karlgren (1950), 254. I read 思 as "thoughts" or "thinking" in the first sentence of each final pair following Zhu Xi 朱熹 (1130–1200 C.E.), *Shi ji zhuan,* 20.2a–3b; and Yuan Mei 袁梅, *Shijing yi zhu,* 603–606. This reading is open to criticism since 思 **sjegh* can also be a meaningless initial particle or a determinative demonstrative in the *Shijing* ("these [horses, chariots] go on endlessly, these are unswerving," etc.). See Dobson (1968), 2.4.1.6.2 (p. 36); 3.8.1 (p. 124); 4.10.1 (p. 168). On the optative use of *si* as I read it in the final verse ("Would that," "may") see Shaughnessy (1997), 191 note 29. The last stanza contains the line *si wu xie* 思無邪, which is quoted by Confucius in the Analects (II.2) to characterise the Odes as a whole. I question whether Confucius simply used this line as a "stimulus" (*xing*) as traditional interpretations have suggested. See Van Zoeren (1991), 37–38. In my view this phrase and its parallels in the preceding stanzas refer to an act of mental concentration. The fact that *si wu xie* is lifted from a poem that focuses on the enumerative and performative use of language may suggest that Confucius saw the recitative use of the Odes as a way to empower one's thoughts and prevent them from "swerving," similar to the way in which the duke in this poem channels his mind on his

horses. This interpretation also tallies with Confucius' admonition in Analects XVII.9 to attain the deeper moral meaning of the Odes and stimulate the mind through studying the names of its fauna and flora. It also allows for a metaphorical reading of the image of herdsmanship as an analogy for apt rulership. On the latter, see Saussy (1993), 67–72.

99. See Chen Zizhan et al. (eds.) (1983), 1157, referring among others to Wang Wufeng's 王梧鳳 (18th cent.) *Shi xue nü wei* 詩學女爲.

100. *Quan shanggu Sandai Qin Han Sanguo Liuchao wen,* 58.3a–b ("Quan Hou Han wen"). For an excellent study of this piece see Harper (1987).

101. Salisbury (1994), 6–7; George and Yapp (1991), 37–41; Hicks (1993), 181–82. Echoing Adam's role as namegiver, claims were made throughout European history for those languages which possessed the linguistic property to approximate animal sounds or name animals to be the Adamic or original language of the human race. See Eco (1997), 80–81, 83–85, 99, 111, 183–85.

102. Liu Xi's 劉熙 (died ca. 219 C.E.) *Shiming* 釋名 contains no entries on animals.

103. *Shuowen jiezi zhu,* 10A.37b–38a. In the *Xunzi,* the "five skills squirrel" symbolizes the idea of having many talents but not being able to bring them to perfection. See *Xunzi jijie,* 1.9–10 ("Quan xue" 勸學).

104. On the Shang origins of some of the main animal graphs see Hopkins (1913); Gibson (1935); Ding Su (1966); Lefeuvre (1990–91); Yang Xiaoneng (2000), 90, 114. For a list of Shang oracle bone graphs related to animals in general see Guo Fu et al. (1999), 23–31; and Ding Su (1993), 267–89.

105. *Shuowen jiezi zhu,* 13B.12b.

106. See also William G. Boltz in Loewe (1993), 430.

107. *Shuowen jiezi zhu,* 11B.16b, 4A.38a, 5A.43b, 10A.37a.

108. *Shuowen jiezi zhu,* 4A.31b, 5A.43b.

109. *Shuowen jiezi zhu,* 10A.1a. The *Bohutong* states that the graph *ma* 馬 rather than *bing* 兵 is used in the title *sima* 司馬, "commander of the army" because it is a *yang* 陽 creature. See *Bohutong shu zheng,* 4.132 ("Feng gong hou" 封公侯). For the horse's association with martiality see also Ying Shao's 應劭 (fl. ca. 140–204 C.E.) commentary to *Hanshu,* 100B.4269; *Hou Hanshu,* 24.840–41; *Dong guan Han ji,* 12.2b–3a.

110. *Shuowen jiezi zhu,* 2A.5a.

111. *Shuowen jiezi zhu,* 10A.36a. Fox demons and fox possession were known at least as early as the third century B.C.E. The hitherto earliest reference to fox possession occurs in two recipes of the *Wushier bing fang* 五十二病方. See *Mawangdui Han mu boshu,* vol. 4, 50 (columns 204, 210); tr. Harper (1998), 261 (no. 124), 264 (no. 128). By Han times imagery of the fox as a crafty cheat was common. See *Xinxu xiang zhu,* 2.42–43 ("Za shi"); *Zhanguo ce,* 14.482. There is an extensive literature on vulpine lore in medieval and late imperial China. See De Groot (1892–1910; rpt. 1964), vol. 4, 188–96; Watters (1874); Johnson (1974); Mathieu (1984c); Hu Kun (1992); Hammond (1996); Huntington (1996), 24–56, 64–76, 78–130, 131–79; Blauth (1996); and Chan (1998).

112. *Shuowen jiezi zhu,* 13B.9a. Xu adds that the tortoise has a bone structure on the outside and flesh at the inside.

113. See *Liji zhushu,* 24.14a ("Li qi" 禮器), 25.12a ("Jiao te sheng" 郊特牲). For a statement that, because of its longevity, the tortoise was preferred above the hoofs of oxen or pig skulls see *Huainanzi,* 17.561 ("Shuo lin"). See also *Bohutong shu zheng,* 7.329 ("Shi gui" 蓍龜).

114. SCC, vol. 6, part 1, 143–44.

115. See Riccardo Fracasso, "Shan hai ching," in Loewe (1993), 357–67.

116. These formula appear predominantly in the first five books of the *Shanhaijing,* the so-called "Wu zang shan jing" 五臧山經. See Fracasso (1983). This study also contains a table with all animals and spirits that figure in the first five books, their dwelling place, the events they foreshadow, and the remedies to counter them. In Fracasso's reading drought occurs most frequently among the foretold events.

117. Hall and Ames have drawn attention to the polysemantic value of the character *ming* 名 meaning both "to mean" and "to name." "Naming" in this sense has a strong connotation of contributing meaning to the object (*wu* 物) to be named. See Hall and Ames (1987), 272–73. The distinctiveness of a name as an identifying property of a creature is evinced in many entries on animal drugs in the *Bencao gangmu* 本草綱目, where Li Shizhen 李時珍 (1518–1593) distinguishes between explaining the name of an animal (*shi ming* 釋名), and explanatory notes on its biological properties (*jijie* 集解).

118. *Shanhaijing jiaozhu,* p. 477.

119. *Shanhaijing jiaozhu,* 16.396. For a similar example see *Shanhaijing jiaozhu,* 16.399.

120. For examples see *Shanhaijing jiaozhu,* 1.9, 1.15, 1.18, 2.35, 2.52, 2.65, 3.67, 3.72, 3.73, 3.74, 3.85, 3.86, 3.88, 3.89, 3.91, 3.92, 3.95, 3.97, 4.107, 4.108, 4.111, 4.115, 5.123, 5.137, 5.166, 5.167. Formula include: 其鳴自叫, 其鳴自詨, 其名自叫, 其名自號, 其名自呼, 其鳴自呼, 其音如呼, 其音如號.

121. *Shanhaijing jiaozhu,* 1.1.

122. *Yilin,* 1.7a. For variora see *Yilin,* 2.21b, 11.6b.

123. *Han Feizi jishi,* 1.67 ("Zhu dao" 主道): "The enlightened ruler . . . orders names to name themselves and affairs to settle themselves" (*ling ming zi ming ye, ling shi zi ding ye* 令名自命也, 令事自定也). See also *Han Feizi jishi,* 2.121–22 ("Yang quan" 揚權); *Shiji,* 130.3292; and Makeham (1994), 73–74.

124. *Jing fa,* 42 ("Ming li" 名理, line 11).

125. *Shanhaijing jiaozhu,* 6.186. On the relationship between piscines and reptiles with reference to the south see chapter 6, pp. 176, 189–90.

126. This is well illustrated in a case study of the *tiao* 鰷 fish by Michael Carr (1993). The *tiao* fish [*hemiculter;* cf. Read (1937), no. 157], which appears in the famous *Zhuangzi* dialogue on the happiness of the fish (*Zhuangzi jishi,* 17.606–607, "Qiu shui" 秋水), is associated with happiness in other sources (e.g., *Xunzi jijie,* 4.57, "Rong ru" 榮辱), and figures in the *Shanhaijing* (3.68, 3.80, 4.102) as a medicinal device against melancholy. However later dictionaries frequently explain this by pointing at the homophony of *tiao* (*diegwx) with several other graphs expressing happiness (陶 *degwh; 窕, 跳 *diagwx).

127. *Kong Congzi,* 5.8b ("Zhi jie" 執節); Ariel (1996), 58. Although this text was most

likely shaped during the course of several centuries, as a collection the work was probably not extant prior to the mid-third century C.E.

128. *Xinlun*, 17b; cf. *Yiwen leiju*, 94.1626.

129. For King Mu's association with horses and his legendary charioteer Zaofu 造父, see *Mu Tianzi zhuan*, 1.4a–b; *Shiji*, 5.175, 43.1779, 130.3310; *Hanshu*, 28B.1641; *Liezi*, 3.3b ("Zhou Mu wang" 周穆王), tr. Graham (1991), 63–64; *Bowuzhi*, 4.3a; *Shiyiji*, 3.1a–2b. See also Cahill (1987).

130. For a review of these theories see Granet (1934; rpt. 1999), 363–72; Schwartz (1985), 92–94; Gassmann (1988), 88–93, 143–54; A. C. Graham (1989), 23–25, 147–55, 261–67, 282–85, 288; Defoort (1997), 165–86; Lewis (1999), 31–35; and William G. Boltz, "Language and Writing," in Loewe and Shaughnessy (1999), 95–98.

131. For theoretical expositions on the "correction of names" and "forms and names" as a tool in the art of rulership, see *Lunyu zhushu*, 13.1b–2a (XIII.3, "Zi Lu" 子路); *Shenzi*, fragments 1(4), 1(6), 1(8) and Creel's discussion pp. 106–24, 186–190; *Xunzi jijie*, chapter 22 ("Zheng ming" 正名); *Lüshi chunqiu jiaoshi*, 16.1019 ("Zheng ming"), 17.1030 ("Shen fen" 審分); *Guanzi jiaoshi* 12 ("Shu yan" 樞言), 4.112, 38 ("Bai xin" 白心), 13.337; *Shizi*, 1.6a; *Jingfa*, 2 (lines 1–6), 3 (lines 5–7), 29–30 (lines 8–10, 17–20), 39 (lines 1–3), 42 (lines 4–7), 73 (lines 4–6); *Huainanzi*, 10.326, 10.330 ("Miu cheng").

132. Graham (1989), 384.

133. Gou Cuihua notes that the term *fenlei*, "distinguishing the species," occurs for the first time in the *Shangshu*, where it refers to differentiation according to clan lineage. See *Jinwen Shangshu kaozheng*, 30.485. Gou defines *bian ming wu* as a "notion of classification in which general reference is made to all objects" and points out that *bian ming wu* as a concept of biological categorization should be distinguished from the notion of *lei* (as a general referent to a group of objects). See Gou Cuihua (1989), 28. I concur with the idea that the notion of *lei* as adopted in modern biology should not be congruent with the expression "to distinguish names and things." However it seems more confusing than illuminating to me to read modern biological notions of species into the classical terminology. In my view *lei* refers to a group, species, or category and *bian ming wu* is not an act of zoological taxonomization but the association of names with creatures and objects in general. Hence modern biological taxonomization (*fenlei*) and *bian ming wu* are not the same process. The modern Chinese term for taxology or (zoo)taxonomy is *(dongwu) fenleixue* (動物) 分類學.

134. *Zhouli zhushu*, 4.6b; *Zhouli zhengyi*, 7.257–58.

135. *Zhouli zhushu*, 4.17a; *Zhouli zhengyi*, 8.296–97 (*bian qi ming wu*).

136. *Zhouli zhushu*, 19.4a; *Zhouli zhengyi*, 36.1440 (*bian qi ming wu*).

137. *Zhouli zhushu*, 20.1a; *Zhouli zhengyi*, 37.1510 (*bian qi wu*).

138. *Zhouli zhushu*, 24.19a; *Zhouli zhengyi*, 48.1950.

139. *Guoyu*, 18.565 ("Chu yu xia" 楚語下).

140. *Zuozhuan zhu*, p. 486 (Lord Xi, year 31). The evening or day before a sacrifice when the sacrificial animals and implements are set out for inspection was known as the *xi sheng ri* 夕牲日. See *Hanshu*, 74.3148; *Hou Hanshu*, "zhi" 志, 4.3105; *Han jiu yi*, 2.3b.

141. *Zuozhuan zhu*, p. 950 (Lord Xiang, year 7). In 629 B.C.E. a similar release took place after four divinations. See *Zuozhuan zhu*, p. 486 (Lord Xi, year 31).

142. *Zhouli zhushu*, 25.10a.

143. *Liji zhushu*, 5.19b ("Qu li xia" 曲禮下), *yi yuan da wu* 一元大武, with *yuan* 元 glossed as *tou* 頭, and *wu* 武 as *ji* 迹 by Zheng Xuan.

144. The Houma variant is *yi yuan* 一元. See Weld (1997), 144. (Variants of) this term also occur in Huan Lin's 桓麟 (fl. second cent. C.E.) rhapsody entitled "Qi shuo" 七說 and in a piece by his son Huan Bin 桓彬 entitled "Qi she" 七設. See *Quan Han fu*, pp. 550, 564. For the role of oaths and covenants in the Warring States period, see Lewis (1990), 45–46, 67–71, 264–65 note 129 ff.

145. For the use of chickens, dogs, and horses in covenants, see *Shiji*, 39.1681, 69.2249, 76.2367. See also Kong Yingda's commentary in *Liji zhushu*, 5.8b ("Qu li xia"); and Weld (1997), 156–160. Animal victims (pigs, dogs, and fowl) were also used to conjure a curse upon an enemy. See *Zuozhuan zhu*, p. 76 (Lord Yin, year 11); *Mao shi zhengyi*, 12C.17a ("He ren si" 何人斯, Mao 199).

146. *Liji zhushu*, 5.19b ("Qu li xia"); *Yili zhushu*, 43.4b ("Shi yu li" 士虞禮).

147. *Liji zhushu*, 5.19b ("Qu li xia").

148. *Fengsu tongyi jiaoshi*, 8.312 ("Si dian" 祀典); *Shuowen jiezi zhu*, 4A.55b. For the association of the chicken with the sun, *yang*, fire, red, and the south see "Shi wen" 十問 in *Mawangdui Han mu boshu*, vol. 4, 150 (slip 83); *Chunqiu shuo ti ci* 春秋說題辭 in *Weishu jicheng*, 865; *Chunqiu kao yi you* 春秋考異郵 in *Weishu jicheng*, 804. For the chicken as the harbinger of dawn see *Huainanzi*, 16.530 ("Shuo shan" 說山); *Chunqiu kao yi you* in *Weishu jicheng*, 790. Liu Xiang associates the fowl (*zhi* 雉) with red. See *Hanshu*, 27.1411. Such evidence favors the explanation of *hanyin* 翰音 "red shriek" as referring to red feathers or plumage. Zheng Xuan suggests to read *chang* 長 for *han* 翰, the idea being that a well-fed chicken has a persevering cry. See *Liji zhushu*, 5.19b ("Qu li xia"). Wooden chicken figurines as well as chicken-shaped headrests have been found in post-Han tombs. They may have had an apotropaic function. See Tan Chanxue (1998).

149. *Fengsu tongyi jiaoshi*, 431 ("yi wen" 佚文). In another version of the story this figure is identified as Zhuji Gong 祝雞公, or "Lord Chicken-Invocator," who is also known as the immortal Zhuji Weng 祝雞翁 "The Old Man Who Beguiled Chickens." See Kaltenmark (1953), 127–28; *Yiwen leiju*, 91.1585 (quoting the *Bowuzhi*).

150. *Duduan*, 1.15a–b. The names of victim animals were not to be used for naming a child. See *Zuozhuan zhu*, p. 116 (Lord Huan, year 6).

Chapter Two. Animals and Officers

1. For "dog keepers," *quan* 犬 and *shouzheng* 獸正, on Shang oracle bones, see Zuo Yandong (1994), p. 25 no. 19. David Keithley reports similar Shang officers (Duo Quan 多犬 "Many Dog," Duo Ma 多馬 "Many Horse") involved in animal management. See "The Shang," in Loewe and Shaughnessy (1999), 280. For oracle bone graphs

on husbandry see Guo Fu, Li Yuese, and Cheng Qingtai (1999), 25–26. Some groups among the Shang's enemy tribe of the Qiang 羌 were linked to horse breeding. See Nicola Di Cosmo, "The Northern Frontier in Pre-Imperial China," in Loewe and Shaughnessy (1999), 908. Records on Shang royal hunts make up a significant share of the presently recovered bone inscriptions, which document a large array of game animals and hunting techniques. For a survey of faunal remains in (late) Shang burials and a discussion of oracle bone evidence on the hunt, see Fiskesjö (1994); and Childs-Johnson (1998), 32–42. For examples of animal officers in Zhou bronze inscriptions, see Zuo Yandong (1994), p. 43 no. 25 (*muniu* 牧牛), p. 74 no. 37 (*zouma* 趣馬); Creel (1970), 118, 303; and Zhao Fulin (1996), 193.

2. See Broman (1961), 1–89, especially nos. 12–14, 133, 177–79, 218, 221, 230–33, 262–68, 280–81, 319–30. A document similar to the *Zhouli* description of government is a paragraph entitled "Xu guan" 序官 ("Precedence of Officers") in the *Xunzi* (most likely inserted by a later editor). It contains descriptions of a director of fields (*zhi tian* 治田) and a master of forests and game (*yu shi* 虞師). See *Xunzi jijie*, 9.166–71 ("Wang zhi" 王制).

3. *Zhouli zhushu*, 13.5b–6b.

4. *Zhouli zhushu*, 13.3a–5b.

5. *Zhouli zhushu*, 12.16a–18b (*fengren* 封人). For the capping of the horns of sacrificial bulls, see *Mao shi zhengyi*, 20B.6a ("Bi gong" 閟宮, Mao 300); Zhang Heng 張衡 (78–139 C.E.), "Dong jing fu" 東京賦 in *Wenxuan*, 3.116. For the decoration of sacrificial calves, see *Zhuangzi jishi*, 32.1062 ("Lie Yukou" 列禦寇).

6. *Zhouli zhushu*, 30.24a–b, *zhangchu* 掌畜 "keeper of domestic animals"; 33.6a, *zouma* 趣馬 "horse trainer"; 33.7b, *souren* 廋人 "horse surveyor"; 30.4a, *mazhi* 馬質 "horse appraiser"; 13.1a–3a, *muren* 牧人 "breeder of sacrificial animals" (cf. *mushi* 牧師 in *Han guan yi*, 1.9b). In *Hanshu*, 99B.4102, the grand minister of works (*sikong* 司空) is said to be in charge of "multiplying and fattening birds and beasts."

7. *Zhouli zhushu*, 16.17b–18a, *youren* 囿人 "animal keeper"; 33.8a, *yushi* 圉師 "chief of parks"; 33.8b, *yuren* 圉人 "stable keeper." See also *Zuozhuan zhu*, p. 253 (Lord Zhuang, year 32). An officer entitled *daluoshi* 大羅氏 "great netter" is attested in the *Liji*. He is in charge of the emperor's animals and tribute animals sent by the feudal lords. See *Liji zhushu*, 26.10a ("Jiao te sheng" 郊特牲). In the *Xunzi* an official named *zaijue* 宰爵 "intendant of the noble ranks" is said to take care of sacrificial animals. See *Xunzi jijie*, 9.166 ("Wang zhi").

8. *Zhouli zhushu*, 16.15b, *yuren* 羽人 "plume gatherer" (cf. *Yanzi chunqiu jishi*, 8.510–11); *Zhouli zhushu*, 16.15a, *jiaoren* 角人 "horn collector"; 7.5b–11a, *siqiu* 司裘 "manager of furs"; 7.11a–b, *zhangpi* 掌皮 "keeper of hides." Taxes were also levied in the form of sacrificial animals. This was the so-called victim tax (*xi fu* 犧賦). See *Liji zhushu*, 4.11a ("Qu li xia"), 17.24b–25a ("Yue ling" 月令). For a (military) tax levy consisting of turtles, pearls, horns, teeth, skin, hides, feathers, and pelts, see *Guoyu*, 18.580 ("Chu yu xia").

9. *Zhouli zhushu*, 14.10b–11a, *tiaoren* 調人 "arbitrator," official who mediates in cases of injury or death caused by wild animals.

10. *Zhouli zhushu*, 32.17b–18a, *tianpu* 田僕 "hunting charioteer"; 4.17a–19a, *shouren*

獸人 "hunter"; 4.19a–b, *yuren* 獻人 "fisherman"; 4.20b–21a, *xiren* 腊人 "keeper of dried meats"; 26.5a–6a, *dianzhu* 甸祝 "invocator at the hunt"; 16.14a, *jiren* 迹人 "tracker" (cf. *Zuozhuan zhu*, p. 1687 [Lord Ai, year 14]). In the Han an official entitled *goujian* 狗監 "director of the palace kennels" was responsible for raising the emperor's hunting dogs. See *Hanshu*, 57A.2533, 93.3725. Two similar officers, the *gongjiaoshi* 宮狡 士 "palace hounds constable" and *waijiaoshi* 外狡士 "outside hounds constable" responsible for the king's dogs are recorded in Qin legal documents. See *Shuihudi Qin mu zhujian*, 138; Hulsewé (1985), 175 (D168). Wang Fu 王符 (ca. 90–165 c.e.) associates a *siyuanshi* 司原氏 "supervisor of the plains" with the hunt. See *Qianfu lun*, 1.55 ("Xian nan" 賢難). Bamboo slips excavated at Baoshan 包山 (Jingmen, Hubei; dated to the fourth cent. b.c.e.) mention an "animal tracker" (*jiren*). See Liu Xinfang (1997), no. 16.

11. Lewis (1999), 43–45.

12. *Zhouli zhushu*, 4.19a–b.

13. *Shiji*, 30.1417.

14. *Shiji*, 30.1420.

15. *Zhouli zhushu*, 33.1a; *Zhouli zhengyi*, 62.2604–605. One commentator suggests that *wu* here could refer to the color of the horses. Given that the entry does not use color terms in its classification it is unlikely that *wu* is used here in this narrow sense. A statement attributed to Confucius mentions that labor horses (i.e. the lowest category of horses) were to be ridden during inauspicious years. See *Liji zhushu*, 43.7a ("Za ji xia" 雜 記下).

16. *Zhouli zhushu*, 30.4a.

17. The "hunter" (*Zhouli zhushu*, 4.17b) classifies victims in function of seasonal sacrifice (winter: wolves; summer: elaphures; spring and autumn: various kinds of wild animals). The "tortoise catcher" (*Zhouli zhushu*, 4.19b) differentiates fishy creatures into "fresh" or "dried" to prepare the royal dishes and sacrificial foodstuffs.

18. *Zhouli zhushu*, 37.3a, 37.3b, 30.23a, 37.5b–8b; *Zhouli zhengyi*, 70.2924, 70.2926, 58.2446–48, 70.2931–40.

19. For examples of this approach, see Wen Renjun (1988), 98–106; Zou Shuwen (1982), 517–18; Gou Cuihua (1989), 28–29; Wang Zichun and Cheng Baochao (1997), 22–24; Guo Fu, Li Yuese et al. (1999), 135–37.

20. *Zhouli zhushu*, 42.14b–16a; *Zhouli zhengyi*, 86.3535–39 ("Xiang jiao" 相角). This passage is followed by a section on glue used in the fabrication of bows. It lists the various colors of glue obtained by boiling the skin or horns of animals. For the use of cow horn, elaphure sinews, and fish glue to fabricate bows, see *Lienü zhuan*, 6.3a ("Bian tong" 辯通).

21. Although the present text of the *Kaogong ji*, which substitutes the original *Zhouli* part that was lost at the beginning of the Han, took its form in the early Han (collected by Liu De 劉德 ca. 130 b.c.e.), it incorporates material that came down from the Warring States period. See Needham, SCC, vol. 4, part 2, 11–17. Glosses and commentaries on its animal references are collated in Chen Zongqi's 陳宗起 *Kaogong ji niaoshou chongyu shi* 考工記鳥獸蟲魚釋 (1885).

22. *Zhouli zhushu*, 41.13a–16a.

23. See Sterckx (2000), 18–19. Needham's contention that the grouping of amphibians and reptiles with invertebrates in this passage was "an unfortunate mistake" (SCC, vol. 6, part 1, 471) is illustrative of the unjustified search for Western taxonomy in early Chinese classificatory schemes.

24. *Zhouli zhushu*, 4.11b. A similar passage occurs in *Liji zhushu*, 28.1b ("Nei ze" 內則), adding that pullets whose tails could not be grasped by the hand were not eaten. A passage in the *Lüshi chunqiu* divides animals into three groups according to their taste: aquatic animals, which have a fetid smell, carnivores, with a putrid scent, and herbivores, with a frowsy odor. See *Lüshi chunqiu jiaoshi*, 14.740 ("Ben wei" 本味).

25. *Zuozhuan zhu*, pp. 1386–89 (Lord Zhao, year 17). For other references to this story, see *Qianfu lun*, 8.452, 8.462–63 ("Wu de zhi" 五德志); *Kongzi jiayu*, 4.6b ("Bian wu" 辯物); *Hanshu*, 19A.721, which also states that Fuxi gave his officers the names of dragons. According to *Hou Hanshu*, 85.2811, the eastern barbarians named their officials after the six domestic animals.

26. *Bao Puzi nei pian jiaoshi*, 12.228 ("Bian wen" 辯問).

27. *Zuozhuan zhu*, pp. 1500–1502 (Lord Zhao, year 29). See also *Zhushu jinian*, 1.9a; *Shiji*, 2.86, 28.1356; *Hanshu*, 1B.81, 25A.1192; *Qianfu lun*, 9.486, 9.498 ("Zhi shi xing" 志氏姓); *Lunheng jiaoshi*, 19.253 ("Gan xu" 感虛). Wang Chong quotes this story and argues that because the dragon had been domesticated and fed in antiquity it cannot be considered spiritlike. See *Lunheng jiaoshi*, 22.287–89 ("Long xu" 龍虛).

28. Whalen Lai, omitting the *Zuozhuan* account, interprets the Kong Jia myth as China's first myth of anthropogony. According to Lai, Kong Jia is the embodiment of the rise of man from beast, the first mortal ruler without supernatural powers (hence his failure to feed the dragons). See Lai (1984), 333–41. See also Birrell (1993), 60–61, who likewise does not quote the *Zuozhuan*.

29. Following Du Yu's gloss *bu shi lu* 不食祿 "does not draw pay."

30. Schwartz (1985), 373; Lévi (1987), 42; Lewis (1999), 46–47, 50, 314. On the importance of Cai Mo's speech for the development of the "five processes," see Harper, "Warring States Natural Philosophy," in Loewe and Shaughnessy (1999), 864.

31. The *Liji* notes that anciently, the Son of Heaven and the feudal lords had to have officers who took care of raising their animals and that the selection of perfect animal victims was considered "the utmost expression of reverence." See *Liji zhushu*, 48.1b ("Ji yi" 祭義).

32. See for instance Zhan Yinxin (1992), 90–91, 116, 157–58; Luo Guihuan et al. (1995), 19–20; and Wang Dayou (1988), 31–32, 37. A totemic interpretation is given to the *Zuozhuan* material in Zhang Hongxun (1992). This paper discusses a Dunhuang manuscript entitled *Bai niao ming* 百鳥名 "The Names of the Hundred Birds" (S.5752; S.3835; P. 3716) (dated to ca. 750–60 C.E.), which portrays the bird kingdom organized as a systematic bureaucracy. See also Mayo (2000).

33. *Shangshu zhengyi*, 5.4b ("Yi Ji" 益稷). The *Sima Fa* 司馬法 states that for insignia the sun and moon were used by the Xia valuing brightness, the Shang used the tiger

valuing awesomeness, and the Zhou used the dragon esteeming culture. See *Sima Fa*, 1.4b ("Tianzi zhi yi" 天子之義); tr. Sawyer (1993), 131.

34. Meanwhile, theories of totemism have been critically put to rest by historians of religion and anthropologists in the West. Cf. Claude Lévi-Strauss' comments on the "totemic illusion" in Lévi-Strauss (1969), 86.

35. Chun (1990), 33–38.

36. *Zuozhuan zhu*, p. 62 (Lord Yin, year 9).

37. *Shiji*, 102.2752; *Hanshu*, 50.2307–8. The official in question is Zhang Shizhi 張釋之. Besides registering the human and animal population in the forest parks, the Shanglin commander was also responsible for catching animals to supply the palace provisioners. Cf. *Dong Han huiyao*, 19.284. The emperor hunted in the Shanglin compound in autumn and winter. See *Han jiu yi*, 2.5b.

38. *Huainanzi*, 18.619 ("Ren jian" 人間).

39. *Lunyu zhushu*, 10.10a ("Xiang dang" 鄉黨).

40. *Lüshi chunqiu jiaoshi*, 14.830 ("Bi ji" 必己).

41. *Zhouli zhushu*, 18.22b–23a (*da zong bo* 大宗伯); *Zhouli zhengyi*, 35.1383–84.

42. *Zhouli zhushu*, 19.4a (*xiao zong bo* 小宗伯); *Zhouli zhengyi*, 36.1440.

43. *Yili zhushu*, 7.6b–7a ("Shi xiang jian li" 士相見禮).

44. *Chunqiu fanlu*, 16.394 ("Zhi zhi"). For the suckling lamb as symbol of obedience, see also *Bohutong shu zheng*, 9.434 ("Yi shang").

45. *Shuoyuan jiaozheng*, 19.485 ("Xiu wen" 修文); *Bohutong shu zheng*, 8.356–57 ("Rui zhi" 瑞贄). See also *Liji zhushu*, 5.25a ("Qu li xia").

46. The *Zuozhuan* refers to a "crane formation" and "goose formation." See *Zuozhuan zhu*, p. 1429 (Lord Zhao, year 21). The *Mozi* mentions Shang king Tang 湯 lining up chariots to form a "bird formation" and "wild goose march." See *Mozi jiaozhu*, 31.342 ("Ming gui xia" 明鬼下). See also *Han Feizi jishi*, 1.43 ("Cun Han" 存韓); and *Wenxuan*, 3.121–22 ("Dong jing fu") where warrior-hunters are said to attack in "goose and stork formations" and in "fish file." On the use of animal imagery in military tactics and troop formation, see also Kubuki Shigehiro (1993), 7–17. Depictions of flying geese formations are preserved on third-century-B.C.E. pottery tiles from tombs in western Henan. See W. C. White (1939), plates 7–12, 16–19.

47. *Bohutong shu zheng*, 10.457 ("Jia qu" 嫁娶). For the use of the goose as a wedding gift, see *Mao shi zhengyi*, 2B.8b–9a ("Pao you ku ye" 匏有苦葉, Mao 34); *Yili zhushu*, 4.4a, 4.8a, 5.3b, 6.4a ("Shi hun li" 士昏禮). The goose as a symbol of marital separation figures prominently in the *Zhouyi*. See *Zhouyi zhengyi*, 5.29a–31b (hex. 53, *jian* 漸 "advance"). See also Shaughnessy (1992), 593–95. For the goose as a messenger carrying a silk note tied to its feet, see *Hanshu*, 54.2466.

48. For a comparative view of the role of ritualized blood slaughter in Chinese and other early religions, see Kleeman (1994).

49. See Chang Tsung-Tung (1970), 65–73.

50. For a discussion of these victims and the spirits they address, see Chen Wei (1996), 175–180; and Chen Wei (1999), 57–59.

51. *Guoyu*, 17.533 ("Chu yu shang"). For regulations regarding the sacrifice and consumption of animals at sacrificial ceremonies and banquets, see also *Guoyu*, 18.564–65 ("Chu yu xia").

52. *Liji zhushu*, 12.21a ("Wang zhi").

53. *Bohutong shu zheng*, 2.81 ("Wu si" 五祀).

54. *Da Dai Liji*, 5.9b ("Zengzi tian yuan" 曾子天圓).

55. *Liji zhushu*, 28.12b ("Nei ze").

56. For the use of bulls as sacrificial victims, see Bodde (1975), 201–209; Bilsky (1975), 117–18, 137, 140, 268–69; and Armstrong (1945).

57. *Zhouli zhushu*, 13.1a–2b.

58. *Mozi jiaozhu*, 31.340 ("Ming gui xia"). Criteria for assessing the suitability of an animal for ritual slaughter are as old as sacrificial practice itself. For instance, an inscription on a bronze basin known as the "Shi Qiang *pan*" 史墙盤, composed shortly before 900 B.C.E., praises the sacrificial victims as "even-horned and redly gleaming." See Shaughnessy (1991), 1–4, 190.

59. The *Chunqiu* and *Zuozhuan* record several instances in which the sacrificial bull is dismissed because of injury or set free because of the failure to obtain a favorable divination for the sacrifice. See *Chunqiu Zuozhuan zhu*, p. 667 (Lord Xuan, year 3), p. 831 (Lord Cheng, year 7), p. 950 (Lord Xiang, year 7), p. 1598 (Lord Ding, year 15), p. 1604 (Lord Ai, year 1). See also *Gongyang zhuan*, 12.18b–20b, 15.6b, 17.13b, 19.10b, 26.17a, 27.1b. See further *Chunqiu fanlu*, 15.387 ("Shun ming" 順命). Some of these cases refer to minute mice undermining the numinous efficacy of the sacrificial bull by gnawing away its most potent symbol of power, the horns. As the mouse is very small, the bull would not feel any pain while this rodent was eating its horns away. See also *Bowuzhi*, 3.4b.

60. *Zuozhuan zhu*, p. 1434 (Lord Zhao, year 22); *Guoyu*, 3.142–43 ("Zhou yu xia"); *Hanshu*, 27.1369; *Fengsu tongyi jiaoshi*, 8.312 ("Si dian").

61. *Zuozhuan zhu*, p. 678 (Lord Xuan, year 4), p. 903 (Lord Cheng year 17); *Guoyu*, 12.426 ("Jin yu" 晉語). Animals that were destined for sacrifice but died before the actual ceremony had to be interred. See *Liji zhushu*, 3.12a ("Qu li shang").

62. *Liji zhushu*, 5.19a ("Qu li xia").

63. *jianli* 繭栗 is a standard term to describe the small, cocoonlike, chestnut shape of the budding horns of a sacrificial calf. See *Guoyu*, 18.565 ("Chu yu xia"); *Hanshu*, 22.1052, 25B.1266; *Shiji*, 12.461, 28.1389; *Yilin*, 1.6a.

64. *Liji zhushu*, 12.21a–b ("Wang zhi"). For similar statements, see *Guoyu*, 18.564–71 ("Chu yu xia"); *Chunqiu fanlu*, 15.390 ("Jiao shi dui" 郊事對); *Hanshu*, 25A.1221; *Li ji ming zheng* 禮稽命徵 in *Weishu jicheng*, 514; *Li wei* 禮緯 in *Weishu jicheng*, 533. The preference for animals with small horns was possibly related to the notion that short horns had a better supply of vital energy since their ends were closer to the animal's brain. The *Zhouli* states that in physiognomizing horns of oxen one wants them to be blue-white with the ends well developed since the root of the horn lies close to the brain and is stimulated by its *qi*. See *Zhouli zhushu*, 42.14b–15b; *Zhouli zhengyi*, 86.3537.

65. *Liji zhushu*, 26.6b ("Jiao te sheng"). See also *Kongzi jiayu*, 7.2b ("Jiao wen" 郊問).

According to one account, bull victims for the sacrifice to Heaven were fed over a five-year period until they reached a weight of 3000 *jin* (ca. 700 kg). See *Han jiu yi*, 2.2a; *Hanshu*, 25A.1231 note 5.

66. The story is set in Kuaiji 會稽 commandery ca. 52 C.E. An official named Di Wulun 第五倫 was dispatched to the region as governor to remedy the cult and put a halt to the power of local shamans. The unwanted butchering of cattle was severely punished. See *Hou Hanshu*, 41.1397; *Fengsu tongyi jiaoshi*, 9.339 ("Guai shen" 怪神).

67. *Hanshu*, 25B.1270. I follow Schafer's identification of *mi* 麋 as "elaphure" (*elaphurus davidianus*). See Schafer (1956).

68. *Liji zhushu*, 3.22b ("Qu li shang"). For the ritual washing or cleansing of the victim, see *Mao shi zhengyi*, 13B.7b ("Chu ci" 楚茨, Mao 209); *Mu Tianzi zhuan*, 2.1b; *Liji zhushu*, 48.1b ("Ji yi"); *Zhouli zhushu*, 12.17b; *Han jiu yi*, 2.3b–4a.

69. *Liji zhushu*, 13.9b–10a ("Wang zhi"); *Kongzi jiayu*, 7.6a ("Xing zheng" 刑政).

70. To use an expression from Noëlie Vialles's anthropological study of abattoirs. See Vialles (1994).

71. For the worship of spirits connected with husbandry, see for instance the "Fu tian" 甫田 (Mao 211) and "Da tian" 大田 (Mao 212) odes in the *Shijing*.

72. On these sacred animals in Western antiquity, see Prieur (1988), 33–72, 121–35, 135–49; and Bodson (1978).

73. See Kuhn (1988), SCC, vol. 5, part 9, 250–52.

74. *Guoyu*, 4.165–70 ("Lu yu shang"). The bird in question was named *yuanju* 爰居. See also *Zhuangzi jishi*, 18.621–22 ("Zhi le" 至樂), 19.665–66 ("Da sheng"); *Zuozhuan zhu*, pp. 525–26 (Lord Wen, year 2); *Hou Hanshu*, 43.1480.

75. For reference to and critiques of the (sacrificial) worship of animals and animal spirits, see *Zuozhuan zhu*, p. 1405 (Lord Zhao, year 19). This passage is a critique of deprecatory sacrifices to dragons. For a cat and tiger spirit, see *Liji zhushu*, 26.8b ("Jiao te sheng"). The sacrificial worship of these natural predators for the expulsion of harmful species is discussed in Liu Dunyuan (1980), 219–24. For other animal spirits, see *Shiji*, 28.1386, and *Hanshu*, 25A.1218 (spirits named "horse traveler" and "dark ram"); *Zhouli zhushu*, 33.3b–4a (spirits named "horse ancestor," "first herdsman," "first equestrian," and "horse walk demon"); *Hanshu*, 25A.1195, *Shiji*, 28.1359, 28.1376 (the Chen Bao 陳寶 spirit which manifests itself in the form of a stone with the head of a cock pheasant, also known as Tian Bao 天寶, cf. *Hanshu*, 87A.3548); *Hanshu*, 25B.1250, 25B.1258; *Hanshu*, 64B.2830; *Liexian zhuan* in Kaltenmark (1953), 171; *Hou Hanshu*, 86.2852 (Golden Horse 金馬 and Azure Chicken 碧雞 spirits). The spirit of the stove has been tentatively identified with a frog or toad. For a critical assessment of this hypothesis, see Chard (1990), 127–39.

76. *Han jiu yi*, 2.1b (*canshen* 蠶神 "bambix mori spirit"); *Hou Hanshu*, "zhi," 4.3110 (*xiancan* 先蠶 "silkworm ancestor").

77. *Hanshu*, 25B.1249–50. The Ba 巴 tribe worshipped the white tiger with the sacrifice of human victims. See *Hou Hanshu*, 86.2840. See also Liu Hong (1988). The Huimo 濊貊 in Chaoxian 朝鮮 worshipped the tiger as a spirit. See *Hou Hanshu*, 85.2818.

78. For this suggestion, see Wu Xiaoqiang (1992).

79. For auspicious and tabooed animal days, see *Shuihudi Qin mu zhujian*, 194, 235.

80. See Harper (1994); and Harper, "Warring States Natural Philosophy and Occult Thought," in Loewe and Shaughnessy (1999), 869.

81. *Zhouli zhushu*, 14.13b–17b; *Zhouli zhengyi*, 26.1033–53.

82. *Shuihudi Qin mu zhujian*, 227–28 (Plates, 115–16). For a full translation and study of this fragment, see Sterckx (1996). Dunhuang manuscripts confirm that several horse spirits identified for the late Warring States period continued to be worshiped in Tang times. See Tan Chanxue (1996).

83. For a transcription of the manuscript text, see Li Xueqin (1990); and Li Xueqin (1994), 181–90. The story is translated in Harper (1994), 14.

84. *Shanhaijing jiaozhu*, 2.47, 10.366.

85. *Shiji*, 117.3060; *Hanshu*, 57B.2596; and *Yilin*, 8.6a ("The lonesome three-legged bird/ cries efficaciously to the Local Inspector / It presides over mistakes and punishes evil / but ruin and destruction have caused it to grieve" [variant at 3.6b]). For the (three-legged) crow residing in the sun, see *Shiji*, 128.3237; *Huainanzi*, 7.221 ("Jing shen" 精神), 17.556 ("Shuo lin"); *Shuowen jiezi zhu*, 4A.57a; *Lunheng jiaoshi*, 32.502–504 ("Shuo ri" 說日); *Qu Yuan ji jiaozhu*, p. 319 ("Tian wen" 天問); *Chunqiu yun dou shu* in *Weishu jicheng*, 716; *Yi wei tong gua yan* 易緯通卦驗 in *Weishu jicheng*, 260. For the crow as essence of the sun, see *Chunqiu yuan ming bao* 春秋元命包 in *Weishu jicheng*, 600, 606; *He tu* 河圖 in *Weishu jicheng*, 1248. For depictions of this motif in tomb art, see Hayashi Minao (1989), plates pp. 233, 249, 251, 282, 289, 291, 293, 303, 305, 323. See also Allan (1991), 30–33.

86. *Guoyu*, 8.295–96 ("Jin yu"). See also *Shuoyuan jiaozheng*, 18.466 ("Bian wu"). Similarly in the *Mozi* the bird-bodied spirit Goumang 句芒 is commissioned by the Thearch to add nineteen years to the lifespan of Duke Mu 穆 of Zheng 鄭 (627–606 B.C.E.). See *Mozi jiaozhu*, 31.337–38 ("Ming gui xia"); and Riegel (1989–90), 58.

87. Titles of later calendars and divination manuals refer to the observation of birds, for instance a work entitled *Huangdi feiniao li* 黃帝飛鳥歷 ("The Yellow Emperor's Calendar [Based on] the Flight of Birds") attributed to Zhang Heng. See *Suishu*, 34.1026, 34.1029; *Jiu Tangshu*, 47.2043.

88. *Mao shi zhengyi*, 8A.11b–23a. It is uncertain which calendar, and hence which months, this poem is referring to.

89. *Zuozhuan zhu*, pp. 106–108 (Lord Huan, year 5). See also *Fengsu tongyi jiaoshi*, 8.294 ("Si dian").

90. *Longyu hetu* 龍魚河圖 in *Gu weishu*, 34.670; *Weishu jicheng*, 1157; *Quan shanggu Sandai Qin Han Sanguo Liuchao wen*, 14.15a ("que ming" 闕名); *Qimin yaoshu*, ch. 5, 45.53.1. Later texts confirm the performance of rat excorcisms in the first calendar month. For instance Han E's 韓鄂 (ca. 750 C.E.) *Si shi zuan yao* 四時纂要 ("Important Rules for the Four Seasons") contains the following instructions for "rat expulsion days" (*rang shu ri* 禳鼠日):

On a *chen* 辰 day in this month, block up the crevices, and the rats will die of themselves. Also, gather the tails of rats killed during the preceding month and, on the first day of the month before sunrise, have the head of the family perform the following prayer in the "silkworm chamber": "(We) cut down the rat vermin. On no account will it be able to squirm around." Perform the incantation three times and put (the rat tails) on the walls. No longer will there be rat calamities.

See *Si shi zuan yao jiaoshi*, p. 18. A recurrent trope illustrating the pernicious damage caused by rats is the reference to "altar rats" (*she shu* 社鼠), who dwell around the sacrificial altars and hide away inside shrines where they cannot be caught without destroying the entire shrine. Rats and "altar rats" are also a metaphor for corrupt officials. See *Zuozhuan zhu*, p. 1085 (Lord Xiang, year 23); *Yanzi chunqiu jishi*, 3.196–97; *Han Feizi jishi*, 13.737 ("Wai chu shuo you shang"); *Han shi waizhuan jishi*, 7.249, 8.305; *Hanshu*, 53.2424; *Yi wei tong gua yan* in *Weishu jicheng*, 253. The hidden nature and inauspicious influence of rats may have been the subject for the decorum of sacrificial vessels. The *Lüshi chunqiu* states that the Zhou tripods were decorated with a motif of a rat trampled by a horse since rats "were not of a *yang* nature. Not being of a *yang* nature (i.e. not "rising up") is customary in a perishing state." See *Lüshi chunqiu jiaoshi*, 20.1374 ("Da yu" 達鬱). The power of the minute rat over the majesty of embellished sacrificial victims and implements is also epitomized in a saying quoted by Jia Yi 賈誼 (201–168 B.C.E.): "I wish to throw (stones) at the rats (on the vessels) but I am concerned about (damaging) the vessel." See *Hanshu*, 48.2254. See also *Hou Hanshu*, 70.2269.

91. *Shuihudi Qin mu zhujian*, 186; Liu Lexian (1994), 67–68.

92. *Huainanzi*, 5.171 ("Shi ze" 時則), *yuren* 漁人; cf. Major (1993), 239. A variant, *yushi* 漁師, occurs in *Lüshi chunqiu jiaoshi*, 6.311 ("Ji xia ji" 季夏紀); *Yi Zhoushu*, 6.10b ("Yue ling jie" 月令解); and *Liji zhushu*, 16.9a ("Yue ling").

93. *Huainanzi*, 5.178 ("Shi ze"), *zhuci* 主祠; cf. Major (1993), 247. See also *Lüshi chunqiu jiaoshi*, 9.468 ("Ji qiu ji" 季秋紀); *Yi Zhoushu*, 6.14a ("Yue ling jie"); and *Liji zhushu*, 17.6b ("Yue ling"). Qiu Xigui speculates that these sacrifices prior to the hunt were directed at the animal spirits out of fear for retribution. See Qiu Xigui (1992), 142–43.

94. *Huainanzi*, 5.182 ("Shi ze"), *yeyu* 野虞; cf. Major (1993), 253. See also *Lüshi chunqiu jiaoshi*, 11.568 ("Zhong dong ji" 仲冬紀); *Yi Zhoushu*, 6.16a ("Yue ling jie"); and *Liji zhushu*, 17.19a ("Yue ling"). Officers in charge of the land were also in charge of the animal species that inhabited it. Early evidence of this occurs in the *Zuozhuan* which records a *shouchen* 獸臣, glossed as a "forester" (*yuren* 虞人) by Du Yu. See *Zuozhuan zhu*, p. 939 (Lord Xiang, year 4). In the "Shun dian" 舜典, Yi 益 is commissioned to be the forester 虞 supervising the plants and trees, birds and beasts in the highlands and lowlands. See *Shangshu zhengyi*, 3.24b–25a. See also *Hanshu*, 19A.721. The *Guoyu* records officials named *shouyu* 獸虞 and *shuiyu* 水虞 in charge of hunting and fishing regulations. See *Guoyu*, 4.178 ("Lu yu shang").

95. *Huainanzi*, 5.184 ("Shi ze"), *yushi* 漁師; cf. Major (1993), 256–57. Major suggests that organized fishing may be seen as a "final ritual obeisance to the power of water in the winter season." See also *Lüshi chunqiu jiaoshi*, 12.615 ("Ji dong ji" 季冬紀); *Yi Zhoushu*, 6.16b ("Yue ling jie"); and *Liji zhushu*, 17.22b ("Yue ling"). The Master of Fish-

eries also collected tax revenues from rivers, springs, ponds, and marshes in the tenth month. See *Liji zhushu*, 17.15b ("Yue ling").

96. *Huainanzi*, 5.166, 5.169 ("Shi ze"); cf. Major (1993), 231, 236. See also *Lüshi chunqiu jiaoshi*, 3.122 ("Ji chun ji" 季春紀), 5.242 ("Zhong xia ji" 仲夏紀); *Liji zhushu*, 17.4b ("Yue ling"); and *Yi Zhoushu*, 6.8a ("Yue ling jie").

97. *Hanshu*, 95.3851. See also *Shiji*, 113.2969.

98. *Hanshu*, 5.147.

99. *Shiji*, 30.1419.

100. *Shiji*, 30.1438. According to the *Zhouli* the director of stables reserved one stallion for every three mares. See *Zhouli zhushu*, 33.3b.

101. *Shiji*, 30.1439.

102. *Xunzi jijie*, 9.165 ("Wang zhi"); tr. Knoblock (1990), vol. 2, 104–105 [modified].

103. Chavannes (1906). Alfred Forke (1911) argued in favor of the Chinese origin of the cycle, assimilated by the Turks. The Central Asia hypothesis, which was proposed first by Zhao Yi 趙翼 (1727–1814), is also reiterated in Chen Anli (1988).

104. *Lunheng jiaoshi*, 14.148–50 ("Wu shi" 物勢), 66.957 ("Yan du" 言毒), 70.994 ("Ji ri" 譏日).

105. Boodberg (1940), 131–35.

106. See *Shuihudi Qin mu zhujian*, 219–20. A punctuated transcription of the Fangmatan version has appeared in Li Xueqin (1994), 166. For the suggestion that these calendars could be forebears to a tradition of name-selecting according to the duodenary animal cycle, see Li Ling (1993a), 204–17. For further discussions, see Kalinowski (1986), 208–209; Zhan Yinxin (1992), 107–11; and Judy Chungwa Ho (1991).

Chapter 3. Categorizing Animals

1. Hicks (1993), 106–11.

2. Lloyd (1983), 11.

3. On the relationship between lay taxonomy and scientific classification, see S. Clark, "Is Humanity a Natural Kind?" in Tim Ingold (1988), 17–23; Atran (1990), chapters 2 and 3; and Atran (1999).

4. Sperber (1975), 22–23; Albert-Llorca (1991), 69–70.

5. The ethnozoologist Roy Ellen holds that "categories of natural kinds are about as rooted in the empirical world as categories can ever get, and in a way that those applied to the world of people and social phenomena can never be." See Ellen (1993), 216. While this may apply to so-called primitive societies that lack a textual tradition, I question whether the premise of natural kinds as the most pure form of classification can be applied stringently across different cultures. This would imply a universal acceptance of a clear-cut divide between nature and culture and assume that the reality understood as empirical is uniform and invariable. It also does not take into account the medium through which information reaches the subject(s) who draw up categories. As we have

seen, early Chinese lexicographers were perfectly capable of classifying animals in a textual realm without necessarily observing real animals in their natural setting.

6. *Xunzi jijie*, 22.419 ("Zheng ming").

7. Eno (1990), 145–47. For a recent (unconvincing) argument that presents the "Zheng ming" chapter of the *Xunzi* as one of the philosophical bases of animal taxonomy in China, see Guo Fu, Li Yuese, and Cheng Qingtai (1999), 138–40.

8. *Daodejing jiangyi*, 2.42. Similar cosmogonies occur in the "Yuan dao" 原道 chapter of the *Huainanzi*, the Mawangdui "Dao yuan" 道原, and the "Dao yuan" chapter in the *Wenzi*. See also the introduction of the "Jiu shou" 九守 chapter in the *Wenzi*.

9. *Huainanzi*, 14.463 ("Quan yan" 詮言). To my knowledge the earliest numerical reference to the whole of the animal species occurs in the ninth-century *Youyang zazu*, 16.151, which states that there are 4500 kinds of birds and 2400 kinds of other animals.

10. *Shangshu zhengyi*, 11.4a.

11. *Qianfu lun*, 6.353 ("Bu lie" 卜列).

12. Porkert (1974), 185–86.

13. This date is suggested in Harper, "Warring States Natural Philosophy," in Loewe and Shaughnessy (1999), 861. For reference to "blood and *qi*" in late-fourth-century and early-third-century sources, see *Guoyu*, 2.62 ("Zhou yu zhong" 周語中), 4.175 ("Lu yu shang" 魯語上); *Guanzi jiaoshi* 49 ("Nei ye" 內業), 16.405. The term also occurs in a late chapter of the *Lunyu* and is used throughout the *Xunzi*. See *Lunyu zhushu*, 16.7a ("Ji Shi" 季氏); *Xunzi jijie*, 2.22, 2.25, 2.35 ("Xiu shen" 修身), 5.76 ("Fei xiang" 非相), 12.234 ("Jun dao" 君道), 18.333 ("Zheng lun" 正論), 20.382 ("Yue lun" 樂論).

14. *Guanzi jiaoshi* 39 ("Shui di" 水地), 14.347 (describing water as the "blood and *qi* of the earth"); *Zuozhuan zhu*, p. 355 (Lord Xi, year 15). The most thorough discussion of Warring States and Han physiology is set forth in Harper (1998), 77–90; and Harper, "Warring States Natural Philosophy," in Loewe and Shaughnessy (1999), 876–79.

15. *Huainanzi*, 7.218 ("Jing shen").

16. *Wenzi*, 1.14b ("Jiu shou").

17. *Guoyu*, 2.62 ("Zhou yu zhong").

18. *Liezi*, 2.21b ("Huang di"); tr. Graham (1991), 53–54.

19. *Liezi*, 2.23a ("Huang di"); tr. Graham (1991), 55 [modified]. *Chimei* may be read as a binome or the name of two different creatures. They were spectral creatures sometimes associated with mountains. See Knechtges (1982), vol. 1, 216, note to line 509.

20. For the idea that man's nature is composed of "blood and *qi*," mind and intelligence, see also *Liji zhushu*, 38.5a ("Yue ji" 樂記); *Shiji*, 24.1206. For the idea that the sage commands the respect of all "blood and *qi*" creatures, see also *Zhongyong zhu*, p. 229. Xunzi attributes "blood and *qi*," will and ambition, knowledge and reflection to humans. See *Xunzi jijie*, 2.22, 2.25 ("Xiu shen").

21. *Lunheng jiaoshi*, 62.871 ("Lun si" 論死).

22. *Lunheng jiaoshi*, 62.874–75 ("Lun si").

23. For the first expression, see *Lunheng jiaoshi*, 49.716 ("Shang chong" 商蟲); cf. *Hanshu*, 64B.2831. For the second, see *Lunheng jiaoshi*, 15.161 ("Qi guai" 奇怪).

24. *Lunheng jiaoshi*, 48.710 ("Zao hu" 遭虎).

25. *Lunheng jiaoshi*, 68.976 ("Si hui" 四諱).

26. *Lunheng jiaoshi*, 24.334 ("Dao xu" 道虛), 54.775 ("Zi ran" 自然).

27. *Liji zhushu*, 58.2a ("San nian wen" 三年問); variant in *Xunzi jijie*, 19.372 ("Li lun" 禮論); cf. *Hou Hanshu*, 74A.2386 note 6. The image of a bird uttering its emotional loss over a companion also occurs in the *Lunyu*, where one of Confucius's disciples, Zengzi 曾子, states that birds display a wailing cry when they are moribund. See *Lunyu zhushu*, 8.2b ("Tai bo" 泰伯). See also *Xinxu xiang zhu*, 1.9–10 ("Za shi" 雜事); *Shuoyuan jiaozheng*, 19.498 ("Xiu wen"); *Shiji*, 126.3208. After a discomforting sojourn in the state of Song, Confucius was said to look forlorn like "a dog of a household in mourning." See *Shiji*, 47.1922; *Kongzi jiayu*, 5.11a ("Kun shi" 困誓); *Han shi waizhuan jishi*, 9.323–24. Mortuary terminology for animals is attested in the *Liji*, where the death of birds is called *jiang* 降 "falling down," and that of quadrupeds *zi* 漬 "dying from infection." See *Liji zhushu*, 5.21b ("Qu li xia").

28. *Liji zhushu*, 53.13b ("Zhong yong" 中庸); *Xunzi jijie*, 19.373 ("Li lun").

29. For the idea that "kind loves kind" in the animal kingdom, see also *Huainanzi*, 17.574 ("Shuo lin"); *Zhanguo ce*, 10.388; *Xunzi jijie*, 4.55 ("Rong ru"). For the spontaneous resonance between neighing horses and lowing cows, see *Xunzi jijie*, 3.45 ("Bu gou" 不苟).

30. *Zuozhuan zhu*, p. 1317 (Lord Zhao, year 10). For the attribution of "anger" (*nu* 怒) to "blood and *qi*," see the Mawangdui *Jing* 經, in *Jing fa*, p. 54 ("Wu zheng" 五政, line 13). A passage in the Guodian texts states that "all creatures that possess 'blood and *qi*' have feelings of pleasure, anger, caution and indulgence (?); their bodies have composure, color, sound, smell, taste, *qi*, and resolve." See "Yu cong" 語叢 I in *Guodian Chu mu zhujian*, 195 (slip 45, graphic variant 血戜). For "blood and *qi*," see also "Tang Yu zhi dao" 唐虞之道 and "Liu de" 六德 in *Guodian Chu mu zhujian*, 157 (slip 11, graphic variant 血戜), 187 (slip 15).

31. *Huainanzi*, 19.645 ("Xiu wu" 修務), 7.221 ("Jing shen"). The image of "blood and *qi*" as the bodily analogue of wind and rain also occurs in *Wenzi*, 1.15b ("Jiu shou").

32. *Huainanzi*, 15.489 ("Bing lüe" 兵略).

33. *Shiji*, 25.1240.

34. *Liezi*, 2.10a ("Huang di").

35. *Shuowen jiezi zhu*, 5A.50b.

36. *Mao shi zhengyi*, 13B.20b ("Xin nan shan" 信南山, Mao 210, stanza 5). For hair and blood as signs of the interior and exterior purity of the victim, see also *Liji zhushu*, 26.22b ("Jiao te sheng"). For the presentation of hair and blood as fixed elements of sacrificial procedure, see *Liji zhushu*, 21.16a ("Li yun"), 24.12a ("Li qi"); *Chunqiu fanlu*, 7.178 ("San dai gai zhi zhi wen" 三代改制質文); *Kongzi jiayu*, 1.9b–10a ("Wen li" 問禮); *Han jiu yi*, 2.4a.

37. *Liji zhushu*, 43.13a–b ("Za ji xia"). A similar description is incorporated (as chapter 73) in *Da Dai Liji*, 10.10a–b ("Zhu hou xin miao" 諸侯釁廟).

38. *Liji zhushu*, 47.11a ("Ji yi").

39. That ears were seen as an identifying feature of victim animals is illustrated in

another anecdote. There a lord orders a pig destined for sacrifice to be replaced because it was in his opinion too small. When his servant brought on a substitute pig, his master recognised that it was the same pig and ordered the servant to be punished. He then explains that the ears enabled him to notice that he had been cheated with the same pig. See *Lüshi chunqiu jiaoshi,* 17.1065 ("Ren shu" 任數).

40. *Zuozhuan zhu,* p. 1566 (Lord Ding, year 8), p. 1711 (Lord Ai, year 17).

41. *Guoyu,* 18.564 ("Chu yu xia").

42. *Liji zhushu,* 29.8b ("Yu zao" 玉藻). For the idea that the ancients never killed and cooked animals without adequate reason, see also *Yantie lun jiaozhu,* 6.202 ("San bu zu" 散不足). For the idea that the ruler ought to stay away from the abattoir, see chapter 5, note 192. Important from the ritualist's point of view was that the act of killing was to be witnessed at the sacrificial locus. John Steele, in his translation of the *Yili* published in 1917, noticed the importance of the notion of life taking in animal sacrifice throughout this work: "Although it is true that there is no trace of expiation evident, there are several indications that the view of 祭 [*ji*] is based upon the offering of life, an earlier theory of sacrifice common to all nations. The animals whose carcasses take the most prominent place are those which have been brought alive to the scene of the ceremony, and not those already slain in the chase, or which have died after leaving the stream. At the supreme moments the game and fish were not presented." See Steele (1917), vol. 1, xxii.

43. *Liji zhushu,* 26.22b ("Jiao te sheng"). For blood, dried meat and broiled meat as offerings conveying *qi* to the spirits, see also *Liji zhushu,* 26.21a. For the lungs as the seat of *qi,* see Zheng Xuan's commentary in *Yili zhushu,* 4.8b ("Shi hun li"). For the lungs and liver as storehouses of blood and *qi,* see *Huangdi neijing ling shu,* 2.11a–b ("Ben shen" 本神).

44. Vialles (1994), 73. Maurice Bloch describes this radical transition in a discussion of cattle sacrifice among the Dinka in southern Sudan. According to Bloch, after the kill meat no longer represents the animal or "vital side of the sacrificer; it has become, by the simple fact of killing, the meat of an animal which, because it is an animal, is by nature alien to humans. Its vitality can be consumed without problem by those present in order that, like all meat, it will restrengthen them through its nutritive value." See Bloch (1992), 36.

45. See Graham (1986), 70–92; Major (1993), 28–32; Schwartz (1985) chapter 9; Harper, "Warring States Natural Philosophy," in Loewe and Shaughnessy (1999), 860–66.

46. Schwartz (1985), 368.

47. This simplified table is based on the *yue ling* model in *Huainanzi* 5 ("Shi ze"). For a similar table of the *Lüshi chunqiu* calendar, see Graham (1986) 48. According to an apocryphal source, each of the five classes of animals contained 360 species. See *Yue ji yao jia* 樂稽耀嘉 in *Weishu jicheng,* 549.

48. See chapter 1, note 26.

49. Zou Shuwen believes that the introduction of humans into the taxonomy of five classes was an innovation by Liu An 劉安 (?179–122 B.C.E.) and argues that Dong Zhongshu introduced the *luo* 倮 variant for 臝. See Zou Shuwen (1982), 515.

50. *Guanzi jiaoshi,* 9 ("Xuan gong tu"), 3.91. Rickett proposes the mid-third century B.C.E. as the earliest date for both the calendar and the essay portions of this text.

The organization of the calendar and essay into chart form is most likely Han. See Rickett (1965), 196–98.

51. One of the Shuihudi almanacs associates the north with the use of red animal victims, the south with black, east with white, and the west with green victims. See *Shuihudi Qin mu zhujian,* 195. The *Mozi* combines east-chicken-green, south-dog-red, west-sheep-white, north-pig-black. See *Mozi jiaozhu,* 68.894–95 ("Ying di ci" 迎敵祠). *Huangdi neijing suwen,* 1.23–25 ("Jin gui zhen yan lun" 金匱眞言論), correlates east-chicken-green, south-sheep-red, center-ox-yellow, west-horse-white, and north-pig-black. Jia Yi associates the ox with the center. See *Xinshu,* 10.4a–b ("Tai jiao" 胎教).

52. Cf. Graham (1989), 320.

53. *Lei* covers the meaning of "animal class" or "species." According to Xu Shen the graph takes its etymological origins from the idea that dogs highly resemble each other. See *Shuowen jiezi zhu,* 10A.33a.

54. *Shiji,* 74.2344; tr. Needham, SCC, vol. 2, 233 [modified]. For Zou Yan, see Graham (1986), 12–15; and Harper, "Warring States Natural Philosophy," in Loewe and Shaughnessy (1999), 824–25.

55. *Ru fan,* 1.1 ("Wu li" 物理). A narrative in the *Shangshu* in which Yao 堯 commands Xi 羲 and He 和 to regulate the seasons for the people notes the seasonal changes of the coats of birds and beasts. See *Shangshu zhengyi,* 2.9a–10b ("Yao dian" 堯典). See also *Shiji,* 1.16–17. Seasonal transitions symbolized by an animal's coating are also attested in the *Zhouli* where the Officer of Furs (*siqiu* 司裘) distributes feathered species to his officials in mid-autumn to respond to the autumn vapors. See *Zhouli zhushu,* 7.5b–6a; *Zhouli zhengyi,* 13.493.

56. *Lüshi chunqiu jiaoshi,* 2.63 ("Zhong chun ji"), 3.121 ("Ji chun ji"), 9.467 ("Ji qiu ji"), 10.515 ("Meng dong ji"); *Liji zhushu,* 15.2b, 15.10a, 17.1b, 17.9b; *Huainanzi,* 5.162, 5.164, 5.177, 5.179 ("Shi ze"); *Yi Zhoushu,* 6.2a, 6.2b, 6.3a (this passage adds rotten weeds changing into glowworms in mid-summer), 6.3b, 6.4a ("Shi xun jie" 時訓解); *Da Dai Liji,* 2.4b, 2.6b, 2.9b ("Xia xiao zheng"). See also *Yi wei tong gua yan* in *Weishu jicheng,* 229, 242, 243.

57. Hall and Ames (1995), 253, 254, 257, 264.

58. French (1994), 15–16, 43–49.

59. These rules occur in the calendrical prescriptions in *Huainanzi* 5. See also *Liji zhushu,* 27.14a–b ("Nei ze," suited meats according to the seasons).

60. *Huainanzi,* 3.81–82 ("Tian wen" 天文); tr. Graham (1989), 333, 336–37 [modified]; cf. Major (1993), 65–66. For the association of *yin* and *yang* animals with winter and summer, see also *Lunheng jiaoshi,* 48.708 ("Zao hu"): "*Yin* creatures appear in winter, *yang* animals come out in summer. Their appearance corresponds to their *qi,* their *qi* stirs its species." Oysters were governed by the phases of the moon and thought to share the same *yin* vapor. See *Huainanzi,* 16.529 ("Shuo shan"); *Lunheng jiaoshi,* 10.102 ("Ou hui" 偶會), 32.503 ("Shuo ri"); *Yantie lun jiaozhu,* 9.335 ("Lun zai" 論菑).

61. *Huainanzi,* 4.142–43 ("Di xing"); Major (1993), 172–74.

62. Cf. *Lüshi chunqiu jiaoshi,* 24.1618 ("Bo zhi" 博志); *Chunqiu fanlu,* 8.206 ("Du zhi" 度制).

63. *Huainanzi,* 4.143–44 ("Di xing"); tr. Major (1993), 179 [modified]. Parallel passages occur in *Da Dai Liji,* 13.7b–8a ("Yi ben ming"); *Kongzi jiayu,* 6.4a–5a ("Zhi pei" 執轡); and *Chunqiu kao yi you* in *Weishu jicheng,* 790.

64. Major (1993), 179–82. For a similar interpretation, see Needham, SCC, vol. 2, 268–72.

65. *Huainanzi,* 4.154–55 ("Di xing"); tr. based on Major (1993), 208–209. For a chart of this scheme, see Gou Cuihua (1989), 32.

66. Luo Yuan, *Erya yi,* 28.297. See also Diény (1987), 212–13.

67. Another significant point of difference with Aristotle, as Geoffrey Lloyd points out in a comparative excursion. See Lloyd (1996b), 106–12, 124. For the *Zhuangzi* passage in question, see *Zhuangzi jishi,* 18.624–25 ("Zhi le" 至樂).

68. Slip 1165; Yates (1994), 91 [tr. modified].

69. Slip 0733; Yates (1994), 91 [tr. modified].

70. Slips 0993/1246/4917; Yates (1994), 92 [tr. modified].

71. *Da Dai Liji,* 5.8b–9a ("Zengzi tian yuan"); cf. Needham, SCC, vol. 2, 269–70. See also *Lunheng jiaoshi,* 22.284 ("Long xu"). For the phoenix as the essence of *yang,* the *qilin* as essence of *yin,* and the myriad human beings as the essence of virtue (*de*), see *Heguanzi,* 8.44 ("Du wan" 度萬). For the accumulation of *jingqi* as the cause for birds to fly and quadrupeds to run, see *Lüshi chunqiu jiaoshi,* 3.136 ("Jin shu" 盡數).

72. *Qianfu lun,* 8.433 ("Ben xun" 本訓).

73. See Sterckx (1996), 70–72. For associations of the dog with *yang qi,* see *Liji zhushu,* 61.22a ("Guan yi" 冠義); and Zheng Xuan's commentary in *Yili zhushu,* 10.10a ("Xiang yin jiu li" 鄉飲酒禮), 13.7b ("Xiang she li" 鄉射禮). Wei Zhao 韋昭 (204–73 C.E.) identifies the dog as a *yang* animal because it catches people while the pig is said to take care of the domestic sphere and belongs to *yin.* See his commentary to *Guoyu,* 20.635–36 ("Yue yu shang"), note 10.

74. For a review, see Graham (1986); Hall and Ames (1995), 256–68.

75. *Mengzi zhushu,* 8A.10a ("Li Lou xia" 離婁下).

76. *Lunyu zhushu,* 18.4a ("Wei zi" 微子). See also *Shiji,* 47.1929. This maxim is also quoted by Zhi Yun 郅惲 (first cent. C.E.) in *Hou Hanshu,* 29.1029; and *Dong guan Han ji,* 15.4a.

77. *Xunzi jijie,* 5.79 ("Fei xiang"). See also *Shuoyuan jiaozheng,* 13.317 ("Quan mou" 權謀). For the idea that the failure to be aware of distinctions (*bian* 辨) equals man to beasts, see also *Shiji,* 128.3232.

78. Hall and Ames (1998), 97.

79. *Xunzi jijie,* 9.164 ("Wang zhi"). The term "ladder of souls" is used in Needham, SCC, vol. 2, 21–24.

80. SCC, vol. 2, 23.

81. Other texts limit themselves to the faculty of cognition as the distinguishing factor between humans and animals. The *Liezi* states that "it is knowledge and foresight that makes man nobler than birds and beasts." See *Liezi,* 7.5b ("Yang Zhu" 楊朱). While frequently emphasizing the many ways in which humans are creatures like any other, Wang Chong notes

that "among the three hundred naked creatures, man takes the first place . . . a superiority he owes to his knowledge (*shi zhi* 識知)." See *Lunheng jiaoshi*, 38.600 ("Bie tong" 別通).

82. *Xunzi jijie*, 9.164–65 ("Wang zhi"). See also *Shuoyuan jiaozheng*, 13.317 ("Quan mou").

83. *Lüshi chunqiu jiaoshi*, 20.1321 ("Shi jun" 恃君).

84. *Gujin zhu*, 3.28 ("Wen da shi yi" 問答釋義).

85. *Guanzi jiaoshi* 2 ("Xing shi" 形勢), 1.17. For the idea that predatory animals do not couple or flock, see *Huainanzi*, 17.568 ("Shuo lin"); *Wenzi*, 1.37b ("Shang de" 上德); *Qu Yuan ji jiaozhu*, "Li sao," p. 39.

86. *Huainanzi*, 9.286 ("Zhu shu" 主術).

87. *Guanzi jiaoshi* 65 ("Li zheng jiu bai jie" 立政九敗解), 21.508. For the absence of gender distinctions as "the way of wild birds and beasts," see also *Liji zhushu*, 26.19a ("Jiao te sheng").

88. *Xunzi jijie*, 2.21 ("Xiu shen"), 4.61 ("Rong ru"), 5.79 ("Fei xiang"), 13.255 ("Chen dao" 臣道).

89. *Bohutong shu zheng*, 9.401 ("Xing ming" 姓名). For statements describing antiquity as an age without proper distinctions of gender, parental, and other kin relationships, see also *Guanzi jiaoshi* 31 ("Jun chen xia" 君臣下), 11.259; *Zhuangzi jishi*, 29.995 ("Dao Zhi" 盜跖). For bestiality as neglecting one's kin, see *Shiji*, 44.1857.

90. *Mengzi zhushu*, 5B.3b ("Teng Wen Gong shang" 藤文公上), 8B.5a–b ("Li Lou xia").

91. *Guanzi jiaoshi* 12 ("Shu yan"), 4.118.

92. *Yanzi chunqiu jishi*, 2.170, 4.241.

93. *Han shi waizhuan jishi*, 4.153.

94. *Yanzi chunqiu jishi*, 1.6, 7.430; *Liji zhushu*, 1.11a ("Qu li shang"); *Xinxu xiang zhu*, 6.185 ("Ci she" 刺奢); *Lüshi chunqiu jiaoshi*, 16.946 ("Xian shi" 先識), 20.1322 ("Shi jun"). In the *Hanshu*, the appearance of *mi* 麋 "elaphures" in the *Chunqiu* (cf. *Chunqiu Zuozhuan zhu*, p. 204 [Lord Zhuang, year 17]) is interpreted as an indication for lewd sexual behavior which "deludes" (*mi* 迷) the state. See *Hanshu*, 27.1396. For a statement that people without filial piety, food and clothes, rites and music are like deer following their instincts, see *Chunqiu fanlu*, 6.156 ("Li yuan shen" 立元神). In *Hanshu*, 94A.3780, the Xiongnu's practice of marrying one's step-mother is condemned as bestial conduct. For a comparison of the Xiongnu's way of life to that of deer in the Middle Kingdom, see *Yantie lun jiaozhu*, 7.262 ("Bei Hu" 備胡). For a statement that a lack of filial piety means having a "heart-mind like birds and beasts," see *Shiji*, 60.2117.

95. *Da Dai Liji*, 3.7b ("Bao fu" 保傅). See also *Xinshu*, 10.3b ("Tai jiao").

Chapter Four. The Animal and Territory

1. My use of the term "sociobiology" is inspired by the reinterrogation of the nature-culture divide proposed by scholars who engage in the scientific study of the bio-

logical basis of social behavior in all kinds of organisms, including humans. The discipline was pioneered by Edward O. Wilson in his influential works *The Insect Societies* (1971) and *Sociobiology: The New Synthesis* (1975). In using the term I refer to an organic mode of thought that seeks to fuse social and biological patterns in its analysis of the world.

2. Han Dongyu (1989); Lewis (1990), 169–74; and Lewis (1999), 127–29.

3. *Mengzi zhushu,* 13A.10a ("Jin xin shang" 盡心上).

4. *Mozi jiaozhu,* 2.109–10 ("Shang tong shang" 尚同上), 3.116 ("Shang tong zhong" 中), 6.255 ("Jie yong zhong" 節用中), 8.382 ("Fei yue shang" 非樂上).

5. Hall and Ames (1998), 273–74.

6. *Han Feizi jishi,* 19.1040 ("Wu du" 五蠹). See also *Zhuangzi jishi,* 29.994–95 ("Dao Zhi"). For a Song account of the edifying works of Nest Dweller, see *Lu shi,* 23–24.

7. For versions of these civilization histories, see *Zhouyi zhengyi,* 8.4b–8a; *Mengzi zhushu,* 5B.2b–3b ("Teng Wen Gong shang"), 6B.3a–4a ("Teng Wen Gong xia"); *Xinyu,* 1.1–21 ("Dao ji" 道基); *Huainanzi,* 13.421–24 ("Fan lun" 氾論), 19.629–31 ("Xiu wu"), 18.596 ("Ren jian"); *Bohutong shu zheng,* 2.49–52 ("Hao" 號); *Hanshu,* 91.3679–80; *Fengsu tongyi jiaoshi,* 1.1–15 ("Huang ba" 皇霸); *Liji zhushu,* 21.11a–b ("Li yun"). For an excellent discussion of Shennong as the patron deity of agriculture and philosophical ideal of an agricultural utopia, see Graham (1986b). For ancient culture heroes and their inventions, see Chang Kwang-Chih's list in Loewe and Shaughnessy (1999), 69, which includes Hai 胲 as the domesticator of cattle and Xiangtu 相土 as the inventor of the horse carriage.

8. *Zuozhuan zhu,* p. 1210 (Lord Zhao, year 1); *Hanshu,* 29.1698. See also Mathieu (1992), 179.

9. *Fengsu tongyi jiaoshi,* 400 ("yi wen").

10. Thomas (1983), 15.

11. For Cheng Ya and Wang Hai, see *Lüshi chunqiu jiaoshi,* 17.1078 ("Wu gong" 勿躬; Wang Hai here is named Wang Bing 冰); *Xunzi jijie,* 21.401 ("Jie bi" 解蔽, variant name Cheng Du 杜); *Shanhaijing jiaozhu,* 9.351; *He tu ting zuo fu* in *Weishu jicheng,* 1109. Another apocryphal source records a bird-bodied spirit named Meng Kui 孟虧 as the first domesticator of birds. See *He tu kuo ti xiang* in *Weishu jicheng,* 1102.

12. Marcel Detienne notes a similar dual attitude in ancient Greece. The Greeks divide the animal world between those that are hunted for the harm that they can cause, and those that are protected because they can serve humans. Aristotle teaches that humans must use animals to their own benefit. If not, they in turn are in danger of leading a bestial life. See "Culinary Practices and the Spirit of Sacrifice," in Detienne and Vernant (1989), 8.

13. The human-animal relationship as portrayed in these narratives is treated in more detail in chapter 5. For a critical study of the general concept of creation in the late Warring States, see Puett (1997).

14. *Zhouyi zhengyi,* 8.4b; tr. Graham (1989), 362 [modified]. This passage is transmitted in its entirety in the Mawangdui manuscript. See "Boshu *Xici* shiwen," 421, lines 3–5; Shaughnessy (1996), 205. See also *Bohutong shu zheng,* 2.51 ("Hao").

15. This has been suggested by a recent translator. See Rutt (1996), 27–28. Tradition

held that the hexagrams were developed out of Fuxi's eight trigrams by King Wen of the Zhou (1171–1122 B.C.E.). See also Lynn (1994), 1–5.

16. Perhaps this image may be traced back to Neolithic times as can be seen in the Yangshao mollusk shell "mosaics" unearthed at Xishuipo 西水坡 in Puyang 濮陽 (Henan). One among these shows a dragon and tiger mosaic placed at the left and right side of the deceased, possibly to symbolize the Blue Dragon and White Tiger constellations. See Yang Xiaoneng (2000), 53–54.

17. In an allusion to the Great Commentary, Lu Jia 陸賈 (ca. 228–140 B.C.E.) describes the perfect cosmic order as one in which all animal and plant species obtain their proper habitat between heaven and earth: "Therefore those who know Heaven look up to the patterns of heaven. Those who know Earth look down and examine the principles of the earth. The species that walk on tiptoe and pant, flinch and fly, wriggle and crawl, those that live in water and those that move over land, plants whose roots stick into the soil or whose foliage grows on the top, all have their hearts appeased and natures content." See *Xinyu*, 1.7 ("Dao ji"). For a similar description of the locomotion of these animals, see *Hanshu*, 94A.3763; and *Jing fa*, 27 ("Lun" 論, lines 11–12).

18. *Chunqiu ming li xu* 春秋命歷序 in *Gu weishu*, 13.256; *Weishu jicheng*, 880.

19. See *Fengsu tongyi jiaoshi*, 1.11 ("Huang ba"). See also *Li han wen jia* 禮含文嘉 in *Gu weishu*, 17.318; *Weishu jicheng*, 494.

20. *Shizi*, 1.15b.

21. *Hou Hanshu*, 62.2053.

22. *Hou Hanshu*, "zhi," 30.3661; Mansvelt Beck (1990), 234 ff. A similar theme is reiterated in the monograph on clothes in the *Jinshu* 晉書. See *Jinshu*, 25.751.

23. *Shuowen jiezi zhu*, 15A.1a–b; *Huainanzi*, 16.538 ("Shuo shan"). For a discussion of Fuxi and Cang Jie as originators of script and writing, see Lewis (1999), 197–202. A colorful early European account on the fashioning of characters based on animals is preserved in an essay by the Sicilian Jesuit Prosper Intorcetta (1625–96):

> If you ask from where Cang Xie [*sic*] took the lineaments and strokes of his characters, the answer is: He formed a great number of them from the traces of birds' claws, left on the earth or the sand—a new and strange idea for a European! . . . Besides Cang Xie at various periods a great number of persons produced new characters in imitation of things they had been contemplating. Thus during the reign of the fourth emperor by name Shao Hao 少昊 an eagle (Phenix bird, *sic*) appeared, and the emperor took the occasion to form new ornamental characters inspired by the sight of its flight and its feathers. In my opinion he wanted to do so because this unusual bird has always been regarded by the Chinese as a hopeful omen of felicity. The following emperor Zhuan Xu 顓頊, having observed swarms of newborn tadpoles swimming in some wine-pots in his royal palace, and the seventh emperor Yao 堯, after having regarded newborn tortoises blindly running around, devised new characters or rather perhaps new ornaments for their scripts. Tr. Lundbaek (1988), 19–21.

24. Lewis (1999), 275.

25. *Huainanzi*, 8.252 ("Ben jing" 本經). See also *Chunqiu yuanming bao* in *Weishu jicheng*, 590; *Lunheng jiaoshi*, 19.249 ("Gan xu"), 55.800 ("Gan lei" 感類). The link between bird tracks and writing is alluded to in Bai Juyi's 白居易 (772–846 C.E.) "Rhapsody on a Cock's Spur Writing Brush" (*Ji ju bi fu* 雞距筆賦). According to Robert J. Cutter the poet "makes his readers see this brush, similar in form to a cock's spur, as the apotheosis of tools at man's disposal in the conquest of dumb nature by human *wen* 文 (implying culture, civilization, and writing)." See Cutter (1989), 80–82.

26. *Shuowen jiezi zhu*, 15A.11a; *Hanshu*, 30.1721.

27. *Shuowen jiezi zhu*, 15A.17a.

28. See Cai Yong's *Zhuan shi* 篆勢 ("Postures of the Seal Script") in Yan Kejun, *Quan shanggu Sandai Qin Han Sanguo Liuchao wen, juan* 80 ("Quan Hou Han wen").

29. DeWoskin (1982), 131–33.

30. Lin Yutang (1936; rpt. 1948), 277–78.

31. *Chunqiu yuanming bao* in *Weishu jicheng*, 589–90; *Jūshū isho shūsei*, 26.

32. Vandermeersch (1977–1980), vol. 2, 290–91.

33. Allan (1991), 103–11. On the turtle species used by Shang diviners and the technical aspects involved in turtle shell divination, see Keithley (1985), ch. 1, 157–60. For the spirit tortoise resembling heaven and earth, see *Luo shu ling zhun ting* 洛書靈準聽 in *Weishu jicheng*, 1259.

34. *Shiji*, 128.3226.

35. *Li han wen jia* in *Gu weishu*, 17.320; *Weishu jicheng*, 494. See also *Songshu*, 28.800. For the river chart, see *Zhouyi zhengyi*, 7.29b. Lewis (1999), 437 note 17, makes reference to an Eastern Han terracotta tortoise with eight trigrams carved on its back.

36. For examples, see *Long yu he tu* 龍魚河圖 in *Weishu jicheng*, 1150; *Chunqiu yun dou shu* in *Weishu jicheng*, 724; *He tu* 河圖 in *Weishu jicheng*, 1219 (includes another version stating that the red markings of a carp formed graphs); *Shangshu zhong hou* 尚書中侯 in *Weishu jicheng*, 400, 402, 404, 405.

37. *Mengzi zhushu*, 5B.2b–3a ("Teng Wen Gong shang").

38. *Yi Zhoushu*, 8.7b–9b ("Zhi fang").

39. *Zhouli zhushu*, 33.10a–14b; *Hanshu*, 28A.1539–42.

40. *Zhouli zhushu*, 10.3b–4a. See also *Shuoyuan jiaozheng*, 18.446 ("Bian wu").

41. *Zhouli zhushu*, 15.11b (*zhangjie* 掌節, "tally keeper"), 37.25a (*xiao xingren* 小行人, "junior messenger").

42. According to Sima Qian, Emperor Wen had tiger tallies cast in bronze in 178 B.C.E. See *Shiji*, 10.424; *Hanshu*, 4.118; *Han guan yi*, 2.9b. For the use of tiger tallies, see also *Shiji*, 106.2836, 114.2980, 122.3151; *Hanshu*, 90.3662; and *Hou Hanshu*, 31.1096–97, where Du Shi 杜詩 (fl. ca. 50 C.E.) pleads for the reinstatement of such tallies as a remedy against the fraudulent use of seals. Three Qin examples are discussed in Li Xueqin (1985), 235–37. For a discussion of tiger tally inscriptions, see Wang Guowei (1923), 15.7a–11a. See further Ōba Osamu (1970), 43–54; Wang Guancheng (1994); Lao Kan (1978), 97; Yang Kuan (1998), 215–17; and Chen Zhaorong (1995).

43. *Guanzi jiaoshi* 17 ("Bing fa"), 6.155.

44. *Shiji*, 32.1479. The identification of the *si* remains problematic. Jean Lefeuvre (1990–91) has suggested that in Shang records it probably refers to a wild buffalo rather than a rhinoceros.

45. *Lunheng jiaoshi*, 52.762–63 ("Shi ying" 是應).

46. *Zhushu jinian*, 2.4a.

47. *Liji zhushu*, 3.8a–b ("Qu li shang").

48. A common title for military men guarding the ruler was *hu ben* 虎賁 "brave as tigers." See *Shangshu zhengyi*, 11.13b ("Mu shi" 牡誓); *Guoyu*, 5.195 ("Lu yu xia"); *Shiji*, 70.2289, 70.2293. *Hu ya* 虎牙 "tiger tooth" occurs as the epitheton for a military general. See for example *Hanshu*, 8.244; *Hou Hanshu*, 15.588, 18.686, 20.732. *Pi hu* 貔虎 "like a leopard and tiger" likewise denoted military bravery. See *Shangshu zhengyi*, 11.18a ("Mu shi"); *Hanshu*, 100B.4264. For the tiger, leopard, and bear as natural warriors and image of martial bravery, see *Mao shi zhengyi*, 4C.1b ("Gao qiu" 羔裘, Mao 80), 18E.5a ("Chang wu" 常武, Mao 263), 20A.17a ("Pan shui" 泮水, Mao 299); *Zuozhuan zhu*, p. 975 (Lord Xiang, year 10); *Shang jun shu jiaoshi*, 18.121 ("Hua ce" 畫策); *Shiji*, 1.3; *Da Dai Liji*, 7.1b ("Wu Di de" 五帝德); *Yantie lun jiaozhu*, 9.313 ("Xian gu" 險固), this last passage compares the state of Qin with bestial violence.

49. *Zuozhuan zhu*, p. 461 (Lord Xi, year 28). See also *Zuozhuan zhu*, p. 184 (Lord Zhuang, year 10). Zhang Heng's "Xi jing fu" 西京賦 describes how Chiyou 蚩尤 dishevels his hair and puts on a tiger skin to fend off malign spirits. See *Wenxuan*, 2.68.

50. They are specified as constellations in *Huainanzi*, 3.88–89 ("Tian wen"); as emblems of the four seasons in *Heguanzi*, 17.108 ("Tian quan" 天權).

51. See the commentaries and subcommentaries by Zheng Xuan and Kong Yingda in *Liji zhushu*, 3.8b ("Qu li shang").

52. *Lunheng jiaoshi*, 14.150–51 ("Wu shi" 物勢), 22.284 ("Long xu"). In the *Chunqiu fanlu* the four spirits are connected to dress ornaments: a sword is worn at the left side to symbolize the Green Dragon, a knife to the right side symbolizes the White Tiger, a leather knee-pad in front of the body symbolizes the Vermilion Bird and a cap on the head symbolizes the Dark Warrior. See *Chunqiu fanlu*, 6.143 ("Fu zhi xiang" 服制像). It has been suggested that the talismanic power of the four directional animals was thought to invigorate the troops' warrior spirit. See Mitarai Misaru (1987), 39. See further Ni Run-an (1999); and chapter 5, pp. 153–55.

53. In addition to determining the shape of tallies or being depicted on banners, animal *wen* also figured on Han coinage. Ca. 120 B.C.E. three types of white metal coinage were minted of an alloy of tin and silver. Both shape and value were determined by a Heaven-Earth-Man symbolism combined with an animal design: the most valuable coin was round and figured a dragon (*qi wen long* 其文龍), the second in value was square with a horse design (*qi wen ma* 其文馬), the third oblong figuring a tortoise (*qi wen gui* 其文龜). See *Shiji*, 30.1427; *Hanshu*, 24B.1164.

54. For a systematic discussion of natural philosophies of violence, see Lewis (1990), 213–26.

55. *Huainanzi,* 4.140, 4.145–46 ("Di xing"). See also *Da Dai Liji,* 13.8b ("Yi ben ming").

56. *Lunheng jiaoshi,* 7.67 ("Wu xing" 無形).

57. *Shuowen jiezi zhu,* 13B.16a. For the expression *tu qi* 土氣, see *Guoyu,* 1.15 ("Zhou yu shang"), 18.567 ("Chu yu xia"). For *tu qi* as climate, see *Hou Hanshu,* 86.2858.

58. *Shangshu zhengyi,* 13.3b–4a ("Lü ao").

59. For examples, see *Hanshu,* 96A.3889, 96A.3890, 96A.3894, 96B.3910; *Hou Hanshu,* 88.2922.

60. *Fengsu tongyi jiaoshi,* p. 1 ("Xu" 序); tr. Lewis (1990), 216.

61. *Shiji,* 74.2344. See also *Yantie lun jiaozhu,* 9.331 ("Lun Zou" 論鄒).

62. *Huainanzi,* 1.20 ("Yuan dao").

63. *Zhouli zhushu,* 39.5b; *Liezi,* 5.7a–8a ("Tang wen" 湯問); cf. *Shuowen jiezi zhu,* 4A.53a.

64. *Liji zhushu,* 12.26b–27a ("Wang zhi").

65. *Huainanzi,* 9.299 ("Zhu shu"), 18.600 ("Ren jian"). For similar statements and critiques on leaving one's natural habitat, see *Lüshi chunqiu jiaoshi,* 17.1108 ("Shen shi" 慎勢); *Han Feizi jishi,* 8.476 ("Shuo lin xia"); *Wenzi,* 2.23b ("Shang ren" 上 仁); *Shiji,* 84.2495; *Shuoyuan jiaozheng,* 16.408 ("Tan cong" 談叢); *Xinxu xiang zhu,* 2.53 ("Za shi").

66. *Xinlun,* 6b.

67. *Han shi waizhuan jishi,* 4.157; tr. Hightower (1952), 152.

68. *Huainanzi,* 7.242 ("Jing shen"). Monkeys were not eaten in the state of Chu where dog was consumed. See *Huainanzi,* 19.654 ("Xiu wu" 修務). Lin Cen (1989) has suggested that snakes were introduced as foodstuff from southern regions around the first cent. B.C.E.

69. The story is transmitted in a critique by Huan Tan. See *Xinlun,* 19b. Another food taboo held that pregnant women should not look at rabbits or eat their meat so as to avoid their babies being born with harelips. See *Huainanzi,* 16.549 ("Shuo shan"); *Bowuzhi,* 2.1b; and the Mawangdui *Taichan shu* 胎產書 ("Book of the Generation of the Fetus") in Harper (1998), 379.

70. *Yanzi chunqiu jishi,* 2.121. See also *Shuoyuan jiaozheng,* 1.19 ("Jun dao" 君道).

71. *Da Dai Liji,* 9.6b–7a ("Si dai" 四代).

72. According to a third century C.E. lexicon red soil was called "Rat's Liver" because of its color. See *Shiming,* 1.5b ("Shi di" 釋地).

73. *Zhouli zhushu,* 16.7a–8a; *Zhouli zhengyi,* 30.1181–88. For the term *tu hua* 土化 "soil transformation," see also *Zhouli zhushu,* 33.19b (*tufangshi* 土方氏 "land surveyor").

74. For discussions of the different soil types mentioned in the "Yu gong," see Needham, SCC, vol. 6, part 2, 82–98; Yang Kuan (1998), 70–73. An elaborate soil typology is preserved in the "Di yuan" 地員 chapter of the *Guanzi.*

75. *Lunheng jiaoshi,* 49.716–17 ("Shang chong").

76. *Fan Shengzhi shu,* 3.1, 3.1.1, 3.2.1, 3.3, 4.1.2, 4.8.2, 4.10. For depictions in Han murals, see Xia Henglian and Lin Zhengtong (1996), plates A17, A18, A19, A20.

77. "Localities (τόποι) also produce differences in character (ἤθη), for example

mountainous and rough places produce different characters from those in level and soft places: even in their look they are wilder and fiercer, like the pigs on Mount Athos; for even their sows are too much for the lowland boars to face." *Historia Animalium*, VII.29.

78. This will be discussed in greater detail in chapters 5 and 6.

79. *Zuozhuan zhu*, pp. 354–56 (Lord Xi, year 15).

80. *Shiji*, 60.2115; *Hanshu*, 28A.1527; *Fengsu tongyi jiaoshi*, 8.295 ("Si dian," quoting an apocryphal *Xiao jing* text); *Xiao jing wei* 孝經緯 in *Weishu jicheng*, 1057; *Yue ji yao jia* in *Weishu jicheng*, 548; *Bo wu jing yi yi*, 35. For a definition of the *she* as the common spirit of the five soils, see *Xiao jing yuan shen qie* 孝經援神契 in *Weishu jicheng*, 970.

81. For the *she* and *fang* sacrifices, see *Mao shi zhengyi*, 14A.6a ("Fu tian" 甫田, Mao 211), 14A.17b ("Da tian" 大田, Mao 212), 18B.19b ("Yun Han" 雲漢, Mao 258); *Chunqiu zhu*, p. 608 (Lord Wen, year 15), p. 1625 (Lord Ai, year 4, destruction of the altar); *Zuozhuan zhu*, p. 225 (Lord Zhuang, year 23), p. 232 (Lord Zhuang, year 25), p. 246 (Lord Zhuang, year 30). For the definition of *she* as "lord of the earth" and the identification of Houtu 后土 as a deity of the earth, see *Zuozhuan zhu*, p. 1502 (Lord Zhao, year 29); *Guoyu*, 4.166 ("Lu yu shang"); *Liji zhushu*, 25.20a–b ("Jiao te sheng"); *Shuowen jiezi zhu*, 1A.15a. On the origins and purpose of the sacrifices to the altars of the soil and grain, see *Bohutong shu zheng*, 3.83–93 ("She ji" 社稷). Sarah Allan has argued that as early as the Shang period the *fang* were perceived as spiritual entities rather than real lands. The four directions or quadrates may have been seen as spirit lands and homes of the winds which influenced rainfall and harvests. See Allan (1991), 75–86.

82. *Liji zhushu*, 46.4a–b ("Ji fa").

83. *Liji zhushu*, 23.2b ("Li qi").

84. For this principle, see *Zuozhuan zhu*, p. 334 (Lord Xi, year 10), p. 487 (Lord Xi, year 31). Yet one taboo ruled that domestic animals should not be sacrificed for the benefit of animals of the same kind. See *Zuozhuan zhu*, p. 381 (Lord Xi, year 19), p. 1327 (Lord Zhao, year 11); *Fengsu tongyi jiaoshi*, 8.297 ("Si dian").

85. *Yili zhushu*, 27.13b ("Jin li" 覲禮). See also *Zhouli zhushu*, 18.5b, *Liji zhushu*, 46.3b ("Ji fa"). The burial of animals as psychopomps for the deceased was subject to controversy. Upon the death of Emperor Yuan 元帝 (33 B.C.E.), a memorial was passed arguing that the interment of (imperial) chariots, carriages, oxen, horses, birds and beasts was against the rites. See *Hanshu*, 10.302. Imperial counsellor Gong Yu 貢禹 (ca. 44 B.C.E.) made a retrospective critique of state marshal Huo Guang's 霍光 (d. 68 B.C.E.) lavish sacrificial burial of birds, beasts, fish, turtles, oxen, horses, tigers, leopards and living wild animals. See *Hanshu*, 72.3071. The solemn nature of the burial also resulted in special treatment being given to horses used to draw carriages at funerals. According to Huan Tan, ten such horses were kept at the burial ground of Empress Wei 衛 (fl. 128 B.C.E.). They were well fed and watered, could not be ridden, and allegedly lived to the age of sixty. See *Xinlun*, 26a. There are occasional references to the burial of pet animals. Confucius states that worn-out curtains can be used to bury a horse. See *Liji zhushu*, 10.24b–25a ("Tan gong xia"). The *Zuozhuan* notes how aristocrats occasionally wrapped up dead horses for burial. See *Zuozhuan zhu*, pp. 1499–1500 (Lord Zhao, year 29). The *Huainanzi* refers to the burial of meritorious animals,

notably the horse and the ox. Horses were wrapped up in cloth and oxen were interred with their carriage. See *Huainanzi*, 13.460 ("Fan lun"). Another standard topos is that of a ruler being criticised for burying or performing sacrifices to his dead pet animals, which is seen as a sign of neglect for the welfare of his people. See for instance *Yanzi chunqiu jishi*, 2.163. Animal burial in later periods is discussed in Eliasberg (1992), 124–41.

86. For sacrifices to Houtu, see *Shiji*, 28.1389; *Hanshu*, 25A.1221. For the sacrifice of a victim to the earth as recompense for a harvest or to propitiate the earth in the absence of a harvest, see *Lüshi chunqiu jiaoshi*, 26.1732 ("Ren di" 任地). For horse drowning sacrifices to Hebo, see *Hanshu*, 76.3237; *Shiji*, 6.273–74; *Mu Tianzi zhuan*, 1.2b. The Baoshan slips document a horse sacrifice to a spirit named Dashui 大水 ("Great Water"), possibly a Yangzi river spirit. See *Baoshan Chu jian*, 37, slip 248. Chen Wei has suggested that "Great Water" is a spirit of the Huai 淮 river. See Chen Wei (1996), 169.

87. Sterckx (1996), 51, 67.

88. *Zhouli zhushu*, 13.1a.

89. *Zhouli zhushu*, 24.19a; *Zhouli zhengyi*, 84.1950.

90. *Guanzi jiaoshi* 76 ("Shan zhi shu" 山至數), 22.574; Rickett (1998), vol. 2, 417–18.

91. On these functions of the hunt, see the introduction to Yang Xiong's "Rhapsody on the Plume Hunt" ("Yu lie fu" 羽獵賦) in *Wenxuan*, 8.387.

92. *Liji zhushu*, 12.5a ("Wang zhi").

93. *Huainanzi*, 20.673 ("Tai zu").

94. *Zuozhuan zhu*, p. 212 (Lord Zhuang, year 19). Elsewhere the *Chunqiu* makes mention of a "Lu you" 鹿囿 "Deer park" (Lord Cheng, year 18). As Yang Bojun suggests, this is likely to be a place name rather than a park where deer were bred. See *Chunqiu Zuozhuan zhu*, p. 905.

95. *Zuozhuan zhu*, p. 1011 (Lord Xiang, year 14), p. 496 (Lord Xi, year 33).

96. *Hou Hanshu*, "zhi," 5.3123. This ceremony is studied in detail in Bodde (1975), 327–39, 381–86. Bodde also collects Han data on organised hunting competitions. For another passage linking the capture of wild animals with military prowess, see *Shangshu da zhuan*, 3.123 ("Lüe shuo" 略說). While hunting was frequently identified with collective military training in early China, it did not have the formative role in the "Bildung" of the individual character the Greeks had attributed to it. For instance Xenophon's famous hunting treatise, the *Cynegeticus* ("Hunting Man"), concludes with a validation of the hunt as an indispensable element in every young male's education. See Hull (1964), 107–140, esp. 136–38.

97. Lewis (1990), 152.

98. *Shiji*, 3.105; tr. Nienhauser (1994), 50 [modified].

99. The record of this campaign is preserved in the "Shi fu" 世俘 chapter of the *Yi Zhoushu*, a text which Edward Shaughnessy believes to be a document contemporary with the events of the conquest. See *Yi Zhoushu*, 4.11a, 4.12b; Shaughnessy (1997), 35–36.

100. *Mu Tianzi zhuan*, 1.1a, 1.2a, 1.3b, 1.4b, 2.1a, 2.2b. It is unlikely that the *Mu Tianzi zhuan* provides a contemporary record of King Mu's activities. It most probably presents a fictional Warring States account of a symbolic journey undertaken by the king. For an evaluation of the arguments, see Porter (1996), chapter 1.

101. *Shizi*, 2.3b.

102. For racing hounds and cockfights, see *Zuozhuan zhu,* p. 1461 (Lord Zhao, year 25); *Lüshi chunqiu jiaoshi,* 16.1004 ("Cha wei" 察微); *Zhuangzi jishi,* 19.654–55 ("Da sheng"); *Shiji,* 33.1540, 47.1910, 69.2257, 101.2744, 129.3271; *Huainanzi,* 18.612–13 ("Ren jian"); *Hanshu,* 8.237, 24B.1171, 65.2855, 97A.3969. For the hare chase, see *Zhanguo ce,* 10.390; *Shiji,* 53.2015. See also *Yantie lun jiaozhu,* 6.202 ("San bu zu," staged tiger fight); *Hanshu,* 68.2940 (staged pig against tiger fight). For fighting wild animals as punishment, see *Shiji,* 121.3123. See also Wang Zijin (1982). According to the *Shiji,* Li Si and his son reminisced one last time about leading their yellow dog to chase a hare minutes before they were executed. See *Shiji,* 87.2562.

Because of the corrupt influence of animal games on the common people, Han Wudi ordered merchants and sons from aristocratic families to be penalized for engaging in cock fighting, horse racing, hunting, or gambling. A payment to the government however was sufficient to be pardoned. See *Shiji,* 30.1437. For other criticisms of the indulgence in animal games, see *Yantie lun jiaozhu,* 2.65 ("Ci quan" 刺權); *Chunqiu fanlu,* 13.341 ("Wu xing xiang sheng" 五行相勝).

For Han murals depicting a bullfight (County Zou, Shandong) and a rabbit chase (County Nanyang, Henan), see Xia Henglian and Lin Zhengtong (1996), plate B40 (p. 104), plate B15 (p. 78). For depictions of cockfights, see Zhou Dao, Tang Wenguang, and Lü Pin (1985), plates 77, 78, 187. Evidence of falconry occurs on third-century b.c.e. tomb tiles. See W. White (1939) plates 28, 54, 55. See also *Hou Hanshu,* 34.1178, 54.1778. For a criticism of the idea that hunting pheasants should be seen as a pastime unworthy of a ruler, see Pan Yue's 潘岳 (247–300 c.e.) "Rhapsody on Pheasant Shooting" ("She zhi fu" 射雉賦) in *Wenxuan,* 9.422; tr. Knechtges (1987), vol. 2, 163. References to cockfighting are numerous throughout post-Han sources. See Cutter (1989b), chapters 2–5. To my knowledge the only preserved manual that treats the breeding and training of fighting cocks is a work entitled *Ji pu* 雞譜 "Treatise on Cockerels" by an unknown author from the Qianlong 乾隆 period (the received edition is dated to 1787). A recent transcription by Zhao Yunxian 趙云鮮 has appeared in Wang Xianqin (1996), 612–26.

103. For a discussion of imperial hunts and animal combats as an extension of the idea of human violence to the natural world, see Lewis (1990), 150–57.

104. *Mao shi zhengyi,* 16E.5b–6a ("Ling tai" 靈臺; Mao 242, stanza 2); tr. Legge (1991), 457 [modified]. After the removal of the Han capital to Luoyang, a new park resembling this numinous park was built. See Ban Gu, "Dong du fu" 東都賦 in *Wenxuan,* 1.32–33.

105. *Mao shi zhengyi,* 16E.1a.

106. *Mengzi zhushu,* 1A.4b–5a ("Liang Hui Wang shang" 梁惠王上).

107. *Mengzi zhushu,* 2A.4b–5a ("Liang Hui Wang xia").

108. *Xinshu,* 6.3b ("Li" 禮). See also *Xinshu,* 7.7b ("Jun dao" 君道).

109. Han foreign relations were mainly based on exchanges and alliances with foreign tribes rather than on the full-scale occupation of territory. The Han did not transplant their own domestic fauna and flora into newly occupied lands. The latter was a prominent feature of European colonization. See Crosby (1993), ch. 7–8.

110. Sima Xiangru's "Shanglin fu" 上林賦 (also known as the "Rhapsody on the Imperial Hunt" or the "Sir Fantasy Rhapsody") is included in his *Shiji* biography. See *Shiji*, 117.3017–43. Zhang Heng describes the Shanglin park in his "Rhapsody on the Western Capital" ("Xi jing fu" 西京賦). See *Wenxuan*, 1.64 ff. For descriptions of the Lingyou and Shanglin parks, see also *Jiaozheng san fu huang tu*, 4.29–30; and Wu Hung (1995), 165–76. On royal preserves, see also Schafer (1962), 286–88.

111. Hervouet (1964), 324–27. For an analysis of the "Rhapsody on the Shanglin Park" as a textual double of the emperor's all-inclusive cosmic authority, see Lewis (1999), 317–20.

112. *Hanshu*, 96B.3928; cf. Hulsewé and Loewe (1979), 199–201.

113. Rawson (1998). See also Wu Hung's remarks on animal images recovered from the mausoleums of the Zhongshan 中山 kingdom (Hebei, 4th cent. B.C.E.). Wu notes the presence of steppe art motifs such as the animal combat and the emphasis on life motion in a tiger stand from tomb no. 1. See "Art and Architecture of the Warring States Period," in Loewe and Shaughnessy (1999), 689–92. For a survey of the various hypotheses regarding the origins of the animal style in the northern frontier regions, see Du Zhengsheng (1993).

114. *Hou Hanshu*, 40A.1338 ("Xi du fu" 西都賦).

115. The symbolism of the hunt as evinced in Sima Xiangru's rhapsodies is treated in detail in Hervouet (1964), 215–44, 256–58, 271–86 et partim. Parallels can be drawn with the exhibition of captive wild animals during religious processions (πομπαι) in ancient Greece and exotic animal parades and staged animal combats (*venationes*) at the Roman games (*ludi*). See Jennison (1937), 6, 25–26, 42–98.

116. See his "Guang cheng song" 廣成頌 in *Hou Hanshu*, 60A.1959. The Nine Preserves (*jiusou* 九藪), among which the famous Yunmeng 雲夢 marsh, are linked with the Nine Provinces in *Zhouli zhushu*, 33.10a, 11a, 12b, 13a, 13b, 14a, 14b.

117. Rivo (1990), 205.

118. Schafer (1968), 329. See also Hervouet (1964), 268. For an anthropological analysis of how zoos reflect the cultural expression of human identity rather than zoological nuances within the animal realm, see Mullan and Marvin (1987).

119. *Shiji*, 117.3017; tr. Watson (1961), vol. 2, 309–12 [modified]. See also *Hanshu*, 57A.2548; *Wenxuan*, 8.363–64.

120. *Zuozhuan zhu*, p. 1181 (Lord Xiang, year 30).

121. *Zhouli zhushu*, 13.18b. The *Yu liaozi* 尉繚子 states that in the same way that wild animals should not be used as sacrificial offerings, miscellaneous studies do not make an accomplished scholar. See *Yu liaozi*, 2.1b–2a ("Zhi ben" 治本).

122. *Quan shanggu Sandai Qin Han Sanguo Liuchao wen*, "Quan Han wen," 42.11b.

123. *Yunmeng Longgang Qin jian*, 27–34. Unfortunately these slips are severely damaged.

124. *Shiji*, 28.1398; *Hanshu*, 25A.1235.

125. *Xijing zaji*, 1.6b–7a, where the fabrication of these censers is attributed to Ding Huan 丁緩 (fl. ca. 180 C.E.), a craftsman from Chang'an. A nice example was recovered from the tomb of Liu Sheng 劉勝, Prince Jing 靖 of Zhongshan 中山 (died 113 B.C.E.) at Mancheng, Hebei. The mountain motif and the iconology of the hill censers have also been related to the Han interest in immortality, which was reflected in the search for

mountain islands and the performance of rituals at mountains. See Dubs (1959); Hentze (1964), 13–48; Kiyohito Munakata (1991), 28–34; and Erickson (1992).

126. This was Liu Yu 劉餘, King Gong 恭 of Lu. The palace was built ca. 154 B.C.E. See *Hanshu*, 53.2413–14.

127. *Wenxuan*, 11.513–16.

128. See *Shiji*, 28.1402; *Hanshu*, 25B.1245. See also *Jiaozheng san fu huangtu*, 3.23.

129. *Xunzi jijie*, 5.161–62 ("Wang zhi"); tr. Knoblock (1990), vol. 2, 102 [modified].

130. *Zuozhuan zhu*, pp. 669–71 (Lord Xuan, year 3). See also *Shiji*, 40.1700; *Shuowen jiezi zhu*, 7A.35b; and *Lunheng jiaoshi*, 26.375–76 ("Ru zeng" 儒增), where Wang Chong denies the apotropaic power of metal tripods. For the *chimei* demons, see chapter 3, note 19. For the *wangliang*, see chapter 7, note 20.

131. Robert Campany argues that this tradition of "cosmographic collection" inspired the development of post-Han *zhiguai* 志怪 literature. See Campany (1996), 101–42, 157–59.

132. David Hall and Roger Ames have coined the term "focus/field sense of order" in discussing this perception of space. See Hall and Ames (1995), 241–44.

133. *Hanshu*, 96A.3872, 3876, 3883, 3890, 3897, 96B.3901, 52.2401 (This passage also qualifies barbarians in distant and cut-off regions as "people that cannot be shepherded"); *Shiji*, 116.2991. Another image is that of barbarians who wriggle around like worms (*chun ju* 蠢居). See *Hou Hanshu*, 86.2861.

134. *Bohutong shu zheng*, 4.134 ("Feng gong hou"), 6.289 ("Xun shou" 巡狩). For references to the ruler-sage as shepherd of the world, see chapter 5, p. 151.

135. *Wu Yue chunqiu*, 6.105; reiterated in *Lunheng jiaoshi*, 38.597 ("Bie tong"). For Bo Yi's association with the naming of animals, see also *Wenxuan*, 2.64 ("Xi jing fu").

136. See *Shanhaijing jiaozhu*, 477–78. For an alternative discussion of the *Wu Yue chunqiu* passage and the Liu Xin preface, see Campany (1996), 133–37.

137. *Yantie lun jiaozhu*, 6.207 ("San bu zu").

138. *Yantie lun jiaozhu*, 7.257–58 ("Chong li" 崇禮).

139. *Hanshu*, 11.336.

140. The core thirty-two chapters of the *Yi Zhoushu* can be dated to the late fourth or early third cent. B.C.E. The dating of the other chapters, including the "Wang Hui," is speculative (some pre-Han, others Western Han) but the final redaction of the *Yi Zhoushu* was not completed until the early first cent. B.C.E. See Shaughnessy, "I Chou shu," in Loewe (1993), 230–31.

141. *Yi Zhoushu*, 7.8a–11b. The "Wang hui" animal nomenclature are annotated at length in Liu Shipei (1907).

142. *Yi Zhoushu*, 7.11b–12a. For the idea that feudal lords bring goods representative of their state to the court, see also *Liji zhushu*, 24.14b ("Li qi").

Chapter Five. Transforming the Beasts

1. The term *sheng* 聲 ("sound," "reputation" or "aura") occurs as a paronomastic gloss for *sheng* 聖 "human sage." See *Fengsu tongyi jiaoshi*, 415 ("yi wen"); *Bohutong shu zheng*, 7.334 ("Sheng ren" 聖人).

2. For (variora of) this expression, see *Liji zhushu*, 38.4b, 38.11a ("Yue ji"); *Xunzi jijie*, 20.381 ("Yue lun"); *Shiji*, 24.1206, 24.1211, 130.3305; *Hanshu*, 5.153, 28B.1640, 100A.4227; *Bohutong shu zheng*, 3.94 ("Li yue").

3. *Lüshi chunqiu jiaoshi*, 5.284 ("Gu yue"). Ox-tail staffs appear among the insignia for grandees in the *Shijing* (cf. *Mao shi zhengyi*, 3B.3b, 9D.2b); feathered ox tails appear as attributes for civil dances. See for example *Shiji*, 24.1179, 1180 note 6.

4. *Lüshi chunqiu jiaoshi*, 5.284–85 ("Gu yue"). See also *Fengsu tongyi jiaoshi*, 6.218 ("Sheng yin" 聲音); *Huainanzi*, 3.113 ("Tian wen").

5. *Xunzi jijie*, 21.389 ("Jie bi"), quoting a lost *Shijing* ode; *Bohutong shu zheng* ("fu lu" 附錄 1), 603; *Lunheng jiaoshi*, 50.733 ("Jiang rui" 講瑞); and *Songshu*, 28.792–93. The etymological relationship between both *feng* graphs is discussed in Tei Masahiro (1978).

6. *Guanzi jiaoshi* 58 ("Di yuan"), 19.465.

7. *Lüshi chunqiu jiaoshi*, 5.285 ("Gu yue").

8. For archaeological evidence of these drums, see Liu Li (1996), 7–9. I am grateful to the State University of New York Press reviewer for bringing this paper to my attention. For textual evidence, see *Mao shi zhengyi*, 16E.7a ("Ling Tai" 靈臺, Mao 242). See also *Shuowen jiezi zhu*, 13B.11b; *Shiji*, 87.2543; Gao You's commentary to *Huainanzi*, 5.171 ("Shi ze"); and Lu Ji's gloss in *Mao shi caomu niaoshou chongyu shu*, 2.55–56. For the use of the alligator drum in the hunt, see *Shiji*, 117.3014; *Hou Hanshu*, 60A.1964. For further reference to the *tuo* (*alligator sinensis*), see Sterckx (2000), 10, note 24.

9. For the use of horse and oxen hides to cover drums, see *Shiji*, 128.3236; *Yi tong gua yan* 易通卦驗 in *Gu weishu*, 14.276; *Weishu jicheng*, 203. For the use of deer hides, see *Lüshi chunqiu jiaoshi*, 5.285 ("Gu yue").

10. See for instance *Chuci*, 5.9b–10a ("Yuan you" 遠遊); *Shanhaijing jiaozhu*, 3.75 (a "long snake" that makes a noise like "drums and wooden rattles").

11. *Shanhaijing jiaozhu*, 13.329, 14.361; *Huainanzi*, 4.150 ("Di xing").

12. *Shanhaijing jiaozhu*, 14.361; Sterckx (2000), 11–12. For Kui as music master, see *Zuozhuan zhu*, p. 1493 (Lord Zhao, year 28); *Hanshu*, 19A.721. For Kui as originator of drums and dance, see Granet (1926), vol. 2, 505–15; Eberhard (1968), 57–58. Kui is traditionally represented as a one-legged monster. See *Lüshi chunqiu jiaoshi*, 22.1526–27 ("Cha zhuan" 察傳); *Han Feizi jishi*, 12.671, 12.686 ("Wai chu shuo zuo xia" 外儲 說左下); *Fengsu tongyi jiaoshi*, 2.52 ("Zheng shi" 正失); and *Kong Congzi*, 1.5b ("Lun shu" 論書).

13. For drumming like thunder and the identification of thunder as heaven's drumming, see *Lüshi chunqiu jiaoshi*, 21.1447 ("Qi xian" 期賢); *He tu kuo di xiang* in *Weishu jicheng*, 1097. On the thalassic origins of thunder, see *Gujin zhu*, 2.19 ("Yu chong" 魚蟲); and *Yi yu tu zan*, 3.15.

14. *Shangshu da zhuan*, 1.3 ("Yao dian" 堯典). See also *Chunqiu fanlu*, 16.414–15 ("Xun tian zhi dao" 循天之道); *Chunqiu yuan ming bao* in *Weishu jicheng*, 602. For the equation of spring with movement, see also *Shizi*, 2.1b. For the link between drumming (*gu* 鼓) and spring, see *Shuowen jiezi zhu*, 5A.35a; *Fengsu tongyi jiaoshi*, 6.227–28 ("Sheng yin"); and Sterckx (2000), 12–13.

15. *Zhouli zhushu*, 40.24a. For drumming causing insects to move, see *Xiao jing gou*

ming jue 孝經鉤命決 in *Weishu jicheng*, 1013. For the idea that drums excited the spirits of troops to "move" or advance toward the enemy, see *Zuozhuan zhu*, p. 183 (Lord Zhuang, year 10); *Guanzi jiaoshi* 17 ("Bing fa"), 6.155.

16. *Cai Shi yueling zhangju*, 1.9a. For thunder awakening hibernating animals, see also *Lüshi chunqiu jiaoshi*, 2.64 ("Zhong chun ji"), 21.1425 ("Kai chun" 開春).

17. The gloss occurs in *Liji zhushu*, 61.22a ("Guan yi"); *Fengsu tongyi jiaoshi*, 8.320 ("Si dian"); *Shuowen jiezi zhu*, 13B.4a; *Chunqiu yuanming bao* in *Weishu jicheng*, 632.

18. *Da Dai Liji*, 2.6a ("Xia xiao zheng").

19. *Da Dai Liji*, 2.3b–4a ("Xia xiao zheng"). Marcel Granet has linked the image of the "drumming pheasant" with pheasant dances (possibly performed by females) to provoke thunder. See Granet (1926), vol. 2, 570–72. Bird song was also associated with the fertility of the harvest. For an example, see *Quan Han Sanguo Jin Nanbei chao shi*, 4.85 ("Quan Han shi"); and Sterckx (2000), 15.

20. For fish, see *Huainanzi*, 20.663 ("Tai zu"). For birds' prescience of wind and cave dwellers' prescience of rain, see *Huainanzi*, 10.337 ("Miu cheng"), 18.618 ("Ren jian"); *Hanshu*, 75.3173; *Chunqiu Han han zi* 春秋漢含孳 in *Weishu jicheng*, 814; *Chunqiu zuo zhu qi* 春秋佐助期 in *Weishu jicheng*, 823. For ants' foreknowledge of rain, see *Dong guan Han ji*, 7.3b. For other examples of animals with a foreknowledge of the future and the climate or the power to induce climatological phenomena, see *Shuowen jiezi zhu*, 4A.42b, 4A.48a, 13A.55a; *Huainanzi*, 13.445 ("Fan lun") stating that apes know the past and magpies are aware of future events.

21. *Hou Hanshu*, 59.1909; tr. Needham, SCC, vol. 3, 627.

22. *Zhouli zhushu*, 37.2b–3a, 37.7a. Spirit drums featuring propitious animals or hybrid animal parts were also used to expel ghosts and spirits. See Sterckx (2000), 16, note 46.

23. For the inscriptions, see Mattos (1988), 165–66, 195–96 (fishing), 220–21, 239–41. The translation is adapted from Mattos (1988), 165–66; and Waley (1954), 290.

24. *Shiji*, 117.3033; tr. Watson (1961), vol. 2, 315. For the battering of drums during the hunt, see also *Wenxuan*, 2.69 ("Xi jing fu").

25. *Shuoyuan jiaozheng*, 16.384 ("Tan cong"). See also *Hou Hanshu*, "zhi," 29.3643, note 14; *Gujin zhu*, 1.4 ("Yu fu" 輿服). For reference to the *luan* and *he* bells, see *Mao shi zhengyi*, 6C.8a ("Si tie" 駟驖, Mao 127), 10A.8a ("Lu xiao" 蓼蕭 Mao 173), 10B.10a ("Cai qi" 采芑, Mao 178), 11A.5a–b ("Ting liao" 庭燎, Mao 182). See further Fukatsu Tanefusa (1986), 13–15.

26. *Zuozhuan zhu*, pp. 88–89 (Lord Huan, year 2).

27. *Xunzi jijie*, 18.335 ("Zheng lun"); tr. Knoblock (1994) vol. 3, 41–42 [modified]. This passage is repeated in *Xunzi jijie*, 19.347 ("Li lun").

28. *Bohutong shu zheng*, 12.588–89 ("que wen").

29. *Zhouli zhushu*, 41.13a–16a (*ziren* 梓人). See also Sterckx (2000), 18–19.

30. *Shuoyuan jiaozheng*, 18.465 ("Bian wu"); *Kongzi jiayu*, 3.9b ("Bian zheng" 辯政). See also *Lunheng jiaoshi*, 43.649–50 ("Bian dong" 變動); *Yuefu shi ji*, 88.1233 ("Za ge yao ci" 雜歌謠辭, associating the bird with the state of Qi); and *Xian Qin Han Wei Jin Nanbei chao shi*, 3.37–38.

31. For a southern feather dance, see *Bohutong shu zheng*, 3.109 ("Li yue"). For Liu Xi's gloss, see *Shiming*, 1.1b ("Shi tian" 釋天). Liu Xiaonan (1995) has suggested that Liu Xi's gloss originated from matching the sound *yu* 羽 with the element water in five-phase thought, with *yu* representing the sound corresponding to water. Hayashi Minao has argued that the feathered headdress motif on top of facial decorative figures in Liangzhu, Longshan, and Yin artifacts was related to rain magic. See Hayashi Minao (1991), 41–48. Salviati (1994) speculates that these feathers represent the antecedents of feathered immortals in Han art, an argument which is difficult to corroborate.

32. *Chunqiu fanlu*, 16.399–407 ("Qiu yu" 求雨). For the fashioning of clay dragon figurines to invoke rain, see *Xinlun*, 9a. The ritual is discussed at length in Loewe (1987).

33. *Liji zhushu*, 37.7b–8a ("Yue ji" 樂記); *Shiji*, 24.1184 ("Yue shu" 樂書). For the ascending hierarchy of sound-tone-music (*sheng-yin-yue*), see also *Mao shi zhengyi*, 1A.6a–7a ("Da xu" 大序).

34. *Liji zhushu*, 37.8a; cf. *Shiji*, 24.1184 note 3. For another passage defining the transition from rough sounds to tones as a process of transformation or modulation (*bian* 變), see *Liji zhushu*, 37.1b.

35. *Lunheng jiaoshi*, 19.245 ("Gan xu").

36. *Shangshu zhengyi*, 3.26a, 5.14b–15a. See also *Xunzi jijie*, 25.463 ("Cheng xiang" 成相); and *Shiji*, 1.39, 2.81. Another allusion to the slapping of the music stones occurs in a ballad on the southern wind ("Nan feng ge" 南風歌), attributed eponymously to Shun. See *Yuefu shi ji*, 57.824–25.

37. *Fengsu tongyi jiaoshi*, 6.217 ("Sheng yin").

38. These stories occur in several sources. See *Xunzi jijie*, 1.10 ("Quan xue"); *Huainanzi*, 16.521–22 ("Shuo shan"). See also *Da Dai Liji*, 7.8a ("Quan xue" 勸學); *Han shi waizhuan jishi*, 6.217; *Shuowen jiezi zhu*, 11B.22a; *Liezi*, 5.14b ("Tang wen"); *Lunheng jiaoshi*, 8.78 ("Shuai xing" 率性), 19.243–45 ("Gan xu"). For Bo Ya, see also *Lüshi chunqiu jiaoshi*, 14.740 ("Ben wei").

39. *Han Feizi jishi*, 3.171 ("Shi guo"). See also *Shiji*, 24.1236; *Lunheng jiaoshi*, 64.910 ("Ji yao" 紀妖); *Fengsu tongyi jiaoshi*, 6.230 ("Sheng yin"). On the association of the lute with the crane, see Van Gulik (1940), 134–40.

40. *Yantie lun jiaozhu*, 5.143 ("Xiang ci" 相刺). Zengzi is Zeng Can 曾參, one of Confucius's disciples who despite his flawless display of filial piety was detested by his parents. See *Zhuangzi jishi*, 26.920 ("Wai wu" 外物); *Lunheng jiaoshi*, 19.239 ("Gan xu").

41. Kaltenmark (1953), 125–27. See also *Shuijing zhu jiao*, 18.588; and *Yiwen leiju*, 78.1327.

42. *Liji zhushu*, 38.16b–17a ("Yue ji"). Identical passage in *Shiji*, 24.1203.

43. *Wenxuan*, 17.788–89, "Dong xiao fu" 洞簫賦; tr. Knechtges (1996), vol. 3, 241–42.

44. *Wenxuan*, 18.818–820, "Chang di fu" 長笛賦; tr. Knechtges (1996), vol. 3, 273–74.

45. *Hanshu*, 36.1933. See also *Shiji*, 1.43, 2.81; *Hou Hanshu*, 70.2272. These passages all reiterate *Shangshu zhengyi*, 5.14b–15a.

46. For other examples of the hybrid phoenix complying to human morality under the influence of musical harmony, see *Yue xie tu zheng* 樂叶圖徵 in *Gu weishu*, 20.392–

93; *Weishu jicheng*, 560. See also *Yiwen leiju*, 919.1707–1708; *Taiping yulan*, 915.3b; *Chunqiu yan Kong tu* 春秋演孔圖 in *Weishu jicheng*, 585–86.

47. For the Yellow Emperor taming wild beasts, see *Shiji*, 1.3; *Da Dai Liji*, 7.1b ("Wu Di de" 五帝德); *Kongzi jiayu*, 5.12a ("Wu Di de" 五帝德); *Liezi*, 2.22a ("Huang di"); *Lunheng jiaoshi*, 9.84 ("Ji yan" 吉驗). On the role of the Yellow Emperor as creator of warfare through the instruction of animals, see Lewis (1990), 199–203.

48. *Liezi*, 2.22a ("Huang di"); tr. Graham (1991), 54.

49. *Kong Congzi*, 1.5b ("Lun shu" 論書).

50. *Shangshu da zhuan*, 1.32–33 ("Jiu yao mo" 咎繇謨). See also *Han shi waizhuan jishi*, 1.16. A number of slips among the Yinyang texts excavated at Yinqueshan indicate how different animals (among other natural categories such as clouds and rain) would respond to different notes. An example: "If you play the *guxian* 古洗 ('old and purified') pitch, the cricket will climb (into) the halls." See Yates (1994), 129, no. 2436. Another entry (Yates [1994], 129, no. 1949) possibly indicates the return of the *da hao* 大浩 bird as a response to a *lü* 呂 tone.

51. *Huainanzi*, 20.664 ("Tai zu"): "Therefore the sage is someone who cherishes a heart of heaven and is able to move and transform all under heaven in the same way as sounds do."

52. *Huainanzi*, 8.265 ("Ben jing").

53. *Shangshu da zhuan*, 1.33 ("Jiu yao mo").

54. *Gu weishu*, 21.402; *Weishu jicheng*, 540; Sterckx (2000), 30.

55. *Han Feizi jishi*, 3.172 ("Shi guo"). See also *Fengsu tongyi jiaoshi*, 6.230–31 ("Sheng yin"); *Lunheng jiaoshi*, 64.910–11 ("Ji yao").

56. *Shuowen jiezi zhu*, 4A.39b. For hymn music causing the arrival of the phoenix and unicorn, see *Hou Hanshu*, 70.2272. See also Hargett (1989), esp. 247–48.

57. *Lüshi chunqiu jiaoshi*, 6.359 ("Ming li" 明理).

58. *Guoyu*, 14.460 ("Jin yu").

59. *Zhouli zhushu*, 22.15b–16a. See also *Dong guan Han ji*, 5.2a.

60. *Shuihudi Qin mu zhujian*, 213 (lines 13–14); tr. Harper (1996), 246 no. 25.

61. *Zhuangzi jishi*, 18.621 ("Zhi le"). See also *Zhuangzi jishi*, 19.665–66 ("Da sheng"); *Huainanzi*, 11.347 ("Qi su" 齊俗).

62. *Zhuangzi jishi*, 9.334–36 ("Ma ti" 馬蹄). For the image of humans peeping undisturbed into nests, see also *Huainanzi*, 13.421 ("Fan lun"); *Wenzi*, 2.35b ("Shang li" 上禮); *Liji zhushu*, 22.24b ("Li yun"); *Kongzi jiayu*, 7.10a ("Li yun" 禮運); *Xunzi jijie*, 31.542–43 ("Ai Gong" 哀公); *Heguanzi*, 13.90–91 ("Bei zhi" 備知).

63. *Daodejing jiang yi*, 55.28b; tr. Lau (1963), 116. For the idea that wild animals do not attack virtuous persons, see also *Zhuangzi jishi*, 17.588 ("Qiu shui").

64. *Liezi*, 2.23a ("Huang di").

65. *Liezi*, 2.22b ("Huang di").

66. *Huainanzi*, 6.206 ("Lan ming"). A similar narrative appears in *Huainanzi*, 8.253–54 ("Ben jing").

67. *Huainanzi*, 6.208 ("Lan ming").

68. *Huainanzi*, 6.211 ("Lan ming"). Similar passages occur in *Shizi*, 2.11b. See also *Xinshu*, 7.4a ("Er bi" 耳痺).

69. *Zuozhuan zhu*, pp. 938–39 (Lord Xiang, year 4).

70. *Han shi waizhuan jishi*, 10.358–59; *Yanzi chunqiu jishi*, 1.83–84. See also *Huainanzi*, 21.710 ("Yao lüe" 要略).

71. *Lüshi chunqiu jiaoshi*, 25.1681 ("Shen xiao" 慎小); *Shiji*, 37.1596.

72. *Xunzi jijie*, 14.260 ("Zhi shi" 致士).

73. *Zuozhuan zhu*, p. 265 (Lord Min, year 2). See also *Lüshi chunqiu jiaoshi*, 11.588 ("Zhong lian" 忠廉); *Shiji*, 37.1594; *Xinxu xiang zhu*, 8.251 ("Yi yong" 義勇).

74. *Lienü zhuan*, 2.3b ("Xian ming" 賢明).

75. *Huainanzi*, 8.253 ("Ben jing"). Ann Paludan suggests that this image is reflected in a pictorial motif of a man trying to catch the tail of a wild beast, which occurs in Sichuan tower (*que* 闕) decoration. See Paludan (1991), 31, fig. 24.

76. *Da Dai Liji*, 9.12b–13a ("Gao zhi" 誥志). A similar statement that animals lost their predatory instincts under the virtuous rule of the Yellow Emperor and Fuxi is recorded in *Wenzi*, 1.9b ("Jing cheng").

77. "Jian ge hu fu" 諫格虎賦. This *fu* is transmitted in *Kong Congzi*, 7.1a–2a; tr. Ariel (1996), 98–101. The editors of the *Quan Han fu*, p. 115, attribute the authorship to Kong Cang 孔臧 (ca. 201–123 B.C.E.).

78. *Mengzi zhushu*, 1A.10b ("Liang Hui Wang shang"). The same statement reoccurs in *Mengzi zhushu*, 6B.4b–5a ("Teng Wen Gong xia"), where it is attributed to Gongming Yi 公明儀.

79. *Mengzi zhushu*, 1B.5a ("Liang Hui Wang shang").

80. See *Lunheng jiaoshi* 48 ("Zao hu"), esp. 48.707–11.

81. *Hou Hanshu*, 38.1278.

82. *Hou Hanshu*, 41.1412–13; cf. *Fengsu tongyi jiaoshi*, 2.92–93 ("Zheng shi"); *Taiping yulan*, 891.2a–b. Song Jun becomes an exemplary figure in later times. For instance, the Ming dynasty *Hu yuan* 虎苑 opens its first chapter entitled "Virtuous Government" ("De zheng" 德政) with the Song Jun case. See *Hu yuan*, 1.1a (p. 3707). For Song Jun's opposition to shamanic practices, see *Fengsu tongyi jiaoshi*, 9.338 ("Guai shen"). On the theme of the tiger plague in the post-Han period, see Eichhorn (1954), 144–46 et partim.

83. *Hou Hanshu*, 41.1419.

84. *Hou Hanshu*, 76.2482.

85. *Lunheng jiaoshi*, 16.188–89 ("Shu xu" 書虛). Elsewhere Wang states that there cannot be any intellectual intercourse (*xiang zhi* 相知) between man and beast. See *Lunheng jiaoshi*, 51.742–43 ("Zhi rui" 指瑞).

86. *Bohutong shu zheng*, 12.590 ("que wen"). See also *Shangshu da zhuan*, 1.10 ("Tang zhuan" 唐傳); *Chunqiu fanlu*, 10.262 ("Shen cha ming hao" 深察名號); *Gongyang zhuan*, 4.11a. The balance between consumption and preservation has also been a central concern in Western debates on the hunt. As Matt Cartmill notes: "Throughout European history hunters have tended to see themselves as enemies of the individual animals but friends of the animal *kinds*—and by extension as friends of the wild, nonhuman realm that the ani-

mals inhabit." See Cartmill (1993), 31. Although criticisms on the hunt and staged animal games reverberated occasionally in Greek and Roman antiquity, the real questioning of the hunt on moral grounds in Europe emerged only with the early Church fathers, and the Church remained the most vociferous critic of the pleasure hunt until at least the Middle Ages. See Szrabó (1997).

87. *Shiji*, 3.95; tr. Nienhauser (1994), 43. For similar accounts, see *Lüshi chunqiu jiaoshi*, 10.560–61 ("Yi yong" 異用); *Xinshu*, 7.4b–5a ("Yu cheng" 諭誠); *Xinxu xiang zhu*, 5.146 ("Za shi").

88. *Liji*, 12.5a–6a ("Wang zhi").

89. *Wenxuan*, 3.121–22; tr. Knechtges (1982), vol. 1, 289.

90. *Liji zhushu*, 13.10a ("Wang zhi"), 25.1a ("Jiao te sheng").

91. *Xunzi jijie*, 9.165 ("Wang zhi").

92. *Mengzi zhushu*, 1A.7a ("Liang Hui Wang shang").

93. *Lüshi chunqiu jiaoshi*, 18.1226 ("Ju bei" 具備).

94. *Lüshi chunqiu jiaoshi*, 1.2 ("Meng chun ji"). See also *Wenzi*, 2.24a–b ("Shang ren").

95. *Guoyu*, 4.178 ("Lu yu shang"). For statements on animal conservation and hunting regulations, see *Guanzi jiaoshi* 40 ("Si shi" 四時), 14.357; 13 ("Ba guan" 八觀), 5.123, 125; *Lüshi chunqiu jiaoshi*, 14.780 ("Yi shang" 義賞), 26.1711 ("Shang nong" 上農); *Huainanzi*, 9.308–309 ("Zhu shu"); *Yi Zhoushu*, 4.9a ("Da ju" 大聚); *Zhouli zhushu*, 16.14a–b; *Liji zhushu*, 4.15a ("Qu li xia"); *Wenzi*, 2.24b ("Shang ren"; dogs and pigs under the age of one should not be eaten); *Yantie lun jiaozhu*, 6.202 ("San bu zu"; criticizing that hunting prescriptions are not upheld).

96. *Shuihudi Qin mu zhujian*, 20; tr. Hulsewé (1985), A2 (p. 22). See also Yang Kuan (1998), 84–86. The Shuihudi laws on hunting have been hailed recently as the earliest examples of environmental law in China. See Luo Guihuan (1995), 50–52. Laws on animals recur in legal codes throughout later Chinese history. See Ikeda On (1984).

97. *Liji zhushu*, 48.6a ("Ji yi"); *Da Dai Liji*, 4.11b ("Zengzi da xiao" 曾子大孝).

98. *Da Dai Liji*, 5.2a ("Zengzi zhi yan" 曾子制言).

99. *Liji zhushu*, 48.1b ("Ji yi").

100. *Lüshi chunqiu jiaoshi*, 4.221 ("Wu tu" 誣徒).

101. *Lunyu zhushu*, 7.8b ("Shu er" 述而).

102. *Han Feizi jishi*, 12.692 ("Wai chu shuo zuo xia"). For a survey of the technical aspects of the hunt and hunting terminology, see Böttger (1960). On the origins of stringed-arrow hunting, see Song Zhaolin (1981).

103. *Hanshu*, 6.211.

104. *Hanshu*, 8.258.

105. *Zuozhuan zhu*, pp. 41–44 (Duke Yin, year 5). See also *Shiji*, 33.1529.

106. *Yanzi chunqiu jishi*, 5.312–13; *Shuoyuan jiaozheng*, 5.101 ("Gui de" 貴德).

107. *Han Feizi jishi*, 7.436 ("Shuo lin shang"); *Huainanzi*, 18.594 ("Ren jian").

108. *Huainanzi*, 18.622 ("Ren jian"); *Han shi waizhuan jishi*, 8.303. See also *Fuzi*, 1.7a ("Ren lun"仁論).

109. *Liji zhushu*, 12.5b, 14.14a, 16.13a, 17.1b; *Lüshi chunqiu jiaoshi*, 1.1 ("Meng chun ji"), 9.467 ("Ji qiu ji"); *Yi Zhoushu*, 6.2a, 6.3a–b ("Shi xun jie"); *Huainanzi*, 5.160, 5.173, 5.177 ("Shi ze"); *Da Dai Liji*, 2.4b, 2.8a, 2.9b ("Xia xiao zheng"). See also *Shuoyuan jiaozheng*, 19.490 ("Xiu wen"); *Wenzi*, 2.24a–b ("Shang ren"); *Xinshu*, 6.3a ("Li"). The opening lines of both the *Hanshu* and *Hou Hanshu* treatises on sacrifice evoke the innate sense of sacrifice in these animals. See *Hanshu*, 25A.1189; *Hou Hanshu*, "zhi," 7.3157. For the sacrificial behavior of the *zhai* 豺 (*canis hodophilax*) and the otter, see also *Mao shi ming wu jie*, 10.2a–3a. Schafer (1991) identifies the *zhai* with the dhole, a small Asian wild dog.

110. *Kongzi jiayu*, 2.8a ("Hao sheng" 好生). Wang Su's 王肅 (195–256 C.E.) commentary suggests that *yi lei* refers to the "barbaric tribes of the four directions." For a similar passage on Shang kings Tang and Wu, see *Da Dai Liji*, 2.3a ("Li cha" 禮察).

111. *Huainanzi*, 9.276 ("Zhu shu").

112. See "Mu He" 穆和 in *Boshu Zhouyi jiaoshi*, 524; tr. Shaughnessy (1996), 267.

113. On a stele carved in 219 B.C.E. during a tour of the empire and in an inscription on Mount Jieshi 碣石 in 215 B.C.E. See *Shiji*, 6.245, 6.252. For other statements on a ruler's virtue reaching birds and beasts, see *Lüshi chunqiu jiaoshi*, 10.560 ("Yi yong" 異用; king Tang), 8.441 ("Jian xuan" 簡選); *Shiji*, 3.95 (king Tang); *Xinxu xiang zhu*, 5.146 ("Za shi," king Tang); *Xinshu*, 7.5a ("Yu cheng," king Tang); *Hanshu*, 6.160 (Zhou kings Cheng 成 and Kang 康), 48.2253, 49.2293, 64A.2780, 94A.3763; *Hou Hanshu*, 25.874, 25.888; *Qianfu lun*, 8.439 ("De hua" 德化); *Kongzi jiayu*, 5.12a ("Wu Di de"); *Xinyu*, 11.155 ("Ming jie" 明誡); *Bohutong shu zheng*, 6.284 ("Feng shan" 封禪); *Shizi*, 1.12b; *Huang shi gong san lüe jinzhu jinyi*, 3.106 ("When the ruler's munificence reaches the insects then the sages will give their allegiance to him"); *Chunqiu gan jing fu* 春秋感精符 in *Weishu jicheng*, 741; *Xiaojing yuan shen qie* in *Weishu jicheng*, 978. The image of Tang and Wu's kindness reaching the animals is also attested in a story stating that after their victory over the tyrants Jie and Zhou they set free horses and oxen allowing them to grow old without being reassembled for war. See *Shang jun shu jiaoshi*, 17.106 ("Shang xing" 賞刑).

114. *Chunqiu fanlu*, 13.347, 13.348, 13.350, 13.351, 13.352 ("Wu xing ni shun" 五行逆順).

115. *Xijing zaji*, 4.4a ("He fu" 鶴賦); *Quan Han fu*, 41. For the crane as a symbol of escapism, see also *Yilin*, 2.16b. Cranes were said to live long because their bodies do not harbor lethal *qi* and because they eat ice (concentrated vital essence). See *Chunqiu fanlu*, 16.416 ("Xun tian zhi dao").

116. *Mengzi zhushu*, 14A.11b ("Jin xin xia"). For fighting animals with one's bare hands as a sign of raw power and moral shortcoming, see *Shiji*, 3.105; *Huainanzi*, 10.322 ("Miu cheng").

117. *Huainanzi*, 6.194 ("Lan ming"). Bo Juzi was a renowned archer from Chu. Zhan He was a famous angler from Chu said to be so skillful that he managed to catch thousand-year-old carp. See *Huainanzi*, 16.521 ("Shuo shan"); *Liezi*, 5.13a–b ("Tang wen"). For other famous archers, see *Liezi*, 5. 17b–18a ("Tang wen").

118. *Zhanguo ce*, 4.571.

119. *Lüshi chunqiu jiaoshi*, 24.1619 ("Bo zhi"). See also *Huainanzi*, 16.540 ("Shuo shan"). The story appears as a pictorial motif on an Eastern Han stone pillar in Sichuan. See Wu Hung (1987), 102–107.

120. *Zhuangzi jishi*, 3.117–19 ("Yang sheng" 養生); *Lüshi chunqiu jiaoshi*, 9.507 ("Jing tong" 精通).

121. *Liezi*, 2.10a–b ("Huang di"). The *Lüshi chunqiu* records a similar story. It tells of a man at the seaside who was fond of dragonflies. The dragonflies spontaneously flocked around him so that he could play with them all day. However when he was asked to catch some for the entertainment of his father, the dragonflies stayed away. See *Lüshi chunqiu jiaoshi*, 18.1167 ("Jing yu" 精諭). For a variant of this story featuring seagulls, see *Liezi*, 2.13a ("Huangdi").

122. *Zhuangzi jishi*, 4.167 ("Ren jian shi" 人間世).

123. *Huainanzi*, 19.638 ("Xiu wu").

124. *Wuzi*, 1.11b ("Zhi bing" 治兵); tr. Sawyer (1993), 216.

125. *Huainanzi*, 9.298 ("Zhu shu").

126. *Han shi waizhuan jishi*, 2.43. Similar ideas are reflected in narratives on charioteering and the legendary Zaofu, charioteer of King Mu of Zhou. See *Xunzi jijie*, 8.137 ("Ru xiao"); *Lunheng jiaoshi*, 8.71 ("Shuai xing").

127. *Lunyu zhushu*, 14.13b ("Xian wen" 憲問). According to Zheng Xuan, "virtue" here stands for "harmony and excellence." The *Lüshi chunqiu* states that the energy of a speedy horse and the determination of the wild goose and the crane ought to be attributed to their sincerity (*cheng* 誠). See *Lüshi chunqiu jiaoshi*, 26.1690 ("Shi rong" 士容).

128. *Lunyu zhushu*, 10.10a ("Xiang dang"). See also *Yantie lun jiaozhu*, 10.344 ("Xing de" 刑德), where the incident is quoted to show that Confucius held human beings in esteem and looked down on animals.

129. *Lunyu zhushu*, 3.10a ("Ba qiao" 八佾). See also *Lunheng jiaoshi*, 29.433 ("Fei Han" 非韓); *Hanshu*, 81.3350; *Hou Hanshu*, "zhi," 7.3166. Gopal Sukhu comments: "What concerns Confucius is not the sheep as 'fellow' creature or item of exchange, but its transformation in the ritual context into food for spirits." See Sukhu (1999), 155.

130. *Lunyu zhushu*, 10.11a ("Xiang dang").

131. *Liji zhushu*, 10.16b–17a ("Tan gong xia"). See also *Lunheng jiaoshi*, 48.708–709 ("Zao hu"); and *Xinxu xiang zhu*, 5.160 ("Za shi").

132. For examples, see *Guanzi jiaoshi* 64 ("Xing shi" 形勢), 20.493–94; *Shizi*, 2.13a; and *Wenzi*, 2.28b ("Shang yi" 上義).

133. *Huainanzi*, 7.241 ("Jing shen").

134. *Shizi*, 2.10b. For the image of the ruler-sage as the shepherd of the world, see *Guoyu*, 4.182 ("Lu yu shang"); *Guanzi jiaoshi* 30 ("Jun chen shang" 君臣上), 10.253, 257; *Hanshu*, 8.239. The sage as shepherd also appears in the Mawangdui version of *Daodejing* 22. See *Boshu Laozi jiaozhu*, p. 340.

135. *Mengzi zhushu*, 7B.1a ("Li Lou shang").

136. *Shiji*, 30.1431–32. See also *Hanshu*, 24B.1173–75, 58.2624–28.

137. *Lunheng jiaoshi*, 9.85 ("Ji yan"), 47.698 ("Luan long").

138. *Mao shi zhengyi*, 17A.10a ("Sheng min" 生民, Mao 245). See also *Chuci*, 3.21b–22a ("Tian wen"); *Shiji*, 4.111; *Lunheng jiaoshi*, 9.86–87 ("Ji yan"); *Lienü zhuan*, 1.2a–b ("Mu yi" 母儀); *Wu Yue chunqiu*, 1.13.

139. *Hanshu*, 61.2692; *Shiji*, 123.3168; *Lunheng jiaoshi*, 9.87–88 ("Ji yan").

140. The original account is in *Zuozhuan zhu*, p. 683 (Lord Xuan, year 4). See also *Hanshu*, 100A.4197.

141. *Hou Hanshu*, 85.2810–11; *Lunheng jiaoshi*, 9.88–89 ("Ji yan").

142. *Hanshu*, 53.2412; *Shiji*, 59.2094.

143. *Hanshu*, 97B.4004. According to Zhang Hua, on the death of the phoenix and the simurgh, wild birds pick up earth to bury them. See *Shi Kuang Qinjing*, 2a.

144. *Hou Hanshu*, 54.1759–60, 54.1767–68; *Xu Hanshu* 續漢書 as quoted in *Hou Hanshu*, 54.1768 note 2; *Yiwen leiju*, 90.1556. For the stele, see *Li shi*, 12.2a. On the Yang clan's association with birds, see also Kakehata Minoru (1991).

145. *Wu Yue chunqiu*, 6.108; *Yue jue shu*, 8.1a; *Lunheng jiaoshi*, 10.103–104 ("Ou hui"). Elsewhere Wang Chong dismisses that such animal behavior could be the result of "sage virtue" on the grounds that animals did not maintain the burial plot of Yao who surpassed both Shun and Yu in virtue. See *Lunheng jiaoshi*, 16.177–79 ("Shu xu" 書虛). See also Eberhard (1968), 265–66; Zeng Xiongsheng (1990); and Liu Zhi (1991).

146. For Pengzu and Zhuji Weng, see Kaltenmark (1953), 82–83, 127–28. For the crane as symbol of longevity, see *Huainanzi*, 17.579 ("Shuo lin"). The crane as an acolyte of immortals is discussed in Izushi Yoshihiko (1943), 707–22.

147. *Hanshu*, 25A.1204; *Shiji*, 28.1370. See also *Liezi*, 5.4b ("Tang wen").

148. The story is transmitted in a critique by Wang Chong. Wang dismisses it by stating that the dogs and chickens followed their master to Heaven because they had eaten some left-over immortality drugs. See *Lunheng jiaoshi*, 24.317–18, 24.325 ("Dao xu").

149. See Hong Gua, *Li shi*, 3.9b–10b. For discussions of Tang Gongfang's stele, see Campany (1996), 187–92; and Chen Xianyuan (1996). For the development of the cult, see Schipper (1995). The fate of animals after death became a prominent subject after the introduction of Buddhism, which advocated the belief in a reincarnation into animal form. See Eliasberg (1992), 125 ff.; and Gjertson (1980).

150. *Liji zhushu*, 22.11a–14b ("Li yun"). An almost identical passage occurs in *Kongzi jiayu*, 7.8b ("Li yun"). The alignment of the tortoise with humans here seems to be based on the idea that the tortoise understands human feelings, as is evinced in divination. Han sources usually include the white tiger (instead of the *qilin*) among the *si ling*.

151. See for example *Mengzi zhushu*, 3A.12a ("Gongsun Chou shang" 公孫丑上). This passage notes that only Confucius was able to stand out above all. See also *Kong Congzi*, 2.4a ("Ji wen" 記問); *Yangzi fayan*, 6.1b–2a.

152. *Kongzi jiayu*, 5.9b ("Kun shi" 困誓). For similar statements, see *Huainanzi*, 8.245–46 ("Ben jing"); *Lüshi chunqiu jiaoshi*, 13.678 ("Ying tong" 應同); *Da Dai Liji*, 13.9a ("Yi ben ming"); *Shizi*, 1.5b; *Wenzi*, 2.38b ("Shang de"); *Shuoyuan jiaozheng*, 5.104 ("Gui de"), 13.313 ("Quan mou"); *Hanshu*, 51.2371; *Xinshu*, 6.3a ("Li"); *Lunheng jiaoshi*, 51.746 ("Zhi rui"); *Shiji*, 47.1926; *Hou Hanshu*, 61.2038; *Songshu*, 28.791, 792.

153. *Shiji*, 128.3225–28.

154. For the *si ling* as acolytes of the sages, see *Da Dai Liji*, 5.9a ("Zengzi tian yuan").

155. *Shuoyuan jiaozheng*, 18.457 ("Bian wu").

156. The observations made by Hall and Ames concerning the organization of *leishu* 類書 in the Chinese tradition confirm similar structural relations in the organization of knowledge on a wider scale: "The *leishu* illustrates what we should call an 'ethical' or 'aesthetic,' rather than a 'logical,' principle of organization. Individual entries begin with the most 'noble' and conclude with the most 'base': animals begin with 'lion' and 'elephant' and finish with 'rat' and 'fox.'" See Hall and Ames (1995), 254–56.

157. *Shuowen jiezi zhu*, 4A.40a. For physical descriptions of these phoenix acolytes, see *Yue xie tu zheng* in *Weishu jicheng*, 560–61.

158. *Lunheng jiaoshi*, 50.738 ("Jiang rui"). This work is possibly a lost apocryphal text. It is also plausible that Wang (d. ca. 100 C.E.) refers to Xu Shen's (d. ca. 120 C.E.) record.

159. *Zhouli zhushu*, 24.19a. For a discussion of the tortoise species in the *Zhouli* and *Erya*, see Zhang Mengwen (1982), 536–45.

160. *Qimin yaoshu*, 61.1.3. The idea of dragons luring fish to leave the pond can be traced back to the first cent. C.E. at least. Xu Shen notes that putting fish traps into the water keeps the *jiao* dragons out. See *Shuowen jiezi zhu*, 13A.54a.

161. See for instance *Bencao gangmu*, 45.11; *Si shi zuan yao*, p. 115 no. 38; *Ge wu cu tan*, 1.14; and Huang Xingzeng's 黃省曾 (Ming) *Yang yu jing* 養魚經 ("Classic on Fish Farming"), 3b–4a (pp. 3650–51).

162. *Han shi waizhuan jishi*, 5.192–93; tr. Hightower (1952), 183 [modified]. See also *Shuoyuan jiaozheng*, 6.116–17 ("Fu en" 復恩). The *Erya* further mentions "paired-shoulder people" or *bi jian min* 比肩民. They share one eye, one nose, etc. See *Erya zhushu*, 7.6a. The *die* fish is also known as the "paired-eye fish" or *bi mu yu* 比目魚 [*paralichthys olivaceus*; Read (1939), no. 177]. See *Lüshi chunqiu jiaoshi*, 14.815 ("Yu he" 遇合); *Erya zhushu*, 7.5b. See also *Hanshu*, 25A.1197, and *Shiji*, 28.1361, where Guan Zhong 管仲 (fl. ca. 730–645 B.C.E.) includes the spontaneous arrival of these hybrids among the necessary presages for the justification of the *feng* and *shan* sacrifices. For the *bi mu yu* as a symbol of unity and cooperation, see also *Zhanguo ce*, 30.1110. For later references, see *Hou Hanshu*, 40A.1348; *Shangshu zhong hou* in *Weishu jicheng*, 419; *Yi yu tu zan*, 2.7; *Ran xi zhi*, 1.5. The *jian* bird is also known as the "paired-wings bird," or *bi yi niao* 比翼鳥. See *Lüshi chunqiu jiaoshi*, 14.815 ("Yu he"); *Shanhaijing jiaozhu*, 6.186, 16.406; *Erya zhushu*, 7.5b; *Yilin*, 2.4b. The *Shanhaijing* documents another bird named *manman* 蠻蠻 with one eye and one wing. It has to pair itself with another bird to fly. See *Shanhaijing jiaozhu*, 2.39. The *Lüshi chunqiu* and *Huainanzi* connect the *jue* beast with the north. See *Lüshi chunqiu jiaoshi*, 15.917 ("Bu guang" 不廣); *Huainanzi*, 12.387 ("Dao ying" 道應). The *Erya* refers to this animal as the "paired-shoulder beast" or *bi jian shou* 比肩獸. See *Erya zhushu*, 7.5b. A related animal, the *qiongqiong* 蛩蛩, white and in the shape of a horse, appears in *Shanhaijing jiaozhu*, 3.247, and *Hanshu*, 57A.2539. See also *Mu Tianzi zhuan*, 1.3b; *Yi Zhoushu*, 7.10b ("Wang hui"); *Qianfu lun*, 5.340 ("Shi bian" 實邊); *Shuowen jiezi zhu*, 13A.60b–61a; *Ji jiu pian*, 4.260; and the discussion in Namio Egami (1951), 111–23. Depictions of some of these hybrids are found on the murals of the Wu Liang Shrine (ca. 151 C.E.). See Wu Hung (1989), 241, fig.100, 242, fig.101, 243, fig.103; and Powers (1991), 248–49.

163. *Erya zhushu*, 7.6a.

164. Vera Dorofeeva-Lichtmann (1995) has suggested that the *Shanhaijing* not only provides an imaginary or idealized perception of geographical space as a magical landscape, but also, in its textual structure itself, reproduces the cosmographic route it depicts thereby creating a "textual space." The text would thus present a "process-oriented scheme" for moving through the world step by step.

165. *Chu xue ji*, 29.703. See also *Taiping yulan*, 896.5b. Robert E. Harrist Jr. (1997) has noted that horse painters of later times were well aware of the discourse on physiognomy.

166. For an example dealing with the interpretation of *wen* (written graphs) on a horse's nose as an indication of the animal's age, see *Qimin yaoshu*, 56.28.2.

167. *Shuoyuan jiaozheng*, 18.455 ("Bian wu"). See also *Han shi waizhuan jishi*, 8.277.

168. *Shanhaijing jiaozhu*, 1.16.

169. See *Yue xie tu zheng* in *Gu weishu*, 20.393–94; *Weishu jicheng*, 560.

170. *Xinxu xiang zhu*, 5.171–72 ("Za shi"); *Han shi waizhuan jishi*, 2.60–61.

171. *Lunheng jiaoshi*, 82.1149–50 ("Shu jie" 書解).

172. *Zuozhuan zhu*, p. 1038 (Lord Xiang, year 18), p. 242 (Lord Zhuang, year 28). See also *Shuijing zhu jiao*, 8.274.

173. See *Sunzi bingfa jiaoshi*, 9.120 (birds rising in flight as a sign of an ambush). See also *Tai Gong liu tao jinzhu jinyi*, 42.170 ("Lei xu" 壘虛).

174. *Yiwen leiju*, 90.1556, referring to a (lost?) *Shiji* passage. For Qin Zhong, see *Shiji*, 5.178.

175. *Han Feizi jishi*, 6.338 ("Jie Lao"); *Lunheng jiaoshi*, 78.1078 ("Shi zhi" 實知).

176. For Yang Wengzhong, see *Lunheng jiaoshi*, 78.1078–79 ("Shi zhi"); cf. *Yiwen leiju*, 93.1617–18. For Bo Yi, see *Guoyu*, 16.512 ("Zheng yu"); *Shiji*, 5.173, 5.177; *Hanshu*, 28B.1641; *Hou Hanshu*, 60B.1987; Cai Yong, "Shi hui" 釋誨 in *Quan Han fu*, p. 602. Bo Yi is often interchanged with Yi 羿 the Archer. See Henricks (1996), 276–77; and Birrell (1993), 58–59.

177. A work named *Shi Kuang* 師曠 in six scrolls and in eight scrolls is included in the *Hanshu* bibliography. See *Hanshu*, 30.1744, 30.1760. Shi Kuang is also known as the eponymous author of a "Classic of Birds" (*Qinjing* 禽經). See chapter 6, p. 175. The *Suishu* bibliography includes books on the divination of "bird behavior" (*niaoqing zhan* 鳥情占) and the cries of animals, such as a work entitled "Miscellaneous Divination of Bird Behavior and the Language of Birds and Beasts" (*Niaoqing za zhan qinshou yu* 鳥情雜占禽獸語, 1 scroll) and others. See *Suishu*, 34.1030. See also *Jiu Tangshu*, 47.2042; and *Xin Tangshu*, 59.1554. A manuscript recovered at Dunhuang (P. 3106) provides rare evidence for the divination of dog howling. See Morgan (1983). The auspicy of bird calls and movements is also noted by Li Shizhen who states that in antiquity a "Classic of Ravens" (*Yajing* 鴉經) circulated for the purpose of divining luck and misfortune. Still, according to Li, northerners were fond of ravens and disliked magpies while southerners liked magpies but disliked ravens. See *Bencao gangmu*, 49.9. Several works on "crow caw" divination emerged after the Han, some attributed apocryphally to Dongfang Shuo 東方朔 (fl. 130 B.C.E.). See Ogawa Yōichi (1987), 497–502. Crow caw divination is also attested in

Tibetan manuscripts and two tenth(?)-century Chinese manuscripts (P. 3988, P. 3479) found at Dunhuang. See Morgan (1987) and Laufer (1914). Judging from Warring States and Han textual evidence, divinatory practices based on the mantic powers of animals or the examination of animal entrails and organs (extispicium, haruspices) were not as widespread as in the Greek and Roman world.

178. *Sanguo zhi*, 29.815, 816, 822; *Bowuzhi*, 9.3b; and DeWoskin (1983), 91–134.

179. For physical and psychological identifications of barbarians as animals, see *Zuozhuan zhu*, p. 256 (Lord Min, year 1), p. 679 (Lord Xuan, year 4), p. 936 (Lord Xiang, year 4); *Guoyu*, 2.62, 2.50–51 ("Zhou yu"), 13.441 ("Jin yu," Rong, Di); *Lüshi chunqiu jiaoshi*, 20.1322 ("Shi jun" 恃君); *Liji zhushu*, 12.26b–27a ("Wang zhi"); *Huainanzi*, 4.146 ("Di xing," northern tribes), 18.617 ("Ren jian," Yue tribe); *Shiji*, 6.230 (King of Qin), 108.2861, 112.2955 (Xiongnu); *Hanshu*, 28A.1524 (the Bird Yi), 49.2285 (Hu), 52.2398, 52.2401, 94A.3743, 78.3282, 64A.2801 (Xiongnu), 64B.2814–15 (Southern Yue, Northern Hu), 94B.3834 (Man, Yi); *Hou Hanshu*, 38.1286, 47.1586 (Man, Yi), 47.1588 (Xiongnu), 86.2833, 86.2836, 86.2860, 87.2869 (Western Qiang).

180. The canine origin of the Dog Rong (*Quan Rong* 犬戎) is attested in the *Shanhaijing*. See *Shanhaijing jiaozhu*, 17.434. The Man 蠻 allegedly descended from the union between the dog Panhu 槃瓠 and a Chinese princess. See *Hou Hanshu*, 86.2829; *Fengsu tongyi jiaoshi*, 438–39 ("yi wen"). These cases have been studied at length by scholars of mythology, anthropology, and ethnology. See De Groot (1892–1910; rpt. 1964), vol. 4, 263–71; Chungshee L. H. (1940–41), 94–100; Eberhard (1968), 43–50; David G. White (1991), chapter 7; and Lemoine (1987), 73–87.

181. *Hou Hanshu*, 48.1598; *Yangzi fayan*, 13.5b. Similar language is used in *Lunheng jiaoshi*, 57.823 ("Xuan Han" 宣漢).

182. *Hou Hanshu*, 25.876.

183. See for example *Hou Hanshu*, 38.1286, 86.2860.

184. *Zhouli zhushu*, 36.16b.

185. *Zuozhuan zhu*, p. 477 (Lord Xi, year 29); *Lunheng jiaoshi*, 78.1078–79 ("Shi zhi"); *Hou Hanshu*, 60B.1987; *Liezi*, 2.22b ("Huang di"). See also *Taiping yulan*, 889.2a–b.

186. *Hou Hanshu*, 86.2842–43; *Huayang guo zhi*, 1.34–35. See also Kleeman (1998), 39–42, 49, 75.

187. Chen Gui 陳龜 (ca. 140 C.E.) in *Hou Hanshu*, 51.1692.

188. *Han Feizi jishi*, 12.695 ("Wai chu shuo zuo xia"); *Lunheng jiaoshi*, 62.873 ("Lun si"); *Hanshu*, 92.3697, 100B.4246; *Shiji*, 75.2355, 99.2720. For robbers and thieves identified with wild animals, see also *Bohutong shu zheng*, 4.132 ("Feng gong hou").

189. See *Shuihudi Qin mu zhujian*, 219–20; Liu Lexian (1994), 269–78. See also Strätz (1996), 235–39. The hybrid names are unattested in contemporary texts. The 亥 graph appears as a pictogram for a pig on oracle bones and Zhou bronzes. See Erkes (1942b), 71.

190. *Taixuan jing*, 2.3a. The "ape" in this passage is the *xing* 猩 or *xingxing* 猩猩 (狌狌) known as the animal nearest in kind to man. It is the first animal mentioned in the *Shanhaijing*, where it is identified as a human-faced beast that knows the names of humans. See *Shanhaijing jiaozhu*, 10.275, 10.278, 18.452. For a statement that the parrot and

ape's ability to speak does not make them equal to human beings, see *Liji zhushu*, 1.11a ("Qu li shang"). For the parrot's limitation to imitated speech, see *Huainanzi*, 16.524 ("Shuo shan"). Another speaking bird was known as the "hundred tongue" (*baishe* 百 舌, *horornis cantans*). It could alter its tongue and imitate the cries of all birds. See *Huainanzi*, 16.531 ("Shuo shan"). Speech-imitating birds were also known as *fan she niao* 反 舌鳥 "turn-tongue birds," or *neng yan niao* 能言鳥. See *Yi wei tong gua yan* in *Weishu jicheng*, 250; *Hanshu*, 6.176.

191. *Mengzi zhushu*, 1B.2b–3b ("Liang Hui Wang shang"). See also *Lunheng jiaoshi*, 58.828 ("Hui guo" 恢國). While there is no evidence for ideologies advocating animal saving or organised animal compassion in pre-Buddhist China, in later times edifying stories such as that of King Xuan as well as depictions of Confucius as a moral hunter supplied canonical precedents for some who wished to prove the native origins of animal compassion against the imported Buddhist practice of releasing animals (*fang sheng* 放生). See Handlin Smith (1999), 60–61, 63.

192. *Da Dai Liji*, 3.4a ("Bao fu"); *Liji zhushu*, 29.8b ("Yu zao"), 47.11a ("Ji yi"); *Xinshu*, 5.4b ("Bao fu" 保傅), 6.3a ("Li"); *Hanshu*, 48.2249; *Yili zhushu*, 42.16a ("Shi yu li," stating that the Master of Ceremony does not witness the dismembering of the sacrificial pig); *Mozi jiaozhu*, 47.686 ("Gui yi" 貴義, "If one were to order a gentleman of the world to become the butcher of one dog or one pig, he would not be able to do it and refuse").

193. This theory is illustrated at length in a memorial submitted to Han Wudi on the occasion of the capture of a white unicorn. This memorial will be discussed in chapter 7.

Chapter Six. Changing Animals

1. Ohnuki-Tierny (1987), 21.

2. Thomas (1983), 38.

3. Allan (1991), 19–20.

4. De Groot (1892–1910; rpt. 1964), vol. 4, 157. David Gordon White writes: "There doesn't seem to have been a Chinese term that directly translates as monster, perhaps because constant metamorphosis, rather than stasis, was the order of things. No creature was a monster in itself, since it existed somewhere along an ever-changing continuum between one sort of animal and another, or between humanity and animality." See White (1991), 20.

5. *Da Dai Liji*, 13.6b–7a ("Yi ben ming"); cf. *Kongzi jiayu*, 6.4a ("Zhi pei"); tr. Needham, SCC, vol. 2, 271 [modified].

6. *Zhuangzi jishi*, 18.624–25 ("Zhi le"). A similar passage occurs in *Liezi*, 1.6a–8a ("Tian rui" 天瑞). The plants and animals in this passage are glossed in Fukatsu Tane-fusa (1982), 85–97.

7. Needham, SCC, vol. 2, 78; Schwartz (1985), 220. For a discussion of similar species transformations in later sources, see Liu Juncan (1996).

8. *Zhuangzi jishi*, 1.2–4 ("Xiao yao you" 逍遙遊); tr. Graham (1981), 43. See also *Liezi*, 5.6a ("Tang wen").

9. Wu Guangming (1990), 70–72. Birds and fish are often classified together in *yinyang* classifications.

10. For *kun* as "fish roe," see *Erya zhushu*, 9.18a; *Yi yu tu zan*, chapter 1, p. 1. The Ming scholar Xie Zhaozhe 謝肇淛 (1567–1624) notes that this metamorphosis is "nothing but a Zhuangzi metaphor." See *Wu zazu*, 9.257 ("Wu bu" 物部). Robert E. Allinson interprets the image as a transformation from ignorance (fish, darkness) to knowledge (freedom, transcendence). See Allinson (1989), 41–42. On the diffusion of the Great Bird legend in China and other areas, see Yamashita Toraji (1931).

11. *Liezi*, 1.7a–b ("Tian rui"); tr. Graham (1991), 21.

12. Graham (1991), 22.

13. *Zhuangzi jishi*, 6.260–61 ("Da zong shi" 大宗師).

14. For the hermaphrodite *lei*, see also *Shanhaijing jiaozhu*, 1.5; and *Liezi*, 1.7a–b ("Tian rui").

15. *Zhuangzi jishi*, 14.532–34 ("Tian yun").

16. *Zhuangzi jishi*, 23.779 ("Gengsang Chu" 庚桑楚).

17. *Zuozhuan zhu*, p. 289 (Lord Xi, year 4). The idea of wind as a promoter of fertility was also noted in the Roman world, notably by Aelian (170– ca. 230 C.E.): "Moreover sheep know this too, viz. that the north wind and the south wind, no less than the rams which mount them, are their allies in promoting fertility. And this also they know, that whereas the north wind tends to produce males, the south wind produces females. . . . At any rate, when the south wind blows (the shepherds) put the rams to the sheep, in order that their offspring may preferably be female." See *De Nature Animalium*, VII.27.

18. For wind as "germination," see *Bohutong shu zheng*, 7.341 ("Ba feng" 八風); *Li wei* 禮緯 in *Weishu jicheng*, 531; *Chunqiu kao yi you* in *Gu weishu* 10.199; *Weishu jicheng*, 793. For insects as the essence of wind, see *Chunqiu kao yi you* in *Weishu jicheng*, 785.

19. *Shuowen jiezi zhu*, 13B.7a; *Lunheng jiaoshi*, 49.715 ("Shang chong").

20. *Huainanzi*, 20.668 ("Tai zu"). A later source states that the male white heron sings an "upper air" upon which the female is impregnated. See *Bowuzhi*, 2.2a.

21. See for instance *Fangyan jianshu*, 8.278 (under the dialectal gloss for *ji* 雞); and *Huainanzi*, 20.671 ("Tai zu").

22. Some Ming and Qing encyclopaedists took the property of change as a criterion in their classifications of animals. Li Shizhen, for instance, divides insects into three subgroups: oviparous insects, water-born insects, and insects produced by metamorphosis (*huasheng lei* 化生類). Li Yuan's *Ru fan* contains a chapter entitled "wu hua" 物化 which lists animals and plants whose mutual relationship is described according to the formula "X changes into/out from Y." See *Bencao gangmu*, 39.56, 41.1, 42.27; *Ru fan*, 2.27–33. The *Wu zazu* states that a transformation from bird into reptile is a change from "sentient" (*you qing* 有情) to "nonsentient" (*wu qing* 無情); a metamorphosis from plant to insect is said to be a change from nonsentient to sentient. It further distinguishes between animals that change (=reproduce) through form (*xinghua* 形化) and those that change through *qi* (*qihua* 氣化). The latter happens when no semen (*zhong* 種) is involved. See *Wu zazu*, 9.269–270.

23. *Zuozhuan zhu*, pp. 1289–90 (Lord Zhao, year 7). There are several versions of and allusions to Gun's metamorphosis. For Gun's failure to dike the floods, see *Shangshu zhengyi*, 2.19b–20a ("Yao dian"). See further *Shanhaijing jiaozhu*, 18.472; *Qu Yuan ji jiaozhu*, p. 307 ("Tian wen"); *Lüshi chunqiu jiaoshi*, 20.1389 ("Xing lun" 行論); *Guoyu*, 14.478 ("Jin yu"); *Wu Yue chunqiu*, 6.102; *Lunheng jiaoshi*, 7.61 ("Wu xing"). Gun was the untalented son of Zhuan Xu and was part of a quartet of evil monsters banned to the distant regions to be devoured by demons. See *Zuozhuan zhu*, pp. 639–40 (Lord Wen, year 18); *Shiji*, 1.36–37. The reference to a yellow *xiong* 熊 need not necessarily be a bear. According to *Shuowen jiezi zhu*, 10A.39b, a *xiong* is a beast that resembles a pig, lives in mountains and hibernates. Some commentators suggest a metamorphosis into a turtle, reptile, or black fish following an old form of the 鯀 graph. See *Shuowen jiezi zhu*, 11B.18b; Karlgren (1957), no. 419.

24. For the former view, see R. Dragan (1993), 173–77; for the latter, see Sun Zhong-en (1989). For a totemic analysis, see Tu Yuanji (1982). See further Granet (1926), vol. 1, 243–47; Ichikawa Isamu (1944), 27; Allan (1991), 70; Mathieu (1992), 173, note 44.

25. Peng Sheng was killed in 694 B.C.E. and reappeared as a pig in 686 B.C.E. See *Zuozhuan zhu*, p. 152 (Lord Huan, year 18), pp. 175–76 (Lord Zhuang, year 8). See also *Guanzi jiaoshi* 18 ("Da kuang" 大匡), 7.162–63; *Shiji*, 32.1483–84; and *Hanshu*, 27.1436. The *Shiji* version of the story is discussed in Cohen (1979), 103–104. Erkes has suggested that the pig may have been a totem of the Peng clan. See Erkes (1942b); and Erkes (1948), 286–87. This clan possibly ruled over a mini-state called Pig Wei (*Shi Wei* 豕韋). See *Guoyu*, 16.511 ("Zheng yu"). See also *Zuozhuan zhu*, p. 1501 (Lord Zhao, year 29); *Qianfu lun*, 9.498 ("Zhi shi xing"); *Shiji*, 2.86; and *Bohutong shu zheng*, 2.60–61 ("Hao").

26. *Shanhaijing jiaozhu*, 2.42–43. For Qin Pi, see also *Zhuangzi jishi*, 6.247 ("Da zong shi").

27. *Shanhaijing jiaozhu*, 3.92. For later allusions to the *jingwei* story, see *Bowuzhi*, 6.1b; *Bao Puzi nei pian jiaoshi*, 8.155 ("Shi zhi" 釋滯); *Shuyiji*, 1.3b; *Yiwen leiju*, 92.1608. See also Tochio Takeshi (1970). For a mythological identification of this bird as another representation of a solar bird, see Lai (1996), 325–26.

28. *Shanhaijing jiaozhu*, 16.389. See also *Huainanzi*, 17.561 ("Shuo lin").

29. *Shiji*, 9.395, 397, 405; *Hanshu*, 27.1397; *Lunheng jiaoshi*, 63.904–905 ("Si wei" 死偽). Wang Chong refutes the metamorphosis on the grounds that the dead have no knowledge of those who had been enemies during their lifetime. On metamorphosis as punishment in Chinese mythology, see Birrell (1993), 189–200. For animal transformation in Greek myth, see Forbes Irving (1990), chapters 2, 3, 4.

30. *Shuowen jiezi zhu*, 9A.42b. On the etymology of *gui*, see Shen Jieshi (1936–37). For a theory claiming that the top of the graph 甶 represents the spirit mask of the deceased, see Ikeda Suetoshi (1956).

31. *Huainanzi*, 2.47 ("Shu zhen" 俶眞); tr. Sivin (1991), 3 [modified]. For further reference to this story, see *Lunheng jiaoshi*, 7.61 ("Wu xing"), 15.162 ("Qi guai"), 48.709 ("Zao hu"), 62.873 ("Lun si"). Zhang Heng alludes to the incident in his *Si xuan fu* 思玄賦 ("Rhapsody on Contemplating the Mysterious"). See *Hou Hanshu*, 59.1923. See also Li Shan's 李善 (? –689 C.E.) commentary in *Wenxuan*, 15.662.

32. *Shuoyuan jiaozheng*, 9.237–38 ("Zheng jian" 正諫). Although both the *Yiwen leiju*, 96.1662–63, and *Taiping yulan*, 845.3a, quote the *Shuoyuan* as their source, the story is likely to be older. There may be a connection between the white dragon which descends to the Qingling 清泠 springs in the *Shuoyuan* story and the river god Hebo 河伯. The *Zhuangzi* records a dream divination in which a fisherman named Yu Qie 余且 (cf. 豫且 in the *Shuoyuan* tale) catches a white turtle at "the place of Hebo" (Yellow River). See *Zhuangzi jishi*, 26.933–34 ("Wai wu"). The same fisherman figures in the *Shiji*'s tale on the discovery of a spirit tortoise used for divination. See *Shiji*, 128.3229–31. The *Chuci* refers to Hebo "riding a white turtle and chasing the striped fish." See *Chuci*, 2.19a ("Dong jun" 東君). Wang Yi's 王逸 (fl. ca. 114–120 C.E.) commentary to *Chuci*, 17.10a ("Zao e" 遭厄), refers to Hebo transforming into a white dragon and being shot by the Archer Yi. The color white and a piscine shape were associated with the river god. A tall creature with a white face and fishy body was known as the genie of the river (*hejing* 河精). See *Shizi*, 2.14a; *Shangshu zhong hou kao he ming* 尚書中侯考河命 in *Weishu jicheng*, 431. See also *Han Feizi jishi*, 9.530 ("Nei chu shuo shang"), where an altar is built on the river bank prompting the movement of a big fish identified as Hebo. The *Gujin zhu*, 2.19 ("Yu chong"), mentions a Water Lord (*shuijun* 水君) with the shape of a man riding a horse, also known as *Yubo* 魚伯, purportedly seen at the end of the Han. For spirits associated with the Yellow River, see also Wang Xiaolian (1992), 237–65.

33. For a table of animal activity in the *Xia xiao zheng* calendar, see Gou Cuihua (1989), 66. The animals in the *Xia xiao zheng* are discussed in Zhuang Yazhou (1985), 79–105.

34. Some of these metamorphoses occur as early as the *Guoyu*. See *Guoyu*, 14.498 ("Jin yu"). They occur as a standard set, with slight variations, in the *ji* 紀 sections at the beginning of *juan* 1 to 12 in the *Lüshi chunqiu*, the *yue ling* chapters in the *Liji*, the "Xia xiao zheng" in the *Da Dai Liji*, *Huainanzi* 5 ("Shi ze"), and in chapters 52 ("Yue ling jie") and 53 ("Shi xun jie") 時訓解) of the *Yi Zhoushu*. The *yue ling* in its present form dates from about 240 B.C.E. See also later *yue ling* literature such as the *Cai Shi yueling zhangju*, 1.7b, 1.10a, 1.19a; the *Yueling qi-shi-er hou jijie*, pp. 2, 3, 8 et partim; and chapter 3, note 56. A received gloss for *shen* 蜃 reads "something that transforms out of fowl when entering water." See *Shuowen jiezi zhu*, 13A.55a–b. For further reference to these sea mussels, see Eberhard (1968), 292–93.

35. *Da Dai Liji*, 2.4b ("Xia xiao zheng"); Watters (1867), 235–36.

36. *Zhouli zhushu*, 30.24a. For pigeons not choking on their food, see *Hou Hanshu*, "zhi," 5.3124.

37. *Yilin*, 12.5a.

38. See Zheng Xuan's commentary in *Zhouli zhushu*, 30.24a; tr. Bodde (1975), 345 [modified]. On the distribution of the pigeon-staff to the aged during the Later Han and its possible origins, see Bodde (1959); and Bodde (1975), 344–48. Bodde discusses the presentation of doves in the light of a southern practice of releasing pigeons at the New Year recorded in the *Liezi*, 8.14b ("Shuo fu" 說符). He further links this custom to a report claiming that Han founder Gaozu was saved from capture by the Xiongnu because of the presence of doves above his hiding place. For this story, see *Fengsu tongyi jiaoshi*, 407–408

("yi wen"). Wang Chong criticises the entire custom: "If the pigeon is considered auspicious, why not give a pigeon instead of a pigeon-staff?" See *Lunheng jiaoshi*, 36.573 ("Xie duan" 謝短).

39. *Shi Kuang Qinjing*, 13a.

40. Migratory and homing behavior among birds was certainly known. See for instance Zhang Heng's description of the birds in the Shanglin park in *Wenxuan*, 2.66 ("Xi jing fu"). Chinese biologists have suggested that the hawk-to-pigeon metamorphosis may indicate the migration of hawks from the central plains toward the north and the arrival of pigeons from the south to take over the habitat of the migrated hawks. The scientific basis of such hypotheses remains questionable. See Guo Fu et al. (1999), 353. Fukatsu Tanefusa attributes these interpretations to the ancients' confusion regarding the seasonal passage of birds. See Fukatsu Tanefusa (1982), 71–85.

41. *Da Dai Liji*, 13.7b ("Yi ben ming"). Similar passages occur in *Huainanzi*, 4.144 ("Di xing"); and *Kongzi jiayu*, 6.4a ("Zhi pei"). See also Major (1993), 178–180, 208–12.

42. *Lunheng jiaoshi*, 66.955-56 ("Yan du" 言毒).

43. *Dong guan Han ji*, 12.5b. The incident occurred ca. 87 C.E.

44. *Guanzi jiaoshi* 39 ("Shui di"), 14.347–48. Rickett dates this chapter between the end of the third century and the third quarter of the second century B.C.E. and suggests that it was written by an author from the Chu-Song area. See Rickett (1998), vol. 2, 100. For the idea that the dragon's divine power depends on the presence of water, see *Guanzi jiaoshi* 2 ("Xing shi"), 1.9. For discussions on the origins of the dragon as a water (rain) spirit, see Izushi Yoshihiko (1928); Shiratori Kiyoshi (1934); Inoi Makoto (1977); and Luo Shirong (1988). For a survey of theories on the natural origins of the *long* and *jiao* dragon, see Dragan (1993), 33–54. For the idea that the sage transforms by means of water, see *Guanzi jiaoshi* 39 ("Shui di"), 14.353. See further Graham (1989), 356–58. Allan (1997) discusses water as a root metaphor in early Chinese thought.

45. *Guoyu*, 3.102 ("Zhou yu xia").

46. *Guodian Chu mu zhujian*, 125–26 (plates pp. 13–14).

47. *Shanhaijing jiaozhu*, 16.416–17.

48. *Huainanzi*, 4.150 ("Di xing"). John Major suggests a link between demifish, associated with immortality, and the representation of Lady Dai 軑 with a serpent's body on the Mawangdui funerary banner. See Major (1993), 204. Sun Shiwen (1987) suggests that the figure represents Nü Wa. A Qing commentary to the *Huainanzi* quotes a source claiming that the immortals Wang (Zi)Qiao 王喬 and Chisong(zi) 赤松 are of the same species as turtles and fish. See *Huainanzi*, 4.143 ("Di xing").

49. *Liji zhushu*, 2.26b ("Qu li shang").

50. *Lunheng jiaoshi*, 7.60 ("Wu xing"). For the gathering of dragons and snakes as a portent for floods, see *Yilin*, 3.17a.

51. *Mao shi zhengyi*, 12C.18b ("He ren si" 何人斯, Mao 199). A similar animal is attested in the *Chunqiu* and described in the commentaries as a "short fox" or a three-footed turtle. See *Chunqiu Zuozhuan zhu*, p. 206, p. 208 (Lord Zhuang, year 18). Xu Shen states that the "spit-sand" harms people with its *qi* (breath). See *Shuowen jiezi zhu*, 13A.58b–59a.

Zheng Xuan refers to an animal named the (water) fox-imp (*huyu* 狐蜮), exorcised by the Water Jug Sprinkler. See his commentary in *Zhouli zhushu*, 37.7a. Liu Xiang states that *yu* emerge among the Southern Yue people because males and females bathe in the same river and engage in unbridled sexual practices. See *Hanshu*, 27.1462–63. See further *Chuci*, 10.2a–b ("Da zhao" 大招); *Guliang zhuan*, 5.21b–22a; *Hanshu*, 64B.2834; *Yiwen leiju*, 35.616. For possible identifications of the *yu*, see also Schafer (1967; rpt. 1985), 111; Eberhard (1968), 193–95; Bodde (1975), 109–11; and Schmidt (1997). For a survey of references to the *yu* up to the Tang, see Chen Jue (1999), 170–78.

52. *Huainanzi*, 11.345–46 ("Qi su"). See also *Shuoyuan jiaozheng*, 18.442 ("Bian wu"). Metamorphosis into a quail is used in the Later Mohist Canon's definition of *hua*. See Graham (1978), 295, A45.

53. The link between reptiles, serpents, and metamorphosis is also confirmed by evidence from other ancient civilizations. See Mundkur (1983).

54. *Shanhaijing jiaozhu*, 5.122. See also Itō Seiji (1990), 24–25.

55. *Shuowen jiezi zhu*, 9B.44a; Needham, SCC, vol. 2, 221, no. 6. See also Wilhelm (1961), 14.

56. *Lüshi chunqiu jiaoshi*, 14.828 ("Bi ji"); *Huainanzi*, 2.54 ("Shu zhen"). See also *Hou Hanshu*, 28B.985.

57. *Guanzi jiaoshi* 12 ("Shu yan"), 4.114; tr. Rickett (1985), 218.

58. The image of animals tunneling into the earth and resurfacing again was associated with worms, which were said to eat the dry earth above and drink from the Yellow Springs below. See *Mengzi zhushu*, 6B.8a ("Teng Wen Gong xia"); *Xunzi jijie*, 1.8 ("Quan xue"); *Da Dai Liji*, 7.7b ("Quan xue"); *Huainanzi*, 16.522 ("Shuo shan"); *Taixuan jing*, 2.1a; *Lunheng jiaoshi*, 30.463, 30.465 ("Ci meng" 刺孟).

59. *Shuoyuan jiaozheng*, 18.455 ("Bian wu"). The *qilin* is also described as having the feet of a horse. See *Mao shi yi shu* 毛詩義疏, as quoted in *Yiwen leiju*, 98.1706. See further Izushi Yoshihiko (1931) (rpt. in Izushi Yoshihiko [1943], 163–86).

60. *Shuoyuan jiaozheng*, 18.455 ("Bian wu"). See also *Han shi waizhuan jishi*, 8.277; *He tu lu yun fa* 河圖錄運法 in *Weishu jicheng*, 1165. The natural origins of the phoenix in China have been subject to much speculation. Schafer, discussing the southern avifauna of Tang China, describes it as "a composite of many pheasants with the peacock, birds thought to be suitable models for representations of the archaic bird symbol." See Schafer (1967; rpt. 1985), 243. For other hypotheses, see Hachisuka (1924); Ding Su (1968); Paper (1986); and Diény (1989–90).

61. *Shuoyuan jiaozheng*, 18.456–57 ("Bian wu"). Descriptive summaries of the *si ling* and other numinous animals can also be found in the "Treatise on Omens" (*fu rui* 符瑞) in the *Songshu* (28.791–800) of the Liu-Song Dynasty (420–479 C.E.). This treatise very likely predates its incorporation into the *Songshu*. See Powers (1991), 239–42.

62. *Shiji*, 128.3231. For statements on the longevity of the tortoise, see also *Xinlun*, 8b, 24b. For a discussion of the magical and divinatory powers associated with the turtle, see Loewe (1988).

63. *Shuowen jiezi zhu*, 4A.39a–b.

64. *Shi Kuang Qinjing*, 1b.

65. Hentze (1958), 73–75. On the theme of the bird as representative of the soul, see Waterbury (1952), 57–72. Regarding the association of birds with the cycles of life and death, Rémi Mathieu has suggested that the crow or black bird in early China was thought to perform a metamorphosing function by transforming the carrion on which it feeds into renewed vital force. See Mathieu (1984a), 296–99.

66. *Yilin*, 12.15a.

67. For the goose as a *yang* bird, see *Xiao Erya*, in Ariel (1996), appendix 1, no. 170/09. See also *Hanshu*, 28A.1528. For the association of the back with heaven and the belly with earth, see *Lunheng jiaoshi*, 40.620–21 ("Zhuang liu" 狀 留).

68. See for example *Huainanzi*, 18.622 ("Ren jian"; "The reason why the sage is honored is because he can transform like a dragon."); *Hanshu*, 25A.1225; *Shiji*, 49.1983. The *Wenzi* states that the Dao is valued because it is transforming like a dragon. See *Wenzi*, 2.4b ("Wei ming" 微 明). *Hou Hanshu*, 30B.1078, states that the *Zhouyi* compares the dragon to the Great Man because its shape and posture is not uniform and its size is not permanent. Several scholars have speculated on the etymological origins of the dragon graph. Ikeda Suetoshi (1953) suggests an etymological relationship between the character *long* and *gui* 鬼 and takes the dragon to be an ancestor-deity transformed into an animal. For a hypothesis equating the *long* graph with the graphs *hui* 虺 and *jiu* 九, see Guo Guanghong (1995).

69. *Guanzi jiaoshi* 39 ("Shui di"), 14.351.

70. Hay (1994), 132.

71. *Ersanzi wen*, 424, lines 6–7; *Boshu Zhouyi jiaoshi*, 348–49; tr. Shaughnessy (1996), 169. The difficulty in describing the shape of the dragon is borne out in the following remark by Wen Yiduo: "It resembles a horse, and that is why a horse is sometimes called a dragon (*long*). . . . The dragon resembles a dog, which is why a dog is sometimes called a dragon. . . . In addition, there is also a kind of dragon with scales resembling fish, a kind with wings resembling a bird, and a kind with horns resembling a deer. When we come to the various kinds of crawling reptiles most easily confused with the dragon, they need not even be mentioned." See Wen Yiduo (1956), 25.

72. *Erya yi*, 28.297; *Wu zazu*, 9.238 ("Wu bu").

73. See *Wenxuan*, 13.612–16 ("Yingwu fu" 鸚 鵡 賦); tr. W.T. Graham (1979), 39–54. For Mi Heng, see *Hou Hanshu*, 80B.2652–58.

74. For literary imagery associated with the parrot, see Schafer (1959b). For reference to speech imitating birds in Chinese history, see Xie Chengxia (1995), 109–12.

75. *Yilin*, 12.20b, 13.15b (variant). For spirit birds, see for example *Hanshu*, 8.258–59, 25B.1248 (pentachromatic geese), 25B.1249, 25B.1252, 89.3631, 99A.4077; *Hou Hanshu*, 36.1235. For spirit power associated with the five colors as a demonifuge, see *Fengsu tongyi jiaoshi*, 414, 415 ("yi wen").

76. *Lunheng jiaoshi*, 39.609 ("Chao qi" 超 奇).

77. *Shizi*, 2.2a.

78. *Zhouyi zhengyi*, 5.19b–20a. For reference to this passage, see *Lunheng jiaoshi*,

61.865 ("Yi wen" 佚文); *Fengsu tongyi jiaoshi*, 2.92 ("Zheng shi"); *Jing shi yi zhuan*, 1.16a; *Guanyinzi*, 9a; *Taiping yulan*, 891.1a, 892.6a. For "striped skin" (*wen pi* 文皮) as the hides of tigers and leopards, see Gao You's commentary in *Huainanzi*, 4.139 ("Di xing").

79. For *ge*, see *Shuowen jiezi zhu*, 3B.1a; Karlgren (1957), no. 931.

80. *Yangzi fayan*, 2.3b. See also *Hou Hanshu*, 75.2438. The wildcat referred to here is the *li* 貍, a foxlike animal also known as the Asian raccoon-dog (*Nyctereutes procyonoides*). Several Tang tales deal with the domestication of the *li*. See Spring (1993), 53–60.

81. For another analogy describing an animal's outside appearance (*wen*) and inner character (*zhi*), see Gongsun Gui's 公孫詭 (second cent. B.C.E.) "Rhapsody on the Striped Deer" (*Wen lu fu* 文鹿賦), in *Quan shanggu Sandai Qin Han Sanguo Liuchao wen*, 19.6b ("Quan Han wen"); *Xijing zaji*, 4.4a–b.

82. *Lunyu zhushu*, 12.4a ("Yan Yuan" 顏淵).

83. See *Han Feizi jishi*, 7.387 ("Yu Lao" 喻老); *Huainanzi*, 10.337 ("Miu cheng"), 17.566 ("Shuo lin"). This comparison echoes the idea that an elephant's tusks, because of their beauty, are the cause of its downfall. See *Zuozhuan zhu*, p. 1090 (Lord Xiang, year 24).

84. *Duduan*, 2.11b. See also *Hou Hanshu*, "zhi," 29.3649; *Han guan yi*, 2.8a.

85. *Gujin zhu*, 1.4 ("Yu fu"). For the leopard's hide symbolizing frugality, see also *Shoujing*, pp. 10–11.

86. *Taixuan jing*, 4.6a; tr. Nylan (1994), 214.

87. *Yi zhi yi*, 433, lines 1–2; *Boshu Zhouyi jiaoshi*, 471; tr. Shaughnessy (1996), 229 [modified].

88. *Xunzi jijie*, 26.477–79 ("Fu" 賦); tr. Knoblock (1994), vol. 3, 199–200. For the transformation period of the silkworm, see *Huainanzi*, 17.570 ("Shuo lin"). The absence of gender is recurrent in descriptions of hybrids. Three hermaphrodites occur in the *Shanhaijing*, each described as "constituting of themselves both male and female" (*zi wei pinmu* 自爲牝牡). See *Shanhaijing jiaozhu*, 1.5, 3.68, 3.88.

89. *Soushenji*, 14.104. The goddess is also known as Matou Niang 馬頭娘, "The Girl with the Horse's Head." See Bodde (1975), 271; Birrell (1993), 199–200. For a study of this tale within the context of comparative folktale research, see Miller (1995). The same story is also known as the *Taigu canma ji* 太古蠶馬記, attributed to Zhang Yan 張儼 (3rd cent. C.E.).

90. See Waley (1955). See also Izushi Yoshihiko (1943), 187–227; Sukhu (1999), 152. Heavenly Horse imagery figured prominently in Tang descriptions of famous steeds and dancing horse performances. See Kroll (1981), 251–56.

91. Two hymns describing the heavenly horse are among nineteen sacrificial hymns performed at the *jiao* 郊 sacrifice. See *Hanshu*, 22.1060–61; *Shiji*, 24.1178. They may be dated to 120 B.C.E. and 101 B.C.E., and were composed after a horse was reported to have been born from the Wuya 渥洼 river. See further *Hanshu*, 6.176, 6.184, 6.202, 6.206, 61.2693–94, 61.2697–2704, 96A.3894–95, 96B.3928; *Shiji*, 123.3170; *Xinlun*, 16b; *Hou Hanshu*, 42.1439; *Yilin*, 10.4b, 13.5b, 13.22b.

92. See for instance *Hanshu*, 79.3294; *Lunheng jiaoshi*, 22.285 ("Long xu"). For poetic descriptions of the transformatory power of the dragon and the dragonlike features of the

horse, see Liu Wan's 劉琬 (Jin period) "Rhapsody on the Holy Dragon" ("Shen long fu" 神龍賦) and "Horse Rhapsody" ("Ma fu" 馬賦) in *Yiwen leiju*, 96.1663; and *Quan Han fu*, pp. 562–63. A wooden dragon-horse figurine excavated in 1960 from a Han tomb in Xining 西寧 (Qinghai) shows its head and neck resembling that of a dragon, with the body and limbs resembling those of a horse. See Li Lin (1991). Its avian nature is attested in a well-known bronze figurine of a horse standing on a swallow, excavated from an Eastern Han tomb at Wuwei in Gansu province (1969). See Niu Longfei (1984).

93. *Hanshu*, 22.1061.

94. *Zhouli zhushu*, 33.8a; *Shuowen jiezi zhu*, 10A.7b.

95. See Ying Shao, quoting the *Liexian zhuan*, in *Hanshu*, 25A.1204 note 3; Kaltenmark (1953), 109–10. For the stele inscription, see *Cai zhonglang ji*, 1.20a–22a ("Wang Ziqiao bei" 王子喬碑).

96. Kaltenmark (1953), 10–26.

97. *Shuoyuan jiaozheng*, 16.387 ("Tan cong").

98. *Lunyu zhushu*, 14.1b ("Xian wen").

99. Ban Zhao's 班昭 (?48–?116 C.E.) "Rhapsody on the Great Peacock" ("Da que fu" 大雀賦) praises the peacock for its phoenixlike virtues of "roaming and traveling over a distance of ten thousand *li* to gather in the emperor's courtyard and rest." See *Yiwen leiju*, 92.1596; *Quan Han fu*, p. 370.

100. *Fengsu tongyi jiaoshi*, 418 ("yi wen").

101. *Hanshu*, 52.2401.

102. *Chuci*, 8.8a ("Jiu bian" 九辯).

103. For examples, see *Shuihudi Qin mu zhujian*, 212 (slips 48–49), 212 (slip 30, figurines), 213 (slip 27), 213 (slips 34–35, spirit bug), 214 (slip 49), 215 (slip 38).

104. *Shiji*, 105.2809. For Chunyu Yi, see Loewe (1997). In the context of early medicine, Elisabeth Hsü (1994) has proposed to differentiate the notions of *bian* and *hua* according to the observer's perspective. *Hua* could then be understood as invisible change inside the body while *bian* would refer to observable, outward symptoms of change.

105. K. C. Chang (1981), 527–54; and K. C. Chang (1983), 44–80. Yang Xiaoneng has argued recently that many animal motifs on Shang and Zhou vessels fulfill an inscriptional role; that is, the designs function as pictorial inscriptions depicting deified spirits associated with particular clans and cultures of the early Bronze Age. See Yang Xiaoneng (2000), 110–32.

106. *Zuozhuan zhu*, p. 640 (Lord Wen, year 18); *Lüshi chunqiu jiaoshi*, 16.947 ("Xian shi"). For a detailed study of the oracle-bone etymology and textual history of the "two-eyed motif," see Wang Tao (1992). Wang connects a two-eyed graph in Shang oracle bone inscriptions with the idea of trepidation, rashness in action, awe, and anxiety.

107. For a synthesis of the problems surrounding the interpretation of the *taotie* motif, see Allan (1991), 128–57. Rawson (1992) sees the variety of the *taotie* motifs primarily as the result of their ornamental function and as the product of an evolving craft process.

108. Childs-Johnson (1993), esp. 11–15, 17–19; Childs-Johnson (1998), 43–56. Paper (1978) has suggested that the *taotie* mask is derived from a mask helmet signifying power and authority. For a critique, see Allan (1991), 145.

109. *Zhouli zhushu,* 31.12a. See also *Duduan,* 1.13b; *Hou Hanshu,* "zhi," 5.3127–28; *Li ji ming zheng* in *Weishu jicheng,* 512.

110. Kaltenmark (1963), 438–39. The *nuo* ceremony is studied in detail in Bodde (1975), 75–138. For the masked dance, see also Granet (1926), vol. 1, 298–338. Hopkins (1943) has interpreted an inscription of a human figurine with a large "ghost-head" on a Shang bone fragment from Henan as a "Man 蠻 hooded with a bearskin." He suggests that the bearskin refers to a mask and speculates that this Man tribesman as semihuman semianimalistic impersonator may be related to the later *fangxiangshi.*

111. *Xunzi jijie,* 5.74 ("Fei xiang"). See also Granet (1926), vol. 1, 325–26. On the spirit mask, see further Knoblock (1988), vol. 1, 295 note 34; and Lewis (1990), 312–13 note 106.

112. Charles Hammond has identified similar ideas in his research on tiger lore in later times. He points out that Xu Shen's etymology of the *hu* 虎 graph (cf. *Shuowen jiezi zhu,* 5A.43b–44a) identifies its two bottom strokes as the tiger's feet similar to representations of a human's feet, while commentators identify the balance of the character as the patterns on the tiger's skin, suggesting that the skin was conceived of as a separate entity. See Hammond (1992–93), 235–55, esp. 239.

113. *Shiming,* 2.3b ("Shi xing" 釋形).

114. I borrow this term from Jean-Louis Durand, "Greek Animals: toward a Topology of Edible Bodies," in Detienne and Vernant (1989), 104.

115. *Lunheng jiaoshi,* 62.873 ("Lun si").

116. *Fengsu tongyi jiaoshi,* 8.307 ("Si dian").

117. *Hanshu,* 99C.4161, 12.351.

118. *Mu Tianzi zhuan,* 5.4a. For its association with earth, see *Zhouli zhushu,* 12.19b–20a.

119. *Shiji,* 28.1399–1400. See also *Hanshu,* 25B.1241. On the superstitious nature of Chu and Yue people, see *Lüshi chunqiu jiaoshi,* 10.551 ("Yi bao" 異寶); *Liezi,* 8.10a ("Shuo fu"); *Huainanzi,* 18.589 ("Ren jian"); *Hanshu,* 63.2760. For a comprehensive treatment of Chu and Yue magic, see Harper (1998), 159–83.

120. *Yuefu shi ji,* 74.1048; *Gujin zhu,* 2.12 ("Yin yue" 音樂).

121. *Lunheng jiaoshi,* 66.956 ("Yan du"). For *zhen* poisoning, see *Zuozhuan zhu,* p. 254 (Lord Zhuang, year 32), p. 674 (Lord Xuan, year 3); *Guoyu,* 4.161–62 ("Lu yu shang"), 8.289 ("Jin yu"); *Shiji,* 33.1532, 37.1595; *Hanshu,* 38.1987–88, 42.2097, 53.2436, 78.3288, 83.3409, 84.3426, 98.4033. For southern animals associated with poison, see also *Hanshu,* 64A.2779, 64A.2781.

122. See *Hanshu,* 28B.1669; Ying Shao's commentary to *Hanshu,* 28B.1670, note 2; *Shuoyuan jiaozheng,* 12.302–303 ("Feng shi" 奉使); *Hanshu,* 64A.2777, 64A.2778, 64B.2823; *Han shi waizhuan jishi,* 8.271. See also Itō Seiji (1994). I have not been able to examine this paper.

123. *Hanshu,* 87A.3550 ("Jiao lie fu" 校獵賦, composed ca. 11 B.C.E.); tr. based on Knechtges (1976), 70–71.

124. *Hou Hanshu,* 86.2848. See also *Fengsu tongyi jiaoshi,* 439 ("yi wen"); *Huayang guo zhi,* 4.424; *Taiping yulan,* 929.2b.

125. Major (1999), 129–31, 134. Reflecting the aquatic southern environment, Major also notes that Chu hunting scenes are especially replete with depictions of the shooting of waterfowl.

126. Tei Masahiro (1978), 93–94; Eno (1990), 196. For other interpretations, see Childs-Johnson (1998), 55–56.

127. Harper (1985), 487–88.

128. See *Mawangdui Han mu boshu*, vol. 4, 95 (nos. 8, 25, 31, 40, 41, 44). The manuscripts are known as the *He yinyang* 合陰陽 ("Conjoining Yin and Yang") and the *Tian xia zhi dao tan* 天下至道談 ("Discourse on the culminant way in Under Heaven"). Animal postures also occur in another Mawangdui manuscript entitled *Yang sheng fang* 養生方 ("Recipes for Nourishing Life"). See *Mawangdui Han mu boshu*, vol. 4, 155, 165, 116–17; tr. Harper (1998), 418–19, 432. The Zhangjiashan manuscript is known as the *Yin shu* 引書. See Zhangjiashan Han jian zhengli zu (1990), 82 (column 2, lines 7, 19), 83 (column 1, lines 6, 12, 16), 84 (column 2, lines 1–5), 86 (column 1, lines 2, 3). For the Mawangdui *Daoyin tu* 圖, see Xiao Dengfu (1990), 279–85, 304–306. Similar animal postures also occur in the *Huainanzi*. See *Huainanzi*, 7.230 ("Jing shen").

129. *Shuyiji*, 1.2a–b; *Hanshu*, 9.285, 24A.1142; *Yantie lun jiaozhu*, 7.257 ("Chong li"); *Liang Han bo wen*, 2.44. See also Bishop (1925); Rudolph (1960), 242; Lewis (1990), 157–60; Loewe (1994), 236–48.

130. *Han guan yi*, 1.16a–b. See also *Duduan*, 2.14b; *Lunheng jiaoshi*, 52.760 ("Shi ying"); *Taixuan jing*, 6.12b. On possible links between horn butting, goats and the origins of legal procedure, see Lewis (1990), 198–99.

131. See Yan Shigu's commentary in *Hanshu*, 96B.3928–30 note 9. For its gold-spitting habit, see Li Shan's commentary to Zhang Heng's "Rhapsody on the Western Capital" in *Wenxuan*, 2.76. This text gives a variant, *hanli* 含利, which has been tentatively identified as a name of Indian origin (Sillah). Knechtges points out that the *manyan* costume was worn by a large number of performers, thus deriving its name from its prodigious length (the "elongating" or "stretching" beast). See Knechtges (1982), vol. 1, 230, 232.

132. *Wenxuan*, 6.76–77; tr. Knechtges (1982), vol. 1, 231–33.

133. *Hou Hanshu*, 51.1685, 86.2851.

134. See Chūbachi Masakazu (1981). For metamorphosis in popular belief in later periods, see Sawada Mizuho (1982), 374–404.

135. Granet (1926), vol. 1, 259–64.

136. *Guoyu*, 5.195 ("Lu yu xia"). For a story about the use of animal furs as an expression of one's character, see *Shuoyuan jiaozheng*, 11.274–75 ("Shan shuo").

137. *Liji zhushu*, 25.12a ("Jiao te sheng"). Similar symbolism is associated with a white tiger tribute presented to Emperor Yuan as a sign of his wielding power over the western regions. See *Hanshu*, 84.3432, 3433 note 11.

138. *Yili zhushu*, 13.10b ("Xiang she li"); *Bohutong shu zheng*, 5.243 ("Xiang she" 鄉射). See also *Li han wen jia* in *Weishu jicheng*, 502. Chariots were also decorated with animal hides to mark the driver's status. See for instance *Liji zhushu*, 29.10b ("Yu zao"). For arrow stands decorated with dragon heads and intertwined snakes, see *Yili zhushu*, 13.14a ("Xiang she li").

139. Riegel (1982), 3.

140. *Shuowen jiezi zhu*, 5B.23b; *Bohutong shu zheng*, 5.244 ("Xiang she").

141. *Zhouli zhushu*, 7.7a. For leopard and deer hides used as tokens of exchange, see *Guanzi jiaoshi* 18 ("Da kuang" 大匡), 7.171.

142. *Bohutong shu zheng*, 5.244 ("Xiang she"); *Shuowen jiezi zhu*, 5B.23b; *Lunheng jiaoshi*, 47.704–705 ("Luan long").

143. See for instance *Guoyu*, 18.567 ("Chu yu xia"); *Hanshu*, 25A.1225; *Shiji*, 28.1392; *Bohutong shu zheng*, 12.591 ("que wen"). See also *Hou Hanshu*, "zhi," 5.3123, 8.3182.

144. For the association of "target" (侯) with "vassal" (侯), see *Liji zhushu*, 62.8a ("She yi"); and Riegel (1982), 5–10. For a comparison of the subjugation of barbarians with skilfullness in fishing and shooting birds, see *Lüshi chunqiu jiaoshi*, 2.110 ("Gong ming" 功名).

145. *Zhouli zhushu*, 23.3b; *Yili zhushu*, 18.14a–b ("Da she" 大射); *Liji zhushu*, 39.13b–14a ("Yue ji"), 62.2a ("She yi"); *Shiji*, 24.1229; *Hanshu*, 57A.2573; *Kongzi jiayu*, 8.4b ("Bian yue jie" 辯樂解); *Hou Hanshu*, 60A.1956.

146. *Mao shi zhengyi*, 1E.13b–15b ("Zouyu" 騶虞, Mao 25).

147. For descriptions of this creature, see *Shangshu da zhuan*, 1.52; *Mao shi caomu niaoshou chongyu shu*, 2.49–50. For its interpretation as the name of an official, see Jia Yi's comments in *Xinshu*, 6.1b–2a ("Li" 禮). The individual titles *zou* and *yu* also occur as names of officials in charge of horse stables. See *Shang jun shu jiaoshi*, 24.150 ("Jin shi" 禁使). See further, Wang Yitong (1978).

148. *Shiji*, 4.120, 28.1366; *Hanshu*, 25A.1200, 56.2500, 77.3252; *Zhushu jinian*, 1.19b; *Shangshu da zhuan*, 2.56 ("Da shi" 大誓); *Shangshu zhong hou* in *Weishu jicheng*, 412; *Shangshu di ming yan* 尚書帝命驗 in *Weishu jicheng*, 371. See also *Hanshu*, 99B.4106, where Wang Mang alludes to a similar portent to legitimize his own authority.

149. *Shiji*, 8.341, 8.347, 8.350, 28.1378; *Hanshu*, 1A.1, 1A.7, 1B.82, 25A.1210, 100A.4211, 100B.4236. See also *Hou Hanshu*, 80A.2598; *Lunheng jiaoshi*, 64.924–25 ("Ji yao"), 25.343 ("Yu zeng" 語增).

150. *Zhushu jinian*, 1.20a, 2.10a, 2.18b. The *Soushenji* dates the horse-to-fox metamorphosis to the 33rd year of King Xuan 宣 of Zhou (827/25–782 B.C.E.). See *Soushenji*, 6.42. While the entire text of the current Bamboo Annals may not be a faithful historical source for the late Shang and Western Zhou period, Edward Shaughnessy has made a strong case to revalidate at least parts of it as a reliable historical source. See Shaughnessy (1997), 69–100.

151. *Mozi jiaozhu*, 19.221 ("Fei gong xia" 非攻下).

152. Raphals (1998), 207–208. Creatures that move at will between human and animal form still provide the object for cultural narratives in contemporary societies. For example the metamorphosis of fresh-water dolphins into human beings who carry off the objects of their desires to an underwater city from which few will return is a prominent theme in Amazonian folktales. Candace Slater has identified such tales as a response by Amazonians to changes in their physical environment (the rain forests) and socio-economic order. See Slater (1994), 59–117, 138–45, 156–65, 233–34 ff.

153. This is also illustrated in a recurring gloss for the graph *bian* 變 "transformation" as *feichang* 非常 "that which is not regular/constant/continuous." See *Bohutong shu zheng*,

6.269 ("Zai bian" 災變). See also *Hanshu*, 36.1961; and Yan Shigu's gloss in *Hanshu*, 36.1930 note 3.

154. Bielenstein attributes the authorship of this treatise (*Hanshu* 27) to Ban Gu rather than Liu Xiang or Liu Xin. See Bielenstein (1984), 105.

155. *Hanshu*, 27.1353. The *Bohutong* glosses *nie* 孽 as "armored animals growing into abnormal species." See *Bohutong shu zheng*, 6.270 ("Zai bian").

156. *Hanshu*, 27.1369, 27.1372, 27.1447–48, 27.1397–98, 27.1419, 27.1430, 27.1436, 27.1465, 27.1466, 27.1467, 27.1468, 27.1469.

157. *Hanshu*, 27.1370–71. See also *Hanshu*, 99B.4112. For a list of Western Han animal omens, see *Xi Han huiyao*, 29.301–305, 30.323–25.

158. On the Wang clan's rise to power, see Twitchett and Loewe (1986), 224–32.

159. See *Hou Hanshu*, "zhi," 13.3273–74, 60B.2000 note 2. See also *Soushenji*, 6.46–47, 53.

160. *Hou Hanshu*, 60B.1999.

161. *Hanshu*, 27.1472, referring to *Shiji*, 44.1849. Similar interpretations of gender transformations occur in the *Chunqiu qian tan ba* 春秋潛譚巴: "When women change into men, worthies will give up their positions and the gentleman will remain on his own. When males change into females, *yin* energy will obscure things and petty individuals will gather." See *Weishu jicheng*, 840.

162. *Hanshu*, 27.1419. For a similar example, see *Shuoyuan jiaozheng*, 10.247–48 ("Jing shen" 敬慎).

163. *Zhanguo ce*, 32.1157. See also *Xinxu xiang zhu*, 4.138–39 ("Za shi"); *Xinshu*, 6.9b ("Chun qiu"). A sparrow giving birth to a hawk is also recorded in the *Zhushu jinian*. See *Zhushu jinian*, 1.18b (Di Xin 帝辛, year 3, 1152 B.C.E.). See also *Kongzi jiayu*, 1.12b ("Wu yi" 五儀).

164. *Hanshu*, 27.1469. For statements that Qin had the heart of a tiger or wolf and passages comparing its policies with bestial behavior, see *Zhanguo ce*, 24.869; *Shiji*, 44.1857; *Hanshu*, 51.2328. The *Hou Hanshu* reports a horse giving birth to a human in 178 C.E. prefiguring endemic rebellion in the empire. See *Hou Hanshu*, "zhi," 17.3345.

165. For cases of interbreeding or crossbreeding, see *Hanshu*, 27.1398, 27.1399, 27.1464–65, 27.1469 (referring to *Shiji*, 15.725). Oxen interbreeding with horses and prodigies caused by the six domestic animals are listed as *ren yao* 人妖 "prodigies that pertain to humans," in *Han shi waizhuan jishi*, 2.38. The decadent prince of Jiangdu 江都 (fl. ca. 107 B.C.E.) forced his palace ladies to "strip off naked, walk on all fours, and mate with sheep and dogs." See *Hanshu*, 53.2416. For a similar case, see *Hanshu*, 38.2002.

166. *Yilin*, 1.19a; variant at 8.18a–b.

167. *Hanshu*, 27.1353, 27.1397–98, 27.1470, 27.1474. For oxen as a portent for military activity, see *Chunqiu qian tan ba* in *Weishu jicheng*, 832, 848. For oxen sprouting more horns than their number of feet, see *He tu shuo zheng shi* 河圖說徵示 in *Weishu jicheng*, 1177. For horses sprouting horns, see also *Shiji*, 86.2538. Horn-sprouting anomalies from the *Hanshu* portent treatise are collated in *Soushenji*, 6.44, 6.46, 6.49.

168. *Taixuan jing*, 3.1a. See also *Yilin*, 8.13a.

169. See for instance *Hanshu*, 27.1447 (ox with five feet); *Yilin*, 3.22a.

170. See *Hanshu*, 27.1448, 47.2211 (144 B.C.E., ox with a foot growing out of its back).

171. *Hanshu*, 27.1473–74.

172. *Xinyu*, 11.155 ("Ming jie").

173. See Sivin (1991). See also Swanson (1984), 69–76.

174. Graham (1989), 359.

175. *Liji zhushu*, 53.3b–4a ("Zhong yong").

176. *Zhouyi zhengyi*, 7.9b; Shaughnessy (1996), 191.

177. *Hou Hanshu*, 86.2840.

178. De Groot (1892–1910; rpt. 1964), vol. 4, 171–72.

179. *Yuefu shi ji*, 28.408; Lu Qinli, *Han shi*, 9.258. The *Bencao gangmu* mentions a bird named *gui-che-niao* 鬼車鳥 "demon-cart bird" (goatsucker, *caprimulgus stictomus*) said to be the recipient of the human *hun* soul. See *Bencao gangmu*, 49.24. See also Eberhard (1968), 166–68.

180. *Hanshu*, 87A.3549.

181. *Wenxuan*, 2.69 ("Xi jing fu"), 4.158 ("Nan du fu" 南都賦).

182. See *Shiji*, 84.2500 ("Peng niao fu" 鵬鳥賦, written in 174 B.C.E.); *Wenxuan*, 13.607; tr. R. Hightower (1959), 128 [modified].

183. *Lunheng jiaoshi*, 65.934–35 ("Ding gui" 訂鬼); *Lunheng jiaoshi*, 7.59–67 ("Wu xing").

184. *Shuowen jiezi zhu*, 10A.55a; *Huainanzi*, 13.458 ("Fan lun"). Gao You explains that blood essence (*xue jing* 血精) sticks to the earth and when exposed to the sun for a hundred days it turns into a blaze like a fire. See also *Liezi*, 1.7a ("Tian rui"); *Bowuzhi*, 2.1b.

185. *Lunheng jiaoshi*, 50.732–33 ("Jiang rui").

186. *Lunheng jiaoshi*, 24.318 ("Dao xu").

187. *Lunheng jiaoshi*, 7.62–63 ("Wu xing").

188. For the Bao Si story, see *Guoyu*, 16.519 ("Zheng yu"); *Shiji*, 4.147; *Lienü zhuan*, 7.2b–3a ("Nie bi" 孽嬖); *Hanshu*, 27.1464–65. See also *Yilin*, 5.8b, 9.8b.

189. *Lunheng jiaoshi*, 15.161 ("Qi guai"). Elsewhere Wang ascribes the appearance of the two dragons to coincidence and chance. See *Lunheng jiaoshi*, 10.100 ("Ou hui").

190. *Lunheng jiaoshi*, 62.873 ("Lun si"). Gun's metamorphosis into a yellow bear is refuted on the basis that a ghost should resemble the shape of the living. See *Lunheng jiaoshi*, 63.903–904 ("Si wei").

191. *Lunheng jiaoshi*, 24.326 ("Dao xu").

192. Harper (1994) traces the Warring States origins of such beliefs. At the time of emperor Qin Shihuang *fangshi* 方士 from the state of Yan were reported to engage in practices such as the "release of the body and fluxing transformation." See *Shiji*, 28.1368–69; *Hanshu*, 25A.1203; and *Liang Han bo wen*, 1.3.

193. See *Lunheng jiaoshi*, 24.331–32 ("Dao xu"); Harper (1994); and Kameda Ichirō (1984).

194. *Hou Hanshu*, 49.1645. See also Lu Qinli, *Han shi*, 7.205; *Liang Han bo wen*, 10.260. For the image of cicadas shedding their exuviae, see also *Huainanzi*, 7.235 ("Jing shen"); and Zhang Heng's "Si xuan fu" in *Hou Hanshu*, 59.1923.

195. *Bao Puzi nei pian jiaoshi*, 2.14 ("Lun xian" 論 仙). For the woman of Chu, see *Hou Hanshu*, "zhi," 17.3348. For other comments on animal metamorphosis, see *Bao Puzi nei pian jiaoshi*, 2.21 ("Lun xian"; Peng Sheng, Ruyi cases), 3.47–48 ("Dui su" 對俗; animals transforming with age), 16.284 ("Huang bai" 黄白).

Chapter Seven. Strange Animals

1. *Wu zazu* 五雜組, 9.250 (*Jian guai bu guai, qi guai zi huai* 見怪不怪,其怪自壞).

2. See Douglas (1966; rpt. 1996), 38–41, 55–57, 167–70; Douglas (1990); and Albert-Llorca (1991), 113, 119. See also Campany (1996), 2–4, 7–8, 238.

3. Even in ancient Greece, which witnessed a much more developed protoscientific interest in the animal world, the classificatory framework behind the discourse on anomalous animal species often remained implicit. As Geoffrey Lloyd states: "It is assumed and goes unchallenged: it is not the subject of deliberate inquiry or critical reflection." See Lloyd (1983), 205.

4. Wang Chuqing (1986) counts sixty-three references to calamitous events in the *Zuozhuan*.

5. *Zuozhuan zhu*, p. 763 (Lord Xuan, year 15). The word *wu* 物 in this passage ("creatures" in my translation) presumably includes plants and other natural phenomena. *Zheng* 正 and *fa* 乏 look like each other's inverted graphs in small seal script. For a later quotation of this passage, see *Hou Hanshu*, 36.1221.

6. *Zuozhuan zhu*, pp. 196–97 (Lord Zhuang, year 14).

7. See for instance Jing Fang's version in *Hanshu*, 27.1467. For other references to the event, see *Shiji*, 42.1763–64; *Fengsu tongyi jiaoshi*, 9.361 ("Guai shen"); *Soushenji*, 6.43. A similar snake fight reportedly took place beneath Emperor Wen's shrine in the state of Zhao (in the autumn of 93 B.C.E.). See *Hanshu*, 6.207, 27.1468; *Soushenji*, 6.46.

8. *Zuozhuan zhu*, p. 197 (Lord Zhuang, year 14). See also *Qianfu lun*, 6.358 ("Wu lie" 巫列).

9. The direct relationship between the neglect of constancy (*chang*) and the emergence of prodigies (*yao*) also forms the theme of the opening part of a "Rhapsody on the Owl" ("Xiao fu" 鴞賦), attributed to Kong Cang, which reminisces on Jia Yi's famous "Owl Rhapsody":

> On a *gengzi* 庚子 day during the last month of summer,
> I was pondering on the Way in a state of peaceful contemplation.
> Next flew by an owl, which perched on the corner of my roof.
> The arrival of strange creatures is a sign for good or bad fortune.
> I observed the creature with joy and examined the writings of the classics.
> To rest with virtue causes good luck,
> to neglect constancy causes prodigies.

See *Quan Han fu*, p. 120; *Yiwen leiju*, 92.1610.

10. *Lunheng jiaoshi*, 64.925 ("Ji yao").

11. *Xinyu*, 11.155 ("Ming jie").

12. *Hanshu*, 75.3173. Similar arguments are set out in a memorial by Liu Xiang. See *Hanshu*, 36.1935, 1941.

13. *Hou Hanshu*, 54.1776.

14. *Hou Hanshu*, 57.1858–59. See also *Hou Hanshu*, 65.2140, where a frontier general, Zhang Huan 張奐 (fl. ca. 55 C.E.), comments on the same events.

15. For Wang Chong's criticisms of the direct correlation between human office, insect plagues, and physical deformity, see *Lunheng jiaoshi*, 49.713–14, 49.720 ("Shang chong"), 52.761–62 ("Shi ying").

16. *Xunzi jijie*, 17.307, 313–14 ("Tian lun"). See also the discussion on signs and omens in Knoblock (1994), vol 3, 4–5, 12–13, 18–19 [tr. modified]. The contradictions in the Xunzian notion of Heaven in this chapter have been subject to debate. Disagreement exists as to how to explain Xunzi's tendency to present Heaven as being value neutral and separated from humanity on occasions, while on the other hand propounding the complete conflation of nature and culture. The most systematic exposition is in Eno (1990), 154–69. See also Puett (1997), 489 note 47; and Machle (1993), 139–40.

17. *Hanshu*, 25B.1260.

18. *Shanhaijing jiaozhu*, p. 478 (*yi guo zai wo, fei wu yi ye* 異果在我, 非物異也). The concept of *bianhua* in Guo Pu's *Shanhaijing* commentary is discussed in Sakurai Tatsuhiko (1993).

19. *Han shi waizhuan jishi*, 5.172–73. This passage reiterates *Xunzi jijie*, 8.140 ("Ru xiao").

20. The *xiaoyang* (= 梟羊) is glossed by Gao You as a big creature in the shape of a human with black spots on its face, hair on its body and feet with heels turned backwards. When seeing people it laughs. See also *Shanhaijing jiaozhu*, 10.270. The *wangxiang* or *wang-liang* 罔兩 is described as a bogy expelled from graves at burials by masked exorcists. Ying Shao (quoting the *Zhouli*) identifies it as a demon that eats the liver and brains of the deceased. See *Fengsu tongyi jiaoshi*, 428 ("yi wen"). See also *Lunheng jiaoshi*, 75.1043 ("Jie chu" 解除). A variant, *wanghang* 罔行, occurs in the Shuihudi demonography. See *Shuihudi Qin mu zhujian*, 212; Harper (1985), 481–83. See further Bodde (1975), 77–80, 116–17; De Groot (1892–1910; rpt. 1964), vol. 5, 497–98; and Yamada Katsumi (1951). The *bifang* is described as a bird like a crane on one leg. See *Shanhaijing jiaozhu*, 2.52, 6.188; Bodde (1975), 111. The *fenyang* will be discussed below.

21. *Huainanzi*, 13.457–59 ("Fan lun"). Similar ideas are voiced elsewhere in the *Huai-nanzi*: "Water scorpions turn into millipedes, the very small ones become mosquitoes. [Grass] when chewed on by a rabbit turns into a gadfly. The way in which such creatures come about is unintentional. Those who do not know this are frightened, those who know it do not consider it strange." See *Huainanzi*, 17.577–78 ("Shuo lin").

22. *Han Feizi jishi*, 11.633 (Wai chu shuo zuo shang"). Variants of this passage occur in *Huainanzi*, 13.432 ("Fan lun"); and *Fengsu tongyi jiaoshi*, p. 2 ("Xu").

23. See *Shenzi* 申子 in Creel (1974), fragment 15 (p. 363); *Xinxu xiang zhu*, 5.173 ("Za

shi"); *Lunheng jiaoshi*, 47.698–99 ("Luan long"); *Hou Hanshu*, 30B.1082 note 3; *Hou Hanshu*, 52.1719 note 2.

24. *Han Feizi jishi*, 6.368 ("Jie Lao"). See also Lewis (1999), 271.

25. *Huainanzi*, 13.452 ("Fan lun").

26. *Huainanzi*, 13.446 ("Fan lun").

27. *Shanhaijing jiaozhu*, 479.

28. For a definition of dreams as images (*xiang* 象), see *Lunheng jiaoshi*, 63.903 ("Si wei").

29. *Zhuangzi jishi*, 2.112 ("Qi wu lun" 齊物論).

30. *Liezi*, 3.6b–7a ("Zhou Mu wang" 周穆王). For the dream as a medium to connect with the spirits, see also Cai Yong's "Jian yi fu" 檢逸賦 in *Quan Han fu*, p. 596. For traditional dream classifications, see *Zhouli zhushu*, 24.13a–15a; and *Qianfu lun*, ch. 28 ("Meng lie" 夢列). On the relationship between the physiology of the body and the contents of a dream, see *Huangdi neijing ling shu*, 7.4a–5a.

31. *Qianfu lun*, 7.376–77, 378 ("Meng lie").

32. To borrow an expression from Zeitlin (1993), 153.

33. *Mao shi zhengyi*, 11B.9a–b ("Si gan," Mao 189). See also *Qianfu lun*, 7.371 ("Meng lie").

34. *Mao shi zhengyi*, 11B.13b ("Wu yang" 無羊, Mao 190). Other poems featuring fish imagery as symbols for prosperity, fertility, and marital relations include "Yu li" 魚麗 (Mao 170), "Qian" 潛 (Mao 281), "Yu zao" 魚藻 (Mao 221), "Heng men" 衡門 (Mao 138), and "Bi gou" 蔽笱 (Mao 104). The classic treatment of the association of fish with fertility and marital relations in the Odes is Wen Yiduo (1948). On the links between fish, fish sacrifice, and fecundity in agriculture, see also Inoi Makoto (1975).

35. *Fengsu tongyi jiaoshi*, 9.350 ("Guai shen"); *Xinxu xiang zhu*, 2.49–50 ("Za shi"); *Bowuzhi*, 8.2b.

36. *Xinxu xiang zhu*, 1.4 ("Za shi"); *Xinshu*, 6.11b ("Chun qiu"); *Lienü zhuan*, 3.3a ("Ren zhi" 仁智); *Lunheng jiaoshi*, 20.266–67 ("Fu xu" 福虛). Another case where a snake prodigy during childhood is interpreted to signify later career success is recorded for regent Dou Wu 竇武 (r. 168 C.E.), whose mother gave birth to him along with a snake that was set free in the woods. When Dou's mother died, the snake emerged to mourn her, butting its head against the coffin and crying blood. This was interpreted as an auspicious sign for the Dou clan. See *Hou Hanshu*, 69.2245, 2253.

37. *Shiji*, 28.1358; *Hanshu*, 25A.1194.

38. *Shiji*, 6.263.

39. *Shiji*, 6.273–74.

40. *Shiji*, 49.1971.

41. *Hou Hanshu*, 17.645.

42. *Guoyu*, 5.201 ("Lu yu xia"). For references to other versions of this story, see *Shiji*, 47.1912; *Hanshu*, 27.1419; *Kongzi jiayu*, 4.5b ("Bian wu"); *Shuoyuan jiaozheng*, 18.464 ("Bian wu").

43. *Shuihudi Qin mu zhujian*, 220.

44. See *Shizi*, 2.5a. Li Shizhen identifies *di yang* 地羊 "earth sheep" as a name for a dog. See *Bencao gangmu*, 50.43. Reference to demonic doglike creatures that reside in the earth appears in later literature. One of two Dunhuang manuscripts (S.6261) that contains part of a Six Dynasties demonography known as the *Baize jingguai tu* 白澤精怪圖 contains the following entry: "If you find a dog while digging up earth, its name is Ye 耶. It is not a harmful creature. Do not call it a demon but only marvel at it." See Li Ling (1993c), 487.

45. *Shuoyuan jiaozheng*, 18.465 ("Bian wu"). See also chapter 5, pp. 128–29.

46. Foucault (1966, rpt. 1994), 157.

47. See *Fengsu tongyi jiaoshi*, 428–29 ("yi wen"). See also *Shuyiji*, 2.13a.

48. *Liezi*, 8.7b–8a ("Shuo fu"); *Lunheng jiaoshi*, 20.265–66 ("Fu xu"); *Huainanzi*, 18.597 ("Ren jian"). The *Huainanzi* version of the story does not mention Confucius but an anonymous elder.

49. *Chunqiu Zuozhuan zhu*, pp. 1680, 1682 (Lord Ai, year 14). See also *Shiji*, 47.1942, 121.3115; *Bo wu jing yi yi*, 18–20. The event is the subject of a rhyme in the *Yilin*:

> The Lad Chu captured a *lin*,
> The *Chunqiu* made this (event) a first year.
> The "hidden" sage would soon meet his end,
> Father Confucius was grieved in his heart.

See *Yilin*, 2.7b, 4.3b. Another ballad was attributed to an eponymous Confucius and alleged to have been sung by him after identifying the unicorn:

> In the age of Tang (Yao) and Shun (Yu),
> the unicorn and phoenix roamed about.
> Now [the unicorn] has come untimely, what is it looking for?
> unicorn oh unicorn, my heart is in sorrow.

See *Xian Qin shi*, 2.26; *Han shi*, 11.316; and *Yuefu shi ji*, 83.1168 ("Za ge yao ci"). In European history the unicorn was occasionally credited with messianic properties. See Shepard (1930; rpt. 1996). The author's suggestion of a historical link between the unicorn as a symbol of the Messiah in the West and its occurrence as a portent for a sage in China (pp. 94–96) is completely unsubstantiated.

50. *Kong Congzi*, 2.4a ("Ji wen" 記 問). See also *Kongzi jiayu*, 4.8a ("Bian wu").

51. I have emended *zhao ren* 昭 人 in the Huang Hui edition to *ye ren* 野 人 as suggested in Beijing daxue lishi xi, *Lunheng zhu shi* 論衡注釋 (Beijing: Zhonghua, 1979), p. 1495 note 28.

52. *Lunheng jiaoshi*, 78.1079–80 ("Shi zhi").

53. On the ritual origins of a theory of authority through naming, see Lewis (1999), 31–35.

54. *Zhuangzi jishi*, 19.650–54 ("Da sheng"). Ying Shao quotes a work entitled

Guanzi shu 管子書 as the original source of the story. See *Fengsu tongyi jiaoshi*, 9.328 ("Guai shen"). On the identification of the *weiyi*, see also Uehara Jundō (1954).

55. On the *yu* "spit-sand," see chapter 6, note 51.

56. *Mawangdui Han mu boshu*, vol. 4, 128–29 (columns 67–69); tr. Harper (1998), 370–71. For other entries involving the "spit-sand," see *Mawangdui Han mu boshu*, vol. 4, 127 (columns 58, 60), 128 (columns 61, 66).

57. *Guanzi jiaoshi* 39 ("Shui di"), 14.351.

58. *Lunyu zhushu*, 7.7a ("Shu er").

59. The verb *yu* has the connotation of an argumentative exposition. The *Shuowen* states: "To speak in a straightforward manner is called *yan*; to discuss problematic things is called *yu*" (*zhi yan yue yan, lun nan yue yu* 直言曰言, 論難曰語). See *Shuowen jiezi zhu*, 3A.7a.

60. The term is used in Campany (1996), 127. For later interpretations of *Lunyu* VII.21, see Nakamura Kazumoto (1992), 1–4.

61. *Fengsu tongyi jiaoshi*, 9.325 ("Guai shen"). For a translation of this chapter, see Nylan (1982), 519–52.

62. *Fengsu tongyi jiaoshi*, 9.353–54, 9.360–61.

63. *Fengsu tongyi jiaoshi*, 9.350.

64. Campany (1996), 142, 335–340.

65. *Shuowen jiezi zhu*, 10A.26b, 4A.33a, 4A.56a. For another example, see *Shuowen jiezi zhu*, 9B.43b.

66. *Shuowen jiezi zhu*, 4A.43a.

67. *Zuozhuan zhu*, p. 1405 (Lord Zhao, year 19).

68. This has been suggested recently by Yuri Pines. See Pines (1997), 38. Sima Qian notes Confucius's respect for Zi Chan. See *Shiji*, 67.2186.

69. *Zuozhuan zhu*, p. 334 (Lord Xi, year 10), p. 487 (Lord Xi, year 31); *Lunyu zhushu*, 2.10a ("Wei zheng" 爲政).

70. *Shuoyuan jiaozheng*, 18.467–69 ("Bian wu"); *Taiping yulan*, 892.7a–b, 827.3a. For the *bo* as a beast resembling a horse with strong teeth devouring tigers and leopards, see *Shuowen jiezi zhu*, 10A.18a.

71. *Chunqiu Zuozhuan zhu*, pp. 1454, 1459–60 (Lord Zhao, year 25).

72. *Bencao gangmu*, 49.5. See also Read (1932), no. 296. For a survey of textual references to the *quyu*, see *Gujin tushu jicheng*, vol. 52, 63451–54.

73. *Shanhaijing jiaozhu*, 5.162, 5.171. According to Yuan Ke it is not plausible that mount Heng refers to the southern peak suggested in Guo Pu's commentary.

74. *Huainanzi*, 1.20 ("Yuan dao"); *Shuowen jiezi zhu*, 4A.53a; *Zhouli zhushu*, 39.5b; and *Liezi*, 5.7a–8a ("Tang wen"). The observation is repeated in Su Shi's 蘇軾 (1036–1101) *Ge wu cu tan*, 1.12.

75. See Tan Qixiang (1987), vol. 1, maps 17–18, 24–25, 26–27, 35–36.

76. The children's ditty recurs frequently as a genre of prediction or explanation of anomalous events. See for instance *Guoyu*, 8.299 ("Jin yu"); *Hanshu*, 97B.3999; *Hou Hanshu*, "zhi," 13.3281, 3282, 3283, 3284, 3285. This was related to the perception of chil-

dren as agents empowered with magical or shamanic powers. See *Lunheng jiaoshi*, 65.943–44 ("Ding gui"), 78.1082 ("Shi zhi"). Another format for the communication of portents were the accounts of madmen. See *Bao Puzi nei pian jiaoshi*, 2.22 ("Lun xian").

77. Read 甫 for 父 (indication of style or name). Zhou is the name of Duke Zhao. Song is the crown prince in Lu who becomes Duke Ding 定 (509–495 B.C.E.).

78. The ballad is quoted in *Hanshu*, 27.1394. See also *Hanshu*, 27.1414, 36.1937; *Chunqiu fanlu*, 4.90 ("Wang dao" 王道), 6.146 ("Er duan" 二端); *Yuefu shi ji*, 88.1232 ("Za ge yao ci"); *Xian Qin shi*, 3.37; *Hou Hanshu*, 43.1480.

79. *Gongyang zhuan*, 24.5b. See also *Bo wu jing yi yi*, 40–41.

80. *Gongyang zhuan*, 28.7a.

81. *Hanshu*, 27.1414.

82. *Lunheng jiaoshi*, 10.100–101 ("Ou hui"). See also *Lunheng jiaoshi*, 18.214–15 ("Yi xu" 異虛).

83. *Chunqiu kao yi you* in *Weishu jicheng*, 790; *Chunqiu wen yao gou* 春秋文曜鉤 in *Weishu jicheng*, 677.

84. *Li ji ming zheng* in *Weishu jicheng*, 512; *Yue ji yao jia* in *Weishu jicheng*, 551.

85. *Hou Hanshu*, 43.1480. The same argument, with reference to the nesting mynahs, had already been formulated by Lu Jia. See *Xinyu*, 11.155 ("Ming jie").

86. *Shuihudi Qin mu zhujian*, 215 (slip 49), 213 (slips 31–33), 215 (slip 47), 215 (slip 33), 215 (slip 35); tr. Harper (1996), 250 no. 66, 246 no. 25, 249 no. 54, 249 no. 52, 250 no. 64.

87. *Hanshu*, 27.1396. Another anecdote accounts how an imperial combine obstructed a wild bear that had broken out of its cage during a staged animal fight, thus stopping it from getting at the throne of Emperor Yuan. See *Hanshu*, 97B.4005. See also Zhang Maoxian's 張茂先 (=Zhang Hua) "Nü shi zhen" 女史箴 in *Wenxuan*, 56.2404. For imagery of bears gathering inside palace gardens, see also *Chuci*, 16.23a ("Min ming" 愍命).

88. *Hanshu*, 27.1411, 27.1416, 36.1964, 63.2766, 83.3405, 85.3478, 89.3632. Compare similar imagery in one of the Nine Songs ("The Lady of the Xiang" 湘夫人). See *Chuci*, 2.10a; *Qu Yuan ji jiaozhu*, 222, 225 notes 1 and 2. The Song scholar Wang Kui 王逵 (991–1072 C.E.) gave a biological explanation for the difference between domestic, "inner sphere" animals and wild, "outer sphere" species. He argued that the difference between domestic birds (chickens, geese, and ducks) and their inability to fly, and wild, flying avians depended on whether the plumage grows inside or outside the egg. See *Li hai ji*, p. 14 ("Shu wu lei" 庶物類).

89. For pigs running loose, see *Hanshu*, 27.1436, 63.2757. See also *Taixuan jing*, 3.11b. For snakes entering the capital, see *Hanshu*, 27.1468, referring to *Zuozhuan zhu*, p. 616 (Lord Wen, year 16). For dancing rats, see *Hanshu*, 27.1374, 63.2757, 63.2762, 68.2956. For rats nesting in trees, see *Hanshu*, 27.1374, 97B.3979. See also *Soushenji*, 6.46, 6.47.

90. For singing ravens, see *Yilin*, 2.14b, 14.22a. For fighting crows and magpies, see *Hanshu*, 27.1415 (80 B.C.E.). This case is elaborated in *Soushenji*, 6.45. For the owl story, see *Yanzi chunqiu jishi*, 6.375–76. For the owl as a bad augury, see *Mao shi zhengyi*, 7A.11b (Mao 141, "Mu men" 墓門, owls perching on trees at the gates to a tomb), 8B.1b (Mao 155, "Zhi xiao" 鴟鴞, as image for political slander), 18E.9a (Mao 264, "Zhan ang" 瞻卬,

clever women interfering in government are compared to owls), 20A.20a (Mao 299, "Pan shui" 泮水, barbarian tribes compared to owls); *Chuci*, 11.3a ("Xi shi" 惜誓), 13.12b ("Miu jian" 謬諫); *Taixuan jing*, 5.5b; *Mu Tianzi zhuan*, 5.5a; and *Shiji*, 28.1361, 84.2493. For beliefs associated with owls in later times, see Eberhard (1968), 155, 159, 161–62.

91. *Shuihudi Qin mu zhujian*, 213 (slips 59–60), 212 (slips 52–53); tr. Harper (1996), 245 nos. 11 and 15.

92. *Zhouli zhushu*, 37.5b (*zhezushi* 蜇族氏); *Zhouli zhengyi*, 70.2931–32. The exact mantic technique referred to here remains unclear.

93. *Zuozhuan zhu*, p. 244 (Lord Zhuang, year 29; *fan wu bu wei zai bu shu* 凡物不爲災不書). For a similar comment on another cockroach plague, see *Zuozhuan zhu*, p. 18 (Lord Yin, year 1).

94. *Gongyang zhuan*, 9.3a.

95. *Gongyang zhuan*, 7.19b, 8.1b; *Chunqiu zhu*, p. 208 (Lord Zhuang, year 18).

96. *Hou Hanshu*, 30B.1080.

97. Lewis (1999), 297–302.

98. *Xunzi jijie*, 17.316 ("Tian lun"). According to Wang Xianqian 王先謙 (1842–1918), *shu* refers to the Six Classics. See also *Han shi waizhuan jishi*, 2.39.

99. *Huainanzi*, 16.531 ("Shuo shan").

100. *Liji zhushu*, 35.16a ("Shao yi" 少儀). Although dogs were certainly eaten in Warring States and Han times, I have not been able to trace the generic term "foodstuff dogs" (*shi quan* 食犬) prior to a Tang subcommentary by Jia Gongyan in the *Zhouli*. See *Zhouli zhushu*, 36.10b. Discussions of the socioeconomic role of the dog in early China include Gai Shanlin (1989) and Wang Lihua (1992).

101. On this theme, see also David G. White (1991), 12; and Elisséeff (1993), 24–25.

102. *Shuowen jiezi zhu*, 10A.29b.

103. *Fengsu tongyi jiaoshi*, 8.314 ("Si dian"). Xu Shen's paronomastic gloss for the graph *gou* 狗 points at the guardian function of the dog: "Confucius said, *gou* 狗 means *kou* 叩 'to knock.' (The dog) butts the *qi* and barks in order to guard." See *Shuowen jiezi zhu*, 10A.26b. A Mawangdui medical text contains a prescription against intrusion by barking dogs: "When there is a dog that likes to bark in the courtyard and gate, daub mud on the well in a rectangular band five *chi* long." See *Zajin fang* 雜禁方, in Harper (1998), 423.

104. *Shuihudi Qin mu zhujian*, 212 (slips 47–49); tr. Harper (1996), 245 no. 9.

105. *Fengsu tongyi jiaoshi*, 9.348–49.

106. *Fengsu tongyi jiaoshi*, 9.349. The *Hanshu* records a headless white dog resembling a man under its neck and wearing a "Square Mountain Cap." See *Hanshu*, 63.2766.

107. *Fengsu tongyi jiaoshi*, 9.353.

108. *Hanshu*, 27.1399; *Soushenji*, 6.48. See also De Groot (1892–1910; rpt. 1964), vol. 4, 184. Another story tells about a dog entering the central courtyard of a household to devour several of the household geese. See *Hanshu*, 84.3438.

109. See commentaries by Zheng Sinong et al. in *Zhouli zhushu*, 32.15a, 36.10a. According to Zheng Xuan the victim could be either a dog or a sheep. See his commen-

tary in *Yili zhushu*, 24.4b ("Pin li" 聘禮). See also *Shuowen jiezi zhu*, 14A.51b. For the sacrifice of a ram to the road, see *Mao shi zhengyi*, 17A.16a (Mao 245, "Sheng min" 生民). Erkes has suggested that the etymology of the 軷 graph consists of the chariot 車 radical and 犮, a dog on a leash. See Erkes (1944a), 218. Another term for the road sacrifice was *rang* 禳. See *Yili zhushu*, 23.5a ("Pin li"). See further Schindler (1924), 649–56; Ling Chunsheng (1957), 14–16; Bilsky (1975), 54–55; and Höllman (1983), 164–67.

110. *Wangshan Chu jian*, p. 70, slip 28; p. 78, slip 119; *Baoshan Chu jian*, p. 33, slips 208, 210; p. 34, slip 219; p. 36, slip 233. See also Chen Wei (1996), 167.

111. *Liji zhushu*, 4.12a ("Qu li xia"). Commentators note that white dog skin is used as leaving one's state can be likened to a funeral.

112. *Shiji*, 5.184, 14.573, 28.1360.See also *Hanshu*, 25A.1196; *Fengsu tongyi jiaoshi*, 8.314 ("Si dian"). *Gu* refers to a demonic concoction prepared from bugs to poison or sicken the victim. During the *wu si* 五祀 sacrifices, a dog was used to sacrifice to the door. See *Bohutong shu zheng*, 2.81 ("Wu si"). Dog feces was also used as a demonifuge. See *Han Feizi jishi*, 10.579 ("Nei chu shuo xia"); *Shuihudi Qin mu zhujian*, 213, 215.

113. *Hou Hanshu*, 90.2980. A mural at the door of a tomb in Liaoyang 遼陽 (Liaoning, *Sanguo* period) shows a white dog on a leash. See Sugimoto Kenji (1979), 249. Similar dog symbolism is known from Greek and Roman antiquity. The Romans held annual apotropaic sacrifices of red dogs at the "Augurium Canarium." Dog sacrifice was also a common practice among the Greeks where the dog figured prominently as a guardian of the underworld. See Stoltz (1937), 10–12, 31–39; and Mainoldi (1984), 37–51, 68–80.

114. *Xinlun*, 25b.

115. *Zhouli zhushu*, 27.8b–10a.

116. *Hanshu*, 6.174, 25A.1219; *Shiji*, 28.1387, 130.3300. See also *Hanshu*, 62.2720, 62.2722 note 5, 88.3589; *Hou Hanshu*, 40A.1325. Stephen Durrant suggests that, in Sima Qian's project, the white unicorn should be seen as a signal for the appearance of a new uncrowned king; i.e., Sima Qian himself, in the footsteps of Confucius. See Durrant (1995), 7, 12.

117. *Shiji*, 12.461, 28.1389; *Hanshu*, 25A.1221.

118. See *Shiji*, 4.120; *Hanshu*, 56.2500, 77.3252; *Shangshu da zhuan*, 2.55 ("Da shi"); *Lunheng jiaoshi*, 12.124 ("Chu bin" 初稟); *Hou Hanshu*, 20.735, 80A.2607 note 12; *Shangshu zhong hou* in *Weishu jicheng*, 412, 413; *Shangshu xuan ji ling* 尚書璇璣鈴 in *Weishu jicheng*, 377 (this text interprets the feetless and wingless fish as an image of tyrant Zhou who was weakened and easy to attack); *Luo shu ling zhun ting* 洛書靈準聽 in *Weishu jicheng*, 1259; and *Songshu*, 29.852.

119. An event documented in the *Zuozhuan* in the year corresponding to 644 B.C.E. See *Chunqiu Zuozhuan zhu*, pp. 368–69 (Lord Xi, year 16). See also *Gongyang zhuan*, 11.13a–14a, *Guliang zhuan*, 8.14b–15a; *Hanshu*, 27.1442–43, 36.1937; *Shuowen jiezi zhu*, 4A.49b; *Yilin*, 1.6a; and *Kong Congzi*, 4.2a ("Gongsun Long" 公孫龍). According to an apocryphal text, the *yi* 鶂 was both hairy and feathered, born in the *yin* but belonging to *yang*. See *Chunqiu kao yi you* in *Weishu jicheng*, 783.

120. I follow Yan Shigu in interpreting this as Chinese garments (as opposed to barbarian hides).

121. *Hanshu*, 64B.2814–17.

122. *Hanshu*, 22.1068. See also *Hanshu*, 6.174; *Xi Han huiyao*, 29.302; and Kern (1996), 55–58. Kern notes the powerful liturgical expression of political legitimation contained in the white unicorn image and suggests that this hymn is the first passage to associate the color white, emblematic for the west in Han cosmology, with the unicorn.

123. For reference to the alighting pheasant, see *Shangshu zhengyi*, 10.8b ("Gaozong rong ri" 高宗肜日); *Shiji*, 3.103; *Zhushu jinian*, 1.16a. For its explicit association with barbarian submission, see *Shangshu da zhuan*, 1.47 ("Gaozong rong ri"). Elsewhere Jia Kui 賈逵 (fl. ca. 102 C.E.) explains the appearance of pentachromatic spirit birds on the palace grounds as a sign of barbarian submission, an event that prompted the emperor to order the composition of a "Spirit Bird Laudatur" ("Shen que song" 神雀頌). See *Hou Hanshu*, 36.1235.

124. See for instance *Hou Hanshu*, 86.2836.

125. *Hanshu*, 57B.2602. For the unicorn's horn as a symbol for the unified rule of the empire, see also *Chunqiu gan jing fu* in *Weishu jicheng*, 742.

126. For this image, see also *Hanshu*, 64A.2782–83 (note 3), where the expression *xu Yue* 畜越 "to domesticate the Yue" is explained by Li Qi 李奇 (fl. ca. 200 C.E.) as "in the same way people raise the six domestic animals."

127. For the identification of the distant periphery as a demonic region, see also *Hanshu*, 81.3335, where Kuang Heng 匡衡 (d. ca. 30 B.C.E.) refers to Shang king Tang's "transformation of foreign customs and comforting of the Demon Regions 鬼方." Ying Shao comments that *guifang* refers to far-off regions. See further *Yilin*, 14.15a; *Hou Hanshu*, 40B.1380; and Seiwert (1983), 325–26. On the Shang use of the term *fang* as a boundary marker distinguishing alien polities from the central heartland, see Wang (2000), 26–28. *Guifang* was also the name of a specific tribe against which Wu Ding had campaigned. See *Zhouyi zhengyi*, 6.22a; *Zhushu jinian*, 1.16a; *Hou Hanshu*, 90.2990; Wang Guowei, "Guifang Kunyi Xianyun kao" 鬼方昆夷玁狁考, in Wang Guowei (1923), 13.1b–5a; Ikeda Suetoshi (1957), 26; and Nicola Di Cosmo, "The Northern Frontier in Pre-Imperial China," in Loewe and Shaughnessy (1999), 919.

128. *Lunheng jiaoshi*, 50.721 ("Jiang rui")

129. *Lunheng jiaoshi*, 50.722–23 ("Jiang rui").

130. *Lunheng jiaoshi*, 50.725–26 ("Jiang rui").

131. *Lunheng jiaoshi*, 50.726–29, 50.729–32 ("Jiang rui").

132. *Lunheng jiaoshi*, 50.738–39 ("Jiang rui").

133. *Lunheng jiaoshi*, 52.761–62 ("Shi ying").

134. *Lunheng jiaoshi*, 50.737 ("Jiang rui").

Conclusion

1. *Les Essais*, "Apologie de Raimond Sebond"; tr. M. A. Screech, *The Complete Essays: Michel de Montaigne* (London: Penguin, 1991), p. 586.

2. Descola, "Constructing Natures," in Descola and Pálsson (1996), 85–86.

3. Müller-Karpe describes animals as the "augenfällige Verkörperung der natürlichen Umwelt . . . in der übernatürliche Mächte und Harmonien wirksam gesehen werden." See Müller-Karpe (1983), 4.

4. Tambiah (1985), 8–9.

BIBLIOGRAPHY

Primary Sources

Bao Puzi nei pian jiaoshi 抱朴子内篇校釋. Compiled by Ge Hong 葛洪 (ca. 280–342 C.E.). Annotated by Wang Ming 王明. Beijing: Zhonghua, 1985.

Baoshan Chu jian 包山楚簡. Hubei sheng Jing-Sha tielu kaogudui (eds.). Hubei: Wenwu, 1991.

Bencao gangmu 本草綱目. Compiled by Li Shizhen 李時珍 (1518–1593). Hong Kong: Shangwu, 1967, 6 vols.

Bian wu xiaozhi 辨物小志. Compiled by Chen Jiang 陳絳 (fl. ca. 1530). *Congshu jicheng* ed. (Shanghai: Shangwu, 1935–40).

Bohutong shu zheng 白虎通疏證. Compiled by Ban Gu 班固 (32–92 C.E.) et al., annotated by Wu Zeyu 吳則虞. Beijing: Zhonghua, 1994.

Boshu Laozi jiaozhu 帛書老子校注. Edited by Gao Ming 高明. Beijing: Zhonghua, 1996.

"Boshu *Xici* shiwen" 帛書繫辭釋文. Transcribed by Chen Songchang 陳松長 in Chen Guying 陳鼓應 ed., *Daojia wenhua yanjiu* 道家文化研究 3 (Mawangdui special issue; Shanghai: Guji, 1993), 417–23.

Boshu Zhouyi jiaoshi 帛書周易校釋. Edited by Deng Qiubo 鄧球伯. Changsha: Hunan chubanshe, 1996 (2d ed.).

Bo wu jing yi yi 駁五經異義. Compiled by Zheng Xuan 鄭玄 (127–200 C.E.). *Congshu jicheng* ed.

Bowuzhi 博物志. Attributed to Zhang Hua 張華 (232–300 C.E.). *Sibu beiyao* ed.

Cai Shi yueling wen da 蔡氏月令問答. Attributed to Cai Yong 蔡邕 (133–192 C.E.), in *Longxi jingshe congshu* 龍溪精舍叢書.

Cai Shi yueling zhangju 蔡氏月令章句. Attributed to Cai Yong, edited by Zang Yong 臧庸 (1799), in *Bai jing tang congshu* 拜經堂叢書.

Cai zhonglang ji 蔡中郎集. By Cai Yong. *Sibu beiyao* edition.

Chu xue ji 初學記. Edited by Xu Jian 徐堅 (659–729 C.E.). Beijing: Zhonghua, 1962.

Chuci 楚辭. *Sibu beiyao* edition.

Chunqiu fanlu jinzhu jinyi 春秋繁露今註今譯. Annotated by Lai Yanyuan 賴炎元. Taipei: Taiwan shangwu, 1992.

Chunqiu Gongyang zhuan zhushu 春秋公羊傳注疏. Annotated by Xu Yan 徐彥 (Tang dynasty). In *Shisanjing zhushu* 十三經注疏 (collated by Ruan Yuan 阮元 [1764–1849]; rpt. Taizhong: Landeng, n.d.), vol. 7.

Chunqiu Guliang zhuan zhushu 春秋穀梁傳注疏. Annotated by Yang Shixun 楊士勛 (Tang dynasty). In *Shisanjing zhushu*, vol. 7.

Chunqiu kao yi you 春秋考異郵 in *Gu weishu; Weishu jicheng.*

Chunqiu yuanming bao 春秋元命包 in *Gu weishu; Weishu jicheng.*

Chunqiu Zuozhuan zhengyi 春秋左傳正義. Annotated by Du Yu 杜預 (222–284 C.E.). In *Shisanjing zhushu*, vol. 6.

Chunqiu Zuozhuan zhu 春秋左傳注. Annotated by Yang Bojun 楊伯峻. Beijing: Zhonghua, 1995.

Da Dai Liji 大戴禮記. Attributed to Dai De 戴德 (fl. ca. 72 B.C.E.). In *Han Wei congshu* (Shanghai: Shangwu, 1925), vol. 1.

Daodejing jiangyi 道德經講義. Taipei: Sanmin, 1980.

Dong guan Han ji 東觀漢記. Compiled by Liu Zhen 劉珍 (second cent. C.E.) et al. *Sibu beiyao* ed.

Dong Han huiyao 東漢會要. Compiled by Xu Tianlin 徐天麟 (fl. ca. 1205 C.E.). Shanghai: Shanghai guji, 1978.

Duduan 獨斷. Compiled by Cai Yong. In *Han Wei congshu*, vol. 2.

Ersanzi wen 二三子問. Transcribed by Chen Songchang 陳松長 and Liao Mingchun 廖名春, in *Daojia wenhua yanjiu* 3 (Shanghai: Guji, 1993), 424–28.

Erya yi 爾雅翼. Compiled by Luo Yuan 羅願 (1136–1184 C.E.). *Congshu jicheng* ed.

Erya zhushu 爾雅注疏. Annotated by Xing Bing 邢昺 (932–1010 C.E.). In *Shisanjing zhushu*, vol. 8.

Fan Shengzhi shu jin shi 氾勝之書今釋. Compiled late first cent. B.C.E. Annotated by Shi Shenghan 石聲漢. Beijing: Kexue, 1974.

Fangyan jianshu 方言箋疏. Attributed to Yang Xiong 揚雄 (53 B.C.E.–18 C.E.), compiled by Qian Yi 錢繹 (fl. ca. 1851), annotated by Li Fashun 李發舜 and Huang Jianzhong 黃建中. Beijing: Zhonghua, 1991.

Fengsu tongyi jiaoshi 風俗通義校釋. By Ying Shao 應劭 (ca. 140–204 C.E.), annotated by Wu Shuping 吳樹平. Tianjin: Renmin, 1980.

Fuzi 傅子. Attributed to Fu Xuan 傅玄 (217–278 C.E.). *Sibu congkan* ed.

Ge wu cu tan 格物麤談. Compiled by Su Shi 蘇軾 (1036–1101 C.E.). *Congshu jicheng* ed.

Gujin tushu jicheng 古今圖書集成. Compiled by Chen Menglei 陳夢雷 et al. (1726–28); section "Qinchong dian" 禽蟲典 (vols. 52, 53). Chengdu: Zhonghua, 1985.

Gujin zhu 古今注. Attributed to Cui Bao 崔豹 (fl. 290–306 C.E.). Shanghai: Shangwu, 1956.

Gu weishu 古微書. Compiled by Sun Jue 孫瑴 (fl. ca. 1640). *Congshu jicheng* ed.

Guanyinzi 關尹子. *Sibu beiyao* edition.

Guanzi jiaoshi 管子校釋. Annotated by Yan Changyao 顏昌嶢 (1868–1944). Changsha: Yuelu shushe, 1996.

Guangya 廣雅. Compiled by Zhang Yi 張揖 (ca. 230 C.E.). *Congshu jicheng* ed.

Guodian Chu mu zhujian 郭店楚墓竹簡. Edited by the Jingmenshi bowuguan. Beijing: Wenwu, 1998.

Guoyu 國語. Shanghai: Guji, 1978.

Han Feizi jishi 韓非子集釋. Attributed to Han Fei 韓非 (d. 233 B.C.E.). Annotated by Chen Qiyou 陳奇猷. Gaoxiong: Fuwen, 1991.

Han guan yi 漢官儀. Attributed to Ying Shao. *Sibu beiyao* ed.

Han jiu yi 漢舊義. Collated by Wei Hong 衛宏 (first cent. C.E.). *Sibu beiyao* ed.

Han shi waizhuan jishi 韓詩外傳集釋. Attributed to Han Ying 韓嬰 (fl. 150 B.C.E.), annotated by Xu Weiyu 許維遹. Beijing: Zhonghua, 1980.

Hanshu 漢書. Compiled by Ban Gu. Beijing: Zhonghua, 1962.

Heguanzi 鶡冠子. *Congshu jicheng* edition.

Hou Hanshu 後漢書. Compiled by Fan Ye 范曄 (398–445 C.E.) et al. Beijing: Zhonghua, 1965.

Hu yuan 虎苑. Compiled by Wang Zhideng 王稚登 (1525–1612). In *Guang baichuan xuehai* 廣百川學海, vol. 6. Taipei: Xinxing, 1970.

Huayang guo zhi jiaozhu 華陽國志校注. Compiled by Chang Qu 常璩 (fl. ca. 350 C.E.). Annotated by Liu Lin 劉琳. Chengdu: Ba Shu shushe, 1984.

Huainanzi honglie jijie 淮南子鴻烈集解. Edited by Liu Wendian 劉文典. Taipei: Wenshizhe, 1992.

Huangdi neijing ling shu 黄帝内經靈樞. Edited by Huang Yizhou 黄以周 (1828–1899), in *Er shi er zi* 二十二子 (Zhejiang shuju, 1875–1909; rpt. Shanghai: Guji, 1986).

Huangdi neijing suwen 黄帝内經素問. Edited by Wang Bing 王冰 (ca. 710–804 C.E.). Shanghai: Shangwu, 1955.

Huang shi gong san lüe jinzhu jinyi 黄石公三略今註今譯. Edited by Wei Rulin 魏汝霖. Taipei: Taiwan shangwu, 1984.

Ji jiu pian 急就篇. Attributed to Shi You 史游 (ca. 48–33 B.C.E.). *Congshu jicheng* ed.

Jiaozheng san fu huang tu 校正三輔黄圖. Anon., Six Dynasties. Shanghai: Gudian wenxue, 1958.

Jinshu 晉書. Compiled by Fang Xuanling 房玄齡 (578–648 C.E.) et al. Beijing: Zhonghua, 1974.

Jinwen Shangshu kaozheng 今文尚書考證. Compiled by Pi Xirui 皮錫瑞 (1850–1908). Beijing: Zhonghua, 1989.

Jing fa 經法. Annotated by Mawangdui Han mu boshu zhengli xiaozu 馬王堆漢墓帛書整理小組. Beijing: Wenwu, 1976.

Jing Shi Yi zhuan 京氏易傳. Attributed to Jing Fang 京房 (77–37 B.C.E.). *Sibu congkan* ed.

Jiu Tangshu 舊唐書. Compiled by Liu Xu 劉煦 (887–946 C.E.) et al. Beijing: Zhonghua, 1975.

Kaogong ji niaoshou chongyu shi 考工記鳥獸蟲魚釋. Compiled by Chen Zongqi 陳宗起 (fl. ca. 1885). In *Yang zhiju jin cun gao* 養志居僅存稿 (Taipei: Yiwen yinshuguan, 1965), vol. 2.

Kong Congzi 孔叢子. Attributed to Kong Fu 孔鮒 (Han). *Sibu beiyao* ed.

Kongzi jiayu 孔子家語. Annotated by Wang Su 王肅 (195–256 C.E.). *Sibu beiyao* ed.

Li hai ji 蠡海集. Compiled by Wang Kui 王逵 (991–1072 C.E.). *Congshu jicheng* ed.

Li han wen jia 禮含文嘉 in *Gu weishu*; *Weishu jicheng*.

Liji zhushu 禮記注疏. Annotated by Kong Yingda 孔穎達 (574–648 C.E.). In *Shisanjing zhushu*, vol. 5.

Li shi 隸釋. Compiled by Hong Gua 洪适 (fl. ca. 1166 C.E.). Tokyo: Kyokutō shoten, 1966.

Liang Han bowen 兩漢博聞. Compiled by Yang Kan 楊侃 (fl. ca. 1017 C.E.). *Congshu jicheng* ed.

Lienü zhuan 列女傳. Attributed to Liu Xiang 劉向 (ca. 77-6 B.C.E.). *Sibu beiyao* ed.

Liexian zhuan 列仙傳. Attributed to Liu Xiang. See Kaltenmark (1953).

Liezi 列子. *Sibu beiyao* ed.

Lu shi 路史. Compiled by Luo Bi 羅泌 (d. ca. 1176 C.E.). *Congshu jicheng* ed.

Lüshi chunqiu jiaoshi 呂氏春秋校釋. Compiled under the auspices of Lü Buwei 呂不韋 (290-235 B.C.E.). Annotated by Chen Qiyou 陳奇猷. Shanghai: Xuelin, 1995.

Lunheng jiaoshi 論衡校釋. Edited by Huang Hui 黃暉, with commentary by Liu Pansui 劉盼遂. Beijing: Zhonghua, 1990.

Lunyu zhushu 論語注疏. Annotated by Xing Bing 邢昺 (932-1010 C.E.). In *Shisanjing zhushu*, vol. 8.

Mawangdui Han mu boshu 馬王堆漢墓帛書. Edited by Mawangdui Han mu boshu zhengli xiaozu, 3 vols. Beijing: Wenwu, 1980-85.

Mao shi caomu niaoshou chongyu shu 毛詩草木鳥獸蟲魚疏. By Lu Ji 陸璣 (ca. 222-280 C.E.). *Congshu jicheng* ed.

Mao shi ming wu jie 毛詩名物解. Compiled by Cai Bian 蔡卞 (1058-1117 C.E.). *Tongzhi tang jing jie* 通志堂經解 ed., rpt. 1873.

Mao shi zhengyi 毛詩正義. Annotated by Kong Yingda et al. In *Shisanjing zhushu*, vol. 2.

Mengzi zhushu 孟子注疏. In *Shisanjing zhushu*, vol. 8.

Mozi jiaozhu 墨子校注. Annotated by Wu Yujiang 吳毓江 and Sun Qizhi 孫啓治. Beijing: Zhonghua, 1993.

Mu Tianzi zhuan 穆天子傳. Attributed to Guo Pu 郭璞 (276-324 C.E.). *Sibu beiyao* ed.

Pi ya 埤雅. Compiled by Lu Dian 陸佃 (1042-1102 C.E.). *Congshu jicheng* ed.

Qianfu lun 潛夫論. Compiled by Wang Fu 王符 (90-165 C.E.). Annotated by Wang Jipei 汪繼培 (b. 1775 C.E.). Shanghai: Guji, 1978.

Qimin yaoshu 齊民要術. Compiled by Jia Sixie 賈思勰 (ca. 535 C.E.), annotated by Shi Shenghan 石聲漢. Beijing: Kexue, 1957.

[*Shi Kuang*] *Qinjing* 禽經. Attributed to Shi Kuang 師曠 (6th cent. B.C.E.), apocryphal, surviving with commentary by Zhang Hua. In *Baichuan xuehai* 百川學海, vol. 7. Taipei: Xinxing, 1969.

Qu Yuan ji jiaozhu 屈原集校注. Annotated by Jin Kaicheng 金開誠 et al. Beijing: Zhonghua, 1996.

Quan Han fu 全漢賦. Collated by Fei Zhengang 費振剛 et al. Beijing: Beijing daxue, 1997.

Quan Han Sanguo Jin Nanbeichao shi 全漢三國晉南北朝詩. Edited by Ding Fubao 丁福保. Shanghai: Zhonghua, 1959, 2 vols.

Quan shanggu Sandai Qin Han Sanguo Liuchao wen 全上古三代秦漢三國六朝文. Compiled by Yan Kejun 嚴可均 (1765-1837). Beijing: Zhonghua, 1965.

Ran xi zhi 然犀志. Compiled by Li Tiaoyuan 李調元 (1734-1803). *Congshu jicheng* ed.

Ru fan 蠕範. Compiled by Li Yuan 李元 (1816). *Congshu jicheng* ed.

Sanguo zhi 三國志. Compiled by Chen Shou 陳壽 (233-297 C.E.). Beijing: Zhonghua, 1959.

Shanhaijing jiaozhu 山海經校注. Annotated by Yuan Ke 袁珂. Shanghai: Guji, 1980.

Shang jun shu jiaoshi 商君書校釋. Annotated by Chen Qitian 陳啓天. Shanghai: Shangwu, 1935.

Shangshu da zhuan 尚書大傳. Attributed to Fu Sheng 伏勝 (fl. 250–175 B.C.E.), commentary by Zheng Xuan, annotated by Chen Shouqi 陳壽祺 (1771–1834). *Congshu jicheng* ed.

Shangshu zhengyi 尚書正義. Annotated by Kong Yingda et al. In *Shisanjing zhushu*, vol. 1.

Shangshu zhong hou 尚書中侯 in *Gu weishu; Weishu jicheng.*

Shenzi 申子. Text fragments in H. G. Creel, *Shen Pu-Hai. A Chinese Political Philosopher of the Fourth Century B.C.* Chicago: University of Chicago Press, 1974.

Shiji 史記. Begun by Sima Tan 司馬談 (d. 112 B.C.E.), primarily composed by Sima Qian 司馬遷 (ca. 145– ca. 86 B.C.E.). Beijing: Zhonghua, 1959.

Shi ji zhuan 詩集傳. Compiled by Zhu Xi 朱熹 (1130–1200 C.E.). Beijing: Wenxue guji, 1955.

Shiming 釋名. Compiled by Liu Xi 劉熙 (d. ca. 219 C.E.). In *Gujin yishi* 古今逸史, fasc. 3. Shanghai: Shangwu, 1937.

Shiyiji 拾遺記. Attributed to Wang Jia 王嘉 (fl. 335–386 C.E.). *Han Wei congshu* ed.

Shi zhuan ming wu jilan 詩傳名物集覽. Compiled by Chen Dazhang 陳大章 (fl. ca. 1700). *Congshu jicheng* ed.

Shizi 尸子. *Sibu beiyao* ed.

Shoujing 獸經. Compiled by Huang Xingzeng 黃省曾 (1490–1540). *Congshu jicheng* ed.

Shuyiji 述異記. Attributed to Ren Fang 任昉 (460–508 C.E.). In *Han Wei congshu*, vol. 7.

Shuihudi Qin mu zhujian 睡虎地秦墓竹簡. Edited by Shuihudi Qin mu zhujian zhengli xiaozu. Beijing: Wenwu, 1991.

Shuijing zhu jiao 水經注校. Annotated by Wang Guowei 王國維. Shanghai: Shanghai renmin, 1984.

Shuowen jiezi zhu 說文解字注. Annotated by Duan Yucai 段玉裁 (1735–1815). Taipei: Yiwen, 1965.

Shuoyuan jiaozheng 說苑校證. Attributed to Liu Xiang, annotated by Xiang Zonglu 向宗魯. Beijing: Zhonghua, 1987.

Sima Fa 司馬法 (compiled fourth cent. B.C.E.). *Sibu beiyao* edition.

Si shi zuan yao jiaoshi 四時纂要校釋. Attributed to Han E 韓鄂 (ca. 750 C.E.), edited by Miao Qiyu 繆啓愉. Beijing: Nongye chubanshe, 1981.

Songshi 宋史. Compiled by Ouyang Xuan 歐陽玄 (1274–1358 C.E.). Beijing: Zhonghua, 1977.

Songshu 宋書. Compiled by Shen Yue 沈約 (441–513 C.E.). Beijing: Zhonghua, 1974.

Soushenji 搜神記. Compiled by Gan Bao 干寶 (fl. 317–350 C.E.). Shanghai: Shangwu, 1957.

Suishu 隨書. Compiled by Wei Zheng 魏徵 (580–643 C.E.) et al. Beijing: Zhonghua, 1973.

Sunzi bingfa jiaoshi 孫子兵法校釋. Edited by Chen Qitian 陳啓天. Shanghai: Zhonghua, 1947.

Tai Gong liu tao jinzhu jinyi 太公六韜今註今譯. Annotated by Xu Peigen 徐培根. Taipei: Taiwan shangwu, 1993.

Taiping yulan 太平御覽. Compiled by Li Fang 李昉 (925–996 C.E.) et al. *Sibu congkan* ed.

Taixuan jing 太玄經. Attributed to Yang Xiong. *Sibu beiyao* ed.

Tang lü shu yi 唐律疏義. Compiled by Changsun Wuji 長孫無忌 (?-659 C.E.). Beijing: Zhonghua, 1983.

Wangshan Chu jian 望山楚簡. Edited by Hubei sheng wenwu kaogu yanjiusuo. Beijing: Zhonghua, 1995.

Weishu jicheng 緯書集成. Compiled by Yasui Kōzan 安居香山 and Nakamura Shōhachi 中村璋八. Shijiazhuang: Hebei renmin, 1994. Translation of *Jūshū isho shūsei* 重修緯書集成. Tokyo: Meitoku shuppansha, 1988.

Wenxuan 文選. Compiled by Xiao Tong 蕭統 (ca. 501-531 C.E.), commentary by Li Shan 李善 (Tang). Shanghai: Guji, 1986.

Wenzi 文子. *Sibu beiyao* edition.

Wu Yue chunqiu 吳越春秋. Annotated by Zhou Shengchun 周生春. Shanghai: Shanghai Guji, 1997.

Wu za zu 五雜俎. Compiled by Xie Zhaozhe 謝肇淛 (1567-1624). Beijing: Zhonghua, 1959.

Wuzi 吳子. Attributed to Wu Qi 吳起 (ca. 440 - ca. 361 B.C.E.). *Sibu beiyao* edition.

Xi Han huiyao 西漢會要. Compiled by Xu Tianlin 徐天麟 (fl. 1205 C.E.). Shanghai: Renmin, 1977.

Xijing zaji 西京雜紀. Attributed to Ge Hong. In *Gujin yishi* (Shanghai: Shangwu, 1937), fasc. 34.

Xian Qin Han Wei Jin Nanbei chao shi 先秦漢魏晉南北朝詩. Compiled by Lu Qinli 逯欽立 (1910-1973). Beijing: Zhonghua, 1983, 3 vols.

Xiaojing zhushu 孝經注疏. In *Shisanjing zhushu*, vol. 8.

Xinlun 新論. Attributed to Huan Tan 桓譚 (43 B.C.E.- 28 C.E.). *Sibu beiyao* ed.

Xinshu 新書. Compiled by Jia Yi 賈誼 (201-168 B.C.E.). *Sibu beiyao* ed.

Xin Tangshu 新唐書. Compiled by Ouyang Xiu 歐陽修 (1007-1072 C.E.), Song Qi 宋祁 (998-1061 C.E.) et al. Beijing: Zhonghua, 1975.

Xinxu xiang zhu 新序詳註. Attributed to Liu Xiang, annotated by Zhao Zhongyi 趙仲邑. Beijing: Zhonghua, 1997.

Xinyu jiaozhu 新語校注. Attributed to Lu Jia 陸賈 (third to second cent. B.C.E.), annotated by Wang Liqi 王利器. Beijing: Zhonghua, 1986.

Xunzi jijie 荀子集解. Annotated by Wang Xianqian 王先謙 (1842-1918). Beijing: Zhonghua, 1988.

Yantie lun jiaozhu 鹽鐵論校注. Compiled by Huan Kuan 桓寬 (first cent. B.C.E.), annotated by Wang Liqi 王利器. Shanghai: Gudian wenxue, 1958.

Yanzi chunqiu jishi 晏子春秋集釋. Annotated by Wu Zeyu 吳則虞. Beijing: Zhonghua, 1962.

Yang yu jing 養魚經. Compiled by Huang Xingzeng 黃省曾 (1490-1540). In *Guang baichuan xuehai*, vol. 6.

Yangzi fayan 揚子法言. Compiled by Yang Xiong. *Sibu beiyao* ed.

Yili zhushu 儀禮注疏. Annotated by Jia Gongyan 賈公彥 (fl. 650 C.E.). In *Shisanjing zhushu*, vol. 4.

Yilin 易林. Attributed to Jiao Gong 焦贛 (Eastern Han). *Sibu beiyao* ed.

Yi tong gua yan 易通卦驗 in *Gu weishu; Weishu jicheng.*

Yiwen leiju 藝文類聚. Compiled by Ouyang Xun 歐陽詢 (557-641 C.E.) et al. Kyoto: Chūbun, 1980, 2 vols.

Yi yu tu zan 異魚圖贊. Compiled by Yang Shen 楊慎 (1488-1559). *Congshu jicheng* ed.

Yi zhi yi 易之義. Transcribed by Chen Songchang 陳松長 and Liao Mingchun 廖名春 in Chen Guying 陳鼓應 (ed.), *Daojia wenhua yanjiu* 3 (Mawangdui special issue; Shanghai: Guji, 1993), 429-33.

Yi Zhoushu 逸周書. Annotated by Kong Chao 孔晁 (third cent. C.E.). *Sibu beiyao* ed.

Yinqueshan Han jian shiwen 銀雀山漢簡釋文. Edited by Wu Jiulong 吳九龍. Beijing: Wenwu, 1985.

Yinwan Han mu jiandu 尹灣漢墓簡牘. Edited by Lianyungangshi bowuguan and Zhongguo shehui kexueyuan jianbo yanjiu zhongxin. Beijing: Zhonghua, 1997.

Youyang zazu 酉陽雜俎. Compiled by Duan Chengshi 段成式 (803?-863 C.E.). Beijing: Zhonghua, 1981.

Yuhan shanfang ji yishu 玉函山房輯佚書. Compiled by Ma Guohan 馬國翰 (1794-1857). Changsha, 1883.

Yu (Wei) liaozi 尉繚子. In *Bai zi quan shu* 百子全書 (Shanghai: Jiangsu renmin, 1991), vol. 2.

Yuefu shi ji 樂府詩集. Compiled by Guo Maoqian 郭茂倩 (ca. 1150-1200 C.E.), 4 vols. Beijing: Zhonghua, 1979.

Yue jue shu 越絕書. Compiled first cent. C.E. *Sibu beiyao* ed.

Yueling qi-shi-er hou jijie 月令七十二侯集解. Compiled by Wu Cheng 吳澄 (1247-1331 C.E.). *Congshu jicheng* ed.

Yue xie tu zheng 樂叶圖徵 in *Gu weishu; Weishu jicheng.*

Yunmeng Longgang Qin jian 雲夢龍崗秦簡. Edited by Liu Xinfang 劉信芳 and Liang Zhu 梁柱. Beijing: Kexue, 1997.

Zhanguo ce 戰國策. Compiled by Liu Xiang. Shanghai: Guji, 1985.

Zhongyong zhu 中庸注. In Kang Youwei 康有爲 (1858-1927), *Mengzi wei* 孟子微, edited by Lou Yulie 樓宇烈. Beijing: Zhonghua, 1987.

Zhouli zhengyi 周禮正義. Annotated by Sun Yirang 孫詒讓 (1848-1908). Beijing: Zhonghua, 1987.

Zhouli zhushu 周禮注疏. Annotated by Jia Gongyan. In *Shisanjing zhushu*, vol. 3.

Zhouyi zhengyi 周易正義. Annotated by Kong Yingda et al. In *Shisanjing zhushu*, vol. 1.

Zhushu jinian 竹書紀年. *Sibu beiyao* ed.

Zhuangzi jishi 莊子集釋. Annotated by Guo Qingfan 郭慶藩 (1844-1897 C.E.). Taipei: Guanya, 1991.

Secondary Works in Chinese and Japanese

Ai Linong 艾力農 (1985). "Xian Qin zhexue 'wu' fanchou de fazhan" 先秦哲學 '物' 範疇的發展, *Zhongguo zhexueshi yanjiu* 中國哲學史研究 1, 28-35.

Beijing shi wenwu gongzuo dui (1964). "Beijing xi jiao faxian Handai shi que qingli jian-bao" 北京西郊發現漢代石闕清理簡報, *Wenwu* 11, 13-22.

Chen Anli 陳安利 (1988). "Gu wenwu zhong de shi-er sheng xiao" 古文物中的十二生肖, *Wenbo* 文博 2, 41-50.

Chen Enzhi 陳恩志 (1987). "Xiang ma shu yuanliu he gudai yang ma zhi ming" 相馬術源流和古代養馬之明, *Nongye kaogu* 農業考古 2, 339-346.

Chen Wei 陳偉 (1996). *Baoshan Chu jian chu tan* 包山楚簡初探. Wuhan: Wuhan daxue.

———— (1999). "Hubei Jingmen Baoshan bushi Chu jian suo jian shenqi xitong yu xiangji zhidu" 湖北荊門包山卜筮楚簡所見神祇系統與享祭制度, *Kaogu* 4, 51-59.

Chen Wenhua 陳文華 (1994). *Zhongguo nongye kaogu tu lu* 中國農業考古圖錄. Jiangxi kexue jishu chubanshe.

Chen Xianyuan 陳顯遠 (1996). "Han xianren Tang Gongfang bei kao" 漢仙人唐公房碑考, *Wenbo* 2, 27-28/48.

Chen Yaojun 陳躍均 and Yuan Wenqing 院文清 (1983). "Zhenmushou lüe kao" 鎭墓獸略考, *Jiang Han kaogu* 江漢考古 3, 63-67.

Chen Zhaorong 陳昭容 (1995). "Zhanguo zhi Qin de fujie, yi shiwu ziliao wei zhu" 戰國至秦的符節—以實物資料爲主, *Zhongyang yanjiuyuan lishi yuyan yan-jiusuo jikan* 中央研究院歷史語言研究所集刊 66.1, 305-366.

Chen Zizhan 陳子展 et al. (eds.) (1983). *Shijing zhijie* 詩經直解. Shanghai: Fudan daxue.

Chūbachi Masakazu 中鉢雅量 (1981). "Chūgoku kodai no dōbutsushin sūhai ni tsuite" 中國古代の動物神崇拜について, *Tōhōgaku* 東方學 62, 1-12.

Ding Su 丁驌 (1966). "Qiwen shoulei ji shou xing zi shi" 契文獸類及獸形字釋, *Zhong-guo wenzi* 中國文字 21, 1-28.

———— (1968). "Fenghuang yu fengniao" 鳳凰與風鳥, *Zhongyang yanjiuyuan min-zuxue yanjiusuo jikan* 中央研究院民族學研究所集刊 25, 35-43.

———— (1993). *Xia Shang shi yanjiu* 夏商史研究. Taipei: Yiwen yinshuguan.

Dong Yuan 董源 (1995). "*Wanwu* zhong bufen zhiwu mingcheng gujin kao" 萬物中部分植物名稱古今考, *Zhongguo kejishi liao* 中國科技史料 16.4, 77-83.

Du Erwei 杜而未 (1966; rpt. 1971). *Feng lin gui long kao shi* 鳳麟龜龍考釋. Taipei: Tai-wan Shangwu.

Du Yaquan 杜亞泉 et al. (eds.) (1933). *Dongwuxue da cidian* 動物學大辭典. Commer-cial Press, n.p.

Du Zhengsheng 杜正勝 (1993). "Ou-Ya caoyuan dongwu wenshi yu Zhongguo gudai beifang minzu zhi kaocha" 歐亞草原動物文飾與中國古代北方民族之考察, *Zhongyang yanjiuyuan lishi yuyan yanjiusuo jikan* 64.2, 231-408.

Fu Junlian 伏俊連 (1997). "Cong xin chutu de *Shen wu fu* kan minjian gushi fu de chan-sheng, tezheng ji zai wenxueshi shang de yiyi" 從新出土的神烏賦看民間故事賦的產生, 特征及在文學史上的意義, *Xibei Shida xuebao* 西北師大學報 34.6, 11-15.

Fukatsu Tanefusa 深津胤房 (1982). "Kodai Chūgokujin no shisō to seikatsu: 'Ying hua wei jiu' ni tsuite" 古代中國人の思想と生活: 鷹化爲鳩について, *Nishō-*

gakusha daigaku tōyōgaku kenkyūjo shūkan 二松學舍大學東洋學研究所集刊 13, 71–135.

———— (1986). "Kodai Chūgokujin no shisō to seikatsu: On ni yoru harai ni tsuite" 古代中國人の思想と生活: 音による祓について, *Musashi daigaku jimbun gakkai zasshi* 武藏大學人文學會雜誌 17.3, 1–38.

Fuyang Han jian zhengli zu (1983). "Fuyang Han jian jianjie" 阜陽漢簡簡介, *Wenwu* 2, 21–23.

———— (1988). "Fuyang Han jian *Wanwu*" 阜陽漢簡 "萬物," *Wenwu* 4, 36–47.

Gai Shanlin 蓋山林 (1989). "Quan yanhua, quan, quan ji" 犬岩畫, 犬, 犬祭, *Beifang wenwu* 北方文物 3, 58–63.

Gou Cuihua 苟萃華 (1958). "Luo fei shou lei bian" 臝非獸類辨, *Kexueshi jikan* 科學史集刊 8, 55–64.

———— (1989). *Zhongguo gudai shengwuxue shi* 中國古代生物學史. Beijing: Kexue.

Gu Yanlong 顧延龍 (1990). *Erya daodu* 爾雅導讀. Chengdu: Ba-Shu shushe.

Guo Fu 郭郛, Li Yuese 李約瑟 (Joseph Needham), and Cheng Qingtai 成慶泰 (1999). *Zhongguo gudai dongwuxue shi* 中國古代動物學史. Beijing: Kexue.

Guo Guanghong 國光紅 (1995). "Jiu, long ji xiangguan zi shishi" 九, 龍及相關字試釋, *Nanfang wenwu* 南方文物 2, 100–105.

Guo Moruo 郭沫若 (1965). "'Wu huan bu mu' shike de buchong kaoshi" 烏還哺母石刻的補充考釋, *Wenwu* 4, 2–5.

Han Dongyu 韓東育 (1989). "Zhuzi de ren shou lilun yu xueshuo fenhe" 諸子的人獸理論與學說分合, *Dongbei Shida xuebao* 東北師大學報 6, 63–69.

Han Li 韓立 (ed.) (1992). *Han La Ying dongwu yao mingcheng* 漢拉英動物藥名稱. Fuzhou: Fujian kexue.

Hasegawa Michitaka 長谷川道隆 (1991). "Chinbojū zakkō" 鎮墓獸雜考, *Kodai bunka* 古代文化 43.5, 21–31.

Hayashi Minao 林巳奈夫 (1989). *Kan dai no kamigami* 漢代の神神. Kyoto: Rinkawa shoten.

———— (1991). Tr. Yang Meili 楊美莉. "Zhongguo gudai yiwu shang suo biaoshi de qi zhi tuxiangxing biaoxian" 中國古代遺物上所表示的氣之圖像性表現, *Gugong xueshu jikan* 故宮學術季刊 9.2, 31–73.

He Runkun 賀潤坤 (1989a). "Cong Yunmeng Qin jian *Rishu* kan Qin guo de liuchu siyang ye" 從雲夢秦簡日書看秦國的六畜飼養業, *Wenbo* 6, 63–67.

———— (1989b). "Yunmeng Qin jian suo fanyang de Qinguo yulie huodong" 雲夢秦簡所反央的秦國漁獵活動, *Wenbo* 3, 49–50/27.

He Xin 何新 (1990). *Long: shenhua yu zhenxiang* 龍: 神化與眞象. Shanghai: Renmin.

Heian Shinshirō 平安慎思郎 (1978). "Shikyō ni okeru ōchō no kō ni tsuite" 詩經に於ける黃鳥の興について, *Nishō-gakusha daigaku jimbun ronsō* 二松學舍大學人文論叢 13, 57–64.

Hu Kun 胡堃 (1992). "Chūgoku kodai kitsune shinkō genryū kō" 中國古代狐信仰源流考, *Fukuoka kyōiku daigaku kiyō* 福岡教育大學紀要 41, 19–31.

Hu Pingsheng 胡平生 and Han Ziqiang 韓自強 (1988). "*Wanwu* lüeshuo" 萬物略說, *Wenwu* 4, 48–54.

Hunan nongxueyuan 湖南農學院 et al. (eds.) (1978). *Changsha Mawangdui yihao Han mu chutu dongzhiwu biaoben de yanjiu* 長沙馬王堆一號漢墓出土動植物標本的研究. Beijing: Wenwu.

Ichikawa Isamu 市川勇 (1944). "Shina ni okeru hanju hanjin shin sūhai no kigen" 支那に於ける半獸半人神崇拜の起源, *Shien* 史苑 15.2, 12–34.

Ikeda On 池田温 (1984). "Chūgoku kodai no mojū taisaku hōki" 中國古代の猛獸對策法規. In *Ritsuryōsei no shomondai* 律令制の諸問題. Festschrift for Takigawa Masajirō 瀧川政次郎 (Tokyo: Kyūko shoin), 611–37.

Ikeda Suetoshi 池田末利 (1953). "Ryūjin kō—soshin no dōbutsu tenkaku no ichirei" 龍神考—祖神の動物轉格の一例, *Tōhōgaku* 6, 1–7.

——— (1956). "Ki ji kō" 鬼字考. *Hiroshima daigaku bungakubu kiyō* 廣島大學文學部紀要 10, 206–48.

——— (1957). "Kodai Shina ni okeru reiki kannen no seiritsu" 古代支那に於る靈鬼觀念の成立, *Shūkyō kenkyū* 宗教研究 152, 18–35.

Inoi Makoto 家井眞 (1975). "Shikyō ni okeru sakana no kōshi to sono tenkai ni tsuite" 詩經に於ける魚の興詞とその展開に就いて, *Nippon-Chūgoku gakkai hō* 日本中國學會報 27, 4–47.

——— (1977). "Ryū no kigen ni tsuite" 龍の起源について, *Nishō-gakusha daigaku jimbun ronsō* 12, 137–145.

Ishikawa Misao 石川三佐男 (1976). "Chūgoku kodai ni okeru tsubame no shūkyōteki igi to Shikyō *En en* hen no kō ni tsuite" 中國古代に於ける燕の宗教的意義と詩經燕燕篇の興について, *Nishō-gakusha daigaku jimbun ronsō* 9, 37–48.

——— (1977a). "Shikyō ni okeru yōsai ka ni tsuite" 詩經に於ける羊祭歌について, *Nishō-gakusha daigaku jimbun ronsō* 11, 55–70.

——— (1977b). "Shikyō ni okeru basai no fukugen ni tsuite" 詩經に於ける馬祭の復原について, *Nishō-gakusha daigaku jimbun ronsō* 12, 75–84.

——— (1983). "Shikyō ni okeru hoto no kōshi to kon-en no zakyō embu ni tsuite" 詩經に於ける捕兔の興詞と婚宴の座興演舞について, *Nippon-Chūgoku gakkai hō* 日本中國學會報 35, 15–31.

Itō Seiji 伊藤清司 (1959). "Kodai Chūgoku no uma no chōryō jujutsu" 古代中國の馬の調良咒術, *Kodai bunka* 古代文化 24.4, 107–13.

——— (1990). Tr. Liu Yeyuan 劉曄原, *Shanhaijing zhong de guishen shijie* 山海經中的鬼神世界. Beijing: Zhongguo minjian wenyi.

——— (1994). "Kyūjō to irezumi" 鳩杖と文身, *Nitchū bunka kenkyū* 日中文化研究 6.

Izushi Yoshihiko 出石誠彥 (1928). "Ryū no yurai ni tsuite" 龍の由來について, *Tōyō gakuhō* 東洋學報 17.2, 282–98.

——— (1931). "Shina no kobunken ni arawaru kirin ni tsuite" 支那の古文獻に現わる麒麟について, *Shien* 史苑 3.4, 289–313.

——— (1943). *Shina shinwa densetsu no kenkyū* 支那神話傳說の研究. Tokyo: Chūō Kōronsha.

Jiang Weidong 蔣衞東 (1991). "Zhenmushou yi yi bian" 鎮墓獸意義辨, *Jiang Han kaogu* 2, 40–44.

Kakehata Minoru 欠端實 (1991). "Kandai no Yōshi to shinchō" 漢代の楊氏と神鳥, *Shikan* 史觀 (Waseda daigaku shigaku kai 早稻田大學史學會) 125, 15-23.

Kameda Ichirō 龜田一邦 (1984). "Chūgoku kodai ni okeru semi ni tsuite" 中國古代における蟬について. *Nishō-gakusha daigaku jimbun ronsō* 29, 10-23.

Kirimoto Tōta 桐本東太 (1996). "'Chūgen chikuroku' kō" 中原逐鹿考, *Tōyō bunka* 76, 95-109.

Kubuki Shigehiro 久富木成大 (1993). "Rikutō ni okeru dōbutsu mohō o megutte" 六韜における動物模倣をめぐって, *Kanazawa daigaku kyōyōbu ronshū (jimbun kagakuhen)* 金沢大學教養部論集 (人文科學篇) 31.1, 1-21.

Lianyungangshi bowuguan 連云港市博物館 (1996). "Yinwan Hanmu jiandu shiwen xuan" 尹灣漢墓簡牘釋文選, *Wenwu* 8, 26-31.

Li Lin 李琳 (1991). "Cong Qinghai chutu mu longma kan Handai ma shen chongbai" 從青海出土木龍馬看漢代馬神崇拜, *Wenbo* 1, 56-59.

Li Ling 李零 (1993a). *Zhongguo fangshu kao* 中國方術考. Beijing: Renmin.

——— (ed.) (1993b). *Zhongguo fangshu gaiguan* 中國方術概觀. *Xiang shu juan* 相術卷. Beijing: Renmin Zhongguo.

——— (ed.) (1993c). *Zhongguo fangshu gaiguan* 中國方術概觀. *Za shu juan* 雜術卷. Beijing: Renmin Zhongguo.

Li Xueqin 李學勤 (1990). "Fangmatan jian zhong de zhiguai gushi" 放馬灘簡中的志怪故事, *Wenwu* 4, 43-47.

——— (1994). *Jianbo yiji yu xueshu shi* 簡帛佚藉與學術史. Taipei: Shibao chuban.

Li Zhuangying 李壯鷹 (1992). "Yue yu yue shen" 樂與樂神, *Hanazono daigaku kenkyū kiyō* 花園大學研究紀要 24, 217-32.

Lin Cen 林岑 (1989). "Zhongguo gudai dui she de renshi he liyong" 中國古代對蛇的認識和利用, *Nongye kaogu* 1, 273-79/314.

Ling Chunsheng 凌純聲 (1957). "Gudai Zhongguo ji Taipingyang qu de quan ji" 古代中國及太平洋區的犬祭, *Zhongyang yanjiuyuan minzuxue yanjiusuo jikan* 3, 1-40.

——— (1971). "Zhongguo gudai de guiji wenhua" 中國古代的龜祭文化, *Zhongyang yanjiuyuan minzuxue yanjiusuo jikan* 31, 17-46.

Liu Dunyuan 劉敦愿 (1980). "Zhongguo gudai duiyu dongwu tiandi guanxi de renshi he liyong" 中國古代對於動物天敵關係的認識和利用. In *Zhongguo gudai nongye keji* 中國古代農業科技 (Beijing: Nongye), 219-31.

Liu Fude 劉夫德 (1990). "Shitan wo guo gudai guishen guannian de chansheng" 試談我國古代鬼神觀念的產生, *Zhongguoshi yanjiu* 中國史研究 2, 137-45.

Liu Hong 劉弘 (1988). "Ba hu yu kaiming shou" 巴虎與開明獸, *Sichuan wenwu* 4, 57-59.

Liu Juncan 劉君燦 (1996). "Zhongguo chuantong de shengwu zhuanhua sixiang ji qi xingqi lun jichu chutan" 中國傳統的生物轉化思想及其形氣論基礎初探. Paper delivered at the fourth Conference on the History of Science, organized by the International Union of the History and Philosophy of Science. Academia Sinica, Nankang, Taipei.

Liu Lexian 劉樂賢 (1994). *Shuihudi Qin jian Rishu yanjiu* 睡虎地秦簡日書研究. Taipei: Wenjin.

Liu Lexian and Wang Zhiping 王志平 (1997). "Yinwan Han jian *Shen wu fu* yu qin niao duo chao gushi" 尹灣漢簡神烏賦與禽鳥奪巢故事, *Wenwu* 1, 59–61.

Liu Shipei 劉師培 (1907). "Wang hui pian bu shi" 王會篇補釋, *Guo cui xuebao* 國粹學報 3.9, 12.

Liu Xiaonan 劉曉南 (1995). "'Yu, yu ye' yin xun yu yuan bianzheng," "雨，羽也"音訓語源辯正, *Dalu zazhi* 大陸雜志 91.4, 35–36.

Liu Xinfang 劉信芳 (1997). "Baoshan Chu jian zhiguan yu guanfu tongkao (shang)" 包山楚簡職官與官府通考 (上), *Gugong xueshu jikan* 15.1, 45–70.

Liu Zhixiong 劉志雄 and Yang Jingrong 楊靜榮 (1992). *Long yu Zhongguo wenhua* 龍與中國文化. Beijing: Renmin.

Liu Zhi 劉志 (1991). "Xiang tian, wu tian kao" 象田烏田考, *Zhongguo nongshi* 中國農史 2, 1–11.

Luo Guihuan 羅桂環, Yang Chaofei 楊朝飛 et al. (eds.) (1995). *Zhongguo huanjing baohu shigao* 中國環境保護史稿. Beijing: Zhongguo huanjing kexue chubanshe.

Luo Shirong 羅世榮 (1988). "Long de qiyuan ji yanbian" 龍的起源及演變, *Sichuan wenwu* 2, 17–19.

Mawangdui Han mu boshu zhengli xiaozu (1977). "Mawangdui Han mu boshu *Xiangmajing* shiwen" 馬王堆漢墓帛書相馬經釋文, *Wenwu* 8, 17–22.

Mitarai Masaru 御手洗勝 (1987). "Shirei ni tsuite" 四靈について, *Hiroshima daigaku bungakubu kiyō* 廣島大學文學部紀要 46, 38–45.

Nagahiro Toshio 長廣敏雄 (1933). "Kandai o chūshin to seru dōbutsu hyōgen ni tsuite" 漢代を中心とせる動物表現に就いて, *Tōhō gakuhō* 4, 106–47.

Nakamura Kazumoto 中村一基 (1992). "'Shi wa kairiki ran shin o katarazu' kō" 子は怪力亂神を語らず考. *Iwate daigaku kyōiku gakubu kenkyū nempō* 岩手大學教育學部研究年報 52.3, 34–42.

Ni Run-an 倪潤安(1999). "Lun liang Han siling de yuanliu" 論兩漢四靈的源流, *Zhongyuan wenwu* 中原文物 1, 83–91.

Niu Longfei 牛龍菲 (1984). "Shuo Wuwei Leitai chutu zhi tongzhu tian ma" 說武威雷台出土之銅鑄天馬, *Dunhuang xue jikan* 敦煌學輯刊 1, 93–99.

Ōba Osamu 大庭修 (1970). "Kandai no dōkohu to chikushihu" 漢代の銅虎符と竹使符. In *Kamata hakase kanreki kinen rekishigaku ronsō* 鎌田博士還曆記念歷史學論叢 (Tokyo: Kabushiki kaisha), 43–54.

Ogawa Yōichi 小川陽一 (1987). "Oshaku minami ni tobu" 烏鵲南に飛ぶ, in Akizuki Kan'ei 秋月觀暎 (ed.), *Dokyō to shūkyō bunka* 道教と宗教文化 (Tokyo: Hirakawa), 489–507.

Peng Hao 彭浩 (1988). "Zhenmushou xin jie" 鎮墓獸新解, *Jiang Han kaogu* 2, 66–68.

Qiu Donglian 邱東聯 (1994). "Zhenmushou biankao" 鎮墓獸辨考, *Jiang Han kaogu* 2, 54–59.

Qiu Xigui 裘錫圭 (1992). *Gudai wenshi yanjiu xin tan* 古代文史研究新探. Nanjing: Jiangsu guji.

——— (1997). "*Shen wu fu* chutan" 神烏賦初探, *Wenwu* 1, 52–58.

Sakurai Tatsuhiko 櫻井龍彥 (1993). "Sangaikyō chu ni miru Guo Pu no henka ron" 山

海經注にみる郭璞の變化論, *Chūkyō daigaku kyōyō ronsō* 中京大學教養論叢 34.3, 41–76.

Sawada Mizuho 澤田瑞穗 (1982). *Chūgoku no minkan shinkō* 中國の民間信仰. Tokyo: Kōsakusha.

Shao Mingsheng 邵茗生 (1964). "Han Youzhou shuzuo Qin jun shi que shiwen" 漢幽州書佐秦君石闕釋文, *Wenwu* 11, 23–24.

Shenzhen bowuguan (1995). *Zhongguo Handai huaxiang shihua xiangzhuan wenxian mulu* 中國漢代畫象石畫像磚文獻目錄. Shenzhen: Wenwu.

Shi Xiaoshi 施孝適 (1990). "*Erya* chongyu ming jinshi" 爾雅蟲魚名今釋, *Dalu zazhi* 大陸雜誌 81.3, 34–48.

Shiratori Kiyoshi 白鳥清 (1934). "Ryū no keitai ni tsuite no kōsatsu" 龍の形態に就いての考察, *Tōyō gakuhō* 21.2, 105–134.

Song Zhaolin 宋兆麟 (1981). "Zhanguo yishe tu ji qi suyuan" 戰國弋射圖及其溯源, *Wenwu* 6, 75–77.

Sugimoto Kenji 杉本憲司 (1979). "Chūgoku kodai no inu" 中國古代の犬, in *Mori Mikisaburō hakase shōju kinen tōyōgaku ronshū* 森三樹三郎博士頌壽記念東洋學論集 (Kyoto: Hōyū shoten), 235–253.

Sun Shiwen 孫世文 (1987). "Mawangdui yi hao Han mu bohua renshou sheshen tu kao" 馬王堆一號漢墓帛畫人首蛇身圖考, *Dongbei Shida xuebao* 東北師大學報 1, 84–88.

Sun Zhong-en 孫重恩 (1989). "Gun" 鯀, *Zhongyuan wenwu* 中原文物 1, 53–59.

Tan Chanxue 譚蟬雪 (1996). "Dunhuang ma wenhua" 敦煌馬文化, *Dunhuang yanjiu* 1, 113–115.

——— (1998). "Sangzang yong ji tanxi" 喪葬用雞探析, *Dunhuang yanjiu* 1, 75–81.

Tan Qixiang 譚其驤 (ed.) (1987). *Zhongguo lishi ditu ji* 中國歷史地圖集. Shanghai: Ditu chubanshe, vol. 1.

Tei Masahiro 鄭正浩 (1978). "Kaze to hō o meguru ongaku shisō" 風と鳳をめぐる音樂思想, *Okayama daigaku gakujutsu kiyō* 岡山大學學術紀要 39, 84–96.

Teng Zhaozong 滕昭宗 (1996). "Yinwan Han mu jiandu gaishu" 尹灣漢墓簡牘概述, *Wenwu* 8, 32–36.

Tochio Takeshi 栃尾武 (1970). "Seiei no densetsu to sono shiryō" 精衞の傳說とその資料, *Chūgoku bungaku ronsō* 中國文學論叢 (Ōbirin daigaku 櫻美林大學) 2, 1–24.

Tu Yuanji 涂元濟 (1982). "Gun hua huang long kaoshi" 鯀化黃龍考釋, *Minjian wenyi jikan* 民間文藝集刊 3, 35–49.

Uehara Jundō 上原淳道 (1954). "Izui, ida, ida ni tsuite" 委隨, 蝛蛇, 委蛇について, in Mikami Tsugio 三上次男 and Kurihara Tomonobu 栗原朋信 (eds.), *Chūgoku kodaishi no shomondai* 中國古代史の諸問題 (Tokyo: Tokyo University Press), 257–71.

Wang Chuqing 王初慶 (1986). "*Zuozhuan* xin gui hao wu bian—zai yi" 左傳信鬼好巫辯—災異, *Furen xuezhi* 輔仁學誌 15, 99–120.

Wang Dayou 王大有 (1988). *Long feng wenhua yuanliu* 龍鳳文化源流. Beijing: Beijing Gongyi meishu.

Wang Guancheng 王關成 (1994). "Man shuo Qin Han hufu" 漫說秦漢虎符, *Wenshi zhishi* 文史知識 12, 52–56.

Wang Guowei 王國維 (1923). *Guantang jilin* 觀堂集林. N.p.

Wang Lihua 王利華 (1992). "Zaoqi Zhongguo shehui de quan wenhua" 早期中國社會的犬文化, *Nongye kaogu* 農業考古 3, 265–70/74.

Wang Qianjin 汪前進 (ed.) (1996). *Chuan shi cang shu* 傳世藏書. Hainan guoji xinwen chuban zhongxin 海南國際新聞出版中心.

Wang Ruiming 王瑞明 (1979). "Zhenmushou kao" 鎮墓獸考, *Wenwu* 6, 85–87.

Wang Xiaolian 王孝廉 (1992). *Shui yu shui shen* 水與水神. Taipei: Sanmin shuju.

Wang Yitong 王伊同 (1978). "Zouyu kao" 騶虞考, in *Qu Wanli xiansheng qizhi rong-qing lunwen ji* 屈萬里先生七秩榮慶論文集 (Taipei: Lianjing chuban shiye gongsi), 45–49.

Wang Yuhu 王毓瑚 (1958). *Zhongguo xumu shi ziliao* 中國畜牧史資料. Beijing: Kexue chubanshe.

——— (1979). *Zhongguo nongxue shulu* 中國農學書錄. Beijing: Nongye.

Wang Yusong 王毓松 (1992). *Niao shou chong yu shi daguan* 鳥獸虫魚詩大觀. Guilin: Guangxi Shifan daxue.

Wang Zhiping 王志平 (1999). "*Shen wu fu* yu Handai *Shijing* xue" 神烏傳 (賦) 與漢代詩經學, in Lianyungangshi bowuguan et al. (eds.), *Yinwan Han mu jiandu zonglun* 尹灣漢墓簡牘綜論 (Beijing: Kexue); 8–17.

Wang Zichun 汪子春 and Cheng Baochao 程寶綽 (1997). *Zhongguo gudai shengwuxue* 中國古代生物學. Beijing: Shangwu.

Wang Zijin 王子今 (1982). "Handai de dou shou he xun shou" 漢代的鬥獸和馴獸, *Renwen zazhi* 5, 75–79.

Wen Renjun 聞人軍 (1988). *Kaogong ji daodu* 考工記導讀. Sichuan: Ba Shu.

Wen Yiduo 聞一多 (1948). "Shuo yu" 說魚, in *Wen Yiduo quan ji* 聞一多全集 (Shanghai: Kaiming shudian), vol. 1, 117–138.

——— (1956). "Fuxi kao" 伏羲考. In *Shenhua yu shi* 神話與詩 (Beijing: Zhonghua), 3–68.

Wu Jiabi 武家璧 (1998). "Hu zuo niao jia gu bianzheng" 虎座鳥架鼓辯正, *Kaogu yu wenwu* 6, 57–62.

Wu Rongzeng 吳榮曾 (1989). "Zhanguo, Handai de cao she shenguai ji youguan shen-hua mixin de bianyi" 戰國漢代的操蛇神怪及有關神話迷信的變異, *Wenwu* 10, 46–52.

Wu Xiaoqiang 吳小強 (1992). "Lun Qin ren de duoshen chongbai tedian" 論秦人的多神崇拜特點, *Wenbo* 4, 53–57.

Xia Henglian 夏亨廉 and Lin Zhengtong 林正同 (1996). *Handai nongye huaxiang zhuanshi* 漢代農業畫像磚石. Beijing: Nongye.

Xiao Dengfu 蕭登福 (1990). *Xian Qin liang Han mingjie ji shenxian sixiang tanyuan* 先秦兩漢冥界及神仙思想探原. Taipei: Wenjin.

Xie Chengxia 謝成俠 (1959). *Zhongguo yang ma shi* 中國養馬史. Beijing: Kexue.

——— (1977). "Guanyu Changsha Mawangdui Han mu boshu *Xiangmajing* de tantao" 關於長沙馬王堆漢墓帛書相馬經的探討, *Wenwu* 8, 23–26.

———— (1980). "Wo guo gudai jiachu waixing jianding (xiang liuchu) ji qi lilun de fazhan he pingjia" 我國古代家畜外形鑑定 (相六畜) 及其理論的發展和評價, in *Zhongguo gudai nongye keji* 中國古代農業科技 (Beijing: Nongye, 1980), 356-68.

———— (1995). *Zhongguo yang qin shi* 中國養禽史. Beijing: Zhongguo Nongye.

Xu Shan 徐山 (1992). *Leishen chongbai* 雷神崇拜. Shanghai: Sanlian.

Yamada Katsumi 山田勝美 (1951). "Chimi mōryō kō" 螭魅罔兩考, *Nippon-Chūgoku gakkai hō* 3, 53-64.

Yamashita Toraji 山下寅次 (1931). "Taihō densetsu ni tsuite" 大鵬傳說に就いて, *Shigaku kenkyū* 史學研究 1.2, 250-264.

Yang Kuan 楊寬 (1955; rpt. 1998). *Zhanguo shi* 戰國史 (revised ed.). Shanghai: Shanghai renmin.

Yang Shuda 楊樹達 (1955a). "Shi ci xiong" 釋雌雄. In *(Zengding) Jiweiju xiaoxue jinshi luncong* 增訂積微居小學金石論叢 (Beijing: Kexue chubanshe), 1.30-31.

———— (1955b). "Shou zi Duan zhu bo" 臩字段注駁. In *(Zengding) Jiweiju xiaoxue jinshi luncong*, 2.81-82.

Yang Wensheng 楊文勝 (1996). "Shitan *Shijing* zhong de xian Qin che ma" 試探詩經中的先秦車馬, *Zhongyuan wenwu* 中原文物 2, 50-55.

Yu Hangui 余漢桂 (1984). "Cong shuizu zhanggu kuitan wo guo gudai yuxue" 從水族掌故窺探我國古代魚學, *Nongye kaogu* 2, 207-216.

Yu Huaqing 余華青 and Zhang Tinghao 張廷皓 (1982). "Qin Han shiqi de xu mu ye" 秦漢時期的畜牧業, *Zhongguo shi yanjiu* 中國史研究 4, 16-30.

Yu Huaqing (1982). "Qin Han shiqi de yuye" 秦漢時期的漁業, *Renwen zazhi* 人文雜志 5, 58-66.

Yu Wanli 虞萬里 (1997). "Yinwan Han jian *Shen wu fu* jianshi" 尹灣漢簡神烏傅箋釋, in *Di san jie guoji xunguxue xueshu yantaohui lunwen* 第三屆國際訓詁學學術研討會論文 (Taipei, 1997), 833-852.

Yuan Mei 袁梅 (1981). *Shijing yi zhu* 詩經譯注. Qinan: Qi-Lu shushe.

Zeng Xiongsheng 曾雄生 (1990). "Xiang geng wu yun tanlun" 象耕鳥耘探論, *Ziran kexue shi yanjiu* 自然科學史研究 9.1, 67-77.

Zhan Yinxin 詹鄞鑫 (1992). *Shenling yu jisi* 神靈與祭祀. Jiangsu: Xinhua shudian.

Zhang Hongxun 張鴻勛 (1992). "Dunhuang changben *Bai niao ming* de wenhua yiyun ji qi liubian yinxiang" 敦煌唱本百鳥名的文化意蘊及其流變影響, *Dunhuang yanjiu* 敦煌研究 1, 70-80.

Zhangjiashan Han jian zhengli zu (1990). "Zhangjiashan Han jian *Yin shu* shiwen" 張家山漢簡引書釋文, *Wenwu* 10, 82-86.

Zhang Jun 張軍 (1994). *Chu guo shenhua yuanxing yanjiu* 楚國神話原型研究. Taipei: Wenjin.

Zhang Mengwen 張孟聞 (1982). "Si ling kao" 四靈考, in Li Guohao, Zhang Mengwen and Cao Tianjin (eds.), *Explorations in the History of Science and Technology in China* (Shanghai: Chinese Classics Publishing House, 1982), 525-52.

Zhang Zhongge 張仲葛 and Zhu Xianhuang 朱先煌 (eds.) (1986). *Zhongguo xumu shi liao ji* 中國畜牧史料集. Beijing: Kexue chubanshe.

Zhao Fulin 晁福林 (1996). *Xia Shang Xi Zhou de shehui bianqian* 夏商西周的社會變遷. Beijing: Beijing shifan daxue.

Zhao Kuifu 趙逵夫 (1989). "Mawangdui Han mu chutu *Xiangmajing, Da guang po zhang, Gu xun zhuan* fawei" 馬王堆漢墓出土"相馬經大光破章故訓傳" 發微, *Jiang Han kaogu* 3, 48–51.

Zheng Shubin 鄭曙斌 (1996). "Chu mu bohua, zhenmushou de hunpo guannian" 楚墓帛畫, 鎮墓獸的魂魄觀念, *Jiang Han kaogu* 1, 81–85/89.

Zhongguo chumu shouyi xuehui; Zhong shouyi yanjiuhui (1992). *Zhong shouyi xue shi lüe* 中獸醫學史略. Beijing: Nongye.

Zhou Dao 周到, Tang Wenguang 湯文光 and Lü Pin 呂品 (eds.) (1985). *Henan Handai huaxiang zhuan* 河南漢代畫像磚. Shanghai: Shanghai renmin meishu.

Zhou Qingming 周慶明 (1984). "Zhou zu Ji xing hu tuteng kao" 周族姬姓虎圖騰考, *Shijie zongjiao yanjiu* 世界宗教研究 1, 123–30.

Zhuang Yazhou 莊雅州 (1985). *Xia xiao zheng xi lun* 夏小正析論. Taipei: Wenshizhe.

Zou Jiezheng 鄒介正 (1959). "Wo guo xiangma waixing xue fazhan shilüe" 我國相馬外形學發展史略, *Nongshi yanjiu jikan* 農史研究集刊 (Beijing: Kexue), vol. 1, 37–53.

Zou Shuwen 鄒樹文 (1982). "Zhongguo gudai de dongwu fenlei xue" 中國古代的動物分類學, in Li Guohao, Zhang Mengwen and Cao Tianjin (eds.), *Explorations in the History of Science and Technology in China* (Shanghai: Chinese Classics Publishing House, 1982), 511–24.

Zuo Yandong 左言東 (1994). *Xian Qin zhiguan biao* 先秦職官表. Beijing: Shangwu.

Works in Western Languages

Aelian (170– ca. 230 C.E.), *De Nature Animalium*. Tr. A. F. Scholfield, *Aelian: On Animals*. Loeb Classical Library; Cambridge, Mass.: Harvard University Press, 1971.

Albert-Llorca, Marlène (1991). *L'Ordre des Choses: Les Récits d'Origine des Animaux et des Plantes en Europe*. Paris: Editions du Comité des Travaux Historiques et Scientifiques.

Allan, Sarah (1991). *The Shape of the Turtle: Myth, Art and Cosmos in Early China*. Albany: State University of New York Press.

———— (1997). *The Way of Water and the Sprouts of Virtue*. Albany: State University of New York Press.

Allinson, Robert E. (1989). *Chuang-Tzu for Spiritual Transformation. An Analysis of the Inner Chapters*. Albany: State University of New York Press.

Ariel, Yoav (1996). *K'ung-Ts'ung-Tzu. A Study and Translation of Chapters 15–23 with a Reconstruction of the Hsiao Erh-ya Dictionary*. Leiden: E.J. Brill.

Aristotle (384–322 B.C.E.). *Historia Animalium*. Tr. D. M. Balme; Loeb Classical Library; Cambridge, Mass.: Harvard University Press, 1991.

Armstrong, Edward A. (1943). "The Crane Dance in East and West," *Antiquity* 17, 71–76.

———— (1945). "Chinese Bull Ritual and its Affinities," *Folk-lore* 56, 200–207.

Atran, Scott (1990). *Cognitive Foundations of Natural History: Towards an Anthropology of Science.* Cambridge: Cambridge University Press.

———— (1999). "Itzaj Maya Folkbiological Taxonomy: Cognitive Universals and Cultural Particulars," in Douglas L. Medin and Scott Atran (eds.), *Folkbiology* (Cambridge, Mass.: MIT Press), 119–203.

Baker, Steve (1993). *Picturing the Beast. Animals, Identity, and Representation.* Manchester: Manchester University Press.

Barrett, T.H. (1998). "The Religious Affiliations of the Chinese Cat: An Essay Towards an Anthropozoological Approach to Comparative Religion," *Louis Jordan Occasional Papers in Comparative Religion* no. 2. SOAS, University of London.

Bielenstein, H. (1984). "Han Portents and Prognostications," *Bulletin of the Museum of Far Eastern Antiquities* 56, 97–112.

Bilsky, Lester J. (1975). *The State Religion of Ancient China.* Asian Folklore & Social Life Monographs 70. Taipei: The Orient Culture Service.

Birrell, Anne (1993). *Chinese Mythology, an Introduction.* London: Johns Hopkins University Press.

Bishop, Carl W. (1925). "The Ritual Bullfight," *China Journal of Science and Arts* 3, 630–637.

———— (1933). "Rhinoceros and Wild Ox in Ancient China," *China Journal* 18.6, 322–330.

Blauth, Birthe (1996). *Altchinesische Geschichten über Fuchsdämonen.* Berlin: Peter Lang.

Bloch, Maurice (1992). *Prey to Hunter. The Politics of Religious Experience.* Cambridge: Cambridge University Press.

Bodde, Derk (1959). "Lieh-Tzu and the Doves: A Problem of Dating," *Asia Major* 7, 25–31.

———— (1975). *Festivals in Classical China: New Year and Other Annual Observances During the Han Dynasty, 206 B.C.–A.D. 220.* Princeton: Princeton University Press.

———— (1991). *Chinese Thought, Society, and Science. The Intellectual and Social Background of Science and Technology in Pre-modern China.* Honolulu: University of Hawaii Press.

Bodson, Liliane (1978). *Hiera Zoa. Contribution à l'Etude de la Place de l'Animal dans la Religion Grecque Ancienne.* Bruxelles: Académie Royale de Belgique.

Boodberg, Peter A. (1940). "Chinese Zoographic Names as Chronograms," *Harvard Journal of Asiatic Studies* 5, 128–36.

Böttger, Walter (1960). *Die Ursprünglichen Jagdmethoden der Chinesen.* Berlin: Akademie-Verlag.

Bray, Francesca (1984). *Agriculture.* In Needham, SCC, vol. 6, part 2. Cambridge: Cambridge University Press.

Broman, Sven (1961). "Studies on the *Chou li*," *Bulletin of the Museum of Far Eastern Antiquities* 33, 1–89.

Burkert, Walter (1983). Tr. Peter Bing. *Homo Necans: The Anthropology of Ancient Greek Sacrificial Ritual and Myth.* Berkeley: University of California Press.

────── (1996; rpt. 1998). *Creation of the Sacred. Tracks of Biology in Early Religion*. Cambridge, Mass.: Harvard University Press.

Cahill, Suzanne E. (1987). "Reflections, Disputes, and Warnings: Three Medieval Chinese Poems about Paintings of the Eight Horses of King Mu," *T'ang Studies* 5, 87–94.

Campany, Robert Ford (1996). *Strange Writing: Anomaly Accounts in Early Medieval China*. Albany: State University of New York Press.

Carr, Michael (1993). "*Tiao*-Fish through Chinese Dictionaries," *Sino-Platonic Papers* no. 40.

Cartmill, Matt (1993). *A View to a Death in the Morning: Hunting and Nature through History*. Cambridge, Mass.: Harvard University Press.

Chan, Leo Tak-hung (1998). *The Discourse on Foxes and Ghosts. Ji Yun and Eighteenth Century Literati Storytelling*. Hong Kong: Chinese University of Hong Kong Press.

Chang, Kwang-chih (1976). *Early Chinese Civilization: Anthropological Perspectives*. Cambridge, Mass.: Harvard University Press.

────── (ed.) (1977). *Food in Chinese Culture. Anthropological and Historical Perspectives*. New Haven: Yale University Press.

────── (1981). "The Animal in Shang and Chou Bronze Art," *Harvard Journal of Asiatic Studies* 41.2, 527–54.

────── (1983). *Art, Myth, and Ritual: The Path to Political Authority in Ancient China*. Cambridge, Mass.: Harvard University Press.

Chang Tsung-Tung (1970). *Der Kult der Shang-dynastie im Spiegel der Orakel-inschriften*. Wiesbaden: Otto Harrassowitz.

Chard, Robert L. (1990). "Master of the Family: History and Development of the Chinese Cult of the Stove." Ph.D. dissertation, University of California at Berkeley.

Chavannes, Edouard (1906). "Le Cycle Turc des Douze Animaux," *T'oung Pao* 7.1, 51–122.

Chen Jue (1999). "Shooting Sand at People's Shadow. *Yingshe* as a Mode of Representation in Medieval Chinese Literature," *Monumenta Serica* 47, 169–207.

Chen, William Y. (1993). *An Annotated Bibliography of Chinese Agriculture*. Taipei: Chinese Materials Center.

Chen Zhi (1999). "A Study of the Bird Cult of the Shang People," *Monumenta Serica* 47, 127–47.

Cheng T'e-K'un (1963). "Animals in Prehistoric and Shang China," *Bulletin of the Museum of Far Eastern Antiquities* 35, 129–38.

Childs-Johnson, Elizabeth (1993). "The Demon Who Devours but Cannot Swallow: Human to Animal Metamorphosis in Shang Ritual Bronze Imagery." *Chinese Archaeology Enters the Twenty-first Century Symposium Papers*, Beijing University, Department of Archaeology (Ms).

────── (1995). "The Ghost Head Mask and Metamorphic Shang Imagery" (Ms.), abridged version in *Early China* 20 (1995), 79–92.

────── (1998). "The Metamorphic Image: A Predominant Theme in the Ritual Art of Shang China," *Bulletin of the Museum of Far Eastern Antiquities* 70, 5–171.

Chun, Allen J. (1990). "Kinship and Kingship in Classical Chou China," *T'oung Pao* 76, 16–48.

Cohen, Alvin P. (1979). "Avenging Ghosts and Moral Judgment in Ancient Chinese Historiography: Three Examples from *Shih-chi*," in Sarah Allan and Alvin P. Cohen (eds.), *Legend, Lore and Religions in China: Essays in Honor of Wolfram Eberhard on His Seventieth Birthday* (San Francisco: Chinese Materials Center), 97–108.

Cook, Constance A., and John S. Major (eds.) (1999). *Defining Chu. Image and Reality in Ancient China*. Honolulu: University of Hawaii Press.

Creel, Herrlee G. (1970). *The Origins of Statecraft in China*. Chicago: University of Chicago Press.

Crosby, Alfred W. (1993). *Ecological Imperialism. The Biological Expansion of Europe, 900–1900*. Cambridge: Cambridge University Press; Canto editions.

Cutter, Robert J. (1989a). "Brocade and Blood: The Cockfight in Chinese and English Poetry," *Journal of the American Oriental Society* 19, 1–16.

——— (1989b). *The Brush and the Spur. Chinese Culture and the Cockfight*. Hong Kong: Chinese University Press.

Defoort, Carine (1997). *The Pheasant Cap Master: A Rhetorical Reading*. Albany: State University of New York Press.

De Groot, J. J. M. (1892–1910; rpt. 1964). *The Religious System of China*. Taipei: Literary House, 6 vols.

Descola, Philippe (1996). "Constructing Natures," in Ph. Descola and Gísli Pálsson (eds.), *Nature and Society. Anthropological Perspectives* (London: Routledge), 82–102.

Detienne, Marcel, and Jean-Pierre Vernant (1989). Tr. Paula Wissing. *The Cuisine of Sacrifice among the Greeks*. Chicago: University of Chicago Press.

De Visser, M. W. (1913; rpt. 1969). *The Dragon in China and Japan*. Wiesbaden: J. Müller.

DeWoskin, Kenneth J. (1982). *A Song for One or Two: Music and the Concept of Art in Early China*. Michigan Papers in Chinese Studies no. 42. Ann Arbor, Michigan: University of Michigan Center for Chinese Studies.

——— (1983). *Doctors, Diviners, and Magicians of Ancient China: Biographies of Fang-shih*. New York: Columbia University Press.

Diény, Jean-Pierre (1987). *Le Symbolisme du Dragon dans la Chine Antique*. Paris: Bibliothèque de l'Institut des Hautes Etudes Chinoises, vol. 27.

——— (1989–90). "Le Fenghuang et le phénix," *Cahiers d'Extrême-Asie* 5, 1–15.

Dobson, W. A. C. H. (1968). *The Language of the Book of Songs*. Toronto: University of Toronto Press.

Dorofeeva-Lichtmann, Vera V. (1995). "Conception of Terrestrial Organisation in the *Shan hai jing*," *Bulletin de l'Ecole Française d'Extrême-Orient* 82, 57–110.

Douglas, Mary (1966; rpt. 1996). *Purity and Danger. An Analysis of the Concepts of Pollution and Taboo*. London: Routledge.

——— (1990). "The Pangolin Revisited: A New Approach to Animal Symbolism," in R. Willis (ed.), *Signifying Animals: Human Meaning in the Natural World* (London: Unwin Hyman), 25–36.

Dragan, Raymond A. (1993). "The Dragon in Early Imperial China." Ph.D. dissertation, University of Toronto.

Dubs, Homer (1959). "Han Hill Censers," in S. Egerød and E. Glahn (eds.), *Studia Serica Bernhard Karlgren Dedicata* (Copenhagen: Ejnar Munksgaard), 259–64.

Durrant, Stephen W. (1995). *The Cloudy Mirror: Tension and Conflict in the Writings of Sima Qian*. Albany: State University of New York Press.

Easton, Linda L. (1980). "Mapping Animal and Human Transformations: Yüan Apes in China." Ph.D. dissertation, University of Chicago.

Eberhard, Wolfram (1968). Tr. Alide Eberhard. *The Local Cultures of South and East China*. Leiden: E. J. Brill.

Eco, Umberto (1997). *The Search for the Perfect Language*. London: Fontana.

Eichhorn, Werner (1954). "Das Kapitel *Tiger* im T'ai-P'ing Kuang-Chi," *Zeitschrift der Deutschen Morgenländischen Gesellschaft* 104.9, 140–62.

Eliasberg, Danielle (1992). "Pratiques Funéraires Animales en Chine Ancienne et Médiévale," *Journal Asiatique* 280.1–2, 115–144.

Elisséeff, Danielle (1992). "Vers une Zoohistoire Chinoise," *Revue Bibliographique de Sinologie*, 171–76.

———— (1993). "Des Animaux sous une Chape de Plomb," *Anthropozoologica* 18, 17–28.

———— (1998). "L'Anthropozoologie. Un thème nouveau dans quelques revues chinoises," *Revue Bibliographique de Sinologie* 16, 273–81.

Ellen, Roy (1993). *The Cultural Relations of Classification: An Analysis of Nuaulu Animal Categories from Central Seram*. Cambridge: Cambridge University Press.

Eno, Robert (1990). *The Confucian Creation of Heaven. Philosophy and the Defense of Ritual Mastery*. Albany: State University of New York Press.

Erickson, Susan N. (1992). "Boshanlu-Mountain Censers of the Western Han period. A Typological and Iconographic Analysis," *Archives of Asian Art* 45, 6–28.

Erkes, Eduard (1942a). "Das Pferd im Alten China," *T'oung Pao* 36, 26–43.

———— (1942b). "Das Schwein im Alten China," *Monumenta Serica* 7, 68–84.

———— (1944a). "Der Hund im Alten China," *T'oung Pao* 37, 186–225.

———— (1944b). "Vogelzucht im Alten China," *T'oung Pao* 37, 15–34.

———— (1948). "Der Chinese und das Tier," *Sinologica* 1, 273–291.

———— (1954). "Das Schaf im Alten China," in J. Schubert and U. Schneider (eds.), *Asiatica. Festschrift Friedrich Weller* (Leipzig: Otto Harrasowitz), 82–92.

Falkenhausen, Lothar von (1993). *Suspended Music: Chime-Bells in the Culture of Bronze Age China*. Berkeley: University of California Press.

Fèvre, Francine (1993). "Drôles de Bestioles: Qu'est-ce qu'un Chong?" *Anthropozoologica* 18, 57–65.

Finsterbusch, Käte (1952). *Das Verhältnis des Shan-hai-djing zur bildenden Kunst*. Abhandlungen der Sächsischen Akademie der Wissenschaften zu Leipzig 46.1. Berlin: Akademie-Verlag.

Fiskesjö, Magnus (1994). "The Royal Hunt of the Shang Dynasty: Archaeological and Anthropological Perspectives." M.A. dissertation, University of Chicago.

Forbes Irving, Paul M.C. (1990). *Metamorphosis in Greek Myths*. Oxford: Clarendon, 1990.

Forke, Alfred (1911). *Lun-Heng*, Part II (Berlin: Harrasowitch), 479–489: Appendix II, "The Cycle of the Twelve Animals."

Foucault, Michel (1966; rpt. 1994). *The Order of Things*. London: Routledge.

Fracasso, Riccardo (1983). "Teratoscopy or Divination by Monsters: Being a Study on the Wu-tsang Shan-ching," *Hanxue yanjiu* 1.2, 657–700.

French, Roger (1994). *Ancient Natural History. Histories of Nature*. London: Routledge.

Gassmann, Robert H. (1988). *Cheng Ming. Richtigstellung der Bezeichnungen*. Bern: Peter Lang.

George, W., and B. Yapp (1991). *The Naming of the Beasts. Natural History in the Medieval Bestiary*. London: Duckworth.

Gibson, H. E. (1935). "Animals in the Writings of Shang," *The China Journal* 23.6, 342–51.

Gjertson, D. E. (1980). "Rebirth as an Animal in Medieval Chinese Buddhism," *Society for the Study of Chinese Religions Bulletin* 8, 56–69.

Graham, Angus C. (1978). *Later Mohist Logic, Ethics and Science*. Hong Kong: Chinese University Press.

——— (1981). *Chuang-tzu: The Inner Chapters*. London: George Allen & Unwin.

——— (1986a). *Yin-Yang and the Nature of Correlative Thinking*. Singapore: Institute of East Asian Philosophies.

——— (1986b). "The Nung-Chia 'School of the Tillers,'" in Graham, *Studies in Chinese Philosophy and Philosophical Literature* (rpt. Taipei), 67–110.

——— (1989). *Disputers of the Tao. Philosophical Argument in Ancient China*. La Salle: Open Court.

——— (1991). *The Book of Lieh-Tzu*. London: Mandala.

Graham, William T. (1979). "Mi Heng's Rhapsody on a Parrot," *Harvard Journal of Asiatic Studies* 39.1, 39–54.

Granet, Marcel (1926). *Danses et Légendes de la Chine Ancienne*. Paris: Librairie Félix Alcan, 2 vols.

——— (1934; rpt. 1999). *La Pensée Chinoise*. Paris: Albin Michel.

Gulik, R. H. van (1940). *The Lore of the Chinese Lute*. Tokyo: Sophia University.

——— (1967). *The Gibbon in China; an Essay in Chinese Animal Lore*. Leiden: E.J. Brill.

Hachisuka, M. U. (1924). "The Identification of the Chinese Phoenix," *Journal of the Royal Asiatic Society of Great Britain and Ireland*, 585–89.

Hall, David L., and Roger T. Ames (1987). *Thinking through Confucius*. Albany: State University of New York Press.

——— (1995). *Anticipating China: Thinking through the Narratives of Chinese and Western Culture*. Albany: State University of New York Press.

——— (1998). *Thinking from the Han: Self, Truth, and Transcendence in Chinese and Western Culture*. Albany: State University of New York Press.

Hammond, Charles E. (1992–93). "Sacred Metamorphosis: The Weretiger and the Shaman," *Acta Orientalia* 46.2–3, 235–55.

——— (1996). "Vulpine Alchemy," *T'oung Pao* 82 (4–5), 364–80.

Handlin Smith, Joanna F. (1999). "Liberating Animals in Ming-Qing China: Buddhist Inspiration and Elite Imagination," *Journal of Asian Studies* 58.1, 51–84.

Harbsmeier, Christoph (1998). *Language and Logic*, in Needham, SCC, vol. 7, part 1. Cambridge: Cambridge University Press.

Hargett, James M. (1989). "Playing the Second Fiddle: The Luan-bird in Early and Medieval Chinese Literature," *T'oung Pao* 75, 235–62.

Harper, Donald (1985). "A Chinese Demonography of the Third Century B.C.," *Harvard Journal of Asiatic Studies* 45, 459–98.

———— (1987). "Wang Yen-shou's Nightmare Poem," *Harvard Journal of Asiatic Studies* 47.1, 239–83.

———— (1990). "The Conception of Illness in Early Chinese Medicine, as Documented in Newly Discovered 3rd and 2nd Century B.C. Manuscripts," *Sudhoffs Archiv* 74.2, 210–31.

———— (1994). "Resurrection in Warring States Popular Religion," *Taoist Resources* 5.2, 13–28.

———— (1996). "Spellbinding," in Donald S. Lopez Jr. (ed.), *Religions of China in Practice* (Princeton: Princeton University Press), 241–50.

———— (1997). "Warring States, Qin, and Han Manuscripts Related to Natural Philosophy and the Occult," in Edward L. Shaughnessy (ed.), *New Sources of Early Chinese History. An Introduction to the Reading of Inscriptions and Manuscripts* (The Society for the Study of Early China & The Institute of East Asian Studies; Berkeley: University of California), 223–52.

———— (1998). *Early Chinese Medical Literature*. London: Kegan Paul International.

———— (1999). "Warring States Natural Philosophy and Occult Thought," in M. Loewe and E. Shaughnessy (eds.), *The Cambridge History of Ancient China* (Cambridge: Cambridge University Press), 813–84.

Harrist, Robert E. Jr. (1997). "The Legacy of Bole: Physiognomy and Horses in Chinese Painting," *Artibus Asiae* 57 (1–2), 135–56.

Hay, John (1994). "The Persistent Dragon (*Lung*)," in W. L. Petersen, A. H. Plaks, Yu Ying-shih (eds.), *The Power of Culture: Studies in Chinese Cultural History* (Hong Kong: Chinese University Press), 119–49.

Henricks, Robert G. (1996). "The Three-Bodied Shun and the Completion of Creation," *Bulletin of the School of Oriental and African Studies* 59.2, 268–95.

Hentze, Carl (1958). "Le Symbolisme des Oiseaux dans la Chine Ancienne," *Sinologica* 5, 65–92.

———— (1964). "Die Wanderung der Tiere um die Heiligen Berge," *Symbolon* 4, 9–104.

Hervouet, Yves (1964). *Un Poète de Cour sous les Han: Sseu-ma Siang-jou*. Paris: Presses Universitaires de France.

Hicks, Carola (1993). *Animals in Early Medieval Art*. Edinburgh: Edinburgh University Press.

Hightower, James (1952). *Han Shih Wai Chuan: Han Ying's Illustrations of the Didactic Application of the Classic of Songs*. Cambridge, Mass.: Harvard University Press.

Hightower, Robert (1959). "Chia Yi's *Owl Fu*," *Asia Major* 7, 125–30.

Ho, Judy Chungwa (1991). "The Twelve Calendrical Animals in Tang Tombs," in George Kuwayama (ed.), *Ancient Mortuary Traditions of China* (Far Eastern Art Council, Los Angeles County Museum of Art), 60–83.

Höllman, Thomas O. (1983). "Die Stellung des Hundes im alten China," in Müller-Karpe (1983), 157–69.

Hopkins, L. C. (1913). "Dragon and Alligator: Being Notes on Some Ancient Inscribed Bone Carvings," *Journal of the Royal Asiatic Society*, 545–52.

—— (1943). "The Bearskin, Another Pictographic Reconnaissance from Primitive Prophylactic to Present-Day Panache: A Chinese Epigraphic Puzzle," *Journal of the Royal Asiatic Society*, 110–17.

Hsü, Elisabeth (1994). "Change in Chinese Medicine: *Bian* and *Hua*," in V. Alleton and A.Volkov (eds.), *Notions et Perceptions du Changement en Chine*. Mémoirs de l'Institut des Hautes Etudes Chinoises, vol. 36 (Paris: Collège de France, 1994), 41–58.

Hull, Denison B. (1964). *Hounds and Hunting in Ancient Greece*. Chicago: University of Chicago Press.

Hulsewé, A. F. P. and M. Loewe (1979). *China in Central Asia: The Early Stage 125 B.C.–A.D. 23*. Leiden: E.J. Brill, 1979.

—— (1985). *Remnants of Ch'in Law*. Leiden: E. J. Brill.

Huntington, Rania A. (1996). "Foxes and Ming-Qing Fiction." Ph.D. dissertation, Harvard University.

Hyland, Ann (1990). *Equus: The Horse in the Roman World*. London: B. T. Batsford.

Ingold, Tim (ed.) (1988). *What Is an Animal?* London: Unwin Hyman.

Izushi Yoshihiko (1937). "A Study of the Origin of the Qilin and the Fenghuang," *Memoirs of the Research Department of the Tōyō Bunko* 9, 79–109.

Jennison, George (1937). *Animals for Show and Pleasure in Ancient Rome*. Manchester: Manchester University Press.

Johnson, T. W. (1974). "Far Eastern Fox Lore," *Asian Folklore Studies* 33, 35–68.

Johnson, Wallace (1997). *The T'ang Code*, vol. 2. Princeton: Princeton University Press.

Jones, William C. (1994). *The Great Qing Code*. Oxford: Clarendon.

Kalinowski, Marc (1986). "Les traités de Shuihudi et l'hémérologie chinoise à la fin des Royaumes Combattants," *T'oung Pao* 72, 175–228.

Kaltenmark, Max (1953). *Le Lie-Sien Tchouan*. Université de Paris; Publications du Centre d'Etudes Sinologiques de Pékin.

—— (1963). "Les Danses Sacrées en Chine," in *Sources Orientales* 6 (Paris: Editions du Seuil), 413–50.

Karlgren, Bernhard (1950). *The Book of Odes*. Stockholm: Museum of Far Eastern Antiquities.

—— (1957; rpt. 1972). *Grammata Serica Recensa*. Stockholm: Museum of Far Eastern Antiquities.

Keithley, David (1985). *Sources of Shang History*. Berkeley: University of California Press.

Kern, Martin (1996). "In Praise of Political Legitimacy: The Miao and Jiao Hymns of the Western Han," *Oriens Extremus* 39.1, 29–67.

Kiyohito Munakata (1991). *Sacred Mountains in Chinese Art*. Krannert Art Museum; University of Illinois Press.

Kleeman, Terry F. (1994). "Licentious Cults and Bloody Victuals: Sacrifice, Reciprocity, and Violence in Traditional China," *Asia Major* 7.1, 185–211.

———— (1998). *Great Perfection. Religion and Ethnicity in a Chinese Millennial Kingdom.* Honolulu: University of Hawaii Press.

Knechtges, David R. (1976). *The Han Rhapsody: A Study of the Fu of Yang Hsiung (53 B.C.– A.D. 18)*. Cambridge: Cambridge University Press.

———— (1982) vol. 1, (1987) vol. 2, (1996) vol. 3. *Wen xuan or Selections of Refined Literature*. Princeton: Princeton University Press.

Knoblock, John (1988) vol. 1, (1990) vol. 2, (1994) vol. 3. *Xunzi. A Translation and Study of the Complete Works*. Stanford: Stanford University Press.

Kroll, Paul W. (1981). "The Dancing Horses of T'ang," *T'oung Pao* 67, 240–68.

———— (1984). "The Image of the Halcyon Kingfisher in Medieval Chinese Poetry," *Journal of the American Oriental Society* 104.2, 237–51.

Kuhn, Dieter (1988). *Textile Technology: Spinning and Reeling*. In Needham, SCC, vol. 5, part 9. Cambridge: Cambridge University Press.

Lai, T. C. (1998). "Messenger of Spring and Morality: Cuckoo Lore in Chinese Sources," *Journal of the American Oriental Society* 118.4, 530–42.

Lai, Whalen (1984). "Symbolism of Evil in China: The K'ung-chia Myth Analyzed," *History of Religions* 23, 316–43.

———— (1996). "An Anthology of Sources on Chinese Mythology," Review of Birrell (1993). *Asian Folklore Studies* 55, 319–27.

Lao Kan (1978). "The Early Use of the Tally in China," in David T. Roy and Tsuen-hsuin Tsien (eds.), *Ancient China: Studies in Early Civilization* (Hong Kong: Chinese University Press), 91–98.

Lau, D. C. (1963). *Lao Tzu Tao Te Ching*. Harmondsworth: Penguin.

Laufer, Bertold (1914). "Bird Divination among the Tibetans," *T'oung Pao* 15, 1–166.

———— (1962). "Jottings on the Races of Dogs in Ancient China," in *Chinese Pottery of the Han Dynasty* (1909; rpt. Tokyo: Charles E. Tuttle), 247–81.

Lefeuvre, Jean A. (1990–91). "Rhinoceros and Wild Buffaloes North of the Yellow River at the End of the Shang Dynasty: Some Remarks on the Graph 兕 and the Character 兕," *Monumenta Serica* 39, 131–157.

Legge, James (1871; rpt. 1991). *The She King*. Taipei: SMC Publishing.

Lemoine, Jacques (1987). "Mythes d'Origine, Mythes d'Identification," *L'Homme* 101, 58–85.

Lévi, Jean (1987). "Les Fonctions Religieuses de la Bureaucratie Céleste," *L'Homme* 101, 35–57.

Lévi-Strauss, Claude (1962). *La Pensée Sauvage*. Paris: Librairie Plon.

———— (1969). *Totemism*. Harmondsworth: Penguin.

Lewis, Mark Edward (1990). *Sanctioned Violence in Early China*. Albany: State University of New York Press.

———— (1999). *Writing and Authority in Early China*. Albany: State University of New York Press.

Li Xueqin (1985). *Eastern Zhou and Qin Civilizations*. New Haven: Yale University Press.

Lin Yutang (1936; rpt. 1948). *My Country and My People*. London: William Heinemann.

Liu, Chungshee H. (1932). "The Dog-Ancestor Story of the Aboriginal Tribes of Southern China," *Journal of the Royal Anthropological Institute of Great Britain and Ireland* 62, 361–68.

———— (1940–41). "On the Dog Ancestor Myth in Asia," *Studia Serica* 1, 85–109.

Liu Li (1996). "Mortuary Ritual and Social Hierarchy in the Longshan Culture," *Early China* 21, 1–46.

Lloyd, G. E. R. (1983). *Science, Folklore and Ideology: Studies in the Life Sciences in Ancient Greece*. Cambridge: Cambridge University Press.

———— (1996a). *Adversaries and Authorities: Investigations into Ancient Greek and Chinese Science*. Cambridge: Cambridge University Press.

———— (1996b). *Aristotelian Explorations*. Cambridge: Cambridge University Press.

Loewe, Michael (1967). *Records of Han Administration*. Cambridge: Cambridge University Press, 2 vols.

———— (1978). "Man and Beast: The Hybrid in Early Chinese Art and Literature," *Numen* 25.2, 97–117.

———— (1987). "The Cult of the Dragon and the Invocation for Rain," in Charles LeBlanc and Susan Blader (eds.), *Chinese Ideas about Nature and Society. Studies in Honor of Derk Bodde* (Hong Kong: Hong Kong University Press), 195–213.

———— (1988). "Shells, Bones and Stalks during the Han Period," *T'oung Pao* 74, 83–88.

———— (ed.) (1993). *Early Chinese Texts: A Bibliographical Guide*. Berkeley: Society for the Study of Early China and the Institute of East Asian Studies, University of California.

———— (1994). *Divination, Mythology and Monarchy in Han China*. Cambridge: Cambridge University Press.

———— (1997). "The Physician Chunyu Yi and His Historical Background," in Jacques Gernet and Marc Kalinowski (eds.), *En Suivant La Voie Royale. Mélanges offerts en hommage à Léon Vandermeersch* (Paris: Ecole Française de l'Extrême Orient), 297–314.

Loewe, M., and Edward L. Shaughnessy (eds.) (1999). *The Cambridge History of Ancient China. From the Origins of Civilization to 221 B.C.* Cambridge & New York: Cambridge University Press.

Lundbaek, Knud (1988). *The Traditional History of the Chinese Script*. Aarhus: Aarhus University Press.

Lynn, Richard J. (1994). *The Classic of Changes*. New York: Columbia University Press.

Machle, Edward J. (1993). *Nature and Heaven in the Xunzi: A Study of the Tian Lun*. Albany: State University of New York Press.

Mainoldi, Carla (1984). *L'Image du Loup et du Chien dans la Grèce Ancienne d'Homère à Platon*. Paris: Editions Orphys.

Major, John (1993). *Heaven and Earth in Early Han Thought*. Albany: State University of New York Press.

———— (1999). "Characteristics of Late Chu Religion," in Cook and Major (1999), 121–143.

Makeham, John (1994). *Name and Actuality in Early Chinese Thought*. Albany: State University of New York Press.

Malamud, Randy (1998). *Reading Zoos: Representations of Animals and Captivity*. New York: New York University Press.

Mansvelt Beck, B. J. (1990). *The Treatises of Later Han*. Sinica Leidensia, vol. 21. Leiden: E. J. Brill.

Mathieu, Rémi (1984a). "Le Corbeau dans la Mythologie de l'Ancienne Chine," *Revue de l'Histoire des Religions* 201.3, 281–308.

———— (1984b). "La Patte de l'Ours, " *L'Homme* 24.1, 5–42.

———— (1984c). "Aux Origines de la Femme-Renarde de l'Ancienne Chine," *Etudes Mongoles et Sibériennes* 15, 83–109.

———— (1990). "Le Lièvre de la Lune dans l'Antiquité Chinoise, " *Revue de l'Histoire des Religions* 207.4, 339–65.

———— (1992). "Yu le Grand et le Mythe du Déluge dans la Chine Ancienne," *T'oung Pao* 78, 162–90.

Mattos, Gilbert L. (1988). *The Stone Drums of Ch'in*. Monumenta Serica Monograph Series 19. Nettetal: Steyler Verlag.

Mayo, Lewis (2000). "The Order of Birds in Guiyi Jun Dunhuang," *East Asian History* 20, 1–59.

Métailié, Georges (1992). "Des mots, des animaux, des plantes," *Extrême-Orient Extrême-Occident* 14, 169–83.

———— (1993). "Regards de Lettrés Chinois sur les Animaux au XVIème Siècle," *Anthropozoologica* 18, 45–55.

Métailié, Georges, and Fr. Fèvre (1993). "Aperçu des Sources Chinoises pour l'Histoire des Animaux," *Anthropozoologica* 18, 99–103.

Miller, Alan L. (1995). "The Woman Who Married a Horse: Five Ways of Looking at a Chinese Folktale," *Asian Folklore Studies* 54, 275–305.

Morgan, Carole (1983). "Dog Divination from a Dunhuang Manuscript," *Journal of the Hong Kong Branch of the Royal Asiatic Society* 23, 185–93.

———— (1987). "La Divination d'après les Croassements des Corbeaux dans les Manuscrits de Dunhuang," *Cahiers d'Extrême-Asie* 3, 55–76.

Morphy, Howard (ed.) (1989). *Animals into Art*. London: Unwin Hyman.

Mullan, B., and G. Marvin (1987). *Zoo Culture*. London: Weidenfield & Nicolson.

Müller-Karpe, Hermann (1983). *Zur frühen Mensch-Tier Symbiose*. München: Verlag C. H. Beck.

Mundkur, Balaji (1983). *The Cult of the Serpent: An Interdisciplinary Survey of its Manifestations and Origins*. Albany: State University of New York Press.

Namio Egami (1951). "The K'uai-T'i, the T'ao-Yu and the Tan-Hsi, the Strange Domestic Animals of the Hsiung-Nu," *Memoirs of the Research Department of the Tōyō Bunko* 13, 87–123.

Needham, Joseph, and D. Leslie (1952). "Ancient and Mediaeval Chinese Thought on

Evolution," *Proceedings of the National Institute of Sciences of India* (New Delhi) 7, 1–18.

Needham, Joseph (1954–). *Science and Civilisation in China* (Abbreviated SCC). Cambridge: Cambridge University Press.

Nienhauser, William H. Jr. (ed.) (1994). *The Grand Scribe's Records. Volume I: The Basic Annals of Pre-Han China*. Bloomington: Indiana University Press.

Nylan, Michael (1982). "Ying Shao's *Feng su t'ung yi*: An Exploration of Problems in Han Dynasty Political, Philosophical, and Social Unity." Ph.D. dissertation, Princeton University.

——— (1994). *The Elemental Changes*. Albany: State University of New York Press.

Ohnuki-Tierny, Emiko (1987). *The Monkey as Mirror: Symbolic Transformations in Japanese History and Ritual*. Princeton: Princeton University Press.

Paludan, Ann (1991). *The Chinese Spirit Road. The Classical Tradition of Stone Tomb Statuary*. New Haven & London: Yale University Press.

Paper, Jordan (1978). "The Meaning of the T'ao-Tieh," *History of Religions* 18.1, 18–42.

——— (1986). "The *Feng* in Protohistoric Chinese Religion," *History of Religions* 25.3, 213–35.

Petit, G., and J. Théodoridès (1962). *Histoire de la Zoologie*. Paris: Hermann.

Pines, Yuri (1997). "The Search for Stability: Late Ch'un-ch'iu Thinkers," *Asia Major* (Third Series) 10 (1–2), 1–47.

Porkert, Manfred (1974). *The Theoretical Foundations of Chinese Medicine*. Cambridge, Mass.: M.I.T. Press.

Porter, Deborah Lynn (1996). *From Deluge to Discourse*. Albany: State University of New York Press.

Powers, Martin J. (1983). "Hybrid Omens and Public Issues in early Imperial China," *Bulletin of the Museum of Far Eastern Antiquities* 55, 1–56.

——— (1991). *Art and Political Expression in Early China*. New Haven & London: Yale University Press.

Prieur, Jean (1988). *Les Animaux Sacrées dans l'Antiquité*. Rennes: Ouest-France.

Puett, Michael (1997). "Nature and Artifice: Debates in Late Warring States China Concerning the Creation of Culture," *Harvard Journal of Asiatic Studies* 57.2, 471–518.

Queen, Sarah A. (1996). *From Chronicle to Canon: The Hermeneutics of the Spring and Autumn according to Tung Chungshu*. Cambridge: Cambridge University Press.

Raphals, Lisa (1998). *Sharing the Light: Representations of Women and Virtue in early China*. Albany: State University of New York Press.

Rawson, Jessica (1992). "Late Shang Bronze Design: Meaning and Purpose," in R. Whitfield (ed.), *The Problem of Meaning*. London: University of London.

——— (1998). "Strange Creatures," *Oriental Art* 44.2, 44–47.

Read, Bernard E. (1931). *Chinese Materia Medica; Animal Drugs*; (1932) *Avian Drugs*; (1937) *Turtle and Shellfish Drugs*; (1939) *Fish Drugs*; (1941) *Insect Drugs*. Beijing: Peking Natural History Bulletin.

Rickett, Allyn W. (1965). *Kuan-Tzu*. Hong Kong: Hong Kong University Press.

—— (1985, 1998). *Guanzi. Political, Economic, and Philosophical Essays from Early China*, 2 vols. Princeton: Princeton University Press.

Riegel, Jeffrey K. (1982). "Early Chinese Target Magic," *Journal of Chinese Religions* 10, 1–18.

—— (1989–90). "Kou-Mang and Ju-Shou," *Cahiers d'Extrême-Asie* 5, 55–83.

Rivo, Harriet (1990). *The Animal Estate: The English and Other Creatures in the Victorian Age*. London: Penguin.

Robinet, Isabelle (1979). "Metamorphosis and Deliverance from the Corpse in Taoism," *History of Religions* 19.1, 37–71.

Rudolph, Richard C. (1960). "Bull Grappling in Early Chinese Reliefs," *Archaeology* 13, 241–45.

Rutt, Richard (1996). *The Book of Changes*. Durham East-Asia Series no. 1; Richmond: Curzon.

Salisbury, Joyce E. (1994). *The Beast Within. Animals in the Middle Ages*. London: Routledge.

Salmony, Albert (1954). *Antler and Tongue: An Essay on Ancient Chinese Symbolism*. Ascona: Artibus Asiae.

Salviati, F. (1994). "Bird and Bird-Related Motives in the Iconography of the Liangzhu Culture," *Revista degli Studi Orientali* 58 (1–2), 133–60.

Saussy, Haun (1993). *The Problem of a Chinese Aesthetic*. Stanford: Stanford University Press.

Sawyer, Ralph D. (1993). *The Seven Military Classics of Ancient China*. Boulder, Colo.: Westview Press.

Schafer, Edward H. (1956). "Cultural History of the Elaphure," *Sinologica* 4, 250–74.

—— (1950). "The Camel in China down to the Mongol Dynasty," *Sinologica* 4.

—— (1959a). "Falconry in T'ang Times," *T'oung Pao* 46, 293–338.

—— (1959b). "Parrots in Medieval China," in S. Egerød and E. Glahn (eds.), *Studia Serica Bernhard Karlgren Dedicata* (Copenhagen: Ejnar Munksgaard), 271–282.

—— (1962). "The Conservation of Nature under the T'ang Dynasty," *Journal of the Economic and Social History of the Orient* 5, 279–308.

—— (1962). "Eating Turtles in Ancient China," *Journal of the American Oriental Society* 82, 73–74.

—— (1967; rpt. 1985). *The Vermilion Bird: T'ang Images of the South*. Berkeley & Los Angeles: University of California Press.

—— (1968). "Hunting Parks and Animal Enclosures in Ancient China," *Journal of the Economic and Social History of the Orient* 11, 318–43.

—— (1991). "The Chinese Dhole," *Asia Major* (New Series) 4.1, 1–6.

Schindler, Bruno (1924). "On the Travel, Wayside and Wind Offerings in Ancient China," *Asia Major* 1, 624–56.

Schipper, Kristofer (1995). "The Immortal Cult of Tang Gongfang." Paper presented at the Conference on Local Cults in China. Paris, Ecole Française d'Extrême-Orient, 29 May–1 June 1995.

Schmidt, Franz-Rudolph (1997). "Entomologie jenseits der Gewissheit. Die Konzeption vom Kurzen Fuchs," *Oriens Extremus* 40.1, 78–101.

Schnapp-Gourbeillon, Annie (1981). *Lions, Héros, Masques. Les Représentations de l'Animal chez Homère*. Paris: Librairie François Maspero.

Schuessler, Axel (1987). *A Dictionary of Early Zhou Chinese*. Honolulu: University of Hawaii Press.

Schwartz, Benjamin I. (1985). *The World of Thought in Ancient China*. Cambridge Mass.: Harvard University Press.

Seiwert, Hubert (1983). "Ausgrenzung der Dämonen—am Beispiel der Chinesischen Religionsgeschichte," *Saeculum* 34, 316–33.

Shaughnessy, Edward L. (1991). *Sources of Western Zhou History*. Berkeley: University of California Press.

———— (1992). "Marriage, Divorce, and Revolution: Reading between the Lines of the Book of Changes," *Journal of Asian Studies* 51.3, 587–99.

———— (1996). *I Ching. The Classic of Changes*. New York: Ballantine Books.

———— (1997). *Before Confucius. Studies in the Creation of the Chinese Classics*. Albany: State University of New York Press.

Shen, Jieshi (1936–37). "An Essay on the Primitive Meaning of the Character Kuei 鬼," *Monumenta Serica* 2, 1–20.

Shepard, Odell (1930; rpt. 1996). *The Lore of the Unicorn*. London: George Allen & Unwin.

Sivin, Nathan (1991). "Change and Continuity in Early Cosmology: The Great Commentary to the Book of Changes," in Yamada Keiji 山田慶兒 and Tanaka Tan 田中淡 (eds.), *Chūgoku kodai kagakushi ron* 中國古代科學史論 (Kyoto: Jinbun Kagaku Kenkyūsho), 3–43.

Slater, Candace (1994). *Dance of the Dolphin: Transformation and Disenchantment in the Amazonian Imagination*. Chicago: University of Chicago Press.

Sorabji, Richard (1993). *Animal Minds and Human Morals. The Origins of the Western Debate*. London: Gerald Duckworth.

Sowerby, Arthur de Carle (1939). "Some Chinese Animal Myths and Legends," *Journal of the North China Branch of the Royal Asiatic Society* 70, 3–20.

———— (1940). *Nature in Chinese Art*. New York: John Day.

Sperber, D. (1975). "Pourquoi les Animaux Parfaits, les Hybrides, les Monstres sont-ils bons à penser symboliquement?" *L'Homme* 15.2, 5–34.

Spring, Madeline K. (1988). "Fabulous Horses and Worthy Scholars in Ninth-Century China," *T'oung Pao* 74, 173–210.

———— (1993). *Animal Allegories in T'ang China*. American Oriental Series, vol. 76. New Haven: American Oriental Society.

Steele, John (1917). *The I Li, or Book of Etiquette and Ceremonial*. London: Probsthain.

Sterckx, Roel (1996). "An Ancient Chinese Horse Ritual," *Early China* 21, 47–79.

———— (2000). "Transforming the Beasts: Animals and Music in Early China." *T'oung Pao* 86, 1–46.

Stoltz, Herbert (1937). *Der Hund in der griechisch-römischen Magie und Religion*. Berlin: Triltsch & Huther.

Strätz, Volker (1996). "Materialen zu Tierkreisen in China," *Monumenta Serica* 44, 213–65.

Sukhu, Gopal (1999). "Monkeys, Shamans, Emperors, and Poets," in Cook and Major (1999), 145–65.

Swanson, Gerald (1984). "The Concept of Change in the *Great Treatise*," in Henry Rosemont Jr. (ed.), *Explorations in Early Chinese Cosmology* (Chico: Scholars Press), 67–93.

Szrabó, Thomas (1997). "Der Kritik der Jagd von der Antike zum Mittelalter," in Werner Rösener (ed.), *Jagd und höfische Kultur im Mittelalter* (Göttingen: Vandenhoeck & Ruprecht), 116–229.

Tambiah, S. J. (1969; rpt. 1985). "Animals are Good to Think and Good to Prohibit," in *Culture, Thought, and Social Action* (Cambridge, Mass.: Harvard University Press), 169–211.

Taylor, Rodney L. (1986). "Of Animals and Man: The Confucian Perspective," in Tom Regan (ed.), *Animal Sacrifices. Religious Perspectives on the Use of Animals in Science* (Philadelphia: Temple University Press), 237–63.

Thomas, Keith (1983). *Man and the Natural World: Changing Attitudes in England 1500–1800*. London: Allen Lane.

Torrance, John (ed.) (1992). *The Concept of Nature. The Herbert Spencer Lectures*. Oxford: Clarendon Press.

Tournier, Maurice Louis (1991). *L'Imaginaire et la Symbolique dans la Chine Ancienne*. Paris: L'Harmattan.

Toynbee, Jocelyn M. C. (1973; rpt. 1996). *Animals in Roman Life and Art*. Baltimore: Johns Hopkins University Press.

Ts'ao Sung-yeh (1970). "Bullfighting in Chin-Hua (Chekiang Province)," in Wolfram Eberhard (ed.), *Studies in Chinese Folklore and Related Essays* (Bloomington: Indiana University Folklore Institute Monograph series, vol. 23), 73–82.

Tuan, Yi-Fu (1984). *Dominance and Affection: The Making of Pets*. New Haven: Yale University Press.

Twitchett, D., and M. Loewe (eds.) (1986). *The Cambridge History of China. Volume I: The Ch'in and Han Empires (221 B.C.-A.D. 220)*. Cambridge: Cambridge University Press.

Vandermeersch, Léon (1977–1980). *Wangdao ou La Voie Royale*. Paris: Ecole Française d'Extrême-Orient; 2 vols.

Van Zoeren, Steven (1991). *Poetry and Personality. Reading, Exegesis, and Hermeneutics in Traditional China*. Stanford: Stanford University Press.

Vialles, Noëlie (1994). Tr. J.A. Underwood. *Animal to Edible*. Cambridge: Cambridge University Press.

Waley, Arthur (1954). *The Book of Songs*. London: George Allen & Unwin.

——— (1955). "The Heavenly Horses of Ferghana, a New View," *History Today* 5, 95–103.

Wang, Aihe (2000). *Cosmology and Political Culture in Early China*. New York: Cambridge University Press.

Wang, C.H. (1974). *The Bell and the Drum: Shih Ching as Formulaic Poetry in an Oral Tradition*. Berkeley: University of California Press.

Wang Tao (1992). "A Textual Investigation on the Taotie" in R. Whitfield (ed.), *The Problem of Meaning* (London: University of London), 102–118.

Waterbury, Florance (1952). *Bird-Deities in China.* Ascona: Artibus Asiae Suppl. 10.

Watson, Burton (1961). *Records of the Grand Historian of China.* New York: Columbia University Press.

Watters, T. (1867). "Chinese Notions about Pigeons And Doves," *Journal of the North China Branch of the Royal Asiatic Society* 4, 225–242.

——— (1874). "Chinese Fox-Myths," *Journal of the North China Branch of the Royal Asiatic Society* 8.4, 45–65.

Weld, Susan (1997). "The Covenant Texts from Houma and Wenxian," in Edward L. Shaughnessy (ed.), *New Sources of Early Chinese History. An Introduction to the Reading of Inscriptions and Manuscripts* (Berkeley: Society for the Study of Early China & Institute of East Asian Studies), 125–60.

White, David G. (1991). *Myths of the Dog-Man.* Chicago: Chicago University Press.

White, William Ch. (1939). *Tomb Tile Pictures of Ancient China.* Toronto: University of Toronto Press.

Wilhelm, Hellmut (1961). *Change. Eight Lectures on the I Ching.* London: Routledge & Kegan Paul.

Wu Guangming (1990). *The Butterfly as Companion: Meditation on the First Three Chapters of the Chuang Tzu.* Albany: State University of New York Press.

Wu Hung (1987). "The Earliest Pictorial Representations of Ape Tales," *T'oung Pao* 73, 86–112.

——— (1989). *The Wu Liang Shrine: The Ideology of Early Chinese Pictorial Art.* Stanford: Stanford University Press.

——— (1995). *Monumentality in Early Chinese Art and Architecture.* Stanford: Stanford University Press.

Yang Xiaoneng (2000). *Reflections of Early China: Decor, Pictographs, and Pictorial Inscriptions.* Seattle & London: The Nelson-Atkins Museum of Art and University of Washington Press.

Yates, Robin D. S. (1994). "The Yin-Yang Texts from Yinqueshan: An Introduction and Partial Reconstruction, with Notes on their Significance in Relation to Huang-Lao Daoism," *Early China* 19, 75–144.

Young, Robert M. (1985). *Darwin's Metaphor: Nature's Place in Victorian Culture.* Cambridge: Cambridge University Press.

Yu, Pauline (1987). *The Reading of Imagery in the Chinese Poetic Tradition.* Princeton: Princeton University Press.

Zeitlin, Judith (1993). *Historian of the Strange: Pu Songling and the Chinese Classical Tale.* Stanford: Stanford University Press.

INDEX

A

abattoir, 161
Adam, 34
adder, 175
Aelian, 298n. 17
afterlife, 63, 232
aggression, 76, 103
agriculture, 26, 28, 35, 43, 51, 64, 65, 95, 107
    aqua farming, 155
    Qin statutes on, 145
air (*see* wind; *qi*)
Allan, Sarah, 187
allegory, 8–11, 123
alligator, 65, 189, 203
altar, 267n. 90, 300n. 32
    altar to the soil, 109, 135
Ames, Roger, 20, 89
amphibians, 31, 87, 100, 125, 126, 168, 175,
    176, 177, 202
animacy, 16, 76, 78
animal(s) (*see also* classification; names)
    adopting human behavior, 229, 231
    and combat, 101, 102, 108, 132, 190
    and invention of writing, 98–100
    and music, 124–137
    and the spirit world, 61, 63, 135–136
    and sensory perception, 126
    animal behavior, 37, 64, 65, 66, 82–83,
        110, 140–143, 227, 228, 229, 231
    as biological category, 3, 74, 80, 82,
        87, 88, 194, 205, 207
    as foodstuff, 28–29, 106, 153, 174, 176
    as gifts, 57–58, 62, 120, 121 (*see also*
        tribute)

    compassion toward, 141, 142, 144, 145,
        146, 161
    cultural studies of, 1–4
    definitions of, 15–21
    emotions of, 75–76
    in art, 10, 12
    in calendars, 64–67
    instruction of, 74, 76, 148–150
    literature on, 21–29
    military symbolism of, 102–103
animal doctors, 26
animal register, 54
animal tracks, 96, 98, 101
anomaly (*see also* strange), 197
    and the realm of texts, 221, 223, 229–
        230
    definitions of, 206–211, 225
    interpretation of, 211–214
antelope, 28
anthropocentrism, 2
anthropology, 69, 70, 71, 206–207
antiquity, 51, 94–96
    as an idealized era, 137, 138, 139
    as primitive, 94, 98
antlers (*see* horns)
ants, 106, 131, 144
ape, 37, 161, 190
apocryphal literature, 97, 100, 133, 159, 230
aquatic animals, 26, 35, 52, 102, 125, 126,
    144, 189
archaeology, 12, 13, 26
archery, 192–194
    legendary archers, 149
    archery songs, 194

Aristotle, 3, 17, 28, 81, 89, 108, 276n. 12

armored animals (see *jie*)

army formations, 58, 102, 103

arrow, 149

    stringed arrow, 145

attacks, 141–142

avenging ghosts, 172

authority, 1, 3, 5, 7, 40, 45, 55, 65, 74, 93, 95, 109, 111, 112, 115, 120, 122, 139, 142, 147, 151, 161, 167, 177, 179, 184, 194, 198, 235, 239, 240

    and music, 129, 131

    numinous authority, 165, 181

B

badger, 64, 105, 107, 112

Bai Juyi, 277n. 25

bambix mori (see also silkworm), 184

Ban Gu, 114, 152, 195, 197

Ban Zhao, 305n. 99

bandits (see villains)

banners, 99

    signal flags, 102

banquet, 36, 50, 139

Bao Puzi, 51, 203

Bao Si, 201, 202

Baoshan, 59

barbarians (see also Yue), 65–66, 106, 119, 158–161, 162, 191, 233–234

    Ailao, 190

    as expert hunters, 108

    as herdsmen, 161

    Ba, 160, 265n. 77

    Board-Shield Man, 160

    communicating with animals, 159

    Di, 74, 159, 227

    Hu, 233

    identified with animals, 55, 74, 158–161, 235, 274n. 94

    Man, 160

    Miao, 106

    Min, 233

    Mo, 160

    Rong, 74, 159

    Wuhuan, 232

    Wusun, 152

    Xiongnu, 108, 151, 160, 234

    Yi, 160, 227

bat, 31

battle, 108, 200

    of Chengpu, 103

bear, 112, 117, 132, 144, 191, 193, 194, 228

    in dreams, 215

bee, 175

bells, 125, 127–128, 133, 136

    decoration of, 128

bestiary, 8, 37, 38, 153, 155, 156

bi ("comparison"), 207

bifang 畢方, 212

biology, 5, 31, 67, 69–71, 84, 88, 153

biotope, 31, 81, 93, 139, 142, 226

bipeds, 21

birds, 18, 22, 27, 35, 37, 42, 50, 51, 63, 75, 145, 148, 152, 155, 158

    bird cult, 61–62

    bird flight, 57–58, 179

    bird killer, 49, 54

    bird names as official titles, 51–52

    bird people, 104, 185

    bird song, 159, 286n. 19

    determining sex of, 31

    spirit birds, 181

bivalves, 81, 169, 201, 203

bixie 辟邪, 32

blood (see also sacrifice), 41, 200, 212

    "blood and *qi*," 72, 73–78, 103

    and custom, 105

    as physiological concept, 73–76

    bleeding victim animals, 76–78

    blood consecration, 76–77, 161

    blood-sweating horses (see also Heavenly Horse), 251n. 55

    of dogs, 232

boar (see also pig), 59

body, 149, 150
Bo Juzi, 149
Bo Le (*see also* physiognomy), 157, 239, 252n. 66
Bo Ya, 130
Bo Yi, 119, 120, 159
Bodde, Derk, 188
Bohutong, 18, 57, 90, 193
bones, 146
    decoction of, 107
Boodberg, Peter, 67
botany, 70
bream, 115, 197
breeding, 48, 65, 66, 110, 115, 155
    species interbreeding, 135
bronze vessels, 187
    inscriptions on, 46, 58, 190
Bu Shi, 26, 151
Buddhism, 297n. 191
buffalo, 63
bugs, 19, 186
bull (*see* ox; cow)
bureaucracy, 7, 51
    and spirit world, 62–63
    dealing with animals, 47–49
burial, 63, 280n. 85
    of sacrificial animals, 41, 109, 232
Burkert, Walter, 3
butterfly, 168, 215

C

cages, 116, 148
Cai Mo, 52
Cai Yong, 21, 42, 99, 126, 183, 185, 196
calamities, 195
calendar, 43, 51, 79, 82, 144, 146, 160, 229, 233
    animal data in, 27, 64–67
    calendrical metamorphoses, 81, 146, 173–177
calf, 218
calligraphy, 99

camel, 121
Campany, Robert, 223
Cang Jie, 22, 98, 99, 100, 170
cangguang 倉光, 102
Cao Shi Yinyang, 86
carp, 115
    carp breeding, 155
castration, 26
cat, 62
categories (*see* classification)
caterpillar, 170, 221
cavalry, 66
cedar, 218
celestial bodies, 97
center versus periphery, 7, 106, 159–160, 162–163, 235
Central States (Middle Kingdom), 101, 105, 106, 118, 121, 156, 159, 162–163, 227, 228, 235, 236
Chang, Kwang-chih, 10, 187
Chang'an, 25, 114, 197
change (*see also* transformation), 6, 89, 117, 124, 157, 167, 173, 177, 178, 180, 181, 185, 186, 195, 201, 203, 205, 206, 209–210, 212
    adaptation to change, 82, 237
    as paradigm, 6, 123, 165, 166, 225, 241–242
    categories of, 171
    terminology for, 199
Changes (see *Yijing*; *Zhouyi*)
character script, 99–100
charioteering, 128, 150
    as craft analogy, 151
chariots, 127, 183, 232, 233
Chavannes, Edouard, 67
Chen Jiang, 21
Cheng Ya, 95
chicken, 19, 21, 32, 60, 62, 145, 152, 195
    associated with color red, 42, 86, 259n.148
    chicken metamorphosis, 196
    chicken officer, 41

physiognomy of, 158

children, 216, 218
    children's ditty, 226, 315n. 76
    deformed child, 197–198
    protected by animals, 151–152

Childs-Johnson, Elisabeth, 187

chimei 魑魅 (demons), 74, 119

chong 蟲 (animal category), 17, 19, 31

chrysalis, 202

Chu (state), 12, 57, 103, 152, 189, 216, 232

Chu Shaosun, 100, 154

chu 畜 (domestic animal; *see also liu chu*), 18, 30, 31

chuliu 貙劉 (ritual), 112

Chun, Allen J., 54

Chunqiu, 9, 97, 225, 226, 229, 230, 233

Chunqiu fanlu, 22, 57, 86, 147
    and five phase scheme, 23

Chunyu Yi, 186

cicada, 64, 83, 190, 196, 202

civilization narratives, 93–96, 89, 100, 130, 138

clams, 201, 203, 212

clan name (*see also shi*), 90, 91

Classic of Birds, 175

classification (*see also* taxonomy), 19, 69–73, 128
    ritual context of, 56–61

claws, 63

climate, 76, 93, 103, 104, 105, 106, 124, 126, 176, 189

clothing, 53, 98, 159, 161, 192

cockerel (*see also* chicken), 59

cockfighting, 282n. 102

cockroach, 229

coinage, 278n. 53

color, 18, 77, 178
    as identification, 34, 38
    color correspondences, 79, 80
    of horses, 33
    of victim animals, 109–110

colts, 66

Confucian Classics, 12, 35, 223

Confucianism (*see also* Confucius), 1
    and role of naming, 39–40
    attitudes toward animals, 89, 150
    virtues associated with animals, 158

Confucius, 8, 23, 24, 30, 88, 132, 133, 144, 145, 147, 150, 151, 169–70
    and animal offices, 51
    and the unicorn, 9, 230, 233
    as itinerant scholar, 185
    as lexicographer, 223
    as master of the strange, 210, 216–20, 227
    as nomothete, 221
    disregarding animals, 150
    facial complexion of, 188, 270n. 27
    horse of, 55–56
    on dragons, 180
    silence on spirits, 210

consumption (*see also* food), 3, 82, 106, 110

cook, 40, 76
    Cook Ding, 149, 214
    ritual cooking, 47, 48

correlative thought, 78–88

cosmogony, 8, 167–171
    based on water, 175–176
    dyadic, 72

cosmology, 3, 72
    cosmographic collection, 118–120, 210
    Shang vision of, 100

covenants, 41, 77

cow, 121, 159, 195

cowherd, 47
    Cowherd constellation, 17

craft analogies, 149, 151

crane, 26, 29, 106, 130, 145, 152
    and immortality, 291n. 115
    "Rhapsody on the Crane," 148

creation, 2, 70, 94, 95, 96, 166, 167

cricket, 131, 202

crocodile, 189

crow (*see also* three-legged bird), 27, 90, 102, 116, 137, 200, 228, 251n. 63, 303n. 65
   red crow, 194
crustaceans, 31
cuckoo, 9, 169
Cui Bao, 90
culture heroes, 93–96
culture
   versus nature, 3, 240
custom (*see also fengsu*), 103, 106, 124, 131, 132, 185, 233
cynanthropy, 231

D

Da Dai Liji, 64, 84, 86, 91, 140, 167
dace, 115
daemonic, 8, 178, 231
   as *shen*, 175, 180
dance (*see also* music), 171
dance and animal mimicry, 128–129, 190–191
   dance as motion, 133
   dancing animals, 130, 132, 133
   dragon dance, 129
   feather dance, 129, 286n. 19
   rats dancing, 197, 228
   shangyang dance, 129, 190
Dao, 178–79, 201
Daodejing, 72, 137, 140
Daoism, 1, 72
   and craft analogies, 149
   and primitive naturalness, 137–138
daoyin ("guiding and pulling"), 190
Darwin, Charles, 2, 85
daybooks, 19, 66, 136, 160, 229, 231
Dayuan, 114
de (*see also* virtue), 113, 139
definition, 20, 74
   of animal groups, 16–21, 35–36, 74
deformed animals, 195–198
demons (*see also gui*), 27
   demonic intrusion, 47, 228

demonic metamorphosis, 171–173
De Groot, J. J. M., 166, 199, 249n. 27
deer, 21, 29, 46, 60, 83, 109, 111, 116, 132, 127, 146, 194, 201
demon fire, 200, 212
demonography, 136, 220, 228, 229, 231
den, 138
Descola, Philippe, 240
DeWoskin, Kenneth, 99
dhole, 291n. 109
Di (Thearch), 60, 216
Di Wulun, 265n. 66
die 鰈 (paired-eye fish), 156, 191
diet (*see also* consumption; food), 28–29, 83
differentiation (*bie, fen*), 71, 72, 212
Ding Huan, 283n. 125
Director of the Life-mandate, 63
divination, 37, 43, 179, 232
   by turtle plastron, 26, 110, 154, 192
   of activities involving animals, 232
   of bird and animal calls, 159, 160, 296n. 177
   of dreams, 215–216
   of sacrificial victims, 41
   with chicken bones, 189
dog, 18, 19, 21, 26, 27, 28, 32, 50, 57, 107, 145, 195, 213, 217, 223, 231–33
   and afterlife, 63, 232
   as guardian animal, 18, 63, 231–32
   dog demons, 231–32
   dog howling, 295n. 177
   dog sacrifice, 232
   dog thieves, 160
   hunting dogs, 46, 282n. 102
domestic animals (*see also chu; liu chu*), 18, 19, 30, 153
domestic sphere, 62, 232
Dong Zhongshu, 22, 195, 223
Dongfang Shuo, 37
Dongming, 152
dongwu 動物, 17, 242

donkey, 121
Dou Wu, 313n. 36
dragon, 4, 21, 62, 65, 106, 126, 138, 147, 153,
        189, 190, 194, 202, 203, 223–224
    and metamorphosis, 179–80
    and *wen*, 183
    as acolyte of Heaven, 173
    as image of sagehood, 185
    as progenitor, 84–85, 194
    dragon dances, 191
    dragon fight, 223–224
    dragon rearers, 52
    dragon tallies, 102
    Flying Dragon, 32, 125
    Green Dragon, 102, 103
    images of, 213
    in dreams, 216
    jiao 蛟 dragon, 134, 154, 155
    sacrifices to, 223
dragonfly, 177, 203, 292n. 121
dragon-horse, 184, 185, 304n. 92
dreams, 188, 214–16
    animals in, 215–16
    interpretation of, 214–15
drums (*see also* dance; music), 125
    alligator drums, 125
    hides used on, 189
    Qin stone drums, 127
    spirit drum, 189
Du Yu, 41
duck, 57, 60, 116
Duke Ai of Lu, 132
Duke Cheng of Lu, 226
Duke De of Qin, 232
Duke Huan of Qi, 26, 220
Duke Jing of Qi, 106, 139, 140, 146
Duke Li of Zheng, 208
Duke Mu of Qin, 130
Duke Ping of Jin, 130, 134, 224
Duke Shi of Shao, 104
Duke Wen of Jin, 215
Duke Wen of Lu, 226

Duke Wen of Qin, 216
Duke Xi of Lu, 33, 34
Duke Xian of Wei, 139
Duke Yan of Lu, 208
Duke Zhao of Lu, 226, 227
Dunhuang, 262n. 32, 266n. 82, 314n. 44
duodenary animal cycle, 66–67, 160–161,
        217

E
eagle, 4, 51
ears, 77, 270n. 39
earth (*see also* soil), 46, 79, 80, 83, 87, 90,
        96, 97, 100, 101, 103, 104, 105, 109, 126,
        178, 217, 218, 222
    earth spirit, 135, 148, 189, 247n. 30
    earth wolf, 217
    earthquakes, 126, 209
east, 26, 31, 77, 79, 115, 172, 185, 224
    and movement, 126
economic value of animals, 48–49, 60, 110,
        111, 117, 120, 145, 231
eggs, 131, 135, 145, 154, 170
elaphure, 60, 83, 193, 194, 229
elephant, 114, 116, 121, 134, 152, 191, 213
    elephant tusks, 118
emblems, 66, 102
emotions, 72, 75–76
Emperor Ai (Han), 188
Emperor Cheng (Han), 210
Emperor Er Shi (Qin), 216
Emperor Gaozu (Han), 160, 172, 194, 202,
        216, 300n. 38
Emperor Guangwu (Han), 216
Emperor Jing (Han), 66, 117
Emperor Qin Shihuang, 147
Emperor Wen (Han), 54, 216
Emperor Wu (Han), 66, 114, 116, 117, 145,
        151, 223, 235
Emperor Xuan (Han), 62, 145, 188
Emperor Yuan (Han), 32
empire, 43, 48, 106, 116, 192, 194, 235

and conquest, 4
celebration of, 114–115
Empress Ding, 152
Empress Lü, 65, 172
Empress Wei, 280n. 85
enclosures (*see* parks)
encyclopaedists, 70, 298n. 22
Eno, Robert, 71
environmental awareness, 145
Ersanzi wen, 180
Erya, 18, 23, 28, 30–32, 156
European tradition, 2, 166, 245n. 8, 256n. 101, 289n. 86, 314n. 49
evolution, 81
evolutionary thinking, 2, 84–85
excrements, 107
exogenous breeds (*see* exoticism)
exorcism, 42, 49, 63, 65, 127, 136, 152–153, 228, 246n. 13
nuo festival, 188
exoticism, 4, 47, 104, 112, 113, 114, 116, 118, 120, 159
exuviae, 202

F
falcon, 26, 51
falconry, 26, 282n. 102
faming 發明 (bird), 155
Fan Ji, 140
Fan Li, 25
Fan Shengzhi, 107
fang (directional deity), 109
Fangmatan, 63, 67, 160, 232
fangxiangshi (spirit mediator), 188
Fangyan, 30, 34
farming (*see* agriculture; breeding)
fat, 76, 83, 86
fatteners, 47, 264n. 65
fawn, 146
feathered species (*see yu*)
feathers, 129
feces (*see* excrements)

Felicity Forest, 154
felines, 114, 182
feng (*see* wind)
fenghuang 鳳凰 (*see also* phoenix), 37, 51, 117, 148, 153, 178, 185–186, 201
Feng Fu, 148
Fengbo (Wind Sire), 134
fengsu (*see also* custom; wind), 105, 124, 131
"altering wind and customs," 124
Fengsu tongyi, 215, 222
fenyang 羵羊 (clay sheep), 169, 212, 217, 218, 222
Ferghana, 184, 251n. 55
fetus, 154, 170
field mice, 174
fighting (*see also* aggression; military), 228
among animals, 27, 112, 208, 223
bull fighting, 190
with animals, 112
filial piety, 145
of animals, 152
disgorging of food as sign of, 9
fish, 31, 109, 115, 132, 152, 180, 191, 195, 197, 201, 216
as omen, 234
as symbol of fertility, 215
fish farming, 25–26, 46
fish roe, 144, 169
giant, 106, 191, 216
spawning of fish, 144
fishhawk, 234
fishing, 65, 144, 145, 149
five animal classes, 79, 84, 85, 92
five colors, 158, 181
five color birds, 181
Five Deities, 59
Five Emperors, 47, 138
five phases, 7, 52, 53, 147–148
and animal classification, 78–88
and color of tortoises, 110
"Treatise on the Five Phases," 195–198, 230

five skills squirrel, 34–35, 37
fledglings, 146, 182, 212
floods, 172, 177
flounder, 115
fly, 86, 169
    firefly, 203
    gadfly, 140, 312n. 21
    mayfly, 83
    wine-fly, 168
foals, 140, 149, 212
fodder, 48, 130
food (*see also* consumption; sacrifice), 28–
    29, 153, 174, 176
    disgorging of, 9
    dogs as, 231
    food taboos, 106
forester, 139, 267n. 94
Foucault, Michel, 218
fowl, 81, 135, 174
    water fowl, 102
fox, 9, 35, 64, 112, 138, 195, 224
    fox furs, 224
    fox possession, 256n. 111
    nine-tailed fox, 61
Fracasso, Riccardo, 36
French, Roger, 81
frog, 86, 174, 201, 203
Fu Qiugong, 26
furou 鵩鶏 (bird), 31
Fuxi, 96, 97, 98, 100
    inventing animal nomenclature, 97
    inventing trigrams, 96, 100

G
games, 112–113, 282n. 102
Gao You, 98, 176, 213
Ge Hong, 203
Ge Lu, 160
Ge Tianshi, 125
gecko, 31, 131, 177
geography, 93, 101, 157, 184
    spirit geography, 136, 156, 185

Zou Yan's theories, 105
gender change, 195, 196, 197, 201, 203
Genesis, 95
gentleman (*junzi*), 77, 88, 91, 109, 118, 129,
    148, 182, 183, 185, 198, 202
germination, 170
germs, 167, 168
gestation, 84
ghosts (see also *gui*; *shen*; spirits), 32, 60,
    74, 90, 117, 172, 206, 210, 213
gibbon, 28, 191
gifts, 7, 56–58
glow-worms, 272n. 56
gnats, 168
goat, 237
God, 2, 34, 70, 166
Gong Yu, 280n. 85
Gongniu Ai, 172–73, 202, 203
Gongsun Gui, 304n. 81
Gongyang zhuan, 227, 229, 230
goose, 29, 57, 60, 111, 116, 139, 147, 179, 201
    and army formations, 57, 263n. 46
    as marital symbol, 58
    as *yang* bird, 58
    snow-goose, 170
Goumang, 266n. 86
government, 51, 53, 66, 120, 121, 130, 133,
    139, 140, 198, 209, 236
    and the natural world, 148, 150–151,
    194, 200–201, 228, 234
    government monopoly, 110
    negligence of, 138, 141, 196, 208, 216
gracko (*see* mynah)
Graham, Angus, 40, 169, 199
Granet, Marcel, 192, 249n. 27, 286n. 19
grass, 63, 83, 203
    white woolly grass, 228, 234
grasshopper, 64, 128
grave (*see also* burial), 63
Great Commentary (Appended State-
    ments, *Xici*), 96, 97, 98, 199
Greco-Roman tradition, 4, 15, 16, 17, 20,

24, 28, 61, 69–70, 240, 242, 281n. 96,
  283n. 115, 295n. 177, 318n. 113
grub, 86
Gu Yong, 210
guai (*see* anomaly; strange)
Guan Lu, 159
guan (*see* office)
Guanzi, 79, 90, 91, 102, 110, 125, 175, 178, 179
gudgeon, 115
gui (*see also* demon; ghosts; spirits), 99, 172
Guliang zhuan, 230
Gun, 172
Guo Pu, 210, 214
Guodian, 76, 176
Guoyu, 18, 41, 61, 74, 77, 135, 144, 176, 192,
  217

H
habitat, 105–107, 139–140, 146, 175
hair, 77
hairy animals (see *mao*)
Hall, David, 20, 89
Han (dynasty), 9, 43, 120, 121, 194, 195, 198,
  202, 208, 209
Han (state), 226
Han Feizi, 94, 134, 213
Han shi waizhuan, 156, 211
Han Ying, 91, 106
Hanshu, 25, 32, 101, 196, 197, 232
Harbsmeier, Christoph, 20
hare, 42, 61, 117
  harelips, 279n. 69
harmony, 36, 39, 74, 124, 131, 132, 200, 201
  between humans and animals, 96, 132
  musical, 133, 135, 137
Harper, Donald, 1, 62
harrier, 32
hawk, 51, 81, 142, 169, 174, 197, 200
Hay, John, 180
he bell, 127–128
He Chang, 227
He Xiu, 18

heart, 78
Heaven, 10, 17, 21, 46, 60, 63, 72, 73, 75, 91,
  94, 96, 97, 99, 100, 103, 106, 109, 112, 113,
  114, 117, 118, 119, 128, 133, 135, 136, 142,
  149, 152, 168, 173, 179, 183, 200, 201, 207,
  209, 210, 212, 219, 234
  mandate of, 233
Heavenly Horse, 184, 185, 304n. 90
Hebo (river god), 109, 300n. 32
hedgehog, 224
hen, 196
herding (*see also* shepherding), 46, 48, 151
hermaphrodites, 304n. 88
heron, 298n. 20
Hervouet, Yves, 114
hexagrams, 182, 232
hibernation, 64, 83, 126, 144, 175
hides (*see also* skin), 41, 59, 76, 126, 146, 159,
  182
  on targets, 193–194
  symbolism of, 192–194
hierarchy, 54, 56, 62, 115, 166, 178, 197
  of species, 81–82, 155, 167
  ritual hierarchies, 56, 57, 59, 60, 67
hill censers, 116
history of science, 2, 253n. 76
hooves, 150, 233
horns, 50, 59, 83, 131, 237
  as sacrificial criteria, 60
  as symbols of violence, 76, 197
  capping of, 47
  horn butting (*juedi*), 190
  horn injury, 264n 59
  unified horns, 233, 234, 235
horse, 19, 21, 62, 108, 109, 127, 128, 137, 149,
  191, 195, 197, 200, 239
  and martiality, 35
  as symbols of wealth, 48–49
  breeding policy, 65–66
  classification of, 49
  economic value of, 26, 48–49
  horse figurine, 109

horse spirits, 62–63
maintenance of, 150
physiognomy of, 157
piebald, 224
terminology, 33–34, 39
"Horses' Hoofs" (chapter), 239
Hou Hanshu, 98, 232
Hou Ji, 95, 107, 112, 151–152, 176
"Hounds of Lü," 104, 120
Houma, 41
Houtu, 109
Hu Ba, 130
Huainanzi, 55, 64, 65, 72, 74, 82–85, 90, 99,
103, 106, 133, 138, 148, 149, 170, 176, 212,
214, 218
Huan Kuan, 120
Huan Tan, 39
human beings, 1, 5, 19, 55, 72, 73, 74, 75–76,
80, 81, 86, 89, 91, 94, 95, 98, 104, 123, 130,
166, 167, 172, 195, 197, 198, 208
and self-perception, 2, 3
human centered, 1
hunts (*see also* parks; sacrifice), 3, 64, 65,
97, 111–116, 139, 172, 220, 224
and drumming, 127
and rulership, 194
criticism of, 139–142, 144
hunter, 40, 97
number of, 111
regulations on, 28, 142–147
techniques, 143, 145
winter hunt, 18, 143
Huo Guang, 280n. 85
husbandry, 3, 62–63
hybrids, 8, 153–157
interpretation of, 235–236, 237

I
iconography, 10, 187
illness, 60, 186, 190, 195, 220
of animals, 59
image (see *xiang*)

immortality, 61, 63, 83
and the turtle, 178–79
animals obtaining immortality, 152
birds as symbols of, 179
criticism of, 201, 202
islands of, 152
immortals, 148
as bird-people, 103, 185
incantations, 34, 42, 62, 221, 266n. 90
induction (extrapolation, *see also tui lei*),
80, 123, 154, 198
infancy legends, 151–152
inner-outer (see *nei-wai*)
insects, 19, 63, 131, 144, 169, 209
as essence of wind, 170
inspection tours, 115, 119
Intorcetta, Prosper, 276n. 23

J
jackal, 182
jade, 41, 114, 119, 212
Ji (clan), 226
Ji (river), 105
Ji Huanzi, 217
Ji jiu pian, 30, 32–33
Ji Zicheng, 183
Jia Gongyan, 40
Jia Kui, 319n. 123
Jia Yi, 113, 200
jian 鶼 (paired-wing bird), 156
jianke 諫珂 (bird), 224
Jianzhang palace, 117
jiaoming 焦明 (bird), 155
Jie (tribe), 160
Jie (tyrant), 138, 151
jie 介 (armored animals), 19, 79, 82, 84, 85,
133, 148
Jin (state), 52, 103
Jinan commandery, 226
Jing Fang, 195, 197
jing 精 (essence, genie), 86, 87, 213
Jingfa, 38, 76

jingshen (essential spirit), 73
jingwei 精衞 (bird), 172
Jixia academy, 80
Judeo-Christian tradition, 34, 95, 166
jue 蟨 (rabbit-legged rat), 156
jun 鵻 (bird), 172
junyi 鵻鸃 (bird), 224
Juyan, 27

K
"Kaogong ji," 50, 127
Kaltenmark, Max, 185, 188
King Cheng, 234
King Gong of Chu, 149
King Hui of Liang, 113
King Hui of Zhou, 111
King Kang of Song, 197
King Mu of Zhou, 112, 117, 210
King of Linjiang, 152
King Tang, 111, 151, 235
    as moral hunter, 143–144
King Wen, 113, 125, 143, 194
King Wu Ding, 235
King Wu, 104, 139, 194, 234
King Xuan of Qi, 141, 161
King Yan of Xu, 112
King You of Zhou, 201
King Zhaoxiang of Qin, 160
King Zhuang of Chu, 140
kinship, 76, 109
kitchens, 28, 40, 77, 111, 144
kite, 32, 102, 103, 169
Knechtges, David, 143
knowledge, 3, 12, 31, 69, 89, 90, 129, 157, 158,
    179, 181, 222, 236
    as power, 4, 29, 30, 43, 79, 119, 213, 218,
    219
    epistemology, 20, 22–23, 212, 240
Kong Anguo, 73
Kong Cang, 311n. 9
Kong Congzi, 38, 219
Kong Jia, 52, 53

Kong Yingda, 18, 42, 199
Kongzi jiayu, 147
Kuang Heng, 319n. 127
Kui , 125, 130, 132, 133, 190
    as prodigy, 217
Kun 鯤 (leviathan), 168–69
Kunlun, 114

L
la festival, 185
Ladder of Souls, 89
Lady Dai, 301n. 48
lamb, 21, 57–58
landscape, 109, 112, 113, 115, 156, 157
language, 16–17, 20, 34
    animal language, 152, 159–160
    views of, 36, 39
Laozi, 169–70
lei 類 (*see also* species), 11, 22, 75, 79, 81, 90,
    170
legal procedure, 27–28, 116, 144–145, 190
    legal disputes, 47, 260n. 9
    Longgang codes, 27, 28, 116
    Shuihudi Qin codes, 27, 145
legalist, 28
leopard, 107, 168, 193, 224
    leopard skin, 102, 103, 182
    leopard tail chariot, 183
Lévi, Jean, 53
Lévi-Strauss, Claude, 16
Lewis, Mark Edward, 47, 53, 230
lexicography, 6, 29–39, 223
    as classification, 30, 35
Li Qi, 319n. 126
Li Shizhen, 226, 298n. 22
Li Si, 282n. 102
Li Yuan, 81
Liezi, 26, 74, 76, 132, 138, 169, 215, 218
Liji, 21, 29, 41, 64, 75, 77, 102, 103, 109, 111,
    145, 176, 232
lion, 4, 114
Lin Yutang, 99

lin 鱗 (scaly animals), 19, 79, 84, 85, 147, 189
lin 麟 (*see* unicorn)
ling 靈 (spirit power), 73, 113, 100, 154, 181
Linnaeus, 3
liturgy, 62–63
Liu An, 152
liu chu 六畜 (six domestic animals), 17, 19, 25, 32, 59, 66, 86, 95, 136, 142, 145, 160, 198, 228
Liu De, 261n. 21
liu qin 六禽 (six birds), 19, 143
liu sheng 六牲 (six sacrificial animals), 19
Liu Sheng, 283n. 125
liu shou 六獸 (six beasts), 19
Liu Xi, 129
Liu Xiang, 195
Liu Xin, 25, 37, 120, 195
Liu Yu, 284n. 126
liver, 78
lizard, 177
Lloyd, Geoffrey, 15, 70
locality (*see also* soil; territory), 93, 101, 103, 105, 106, 108, 109, 123, 124
locomotion, 34, 180
locusts, 64, 86, 144
    plagues of, 175
longevity (*see* immortality)
lou 嶁 (animal), 156
Lu (state), 33, 54, 225, 226
Lu Gong, 160
Lu Ji, 23–24, 250n. 39
Lu Jia, 198, 276n. 17
Lu Qiaoru, 148
luan bells, 127–128, 134
luan knife, 76, 77
luan 鸞 (bird) (*see* simurgh)
lungs, 78
Lunheng, 24, 67, 86, 193, 218
Lunyu, 23, 29, 30, 88, 145, 150, 183, 210, 217, 221, 224
Luo diagram, 100
luo (naked animals), 19, 79, 148

Lüshi chunqiu, 56, 64, 86, 90, 125, 145, 178, 187
lynx, 132

M

Ma Rong, 115, 131
Ma Shihuang, 26
Ma Yuan, 189
macrura, 177
maggots, 168, 203
magic, 126, 152, 190
magpie, 29, 32, 137, 228, 295n. 177
Major, John, 83, 85
manager of furs, 193
manuals, 25–26, 33, 70, 99, 107, 155, 157, 159, 179, 190, 193, 220
manure, 107, 168
manyan 漫衍 (monster), 191, 192
Mao Heng, 30
mao 毛 (hairy animals), 19, 21, 79, 82, 84, 85, 148, 212
maps, 36
mare, 22, 49, 65, 66
market, 61, 135, 141, 144, 155
marshland, 102, 106, 107, 115, 154
    spirits of, 135, 220
masks, 190, 191
    as bronze motif, 187
    masked dance, 188
Matou Niang, 304n. 89
Mawangdui, 27, 29, 38, 76, 147, 157, 180, 183, 190, 220
meat, 28, 29, 82, 111, 112, 140
    sacrificial meat, 48, 50, 150
    taste of, 50
medicine, 25, 26, 28, 70, 186
    medical literature, 19, 27, 43, 73, 157, 220–221
    poisonous, 144
melody, 125, 129, 131, 134, 135, 136
    as transformation, 129
menageries, 4

Meng Kui, 275n. 11
Mengzi (Mencius), 94, 101, 113, 141, 148, 151, 161
    on fishing, 144
    on human-animal relationship, 88, 161
metamorphosis, 8, 85, 165, 167–171, 177, 179, 183, 186, 188, 190, 196, 198–200, 235, 237
    and moral causation, 172–173
    as portent, 194–198
    criticisms of, 200–202
    fish to bird, 169, 175
    human to animal, 172
    induced by water, 175–176
    pigeon to hawk, 174
metaphor, 3, 8–11, 123, 159, 169, 172, 184, 235
Mi Heng, 181
Middle Kingdom (*see* Central States)
migration, 57, 58, 175
    of birds, 63, 83
    of souls, 166
military, 35, 108, 122, 159, 209, 222
    symbolism, 102–103, 184
    training, 112, 150, 190
millipede, 312n. 21
mimicry of animals, 188, 190–193
ming (*see* names; naming; nomenclature)
model thinking, 87
mole, 169
mollusks, 81, 174
monkey, 21, 67, 117, 149, 169, 190, 191
monopeds, 190, 285n. 12
monster, 8, 32, 36, 38, 102, 189, 190–191, 217, 218, 221
Montaigne, Michel de, 239
moral hybrids, 153–156
moral tales, 27, 173
morality, 3, 35, 43, 58, 68, 74, 77, 94, 113, 118, 121, 165, 170, 172, 176, 183, 205, 207, 212, 215, 217, 240
    moral biology, 72, 75, 93, 104, 108

moral harmony, 101, 108, 110, 123
moral instruction of animals, 123–124, 137–153
moral taxonomy, 88–91
mortuary ritual, 58, 231, 232–233
    mortuary terminology, 270n. 27
mosquito, 140, 312n. 21
moth, 135
mouse, 174, 203
movement, 125, 126, 133
mountain animals, 35, 130, 141, 142
mountains (*see also* hill censer), 23, 53, 72, 80, 94, 100, 101, 102, 103, 106, 109, 116–117, 119, 126, 135, 139, 140, 146, 149, 212, 224, 283n. 125
    Mount Fu, 216
    Mount Heng, 226
    Mount Tai, 116, 134, 150, 234
    Mount Wu, 63
    Mount Youyuan, 226
    mountain spirits, 135, 172
    Red Mountain, 232
    sacrifices to, 109, 116
Mozi, 59, 94, 195, 254n. 84
    Mohist writings, 39
Mu Tianzi zhuan, 117, 188
mule, 121
mulberry, 64, 184
music, 7, 50, 55, 155, 158, 161, 170, 177, 191, 200, 206, 242
    and the spirit world, 135–136
    as transformation, 129–130, 136
    disharmony, 135
    instruments, 128
    origins of, 124–129
    shao music, 55, 132
    transforming animals, 129–137
music masters (*see also* Shi Kuang), 130, 132, 134, 159, 190, 223, 224
muskrat, 189
mussels, 175
mynah, 105, 225–228, 229

N

naked animals (*see also luo*), 21, 79, 86, 127, 148
 humans as, 82, 84, 148, 156, 249n. 26
names (*see also* naming, nomenclature), 6, 23, 45, 51, 56, 67, 69, 97, 99, 114, 160
 enumeration of names, 33–34, 39
 forms and names, 38
 lexicographical classification of, 6, 34–36
 name magic, 34, 220
 origins of animal names, 38
 rectification of names, 36, 39–41, 43, 55
 selection of, 67
naming (*see also* names, nomenclature), 8, 23, 29–42, 71, 221
 and power, 43, 216–225
 in the *Shanhaijing*, 36–38
 linked with Confucius, 216–220
 naming in ritual, 40–42
natural experts, 25
natural philosophy, 2, 25, 103
nature versus culture, 240
Needham, Joseph, 2, 23, 24, 30, 32, 36, 84, 89, 168, 177, 253n 76
nei–wai (*see also* center versus periphery), 208, 225, 226, 228, 229, 231, 235
Neolithic, 276n. 16, 287n. 31
nests, 94, 137, 145, 154, 226, 227
 nest destroyer, 49, 229
 Nest Dweller, 94
nets, 116, 127, 143, 144, 146
 bird netter, 54
 prohibitions on the use of, 145
niao 鳥 (animal category), 31, 35, 85
nine herdsmen, 118, 119
nine provinces, 101, 105, 115, 119, 139, 155, 233
nine resemblances, 180
nine tripods, 118–119
Ning Qi, 26

nomadism, 119, 151
nomenclature (*see also* names; naming), 6, 22, 24, 30, 32, 36, 247n. 31, 253n. 76
 in the *Shijing*, 23
 ritual nomenclature, 41–42
numinous animals, 10, 82, 85, 103, 110, 153, 154, 156, 158, 178
numinous power, 8, 100, 108, 110, 112, 113, 116, 122, 155, 157, 165, 178, 180, 181, 183, 184, 185, 187, 192, 204, 205, 225
 numinous hierarchy, 178
Nü Wa, 138, 172, 301n. 48

O

observation, 6, 19, 47, 84
Odes (see *Shijing*)
odor, 50
office, 7, 45, 47–49, 51–53, 54, 56, 62, 65, 147, 216, 220, 222
 administrative and religious, 48
officials, 27, 38, 56–57, 107, 115, 157
 depravity of, 141, 142, 197, 209
 in charge of animals, 26, 41, 46–56, 65, 127, 144, 149, 160, 193, 229
 in the spirit world, 63
 named after animals, 51
officiants, 40, 42, 76, 77, 109, 188, 192, 221
Ohnuki-Tierney, Emiko, 166
omens (*see also* portents), 91
oneiromancy (*see* dreams)
ontology, 17, 72, 81, 85, 87, 168, 203, 241, 242
oracle bones, 58, 61, 190
order, 4, 6, 7, 8, 40, 45, 49, 67, 69, 71, 72, 74, 86, 92, 96, 101, 105, 109, 111, 115, 119–120, 121, 122, 166, 206, 207, 208, 212
 bureaucratic order, 46
 Great Divine Order, 118
 nominalist order, 30, 39, 43, 56, 69
 ritual order, 48, 58
 sociobiological order, 93, 105, 110, 225
organs, 78
origin narratives, 94–96

oriole, 64

osprey, 8, 172

ostrich, 114

otherness, 4

otter, 146, 151, 189

oviparous, 83, 131, 170, 175

owl, 32, 132, 135, 228, 246n. 13

    as bad augury, 316n. 90

    "Owl Rhapsody," 200, 311n. 9

ox, 17, 18, 21, 35, 57, 107, 191, 200

    as sacrificial victim, 41, 50, 59–60

    as symbol of agriculture, 95

    ox officer, 47

oysters, 83, 168, 203

P

palaces, 117

Paludan, Ann, 10, 289n. 75

Pan Yue, 282n. 102

Panhu, 296n. 180

pan-pipes, 125, 131

panther, 112, 132, 224

parks, 7, 22, 28, 47, 111–115, 117, 118, 120, 122, 125, 140, 148, 192

    as hunting grounds, 93, 111–113

    as microcosm, 4

    Forbidden Parks, 116, 145

    internal layout of, 114–115

    park attendants, 47, 54, 194

    Shanglin park, 54, 115, 127, 151

paronomasia, 36, 143

parrot, 161

partridge, 29, 51

pastures (*see also* agriculture) 62, 66, 110

patterns (see *wen*)

peacock, 130, 152

pelts, 147, 182–183

    molting of, 182

Peng Sheng, 172

Peng 鵬 (bird), 168

Pengzu, 152

pentachromatic birds, 37, 181

pentatonic scale, 125

pets, 280n. 85

pheasant, 29, 57, 98, 125, 201, 203

phoenix (*see also fenghuang*), 9, 32, 51, 84, 86, 91, 103, 117, 125, 132, 134, 138, 147, 148, 153, 154, 155, 157, 158, 178, 179, 180, 181, 185, 201, 224, 236

    and music, 125, 134

    Phoenix Pavilion, 130

    phoenixlike birds, 63, 155

    Shrine of the Phoenix Girl, 130

physiognomy, 156–158

    manuals on, 25, 26, 251n. 52

    of dogs and chickens, 26, 27

    of horns, 264n. 64

    of horses, 25, 27

physiology, 91

pig, 19, 32, 57, 58, 59, 109, 125, 133, 138, 160, 193, 195, 228

pigeon, 32, 51, 81, 142, 174, 201

    and longevity, 174

pigeon staffs, 174

piscines, 31, 155, 176, 180

plagues, 65, 175, 189

    of insects, 107, 229

    of tigers, 141–142

plants, 19, 70, 84, 101, 106

    plant officer, 107

plastromancy, 100

Plato, 16

plowing, 35, 120

pojia 破家 (bird), 37

pojing 破鏡 ("mirror breaker"), 246n.13

poisonous animals, 37, 47, 138, 154, 189, 220

    gu poisoning, 232

ponds, 148, 155

    Divine Pond, 133

portents, 51, 53, 110, 171, 177, 194–198, 215, 216, 230

Powers, Martin, 10

predatory animals, 90, 102, 103, 138, 193

causes for predatory behavior, 140–142

officer of predatory birds, 49

preserves (*see* parks)

prodigies (*see also* anomaly; strange), 117, 207, 208, 212, 229

pullets, 262n. 24

pupa, 202

Pythagoras, 16

Q

Qi (state), 26, 31, 80, 106, 130, 139, 141, 146, 161, 172, 213, 218, 220, 226

qi 氣, 73, 78, 86, 87, 89, 154, 201, 208, 209
   and fear, 220
   influencing living creatures, 103–105, 159–160

qilin 麒麟 (*see* unicorn)

Qimin yaoshu, 155

Qin (state, dynasty), 28, 108, 197

Qin Pi, 172

Qin Xiba, 146

Qin Zhong, 159

qin 禽 (animal category), 17, 18, 21

qingji 慶忌 (marsh demon), 221

qiongqiong juxu 蛩蛩踞虛 (animal), 156

quadrupeds, 18, 21, 136

quail, 32, 63, 135, 174, 177, 201, 203

Queen Mother of the West, 61, 63

quyu 鸜鵒 (*see* mynah)

R

rabbit, 21, 29, 46, 190, 312n. 21
   and writing brush, 99

raccoon dog, 64, 138

rain, 64, 125
   feathers as symbols of, 129
   rain dances, 128–129, 190
   Rain Master ("Yushi"), 134

ram, 59

Raphals, Lisa, 195

rat, 21, 31, 35, 161, 169, 197, 201, 228

altar rats, 267n. 90

and divination, 65

rat exorcism, 64, 65, 152–153, 267n. 90

ravens, 295n. 177

Rawson, Jessica, 114

rectification of names (*see* names; naming)

Red Emperor, 172

release from the corps, 202

religion, 3, 27, 29, 48, 60, 61–63, 76, 108–109, 110, 119, 184, 187, 231
   Chu religion, 190
   religious authority, 53
   religious worship, 61

reptiles, 19, 117, 125, 131, 161, 176, 177, 180, 202

resonance, 127, 130, 131, 135

retribution, 145

rhapsody (*fu* 賦), 27, 34, 43, 114
   "Rhapsody on the Plume Hunt," 281n. 91
   "Nightmare Rhapsody," 34
   "Owl Rhapsody," 200
   "Rhapsody on Remonstrating against Engaging with Tigers in Combat," 140
   "Rhapsody on the Barricade Hunt," 189, 200
   "Rhapsody on the Great Peacock," 305n. 99
   "Rhapsody on the Long Flute," 131
   "Rhapsody on the Numinous Radiance Basilica in Lu," 117
   "Rhapsody on the Pan-pipes," 131
   "Rhapsody on the Parrot," 181
   "Rhapsody on the Shanglin Park," 114, 283n. 110
   "Rhapsody on the Silkworm," 184
   "Rhapsody on the Spirit Crows," 27
   "Rhapsody on the Striped Deer," 304n. 81
   "Rhapsody on the Western Capital," 191, 200

rhinoceros, 102, 112, 116, 118, 121

Riegel, Jeffrey, 193

rishu (*see* daybooks)

ritual, 3, 42, 48, 50, 53, 54, 61, 67, 71, 72, 77,
   82, 108, 110, 112, 115, 116, 145, 150, 171, 187,
   190, 191, 192, 193, 220, 231, 235
     animals and ritual, 56–61
     gifts, 45, 57
     ritual music, 136–137, 194, 234
     ritual vessels, 18, 128, 187, 235
     ritual washing, 47, 61

ritual codes, 56, 78, 144, 176

ritual killing, 58, 59, 76–77, 113

ritual propriety, 90, 91, 94, 158

ritual taxonomies, 46, 56–61, 150

ritual texts, 29, 40, 45, 136

rivers, 23, 72, 80, 100, 105, 109, 119, 135, 189
     River Chart, 100
     river sacrifices, 109, 112, 216

rodents, 65

rooster, 135, 152, 196

Ru, 211, 236

Rushou, 63

S

sacrifice, 3, 18, 19, 36, 47, 48, 49, 59, 61, 64,
   65, 76–78, 82, 109, 111, 112, 115, 117, 122,
   123, 145–146, 161, 187, 191, 193, 195, 213,
   216, 218, 223–224, 228, 231
     by animals, 146
     consecration sacrifice, 76–77, 161
     driving-over sacrifice, 232
     feng and *shan*, 116, 234
     rain sacrifice, 64
     sacrifice and status, 59
     sacrificial officiants, 76, 77
     sacrificial taboos, 144, 161, 224
     sacrificial techniques, 109
     to a horse spirit, 33
     to dragons, 223–224
     to Hebo, 109
     to Hou Ji, 60, 99
     to Houtu, 109, 234
     to the Five Deities, 59
     to the gate, 233
     to the new moon, 150
     to the road, 232

sacrificial appellations, 41–42

sacrificial robe, 53

sacrificial victims, 19, 41, 42, 47, 58–61, 76–
   78, 108, 110, 115, 160
     cleansing of, 61
     criteria for selection, 59–60, 109
     divination of, 41
     hierarchy of, 59, 115
     linked to the soil, 108–110
     preparation and inspection of, 47, 77,
     145

sagehood, 5, 7, 177, 179, 184, 186, 204, 206,
   211, 219, 239, 240, 241

sages, 5, 7, 8, 22, 23, 40, 43, 51, 55, 56, 59, 65,
   74, 84, 87, 89, 91, 94, 95, 97, 98, 101, 106,
   113, 118, 120, 122, 123, 124, 125, 129–130,
   132, 134, 136, 137, 138, 140, 142, 144, 147,
   148, 151, 153, 154, 156, 158, 161, 162, 176,
   180, 182–183, 185, 186, 204, 206, 210, 211–
   214, 216, 218, 219, 221, 223, 225, 230, 233,
   235, 237, 242–243
     as central species, 82
     as interpreters of animal behavior,
     159
     as naked animal, 86, 156, 178
     understanding metamorphosis, 177

salamander, 115, 125, 158

scaly animals (see *lin*)

scapulimancy, 100

Schafer, Edward, 9, 28, 115

Schwartz, Benjamin, 53, 79, 168

science, 1, 2

scorpion, 175, 177, 312n. 21

script (see *wen*; writing)

seagull, 292n. 121

seeds, 107

seminal energy (see *jing*)

sericulture, 26, 184
    goddess of sericulture, 184
seasons, 51, 57, 64–67, 79, 80, 81, 91, 109,
    129, 143, 146, 147–148, 165, 170, 174, 175,
    178, 185, 199, 200, 203, 207
    seasonal breeding, 62, 65, 144
    seasonal consumption, 82
    seasonal hunts, 111, 144
seismograph, 126
sex, 220
    intercourse across species, 197, 198
    of animals, 31, 65, 83
    separation between, 90
    sexual positions, 190
    sexual union of animals and humans,
        159, 194, 201–202
shamanism, 26, 186–189, 220, 223
Shanhaijing, 8, 30, 36–38, 119–120, 125, 156,
    176, 185, 226
    role of naming in, 36–37
Shang (period), 10, 18, 46, 58, 100, 102, 104,
    112, 187, 235, 319n. 127
Shangshu da zhuan, 133
Shangshu, 53, 73, 104, 130, 132, 133
shangyang 商羊 (bird), 128–129, 218
Shaohao, 51, 276n. 23
shaolao 少牢 ("lesser lot"), 59
she (altar of the soil), 109
sheatfish, 115
sheep, 19, 21, 28, 50, 57, 59, 76–77, 86, 110,
    195, 217, 223
sheep farming, 26
sheep sacrifice, 150
sheli 舍利 (beast), 191
Shen Xu, 208
Shen Yue, 10
shen (*see also* numinous power; spirits),
    73, 83, 175
sheng 牲 (sacrificial victim), 41–42
Shennong, 95, 107, 151
shepherding (*see also* Bu Shi; herding), 119
    as craft analogy for rulership, 151

shi 氏 (clan, guild, specialist), 53–54
Shi Ji, 226
Shi Kuang (music master), 130, 134, 159,
    174, 223, 224
Shi You, 32
Shiji, 76, 100, 105, 154, 172, 178
Shijing, 8, 10–11, 23, 29, 30, 33–34, 64, 76,
    113, 125, 165, 176, 194, 207, 209, 215
    and Confucius, 23–24, 217
    and natural imagery, 64
    as source of nomenclature, 23
    "Jiong" 駉 (Mao 297)
Shizi, 151, 181, 217
shooting, 145, 193–194, 216
shou (winter hunt), 143
shou 獸 (animal category), 17, 18, 21, 31, 85
shrike, 51, 64
shrimp, 175
Shuanggudui, 27
Shuihudi, 19, 27, 62, 67, 136, 160, 217, 220,
    228, 229, 231
Shun, 52, 95, 147, 151, 152, 159
Shuowen jiezi, 17, 28, 30, 34–36, 76, 179, 193,
    223
Shuoyuan, 57, 154, 224
si ling 四靈 (four sacred animals), 103,
    153–155, 178–179
silkworm, 83
    silkworm month, 64
    silkworm spirit, 61, 62
Sima Biao, 196
Sima Qian, 23, 48, 102, 105, 112, 120, 143, 151,
    152, 232
Sima Xiangru, 114, 115, 127, 140, 235
simurgh (*luan* 鸞), 37, 86, 134, 179
Sivin, Nathan, 199
six domestic animals (see *liu chu*)
    physiognomy of, 25
skin, 80–81, 102, 103, 118, 171, 188
    and drums, 125–126
    and metamorphosis, 80–81
slaughter, 41, 58, 76–78

slave contract, 115–116

snake, 21, 86, 102, 106, 108, 117, 135, 151, 201, 203, 228
    and metamorphosis, 177–78
    as portent, 194, 208, 209, 216, 222, 228
    as symbol of the female, 215
    bramble-head snake, 156
    in dreams, 215
    mounting snake, 202
    whisker snake, 106

sociobiology, 93, 105, 110, 274n. 1

Socrates, 3, 20

soil (*see also* earth; territory), 80
    and animal markings, 96–97, 101
    and sacrifice, 108–110
    soil fertilizers, 107
    soil vapor (*tu qi*), 103–104, 106, 156
    typology of, 101, 107

solar symbolism, 179

Song Jun, 141–142

soul, 89, 166, 199–200

sound (*see also* music), 37–38, 125

south, 38, 62, 79, 119, 128, 141, 154, 168, 174, 190 220
    associated with chicken, 42
    associated with reptiles, 12, 176, 189
    southern animals, 189
    southern tribes, 65, 106, 108, 121, 189, 233

space, 111, 119
    in parks, 114–115

sparrow, 75, 116, 146, 175, 197, 201, 203

species, 15, 16, 17, 35, 38, 49, 53, 54, 56, 58, 59, 69, 70, 72, 75, 79, 80, 86, 105, 109, 114, 117, 123, 135, 137, 147, 153, 155, 165, 171, 175, 178, 180, 184, 193, 195, 197, 198, 201, 205, 236
    definition of, 6, 20, 31
    differentiation of , 22–23, 40, 48, 58, 71, 74, 76, 83, 85, 166, 167, 212
    hierarchy of, 81–82, 95
    species change, 164–167

speckle bird, 32

speech imitating birds, 161, 297n. 190

spirit birds, 145, 152

spirit medium, 188

spirits (*see also* ghosts; *gui*; *shen*), 109, 134
    animal spirits, 61–63, 265n. 75
    ghosts and spirits, 32–33
    spirit of the grain, 59, 60
    spirit of the soil, 59
    stove spirit, 265n. 75
    thunder spirits, 125, 126, 180

spirit drum, 127

"spirit guardian" (tortoise), 155

"Spiritual Country of the Red Region," 105

spontaneous generation, 167, 168

spring, 126, 145

spurs, 196

stables, 47, 116, 150
    stable officer, 49, 55

stag, 112, 139

stallions, 22, 65, 66, 184
    of Duke Xi of Lu, 33

stele inscriptions, 152, 291n. 113

stork, 263n. 46

strange (*see also* anomaly), 8, 37, 208, 210, 222, 230, 233, 235
    and popular perceptions, 211–214
    and sages, 211–214

sturgeon, 115, 153

Suiren, 97

Sun Shu-ao, 216

sushuang 鷫霜 (bird), 155

swallow, 75, 152, 169

swamps (*see also* marshland), 108, 176, 189

swan, 178, 182

T

taboo, 279n. 69
    consumption taboos, 40, 106

tail, 31, 35, 63, 115, 140, 149, 190, 194
    leopard tail, 183

nine-tailed birds, 51
nine-tailed fox, 61
ox tail, 125, 178
rat tail, 65
tail feathers, 59
tailed barbarians, 190
yak tail, 118
tailao 太牢 ("greater lot"), 59
Taixuan jing, 183
tallies, 99, 102, 211
Tan, Lord of, 51
Tang Gongfang, 152
taotie 饕餮 , 187
Taozhu Gong, 26
targets, 193–194
taste, 50, 106, 161
tattooing, 189, 190
taxation, 47, 48, 142, 160
    victim tax, 260n. 8
taxonomy, 7, 69–73, 84, 87, 88, 206–207,
    258n. 133
    and anomaly, 206–207
    and Xunzi, 71
    based on "blood and *qi*," 73–78
    correlative, 78–88
    culinary taxonomy, 50
    lexicographic taxonomy, 31–32, 34–38
    moral taxonomy, 88–91
    of horses, 49
    ritual taxonomy, 56–61
technical literature, 25–26
    experts, 54
teeth, 66, 76, 83, 146
temples, 76–77, 139, 144
terminology, 16–21
territory (*see also* soil), 101–110
Thearch (*see* Di)
theory of animals, 2, 6, 16, 20, 21, 22, 73, 82,
    165
Thomas, Keith, 2, 166
three-legged bird, 61, 63, 266n. 85
three-sided battue, 143

thunder, 125–126, 180
    Thunder Animal, 126
Tian Zifang, 146
tiger, 21, 62, 76, 91, 106, 108, 134, 148, 149,
    154, 161, 173, 190, 191, 194, 202, 203, 216,
    224
    and immortals, 152
    as symbol for bravery, 103
    graph for, 34, 35
    tiger and wolf attacks, 140–142, 150–
        151
    tiger rearer, 76
    tiger skin, 182, 188
    tiger tallies, 102
    White Tiger, 102, 103
    white tiger, 62, 160
toad, 61, 86, 126, 191
tomb-quelling animals (see *zhenmushou*)
tombs, 152, 232
Tong Hui, 142
topography, 83
tortoise (*see also* turtle), 153, 155, 189, 191,
    203, 237
    and divination, 26, 36, 192
    and longevity, 154, 178–179, 257n. 113
    and transformation, 178
    carapace of, 100
    classification of, 110
    Dark Warrior, 102
    spirit tortoise, 148, 300n. 32
    tortoise keeper, 41, 110
totemism, 53
Toynbee, Jocelyn, 4
trade, 65, 66
training, 46, 47, 93, 124, 160, 162
    animal tamer, 54
    of horses, 149
    of tigers, 149
transformation (*see also* change), 6, 7, 8,
    78, 96, 117, 123, 129–137, 137–153, 161, 165,
    166, 167–171, 171–173, 177–186, 194–198,
    205, 214, 229, 232, 234, 235, 241–242

"transforming like a dragon," 185
and dreams, 214–216
and sound, 125, 129
instructing through, 132
soil transformation, 107
terminology, 198–200
transport, 3, 48
traps, 141
Night-time Trapper, 54, 127
tribute, 36, 62, 147, 192, 193
animals as, 47, 117–118
debates on, 104, 120–122
tripods, 118, 119, 235
trigrams, 93, 96–97, 98
tropics, 108, 189
tui lei 推類, 80, 123, 154
turtle (*see also* tortoise), 25, 65, 109, 148, 152, 178, 201, 237

U

unicorn, 9–10, 148, 153, 178, 201
"Song of the White Unicorn," 234
capture of, 219, 227, 233–36
memorial on, 233–34

V

Van Zoeren, Steven, 24
Vandermeersch, Léon, 100
Vermilion Bird, 102, 103
veterinary practice, 26, 47, 48, 70, 157
Vialles, Noëlie, 78
villains, 160–161, 217
violence, 132
violent animal behavior, 91, 140–142
viper, 19, 151, 175
virtue (*see also de*), 75, 91, 113, 116, 118, 120, 124, 134, 135, 137, 138–139, 141, 154, 155, 157, 161, 175, 178, 180, 181, 197, 207, 209, 216, 224, 228, 229, 235, 236
reaching animals, 142, 147–148
reciprocated by animals, 151–153
viviparous, 83

vulture, 51

W

Wang Bao, 131
Wang Chong, 24–25, 102, 103, 104, 130, 141, 142, 155, 174, 175, 181, 188, 200
criticism of metamorphosis, 200–202
criticism of omens, 208, 209, 236–37
criticism of the sages, 219–20
on "blood and *qi*," 75
on *wen*, 158, 181
Wang Feng, 196
Wang Fu, 73, 86, 180, 215
Wang Guowei, 31
Wang Hai, 95
Wang Kui, 316n. 88
Wang Mang, 60, 152, 196
Wang Su, 140
Wang Yanshou, 24, 117
Wang Ziqiao, 185
Wangshan, 232
wangxiang 罔象 (beast), 119, 212, 217
wasp, 170
water, 51, 80, 81, 83, 90, 102, 105, 106, 108, 109, 125, 136, 142, 144, 150, 151, 154, 179, 184, 212, 217, 221
and the five phases, 52, 79, 148
as transformatory agent, 82, 168,175–76, 201
cosmogony based on, 175–76
water god, 216
Water Lord, 300n. 32
water monsters, 102
Water Jug Sprinkler, 127, 302n. 51
wei 蝛 (serpentine demon), 221
weiyi 委蛇 (demon), 220
well, 212, 213
Wen (river), 105
Wen Yiduo, 303n. 71
wen 文 (pattern, mark), 7, 124, 181, 182, 192
and physiognomy, 156–158
as animal traces, 96–97

as plumage pattern, 98
as script, 99–100, 157
as social pattern, 96–101
versus *zhi*, 182–183
Wenxian, 41
Wenzi, 72, 74
whale, 147
White Emperor, 194, 216
wild animals, 29, 32, 40, 41, 47, 49, 57, 65,
74, 75, 90, 97, 102, 110, 112, 116, 120, 121,
127, 133, 138, 139, 140, 141, 148, 149, 151,
154, 171, 182, 187, 192, 224, 228
and barbarians, 160, 235
as sacrificial offering, 115
versus domestic, 18–19, 40, 71, 115, 118,
119, 123, 132, 225, 228, 229, 231
wildcat, 182, 194
wilderness, 45, 53, 55, 91, 98, 101, 116, 125,
139, 141, 144, 147, 151, 219, 227, 228, 234,
235
conquest of, 8, 93–95, 113, 130, 131, 161,
190, 193–194
wind (*feng*), 84, 103, 105, 124, 125, 135
and sexual attraction, 170
wind transformation, 137
wings, 31, 185
wolf, 91, 132, 134, 138, 151, 152, 154, 228
earth wolf, 217
women (*see also* gender change)
and snakes, 215
subservience of, 98
turning into men, 195
worms, 19, 126, 131, 186, 203
worm specialist, 49
worm vapor, 186
writing, 98–100, 157
Wu Ding, 235
Wu Qi, 150
Wu Yue Chunqiu, 119
Wu Zixu, 173
wu 物 (living being), 17–18, 52, 53
as referent, 40–41, 71
wuxing (*see* five phases)

X
Xia (dynasty), 52, 126, 138, 201
Xia xiao zheng, 126
Xici (*see* Great Commentary)
xiang 象 "image" (*see also* elephant), 213–
214, 215
Xiang Kai, 230
Xiangmajing, 27
Xiangtu, 275n. 7
Xiao Shi, 130
xiaoyang 梟陽, 212
Xie Bi, 209
Xie Zhaozhe, 205
xiezhai 獬豸 (beast), 190
Xing Bing, 30
xing ("stimulus"), 11, 207
xingxing 狌狌 (ape), 37, 220
Xinlun, 232
Xu Shen, 17, 18, 22, 42, 98, 155, 170, 172, 177, 231
Xun Shuang, 97–98
Xunzi, 26, 71, 75, 89, 118, 128, 139–140, 144,
184, 188
"Tian lun," 209–210, 230

Y
yak, 112, 118
Yang clan, 152
Yang Si, 209
Yang Wengzhong, 159
Yang Xiong, 34, 182, 189, 197, 200
Yang Youji, 149
Yang Zhen, 152
Yangzi, 154
Yantie lun, 120, 130
Yanzi (Master Yan), 139, 140, 224
Yanzi chunqiu, 91, 106, 228
Yao, 95, 101, 202
Yellow Emperor, 26, 95, 98, 126, 132, 134, 138
Yellow Turbans, 196
Yi Feng, 208
Yi the Archer, 139
Yi Yin, 121, 122
Yi zhi yi, 183

Yi Zhoushu, 64
    on geography, 101
    on tribute, 121–22
Yijing (see *Zhouyi*; Changes)
Yili, 21, 29, 57, 109
Yilin, 37
Ying Shao, 42, 130, 222, 223, 231
Yinqueshan, 27, 86, 87
Yinwan, 27
yin-yang, 7, 72, 78–88, 131, 174, 176–77, 197, 208, 210, 227
yoke, 149
youchang 幽昌 (bird), 155
Yu Qie, 300n. 32
Yu (the Great), 95, 101, 118, 119, 130, 132, 139, 152, 172
    "Yu gong," 101
yu 羽 (feathered animals), 21, 79, 82, 84, 85, 148, 212
yu 魚 (*see also* fish), 35, 85
yu 蜮 ("spit-sand"), 176, 178, 220, 230, 301n. 51
Yu, Pauline, 11
Yue (state, people), 25, 26, 65, 106, 170, 233
    identified with watery creatures, 189
yue ling (*see also* calendar; daybooks), 21, 64–67, 81, 146
Yunmeng, 116

Z
Zaofu, 292n. 126
Zengzi, 130
Zhan He, 159
Zhang Heng, 114, 126, 143, 191, 200
Zhang Hua, 175, 179
Zhang Qian, 152
Zhangjiashan, 190
Zhanguo ce, 197
zhen 鴆 (falcon), 189
zheng ming (*see* rectification of names)
Zheng Sinong, 56
Zheng Xuan, 18, 42, 102, 106, 110, 126, 129, 174

Zheng (state), 208, 223
zhenmushou 鎮墓獸 (tomb quelling animals), 12, 247n. 30
Zhong Changtong, 202
Zhong Jun, 233, 235
Zhou (period, state), 10, 26, 46, 104, 112, 127, 184, 187, 194, 201, 234, 235
    Duke of Zhou, 120
Zhou (tyrant), 112, 120, 151
Zhouli (Rites of Zhou), 7, 19, 21, 26, 29, 109, 115, 126, 135, 160, 188, 193, 229
    and animal officers, 40–41, 46–50
    on biotope, 101–102, 104
Zhouyi, 100, 104, 147, 180, 182, 183, 199, 217
Zhu Gong (Lord Crimson), 42
Zhuan Xu, 125, 176, 276n. 23
Zhuangzi, 8, 18, 94, 136–137, 141, 149, 167–168, 170, 214, 215, 220, 239
    "Tian yun" chapter, 169–170
    on horses, 239
    on spontaneous generation, 166–169
    skepticism of music, 136–137
Zhuji Weng, 152
Zhushu jinian, 195
Zi Chan, 115, 223–24
Zi Gao, 213
Zi Gong, 55, 150
Zi Lu, 150
zi ran 自然, 15–16
Zi Wen, 152
Zi Xia, 227
zodiac, 66–67
zoolatry, 61–62
zoology, 1, 5, 28, 30, 36, 70, 79, 80, 83, 85, 165, 247n. 31, 253n. 76
    ethnozoology, 70, 268n. 5
zoo, 4, 243 (*see also* parks)
zoomorphism, 10, 187
Zou Yan, 80, 105
zouyu 騶虞 (beast), 194
Zuozhuan, 18, 41, 50–53, 54, 64, 76, 108, 115, 118–119, 128, 140, 145–146, 159, 160, 170, 172, 207, 208, 210, 217, 223– 224, 228, 229

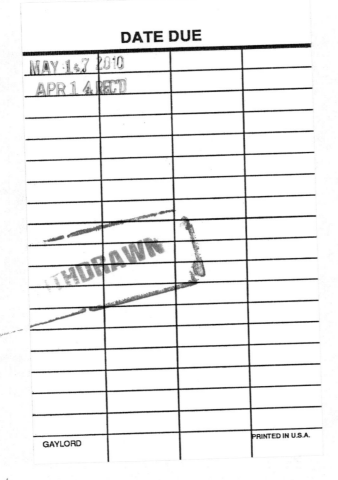